2007 Index
of Economic Freedom

Contributors

Tim Kane, Ph.D., is Director of the Center for International Trade and Economics (CITE) at The Heritage Foundation.

Kim R. Holmes, Ph.D., is Vice President of Foreign and Defense Policy and Director of the Kathryn and Shelby Cullom Davis Institute for International Studies at The Heritage Foundation.

Mary Anastasia O'Grady is a Member of *The Wall Street Journal* Editorial Board and Editor of the Journal's "Americas" column.

William W. Beach is Director of the Center for Data Analysis at The Heritage Foundation.

Ana Isabel Eiras is Senior Policy Analyst in International Economics in the Center for International Trade and Economics (CITE) at The Heritage Foundation. She is also Editor of the Spanish-language edition of the *Index of Economic Freedom*.

Edwin J. Feulner, Ph.D., is President of The Heritage Foundation.

Paul A. Gigot is Editor of *The Wall Street Journal* Editorial Page.

Anthony B. Kim is Research Associate in the Center for International Trade and Economics (CITE) at The Heritage Foundation.

Daniella Markheim is Jay Van Andel Senior Trade Policy Analyst in the Center for International Trade and Economics (CITE) at The Heritage Foundation.

Johnny Munkhammar is a research scholar at the Swedish think tank Timbro.

Andrew L. Peek is Research Assistant in the Center for International Trade and Economics (CITE) at The Heritage Foundation.

Xavier Sala-i-Martin is a professor of economics at Columbia University.

Brett D. Schaefer is Jay Kingham Fellow in the Margaret Thatcher Center for Freedom at The Heritage Foundation.

2007 Index
of Economic Freedom

Tim Kane, Ph.D.

Kim R. Holmes, Ph.D.

Mary Anastasia O'Grady

with Ana Isabel Eiras, Anthony B. Kim, Daniella Markheim,
Andrew L. Peek, and Brett D. Schaefer

The Heritage Foundation   THE WALL STREET JOURNAL.

The Heritage Foundation
214 Massachusetts Avenue, NE
Washington, DC 20002
(202) 546-4400
heritage.org

The Wall Street Journal
Dow Jones & Company, Inc.
200 Liberty Street
New York, NY 10281
(212) 416-2000
www.wsj.com

Cover images by Punchstock, Corbis, World Bank
ISBN: 0-89195-274-8
ISSN: 1095-7308

Table of Contents

Advisory Board

The following members of the Advisory Board for the *2007 Index of Economic Freedom* were consulted as part of the ongoing review of the methodology used in this year's edition. Their advice, insights, and critiques, as well as the efforts of many others who participated in the review process, are gratefully acknowledged.

William W. Beach, co-chairman, *The Heritage Foundation*
Tim Kane, co-chairman, *The Heritage Foundation*

Maria Sophia Aguirre, *Catholic University of America*
Donald J. Boudreaux, *George Mason University*
Ike Brannon, *Economist, Washington, D.C.*
Simeon Djankov, *World Bank*
Axel Dreher, *ETH Zurich*
Clive Granger, *University of California, San Diego*
Douglas Holtz-Eakin, *Council on Foreign Relations*
Garett Jones, *Southern Illinois University Edwardsville*
Mordechai "Max" Kreinin, *Michigan State University*
Philippe Lacoude, *Economist, Paris, France*
Richard Roll, *University of California, Los Angeles*
Xavier Sala-i-Martin, *Columbia University*
Friedrich Schneider, *University of Linz*
Aaron Smith, *University of California, Davis*

Foreword

The world economy has had another stellar year, growing in the neighborhood of 5 percent and continuing what has become the strongest four-year expansion since the 1970s, defying war, terrorism, and $75-a-barrel oil. This is testament in part to the policy lessons highlighted these past 13 years in this *Index of Economic Freedom*. As we greet 2007, however, there are warning signs that adherence to those lessons may be starting to fray.

On the surface, to be sure, the economic news continues to be mostly good. While the United States is shifting to a slower pace of growth following the boom from mid-2003 to early 2006, there continues to be no sign of recession. The major issue in the next year is whether the decline in housing will be so deep that it sinks the larger economy. That answer depends in part on how much the Federal Reserve must raise interest rates to compensate for its mistake of keeping monetary policy so loose for too long in 2003 and 2004. The early evidence is that rising corporate profits and a robust labor

market will offset the housing slump, but that is no certainty.

China and India are roaring ahead, notwithstanding the return of a center-left government in New Delhi that has tried to temper the pace of economic change. Center-left isn't the economic drag it used to be even in India, however, and the emergence of India as a global economic player continues. Japan seems finally to have shaken its decade-long deflation, and even Old Europe left the doldrums in 2006, albeit in relatively modest terms. The pace of world trade and investment continued to accelerate, and millions more of the world's poor entered the middle class.

One lesson of this *Index*, however, is that what really matters is the direction of policy: that is, the change at the margin. And on that score, there is some reason for worry about an erosion in economic freedom. Start with the U.S., where the congressional election campaign created bipartisan policy stampedes against foreign investment from China and

Dubai. Congress, in its lack of wisdom, is also seeking to add even more political hurdles to foreigners who want to create jobs by investing in America.

The election also moved Congress to the left economically, with strong new voices rejecting the free trade consensus of the past 50 years. President Bush retains his office lease and veto pen for two more years, but the most he may be able to accomplish is to prevent any major policy mistakes. He will almost certainly not be able to extend his trade promotion authority, for example, when that expires in mid-2007. Political gridlock is probably the best we can expect until the policy showdown that is likely to take place in the 2008 presidential contest.

This is all the more reason for the world's policymakers to complete the Doha Round of trade talks as soon as possible. At this writing, however, the talks remain caught between a French-led Europe that refuses to reduce its farm subsidies and an assertive bloc of developing nations that won't bend on manufacturing and services without such a European concession. This is short-sighted in the extreme, and one question is whether this is a temporary setback due to weak political leadership, or whether it reflects a larger popular backlash against the dynamic forces of globalization.

My guess is the former, but I would prefer not to test that proposition in the teeth of a global recession.

This policy drama is all the more reason to welcome the refinements in this year's *Index*. The shift to a 0–100 freedom scale allows for more nuanced distinctions among countries. The introduction of a measure for labor freedom is also notable and informative because labor mobility has clearly become crucial to national prosperity and competitiveness. Merely contrast the job creation in the U.S., where labor mobility is high, with the record in France and Germany to prove that point. The slight overall decline in average world economic freedom—down 0.3 percentage point from a year earlier—also suggests the policy setbacks I have described.

There are no permanent victories in politics or economics, which is one reason that this *Index* exists to chronicle annual progress or regression. The next year is one to watch carefully for setbacks and to remind forgetful politicians of the benefits of economic freedom.

Paul A. Gigot
Editorial Page Editor
The Wall Street Journal
November 2006

Preface

If there is a single triumph that history will remember about the 20th century, it is not the defeat of Nazism or the collapse of Soviet Russia, but the West's enduring confidence in freedom as a moral and liberating force for all peoples. The victory of political freedom as a universal ideal is so complete today that even modern tyrannies cloak their countries as "people's republics." Now, as we progress into a new century, countries around the world are adopting new institutions to enhance their economic growth. Thus, history will surely remark that the more fundamental freedoms of property, trade, entrepreneurship, work, and investment served as the foundations of true democracy and revolutionized the world.

The importance of economic freedom—an individual's natural right to own the value of what he or she creates—would seem to be anything but controversial. People crave liberation from poverty, and they hunger for the dignity of free will. Yet the struggle for economic freedom faces timeless opposition. Tariffs, just one example of protectionism, never lack champions or supporters, and the urge to avoid risk will always pressure societies to expand the size and weight of government intervention. It is therefore precisely the importance of economic freedom—and ultimately, as Milton Friedman pointed out, political freedom—that makes our publication of the *Index of Economic Freedom* so necessary.

The *Index of Economic Freedom* has documented the progress of market economics with research and analysis for 13 years and encompasses 161 countries. Published jointly by The Heritage Foundation and *The Wall Street Journal*, the *Index* has created a global portrait of economic freedom and established a benchmark by which to gauge a country's prospects for economic success. It follows the simple tenet that something cannot be improved if it is not measured. Tracing the path to economic prosperity, the annual *Index* continues to serve as a critical tool for students, teachers, policymakers, business leaders, investors, and the media.

In this 13th edition, we have refined the methodology to reflect a clearer picture of economic freedom. Countries are assigned a percent score rather than a 1–5 rating. In addition, labor freedom (something that was simply not measurable before) has been added as a variable, and several other factors have been honed to provide more objectivity and greater attention to detail. Despite these changes, a core of stability remains, starting with our tradition of blending "Ten Freedoms" equally to produce a simple, unbiased overall score. Most of the 20 freest countries from last year are still ranked among the freest, although others, in the middle of the pack, have experienced some shuffling as a result of the greater level of detail in the new methodology.

The *2007 Index* shows that economic freedom worldwide has decreased slightly since last year but remains high. The Middle East's freedom increased to its highest level since 1995. Europe, Asia, and the Americas are the three freest regions, and each has something special worth noting. Asia has both the world's three freest economies and its least free economy. Europe has over half of the top 20 countries, and the Americas are home to both the richest and some of the most dynamic countries in the world.

The *2007 Index* contains two guest chapters written by outside scholars that document the spectacular growth of incomes in the face of globalization, as well as the vital importance of labor freedom in Europe and elsewhere. This edition also contains a description of the new methodology and an entirely new chapter analyzing each of the five geographic regions—a focus that matters for local competition. And of course, this edition includes our traditional country pages, so that each freedom in every economy is explained in detail. Each country page includes new charts highlighting the strengths and weaknesses of each economy.

At the most personal level, however, it may well be that academic methodology and carefully measured charts cannot make the best case for economic freedom. The real world—a walk, perhaps, through downtown Hong Kong—is far more eloquent than we can ever hope to be.

Edwin J. Feulner, Ph.D.
President
The Heritage Foundation
November 2006

Acknowledgments

We wish to express our profound gratitude to the many individuals, especially those at The Heritage Foundation, who have made such valuable contributions to this 13th annual edition of the *Index of Economic Freedom*. The Heritage Foundation's Center for International Trade and Economics (CITE) produces the *Index*, an effort that this year involved Ana Isabel Eiras, Anthony Kim, Daniella Markheim, and Brett Schaefer, as well as research assistant Andrew Peek.

Others at The Heritage Foundation also made invaluable contributions to this year's edition. We are particularly grateful to Center for Data Analysis Director William Beach for his continued support and for his contributions to the methodology chapter. In the Douglas and Sarah Allison Center for Foreign Policy Studies, a division of the Kathryn and Shelby Cullom Davis Institute for International Studies, Ariel Cohen, Stephen Johnson, James Phillips, and Will Schirano wrote introductory paragraphs and provided their expertise. We are especially grateful for the many insightful contributions that Helle C. Dale, Director of the Douglas and Sarah Allison Center for Foreign Policy Studies, made to the content of this year's *Index*. Yvette Campos and Marla Graves provided valuable production support, and Marla did the initial editing of all 161 country introductions.

In the Asian Studies Center, Dana Dillon, Balbina Hwang, and John J. Tkacik, Jr., wrote introductions and provided assistance, and Allison Goodman provided valuable production support. In the Information Technology Department, invaluable help was provided by Vice President of Information Technology Michael Spiller and Michael Smith. We are grateful for their professionalism.

In Publishing Services, Manager Therese Pennefather, Elizabeth Brewer, and Alex Adrianson were responsible for all aspects of the production process, including the extensive design and layout that make this 13th edition the most readable and accessible yet published, as well as for developing the world and country maps and formatting the charts and tables. We are grateful to Director of Online Communications Ted Morgan, Tosan Ogharaerumi, and the other IT staff for placing the entire *Index* on the Heritage Web site (*www.heritage.org/index/*). We also thank James Dean, Alison Fraser, Mike Franc, Rebecca Hagelin, John Sieg, Jan Smith, and Bridgett Wagner for their insightful contributions and support.

Once again, we wish to express our deep appreciation for the work of Senior Editor Richard Odermatt, who was responsible for final review of the completed text, and Senior Copy Editor William T. Poole, who continues to bear the primary responsibility for editing the entire book. Each year, their professionalism, commitment to the project, and attention to detail play a crucial role in making the *Index* a reality. We are likewise grateful to Editor Jon Rodeback, who carefully reviewed every one of the many charts and tables included in the book. In addition, Andrew Peek was responsible for proofreading the English-language drafts and crosschecking the facts and figures, and the dedicated research of Heritage interns Hayley Darden, Peter Farmer, Alana Finley, Sarah MacArthur, and Caroline Walsh did much to make the specialists' in-depth analysis possible.

Countless individuals serving with various accounting firms, businesses, research organizations, U.S. government agencies, foreign embassies, and other organizations cooperated by providing us with the data used in the *Index*. Their assistance is much appreciated. As always, we acknowledge our enduring debt to Heritage Trustee Ambassador J. William Middendorf II, who originally encouraged us to undertake such a study of global economic freedom.

Finally, we would like to express our appreciation to the many people who, year after year, either praise or criticize the *Index of Economic Freedom* so enthusiastically. The support and encouragement of people in all parts of the world continue to serve as a major source of inspiration for The Heritage Foundation and *The Wall Street Journal* in their ongoing collaboration on this important work. We hope this year's effort once again matches the expectations of our supporters, as well as the thoughtful critics who so often have provided the insights that enable us to continue to improve the *Index*.

Tim Kane, Ph.D.
Kim R. Holmes, Ph.D.
Mary Anastasia O'Grady
November 2006

What's New in the 2007 *Index?*

E very year, the editors evaluate the *Index of Economic Freedom* and consider ways to improve the product. This year's edition of the *Index* embodies the most dramatic changes, in both style and substance, that have been made since publication of the inaugural edition in 1995. The book is physically smaller to enhance its usability and portability. An extensive redesign of the country pages includes two new charts to help readers quickly assess each economy's progress. Finally, the methodology has been improved with the help of a newly formed academic advisory board and utilization of new data from the World Bank that have been made available only recently. Previous years' scores have been revised to reflect the more rigorous approach.

These changes continue the Heritage Foundation/*Wall Street Journal* tradition of continuing, year-by-year improvement. Changes in the methodology were instituted in 2000, 2002, 2004, and 2006 to enhance the robustness of one or more of the 10 factors that are used to mea-sure overall economic freedom, and the entire time series was revised so that all scores were and are as consistent as possible, dating back to 1995. The 2001 *Index* saw the publication of a Spanish-language edition in cooperation with several Latin American think tanks. That same edition was the first to suspend countries from grading as a result of insufficient or inapplicable data.

To the extent that the changes are bigger in 2007 than ever before, they are driven by a new process: a fundamental effort to formalize the feedback so that suggestions of friends, scholars, policymakers, and other readers are collected, considered, and acted upon. For example, we conducted an internal survey of scholars at Heritage and an external survey of 375 people from the academic, business, government, and international communities who downloaded the *Index* from our Web site last year to assess our strengths and weaknesses. We also solicited advice from academic scholars before revising the methodology.

10 Factors	10 Freedoms
(Old Methodology)	(New Methodology)
Regulation	Business Freedom
Trade Policy	Trade Freedom
Fiscal Burden	Fiscal Freedom
Government Intervention	Freedom from Government
Monetary Policy	Monetary Freedom (80%)
Wages and Prices	Monetary Freedom (20%)
Foreign Investment	Investment Freedom
Banking and Finance	Financial Freedom
Property Rights	Property Rights
Informal Market	Freedom from Corruption
(N/A)	Labor Freedom

Some of the most common suggestions were (1) to use a new 0–100 percent grading scale rather than 5–1 so that a higher score now represents more freedom, (2) to add regional context to the rankings; (3) to enhance the methodological rigor by using equations instead of brackets where possible; and (4) to add a factor for labor freedom. One example of the increased detail in the new *Index* is the way monetary freedom is measured: Two economies with inflation rates of 1 percent and 2 percent, respectively, traditionally were given identical monetary scores in the *Index* because both economies were in the same bracket, but now we use an equation that allows for finer detail in the scores. In the new methodology for monetary freedom, the closer an inflation rate is to zero—even one-tenth of a percentage point—the higher the monetary freedom score.

A more detailed explanation of what has changed, as well as what has not changed, in the 2007 *Index* follows:

• **Academic Advisory Board.** The methodology is the heart of the entire *Index* project. It gives credibility to the product and is a key tool in fighting claims of bias. While scholars working on different ways to measure economic freedom agree that such an abstract concept can never be measured perfectly, the most important attribute of any approach is that it be unbiased. For this reason, we assembled an academic advisory board to review the methodology with us on a continuing basis, both this year and in future years. Those scholars who approved of the final methodology that was developed then offered their endorsement.

• **Continuous Percentile Scores.** The *Index* is converting to a 0–100 scoring scale that both translates more easily into percentages of freedom and ends the use of discrete brackets (1, 2, 3, 4, and 5) in favor of a continuous scale that allows an economy in many cases to receive, for example, a score of 83.3 percent instead of an 80 or 90. All previous scores back to 1995 have been converted to the new 0–100 scale. The 5–1 rankings in use in the 1995–2006 editions (where a lower number equaled more freedom) were based on the original methodology. As the methodology and precision improved in subsequent editions, it became increasingly obvious that the scoring should be brought into line. In addition, economic freedom is a *positive* quantity, not a mere absence of oppression, and the use of a zero to denote a total lack of freedom seems to epitomize this.

• **New Methodology.** The *Index* methodology is changing substantively in several ways. First, new data from the World Bank's *Doing Business* report that became available only recently are utilized as the basis for the business freedom factor (replacing the old regulation factor) and a new labor freedom factor. Second, an equation-based approach replaces the bracket scores for numerous factor variables, notably inflation and tariffs. The 10 factors have been renamed as described in the accompanying table. It must be emphasized that the new methodology is not only for 2007 scores; rather, it has been implemented for this year and all previous years. An obvious consequence of the new methodology is the effect on each country's overall freedom score and ranking, which is due to the new attention to detail. Small policy changes are detected more easily in the more detailed methodology and can cause a large change in worldwide rank for many countries.

• **A New Labor Freedom Factor.** The recent

labor riots in France and the wide disparity in unemployment rates across countries call for a stronger focus on labor freedom. Labor laws were covered in the previous methodology as a small component of the regulation factor and less-than-equal component of the wages and prices factor, but this was primarily because no consistent data source existed for cross-country comparisons until 2003. The new labor freedom factor is based on objective data from the World Bank's *Doing Business* study, which covers minimum wages, laws inhibiting layoffs, severance requirements, and measurable regulatory burdens on hiring, hours, and so on. These cross-country labor data, though cutting-edge and well-respected, are available only for 2005–2007.

• **New Country Page Design.** The new country page design emphasizes overall economic freedom on the first page and details for each of the 10 areas of economic freedom on the second page. The heading includes the world rank for each economy and a new regional rank. The new approach focuses more precisely on economic policy and the *Index* scores. A paragraph that describes historical background for each country, with political context, remains as an anchor on the first page. The "Quick Facts" box has been revised to include many new variables: unemployment and inflation rates, GDP in terms of purchasing power parity, a five-year compound average annual growth rate, foreign direct investment (FDI), three official development assistance measures, and external debt. The time series chart has been expanded to give a better sense of how a country's economic freedom is evolving, which now includes both time series lines for the world and regional averages from 1995 to the present. Finally, a new second chart created for each economy shows graphically how each of a country's 10 economic freedoms compares to the world average.

• **New Regions.** From this year forward, the *Index* will emphasize a country's regional rank as well as its global rank. For example, the United Kingdom ranks as the 6th freest economy in the world in 2007, but it also ranks as the freest in Europe. Similarly, Israel has the freest economy in the Middle East/North Africa region,

Mauritius is the best in sub-Saharan Africa, and the United States is number one in the Americas. These five regions are consistent with past *Index* groupings with the exception of three countries: Canada, Mexico, and the U.S. are now included in the Americas (which replaces Latin America as a region). As a result, Europe is now a separate region, replacing the old North America and Europe. These regions are not only more geographically consistent; they also represent our long-standing philosophy of human equality. Just because Canada is wealthier than many other New World economies does not necessarily mean that its people are better or that its economy merits inclusion in a different class of countries. We believe (and have always believed) that all peoples have equal potential and that all economies deserve equal liberty.

We hope the changes in the *Index* make it an even better research tool and a more accessible policymaking guide. Despite the new look, however, our goal is and will remain the same: to advance human freedom. We believe that the redesigned *Index* might even make the transition to a better world faster and surer.

One of the editors' paramount concerns is that the *Index* always remains a useful tool for researchers. This means that the integrity of the current-year scores is crucial. During a period of aggressive improvements, there undoubtedly will be mistakes in the scores, based on our errors and errors in source data. We cannot promise perfection, but we do promise objectivity: Our methods and modifications will always be transparent and duplicable by other scholars.

Moreover, even though the *Index* itself is published in January, based on policies and data available as of the previous June, we remain committed to providing the most accurate and up-to-date measures on-line and will make any needed corrections to that source file immediately. For researchers who want to weight the *Index* or consider individual components in statistical analysis, the 10 freedoms and even the raw data are also available transparently on-line. Revised scores of individual factors for all years are available for download at *www.heritage.org/Index*.

Executive Summary

With the publication of this edition, The Heritage Foundation/Wall Street Journal *Index of Economic Freedom* marks its 13th anniversary. The idea of producing a user-friendly "index of economic freedom" as a tool for policymakers and investors was first discussed at The Heritage Foundation in the late 1980s. The goal then, as it is today, was to develop a systematic, empirical measurement of economic freedom in countries throughout the world. To this end, the decision was made to establish a set of objective economic criteria that, since the inaugural edition in 1995, have been used to study and grade various countries for the annual publication of the *Index of Economic Freedom*.

Economic theory dating back to the publication of Adam Smith's *The Wealth of Nations* in 1776 emphasizes the lesson that basic institutions that protect the liberty of individuals to pursue their own economic interests result in greater prosperity for the larger society. Perhaps the idea of freedom is too sophisticated, as popular support for it constantly erodes before the onslaught of populism, whether democratic or autocratic. Yet modern scholars of political economy are rediscovering the centrality of "free institutions" as fundamental ingredients for rapid long-term growth. In other words, the techniques may be new, but they reaffirm classic truths. The objective of the *Index* is to catalog those economic institutions in a quantitative and rigorous manner.

Yet the *Index* is more than a simple ranking based on economic theory and empirical study. It also identifies the variables that comprise economic freedom and analyzes the interaction of freedom with wealth.

The *2007 Index of Economic Freedom* measures 157 countries across 10 specific factors of economic freedom, which are listed below. Chapter 3 explains these factors in detail. High scores approaching 100 represent higher levels of freedom. The higher the score on a factor, the lower the level of government interference in the economy.

The 10 Economic Freedoms
- Business Freedom
- Trade Freedom
- Fiscal Freedom
- Freedom from Government
- Monetary Freedom
- Investment Freedom
- Financial Freedom
- Property Rights
- Freedom from Corruption
- Labor Freedom

HIGHLIGHTS FROM THE 2007 INDEX

Global economic freedom holds steady, but there is much room for improvement. The average economic freedom score is 60.6 percent, the second highest level since the *Index* began in 1995 and down by 0.3 percentage point from last year. Each region has experienced an increase in economic freedom during the past decade.

Former British colonies in Asia lead the world in economic freedom. Hong Kong has the highest level of economic freedom for the 13th straight year. Singapore remains close, ranked second in the world, and Australia is ranked third freest economy in the world, which means that the Asia–Pacific region is home to the top three economies.

Twelve of the top 20 freest economies are European. A majority of the freest economies are in Europe, led by the United Kingdom, Ireland, Luxembourg, and Switzerland. Only five are in the Asia–Pacific region. The remaining three are from the Americas: the United States, Canada, and Chile.

The methodology for measuring economic freedom is significantly upgraded. The new methodology uses a scale of 0–100 rather than the 1–5 brackets of previous years when assessing the 10 component economic freedoms, which means that the new overall scores are

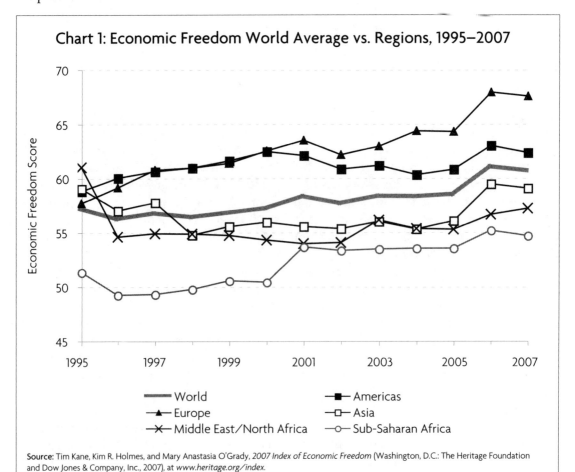

Chart 1: Economic Freedom World Average vs. Regions, 1995–2007

Legend:
— World
—■— Americas
—▲— Europe
—□— Asia
—✕— Middle East/North Africa
—○— Sub-Saharan Africa

Source: Tim Kane, Kim R. Holmes, and Mary Anastasia O'Grady, *2007 Index of Economic Freedom* (Washington, D.C.: The Heritage Foundation and Dow Jones & Company, Inc., 2007), at *www.heritage.org/index.*

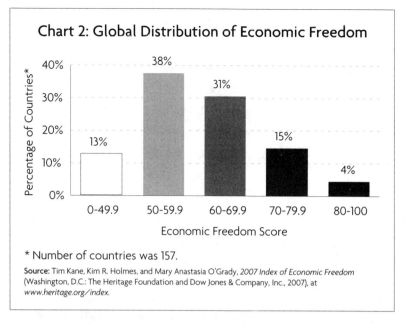

Chart 2: Global Distribution of Economic Freedom

* Number of countries was 157.

Source: Tim Kane, Kim R. Holmes, and Mary Anastasia O'Grady, *2007 Index of Economic Freedom* (Washington, D.C.: The Heritage Foundation and Dow Jones & Company, Inc., 2007), at *www.heritage.org/index.*

Table 1: Global Distribution of Economic Freedom

Scores	Category	Number of Countries
80–100	Free	7
70–79.9	Mostly Free	23
60–69.9	Moderately Free	48
50–59.9	Mostly Unfree	59
0–49.9	Repressed	20

Source: Tim Kane, Kim R. Holmes, and Mary Anastasia O'Grady, *2007 Index of Economic Freedom* (Washington, D.C.: The Heritage Foundation and Dow Jones & Company, Inc., 2007), at *www. heritage.org/index.*

good economic performance. The world's freest countries have twice the average per capita income of the second quintile of countries and over five times the average income of the fifth quintile of countries. The freest economies also have lower rates of unemployment and lower inflation. These relationships hold across each quintile, meaning that every quintile of less free economies has worse average rates of inflation and unemployment than the preceding quintile has.

The top 20 countries have held relatively steady. Even though the methodology used for rating economic freedom has been revised with this edition of the *Index*, the composition and order of the top 20 economies have hardly changed at all. Japan and Belgium moved into the top group (compared to the old methodology, not compared to 2006 scores using the new methodology), whereas Austria and Sweden fell to lower positions.

Progress is universal across all continents. Across the five regions, Europe is clearly the most free using an unweighted average (67.5 percent), followed at some distance by the Americas (62.3 percent). The other three regions fall below the world average: Asia–Pacific (59.1 percent), Middle East/North Africa (57.2 percent), and sub-Saharan Africa (54.7 percent). However, trends in freedom are mirrored closely across all regions. The main distinguishing feature of the regions is that Asia–Pacific countries have the highest variance, which means that there is a much wider gap between the heights of freedom in some economies and

more refined and therefore more accurate. Second, a new labor freedom factor has been added, and entrepreneurship is being emphasized in the business freedom factor. Both of these new categories are based on data that became available from the World Bank only recently. This attention to detail benefits some countries and punishes others, and readers may note some dramatic changes in rankings. The methodology has been vetted with a new academic advisory board and should better reflect the details of each country's economic policies. In order to compare country performances from past years accurately, scores and rankings for all previous years dating back to 1995 have been adjusted to reflect the new methodology.

Economic freedom is strongly related to

the lows in others that is nearly twice as variable as the norm.

Of the 157 countries graded numerically in the 2007 *Index*, only seven have very high freedom scores of 80 percent or more,[1] making them what we categorize as "free" economies. Another 23 are in the 70 percent range, placing them in the "mostly free" category. This means that less than one-fifth of all countries have economic freedom scores higher than 70 percent. The bulk of countries—107 economies—have freedom scores of 50 percent–70 percent. Half are "moderately free" (scores of 60 percent–70 percent), and half are "mostly unfree" (scores of 50 percent–60 percent). Only 20 countries have "repressed economies" with scores below 50 percent.

The typical country has an economy that is 60.6 percent free, down slightly from 60.9 percent in 2006. This decline is caused primarily by monetary freedom scores, which are 2.6 percentage points lower on average due to slightly more extensive price controls and a mild increase in inflation. Even so, the past scores for these two years produced the overall highest scores ever recorded in the *Index*, so the overall trend continues to be positive. As noted, although the methodology used for measuring freedom was revised this year, previous scores were also revised to be consistent across time.[2]

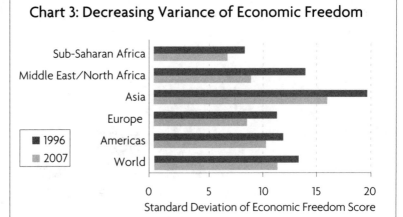

Chart 3: Decreasing Variance of Economic Freedom

Legend:
- 1996
- 2007

Categories (top to bottom): Sub-Saharan Africa, Middle East/North Africa, Asia, Europe, Americas, World

X-axis: Standard Deviation of Economic Freedom Score (0, 5, 10, 15, 20)

Source: Tim Kane, Kim R. Holmes, and Mary Anastasia O'Grady, *2007 Index of Economic Freedom* (Washington, D.C.: The Heritage Foundation and Dow Jones & Company, Inc., 2007), at *www.heritage.org/index*.

Among specific economies during the past year, the scores of 65 countries are now higher, and the scores of 92 countries are worse.

The variation in freedom among all of these countries declined again for the sixth year in a row, and the standard deviation among scores now stands at 11.4, down one-tenth of a percentage point from last year and down two full points since 1996.[3]

THE IMPACT OF ECONOMIC FREEDOM

There is a clear relationship between economic freedom and numerous other cross-country variables, the most prominent being the strong relationship between the level of freedom and the level of prosperity in a given country. Previous editions of the *Index* have confirmed the tangible benefits of living in

---

1   Four countries (the Democratic Republic of Congo, Iraq, Serbia and Montenegro, and Sudan) were suspended from grading again this year because of questions about the accuracy of the data reported by each country or about whether the data truly reflect economic circumstances for most of the country. Data for suspended countries are reviewed annually to ascertain whether the situation has improved. The Democratic Republic of Congo and Sudan were suspended from grading in the 2007 *Index* because in each case, civil unrest or anarchy indicated that official government policies did not apply to large portions of the country. Serbia and Montenegro and Iraq were suspended because reliable data were not available.

2   The minor discontinuity in methodology for three factors may have a slight impact on a handful of countries, but the aggregate effect is nil. Thus, the decline in global economic freedom is real, not a reflection of the new level of methodological detail. See For a more detailed discussion, see Chapter 3, "Methodology: Measuring the 10 Economic Freedoms."
3   The analysis does not extend to the 1995 edition of the *Index* because many fewer countries were graded in that year.

THE 10 ECONOMIC FREEDOMS: A GLOBAL GUIDE

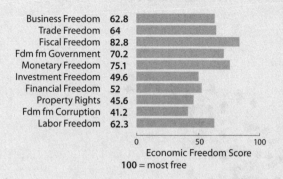

Business Freedom	62.8
Trade Freedom	64
Fiscal Freedom	82.8
Fdm fm Government	70.2
Monetary Freedom	75.1
Investment Freedom	49.6
Financial Freedom	52
Property Rights	45.6
Fdm fm Corruption	41.2
Labor Freedom	62.3

Economic Freedom Score
100 = most free

BUSINESS FREEDOM — *62.8%*

Business freedom is a measure of how free entrepreneurs are to start businesses, how easy it is to obtain licenses, and how easy it is to close a business. Impediments to any of these three components deter business activity and job creation. Globally, starting a business takes an average of 48 days, while getting necessary licenses takes an average of about 215 days.[1] Bankruptcy proceedings take an average of three years.

TRADE FREEDOM — *64%*

Tariffs are the primary obstacle to free trade, but non-tariff barriers like quotas and bureaucratic delays are also significant impediments. Using our equation, which assigns four-fifths of the score based on weighted average tariffs and a full 20 percentage point reduction for the existence of non-tariff barriers, the average trade freedom score is 64 percent. The mean weighted average tariff is 8 percent. Notably, every one of the 157 countries graded was penalized 20 points for its non-tariff barriers.

FISCAL FREEDOM — *82.8%*

The top tax rate on individual income averages 31 percent, and the top tax rate on corporate income averages 27 percent. The total revenue from all forms of taxation (including tariffs) averages 20 percent of country GDP. Mixing the three scores together is the basis of the fiscal freedom score. Using an equation that defines higher freedom with lower taxes and tax rates, the average score is 82.8 percent.

FREEDOM FROM GOVERNMENT — *70.2%*

Government expenditures are the other side of the fiscal intervention coin. The average level of government spending as a portion of GDP is 31 percent.[2] Governments that generate revenue from state-owned enterprises are also penalized.

MONETARY FREEDOM — *75.1%*

The worldwide average of the weighted average rate of inflation from 2003 to 2005 is 7.9 percent. Price stability explains most of the monetary freedom score, although there is also a penalty of up to 20 percentage points for countries that use price controls. The average price control penalty was 9.9 points this year.

INVESTMENT FREEDOM — *49.6%*

Only 13 countries enjoy high investment freedom, earning scores of 80 percent and higher. These countries impose few or no restrictions on foreign investment, which promotes economic expansion and enhances overall economic freedom. Meanwhile, more than one-third of countries earn scores of less than 50 percent.

FINANCIAL FREEDOM — *52%*

The financial freedom factor measures the relative openness of a country's banking and financial system. Burdensome bank regulation still reduces opportunities and restricts economic freedom in the preponderance of countries in all areas of the world.

PROPERTY RIGHTS — *45.6%*

Strong property rights are still a work in progress. Although many Western economies along with Hong Kong and Singapore benefit from secure protection of property rights, earning scores of 80 percent or higher, more than half of the world's countries receive a score of less than 50 percent.

FREEDOM FROM CORRUPTION — *41.2%*

There has been little progress since last year. Only 16 countries earned scores of 80 percent or higher, and 110 countries earned scores of less than 50 percent. Freedom from corruption is the lowest average score among the 10 factors.

LABOR FREEDOM — *62.3%*

The world average of labor freedom is 62.3 percent, reflecting wage, hour, and other restrictions. The average ratio of minimum wage to average wage is 0.32. The average cost of firing equals 54 weeks of salary. Only 22 countries have notably flexible labor market policies that earn scores of 80 percent or higher.

---

1   The global average is based on data for 145 countries that are graded by both the *Index of Economic Freedom* and the 2007 edition of the World Bank's *Doing Business*.

2   In general, freedom from government looks at the general government expenditure data that combine all levels of government. In grading countries for which general government spending data are not available, central government expenditure data are used.

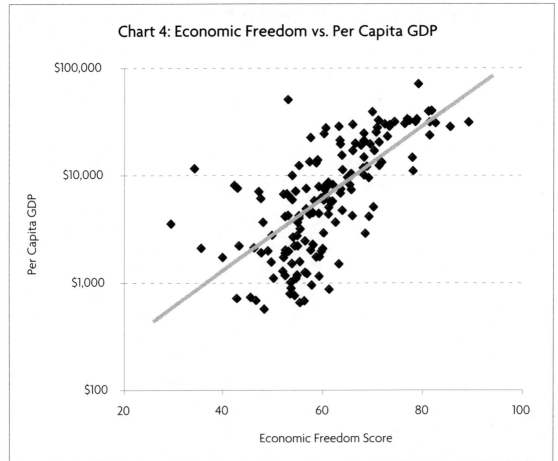

Chart 4: Economic Freedom vs. Per Capita GDP

Per Capita GDP (y-axis): $100,000 / $10,000 / $1,000 / $100

Economic Freedom Score (x-axis): 20, 40, 60, 80, 100

Sources: World Bank, *World Development Indicators Online*, at *publications.worldbank.org/subscriptions/WDI* (October 19, 2006; subscription required); Central Intelligence Agency, *The World Factbook 2005*, at *www.cia.gov/cia/publications/factbook/index.html* (October 19, 2006); International Monetary Fund, World Economic Outlook database, April 2006, at *www.imf.org/external/pubs/ft/weo/2006/01/data/ 24 index.htm* (October 19, 2006); and Tim Kane, Kim R. Holmes, and Mary Anastasia O'Grady, *2007 Index of Economic Freedom* (Washington, D.C.: The Heritage Foundation and Dow Jones & Company, Inc., 2007), at *www.heritage.org/index.*

freer societies. Not only is a higher level of economic freedom clearly associated with a higher level of per capita gross domestic product, but those higher GDP growth rates seem to create a virtuous cycle, triggering further improvements in economic freedom. Our 13 years of *Index* data strongly suggest that countries that increase their levels of freedom experience faster growth rates.

Chart 4 shows a strong relationship between the level of economic freedom in 2007 and the logarithmic value of the most recent data for per capita GDP using 157 countries as data points.

Charts 5–8 illustrate four different relationships using a quintile framework. The top quintile of countries is composed of those that are ranked from 1 to 31 globally (Hong Kong to the Czech Republic), and each subsequent quintile includes the next group of countries. Quintiles are not the same as categorical groups (free, mostly free, etc.) and are used here because each quintile is comparable based on the same number of countries.

Chart 5 shows that four of five quintiles have roughly equal populations, but the fourth quintile alone contains half of the world's population. This is due to the presence of China and India together. This fact suggests that when China and India further open their economies to globalization so that internal economic freedoms are strengthened, the rise in global prosperity is poised for very large increases.

Chart 6 is another look at the relationship between economic freedom and average per capita incomes. The quintiles with higher

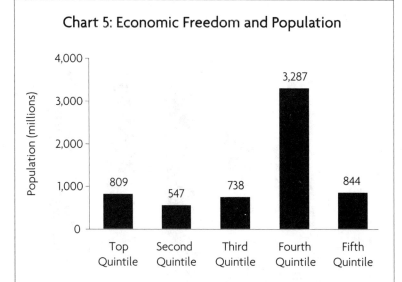

Chart 5: Economic Freedom and Population

Population (millions)

- Top Quintile: 809
- Second Quintile: 547
- Third Quintile: 738
- Fourth Quintile: 3,287
- Fifth Quintile: 844

Sources: World Bank, World Development Indicators Online, at *publications.worldbank.org/ subscriptions/WDI* (October 19, 2006; subscription required); Central Intelligence Agency, *The World Factbook 2005*, at *www.cia.gov/cia/publications/factbook/index.html* (October 19, 2006); International Monetary Fund, World Economic Outlook database, April 2006, at *www.imf.org/external/pubs/ft/weo/2006/01/data/index.htm* (October 19, 2006); and Tim Kane, Kim R. Holmes, and Mary Anastasia O'Grady, *2007 Index of Economic Freedom* (Washington, D.C.: The Heritage Foundation and Dow Jones & Company, Inc., 2007), at *www.heritage.org/index*.

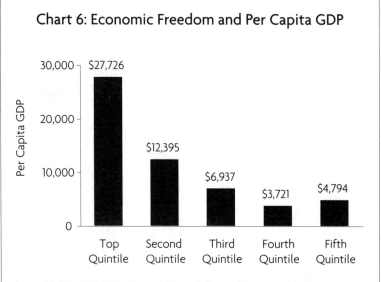

Chart 6: Economic Freedom and Per Capita GDP

Per Capita GDP

- Top Quintile: $27,726
- Second Quintile: $12,395
- Third Quintile: $6,937
- Fourth Quintile: $3,721
- Fifth Quintile: $4,794

Sources: World Bank, World Development Indicators Online, at *publications.worldbank.org/ subscriptions/WDI* (October 19, 2006; subscription required); Central Intelligence Agency, *The World Factbook 2005*, at *www.cia.gov/cia/publications/factbook/index.html* (October 19, 2006); International Monetary Fund, World Economic Outlook database, April 2006, at *www.imf.org/external/pubs/ft/weo/2006/01/data/index.htm* (October 19, 2006); and Tim Kane, Kim R. Holmes, and Mary Anastasia O'Grady, *2007 Index of Economic Freedom* (Washington, D.C.: The Heritage Foundation and Dow Jones & Company, Inc., 2007), at *www.heritage.org/index*.

nomic freedom. Likewise, inflation rates rise on average as economic freedom declines.

The lesson from these charts is simple. Economic repression is a sad consequence of other events. Countries that are able to reflect the desires of their people for better lives will adopt economic freedom, and countries that repress their people for political reasons will cause economic suffering.

In other words, the claim that the suspension of economic freedom is done for the good of the people is no longer tenable.

economic freedom have dramatically higher incomes per person.

Charts 7 and 8 show that unemployment rates are higher for each quintile of lower eco-

Chart 7: Economic Freedom and Unemployment

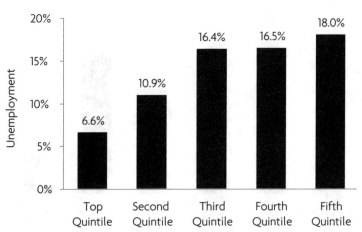

Sources: World Bank, World Development Indicators Online, at *publications.worldbank.org/ subscriptions/WDI* (October 19, 2006; subscription required); Central Intelligence Agency, *The World Factbook 2005,* at *www.cia.gov/cia/publications/factbook/index.html* (October 19, 2006); International Monetary Fund, World Economic Outlook database, April 2006, at *www.imf.org/external/pubs/ft/weo/2006/01/data/index.htm* (October 19, 2006); and Tim Kane, Kim R. Holmes, and Mary Anastasia O'Grady, *2007 Index of Economic Freedom* (Washington, D.C.: The Heritage Foundation and Dow Jones & Company, Inc., 2007), at *www.heritage.org/index.*

Chart 8: Economic Freedom and Inflation

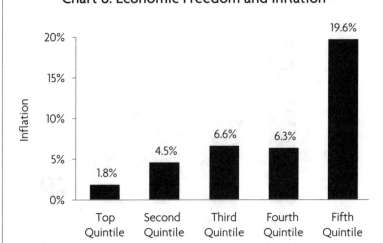

Sources: World Bank, World Development Indicators Online, at *publications.worldbank.org/ subscriptions/WDI* (October 19, 2006; subscription required); Central Intelligence Agency, *The World Factbook 2005,* at *www.cia.gov/cia/publications/factbook/index.html* (October 19, 2006); International Monetary Fund, World Economic Outlook database, April 2006, at *www.imf.org/external/pubs/ft/weo/2006/01/data/index.htm* (October 19, 2006); and Tim Kane, Kim R. Holmes, and Mary Anastasia O'Grady, *2007 Index of Economic Freedom* (Washington, D.C.: The Heritage Foundation and Dow Jones & Company, Inc., 2007), at *www.heritage.org/index.*

Index of Economic Freedom World Rankings

2007 Rank	Country	Economic Freedom 2007	Business Freedom	Trade Freedom	Fiscal Freedom	Freedom from Government	Monetary Freedom	Investment Freedom	Financial Freedom	Property Rights	Freedom from Corruption	Labor Freedom
1	Hong Kong	89.29	88.3	80.0	95.3	91.6	91.1	90	90	90	83	93.6
2	Singapore	85.65	94.6	80.0	93.0	86.2	89.5	80	50	90	94	99.3
3	Australia	82.69	91.7	73.8	75.4	70.1	84.8	70	90	90	88	93.1
4	United States	81.98	94.5	76.6	79.4	67.5	83.8	80	80	90	76	92.1
5	New Zealand	81.59	93.7	74.0	74.2	63.6	84.5	70	80	90	96	89.9
6	United Kingdom	81.55	92.1	76.6	74.6	54.2	79.3	90	90	90	86	82.7
7	Ireland	81.31	92.8	76.6	81.1	73.1	85.1	90	90	90	74	60.4
8	Luxembourg	79.31	90.0	76.6	75.4	55.9	80.2	90	80	90	85	70.0
9	Switzerland	79.05	83.3	77.0	78.6	68.6	83.6	70	70	90	91	78.4
10	Canada	78.72	96.1	78.2	83.9	61.8	80.6	60	70	90	84	82.7
11	Chile	78.29	68.9	72.4	85.7	87.6	79.9	70	70	90	73	85.3
12	Estonia	78.13	80.0	76.6	89.7	66.8	83.0	90	90	90	64	51.2
13	Denmark	77.56	95.3	76.6	55.2	32.1	86.8	80	90	90	95	74.7
14	Netherlands	77.08	88.3	76.6	65.8	47.8	87.0	90	80	90	86	59.2
15	Iceland	77.06	94.1	74.0	82.4	50.3	82.9	60	70	90	97	69.9
16	Finland	76.55	95.3	76.6	75.4	39.0	89.7	70	80	90	96	53.4
17	Belgium	74.53	90.8	76.6	62.2	41.2	80.0	90	80	80	74	70.5
18	Japan	73.57	94.3	75.2	80.6	67.2	92.0	60	50	70	73	73.4
19	Germany	73.52	88.2	76.6	74.3	48.0	81.5	90	50	90	82	54.6
20	Cyprus	73.10	70.0	76.6	87.8	54.9	84.7	70	70	90	57	70.0
21	Sweden	72.59	95.0	76.6	53.6	31.5	85.2	80	70	90	92	52.0
22	Lithuania	72.00	86.4	76.6	91.0	76.6	81.2	70	80	50	48	60.1
23	Trinidad and Tobago	71.44	61.8	69.0	88.0	83.7	74.7	70	70	70	38	89.2
24	Bahamas	71.43	80.0	28.8	98.3	89.9	77.3	40	70	80	70	80.0
25	Austria	71.33	79.8	76.6	66.9	40.5	85.7	70	70	90	87	46.8
26	Taiwan	71.12	73.0	76.7	84.7	89.8	81.3	70	50	70	59	56.7
27	Spain	70.87	77.1	76.6	70.1	63.6	78.6	70	80	70	70	52.7
28	Barbados	70.52	90.0	47.0	78.3	64.4	76.5	50	60	90	69	80.0
29	El Salvador	70.31	62.6	66.6	90.9	95.1	76.7	70	70	50	42	79.2
30	Norway	70.09	97.0	79.2	66.1	45.9	82.6	50	50	90	89	51.1
31	Czech Republic	69.68	61.2	76.6	79.9	52.7	86.2	70	80	70	43	77.2
32	Armenia	69.43	84.5	75.6	93.1	91.6	79.7	60	70	30	29	80.9
33	Uruguay	69.33	68.1	71.6	90.8	81.7	73.1	70	30	70	59	79.0
34	Mauritius	68.96	74.5	70.0	87.5	82.0	76.2	70	60	60	42	67.4
35	Georgia	68.70	78.9	61.8	94.2	91.3	77.9	60	70	30	23	99.9

Index of Economic Freedom World Rankings

2007 Rank	Country	Economic Freedom 2007	Business Freedom	Trade Freedom	Fiscal Freedom	Freedom from Government	Monetary Freedom	Investment Freedom	Financial Freedom	Property Rights	Freedom from Corruption	Labor Freedom
36	Korea, South (ROK)	68.65	83.1	64.2	81.0	81.5	79.0	70	50	70	50	57.7
37	Israel	68.42	69.7	75.2	72.0	60.0	84.2	70	50	70	63	70.1
38	Botswana	68.40	66.6	59.6	82.6	54.5	76.8	70	70	70	59	74.9
39	Bahrain	68.40	80.0	69.6	99.6	56.7	80.1	50	90	60	58	40.0
40	Slovakia	68.37	71.1	76.6	93.0	60.8	76.7	70	80	50	43	62.5
41	Latvia	68.21	76.8	76.6	89.3	69.2	74.1	70	70	50	42	64.1
42	Malta	67.80	70.0	76.6	74.0	42.2	79.2	50	70	90	66	60.0
43	Portugal	66.66	79.6	76.6	79.6	49.6	80.2	70	50	70	65	46.0
44	Hungary	66.15	71.2	76.6	79.2	41.8	76.7	70	60	70	50	66.1
45	France	66.11	86.1	76.6	64.2	32.0	81.3	50	60	70	75	65.9
46	Jamaica	66.05	78.3	60.4	83.4	67.4	70.9	80	60	50	36	74.1
47	Panama	65.87	75.1	66.2	88.7	86.8	85.8	70	60	30	35	61.2
48	Malaysia	65.85	68.6	71.8	87.8	79.8	80.0	40	40	50	51	89.5
49	Mexico	65.80	82.1	72.6	88.1	77.2	77.0	50	60	50	35	66.0
50	Thailand	65.56	76.1	69.2	83.2	91.2	77.6	30	50	50	38	90.4
51	Costa Rica	65.12	63.5	72.4	88.6	92.3	67.1	70	40	50	42	65.4
52	South Africa	64.10	70.8	68.8	79.8	79.3	78.8	50	60	50	45	58.5
53	Jordan	64.02	54.8	64.2	88.8	64.1	83.5	50	60	50	57	67.9
54	Oman	63.94	63.6	73.8	99.0	37.7	79.1	50	50	50	63	73.2
55	Namibia	63.76	76.7	79.0	78.6	70.5	78.6	40	60	30	43	81.2
56	Belize	63.71	76.7	57.2	79.8	80.1	73.5	50	50	50	37	82.8
57	Kuwait	63.66	67.9	72.2	99.9	39.2	78.8	50	50	50	47	81.7
58	Slovenia	63.60	74.2	76.6	69.7	56.8	79.0	70	50	50	61	48.7
59	Uganda	63.41	54.1	58.8	87.1	86.7	78.3	50	70	30	25	94.0
60	Italy	63.36	73.7	76.6	68.5	46.4	80.8	70	60	50	50	57.6
61	Nicaragua	62.70	59.7	72.4	86.4	85.6	71.2	70	60	30	26	65.7
62	Bulgaria	62.17	66.9	60.8	91.3	65.6	75.7	60	60	30	40	71.5
63	Peru	62.07	65.1	62.6	86.8	92.2	85.7	50	60	40	35	43.3
64	Swaziland	61.58	71.5	59.0	81.5	73.3	76.3	50	50	50	27	77.2
65	Madagascar	61.43	51.2	72.8	87.2	85.0	70.0	70	50	50	28	50.1
66	Albania	61.38	56.1	63.2	91.5	77.7	80.7	60	70	30	24	60.6
67	Romania	61.26	70.9	74.0	91.7	74.9	69.7	50	60	30	30	61.4
68	Guatemala	61.25	54.1	70.2	86.5	96.4	72.2	50	60	30	25	68.0
69	Tunisia	60.99	78.3	61.8	80.8	82.1	80.0	30	30	50	49	67.9
70	Brazil	60.89	53.3	64.8	88.6	88.8	72.6	50	40	50	37	63.8

Index of Economic Freedom World Rankings

2007 Rank	Country	Economic Freedom 2007	Business Freedom	Trade Freedom	Fiscal Freedom	Freedom from Government	Monetary Freedom	Investment Freedom	Financial Freedom	Property Rights	Freedom from Corruption	Labor Freedom
71	Macedonia	60.84	60.9	73.4	90.0	67.8	91.1	50	60	30	27	58.1
72	Qatar	60.73	60.0	71.4	99.9	54.6	72.4	30	50	50	59	60.0
73	Colombia	60.54	71.4	61.4	82.4	87.0	70.2	50	60	30	40	53.0
74	United Arab Emirates	60.39	49.2	70.0	99.9	60.3	75.3	30	40	40	62	77.2
75	Kazakhstan	60.35	66.5	64.2	87.6	85.9	72.9	30	60	30	26	80.5
76	Honduras	60.32	56.6	69.2	87.8	82.9	71.5	50	70	30	26	59.2
77	Lebanon	60.27	56.2	67.4	95.9	64.3	83.5	30	70	30	31	74.4
78	Mongolia	60.12	73.1	70.0	81.0	56.9	74.3	60	60	30	30	65.9
79	Kyrgyzstan	59.87	61.4	71.4	95.1	76.3	77.1	40	50	30	23	74.4
80	Fiji	59.80	70.4	61.8	86.3	74.3	74.7	30	60	30	40	70.5
81	Moldova	59.47	70.0	74.4	90.4	71.7	68.0	30	50	50	29	61.2
82	Kenya	59.41	58.9	65.0	85.9	83.6	74.4	50	50	40	21	65.2
83	Turkey	59.33	67.4	76.0	79.4	69.9	70.2	50	50	50	35	45.4
84	Sri Lanka	59.30	69.2	66.6	85.7	85.7	69.8	30	40	50	32	63.9
85	Saudi Arabia	59.10	52.9	65.4	99.6	46.1	80.1	30	40	50	34	92.9
86	Senegal	58.79	56.4	61.6	73.9	85.9	82.9	50	50	50	32	45.2
87	Poland	58.77	56.1	76.6	79.1	55.3	80.3	50	50	50	34	56.2
88	Cape Verde	58.41	50.5	31.2	78.0	77.7	84.2	50	50	70	30	62.5
89	Pakistan	58.20	70.9	53.6	82.0	89.3	72.0	50	40	30	21	73.2
90	Guyana	58.16	57.0	57.0	78.5	66.1	74.0	50	60	40	25	74.1
91	Ghana	58.15	54.9	58.0	88.4	72.0	70.0	50	50	50	40	48.2
92	Zambia	57.91	63.6	60.8	80.4	81.9	57.8	50	50	40	26	68.6
93	Gambia	57.65	59.0	54.6	81.4	76.4	67.2	50	60	30	27	70.9
94	Greece	57.65	70.2	76.6	74.5	45.3	78.3	50	40	50	43	48.5
95	Argentina	57.47	65.5	61.4	82.3	89.6	71.3	50	40	30	28	56.6
96	Morocco	57.43	74.3	51.0	75.5	76.3	83.3	70	40	30	32	41.9
97	Philippines	57.35	54.2	74.8	84.0	91.4	73.4	30	50	30	25	60.7
98	Tajikistan	56.91	53.2	66.0	93.2	86.8	67.2	30	40	30	21	81.7
99	Paraguay	56.81	47.0	67.4	97.8	79.8	78.4	50	40	30	21	36.7
100	Dominican Republic	56.75	57.6	63.8	86.5	91.5	63.2	50	40	30	30	54.9
101	Mozambique	56.55	51.5	60.2	85.5	86.2	75.9	50	50	30	28	48.2
102	Cambodia	56.54	37.1	47.2	94.2	85.1	81.1	50	50	30	23	67.7
103	Tanzania	56.40	44.8	63.6	87.1	85.7	74.4	50	50	30	29	49.4
104	India	55.60	49.6	51.2	84.8	89.0	77.2	40	30	50	29	55.1
105	Ivory Coast	55.52	48.1	58.6	66.3	86.2	78.6	40	70	30	19	58.4

Index of Economic Freedom World Rankings

2007 Rank	Country	Economic Freedom 2007	Business Freedom	Trade Freedom	Fiscal Freedom	Freedom from Government	Monetary Freedom	Investment Freedom	Financial Freedom	Property Rights	Freedom from Corruption	Labor Freedom
106	Malawi	55.50	54.4	59.6	80.6	53.3	66.4	50	50	40	28	72.8
107	Azerbaijan	55.36	58.0	67.6	87.2	86.6	76.8	30	30	30	22	65.4
108	Ecuador	55.33	57.1	62.0	85.7	85.2	74.1	30	60	30	25	44.2
109	Croatia	55.32	53.8	77.8	79.9	36.5	79.3	50	60	30	34	52.0
110	Indonesia	55.08	45.7	69.0	85.0	90.7	70.9	30	40	30	22	67.5
111	Guinea	55.06	39.3	54.6	83.3	92.4	57.5	30	60	30	30	73.5
112	Bolivia	54.99	62.3	69.2	93.2	74.3	70.9	30	60	30	25	35.0
113	Burkina Faso	54.96	42.7	57.2	84.9	88.9	76.8	40	50	30	34	45.1
114	Benin	54.79	47.2	54.6	78.5	87.9	82.5	30	60	30	29	48.2
115	Bosnia & Herzegovina	54.70	53.8	70.2	90.0	45.6	81.1	50	60	10	29	57.3
116	Ethiopia	54.44	59.4	53.0	84.8	83.0	69.9	50	20	30	22	72.3
117	Cameroon	54.43	41.0	50.0	79.7	86.5	77.4	50	60	30	22	47.6
118	Lesotho	54.14	68.2	44.4	79.5	53.7	76.7	30	50	40	34	64.9
119	China	54.02	54.9	68.0	77.7	88.6	75.5	30	30	20	32	63.5
120	Russia	54.01	66.6	62.6	86.3	71.6	62.8	30	40	30	24	66.2
121	Nepal	53.95	59.6	51.4	91.0	91.0	77.6	30	30	30	25	54.0
122	Yemen	53.79	52.7	56.4	88.8	65.1	68.2	50	30	30	27	69.7
123	Mali	53.70	37.1	58.6	79.5	84.6	78.4	50	40	30	29	49.7
124	Niger	53.53	38.4	52.4	77.5	89.2	80.7	50	50	30	24	43.1
125	Ukraine	53.35	54.0	72.2	89.1	61.9	68.4	30	50	30	26	51.8
126	Mauritania	53.25	37.5	61.4	83.7	60.4	73.9	60	50	30	30	45.5
127	Egypt	53.21	39.9	52.2	93.6	73.6	69.0	50	30	40	34	49.8
128	Equatorial Guinea	53.20	44.7	47.6	82.1	81.8	79.3	30	60	30	19	57.4
129	Gabon	52.97	52.1	46.4	74.2	71.0	81.3	40	40	40	29	55.7
130	Djibouti	52.63	37.1	26.4	87.0	53.4	79.0	50	60	30	30	73.5
131	Nigeria	52.57	63.1	56.6	89.5	41.7	70.5	30	50	30	19	75.2
132	Uzbekistan	52.57	66.1	68.2	90.0	66.1	58.6	30	20	30	22	74.7
133	Suriname	52.56	42.0	55.0	76.3	65.3	69.1	30	30	50	32	75.9
134	Algeria	52.25	73.7	56.0	82.6	47.9	80.6	50	20	30	28	53.7
135	Haiti	52.25	37.6	74.2	85.3	95.2	62.0	30	40	10	18	70.2
136	Rwanda	52.13	50.8	60.6	82.6	80.3	70.2	30	40	30	21	55.9
137	Central African Rep.	50.27	38.9	44.2	77.1	90.2	76.4	40	40	20	30	45.9
138	Vietnam	49.95	62.0	51.0	82.9	80.8	67.5	30	30	10	26	59.3
139	Togo	49.83	37.5	58.4	69.8	90.6	76.5	30	30	30	30	45.5
140	Laos	49.15	51.0	55.8	80.6	86.3	71.3	30	20	10	33	53.5

Index of Economic Freedom World Rankings

2007 Rank	Country	Economic Freedom 2007	Business Freedom	Trade Freedom	Fiscal Freedom	Freedom from Government	Monetary Freedom	Investment Freedom	Financial Freedom	Property Rights	Freedom from Corruption	Labor Freedom
141	Sierra Leone	48.37	50.5	50.2	82.0	83.8	72.9	30	40	10	24	40.2
142	Syria	48.17	56.6	49.0	88.3	57.5	68.9	30	10	30	34	57.4
143	Bangladesh	47.80	64.3	–	89.4	91.5	68.7	30	20	30	17	67.0
144	Venezuela	47.68	48.8	56.2	83.7	69.5	57.6	20	40	30	23	48.0
145	Belarus	47.36	54.5	62.2	87.9	66.9	61.4	20	10	20	26	64.7
146	Burundi	46.77	40.9	50.6	80.0	60.0	68.1	30	30	30	23	55.2
147	Chad	46.38	25.1	54.2	57.7	81.9	77.7	40	50	20	17	40.2
148	Guinea-Bissau	45.71	27.2	52.8	88.6	59.9	80.7	40	40	20	10	37.9
149	Angola	43.47	33.9	68.0	90.0	38.4	47.7	20	40	20	20	56.7
150	Iran	43.13	54.9	50.4	84.8	59.8	61.3	10	10	10	29	61.2
151	Congo, Republic of	43.00	40.4	44.4	73.2	56.9	77.3	30	30	10	23	44.8
152	Turkmenistan	42.54	30.0	74.2	94.4	82.9	65.9	10	10	10	18	30.0
153	Burma	40.14	20.0	71.8	87.9	88.3	65.4	10	10	10	18	20.0
154	Zimbabwe	35.81	42.9	42.6	79.5	83.9	–	10	20	10	26	43.2
155	Libya	34.48	20.0	29.6	87.8	23.5	78.9	30	20	10	25	20.0
156	Cuba	29.68	10.0	60.2	62.8	10.0	65.8	10	10	10	38	20.0
157	Korea, North (DPRK)	3.00	–	–	–	–	–	10	–	10	10	–

Source: Tim Kane, Kim R. Holmes, and Mary Anastasia O'Grady, *2007 Index of Economic Freedom* (Washington, D.C.: The Heritage Foundation and Dow Jones & Company, Inc., 2007), at *www.heritage.org/index*.

Chapter 1

Global Inequality Fades as the Global Economy Grows

Xavier Sala-i-Martin

In this "age of globalization," countless studies offer conflicting conclusions about overall poverty rates and income inequality worldwide. All observers agree that the rapid integration of international economies is one of the dominant experiences of the post–Cold War world.

Many critics have assailed globalization as a form of extreme capitalism that is leaving the world's poor behind. At a conference in the fall of 2001, for example, Noam Chomsky declared that "Inequality is soaring through the globalization period—within countries and across countries."[1] To substantiate their claims, however, such anti-globalization activists rely on the United Nations Development Programme's Human Development Report *for 1999, which claims that:*

> *Gaps in income between the poorest and richest countries have continued to widen. In 1960, the 20% of the world's*

people in the richest countries had 30 times the income of the poorest 20%— in 1997, 74 times as much.[2]

How could it be true that globalization has helped rather than hurt the world's poor?

Xavier Sala-i-Martin, a professor of economics at Columbia University, is a renowned expert on economic growth who in recent years has published authoritative research on global incomes. Here, in his own words, he reviews the latest evidence. He notes that the confusion about growing global inequality among individuals is based on a logical misunderstanding. Comparing countries and comparing individuals within those countries is akin to the classic problem of mixing apples and oranges. The correct analysis is to integrate apples and apple trees, and that is what Professor Sala-i-Martin does with powerful lessons for all of us.

— The Editors

---

1   Virginia Postrel, "The Rich Get Rich and Poor Get Poorer. Right? Let's Take Another Look," *The New York Times*, August 15, 2002.

2   United Nations Development Programme, *Human Development Report 1999*, at *http://hdr.undp. org/reports/global/1999/en/*.

Looking at the planet as a whole, never in history has poverty been eradicated so rapidly as it has been during our lifetimes. Moreover, individual income inequalities have been falling, and this is the first time they have fallen since the eve of the Industrial Revolution. The aggregate numbers have never looked better. Looking at the world distribution of income (WDI), the world is a better place.

Poverty and inequality are, of course, difficult to measure because of the arduousness of collecting data, the ambiguity of the definition of poverty, and debate concerning the proper unit of measures of both poverty and inequality. However, the mounting empirical evidence points to significant improvements in these two dimensions over the past two to three decades.

Although this is certainly good news, the analysis presented in this discussion also shows that, alongside these positive global trends, the continued deterioration of the economic situation of African countries is pushing up our measures of poverty rates and head counts in that continent. The positive economic income growth experienced by billions of Asian citizens, along with the negative growth experienced by the majority of Africans, has turned poverty, which used to be an essentially Asian phenomenon, into an essentially African problem.

MEASURING POVERTY

The empirical literature on cross-country convergence shows that the dispersion of incomes per capita across countries tends to increase over time, a phenomenon that Robert Barro and I have called σ-divergence.[3] Countries are useful units if we want to test growth theories because many of the policies or institutions considered by the theories are country-wide.

If we are interested in whether poor people's standards of living improve more rapidly than rich people's, however, then the correct unit is a person rather than a country: The evolution of China's per capita income is more important than the evolution of Lesotho's because China has a lot more people. In fact, China has almost twice as many citizens as all African countries combined, even though Africa has around 35 independent states. There is no reason to downweight the well-being of a Chinese peasant relative to a Senegalese farmer just because China's population is larger than Senegal's. The country analysis of the traditional convergence literature does not help to answer such questions as how many people in the world live in poverty, how poverty rates have changed over the past few decades, or whether inequalities across citizens are growing over time.

A better measure of the evolution of personal inequality is the population-weighted variance of the log of income per capita, as opposed to the simple variance of the log of income per capita, which gives the same weight to all countries regardless of population. The striking result is that the weighted variance does *not* increase monotonically over time. As shown by T. Paul Schultz and by Steve Dowrick and Muhammad Akmal,[4] the weighted variance increases for most of the 1960s and 1970s but peaks in 1978. After that, the weighted variance declines, and this is rooted in the fact that China, with 20 percent of the world's population, has experienced large increases in per capita income. This effect was reinforced in the 1990s when India, with another 1 billion inhabitants, started its process of rapid growth.

Using population-weighted distributions of per capita income (from national accounts) is a step in the right direction, but it is not sufficient to provide accurate estimates of concepts like poverty rates or indexes of income inequality. These measures still miss within-country dispersion, a factor that needs to be included if sensible estimates of the WDI are to be constructed.

---

3   Robert J. Barro and Xavier Sala-i-Martin, "Convergence," *Journal of Political Economy*, Vol. 100, No. 2 (April 1992), pp. 223–251.

4   T. Paul Schultz, "Inequality and the Distribution of Personal Income in the World: How It Is Changing and Why," *Journal of Population Economics*, Vol. 11, No. 3 (1998), pp. 307–344; Steve Dowrick and Muhammad Akmal, "Contradictory Trends in Global Income Inequality: A Tale of Two Biases," mimeographed, Australian National University, March 2003.

By using population weights, researchers recognize that different countries have different population sizes, but this alone is insufficient because it still implicitly assumes that all citizens of a country have the same level of income. This can yield misleading results. If the per capita income in a country were a couple of dollars above the poverty line, for example, researchers would conclude that no poor citizens lived in that country. Similarly, they would tend to find dramatic declines in poverty rates as the income per capita of very populated countries grew from a few dollars below to a few dollars above the poverty line. Additionally, in terms of inequality, population-weighted indexes of inequality could show a decline in overall global inequality, while the true individual inequalities could be rising if within-country inequalities increased sufficiently.

Incorporating information about within-country income dispersion is problematic, however, because such information is not readily available—but there is hope. Klaus Deininger and Lyn Squire, for example, collected data from a large number of microeconomic surveys conducted in a variety of countries over a period of 30 years,[5] and the United Nations University's World Institute for Development Research (UNU-WIDER) keeps an update of this collection. Although these surveys contain a large amount of information about the distribution of income (or expenditure) within many countries, however, they are still incomplete. Surveys do not exist for a number of economies, and for the countries for which surveys do exist, many years are missing. Nevertheless, this information can and should be used to complement the population-weighted national accounts and to construct estimates of the WDI.

MEASURING THE WORLD DISTRIBUTION OF INCOME

I construct a WDI by estimating an annual income distribution for each of 138 countries and then integrating these country distributions for all levels of income.[6] The starting point of the analysis is the population-weighted income per capita, which we will use as the mean of each country's distribution. As a measure of income, I use the purchasing power parity–adjusted GDP per capita from the Penn World Tables.[7] One could anchor the country distributions to other measures of average income, such as the mean income from surveys. I choose not to do so for a variety of reasons, including (but not limited to) the lack of survey data for many countries and time periods. Since surveys are not available every year, if one used the mean income of those surveys to anchor the mean of the distribution, then one would have to "forecast" the means for missing years. National accounts data, on the other hand, are reported by the Penn World Tables for all countries during our sample period.

The mean of the distribution can be complemented by adding within-country information on income distribution contained in microeconomic income surveys reported by Deininger and Squire[8] and extended with UNU-WIDER compilation. Non-parametric kernel density analysis is used to determine annual income distribution data for the various countries.

Once a distribution of income has been estimated for each country/year, I construct an annual world distribution of income by integrating all of the country distributions.[9] Charts 1 and 2 report the estimates of the density function for some of the largest countries as well as WDI for 1970 and 2000, respectively. For convenience, the charts also include a vertical line representing the equivalent annual income of $1 per day, a widely used measure of poverty that will be discussed below.

5 Klaus Deininger and Lyn Squire, "A New Data Set Measuring Income Inequality," World Bank Economic Review, Vol. 10 (1996), pp. 565–591.

6 Xavier Sala-i-Martin, "The World Distribution of Income: Falling Poverty and…Convergence, Period," Quarterly Journal of Economics, Vol. 121, No. 2 (May 2006), pp. 351–397.
7 Allan Heston, Robert Summers, and Bettina Aten, Penn World Table Version 6.1, Center for International Comparisons at the University of Pennsylvania, December 2002.
8 Deininger and Squire, "A New Data Set Measuring Income Inequality."
9 Sala-i-Martin, "The World Distribution of Income."

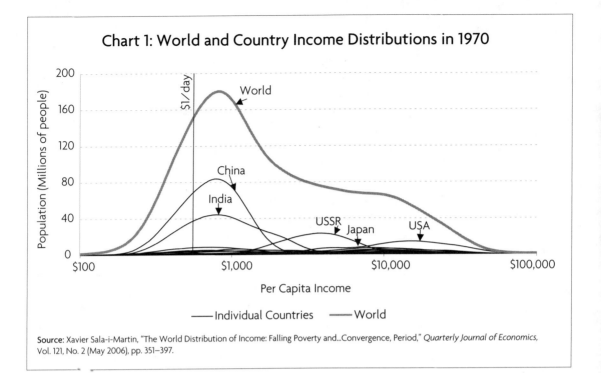

Chart 1: World and Country Income Distributions in 1970

Per Capita Income

—— Individual Countries ——— World

Source: Xavier Sala-i-Martin, "The World Distribution of Income: Falling Poverty and...Convergence, Period," *Quarterly Journal of Economics*, Vol. 121, No. 2 (May 2006), pp. 351–397.

An interesting aspect of the charts is that one can visually appreciate that a substantial part of individual income inequality across the world comes from differences in per capita incomes across countries rather than differences within countries. In other words, the distance between country distributions (say, the difference between the mean of the United States and China) seems to be much larger than the differences between rich and poor Americans or rich and poor Chinese.

A quick comparison of Chart 1 and Chart 2 reveals the following features. First, the WDI has shifted to the right. This, of course, reflects the fact that per capita GDP is much larger in 2000 than in 1970. Second, it is not visually evident whether the WDI is more dispersed in 1970 than in 2000. Third, if we analyze the reasons for the WDI's change in shape, we observe that a major change occurs in China, whose distribution both shifts dramatically to the right (China is getting richer) and increases in dispersion (China is becoming more unequal).

To see the evolution of the WDI over time, Chart 3 plots together the global distributions (without individual country functions) for 1970, 1980, 1990, and 2000. It is now apparent that the distribution shifts rightward, implying

that the incomes of the majority of the world's citizens increased over time. It is also clear that the fraction of the overall area that lies to the left of the poverty line declines, which indicates a reduction in poverty rates, and that the absolute area to the left of the poverty line also diminishes, which indicates an overall reduction in the number of poor citizens in the world. Again, the chart does not show clearly whether world income inequality increased or decreased, so precise measures of income inequality will have to be used if we want to discuss the evolution of inequality over the last three decades.

DEFINING POVERTY

Once we have a good estimate of the WDI, we can use it to estimate poverty rates and head counts. The first problem we encounter, however, is defining what we mean by poverty. For a long time, analysts identified poverty with the lack of physical means for survival. Thus, some attempted to define poverty in terms of a minimum required caloric intake. Other analysts define poverty in monetary terms: Poor people are those whose income (or consumption) is less than a specified amount. Some attempts have been made to reconcile the two

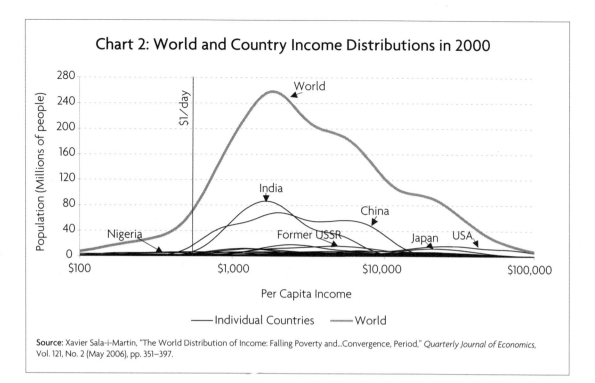

Chart 2: World and Country Income Distributions in 2000

Source: Xavier Sala-i-Martin, "The World Distribution of Income: Falling Poverty and...Convergence, Period," *Quarterly Journal of Economics*, Vol. 121, No. 2 (May 2006), pp. 351–397.

definitions by putting a monetary value on the minimum caloric intake.

Even if we agree that poverty should be defined in monetary terms, however, we would define a poverty threshold. In other words, at what level of income (or consumption) do we say that a person is poor? For example, the poverty line used by the United Nations when it first proposed the Millennium Goals was $1 a day. The World Bank uses both $1-a-day and $2-a-day lines. Surjit Bhalla settles in the middle and prefers $1.50 per day.[10] Lant Pritchett is more extreme and argues that the poverty line should be put at $15 per day.[11]

An additional problem concerns the "baseline year." If we are to compare poverty rates over time, we need to specify a particular poverty line in constant prices—but with which baseline? The lack of precision as to what baseline year a particular definition applies has enormous implications for estimates of pov-

erty rates and head counts and their evolution over time; the difference between the number of people who live with less than $340 and the number who live with less than $495 is in the hundreds of millions.

The fundamental problem is that the answers to all these questions deliver many possible definitions. All of them are reasonable and, to some extent, arbitrary. If we settle on a poverty line, then the number of poor people in the world can be readily estimated by integrating the estimated WDI from minus infinity to a predetermined income threshold, known as the poverty line. Poverty rates can then be computed by dividing the total number of poor by the overall population.

POVERTY ESTIMATES

Since, as explained above, there is no agreement on the level of income below which people are poor, we use four different lines. The first is the most widely publicized poverty line: the World Bank's $1-a-day line. Since the World Bank's original poverty line was expressed in 1985 prices, and given that our baseline year is 1996, the corresponding annual income in our analysis is $495.

The survey data used to construct our WDI

---

10   Surjit S. Bhalla, *Imagine There Is No Country* (Washington, D.C.: Institute for International Economics, 2002).
11   Lant Pritchett, "One World, One World Bank, One Poverty Line: Proposing A New Standard for Poverty Reduction," mimeographed, Center for Global Development, 2003.

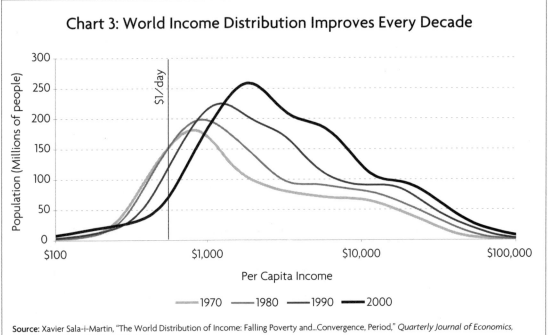

Chart 3: World Income Distribution Improves Every Decade

Source: Xavier Sala-i-Martin, "The World Distribution of Income: Falling Poverty and...Convergence, Period," *Quarterly Journal of Economics,* Vol. 121, No. 2 (May 2006), pp. 351–397.

are said to include systematic errors. In particular, it is believed that the rich tend to underreport their income relatively more than the poor do. If this is the case, then reanchoring the survey mean to the national accounts mean, as we do here, biases poverty estimates downwards, although it is not clear whether there are biases in the trend. Bhalla argues that this bias is best corrected not by using survey means, as done by the World Bank, but by adjusting the poverty line by roughly 15 percent.[12] If we increase the $495 poverty line by 15 percent, we get an annual income of $570.

We finally report two additional poverty lines: an annual income of $730 (roughly $2 a day in 1996 prices) and $1,140 per year (which is twice $570; since $570 was labeled the $1.50-a-day line, we call this the $3-a-day line).

Using the original World Bank definition ($495 annual income), the poverty rate declined from 15.4 percent of the world population in 1970 to 5.7 percent in 2000, a decline of a factor of almost three. This is especially impressive given that, during the same period, world population increased by almost 50 percent, from 3.5

billion to 5.5 billion. The implication is that the total number of poor citizens went from 534 million to 322 million, a decline of 50 percent. It is interesting to note that the total number of people whose income is less than $1 a day is nowhere near the widely cited number of 1.2 billion. Our estimates of $1 a day are between 33 percent and 40 percent lower.

Using the $1.50-a-day line, we see a similar picture. The poverty rate fell from 20 percent to 7 percent, a decline of a factor close to 3. The poverty head count declined by about 300 million people, from 700 million to a little less than 400 million. In other words, the total number of poor people declined by about 56 percent in a period during which world population increased by 50 percent.

With the $2-a-day definition ($730 a year), the poverty rate was close to 30 percent in 1970 and a little below 11 percent in 2000. Again, the poverty rate declined by a factor close to 3. The number of people whose income was less than $2 a day was just above 1 billion in 1970 and about 600 million in 2000, a decline of 400 million, or 54 percent.

Finally, using the $3-a-day definition ($1,140 a year), the poverty rate was 47 percent in

---

12   Bhalla, *Imagine There Is No Country.*

1970 and 21 percent in 2000—again, a healthy decline over the past 30 years. The overall poverty head count declined by more than 400 million people, from 1.6 billion in 1970 to 1.2 billion in 2000.

REGIONAL TRENDS IN POVERTY RATES

Despite the overall decline of global poverty rates, regional trends vary. With over 1.7 billion people in 2000, East Asia is the world's most populous region, accounting for 30 percent of world population. Poverty rates in East Asia were close to one-third in 1970. By 2000, poverty rates had declined to a little less than 2.4 percent. In other words, poverty rates in East Asia were cut by a factor of 10. The poverty head count was reduced by over 300 million, from 350 million in 1970 to 41 million in 2000. In 1970, 54 percent of the world's poor lived in East Asia; by 2000, this fraction had fallen to only 9.4 percent.

The exact growth of income per capita in China is a key determinant of the reduction of worldwide poverty, given its large size and the remarkable rate at which it has reduced poverty. Using only survey data, the World Bank estimates that $1-a-day consumption poverty in China fell from 53 percent in 1980 to 8 percent in 2000.[13]

Although China is an important part of this success story with a decline in the poverty rate from 32 percent in 1970 to 3.1 percent in 2000, which accounts for 251 million people escaping poverty, it is by no means the whole story. Indonesia's poverty rate declined from 35 percent in 1970 to 0.1 percent in 2000. Thailand, with a poverty rate over 23 percent in 1970, had practically eliminated poverty by 2000. In fact, with one exception, all of the countries in this region experienced reduction in poverty rates; the only country in which the poverty head count increased was Papua New Guinea.

South Asia is the second most populous region in the world, with 1.3 billion people in 2000, or 24 percent of the world's popula-

tion. The evolution of poverty in South Asia is similar to that in East Asia; the poverty rate fell from 30 percent in 1970 to 2.5 percent in 2000. Most of the decline in the poverty head count can be attributed to the success of the post-1980 Indian economy; between 1970 and 1980, the total number of poor Indians actually increased by 15 million. This is not to say that the other countries in the region did not improve. With the exception of Nepal, all of the other countries also experienced a positive evolution of overall poverty.

The great Asian success contrasts dramatically with the African tragedy. With a total population of just over 608 million, sub-Saharan Africa is the third most populated region in our data set. In all, 41 countries are analyzed. Most of them had such dismal growth performances that poverty increased throughout the continent. Overall, poverty rates in 1970 were similar to those in South Asia and East Asia at 35 percent. By 2000, poverty rates in Africa had reached close to 50 percent, while those in Asia had declined to less than 3 percent. The three decades have been almost equally terrible; the poverty rate increased from 35.1 percent to 37.2 percent in the 1970s, 43.7 percent in 1990, and 48.8 percent in 2000. Within Africa, poverty head counts increased in all countries with the exception of Botswana, the Republic of Congo, and the islands of Mauritius, Cape Verde, and the Seychelles.

This disappointing performance, together with the great success of the other two poor regions of the world (East Asia and South Asia) means that the majority of the world's poor now live in Africa. Indeed, Africa accounted for only 14.5 percent of the world's poor in 1970. Today, despite the fact that Africa accounts for only 10 percent of the world's population, it accounts for 67.8 percent of the world's poor. As noted, poverty, once an essentially Asian phenomenon, has become an essentially African phenomenon.

With close to 500 million people—about 9 percent of the world's population—Latin America has had a mixed performance over the past three decades. Poverty rates were cut by more than one-half between 1970 (poverty

---

13 Shaoua Chen and Martin Ravallion, "How Did the World's Poorest Fare Since the Early 1980s?" World Bank *Research Observer*, Vol. 19, No. 2 (2004), pp. 141–170.

rate of 10.3 percent) and 2000 (poverty rate of 4.2 percent). This would be an optimistic picture were it not for the fact that all of the gains occurred during the first decade. Little progress has been achieved since then. Indeed, the poverty rate in Latin America grew from 3 percent in 1980 to 4.1 percent in 1990. This mixed performance has meant that, although Latin America started from a superior position relative to both East Asia and South Asia, where poverty rates were well above 30 percent in 1970, we see that poverty rates were larger in Latin America than in both Asian regions by 2000. The fraction of the world's poor that live in Latin America declined from 4.3 percent in 1970 to 1.7 percent in 1980. It then increased to 3.7 percent in 1990 and 4.8 percent by 2000.

Our sample of Middle Eastern and North African (MENA) countries has 220 million people, or 7.7 percent of the world's sampled population in 2000. Poverty rates in MENA countries have declined over the past three decades. Although the starting point was better than those for East Asia, South Asia, and sub-Saharan Africa, MENA has nevertheless managed to reduce those rates even further.

Our final region is Eastern Europe and Central Asia, which includes the USSR and (after 1990) the former Soviet Republics. About 436 million people inhabited this region in 2000. A lot has been written about the deterioration of living conditions in this region after the fall of Communism. The fact, however, is that, although poverty has increased since 1990, the level of income in this region was so high to begin with that poverty rates were a lot smaller than they were in any of the regions analyzed up until now. The rate, which was at the already low level of 1.3 percent in 1970, had declined to 0.4 percent by 1980. It did not change at all during the 1980s and then more than doubled during the decade that followed the fall of Communism. The increase in poverty was the result of both a decline in per capita income and an increase in inequality within countries, but the starting level was so small in magnitude that, despite its doubling, the rate remained at 0.1 percent in 2000.

CONVERGENCE, PERIOD!

Researchers have long worried about world income inequality. Recently, policymakers have joined the debate. For example, in its 2001 *Human Development Report*, the United Nations Development Programme (UNDP) argues that global income inequality has risen based on the following logic:[14]

- Claim 1: "Income inequalities within countries have increased."
- Claim 2: "Income inequalities across countries have increased."
- Conclusion: "Global income inequalities have also increased."

To document Claim 1, analysts collect the Gini coefficients, which measure inequality, for a number of countries. They notice that the Gini "increased in 45 countries and fell in 16." To document the second claim, analysts go to the convergence/divergence literature and show that the Gini coefficient of per capita GDP across countries has been increasing unambiguously over the past 30 years. This increasing difference in per capita income across countries is a well-known phenomenon that empirical growth economists call "absolute divergence."

Although it is true that within-country inequalities are increasing on average, and although it is also true that income per capita across countries has been diverging, the conclusion that global income inequality has risen does not follow logically from these premises. The reason is that Claim 1 refers to the income of "individuals" and Claim 2 refers to per capita incomes of "countries." By adding two different concepts of inequality to analyze the evolution of world income inequality, the UNDP falls into the fallacy of comparing apples to oranges.

The argument would be correct if the concept of inequality implicit in Claim 2 was not the level of income inequality across *countries* but, instead, the inequality across *individuals* that would exist in the world if all citizens in

---

14   United Nations Development Programme, *Human Development Report 2001*, at *http://hdr.undp.org/reports/global/2001/en/*.

each country had the same level of income but different countries had different levels of per capita income. The difference is that the correct statement would recognize that there are four Chinese citizens for every American so that the income per capita of China is assigned four times the weight. In other words, instead of using a measure of inequality in which each country's income per capita is one data point, the correct measure would weight by the size of the country. The problem for the UNDP is that population-weighted measures of income inequality show a downward trend over the past 20 years. The question, then, is whether the decline in across-country individual inequality, correctly weighted by population, more than offsets the population-weighted average increase in within-country individual inequality.

Since we have estimated the WDI, we are well equipped to answer this question. Our analysis shows that, after having stagnated during the 1970s, global income inequality started a two-decades-long process of decline. This change in trend is surprising because, according to François Bourguignon and Christian Morrison, world income inequality had increased continuously over the preceding century and a half.[15] What caused this reversal? The answer is the growth rate of some of the largest yet poorest countries: China, India, and the rest of Asia. We could say that in 1820, the whole world was poor. Slowly, the incomes of the 1 billion people (in population size in 2000) in what is today the Organisation for Economic Co-operation and Development (OECD) grew and diverged away from the incomes of the 5 billion people in the developing world. The dramatic growth rates of China, India, and the rest of Asia from the 1970s meant that the incomes of 3 billion to 4 billion people started to converge with those of the OECD. This reduced worldwide income inequality for the first time in centuries because it more than offset the divergent incomes of 608 million Africans.

In sum, the correct decomposition of inequality into "within-country" and "across-country" components reflects that within-country inequality increased over the sample period, as suggested by the UNDP reports. However, the decline in the correct measure of across-country inequality more than offset the first effect and delivered an overall reduction in global income inequality.

In 1997, Lant Pritchett famously described the evolution of income per capita across countries with the expression "divergence, big time."[16] Using a similarly spirited expression, we could say that our analysis shows that, if rather than considering GDP per capita across countries we analyze the incomes of individual citizens, the past two decades have witnessed an unambiguous process of "convergence, period!"

IS IT ALL ABOUT CHINA?

Critics have argued that the above results are all driven by China. They argue that when China is excluded from the analysis, worldwide individual income inequalities increase. This is true: They increase by 4.4 percent. However, eliminating 22 percent of the data points (that is, excluding 1.58 billion citizens out of 5.66 billion) in any empirical analysis can overturn *any* result. Moreover, this is not an exception: If we exclude the incomes of 22 percent of the citizens that have converged, the remaining incomes have obviously diverged.

We should not conclude, however, that all of our results are driven solely by China. They are driven by China—and all of the other people of the world. For example, if we exclude the United States (5 percent of the data points) from the analysis, the tendency for incomes to converge is reinforced. If we instead exclude the people of Africa (Africa has a total of 41 countries but, with 608 million people, only half as many people as China and thus accounts for 11 percent of the data points), the decline in inequality is also reinforced. Finally, if we exclude

15   François Bourguignon and Christian Morrison, "Inequality Among World Citizens: 1820–1992," *American Economic Review*, Vol. 92, No. 4 (2002), pp. 727–744.

16   Lant Pritchett, "Divergence, Big Time," *Journal of Economic Perspectives*, Vol. 11, No. 3 (Summer 1997), pp. 3–17.

TABLE I: Poverty Rates and Headcounts for Various Poverty Lines

Poverty Rates

Poverty Line Definition	1970	1975	1980	1985	1990	1995	2000	Change, 1970–2000
$495 ($1/day)*	15.4%	14.0%	11.9%	8.8%	7.3%	6.2%	5.7%	-0.01
$570 ($1.5/day)	20.2%	18.5%	15.9%	12.1%	10.0%	8.0%	7.0%	-0.13
$730 ($2/day)	29.6%	27.5%	24.2%	19.3%	16.2%	12.6%	10.6%	-0.19
$1,140 ($3/day)	46.6%	44.2%	40.3%	34.7%	30.7%	25.0%	21.1%	-0.25

Poverty Headcounts (thousands of people)

	1970	1975	1980	1985	1990	1995	2000	Change, 1970–2000
World Population	3,472,485	3,830,514	4,175,420	4,539,477	4,938,177	5,305,563	5,660,343	2,187,858
Poverty Line Definition								
$495 ($1/day)*	533,861	536,379	498,032	399,527	362,902	327,943	321,518	-212,343
$570 ($1.5/day)	699,896	708,825	665,781	548,533	495,221	424,627	398,403	-301,493
$730 ($2/day)	1,028,532	1,052,761	1,008,789	874,115	798,945	671,069	600,275	-428,257
$1,140 ($3/day)	1,616,772	1,691,184	1,681,712	1,575,415	1,517,778	1,327,635	1,197,080	-419,691

* World Bank poverty line.

Source: Xavier Sala-i-Martin, "The World Distribution of Income: Falling Poverty and...Convergence, Period," *Quarterly Journal of Economics*, Vol. 121, No. 2 (May 2006), pp. 351–397.

China, the United States, and Africa (which overall account for 2.1 billion people or 38 percent of the data points), the Gini coefficient still declines by 1.32 percent. In other words, if we exclude the "main convergers" (namely China) and the "main divergers" (Africa and the United States), we still reach the conclusion that world income inequality has decreased over the past three decades.

The problem, therefore, is that unless the incomes of these African citizens begin to grow, and grow rapidly, world income inequality will start to rise again in a few years' time.

THE WORLD IS A BETTER PLACE

The estimates of a WDI for the 1970–2000 period result in a number of interesting lessons.

First, global poverty rates, defined as the fraction of the WDI below a certain poverty line, declined significantly over the past three decades. We have documented this claim for the four most widely used poverty thresholds.

Poverty rates were cut by a factor of almost three, according to all four poverty lines, and the total decline in poverty head counts was between 212 million and 428 million people. We have shown that this is also true for all conceivable poverty lines. (See Table 1.)

Second, the spectacular reduction of worldwide poverty hides the uneven performance of various regions in the world. East and South Asia account for a large fraction of this success. Africa, on the other hand, seems to have moved in the opposite direction.

Third, after remaining constant during the 1970s, inequality declined substantially during the past two decades. The main reason is that incomes of some of the world's poorest and most populated countries (most notably China and India, but also many other countries in Asia) converged rapidly with the incomes of OECD citizens. This force has been larger than the divergence effect caused by the dismal performance of African countries.

Fourth, the decomposition of inequality into

"within-country" and "across-country" components reflects that within-country inequality increased over the sample period. However, the decline in across-country inequality more than offset the first effect and delivered an overall reduction in global income inequality.

In 2000, the United Nations established the Millennium Development Goals. Kofi Annan challenged national leaders around the world to adopt the target "of halving the proportion of people living in extreme poverty, and so lifting more than 1 billion people out of it, by 2015."[17] Table I shows that the $1.50 per day poverty rate in 1990 was 10 percent. The Millennium Development Goals will be achieved, therefore, when poverty rates are 5 percent, and we have seen that the poverty rate in 2000 was 7 percent. Thus, when the goal was established in 2000, the world was already 60 percent of the way toward achieving it. The world might just be in better shape than many of our leaders believe.

_____

17 See United Nations Web site at *www.un.org/ millennium/sg/report/ch2.pdf.*

Chapter 2

The Urgent Need for Labor Freedom in Europe— and the World

Johnny Munkhammar

For several weeks during the autumn of 2005, riots raged in the streets of Paris. Every night, hundreds of cars were burned, shops were vandalized, and violence ruled. French President Jacques Chirac concluded that his nation was suffering from a profound "malaise," a word that indeed captures the reality of economic and social problems in many European countries. After centuries of economic leadership, Europe must now face the truth that its governing institutions—especially its labor markets—are deeply flawed. Those who finally took to the streets, native and immigrant citizens alike, were severely affected by unemployment.

France may be the most stubborn defender of the so-called European social model, characterized by vast government intervention in the economy, but many other governments in Western Europe are committed to the same philosophy. Presidents and prime ministers devote speeches to nostalgic messages and promise to maintain and protect the existing social model.

Their rhetoric translates into policies that are a new kind of protectionism for traditional jobs, a protectionism that is reflected in the widespread official resistance to a single European Union (EU) market in services, disapprovals of business mergers, and an anxious debate about the "Polish plumber" representing free flows of labor within the EU.

We Europeans are clearly at a crossroads. Either we look to the future and learn from successful market-oriented reforms, or we look back to the past and continue trying to shield old occupations from international economics. It is a choice between openness and protectionism, between modernization and nostalgia—indeed, between government intervention and freedom itself. The problems of Europe are not born overseas, but are innate to the process of internal economic development and change. That is why a tighter adherence to a failing model will only exacerbate current problems and lead to more unrest in European cities. Rioting and decline is a destiny that no European wants to face.

Yet there is reason for optimism. Never before have so many countries been so deeply involved in the global economy, and the benefits of globalization—economic growth, employment, and competition—are ever clearer. Never before have so many countries made successful free-market reforms, which is an inspiration for others. Almost all European countries can point to at least one successful reform, and as we copy each other's successes, the future should rapidly become much brighter.

In my view, of all the areas that are still in need of substantial reform, the most important is the labor market. People—especially the young—want jobs and freedom, not dependence on government.

THE LABOR MARKET AND OTHER MARKETS: A FUNDAMENTAL DIFFERENCE?

Critics have difficulty seeing labor as a market like other markets. In the public debate, it is often assumed that there is a fundamental difference between the labor market and other markets. "Bananas can be traded freely in the market," the argument goes, "but people are not bananas. In the labor market, we need government intervention." Even assuming there is a difference, however, one might ask: Should bananas have more freedom than workers? Is the market for labor truly unique in the way that critics suggest?

My answer is no. The free market is a superior institution for labor, yielding the best results for society and workers, just as the free market has proven superior for virtually all other fields. Furthermore, government intervention produces the same problems in the labor market that it produces in any other market. Finally, in a globalized world, a free labor market is increasingly important as a way to make workers more competitive and, ultimately, better compensated.

The addition of the new labor freedom factor to the 2007 *Index of Economic Freedom* is thus highly relevant. The elements that comprise this new category encompass several common restrictions on freedom that produce consequences for the labor market. Freedom is just as essential in the labor market as it is in any other market; indeed, it is fundamental to the concept of economic freedom.

MARKET PRINCIPLES AND DEREGULATION

The core principle of a market is free, voluntary exchange. That principle has several components: free choice, free pricing, and free competition. Today, in scholarly research or policy debates, it is generally accepted that the free market leads to constant improvements. A thousand consumer goods compared over time reveal the relentless impact of competitive pressure for innovation, price reduction, and consumer prosperity. Consider the DVD disc technology now sweeping away the VHS tape, which itself was an innovation two decades ago.

A more profound lesson is that whole societies are similarly superior to others, at least in purely economic terms. A comparison between the free economies in Europe versus the centrally planned economies reveals much. A BMW is better than a Trabant, the poorly manufactured, expensive, and polluting cars made in the former East Germany.

Innovators and entrepreneurs compete to satisfy consumers. Free exchange is good in a town, better in a country, and best in every country: more minds, more ideas, more people that want to create something new. The globalized economy has enlarged markets and increased specialization. Competition means lower consumer prices, a broader supply, and better quality. Improvements in everyday life on a global scale constantly confirm the textbook theories.

The free market unleashes creativity and change. It has been estimated that three-quarters of all products today did not exist in any form 100 years ago.[1] Joseph Schumpeter's point about destruction of the old being a nec-

---

1   William D. Nordhaus, "Do Real-Output and Real-Wage Measures Capture Reality? The History of Lighting Suggests Not," in Timothy F. Bresnahan and Robert J. Gordon, eds., *The Economics of New Goods* (Chicago: University of Chicago Press, 1997).

essary condition for creation of the new is both relevant and visible in society.[2] Some 150 years ago in Western Europe, three-quarters of the population was employed in agriculture versus about 3 percent today, and today's farmers produce more total output. Innovation in economic efficiency is therefore interwoven with the changing composition of the labor force.

LABOR MARKET INTERVENTION IN THEORY

As the types of work and jobs changed during the Industrial Revolution, governments required better general treatment of workers. A minimum wage became common, as did other regulations mandating that businesses limit the number of hours each worker could contribute per week. As prosperity advanced, so did the multitude and variety of labor regulations.

Government interventions in the labor market are not limited to wages or hours; they also affect hiring and firing practices, workplace rules, safety, and even the kind of language allowed. In various ways, the interventions also decide how, with what, where, and when people work. Government also affects pricing through taxation and trade union privileges, notably collective bargaining. Finally, governments often mandate social insurance systems, such as pensions. Unlike many other government programs, regulatory structures normally impose costs that are invisible to the public simply because they do not show up on government budgets.

Why do governments intervene in labor markets? Three possible explanations are commonly cited: (a) to make the labor market more efficient, implying greater per capita incomes; (b) to gain political power; or (c) as a natural consequence of different legal systems. A 2004 Harvard study of 85 countries empirically tested the three theories and found no support for the efficiency theory. On the contrary, the researchers showed that heavy regulations in the labor market produced adverse consequences for employment. But they did find significant support for the other explanations: a clear connection between higher regulation and leftist governments and substantial evidence that legal origin countries have more labor market regulations than common law countries.[3]

Countries with more left-leaning governments tend to enact stricter labor regulations, which yield adverse efficiency results. The main reason behind most of the interventions, however, is a perception of reality: the fear of a "race to the bottom." In other words, preventing "social dumping" motivates intervention. Skeptics have long warned that wages and other working conditions will decline in a pure free market. This skepticism has roots in the Marxist notion of capitalism, which retains its appeal even though economic history has hardly been kind to the theory in practice.

In Western Europe, on average, wages are roughly 10 times higher today than they were a hundred years ago because our productivity today is that much higher. We produce, per person, 10 times more value, which is why we get more pay. If we had not increased productivity, no regulations or trade unions in the world could have created such tenfold wage increases. Moreover, if wages in a free market are set below productivity, a competitor will benefit from offering the employees a higher wage. Thus, "social dumping" is largely a myth. Those who argue that labor protections are essential for a higher quality of life should ponder this point, as well as the material misery of countries that embrace such policies.

Why else would the world's highest wages be found in the United States, where the labor market is relatively free and only some 10 percent of the labor force are members of trade unions?[4] Why else would multinational companies voluntarily pay workers in, for example, China 30 percent higher wages on average than old, state-owned, industries do? And why did the average

2   Joseph Schumpeter, *Capitalism, Socialism and Democracy* (New York: Harper, 1975).

3   Juan C. Botero, Simeon Djankov, Rafael La Porta, Florencio Lopez De Silanes, and Andrei Schleifer, "The Regulation of Labor," *The Quarterly Journal of Economics*, November 2004.
4   See International Labor Organization Web site at *http://laborsta.ilo.org/*.

wages rise by three times in foreign-owned companies during the past 10 years?[5] The desire to make a profit in a free market benefits not only consumers, but also workers.

Karl Marx and Friedrich Engels pointed out that capitalism—in 1848—had created more wealth than had been experienced by all previous human generations combined,[6] but they thought that an elite group of capitalists would eventually capture all the wealth and leave workers poor. They were proven totally wrong. The global explosion of living standards—for all people, not just the rich—since that time is breathtaking, and it has happened to the largest extent in countries that followed Marx's and Engels' recommendations the least.

RESULTS OF FREE MARKETS VS. INTERVENTION

Massive state interventions in the labor market are thus founded on a romantically appealing but scientifically void theory of how the market works. In practice, the distortions generated by limiting labor freedom follow suit. Europe happens to be a very telling showcase for both regulation and deregulation in the labor market.

In Western Europe, the labor market is often highly regulated. The share of the working-age population employed in EU countries is only 64 percent,[7] and this really says little. "Working age" between the ages of 15 and 64 really should be redefined because people live very long and healthy lives today, compared to when the definition was established decades ago. The U.S., of course, is far from a free-market heaven, but its labor market is freer than those found in most of Western Europe, and the U.S. employment rate is 72 percent.

Consider that between 1970 and 2003, employment in the U.S. increased by 75 percent. In France, Germany, and Italy, it increased by 26 percent.[8] In 2004, only 13 percent of unemployed workers in the U.S. were unable to find a new job within 12 months; in the EU, the figure was 44 percent.[9] In the EU, average youth unemployment is 17 percent. In the U.S., it is 10 percent.[10]

But the best comparisons can be made within Europe itself. Denmark has an employment rate of 76 percent, but Poland is far lower at 53 percent. Youth unemployment is above 20 percent in Greece, Italy, Sweden, France, Belgium, and Finland and below 8 percent in Ireland, the Netherlands, and Denmark.[11] In the EU's 15 member states, between 1995 and 2004, the development of employment was also very different between the countries. In Ireland, the Netherlands, and Spain, the increase in employment was the highest; in Germany and Austria, it was almost zero.[12]

What were the differences between the successful countries and the others? First of all, the labor market was substantially freer in the countries that succeeded in creating new jobs.[13] Second, payroll and income taxes were more than 10 percentage points lower in the five best economies (in terms of job creation) compared to the five worst.[14] Third, the levels of contri-

5   Nicholas Lardy, "Do China's Abusive Labor Practices Encourage Outsourcing and Drive Down American Wages?" testimony before the Senate Democratic Policy Committee, March 29, 2004.
6   Karl Marx and Friedrich Engels, *The Communist Manifesto*, 1848.
7   See European Commission, Eurostat Web site, at *http://epp.eurostat.ec.europa.eu/portal/page?_pageid=1996,39140985&_dad=portal&_schema=PORTAL&screen=detailref&language=en&product=STRIND_EMPLOI&root=STRIND_EMPLOI/emploi/em011*.

8   Olaf Gersemann, *Cowboy Capitalism: European Myths, American Reality* (Washington, D.C.: Cato Institute, 2004).
9   Diana Furchtgott-Roth, "What US Labor Laws Can Teach Europe," *Financial Times*, August 11, 2005.
10 See European Commission, Eurostat Web site, at *http://epp.eurostat.ec.europa.eu/portal/page?_pageid=1996,39140985&_dad=portal&_schema=PORTAL&screen=detailref&language=en&product=Yearlies_new_population&root=Yearlies_new_population/C/C4/C42/ccb30992*.
11 *Ibid.*
12 European Commission, *Employment in Europe 2005*, at *http://ec.europa.eu/employment_social/employment_analysis/employ_2005_en.htm*.
13 Marc A. Miles, Edwin J. Feulner, and Mary Anastasia O'Grady, *2005 Index of Economic Freedom* (Washington, D.C.: The Heritage Foundation and Dow Jones & Company, Inc., 2005).
14 Organisation for Economic Co-operation and Development, *Taxing Wages 2004–2005*, at *http://*

Table 1: Labor Freedom in Europe

EU15/EU25	Nation	Labor Freedom
	Georgia	99.9
EU-15	United Kingdom	82.7
	Armenia	80.9
	Switzerland	78.4
EU-25	Czech Republic	77.2
EU-15	Denmark	74.7
	Bulgaria	71.5
EU-15	Belgium	70.5
EU-15	Luxembourg	70.0
EU-25	Cyprus	70.0
	Iceland	69.9
	Russia	66.2
EU-25	Hungary	66.1
EU-15	France	65.9
	Belarus	64.7
EU-25	Latvia	64.1
EU-25	Slovakia	62.5
	Romania	61.4
	Moldova	61.2
	Albania	60.6
EU-15	Ireland	60.4
EU-25	Lithuania	60.1
EU-25	Malta	60.0
EU-15	Netherlands	59.2
	Macedonia	58.1
EU-15	Italy	57.6
	Bosnia and Herzegovina	57.3
EU-25	Poland	56.2
EU-15	Germany	54.6
EU-15	Finland	53.4
EU-15	Spain	52.7
EU-15	Sweden	52.0
	Croatia	52.0
	Ukraine	51.8
EU-25	Estonia	51.2
	Norway	51.1
EU-25	Slovenia	48.7
EU-15	Greece	48.5
EU-15	Austria	46.8
EU-15	Portugal	46.0
	Turkey	45.4
Averages		
	EU-15	59.7
	EU-25	60.4
	Non-EU	64.4
	Europe	62.0

Source: Tim Kane, Kim R. Holmes, and Mary Anastasia O'Grady, *2007 Index of Economic Freedom* (Washington, D.C.: The Heritage Foundation and Dow Jones & Company, Inc., 2007), at *www.heritage.org/index*.

bution from the state for unemployment and sick leave were lower in the best economies.[15] What the successful countries have in common are freer labor markets, lower taxes, and lower contributions.

A look at the results for various countries in the labor freedom category in the *Index* provides further proof of the connection between labor freedom and employment. Table 1 shows all of the nations of Europe, including their EU affiliations, ranked according to their labor freedom scores in the 2007 *Index*.

Countries like Georgia, the U.K., Switzerland, and Denmark enjoy higher scores in labor freedom and have experienced better employment outcomes generally. Countries with low scores like Germany, Italy, Portugal, and Sweden have suffered weak employment and outright stagnation.

Comparing the 15 countries that were members of the EU in 1995–2004 to EU-25 and non-EU countries is illustrative. In Britain, the labor market is relatively free and earns a score of 82.7 percent, whereas in Sweden, it is highly regulated and earns a score of 52 percent, compared to the EU-15 average of 59.7 percent. The 10 countries that recently joined the EU have raised their average labor freedom by nearly a full point, but the scores of non-EU economies average nearly five full percentage points higher. Yet the average income between 1995 and 2004 grew by 29 percent in Sweden, 37 percent in EU-15 countries, and 72 percent in Britain. The income of the poorest 10 percent of the population grew by only 10 percent in Sweden, compared to 59 percent in Britain.[16] The worst off were better off where the labor market was freer.

The larger lesson is that Europe's more "advanced" economies have generally created more complex restrictions on labor freedom in the name of protecting workers. This

---

www.oecd.org/document/40/0,2340,en_2649_37427_36330280_1_1_1_37427,00.html.

15 European Commission, MISSOC (Mutual Information System on Social Protection in the European Union), 2004.

16 Euromonitor, "World Income Distribution 2006/2007," at *www.euromonitor.com/World_Income_Distribution*.

relative wealth has been a convenient excuse for stagnant growth and higher unemployment, but the apology is losing its validity as many Eastern and Middle European countries experiment successfully with freedom.

WHY REGULATION CREATES PROBLEMS

The problems in the countries with substantial state interventions in the labor market are no coincidence. Despite numerous differences between all countries, there are many common features. One common experience is a mismatch between labor supply and demand when restrictions and protections are forced onto the market by government. A highly simplified image of a local labor market may help to shed some light on causes and consequences.

Imagine that your neighbor, having broken a leg, wants your son's help to mow his lawn. He is prepared to pay 20 euros, and your son is willing to do the work for as little as 15 euros. But imagine the state demanding a 50 percent tax. The deal (and work) are taxed out of existence. Or suppose the government demands that the service be performed by a public monopoly, which perhaps charges above 20 euros. Again, your son is without work. Or a labor market regulation demands a minimum wage of 50 euros, and the neighbor is not willing to pay that much. Again, nothing happens. Or a trade union is allowed to deny your son access to your neighbor's lawn because he is not a member of their organization. The result: no job.

Reality, of course, is more complicated, but this example describes in principle some of the most common barriers created by governments in the labor market. The state uses force to raise barriers against free exchange and thereby creates unemployment—all in the name of some "social" policy. It is not difficult to understand why such limitations in the name of protection generate widespread youth unemployment and resentment, resulting in such outcomes as the Paris riots. And there are several ticking bombs like Paris in Western Europe.

In recent years, the Organisation for Economic Co-operation and Development (OECD) has published a number of studies that confirm

these connections in its member countries.[17] Government interventions in the labor market produce serious negative effects in terms of unemployment, especially among young people and immigrants. To some extent, this is also the intention. Trade unions are a cartel dedicated to limiting competition. Regulations against firing workers prevent old jobs from being replaced by new ones. It is common knowledge that allowing such interventions does produce adverse effects, but some people seem ready to accept those effects—for example, in order to win elections.

OBSTACLES TO FREE-MARKET REFORM

When the government of France proposed a limited deregulation of the labor market, there were massive protests. Young people demonstrated under slogans like "Regulation!" despite a youth unemployment rate of 22 percent. Fears of neoliberalism were frequently mentioned. Some interpreted this as a lack of understanding among the young French, but there is every reason to believe that many of them knew exactly what they were saying. Many of them were educated and might well have felt certain that they would belong to the privileged group that would have secure jobs in the future, even if others did not.

This well-known phenomenon has been referred to as "insiders and outsiders." Those on the inside are well protected and care more about remaining so than they do about the vast numbers of people on the outside. They

---

17 Giuseppe Nicoletti and Stefano Scarpetta, "Product Market Reforms and Employment in OECD Countries," Organisation for Economic Co-operation and Development, *Economics Department Working Paper* No. 472, December 21, 2005; Andrea Bassanini and Romain Duval, "Employment Patterns in OECD Countries; Reassessing the Role of Policies and Institutions," Organisation for Economic Co-operation and Development, *Social, Employment and Migration Working Paper* No. 35, June 2006; *Boosting Jobs and Incomes—Policy Lessons from Reassessing the OECD Jobs Strategy*, Organisation for Economic Co-operation and Development, June 15–16, 2006, at *www.oecd. org/document/19/0,2340,en_21571361_36276310_ 36276371_1_1_1_1,00.html*.

do not want to give up their own "cradle to the grave" security so that others can have a job. But in a global economy characterized by rapid change and constant restructuring, even formerly secure jobs become insecure; and in a regulated labor market with few new jobs, it is hard to find a new one. Labor market regulations thus tend to create a double insecurity, both for insiders and outsiders.

A broader issue is that labor problems are largely the result of these policies, not something evil created by invisible forces. High taxes on workers make hiring more expensive and working less profitable. Fewer can afford to hire, and the desire to work decreases. Combine that with the possibility of getting contributions from the state for unemployment or sick leave at 80 percent–90 percent of the previous salary, and the result is a so-called unemployment trap in which the economic benefit of going from government support to work is very limited. Those who are permanently on the outside, however, such as people in early retirement, get lower amounts. The government takes a lot of money from those who work to pay millions to those who do not work, and the result should not surprise anyone: fewer people working to support a growing number of people who are dependent on the government.

FORCE LEADS TO MORE FORCE

A central idea of those who favor intervention in the labor market is that people should not work for low wages. Subsidies, minimum wages, and collective bargaining are said to avoid this. The ultimate effect, however, is that people with low productivity become unemployed. These groups, which have grown in size in Western Europe, are often labelled something like "early retired" rather than "unemployed," but no matter what they are called, the effect is the same: They are not allowed to work for low wages, so they have to live their lives dependent instead on low contributions from the state. In many reforming countries, such people are allowed to work and, unlike their counterparts in regulated countries, may rise in competence and salary over time.

There is a tendency in Western Europe to ignore the fact that this system is the cause of many problems, and thus to avoid gradually liberalizing it. Instead, regulation tends to create more regulation, and government force leads to more force. It has become clear to most politicians that productive activities create wealth, but since the current system puts barriers in the way, too little work is performed. Many politicians also understand that big public welfare monopolies and social security will be hard to finance in the future, so they talk with increasing frequency about people "having to work more." Instead of deregulating and making work more profitable, which would boost people's willingness to work, they keep the regulations and talk about duty and discipline. This is contrary to national survival, not just to economic freedom.

PROTECTIONISM OR FREE MARKETS?

In Western Europe, the two most common fears are of companies moving out and people moving in. In turn, this triggers various protectionist opinions and policies. In France, such policies have been labelled "economic patriotism," which is in fact a continuing *de facto* endorsement of big government, more intrusive regulations, and more barriers to the world. To a large extent, the fears are exaggerated: Not many jobs have left, and immigration has been limited, though both are likely to increase. Mainly, these fears are founded on a misunderstanding of the market and the effects of regulation.

It might be regarded as a weakness of free economies that it is impossible to say exactly which new goods, services, and jobs will replace the old. In a centrally planned economy, bureaucrats can pretend to know exactly how many people they will put in different factories next year. But the illusion of certainty is not a strength, and uncertainty is not necessarily a weakness. Innovation and the uncoordinated demand of free people are a solid foundation in fact. Nor does this mean the future is impossible to know. We can see broadly what kinds of production have increased as traditional manufacturing employment has declined: in one word, services.

THE NEW JOBS

In recent decades, companies have rapidly been shedding manufacturing jobs throughout Western Europe. What emerges in their stead are service-sector occupations. About 70 percent of the work force in Western Europe today is employed in the service sector. In Ireland, for example, employment in manufacturing has decreased by 10 percent since 2000, but total employment has risen by 10 percent. For every job lost, two new ones have been created; and as before, the new jobs are better, and wages are higher. We know now that the larger the share of services is in the economy, the higher the level of GDP per capita and the lower the level of unemployment.[18]

The single market for goods within the EU has created enormous prosperity and new jobs. A next logical step would be a single market in services, but the European Parliament has approved only a watered-down services directive. Parliament removed sectors that would benefit the most from free trade in services—health care and education—as well as the important and simplifying principle that allows countries to follow the regulations of their countries of origin. The gains could have been substantial indeed; studies have pointed to substantial gains in terms of increased economic growth and employment. The watered-down directive illustrates what happens when protectionism gains ground.

We have every reason to welcome the new. Logic dictates that the old must make way. If we lock up productive resources in the old sectors, the new economy cannot expand. This is always a painful process in the short run for those who are affected. What is a metal worker going to do when his job vanishes, whether it leaves the country or gets taken by a foreigner? We still do not have a society that makes gaining new competence and change

profitable enough. The painful fact is that people throughout Western Europe do not have enough new job opportunities. If their governments stopped focusing on how to protect old jobs, we could think more about how to facilitate change to the new.

The prime example of extreme protectionism is the European Agricultural Policy. It is a system of massive tax-paid subsidies, quotas, tariffs, and regulations. What could have been a productive part of society, as agriculture became in New Zealand after deregulation, has instead become a burden. As industrial manufacturing has evolved to utilize less labor, a terrible precedent has been established, and it haunts the policy debate. Manufacturing is, in that sense, the agriculture of our time.

GLOBALIZATION AND CHANGE

The global economy is a consequence of the fact that market theory has been spread to more parts of the world than ever before. International trade and investment have increased sharply during the past 20 years. Barriers to trade and capital have been reduced. The global economy has been growing steadily.

The economic rise of China and India (with GDPs, respectively, that are 650 percent and 350 percent higher today than they were in 1980) has been analyzed extensively.[19] So far, the number of Chinese that have entered the global work force has equaled the size of the U.S. work force, with 80 percent more Chinese on the way. Global poverty has been cut in half in 20 years, from 40 percent to 20 percent of the world's population, using conservative estimates from the World Bank[20] or distributional estimates from Xavier Sala-i-Martin.[21] GDP growth in poor countries that opened up

---

18 World Bank, *World Development Indicators 2005*, at *http://publications.worldbank.org/ecommerce/catalog/product?item_id=631625*.

19 Statistics from Central Statistical Organisation, India, International Monetary Fund, and Organisation for Economic Co-operation and Development.

20 Shaohua Chen and Martin Ravaillon, "How Have the World's Poorest Fared Since the Early 1980s?" World Bank *Policy Research Working Paper* No. 3341, 2004.

21 See, for example, Chapter 1, "Global Inequality Fades as the Global Economy Grows," in this volume.

to the global economy averaged 5 percent during the 1990s, whereas GDP in poor countries that were protectionist decreased by 1 percent a year.[22]

This has an obvious effect on Western labor markets. The emergence of developing countries creates new and wealthy markets for products from the U.S. and Europe. The fact that these countries gain competence and create healthy business climates implies that they will be able to produce goods and services that they can make available to consumers in the U.S. and Europe. In turn, this enhances global specialization. Currently, quite a few manufacturing, information technology, and service jobs are moving to Southeast Asia. As the productivity of the people in these countries increases, even more high-skilled jobs are likely to depart. It is essential to recognize, however, that rising Asia is not stealing jobs, as in a zero sum game. Rather, the process of development is leading to gains in efficiency that result in less industrial employment on net. Already, China has lost millions of manufacturing jobs.[23]

In a growing global economy, every country can become wealthier, but a country cannot continue to produce the same goods and services when hundreds of millions of Chinese can do it for a fraction of the price. The same restructuring of the business sector and the labor market that has been going on for centuries will accelerate, and a country that wants to be successful must have policies that facilitate that development as much as possible. Public monopolies, high taxes, labor market regulations, and high public contributions to people who don't work do the opposite.

DEMOGRAPHY AND CHANGE

The current problems in the labor market of Western Europe as a consequence of government intervention may grow worse in a time of globalization. The other main trend, which makes reform even more important, is the demographic situation. The average European simply gets older. Fewer people are born, and we live longer. Some politicians seem to deplore this, because they oppose reform. Of course, the fact that we live longer and healthier lives on average is a sign of great progress, but it will nevertheless affect the labor market and government interventions, such as pensions and health care.

In Germany, for example, it is estimated that the population will decrease from today's 82 million to 72 million in 2050. A similar trend is visible in many other European countries. If the same definition of "working age" is applied in the future, the population of working age in Germany will decrease from 56 million to 41 million during the same period, and the population of working age in Italy will decrease from 39 million to 22 million. It might be said that it is hard to predict what the world will be like in 45 years, but in fact everyone who will retire in 2050 is already born. This has effects not only in terms of the number that work and how many they will have to support, but also in terms of growth. If the population decreases by 0.5 percent a year and productivity rises by 0.5 percent a year, growth is zero.[24] Public expenditure would explode in several countries if nothing is done; in Spain, pension costs today amount to 50 percent of public expenditure and would be 80 percent by 2030 if nothing is done.[25]

Greater openness to immigration is often mentioned in this context, and of course it could increase the labor supply. But in time, immigrants also grow older. The real challenge is how older workers are treated and whether they have incentives to continue working if they are healthy in their later years. Today, when workers retire later than the mandatory age, they lose benefits. The OECD has calculated the size of

22   Paul Collier and David Dollar, *Globalization, Growth and Poverty: Building an Inclusive World Economy*, World Bank, 2002.
23   John E. Hilsenrath and Rebecca Buckman, "Factory Employment Is Falling World-Wide," *The Wall Street Journal*, October 20, 2003.

24   Gabriel Stein and Brian Reading, "Baby Boomer's Poverty Trap: Continental/Japanese Ageing," *Monthly International Review*, September 2003.
25   Tito Boeri, "What Are the Options for Pension and Social Security Reforms in Europe?" paper presented at the 747th Wilton Park Conference, Germany, May 17–19, 2004.

this loss, calling it a tax that amounts to between 50 percent and 90 percent in various Western European countries. A free retirement age where the pension rises with the age of retirement does not punish people who want to work longer. In addition, the funding of health care and elderly care turns out to be a problem only if the government continues to demand that those services be tax-funded. To the extent that such programs are funded privately, higher spending ceases to be a major concern. In other words, the perceived difficulties of funding programs for older workers come not from the market, but from government intervention. Fortunately, reforms can solve that.

CONCLUSION

Labor freedom is in turmoil throughout Europe as the nations of the EU are forced to confront inefficiencies in their protectionist policies. In all relevant respects, the labor market is not fundamentally different from other markets. Just as it is in so many other areas of human endeavor, the free market is superior when it comes to labor. Numerous theories and empirical studies confirm the counterproductive results of government intervention and the successes of deregulation.

In Western Europe, reality shows that there is a great need for liberalization in the labor market to allow more new jobs and prosperity to develop. Viewed within the context of globalization and demographics, the need for reform is even stronger. It is also apparent that freedom in the labor market and better social conditions are not opposites. In fact, if the world wants to achieve both more jobs *and* better living standards, freedom is essential.

Chapter 3

Methodology: Measuring the 10 Economic Freedoms

William W. Beach and Tim Kane, Ph.D.

The *Index of Economic Freedom* is a simple average of 10 individual freedoms, each of which is vital to the development of personal and national prosperity. The fundamental right of property, for example, has been recognized for centuries by the great philosophers of liberty such as Locke and Montesquieu as a bulwark of free people. Over time, scholars and practitioners have recognized many other freedoms as essential to economic liberty, including free trade, investment rights, and labor freedom.

As the first comprehensive study of economic freedom ever published, the 1995 *Index of Economic Freedom* defined a method by which economic freedom could be rated and ranked in such vastly different places as Hong Kong and North Korea. It did so by identifying 10 measurable freedoms for each country that in concert seem to matter most for the creation of wealth. Some of these freedoms are international in nature, measuring the extent of an economy's openness to investment or trade.

Most are internal in nature, assessing the liberty of individuals to use their labor or finances without restraint.

Since 1995, the *Index* has grown and improved; other, similar studies have added to the effort. Each cross-country study offers a unique and profound contribution that has helped to shape the world being measured.[1]

DEFINING ECONOMIC FREEDOM

Economic freedom is that part of freedom that is concerned with the material autonomy of the individual in relation to the state and other organized groups. An individual is economically free who can fully control his or her labor and property. This economic component

---

1   See, for example, James D. Gwartney and Robert A. Lawson with Erik Gartzke, *Economic Freedom of the World, 2005 Annual Report* (Vancouver, Canada: Fraser Institute, 2005), and Richard E. Messick, *World Survey of Economic Freedom: 1995–1996* (New Brunswick, N.J.: Transaction Publishers, 1996).

of human liberty is related to—and perhaps a necessary condition for—political freedom, but it is also valuable as an end in itself.

The authors of the *Index* perceive economic freedom as a positive concept, recognizing that its traditional definition as an *absence of government coercion or constraint* must also include a sense of liberty as distinct from anarchy. Governments are instituted to create basic protections against the ravages of nature, so that positive economic rights such as property and contract are given social as well as individual defense against the destructive tendencies of others. The definition of economic freedom therefore *encompasses all liberties and rights of production, distribution, or consumption of goods and services. The highest form of economic freedom provides an absolute right of property ownership, fully realized freedoms of movement for labor, capital, and goods, and an absolute absence of coercion or constraint of economic liberty beyond the extent necessary for citizens to protect and maintain liberty itself.* In other words, individuals are free to work, produce, consume, and invest in any way they please, and that freedom is both protected by the state and unconstrained by the state.

All government action involves coercion. Some minimal coercion is necessary for the citizens of a community or nation to defend themselves, promote the evolution of civil society, and enjoy the fruits of their labor. This Lockean idea is embodied in the U.S. Constitution. For example, citizens are taxed to provide revenue for the protection of person and property as well as for a common defense. Most political theorists also accept that certain goods—what economists call "public goods"—can be supplied more conveniently by government than through private means. Of particular interest are those economic freedoms that are also public goods, such as the maintenance of a police force to protect property rights, a monetary authority to maintain a sound currency, and an impartial judiciary to enforce contracts among parties.

When government coercion rises beyond the minimal level, however, it becomes corrosive to freedom—and the first freedom affected is economic freedom. Logically, an expansion of state power requires enforcement and there-

fore funding, which is extracted from the people. Exactly where that line is crossed is open to reasoned debate.

Throughout history, governments have imposed a wide array of constraints on economic activity. Constraining economic choice distorts and diminishes the production, distribution, and consumption of goods and services (including, of course, labor services).[2] The establishment of a price control is perhaps the clearest example of the distortionary effect of state coercion because of its well-known disruption of the equilibrium of supply and demand.

The 10 Economic Freedoms. Overall economic freedom, defined by multiple rights and liberties, can be quantified as an index of less abstract components. The index we conceive uses 10 specific freedoms, some as composites of even further detailed and quantifiable components. A detailed discussion of each of these factors and their component variables follows this overview.

- **Business freedom** is the ability to create, operate, and close an enterprise quickly and easily. Burdensome, redundant regulatory rules are the most harmful barriers to business freedom.
- **Trade freedom** is a composite measure of the absence of tariff and non-tariff barriers that affect imports and exports of goods and services.
- **Monetary freedom** combines a measure of price stability with an assessment of price controls. Both inflation and price controls distort market activity. Price stability without microeconomic intervention is the ideal state for the free market.
- **Freedom from government** is defined to include all government expenditures—including consumption and transfers—and state-owned enterprises. Ideally, the state will

2   "The property which every man has in his own labour, as it is the original foundation of all other property, so it is the most sacred and inviolable." Adam Smith, *An Inquiry into the Nature and Causes of the Wealth of Nations* (New York: The Modern Library, 1937), pp. 121–122; first published in 1776.

provide only true public goods, with an absolute minimum of expenditure.

- **Fiscal freedom** is a measure of the burden of government from the revenue side. It includes both the tax burden in terms of the top tax rate on income (individual and corporate separately) and the overall amount of tax revenue as portion of GDP.
- **Property rights** is an assessment of the ability of individuals to accumulate private property, secured by clear laws that are fully enforced by the state.
- **Investment freedom** is an assessment of the free flow of capital, especially foreign capital.
- **Financial freedom** is a measure of banking security as well as independence from government control. State ownership of banks and other financial institutions such as insurer and capital markets is an inefficient burden, and political favoritism has no place in a free capital market.
- **Freedom from corruption** is based on quantitative data that assess the perception of corruption in the business environment, including levels of governmental legal, judicial, and administrative corruption.
- **Labor freedom** is a composite measure of the ability of workers and businesses to interact without restriction by the state.

Equal Weight. In the *Index of Economic Freedom*, all 10 factors are equally weighted in order not to bias the overall score toward any one factor or policy direction. As described earlier, economic freedom is an end in itself. The ability of economic freedom to establish a foundation for the rapid development of wealth for the average citizen explains contemporary interest, but it is not a valid rationale to weight some components over others. Nor would it be proper to weight the *Index* in a manner that caused the relation between democracy and economic freedom to be statistically stronger.

This is a common-sense approach. It is also consistent with the purpose of the *Index*: to reflect the balanced economic environment in every country surveyed. The *Index* has never been designed specifically to explain economic

growth or any other dependent variable; that is ably done by empirical econometricians elsewhere.

Nor is it clear how the 10 economic freedoms interact. Is a minimum threshold for each one essential? Is it possible for one to maximize if others are minimized? Are they dependent or exclusive, complements or supplements? These are valid questions, and they are beyond the scope of our more fundamental mission. The *Index*, then, offers a simple composite based on an average of the 10 freedoms. It also offers the raw data for each factor so that others can study and weight and integrate as they see fit.

The Grading Scale. Each one of the 10 freedoms is graded using a scale from 0 to 100, where 100 represents the maximum freedom. A score of 100 signifies an economic environment or set of policies that is most conducive to economic freedom. The grading scale is continuous, meaning that scores with decimals are possible. For example, a country could have a trade freedom score of 50.33. Many of the 10 freedoms are based on quantitative data that are converted directly into a score. In the case of trade, a country with zero tariffs and zero nontariff barriers will have a trade freedom score of 100. This will often be described using percent terminology.

In previous years, the *Index* used a scale of 1 to 5, in which 1 represented the best score. All of the old scores have been converted seamlessly to the new scale. If a country had an overall score of 3.00 and a trade freedom score of 2.00 in the year 1997, for example, those have been converted to 50 percent and 75 percent, respectively.[3]

Period of Study. For the current *Index of Economic Freedom*, the authors generally examined data for the period covering the second half of 2005 through the first half of 2006. To the extent possible, the information considered for each factor was current as of June 30, 2006. It is important to understand, however, that some factors are based on historical information.

---

3   For detailed guidance on how the data in the *Index* can be used in statistical research, see *www.heritage.org/research/features/index/downloads. cfm#methodology.*

For example, the monetary freedom factor is a three-year weighted average rate of inflation from January 1, 2003, to December 31, 2005.

Sources. In evaluating the criteria for each factor, the authors have used a range of authoritative sources. Because it would be unnecessarily cumbersome to cite all the sources used in scoring every single variable of each factor, unless otherwise noted, the major sources used in preparing the country summaries may be found below, in the introduction to Chapter 5, and in the list of Major Works Cited.

METHODOLOGY FOR THE 10 ECONOMIC FREEDOMS

Freedom #1: Business Freedom

Business freedom is a quantitative measure of the ability to start, operate, and close a business that represents the overall burden as well as the efficiency of government regulations. Regulations are a form of taxation that make it difficult for entrepreneurs to create value. Although many regulations hinder businesses, the most important are associated with licensing new companies and businesses. In some countries, as well as many states in the United States, the procedure for obtaining a business license can be as simple as mailing in a registration form with a minimal fee. In Hong Kong, for example, obtaining a business license requires filling out a single form, and the process can be completed in a few hours. In other countries, such as India and countries in parts of South America, the process involved in obtaining a business license requires endless trips to government offices and can take a year or more.

Once a business is open, government regulation does not always subside; in some cases, it increases. Interestingly, two countries with the same set of regulations can impose different regulatory burdens. If one country, for instance, applies its regulations evenly and transparently, it lowers the regulatory burden because it enables businesses to make long-term plans more easily. If the other applies regulations inconsistently, it raises the regulatory burden by creating an unpredictable business environment. Finally, regulations that make it difficult and expensive to close businesses are disincentives for entrepreneurs to start them in the first place.

Methodology. The business freedom score for each country is a number between 0 and 100 percent, with 100 equaling the freest business environment. The score is based on 10 components, all weighted equally, based on objective data from the World Bank's *Doing Business* study:

- Starting a business—procedures (number);
- Starting a business—time (days);
- Starting a business—cost (% of income per capita);
- Starting a business—minimum capital (% of income per capita);
- Obtaining a license—procedures (number);
- Obtaining a license—time (days);
- Obtaining a license—cost (% of income per capita);
- Closing a business—time (years);
- Closing a business—cost (% of estate); and
- Closing a business—recovery rate (cents on the dollar).[4]

Each of these raw components is converted to a 0 to 100 scale, after which the average of the converted values is computed. The result represents the country's business freedom score. For example, even if a country requires the highest number of procedures for starting a business, which yields a score of zero in that component, it could still receive a score as high as 90 based on scores in the other nine components.

Norway, for example, has the world's highest business freedom score (97 percent), even though it is ranked 30th in overall freedom worldwide. Indeed, Norway receives scores of 100 in nine of the 10 components, the exception being the 13 procedures required by the government for closing a business, which equates to a score of 69.8 percent for that component.

---

4   The recovery rate is a function of time and cost. However, the business freedom factor uses all three subvariables to emphasize closing a business, starting a business, and dealing with licenses equally.

Each component is converted to a 100 percent scale using the following equation:

$$Component\ Score_i = 50\frac{component_{average}}{component_i}$$

which is based on the ratio of the country data for each component relative to the world average, multiplied by 50. For example, on average worldwide, there are 18.16 procedures to close a business. Norway's 13 procedures is a component value better than the average, resulting in a ratio of 1.397. That ratio multiplied by 50 equals the final component score of 69.8 percent. The average country will receive a component score of 50 percent, whereas a country's maximum component score is limited to 100 percent.

For the 12 countries that are not covered by the World Bank's *Doing Business* study, the business freedom factor is scored by looking into business regulations based on qualitative information from reliable and internationally recognized sources.[5]

Sources. Unless otherwise noted, the authors used the following sources in determining business freedom scores, in order of priority: World Bank, *Doing Business 2007: How to Reform*; Economist Intelligence Unit, *Country Report* and *Country Profile*, 2004–2006; U.S. Department of Commerce, *Country Commercial Guide*, 2003, 2004, 2005, and 2006.

Freedom #2: Trade Freedom

Trade restrictions can take the form of taxes on imports and exports (known as tariffs), quotas or outright bans on trade, and regulatory barriers. The degree to which government hinders access to and the free flow of foreign commerce can have a direct bearing on the ability of individuals to pursue their economic goals.

Tariffs immediately and directly increase the prices that local consumers pay for foreign imports, and these price distortions change incentives, often indirectly pulling producers away from specializing in some goods

---

5   Twelve countries are not covered by the World Bank's *Doing Business* study: Bahamas, Bahrain, Barbados, Burma, Cuba, Cyprus, North Korea, Libya, Luxembourg, Malta, Qatar, and Turkmenistan.

and toward the blocked goods. By interfering with comparative advantage, trade restrictions impede economic growth. Also, tariffs make local citizens poorer by raising prices. In many cases, trade limitations put advanced technology products and services beyond the reach of local people, limiting their own productive development.

Methodology. The trade freedom score is based two inputs:

• The trade-weighted average tariff rate and
• Non-tariff barriers (NTBs).

Weighted average tariffs are a purely quantitative measure and account for the basic calculation of the score using an equation that is described below. The presence of NTBs in a country affects its trade freedom score by incurring a penalty of up to 20 percentage points, or one-fifth of the maximum score.

Different imports entering a country can, and often do, face different tariffs. The weighted average tariff uses weights for each tariff based on the share of imports for each good. This can be calculated by dividing the country's total tariff revenue by the total value of imports. This weighted measure may understate the level of tariff protection because goods with high tariffs will have low trade weights. Furthermore, a tariff is counted toward the average level of protection only if an import actually occurred; thus, tariffs that are so high as to fully prevent imports are not captured. In contrast, the simple average tariff makes no distinction as to how much of each product is actually imported.

The weighted average tariff rate is converted to the base trade freedom score using this equation:

$$TF_i = \frac{Tariff_{max} - Tariff_i}{Tariff_{max} - Tariff_{min}} - NTB_i$$

where TF_i represents the trade freedom in country *i*, $Tariff_{max}$ and $Tariff_{min}$ represent the upper and lower bounds for tariff rates, and $Tariff_i$ represents the weighted average tariff rate in country *i*. The minimum tariff is naturally zero, and the upper bound was set as 50 percent. If applicable to country i, the NTB penalty of 20 percentage points is then subtracted from the base score. The equation simplifies to:

$$TF_i = \frac{50 - Tariff_i}{50} - NTB_i$$

As an example, France received a trade freedom score of 76.6 percent, as did over 20 other European Union countries that share a unified trade policy. The weighted average tariff of 1.7 percent yields a base score 96.6 percent. The existence of significant NTBs, however, reduces the score by 20 percentage points.

Gathering data on tariffs to make a consistent cross-country comparison can be a challenging task. Unlike data on inflation, for instance, countries do not report their weighted average tariff rate or simple average tariff rate every year; in some cases, the most recent time a country reported its tariff data could have been as far back as 1993. To preserve consistency in grading the trade policy factor, the authors have decided to use the most recently reported weighted average tariff rate for a country from our primary source. If another reliable source reports more updated information on the country's tariff rate, the authors note this fact and may review the grading of this factor if there is strong evidence that the most recently reported weighted average tariff rate is outdated.

The World Bank produces the world's most comprehensive and consistent information on weighted average applied tariff rates. When the weighted average applied tariff rate is not available, the authors use the country's average applied tariff rate; and when the country's average applied tariff rate is not available, the authors use the weighted average or the simple average of most favored nation (MFN) tariff rates.[6] The

data for customs revenues and total imports may not be consolidated in just one source. In addition, in the very few cases in which data on duties and customs revenues are not available, the authors use data on international trade taxes instead. In all cases, the authors clarify the type of data used and the different sources for those data in the corresponding write-up for the trade policy factor. Sometimes, when none of this information is available, the authors simply analyze the overall tariff structure and estimate an effective tariff rate.

Sources. Unless otherwise noted, the authors used the following sources to determine scores for trade policy, in order of priority: World Bank, *World Development Indicators 2005* and *Data on Trade and Import Barriers: Trends in Average Tariff Rates for Developing and Industrial Countries 1981–2003*; World Trade Organization, *Trade Policy Reviews*, 1995 to March 2005; Office of the U.S. Trade Representative, 2005 *National Trade Estimate Report on Foreign Trade Barriers*; U.S. Department of Commerce, *Country Commercial Guide*, 2004 and 2005; Economist Intelligence Unit, *Country Report, Country Profile*, and *Country Commerce*, 2004–2005 and 2005–2006; and official government publications of each country.

Freedom #3: Fiscal Freedom

A government can impose fiscal burdens on economic activity by generating revenue for itself, primarily through taxation but also from debt that ultimately must be paid off through taxation. Fiscal freedom is a quantitative measure of these burdens in which lower taxation translates as a higher level of fiscal freedom. The *Index* methodology includes the top marginal tax rates on individual and corporate income, as well as a measure of total tax revenue as a portion of gross domestic product (GDP).

The marginal tax rate confronting an individual is, in effect, the price paid for supplying the next economic effort or engagement in an entrepreneurial venture. What remains after the tax is subtracted are the rewards of the effort. The higher the price of effort or entrepreneurship, the lower the rewards—and the less often such effort will be undertaken. Higher tax

---

6   The most favored nation tariff rate is the "normal," non-discriminatory tariff charged on imports of a good. In commercial diplomacy, exporters seek MFN treatment; that is, the promise that they will be treated as well as the most favored exporter. The MFN rule requires that the concession be extended to all other members of the World Trade Organization. MFN is now referred to as permanent normal trade relations (PNTR).

rates interfere with the ability of individuals to pursue their goals in the marketplace.

While individual and corporate income tax rates are important to economic freedom, they are not a comprehensive measure of the tax burden. First, they do not include the many other taxes such as payroll, sales, and excise taxes, tariffs, and the value-added tax (VAT). One way to capture all taxation is to measure total government revenues from all forms of taxation as a percentage of total GDP.

Methodology. Fiscal freedom is composed of three quantitative components in equal measure:

- The top tax rate on individual income,
- The top tax rate on corporate income, and
- Total tax revenue as a percentage of GDP.

In scoring the fiscal freedom factor, each of these numerical variables is weighted equally as one-third of the factor. This equal weighting allows a country to achieve a score as high as 67 percent based on two of the components even if it receives a score of 0 percent on the third.

The economics of public finance are unambiguous on the effect of taxation, using simple supply and demand. A doubling of the tax rate quadruples the economic cost to society of lost market activity. This is known as deadweight loss because it is not value gained by government, but simply prosperity that is destroyed. This happens because the price wedge created by taxation separates optimal supply and demand and diminishes the quantity of goods exchanged. In the extreme, raising tax rates will decrease tax revenue itself, as famously demonstrated by the Laffer curve. Therefore, the scoring of fiscal freedom is calculated with a quadratic cost function. Each of the component pieces of data is converted to a 100-point scale using this quadratic equation:

$$FF_{ij} = 100 - 200 \left(Component_{ij} \right)^2$$

where FF_{ij} represents the fiscal freedom in country i for component j and $Component_{ij}$ represents the raw percentage value (a number between 0 and 1) in country i for component

j. The minimum score for each component is zero, which is not represented in the printed equation but was utilized because it means that no single high tax burden will make the other two components irrelevant.

As an example, in the 2007 *Index*, the Bahamas has no tax on individual or corporate income, so two of the components equal 100. However, overall tax revenue as a portion of GDP in the Bahamas is 16 percent, or 0.16, yielding a revenue component score of 94.9. When the three component freedoms are averaged together, you get the Bahamas' overall fiscal freedom score of 98.3 percent, which is the world's 7th best fiscal freedom score.

Sources. Unless otherwise noted, the authors used the following sources for information on taxation, in order of priority: Ernst & Young, *The Global Executive* and *Worldwide Corporate Tax Guide 2005–2006*; Deloitte, *Country Snapshot*, 2005–2006, and *Corporate Tax Rates at a Glance*; International Monetary Fund (IMF), Staff Country Report, *Selected Issues and Statistical Appendix*, 2002 to 2006; investment agencies; and other governmental authorities (i.e., embassy confirmations and/or the country's treasury or tax authority). For information on tax revenue as a percentage of GDP, the authors' primary sources were Organisation for Economic Co-operation and Development data (for member countries); African Development Bank; International Monetary Fund, Staff Country Report, *Selected Issues and Statistical Appendix*, 2002 to 2006; Asian Development Bank, *Key Indicators of Developing Asian and Pacific Countries 2005*; official government publications of each country; and individual contacts from government agencies and multinational organizations such as the IMF and World Bank.

Freedom #4: Freedom from Government

The burden of excessive government is a central issue in economic freedom, both in terms of generating revenue (see fiscal freedom) and in terms of expenditure. After a major methodology review, the 2007 *Index* is adopting the newly named freedom from government factor to measure the level of government spending and control in one place.[7] The revised factor considers both the level of government expenditures as a percentage of GDP and the share of government revenue from state-owned enterprises and property. Government expenditures—including consumption and transfers—account for two-thirds of the score, and revenue from state-owned enterprises and properties accounts for the remainder.

Government expenditures are often justified in terms of "public goods" that are provided efficiently by the state rather than by the market. There is also a justification for correcting market failures through government action. Economists recognize another kind of systemic failure as well: a tendency for government failure whereby the state becomes inefficient, bureaucratic, and even harmful to productivity. Government expenditures necessarily compete with private agents and interfere in market prices by overstimulating demand and potentially diverting resources through a crowding-out effect. In extreme cases, governments can coerce goods and capital out of markets altogether, driving up interest rates and inflation. Distortions in markets occur whenever the purpose of the government's expenditure is to acquire resources for its own purposes (government consumption) or for transfer payments.

For these reasons, the new methodology treats zero government spending as the ideal level. Since some level of government expenditures represents public goods, setting the ideal level greater than zero, where anything more or less than this ideal level of government expenditures (e.g., 10 percent) would receive a lower score, was considered. Ultimately, choosing a non-zero ideal level seems too arbitrary, static, and difficult to apply universally. Moreover, governments with no public goods will be penalized by lower scores in the other factors (such as property rights and financial freedom) that measure public goods institutions. As a compromise, the new scale for scoring govern-

ment spending is non-linear, which means that government spending that is close to zero is not significantly penalized, while levels of government exceeding 30 percent of GDP receive much worse scores in a quadratic fashion (e.g., doubling spending yields four times less freedom), so that only really large governments receive very negative scores.

The government's appetite for private resources affects both economic freedom and economic growth. Even if a state-managed economy achieves fast growth through heavy expenditure, it diminishes freedom in the process and can create long-term damage to a country's growth potential.

Methodology. Scoring of the freedom from government factor is based on two components:

- Government expenditures as a percentage of GDP and
- Revenues generated by state-owned enterprises (SOEs) and property as a percentage of total government revenue.

Government expenditure as a percentage of GDP is weighted as two-thirds of the freedom from government factor score, and revenue from SOEs is weighted as one-third. In cases where SOE data do not exist, the data are excluded from the factor score.

A non-linear quadratic cost function is used to calculate the expenditures score, and a simple subtraction function is used for the SOE score. The expenditure equation is:

$$GE_i = 100 - C(Expenditures_i)^2$$

where GE_i represents the government expenditure score in country i, Expenditures$_i$ represents the total amount of government spending at all levels as a portion of GDP (between 0 and 1), and C is a constant to control for variation among scores (set at 3500). The minimum component score is zero.

For example, Israel has a freedom from government score of 60.0 percent, which is driven largely by high government expenditures that equal 40.8 percent of GDP, yielding a compo-

7 In previous years' *Index* methodology, expenditure measures were considered in two different places: the fiscal burden of government factor and the government intervention factor.

nent score of 41.7. The other component for SOE has a score of 96.5, which is 100 minus the 3.5 percent of SOE revenue collected. In contrast, Hong Kong has an expenditure level of 18.3 percent of GDP, for a component score of 88.3, but its SOE is so low that its overall freedom from government score is 91.6 percent—the 8th highest in the world.

In most cases, general government expenditure data include all levels of government such as federal, state, and local. In cases where general government spending data are not available, data on central government expenditure are used instead. Often, data for the share of total revenues from state-owned enterprises and government ownership of property are not readily available. In these cases, the authors look both for data on total revenues from state-owned enterprises and property and for data on total government revenues and then calculate the percentage of total revenues that is attributable to revenues from state-owned enterprises and property.

Sources. Unless otherwise noted, the authors used the following sources for information on government intervention in the economy, in order of priority: World Bank, *World Development Indicators 2006* and *Country at a Glance* tables; official government publications of each country; Economist Intelligence Unit, *Country Report* and *Country Profile*, 2004–2006; International Monetary Fund, *Government Finance Statistics April 2006* on CD–ROM; Organisation for Economic Co-operation and Development data (for member countries); African Development Bank; International Monetary Fund, Staff Country Report, *Selected Issues and Statistical Appendix*, 2002 to 2006; Asian Development Bank, *Key Indicators 2005*; and U.S. Department of Commerce, *Country Commercial Guide*, 2003, 2004, 2005, and 2006.

Freedom #5: Monetary Freedom

Monetary freedom is to market economics what free speech is to democracy. Free people need a steady and reliable currency as a medium of exchange and store of value. Without monetary freedom, it is difficult to create long-term value.

A country's currency is controlled largely by the monetary policy of its government. With a monetary policy that endeavors to maintain stability, people can rely on market prices for the foreseeable future. Investment, savings, and other longer-term plans are easier to make, and individuals enjoy greater economic freedom. Inflation not only confiscates wealth like an invisible tax, but also distorts pricing, misallocates resources, raises the cost of doing business, and undermines a free society.

There is no singularly accepted theory of the right monetary institutions for a free society. At one time, the gold standard enjoyed widespread support, but this is no longer the case. What characterizes almost all monetary theorists today, however, is support for low inflation and an independent central bank. There is a powerful consensus among economists that price controls corrupt market efficiency and that measured inflation in the face of widespread price controls is essentially impossible since the price signal can no longer equate supply and demand.

Methodology. The score for the monetary freedom factor is based on two components:

- The weighted average inflation rate for the most recent three years and
- Price controls.

The weighted average inflation (WAI) rate for the most recent three years serves as the primary input into an equation that generates the base score for monetary freedom (MF). The extent of price controls is then assessed as a penalty of up to 20 percent subtracted from the base score. The two equations used to convert inflation into the policy score for a given year are:

$$WAI_i = \Theta_1 Inflation_{it} + \Theta_2 Inflation_{it-1} + \Theta_3 Inflation_{it-2}$$

$$MF_i = 100 - d\sqrt{WAI_i} - PC_i$$

where Θ_1 through Θ_3 (thetas 1–3) represent three numbers that sum to 1 and are exponentially smaller in sequence (in this case, values of

0.665, 0.245, and 0.090, respectively); Inflation$_{it}$ is the absolute value of the annual inflation rate in country i during year t as measured by the consumer price index; d represents a constant that stabilizes the variance of scores; and the PC penalty is an assigned value of 0–20 percentage points based on the extent of price controls. The convex (square root) functional form was chosen to create separation among countries with low inflation rates; 128 of 161 countries had weighted average inflation under 10 percent in absolute value. A concave functional form would essentially treat all hyperinflations as equally bad, whether they were 100 percent price increases annually or 100,000 percent, whereas the square root provides much more gradation. The constant d is set to equal 6.333, which converts a 10 percent inflation rate into a freedom score of 80.0 and a 2 percent inflation rate into a score of 91.0.

Sources. Unless otherwise noted, the authors used the following sources for data on monetary policy, in order of priority: International Monetary Fund, *International Financial Statistics On-line*; International Monetary Fund, *2006 World Economic Outlook*; and Economist Intelligence Unit, *Country Report*, 1999 to 2006, and *Country Profile*, 2004–2006.

Freedom #6: Investment Freedom

Restrictions on foreign investment limit the inflow of capital and thus limit economic freedom. By contrast, little or no restriction of foreign investment enhances economic freedom because foreign investment provides funds for economic expansion. By its nature, capital will flow to where it is most needed and the returns are greatest. State action to redirect the flow of capital is an imposition on both the freedom of the investor and the people seeking capital. For this factor, the more restrictions a country imposes on foreign and domestic investment, the lower its level of economic freedom.

Methodology. This factor scrutinizes each country's policies toward foreign investment, as well as its policies toward capital flows internally, in order to determine its overall investment climate. The authors assess all countries using the same rubric.

Questions examined include whether there is a foreign investment code that defines the country's investment laws and procedures; whether the government encourages foreign investment through fair and equitable treatment of investors; whether there are restrictions on access to foreign exchange; whether foreign firms are treated the same as domestic firms under the law; whether the government imposes restrictions on payments, transfers, and capital transactions; and whether specific industries are closed to foreign investment. The following criteria are used:

- **100%**—Foreign investment (FI) is encouraged and treated the same as domestic investment, with a simple and transparent FI code and a professional, efficient bureaucracy. There are no restrictions in sectors related to national security or real estate. No expropriation is allowed. Both residents and non-residents have access to foreign exchange and may conduct international payments. Transfers or capital transactions face no restrictions.
- **90%**—Same as above with the following exceptions: There are very few restrictions on FI in sectors related to national security. There are legal guarantees against expropriation of property. Transfers or capital transactions are subject to virtually no restrictions.
- **80%**—Same as above with the following exceptions: A transparent FI code is subject to minimal bureaucratic or other informal impediments. There are very few restrictions on foreign exchange. Transfers or capital transactions are subject to very few restrictions.
- **70%**—Same as above with the following exceptions: There are some restrictions on FI through general rules or in a few sectors such as utilities, natural resources, or national security. There are a few restrictions on access to foreign exchange or the ability to conduct international payments.
- **60%**—Same as above with the following exceptions: FI is generally encouraged but may not receive equal treatment in a few sectors. The FI code is somewhat non-transparent and/or FI faces bureaucratic impediments.

Expropriation of property is highly unlikely, and the government guarantees compensation. Transfers or capital transactions are subject to some restrictions.

- **50%**—Same as above with the following exceptions: Foreign investors face restrictions on their ability to purchase real estate. All investors face bureaucratic impediments and corruption. Residents and/or non-residents face some restrictions on access to foreign exchange or their ability to conduct international payments. Transfers or capital transactions are subject to obvious restrictions.
- **40%**—Same as above with the following exceptions: FI is somewhat restricted, the FI code is somewhat discriminatory, and FI is restricted outright in some sectors. Expropriation of property is rare. Transfers and capital transactions are subject to significant restrictions.
- **30%**—Same as above with the following exceptions: FI is significantly restricted, the FI code is discriminatory, and foreign investors may purchase real estate only in limited circumstances. All investors face significant bureaucratic impediments and corruption. Residents and non-residents face strict restrictions on access to foreign exchange, and the government imposes many controls on international payments.
- **20%**—Same as above with the following exceptions: FI is discouraged and prohibited in many sectors, the FI code is discriminatory, and the approval process is opaque and subject to widespread corruption. Few sectors are open to FI. Expropriation of property is common. The government imposes extensive controls on international payments, transfers, and capital transactions.
- **10%**—Same as above with the following exceptions: Foreign investors may not purchase real estate. The government controls or prohibits most international payments, transfers, and capital transactions.
- **0%**—Same as above with the following exceptions: FI is prohibited, foreigners may not own real estate, and the government prohibits international payments, transfers, and capital transactions.

Sources. Unless otherwise noted, the authors used the following sources for data on capital flows and foreign investment, in order of priority: International Monetary Fund, *Annual Report on Exchange Arrangements and Exchange Restrictions 2005*; official government publications of each country; Economist Intelligence Unit, *Country Commerce, Country Profile*, and *Country Report*, 2005 and 2006; Office of the U.S. Trade Representative, *2006 National Trade Estimate Report on Foreign Trade Barriers*; and U.S. Department of Commerce, *Country Commercial Guide*, 2005 and 2006.

Freedom #7: Financial Freedom

In most countries, banks provide the essential financial services that facilitate economic growth; they lend money to start businesses, purchase homes, and secure credit for the purchase of durable consumer goods. Banks also furnish a safe place in which individuals can store their savings. Greater direct control of banks by government is a threat to these functions because government interference can introduce inefficiencies and outright corruption. Heavy bank regulation reduces opportunities and restricts economic freedom; therefore, the more a government restricts its banking sector, the lower its economic freedom score will be.

It should be noted that virtually all countries provide some type of prudential supervision of banks and other financial services. This supervision serves two major purposes: ensuring the safety and soundness of the financial system and ensuring that financial services firms meet basic fiduciary responsibilities. Ultimately, this task falls under a government's duty to enforce contracts and protect its citizens against fraud by requiring financial institutions to publish their financial statements and relevant data, verified by independent audit, so that borrowers, depositors, and other financial actors can make informed choices.

In a free banking environment, the marketplace should be the primary source of protection through such institutions as independent auditors and information services. Such oversight is distinguished from burdensome or intrusive government regulation or government ownership of banks, both of which interfere with market provision of financial services to consumers. It is such government intervention in the market, not the market itself, that limits economic freedom and causes a country's grade for this factor to be worse than it might otherwise be.

Increasingly, the central role played by banks is being complemented by other financial services that offer alternative means for raising capital or diversifying risk. As a result, the authors take related non-banking financial services, such as insurance and securities, into consideration when grading this factor. As with the banking system, aside from basic provisions to enforce contractual obligations and prevent fraud, increased government intervention in these areas undermines economic freedom and inhibits the ability of non-banking financial services to contribute to economic growth. If the government intervenes in the stock market, it contravenes the choices of millions of individuals by interfering with the pricing of capital—the most critical function of a market economy. Equity markets measure, on a continual basis, the expected profits and losses in publicly held companies. This measurement is essential in allocating capital resources to their highest-valued uses and thereby satisfying consumers' most urgent requirements. Similarly, government ownership or intervention in the insurance sector undermines the ability of providers to make available those services at prices based on risk and market conditions.

Methodology. The financial freedom factor measures the relative openness of each country's banking and financial system. The authors score this factor by determining the extent of government regulation of financial services; the extent of state intervention in banks and other financial services; the difficulty of opening and operating financial services firms (for both domestic and foreign individuals); and government influence on the allocation of credit. The authors use this analysis to develop a description of the country's financial climate and assign it an overall score between 0 percent and 100 percent. The following criteria are used in determining a country's score for this factor:

- **100%—Negligible government influence.** Independent central bank supervision and regulation of financial institutions are limited to enforcing contractual obligations and preventing fraud. Credit is allocated on market terms. The government does not own financial institutions. Financial institutions may engage in all types of financial services. Banks are free to issue competitive notes, extend credit and accept deposits, and conduct operations in foreign currencies. Foreign financial institutions operate freely and are treated the same as domestic institutions.
- **90%—Minimal government influence.** Same as above with the following exceptions: Independent central bank supervision and regulation of financial institutions are minimal but may extend beyond enforcing contractual obligations and preventing fraud.
- **80%—Nominal government influence.** Same as above with the following exceptions: Independent central bank supervision and regulation are straightforward and transparent but extend beyond enforcing contractual obligations and preventing fraud. Government ownership of financial institutions is a small share of overall sector assets. Financial institutions face almost no restrictions on their ability to offer financial services.
- **70%—Limited government influence.** Same as above with the following exceptions: Credit allocation is slightly influenced by the government, and private allocation of credit faces almost no restrictions. Foreign financial institutions are subject to few restrictions.
- **60%—Significant government influence.** Same as above with the following exceptions: The central bank is not fully independent, its supervision and regulation of financial institutions are somewhat burdensome, and its ability to enforce contracts and prevent fraud is insufficient. The government exercises active ownership and control of financial institutions with a significant share of overall sector assets. The ability of financial institutions to offer financial services is subject to some restrictions.
- **50%—Considerable government influence.** Same as above with the following exceptions: Credit allocation is significantly influenced

by the government, and private allocation of credit faces significant barriers. The ability of financial institutions to offer financial services is subject to significant restrictions. Foreign financial institutions are subject to some restrictions.

- **40%—Strong government influence.** Same as above with the following exceptions: The central bank is subject to government influence, its supervision and regulation of financial institutions are heavy, and its ability to enforce contracts and prevent fraud is weak. The government exercises active ownership and control of financial institutions with a large minority share of overall sector assets.
- **30%—Extensive government influence.** Same as above with the following exceptions: Credit allocation is extensively influenced by the government. The government owns or controls a majority of financial institutions or is in a dominant position. Financial institutions are heavily restricted, and bank formation faces significant barriers. Foreign financial institutions are subject to significant restrictions.
- **20%—Heavy government influence.** Same as above with the following exceptions: The central bank is not independent, and its supervision and regulation of financial institutions are repressive. Foreign financial institutions are discouraged or highly constrained.
- **10%—Near repressive.** Same as above with the following exceptions: Credit allocation is controlled by the government. Bank formation is restricted. Foreign financial institutions are prohibited.
- **0%—Repressive.** Same as above with the following exceptions: Supervision and regulation are designed to prevent private financial institutions. Private financial institutions are prohibited.

Sources. Unless otherwise noted, the authors used the following sources for data on banking and finance, in order of priority: The Financial Sector Reform and Strengthening (FIRST) Initiative jointly undertaken by the Department for International Development of the United Kingdom (DFID), the International Development Agency of Canada, the State Secretariat for Economic Affairs of Switzerland, the Ministry of Foreign Affairs of the Netherlands, the International Bank for Reconstruction and Development (IBRD or World Bank), and the International Monetary Fund; Economist Intelligence Unit, *Country Commerce*, *Country Profile*, and *Country Report*, 2005 and 2006; official government publications of each country; U.S. Department of Commerce, *Country Commercial Guide*, 2005 and 2006; Office of the U.S. Trade Representative, *2006 National Trade Estimate Report on Foreign Trade Barriers*; and World Bank, *World Development Indicators 2006*.

Freedom #8: Property Rights

The ability to accumulate private property is the main motivating force in a market economy, and the rule of law is vital to a fully functioning free-market economy. Secure property rights give citizens the confidence to undertake commercial activities, save their income, and make long-term plans because they know that their income and savings are safe from expropriation.

Methodology. This factor scores the degree to which a country's laws protect private property rights and the degree to which its government enforces those laws. It also assesses the likelihood that private property will be expropriated and analyzes the independence of the judiciary, the existence of corruption within the judiciary, and the ability of individuals and businesses to enforce contracts.

The authors grade each country according to the following criteria:

- **100%—Private property** is guaranteed by the government. The court system enforces contracts efficiently and quickly. The justice system punishes those who unlawfully confiscate private property. There is no corruption or expropriation.
- **90%—Private property** is guaranteed by the government. The court system enforces contracts efficiently. The justice system punishes those who unlawfully confiscate private property. Corruption is nearly nonexistent, and expropriation is highly unlikely.
- **80%—Private property** is guaranteed by

the government. The court system enforces contracts efficiently but with some delays. Corruption is minimal, and expropriation is highly unlikely.

- **70%**—Private property is guaranteed by the government. The court system is subject to delays and is lax in enforcing contracts. Corruption is possible but rare, and expropriation is unlikely.
- **60%**—Enforcement of property rights is lax and subject to delays. Corruption is possible but rare, and the judiciary may be influenced by other branches of government. Expropriation is unlikely.
- **50%**—The court system is inefficient and subject to delays. Corruption may be present, and the judiciary may be influenced by other branches of government. Expropriation is possible but rare.
- **40%**—The court system is highly inefficient, and delays are so long that they deter the use of the court system. Corruption is present, and the judiciary is influenced by other branches of government. Expropriation is possible.
- **30%**—Property ownership is weakly protected. The court system is highly inefficient. Corruption is extensive, and the judiciary is strongly influenced by other branches of government. Expropriation is possible.
- **20%**—Private property is weakly protected. The court system is so inefficient and corrupt that outside settlement and arbitration is the norm. Property rights are difficult to enforce. Judicial corruption is extensive. Expropriation is common.
- **10%**—Private property is rarely protected, and almost all property belongs to the state. The country is in such chaos (for example, because of ongoing war) that protection of property is almost impossible to enforce. The judiciary so corrupt that property is not protected effectively. Expropriation is common.
- **0%**—Private property is outlawed, and all property belongs to the state. People do not have the right to sue others and do not have access to the courts. Corruption is endemic.

Sources. Unless otherwise noted, the authors used the following sources for information on property rights, in order of priority: Economist Intelligence Unit, *Country Commerce*, *Country Profile*, and *Country Report*, 2005 and 2006; U.S. Department of Commerce, *Country Commercial Guide*, 2005 and 2006; and U.S. Department of State, *Country Reports on Human Rights Practices*, 2005 and 2006.

Freedom #9: Freedom from Corruption

Corruption is defined as dishonesty or decay. In the context of governance, it can be defined as the failure of integrity in the system, a distortion by which individuals are able to gain personally at the expense of the whole. Political corruption is a sad part of human history and manifests itself in many forms such as bribery, extortion, nepotism, cronyism, patronage, embezzlement, and (most commonly) graft, whereby public officials steal or profit illegitimately from public funds.

Corruption infects all parts of an economy unless the market is allowed to develop transparency and effective policing. As a general rule, a higher level of corruption equates to a greater corrosion of economic freedom, although this may not hold in extreme cases. "In some circumstances," notes Harvard economist Robert Barro, "corruption may be preferable to honest enforcement of bad rules. For example, outcomes may be worse if a regulation that prohibits some useful economic activity is thoroughly enforced rather than circumvented through bribes."[8]

Many societies, of course, outlaw such activities as trafficking in illicit drugs, but others frequently limit individual liberty by outlawing such activities as private transportation and construction services. A government regulation or restriction in one area may create an informal market in another. For example, a country with high barriers to trade may have laws that

---

8   Robert J. Barro, "Rule of Law, Democracy, and Economic Performance," Chapter 2 in Gerald P. O'Driscoll, Jr., Kim R. Holmes, and Melanie Kirkpatrick, *2000 Index of Economic Freedom* (Washington, D.C.: The Heritage Foundation and Dow Jones & Company, Inc., 2000), p. 36.

protect its domestic market and prevent the import of foreign goods, but these barriers create incentives for smuggling and an informal market for the barred products.

Methodology. This factor relies on Transparency International's Corruption Perceptions Index (CPI), which measures the level of corruption in 152 countries, to determine the freedom from corruption scores of countries that are also listed in the *Index of Economic Freedom*.

The CPI is based on a 10-point scale in which a score of 10 indicates very little corruption and a score of 1 indicates a very corrupt government. In scoring freedom from corruption, the authors convert each of these raw CPI data to a 0 to 100 scale by multiplying the CPI score by 10. For example, if a country's raw CPI data score is 5.5, the country's overall freedom from corruption score is 55.

For countries that are not covered in the CPI, the freedom from corruption score is determined by using the qualitative information from internationally recognized and reliable sources. This procedure considers the extent to which corruption prevails in a country.

Sources. Unless otherwise noted, the authors used the following sources for information on informal market activities, in order of priority: Transparency International, *Corruption Perceptions Index*, 2002, 2003, 2004, and 2005; U.S. Department of Commerce, *Country Commercial Guide*, 2004, 2005, and 2006; Economist Intelligence Unit, *Country Commerce, Country Profile*, and *Country Report*, 2004, 2005, and 2006; Office of the U.S. Trade Representative, *2006 National Trade Estimate Report on Foreign Trade Barriers*; and official government publications of each country.

Freedom #10: Labor Freedom

Labor policy has been a key variable in the *Index of Economic Freedom* since its inception in 1995 as part of the wages and prices factor as well as the regulation factor. However, coverage on labor market flexibility in the previous methodology was limited by the lack of data on labor regulation that were available across countries in a consistent manner.

In light of the growing importance of labor market flexibility in today's economy and the increased availability of consistent labor policy data across countries, the 2007 *Index* has adopted an independent labor freedom factor that is designed to measure countries' labor market regulations more adequately.

Methodology. The new labor freedom factor is a quantitative factor based on objective data from the World Bank's *Doing Business* study. It provides reliable cross-country data on regulations concerning minimum wages, laws inhibiting layoffs, severance requirements, and measurable regulatory burdens on hiring, hours, and so on.

Specifically, four quantitative components are equally weighted as 25 percent of the labor freedom factor:

- Minimum wage,
- Rigidity of hours,
- Difficulty of firing redundant employees, and
- Cost of firing redundant employees.

The minimum wage component is basically a single quantitative measure: each country's mandatory minimum wage as a percentage of the average value added per worker. A higher minimum wage makes hiring unskilled workers more difficult.

Rigidity of hours is an index measure, calculated by *Doing Business*, that includes five components:

(i) whether night work is unrestricted; (ii) whether weekend work is unrestricted; (iii) whether the workweek can consist of 5.5 days; (iv) whether the workweek can extend to 50 hours or more (including overtime) for 2 months a year; and (v) whether paid annual vacation is 21 working days or fewer.[9]

Difficulty of firing is also an index measure calculated by *Doing Business*. It represents a simple issue: whether employers have the

---

9   World Bank, *Doing Business 2007: How to Reform*, p. 81.

legal authority to lay off workers efficiently, or whether that act has to be justified to the government or third parties. It has eight components:

(i) whether redundancy is disallowed as a basis for terminating workers; (ii) whether the employer needs to notify a third party (such as a government agency) to terminate 1 redundant worker; (iii) whether the employer needs to notify a third party to terminate a group of more than 20 redundant workers; (iv) whether the employer needs approval from a third party to terminate 1 redundant worker; (v) whether the employer needs approval from a third party to terminate a group of more than 20 redundant workers; (vi) whether the law requires the employer to consider reassignment or retraining options before redundancy termination; (vii) whether priority rules apply for redundancies; and (viii) whether priority rules apply for reemployment.[10]

The cost of firing is a composite of three quantitative subcomponents related to dismissals: the legally mandated notice period, mandatory severance pay, and a penalty the employer must pay when dismissing a worker.

In constructing the labor freedom score, each of the four components is converted to a 0 to 100 scale, based on the following equation:

$$Component\ Score_i = 50 \frac{component_{average}}{component_i}$$

where country i data are calculated relative to the world average and then multiplied by 50. The average country will receive a component score of 50 percent, whereas a country's maximum component score is limited to 100 percent. The four component scores are then averaged for each country, yielding a labor freedom score.

As an example, Turkey's average minimum wage as a ratio of the average wage is 0.62, which is double the average of 0.32 globally,

yielding a component score of 25.2 percent. Turkey's overall score is 45.4 percent, which is higher because the other three components represent a higher level of freedom than its minimum wage represents.

The simple average of the converted values for these four variables is computed for the country's labor freedom score. For example, even if a country has the worst rigidity of hours in the world, with a zero score for the component, it could still get a score as high as 75 based on the other three components.

For the 12 countries that are not covered by the World Bank's *Doing Business* study, the labor freedom factor is scored by looking into labor market flexibility based on qualitative information from other reliable and internationally recognized sources.[11]

Sources. Unless otherwise noted, the authors relied on the following sources for data on labor freedom, in order of priority: World Bank, *Doing Business 2007: How to Reform*; Economist Intelligence Unit, *Country Report* and *Country Profile*, 2004–2006; U.S. Department of Commerce, *Country Commercial Guide*, 2004, 2005, and 2006.

CONTINUITY AND CHANGE

With over a decade's experience measuring freedom in over a hundred nations annually, two issues regularly challenge our methodology. The first challenge has to do with outdated data. Country data in the most up-to-date sources are often behind by years. A few months before this publication went to press, for example, the World Bank revised tariff data for numerous countries, and this affected their trade freedom scores as we incorporated the new tariff rates. But countries often make policy changes during the year of grading. Sometimes the policy changes are not reflected in official data, and sometimes the changes are proposed but not made law, or made law but not enforced. Additionally, a country can experience a violent conflict or catastrophe that interrupts all efforts to measure the economy.

The second challenge is the balance between

---

10 *Ibid.*

11 See note 5.

quality and consistency of the *Index* itself. The authors aim for methodological consistency from one year to the next, balanced against opportunities to incorporate new data and methods that improve the quality of the current year's scores.

Most Current Information. Analyzing economic freedom annually permits the authors of the *Index* to include the most recent information as it becomes available country by country. A cutoff date is utilized so that all countries are treated fairly. As described above, the period of study for the current year's *Index* considers all information as of the last day of June of the previous year (June 30, 2006). Any changes in law effective after that date have no positive or negative impact; nor do new constitutions, election results, or democratic initiatives.

Occasionally, because the *Index* is published several months after the cutoff date for evaluation, major economic events occur that cannot be factored into the scores. In the past, such occurrences have been uncommon and isolated to one region of the world. The Asian financial crisis, for example, erupted at the end of 1997 just as the *1998 Index of Economic Freedom* was going to print. The policy changes in response to that crisis therefore were not considered in that year's scoring but were included in the next year's scores.

Changes in government policy are occurring at a rapid rate in many less-developed countries. The *Index of Economic Freedom*, because it is published each year, enables readers around the world to see how recent changes in government policy affect economic freedom in any of 161 specific countries. Each country page includes a time series graph of the country's overall score for each year from the present back to 1995.

In 2006, numerical grading was suspended for four countries: the Democratic Republic of Congo and Sudan, which are in a state of civil unrest or anarchy, and Iraq and Serbia–Montenegro, for which data necessary to grade the country are not available. Grading was resumed in 2006 for Angola and Burundi, which had been suspended since 2001 because of civil unrest or anarchy.

New Methodology. This year, every one of the 10 factors of freedom has been revised, and only a few—those that are purely quantitative—are 100 percent continuous back to 1995. Most have a discontinuity of some degree for one year in the overall series. For example, business freedom uses inputs from the World Bank's *Doing Business* for the 2006 and 2007 *Indices* but uses graders' assessments of the regulatory environment for the years 1995–2005. The correlation between these methods is high, but the methods themselves are clearly distinct.

The changes introduced in the 2007 *Index* include very minor discontinuities for comparisons between 2006 and 2007 scores because the 2006 scores have been revised as well. The following table defines how the *Index* time series changed over time.

The inclusion of labor freedom is the only radical departure from the old methodology. With the publication of the World Bank's *Doing Business* report, there exists for the first time a way to compare the restrictions placed on labor freedom in a quantitative way. Regrettably, this information is new and extends back only to 2005.

The other discontinuities are really just changes in the method, not adoptions of new data that have no relation to the previous data. High correlations exist between old and new data sources for the business freedom and freedom from corruption factors.

The three qualitative freedoms (investment, financial, and property) present an interesting dilemma. Though the methodology for the qualitative freedoms is not changed, the scaling is changed, from a five-bracket scale to a 0–100 scale. Old 1–5 scores for 1995–2006 were converted using a simple equation—e.g., using 100, 75, 50, 25, and 0, respectively, for 1–5—but the new detail allowed for 2007 scores means that there will be a one-time adjustment in these four factor series. For example, a country that received a 2 for property rights in 2006—which is now transformed to 75—may get a score of 80 in 2007 even if its laws are unchanged.

An attempt to regrade qualitative factor scores in previous years is problematic given

Time Series Continuity

	2006–2007 *Index*		1995–2007 *Index*	
	Continuity (100 = no change)	Explanation	Continuity (100 = no change)	Explanation
Business Freedom	100		50	New data in 2006
Trade Freedom	100		100	
Fiscal Freedom	100		100	
Freedom from Government	100		100	
Monetary Freedom	95	New data in 2007	95	New data in 2007
Investment Freedom	90	New scale in 2007	90	New scale in 2007
Financial Freedom	90	New scale in 2007	90	New scale in 2007
Property Rights	90	New scale in 2007	90	New scale in 2007
Freedom from Corruption	100		50	New data in 2002
Labor Freedom	100		0	Introduced in 2005

Source: Tim Kane, Kim R. Holmes, and Mary Anastasia O'Grady, *2007 Index of Economic Freedom* (Washington, D.C.: The Heritage Foundation and Dow Jones & Company, Inc., 2007), at *www.heritage.org/index*.

their qualitative/subjective nature, and we think it is fairest to leave them as is. While the new level of detail is clearly superior, the breaks mean that overall score changes between 2006 and 2007 will partially be the result of methodological detail in the *Index* and partially due to policy changes in the country.

Continuity. Ideally, the methodology used for the *Index of Economic Freedom* should not change over time. Instead, the scores for various countries would improve as the institutions of freedom improved as measured against a constant standard of measurable liberty. However, the increased quality of data available allows researchers to create more detailed measures of institutions as well as economic performance. The happy consequence of progress is an enhanced ability to measure progress.

Over time, therefore, the *Index of Economic Freedom* has been continually revised and improved; but we also aim for continuity, so each time a methodology change is implemented, we

also attempt to make the scores continuous back to 1995. In this way, country performance from one year to the next is comparable.

Nevertheless, there are still some cases for which new data are not available going back to the first year, at least not in the same level of detail. There is a natural tension between the quality of the *Index* and the continuity of the *Index*. It would be easy to maintain perfect continuity if no changes were ever made, or vice versa, but we are committed to incorporating innovations into the methodology to optimize both the quality and continuity of the *Index* rather than simply maximizing one at the expense of the other.

It is important to remember that the *Index* has been an effort to quantify subjective factors, not the measure of a singular, natural data-generating process (such as temperature), and has inevitably relied on the assessments of human beings. It is a policy tool with uses for current year analysis and time series analysis.

Discontinuities in any one of the 10 factors tend to be minor, with negligible impact on the overall score. For example, in 2002, the authors began to use a measure of corruption reflecting survey data rather than expert judgment. The change made sense, and the discontinuity of time series was justified by a high correlation between the methods. Another theoretical discontinuity is the fact that different human graders are used to judge the same factor in different years, although the graders make every effort to use the same standards.

In the end, both the addition of an academic advisory board and the effort to improve the methodology are intended to help people achieve greater personal freedom. As a tool to compare economic institutions across countries, the *Index* should therefore be better than ever.

Chapter 4

Economic Freedom in Five Regions

Tim Kane, Ph.D.

This chapter summarizes data on the five geographic regions used in scoring the countries included in the *Index of Economic Freedom*. Each region has features that are unlike any other, such as the generally high levels of wealth and freedom in Europe, the huge populations of Asia, and the punishing unemployment and inflation rates throughout sub-Saharan Africa.

Yet one relationship remains constant for all to see: In each region, the richest countries tend to be those with the strongest economic freedoms.

Table 1: Economic Freedom and Performance by Region

	Average Economic Freedom 2007 Score		Population	GDP per Capita (PPP)*	GDP 5-Year Growth Rate*	Unemployment Rate*	Inflation Rate*
	Simple	Weighted*					
Asia–Pacific	59.1	55.6	3,578,391,533	$5,784	6.7	8.7	4.2
Europe	67.5	64.5	797,644,407	$19,128	4.0	9.1	5.5
Americas	62.3	68.5	871,285,637	$19,503	2.5	8.4	5.5
Middle East/N. Africa	57.2	52.4	306,947,553	$7,002	4.3	13.6	7.8
Sub-Saharan Africa	54.7	54.2	670,760,171	$1,984	4.1	10.5	15.1
World	60.6	58.2	6,225,029,301	$9,065	5.4	9.1	5.9

* Weighted by population.

Sources: World Bank, World Development Indicators Online, at *publications.worldbank.org/subscriptions/WDI* (October 19, 2006; subscription required); Central Intelligence Agency, *The World Factbook 2005*, at *www.cia.gov/cia/publications/factbook/index.html* (October 19, 2006); International Monetary Fund, World Economic Outlook database, April 2006, at *www.imf.org/external/pubs/ft/weo/2006/01/data/index.htm* (October 19, 2006); and Tim Kane, Kim R. Holmes, and Mary Anastasia O'Grady, *2007 Index of Economic Freedom* (Washington, D.C.: The Heritage Foundation and Dow Jones & Company, Inc., 2007), at *www.heritage.org/index*.

ASIA–PACIFIC (REGION A)

The Asia–Pacific region spans the world's largest surface area, stretching from Japan and New Zealand in the East to Azerbaijan in the West. With 3.6 billion inhabitants, this region contains over half of the world's population: one-third in China and nearly another third in India. Yet there are only 30 countries in the region, compared to 41 in Europe and 40 in sub-Saharan Africa.

Despite having one of the world's poorest populations—the population-weighted average GDP per capita is $5,784—the Asia–Pacific region has far and away the fastest five-year per-capita growth rate at 6.7 percent. It also has one of the lowest average unemployment rates (8.7 percent) and the lowest average inflation rate (4.2 percent).

Chart A1 shows the 1995–2007 time series of the average economic freedom score for the region, compared to the world average. Chart A2 shows the clear relationship between high levels of economic freedom and high GDP per capita.

The fast growth cannot be explained by a high level of economic freedom alone, given that the average economic freedom score is below the world average at 59.1 percent. What makes Asia quite different from other regions is the extraordinary disparity in levels of economic freedom. The world's three freest economies—Hong Kong, Singapore, and Australia—are in Asia, in contrast with regional neighbors like Turkmenistan, Vietnam, Laos, Bangladesh, and Burma, all of which are categorized as "repressed," and North Korea, which has been the world's most economically repressed society for over a decade.

Table A1 ranks the countries in the region from most free to least free based on their overall freedom scores. It also includes the change from last year's score, the country's world rank, and each country's 2007 scores for each of the 10 economic freedoms. Chart A3 shows the distribution of countries across five different categories.

India and China are ranked 19 and 22 in the region, and both giants are categorized as "mostly unfree." Despite these seemingly low

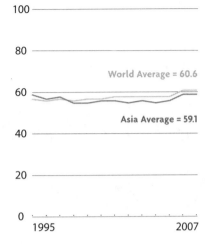

Chart A1: Asia-Pacific Average Economic Freedom

World Average = 60.6

Asia Average = 59.1

1995   2007

Source: Tim Kane, Kim R. Holmes, and Mary Anastasia O'Grady, *2007 Index of Economic Freedom* (Washington, D.C.: The Heritage Foundation and Dow Jones & Company, Inc., 2007), at *www.heritage.org/index*.

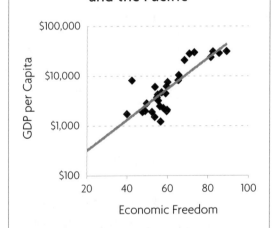

Chart A2: Economic Freedom vs. GDP per Capita in Asia and the Pacific

GDP per Capita

Economic Freedom

Sources: World Bank, World Development Indicators Online, at *publications.worldbank.org/subscriptions/WDI* (October 19, 2006; subscription required); Central Intelligence Agency, The World Factbook 2005, at *www.cia.gov/cia/publications/factbook/index.html* (October 19, 2006); International Monetary Fund, World Economic Outlook database, April 2006, at *www.imf.org/external/pubs/ft/weo/2006/01/data/index.htm* (October 19, 2006); and Tim Kane, Kim R. Holmes, and Mary Anastasia O'Grady, *2007 Index of Economic Freedom* (Washington, D.C.: The Heritage Foundation and Dow Jones & Company, Inc., 2007), at *www.heritage.org/index*.

scores, there is no denying that the winds of change are blowing in Asia, particularly in

Table A1: Economic Freedom Scores for Asia and the Pacific

2007 World Rank	2007 Regional Rank	Country	Economic Freedom 2007	Change from 2006	Business Freedom	Trade Freedom	Fiscal Freedom	Freedom from Government	Monetary Freedom	Investment Freedom	Financial Freedom	Property Rights	Freedom from Corruption	Labor Freedom
1	1	Hong Kong	89.3	-1.6	88.3	80.0	95.3	91.6	91.1	90.0	90.0	90.0	83.0	93.6
2	2	Singapore	85.7	-2.8	94.6	80.0	93.0	86.2	89.5	80.0	50.0	90.0	94.0	99.3
3	3	Australia	82.7	1.2	91.7	73.8	75.4	70.1	84.8	70.0	90.0	90.0	88.0	93.1
5	4	New Zealand	81.6	-2.4	93.7	74.0	74.2	63.6	84.5	70.0	80.0	90.0	96.0	89.9
18	5	Japan	73.6	-1.0	94.3	75.2	80.6	67.2	92.0	60.0	50.0	70.0	73.0	73.4
26	6	Taiwan	71.1	0.5	73.0	76.7	84.7	89.8	81.3	70.0	50.0	70.0	59.0	56.7
36	7	Korea, South	68.6	0.6	83.1	64.2	81.0	81.5	79.0	70.0	50.0	70.0	50.0	57.7
48	8	Malaysia	65.8	2.1	68.6	71.8	87.8	79.8	80.0	40.0	40.0	50.0	51.0	89.5
50	9	Thailand	65.6	0.5	76.1	69.2	83.2	91.2	77.6	30.0	50.0	50.0	38.0	90.4
75	10	Kazakhstan	60.4	-0.8	66.5	64.2	87.6	85.9	72.9	30.0	60.0	30.0	26.0	80.5
78	11	Mongolia	60.1	-3.1	73.1	70.0	81.0	56.9	74.3	60.0	60.0	30.0	30.0	65.9
79	12	Kyrgyzstan	59.9	-3.0	61.4	71.4	95.1	76.3	77.1	40.0	50.0	30.0	23.0	74.4
80	13	Fiji	59.8	2.8	70.4	61.8	86.3	74.3	74.7	30.0	60.0	30.0	40.0	70.5
84	14	Sri Lanka	59.3	-0.8	69.2	66.6	85.7	85.7	69.8	30.0	40.0	50.0	32.0	63.9
89	15	Pakistan	58.2	-1.3	70.9	53.6	82.0	89.3	72.0	50.0	40.0	30.0	21.0	73.2
97	16	Philippines	57.4	-0.2	54.2	74.8	84.0	91.4	73.4	30.0	50.0	30.0	25.0	60.7
98	17	Tajikistan	56.9	1.1	53.2	66.0	93.2	86.8	67.2	30.0	40.0	30.0	21.0	81.7
102	18	Cambodia	56.5	-2.7	37.1	47.2	94.2	85.1	81.1	50.0	50.0	30.0	23.0	67.7
104	19	India	55.6	3.3	49.6	51.2	84.8	89.0	77.2	40.0	30.0	50.0	29.0	55.1
107	20	Azerbaijan	55.4	1.4	58.0	67.6	87.2	86.6	76.8	30.0	30.0	30.0	22.0	65.4
110	21	Indonesia	55.1	1.0	45.7	69.0	85.0	90.7	70.9	30.0	40.0	30.0	22.0	67.5
119	22	China	54.0	-1.4	54.9	68.0	77.7	88.6	75.5	30.0	30.0	20.0	32.0	63.5
121	23	Nepal	54.0	-1.5	59.6	51.4	91.0	91.0	77.6	30.0	30.0	30.0	25.0	54.0
132	24	Uzbekistan	52.6	2.2	66.1	68.2	90.0	66.1	58.6	30.0	20.0	30.0	22.0	74.7
138	25	Vietnam	50.0	-0.0	62.0	51.0	82.9	80.8	67.5	30.0	30.0	10.0	26.0	59.3
140	26	Laos	49.1	2.4	51.0	55.8	80.6	86.3	71.3	30.0	20.0	10.0	33.0	53.5
143	27	Bangladesh	47.8	-6.6	64.3	0.0	89.4	91.5	68.7	30.0	20.0	30.0	17.0	67.0
152	28	Turkmenistan	42.5	-1.3	30.0	74.2	94.4	82.9	65.9	10.0	10.0	10.0	18.0	30.0
153	29	Burma	40.1	0.5	20.0	71.8	87.9	88.3	65.4	10.0	10.0	10.0	18.0	20.0
157	30	Korea, North	3.0	-1.0	0.0	0.0	0.0	0.0	0.0	10.0	0.0	10.0	10.0	0.0

Source: Tim Kane, Kim R. Holmes, and Mary Anastasia O'Grady, *2007 Index of Economic Freedom* (Washington, D.C.: The Heritage Foundation and Dow Jones & Company, Inc., 2007), at *www.heritage.org/index*.

India and China. The economic success enjoyed by Taiwan, South Korea, and Japan in particular are an inspiration for other Asian countries—and for the rest of the world as well. Meanwhile, major reforms in New Zealand and Australia have raised their economic freedom scores and contributed to superior economic performance.

Asia–Pacific countries are significantly stronger than the world average in two of the 10 economic freedoms: labor freedom and freedom from government. Lower government expenditures result in a government score that is almost a full 10 percentage points better than the world average, whereas labor freedom is 4 percentage points better.

However, the typical Asian country has notably lower scores in four factors: investment freedom, financial freedom, property rights, and freedom from corruption. This suggests that countries could make the most progress by strengthening their banking and investment institutions, perhaps by allowing greater foreign investment by overseas financial firms, including insurance and banking firms.

Hong Kong is clearly blazing a trail for others to follow. Hong Kong has the top score in six of the 10 factors. Singapore is the top country in business freedom and labor freedom, meaning that it is easiest to start, operate, and close a firm there, and also allows firms the most flexibility in hiring and firing workers. Japan enjoys the strongest monetary freedom, thanks largely to its low inflation rate, and New Zealand sets the standard for clean government.

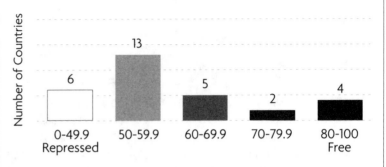

Chart A3: Distribution of Economic Freedom in Asia and the Pacific

Source: Tim Kane, Kim R. Holmes, and Mary Anastasia O'Grady, *2007 Index of Economic Freedom* (Washington, D.C.: The Heritage Foundation and Dow Jones & Company, Inc., 2007), at *www.heritage.org/index*.

Chart A4: Asia and the Pacific Ten Economic Freedoms

Source: Tim Kane, Kim R. Holmes, and Mary Anastasia O'Grady, *2007 Index of Economic Freedom* (Washington, D.C.: The Heritage Foundation and Dow Jones & Company, Inc., 2007), at *www.heritage.org/index*.

EUROPE (REGION B)

Europe is the birthplace of the modern industrial economy. It also served as the testing ground for the two great economic philosophies of the past century and witnessed the collapse of Communism. Now that Cold War contrast has been eclipsed by a new technology-driven globalization. The contemporary European Union consensus, which is built around a quasi-market welfare state, is itself looking like a relic of the past century in contrast with fast-growing tigers like Ireland and Estonia.

The 41 countries in Europe are the most of any region and include nations as diverse as Russia, Switzerland, Iceland, and Greece. Most people around the world see Europe and prosperity as synonymous because the people of most European countries enjoy incomes that average $19,128 per capita annually, or more than twice the world average.

The European continent produces one-quarter of the world's economic product and is doubly more active in export and import than other regions (though much of this activity is internal trade). It enjoys moderate growth and inflation but has been plagued by higher unemployment rates than it should naturally endure—which means, put another way, that its economic model is failing to generate jobs year after year for almost one-tenth of willing workers.

Chart B1 shows the 1995–2007 time series of the average economic freedom score for the region, compared to the world average. Chart B2 shows the clear relationship between high levels of economic freedom and high GDP per capita.

The overall statistical picture of Europe is one of prosperity and of stability. The heavy business and labor regulations that are in place are intended to protect traditional sectors and occupations. If there is one lesson about economics from the past 300 years, it is that capital does not stand still. The restrictions on labor, the lack of fiscal and governmental freedom, and the distortionary subsidies in many parts of Europe hinder its growth.

Table B1 ranks the countries in the region from most free to least free based on their over-

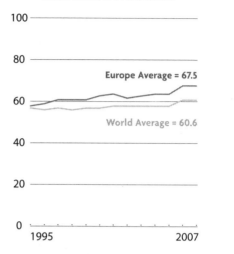

Chart B1: Europe Average Economic Freedom

Europe Average = 67.5

World Average = 60.6

Source: Tim Kane, Kim R. Holmes, and Mary Anastasia O'Grady, *2007 Index of Economic Freedom* (Washington, D.C.: The Heritage Foundation and Dow Jones & Company, Inc., 2007), at *www.heritage.org/index*.

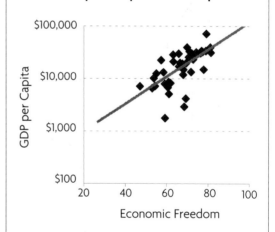

Chart B2: Economic Freedom vs. GDP per Capita in Europe

Sources: World Bank, World Development Indicators Online, at *publications.worldbank.org/subscriptions/WDI* (October 19, 2006; subscription required); Central Intelligence Agency, The World Factbook 2005, at *www.cia.gov/cia/publications/factbook/index.html* (October 19, 2006); International Monetary Fund, World Economic Outlook database, April 2006, at *www.imf.org/external/pubs/ft/weo/2006/01/data/index.htm* (October 19, 2006); and Tim Kane, Kim R. Holmes, and Mary Anastasia O'Grady, *2007 Index of Economic Freedom* (Washington, D.C.: The Heritage Foundation and Dow Jones & Company, Inc., 2007), at *www.heritage.org/index*.

all freedom scores. It also includes the change from last year's score, the country's world

Table B1: Economic Freedom Scores for Europe

2007 World Rank	2007 Regional Rank	Country	Economic Freedom 2007	Change from 2006	Business Freedom	Trade Freedom	Fiscal Freedom	Freedom from Government	Monetary Freedom	Investment Freedom	Financial Freedom	Property Rights	Freedom from Corruption	Labor Freedom
6	1	United Kingdom	81.6	-0.7	92.1	76.6	74.6	54.2	79.3	90	90	90	86	82.7
7	2	Ireland	81.3	0.1	92.8	76.6	81.1	73.1	85.1	90	90	90	74	60.4
8	3	Luxembourg	79.3	-1.0	90.0	76.6	75.4	55.9	80.2	90	80	90	85	70.0
9	4	Switzerland	79.1	-1.0	83.3	77.0	78.6	68.6	83.6	70	70	90	91	78.4
12	5	Estonia	78.1	2.2	80.0	76.6	89.7	66.8	83.0	90	90	90	64	51.2
13	6	Denmark	77.6	1.4	95.3	76.6	55.2	32.1	86.8	80	90	90	95	74.7
14	7	Netherlands	77.1	0.1	88.3	76.6	65.8	47.8	87.0	90	80	90	86	59.2
15	8	Iceland	77.1	-0.6	94.1	74.0	82.4	50.3	82.9	60	70	90	97	69.9
16	9	Finland	76.5	0.9	95.3	76.6	75.4	39.0	89.7	70	80	90	96	53.4
17	10	Belgium	74.5	0.3	90.8	76.6	62.2	41.2	80.0	90	80	80	74	70.5
19	11	Germany	73.5	-0.5	88.2	76.6	74.3	48.0	81.5	90	50	90	82	54.6
20	12	Cyprus	73.1	-0.2	70.0	76.6	87.8	54.9	84.7	70	70	90	57	70.0
21	13	Sweden	72.6	-1.4	95.0	76.6	53.6	31.5	85.2	80	70	90	92	52.0
22	14	Lithuania	72.0	-1.0	86.4	76.6	91.0	76.6	81.2	70	80	50	48	60.1
25	15	Austria	71.3	-0.1	79.8	76.6	66.9	40.5	85.7	70	70	90	87	46.8
27	16	Spain	70.9	0.3	77.1	76.6	70.1	63.6	78.6	70	80	70	70	52.7
30	17	Norway	70.1	-0.7	97.0	79.2	66.1	45.9	82.6	50	50	90	89	51.1
31	18	Czech Republic	69.7	-0.3	61.2	76.6	79.9	52.7	86.2	70	80	70	43	77.2
32	19	Armenia	69.4	-5.1	84.5	75.6	93.1	91.6	79.7	60	70	30	29	80.9
35	20	Georgia	68.7	3.9	78.9	61.8	94.2	91.3	77.9	60	70	30	23	99.9
40	21	Slovakia	68.4	-0.8	71.1	76.6	93.0	60.8	76.7	70	80	50	43	62.5
41	22	Latvia	68.2	-1.0	76.8	76.6	89.3	69.2	74.1	70	70	50	42	64.1
42	23	Malta	67.8	-1.6	70.0	76.6	74.0	42.2	79.2	50	70	90	66	60.0
43	24	Portugal	66.7	1.1	79.6	76.6	79.6	49.6	80.2	70	50	70	65	46.0
44	25	Hungary	66.2	-0.9	71.2	76.6	79.2	41.8	76.7	70	60	70	50	66.1
45	26	France	66.1	0.9	86.1	76.6	64.2	32.0	81.3	50	60	70	75	65.9
58	27	Slovenia	63.6	0.1	74.2	76.6	69.7	56.8	79.0	70	50	50	61	48.7
60	28	Italy	63.4	0.7	73.7	76.6	68.5	46.4	80.8	70	60	50	50	57.6
62	29	Bulgaria	62.2	-2.1	66.9	60.8	91.3	65.6	75.7	60	60	30	40	71.5
66	30	Albania	61.4	-0.6	56.1	63.2	91.5	77.7	80.7	60	70	30	24	60.6
67	31	Romania	61.3	2.3	70.9	74.0	91.7	74.9	69.7	50	60	30	30	61.4
71	32	Macedonia	60.8	0.2	60.9	73.4	90.0	67.8	91.1	50	60	30	27	58.1
81	33	Moldova	59.5	-0.1	70.0	74.4	90.4	71.7	68.0	30	50	50	29	61.2
83	34	Turkey	59.3	0.9	67.4	76.0	79.4	69.9	70.2	50	50	50	35	45.4
87	35	Poland	58.8	-2.8	56.1	76.6	79.1	55.3	80.3	50	50	50	34	56.2
94	36	Greece	57.6	-0.5	70.2	76.6	74.5	45.3	78.3	50	40	50	43	48.5
109	37	Croatia	55.3	-0.9	53.8	77.8	79.9	36.5	79.3	50	60	30	34	52.0
115	38	Bosnia & Herzegovina	54.7	-2.2	53.8	70.2	90.0	45.6	81.1	50	60	10	29	57.3
120	39	Russia	54.0	-0.3	66.6	62.6	86.3	71.6	62.8	30	40	30	24	66.2
125	40	Ukraine	53.3	-2.2	54.0	72.2	89.1	61.9	68.4	30	50	30	26	51.8
145	41	Belarus	47.4	-1.2	54.5	62.2	87.9	66.9	61.4	20	10	20	26	64.7

Source: Tim Kane, Kim R. Holmes, and Mary Anastasia O'Grady, *2007 Index of Economic Freedom* (Washington, D.C.: The Heritage Foundation and Dow Jones & Company, Inc., 2007), at *www.heritage.org/index*.

2007 Index of Economic Freedom

rank, and each country's 2007 scores for each of the 10 economic freedoms. Chart B3 shows the distribution of countries across five different categories.

A majority of the world's 20 freest countries are in Europe, which is the only region to have a distribution of economies that is skewed toward freedom. The United Kingdom is the highest-ranking European country, ranked 6 worldwide,

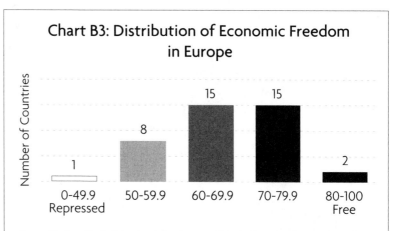

Chart B3: Distribution of Economic Freedom in Europe

Source: Tim Kane, Kim R. Holmes, and Mary Anastasia O'Grady, *2007 Index of Economic Freedom* (Washington, D.C.: The Heritage Foundation and Dow Jones & Company, Inc., 2007), at *www.heritage.org/index*.

followed immediately by Ireland at 7, Luxembourg at 8, and Switzerland at 9. Scandinavian and Baltic countries, primarily, round out the top 20, along with Germany, Holland, Belgium, and Cyprus. Europe has definitely benefited from economic competition over the centuries, which may explain why economic repression is so rare in the West.

With its extensive free-market institutions, Europe has higher than average scores in seven of the 10 economic freedoms. Its average score in business freedom is an impressive 13 percentage points ahead of any other region. It is 12 points ahead in investment freedom, 11 in financial freedom, 13 in freedom from corruption, and 15 in property rights. However, Europe suffers from the second-worst regional score in labor freedom and is dead last in fiscal freedom and freedom from government—the price of welfare states that are so large as a percentage of GDP. Strong state sectors and rigid labor markets have already prompted significant social turmoil, not least in France.

Norway leads in business and trade freedom. Impressively for a post-Communist state, Georgia leads in labor freedom and fiscal freedom because of a combination of low taxes and a highly flexible labor market. Armenia and Macedonia—leaders in freedom from government and monetary freedom, respectively—are other former Communist nations that are rebuilding their economies.

Many nations are tied with the top scores in

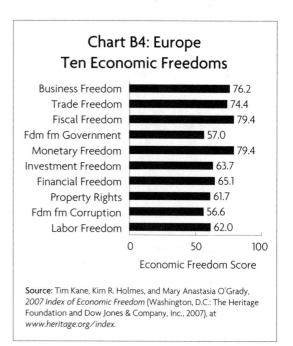

Chart B4: Europe Ten Economic Freedoms

Source: Tim Kane, Kim R. Holmes, and Mary Anastasia O'Grady, *2007 Index of Economic Freedom* (Washington, D.C.: The Heritage Foundation and Dow Jones & Company, Inc., 2007), at *www.heritage.org/index*.

property rights and financial freedom, which confirms how widespread good intentions are throughout the region.

THE AMERICAS (REGION C)

The Americas is one of the most economically diverse regions and presents a puzzle. Countries range from the hyperwealthy United States and developing powerhouse Brazil to the small island economies of the Caribbean and poor nations of Central America. The average population for each country is 30 million people, and the overall regional population is 871 million: second only to Asia on both counts. With the world's lowest average unemployment rate and peaceful relationships, it would seem poised for broadly shared economic success.

Chart C1 shows the 1995–2007 time series of the average economic freedom score for the region, compared to the world average. On that simple basis, the region has performed well.

Across the region, however, the reality is that economies are stagnating. Among the five regions, the Americas has one of the lowest average per capita incomes and by far the slowest compound five-year growth rate. The puzzle is that the income rank is inverted if a population-weighted average is used instead of a simple average. Once population is taken into account, income per capita is higher in the Americas than in any other region, even Europe. All this statistical evidence means that the smaller nations around the Western Hemisphere seem to be stuck in poverty traps.

Chart C2 shows the clear relationship between high levels of economic freedom and high GDP per capita, implying a large freedom gap. The recent rise of populists like Evo Morales and Hugo Chávez threatens to widen the freedom gap in the Americas even more.

The Americas has been the second-highest region in terms of freedom since 1999, when it was the world leader. That was before Argentina's economic implosion and the protectionist policy responses that followed, notably the weakened average trade score.

Table C1 ranks the countries in the region from most free to least free based on their overall freedom scores. It also includes the change from last year's score, the country's world rank, and each country's 2007 scores for each of the 10 economic freedoms. Chart C3 shows

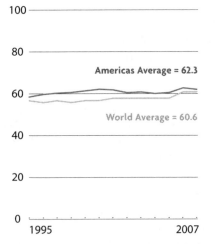

Chart C1: The Americas Average Economic Freedom

Americas Average = 62.3

World Average = 60.6

Source: Tim Kane, Kim R. Holmes, and Mary Anastasia O'Grady, *2007 Index of Economic Freedom* (Washington, D.C.: The Heritage Foundation and Dow Jones & Company, Inc., 2007), at *www.heritage.org/index.*

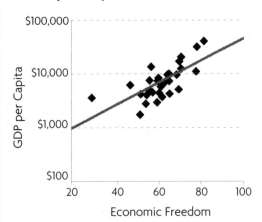

Chart C2: Economic Freedom vs. GDP per Capita in the Americas

Sources: World Bank, World Development Indicators Online, at *publications.worldbank.org/subscriptions/WDI* (October 19, 2006; subscription required); Central Intelligence Agency, The World Factbook 2005, at *www.cia.gov/cia/publications/factbook/index.html* (October 19, 2006); International Monetary Fund, World Economic Outlook database, April 2006, at *www.imf.org/external/pubs/ft/weo/2006/01/data/index.htm* (October 19, 2006); and Tim Kane, Kim R. Holmes, and Mary Anastasia O'Grady, *2007 Index of Economic Freedom* (Washington, D.C.: The Heritage Foundation and Dow Jones & Company, Inc., 2007), at *www.heritage.org/index.*

the distribution of countries across five different categories.

Only three countries from the Americas rank

Table C1: Economic Freedom Scores for the Americas

2007 World Rank	2007 Regional Rank	Country	Economic Freedom 2007	Change from 2006	Business Freedom	Trade Freedom	Fiscal Freedom	Freedom from Government	Monetary Freedom	Investment Freedom	Financial Freedom	Property Rights	Freedom from Corruption	Labor Freedom
4	1	United States	82.0	-0.4	94.5	76.6	79.4	67.5	83.8	80	80	90	76	92.1
10	2	Canada	78.7	-0.0	96.1	78.2	83.9	61.8	80.6	60	70	90	84	82.7
11	3	Chile	78.3	-2.9	68.9	72.4	85.7	87.6	79.9	70	70	90	73	85.3
23	4	Trinidad and Tobago	71.4	-0.4	61.8	69.0	88.0	83.7	74.7	70	70	70	38	89.2
24	5	Bahamas	71.4	-1.2	80.0	28.8	98.3	89.9	77.3	40	70	80	70	80.0
28	6	Barbados	70.5	-4.7	90.0	47.0	78.3	64.4	76.5	50	60	90	69	80.0
29	7	El Salvador	70.3	-0.7	62.6	66.6	90.9	95.1	76.7	70	70	50	42	79.2
33	8	Uruguay	69.3	1.8	68.1	71.6	90.8	81.7	73.1	70	30	70	59	79.0
46	9	Jamaica	66.1	-1.6	78.3	60.4	83.4	67.4	70.9	80	60	50	36	74.1
47	10	Panama	65.9	-1.3	75.1	66.2	88.7	86.8	85.8	70	60	30	35	61.2
49	11	Mexico	65.8	1.2	82.1	72.6	88.1	77.2	77.0	50	60	50	35	66.0
51	12	Costa Rica	65.1	-2.3	63.5	72.4	88.6	92.3	67.1	70	40	50	42	65.4
56	13	Belize	63.7	-1.8	76.7	57.2	79.8	80.1	73.5	50	50	50	37	82.8
61	14	Nicaragua	62.7	-1.7	59.7	72.4	86.4	85.6	71.2	70	60	30	26	65.7
63	15	Peru	62.1	1.2	65.1	62.6	86.8	92.2	85.7	50	60	40	35	43.3
68	16	Guatemala	61.2	0.6	54.1	70.2	86.5	96.4	72.2	50	60	30	25	68.0
70	17	Brazil	60.9	-0.8	53.3	64.8	88.6	88.8	72.6	50	40	50	37	63.8
73	18	Colombia	60.5	-2.4	71.4	61.4	82.4	87.0	70.2	50	60	30	40	53.0
76	19	Honduras	60.3	0.7	56.6	69.2	87.8	82.9	71.5	50	70	30	26	59.2
90	20	Guyana	58.2	-1.4	57.0	57.0	78.5	66.1	74.0	50	60	40	25	74.1
95	21	Argentina	57.5	0.2	65.5	61.4	82.3	89.6	71.3	50	40	30	28	56.6
99	22	Paraguay	56.8	1.4	47.0	67.4	97.8	79.8	78.4	50	60	30	21	36.7
100	23	Dominican Republic	56.7	0.1	57.6	63.8	86.5	91.5	63.2	50	40	30	30	54.9
108	24	Ecuador	55.3	-0.3	57.1	62.0	85.7	85.2	74.1	30	60	30	25	44.2
112	25	Bolivia	55.0	-4.1	62.3	69.2	93.2	74.3	70.9	30	60	30	25	35.0
133	26	Suriname	52.6	-0.6	42.0	55.0	76.3	65.3	69.1	30	30	50	32	75.9
135	27	Haiti	52.2	2.4	37.6	74.2	85.3	95.2	62.0	30	40	10	18	70.2
144	28	Venezuela	47.7	2.6	48.8	56.2	83.7	69.5	57.6	20	40	30	23	48.0
156	29	Cuba	29.7	-2.5	10.0	60.2	62.8	10.0	65.8	10	10	10	38	20.0

Source: Tim Kane, Kim R. Holmes, and Mary Anastasia O'Grady, *2007 Index of Economic Freedom* (Washington, D.C.: The Heritage Foundation and Dow Jones & Company, Inc., 2007), at *www.heritage.org/index*.

among the top 20 in the world: the United States (4), Canada (10), and Chile (11). Indeed, the region's countries are distributed in a more balanced fashion than are the countries of any other region, almost like a bell curve. All but three countries receive an economic freedom score between 50 percent and 80 percent, and roughly half fall in the middle category of "moderately free."

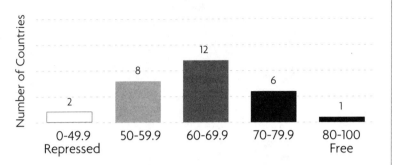

Chart C3: Distribution of Economic Freedom in the Americas

Number of Countries

2 — 0-49.9 Repressed
8 — 50-59.9
12 — 60-69.9
6 — 70-79.9
1 — 80-100 Free

Source: Tim Kane, Kim R. Holmes, and Mary Anastasia O'Grady, *2007 Index of Economic Freedom* (Washington, D.C.: The Heritage Foundation and Dow Jones & Company, Inc., 2007), at *www.heritage.org/index.*

Looking at each of the specific economic freedoms, countries in the Americas perform better than the world average in eight of 10. Corruption and inflation are the problem areas, representing weaker monetary policy and rule of law. The deficits in freedom from corruption and monetary freedom are due to a few outliers, such as Suriname for corruption and the Dominican Republic, which is suffering from over 50 percent annual inflation.

The typical North/Central/South American nation stands out positively in terms of limited government taxation and expenditures, as well as strong labor freedoms. The other five freedoms are also slightly stronger in the Americas than they are elsewhere, with lighter trade, investment, financial, and regulatory burdens.

The United States and Canada are the leaders in most of the 10 categories. The U.S. is most free in investment freedom, financial freedom, property rights, and labor freedom. The result: a flexible, adaptive economy that remains one of the world's premier financial markets. Canada leads in freedom from corruption and (deviating from the European model) trade and business freedom. Guatemala (for its low government expenditures), Panama (for its low inflation rate), and the Bahamas (for low taxes) round out the rest of the best.

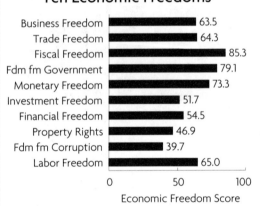

Chart C4: The Americas Ten Economic Freedoms

	Economic Freedom Score
Business Freedom	63.5
Trade Freedom	64.3
Fiscal Freedom	85.3
Fdm fm Government	79.1
Monetary Freedom	73.3
Investment Freedom	51.7
Financial Freedom	54.5
Property Rights	46.9
Fdm fm Corruption	39.7
Labor Freedom	65.0

Source: Tim Kane, Kim R. Holmes, and Mary Anastasia O'Grady, *2007 Index of Economic Freedom* (Washington, D.C.: The Heritage Foundation and Dow Jones & Company, Inc., 2007), at *www.heritage.org/index.*

MIDDLE EAST/NORTH AFRICA (REGION D)

The Middle East/North Africa region encompasses some of the world's most ancient civilizations. Stretching from Morocco's Atlantic shores to Iran and Yemen's beaches on the Arabian Sea, the Middle East remains central in the world's affairs. Today, however, most of the economies in this region are not free. Cursed in some ways by enormous natural oil resources, the local populations experience extreme concentrations of wealth and poverty.

The Middle East has a comparatively high GDP per capita. At $7,002 per person, the regional GDP is dead center: lower than Europe and the Americas but higher than Asia and sub-Saharan Africa. The difference between the highest GDP per capita and the lowest is enormous: an estimated $27,400 in Qatar versus $879 in Yemen. Structural problems clearly abound, as the regional unemployment rate, which averages 13.6 percent, is the highest in the world. Despite the outflow of crude oil, the Middle East is also second worst among the regions in exports and imports ($24 billion and $21 billion, respectively), indicating a lack of economic dynamism.

Chart D1 shows the 1995–2007 time series of the simple average economic freedom score for the region, compared to the world average. Using a population-weighted average, the people of the Middle East/North Africa region have the least economic freedom in the world. Paradoxically, the Middle East/North Africa region is also the only *Index* area to increase its average economic freedom over the past year. Yemen and Morocco made the biggest leaps forward with 3.0 percent and 4.4 percent increases, respectively. The United Arab Emirates (UAE), Tunisia, Qatar, Jordan, Libya, Kuwait, Lebanon, Israel, and Egypt also improved their economic freedom scores, marking a definite regional trend.

Yet even in this region, there is a correlation between freedom and prosperity. Chart D2 shows the positive relationship between high levels of economic freedom and high GDP per capita. The ongoing transformation of innovative states in Bahrain, Qatar, and the UAE

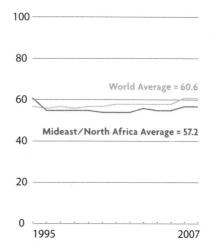

Chart D1: Middle East/N. Africa Average Economic Freedom

World Average = 60.6

Mideast/North Africa Average = 57.2

Source: Tim Kane, Kim R. Holmes, and Mary Anastasia O'Grady, *2007 Index of Economic Freedom* (Washington, D.C.: The Heritage Foundation and Dow Jones & Company, Inc., 2007), at *www.heritage.org/index*.

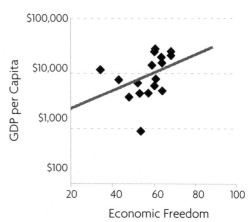

Chart D2: Economic Freedom vs. GDP per Capita in the Middle East and North Africa

Sources: World Bank, World Development Indicators Online, at *publications.worldbank.org/subscriptions/WDI* (October 19, 2006; subscription required); Central Intelligence Agency, The World Factbook 2005, at *www.cia.gov/cia/publications/factbook/index.html* (October 19, 2006); International Monetary Fund, World Economic Outlook database, April 2006, at *www.imf.org/external/pubs/ft/weo/2006/01/data/index.htm* (October 19, 2006); and Tim Kane, Kim R. Holmes, and Mary Anastasia O'Grady, *2007 Index of Economic Freedom* (Washington, D.C.: The Heritage Foundation and Dow Jones & Company, Inc., 2007), at *www.heritage.org/index*.

Table D1: Economic Freedom Scores for the Middle East and North Africa

2007 World Rank	2007 Regional Rank	Country	Economic Freedom 2007	Change from 2006	Business Freedom	Trade Freedom	Fiscal Freedom	Freedom from Government	Monetary Freedom	Investment Freedom	Financial Freedom	Property Rights	Freedom from Corruption	Labor Freedom
37	1	Israel	68.4	1.7	69.7	75.2	72.0	60.0	84.2	70	50	70	63	70.1
39	2	Bahrain	68.4	-2.6	80.0	69.6	99.6	56.7	80.1	50	90	60	58	40.0
53	3	Jordan	64.0	0.2	54.8	64.2	88.8	64.1	83.5	50	60	50	57	67.9
54	4	Oman	63.9	1.6	63.6	73.8	99.0	37.7	79.1	50	50	50	63	73.2
57	5	Kuwait	63.7	1.1	67.9	72.2	99.9	39.2	78.8	50	50	50	47	81.7
69	6	Tunisia	61.0	1.8	78.3	61.8	80.8	82.1	80.0	30	30	50	49	67.9
72	7	Qatar	60.7	0.3	60.0	71.4	99.9	54.6	72.4	30	50	50	59	60.0
74	8	UAE	60.4	0.7	49.2	70.0	99.9	60.3	75.3	30	40	40	62	77.2
77	9	Lebanon	60.3	1.8	56.2	67.4	95.9	64.3	83.5	30	70	30	31	74.4
85	10	Saudi Arabia	59.1	-2.3	52.9	65.4	99.6	46.1	80.1	30	40	50	34	92.9
96	11	Morocco	57.4	1.4	74.3	51.0	75.5	76.3	83.3	70	40	30	32	41.9
122	12	Yemen	53.8	3.0	52.7	56.4	88.8	65.1	68.2	50	30	30	27	69.7
127	13	Egypt	53.2	1.0	39.9	52.2	93.6	73.6	69.0	50	30	40	34	49.8
134	14	Algeria	52.2	-1.1	73.7	56.0	82.6	47.9	80.6	50	20	30	28	53.7
142	15	Syria	48.2	-2.3	56.6	49.0	88.3	57.5	68.9	30	10	30	34	57.4
150	16	Iran	43.1	-0.2	54.9	50.4	84.8	59.8	61.3	10	10	10	29	61.2
155	17	Libya	34.5	0.2	20.0	29.6	87.8	23.5	78.9	30	20	10	25	20.0

Source: Tim Kane, Kim R. Holmes, and Mary Anastasia O'Grady, *2007 Index of Economic Freedom* (Washington, D.C.: The Heritage Foundation and Dow Jones & Company, Inc., 2007), at *www.heritage.org/index*.

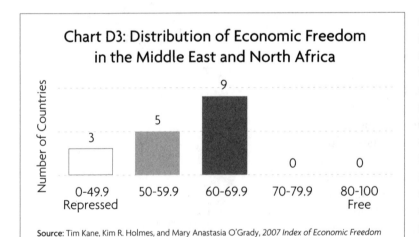

Chart D3: Distribution of Economic Freedom in the Middle East and North Africa

Number of Countries

- 0-49.9 Repressed: 3
- 50-59.9: 5
- 60-69.9: 9
- 70-79.9: 0
- 80-100 Free: 0

Source: Tim Kane, Kim R. Holmes, and Mary Anastasia O'Grady, *2007 Index of Economic Freedom* (Washington, D.C.: The Heritage Foundation and Dow Jones & Company, Inc., 2007), at *www.heritage.org/index*.

overall freedom scores. It also includes the change from last year's score, the country's world rank, and each country's 2007 scores for each of the 10 economic freedoms. Israel, Bahrain, and Jordan—three nations that are radically different politically but all have made a commitment to economic freedom—rank highest. Two leading oil-producing nations—Oman and Kuwait—round out the top five. The lowest ranking countries are Syria, Iran, and Libya, a group of fairly disparate nations that are united by their lack of economic or political liberalism. Chart D3 shows may yet light the way for economic growth regionally.

Table D1 ranks the countries in the region from most free to least free based on their

the distribution of countries across five different categories.

The Middle East does not have any countries in the ranks of the world's 20 most free. Israel, the region's most free nation, is ranked 37 globally, Bahrain is ranked 39, and Jordan is ranked 53. Oman, Kuwait, and Tunisia are the last countries in the top 70. The lack of economic freedom reflects the region's sluggish economic growth and hints at the reason why its GDP per capita lags behind the rest of the world.

The Middle East's stunted economic growth may be due to its over-reliance on oil wealth. To determine whether this is so, we divided the region into two halves, categorizing 12 of the 17 countries as oil exporters (with such exports in excess of 10 percent of total GDP) and the other five as non-oil countries. The most oil-dependent economies in the Middle East are Qatar (60 percent), Oman (49 percent), Algeria (45 percent), Saudi Arabia (43 percent), Libya (33 percent), and the UAE (32 percent). Our analysis reveals that the non-oil countries have 10 percentage points more economic freedom, using a population-weighted average. They also have lower inflation and slightly better employment and income levels, although their growth rates have been insignificantly lower.

Economists subscribe to a theory known as the "Dutch disease," which holds that natural resource wealth can inhibit the development of other sectors by skewing wages. In contrast, resource-poor countries must give their citizens a certain amount of economic freedom in order to create a living for themselves, developing human capital in order to create value. This means that people must be invested with skills.

Oil revenue, on the other hand, comes from the ground. In most Gulf states, even the process of extracting the oil is in the hands of foreigners. It requires no investment in labor, no investment in humans, and only a marginal amount of investment in the land. People need different freedoms to be productive, but oil does not generate the incentives needed for societies to create those freedoms.

The Middle East is the absolute world leader in only one category: fiscal freedom. Fiscally,

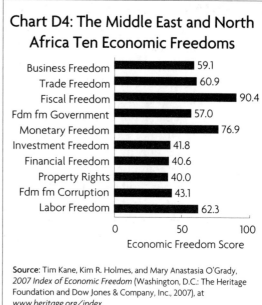

Chart D4: The Middle East and North Africa Ten Economic Freedoms

	Economic Freedom Score
Business Freedom	59.1
Trade Freedom	60.9
Fiscal Freedom	90.4
Fdm fm Government	57.0
Monetary Freedom	76.9
Investment Freedom	41.8
Financial Freedom	40.6
Property Rights	40.0
Fdm fm Corruption	43.1
Labor Freedom	62.3

Source: Tim Kane, Kim R. Holmes, and Mary Anastasia O'Grady, *2007 Index of Economic Freedom* (Washington, D.C.: The Heritage Foundation and Dow Jones & Company, Inc., 2007), at *www.heritage.org/index*.

its 90.4 percent average score is well above the world average of 82.8 percent, a level reached because of the extremely low income taxes common to oil kingdoms. The region does score above the world average in other areas, however, such as monetary freedom and freedom from corruption—a result that may reflect the measures regional leaders are taking to cut back on bribery and government malfeasance.

Israel is the leader in half of the categories. Oil-exporting states top the five factors, with Kuwait as the leader in fiscal freedom. Oil states need flexible labor markets to hire foreign workers, and their governments require little tax revenue. Bahrain is moving toward a more business-friendly environment, possibly influenced by the success of the Dubai model.

SUB-SAHARAN AFRICA (REGION E)

Sub-Saharan Africa is well known as the poorest and most violent region of the world. It also seems to be the one region that has been slipping further behind over the past half-century rather than advancing in terms of popular material well-being. Civil war flares sporadically from the Horn of Africa to the Atlantic Coast. AIDS is a continuing burden. Mass unemployment is common.

Average GDP per capita is only $1,984—the lowest of any region and barely one-tenth of the average incomes in Europe and the Americas. Unemployment hovers at 10.5 percent, and the 15 percent average inflation rate is twice as high as that of the next worst region. Unsurprisingly, Africa receives more absolute foreign aid, both multilateral and bilateral, than any other region even though it has just one-fifth the population of Asia.

Chart E1 shows the 1995–2007 time series of the average economic freedom score for the region, compared with the world average. Africa's overall level of economic freedom is weaker than any other region's and has even declined over the past year. Nevertheless, there are some success stories, and they usually involve countries with greater freedom. Chart E2 shows the clear relationship between high levels of economic freedom and high GDP per capita.

Table E1 ranks the countries in the region from most free to least free based on their overall freedom scores. It also includes the change from last year's score, the country's world rank, and each country's 2007 scores for each of the 10 economic freedoms. Chart E3 shows the distribution of countries across five different categories.

Unlike regions that have a diverse range of free-market economies, in sub-Saharan Africa there are only distinctions among less free economies. A majority of nations are ranked "mostly unfree," with the balance split evenly between "moderately free" and "repressed." Reflecting the consistency of Africa's chronic problems is a standard deviation of 6.7 points among freedom scores, which is the smallest deviation of any region. Africa's most free countries, Mauri-

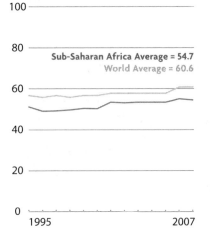

Chart E1: Sub-Saharan Africa Average Economic Freedom

Sub-Saharan Africa Average = 54.7
World Average = 60.6

Source: Tim Kane, Kim R. Holmes, and Mary Anastasia O'Grady, *2007 Index of Economic Freedom* (Washington, D.C.: The Heritage Foundation and Dow Jones & Company, Inc., 2007), at *www.heritage.org/index*.

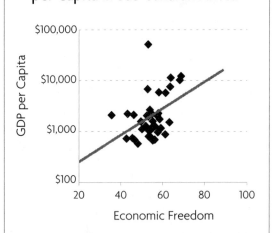

Chart E2: Economic Freedom vs. GDP per Capita in Sub-Saharan Africa

Sources: World Bank, World Development Indicators Online, at *publications.worldbank.org/subscriptions/WDI* (October 19, 2006; subscription required); Central Intelligence Agency, The World Factbook 2005, at *www.cia.gov/cia/publications/factbook/index.html* (October 19, 2006); International Monetary Fund, World Economic Outlook database, April 2006, at *www.imf.org/external/pubs/ft/weo/2006/01/data/index.htm* (October 19, 2006); and Tim Kane, Kim R. Holmes, and Mary Anastasia O'Grady, *2007 Index of Economic Freedom* (Washington, D.C.: The Heritage Foundation and Dow Jones & Company, Inc., 2007), at *www.heritage.org/index*.

tius and Botswana, are globally ranked 34 and 38, respectively. South Africa, the third-highest ranked African nation, is ranked 52 globally.

Table E1: Economic Freedom Scores for Sub-Saharan Africa

2007 World Rank	2007 Regional Rank	Country	Economic Freedom 2007	Change from 2006	Business Freedom	Trade Freedom	Fiscal Freedom	Freedom from Government	Monetary Freedom	Investment Freedom	Financial Freedom	Property Rights	Freedom from Corruption	Labor Freedom
34	1	Mauritius	69.0	2.5	74.5	70.0	87.5	82.0	76.2	70	60	60	42	67.4
38	2	Botswana	68.4	-1.9	66.6	59.6	82.6	54.5	76.8	70	70	70	59	74.9
52	3	South Africa	64.1	-2.2	70.8	68.8	79.8	79.3	78.8	50	60	50	45	58.5
55	4	Namibia	63.8	2.9	76.7	79.0	78.6	70.5	78.6	40	60	30	43	81.2
59	5	Uganda	63.4	-1.5	54.1	58.8	87.1	86.7	78.3	50	70	30	25	94.0
64	6	Swaziland	61.6	-0.6	71.5	59.0	81.5	73.3	76.3	50	50	50	27	77.2
65	7	Madagascar	61.4	-1.6	51.2	72.8	87.2	85.0	70.0	70	50	50	28	50.1
82	8	Kenya	59.4	-0.6	58.9	65.0	85.9	83.6	74.4	50	50	40	21	65.2
86	9	Senegal	58.8	1.4	56.4	61.6	73.9	85.9	82.9	50	50	50	32	45.2
88	10	Cape Verde	58.4	-1.8	50.5	31.2	78.0	77.7	84.2	50	50	70	30	62.5
91	11	Ghana	58.1	1.5	54.9	58.0	88.4	72.0	70.0	50	50	50	40	48.2
92	12	Zambia	57.9	-1.2	63.6	60.8	80.4	81.9	57.8	50	50	40	26	68.6
93	13	Gambia	57.6	-0.3	59.0	54.6	81.4	76.4	67.2	50	60	30	27	70.9
101	14	Mozambique	56.6	1.4	51.5	60.2	85.5	86.2	75.9	50	30	30	28	48.2
103	15	Tanzania	56.4	-2.9	44.8	63.6	87.1	85.7	74.4	50	50	30	29	49.4
105	16	Ivory Coast	55.5	-1.3	48.1	58.6	66.3	86.2	78.6	40	70	30	19	58.4
106	17	Malawi	55.5	-2.4	54.4	59.6	80.6	53.3	66.4	50	50	40	28	72.8
111	18	Guinea	55.1	1.4	39.3	54.6	83.3	92.4	57.5	30	60	30	30	73.5
113	19	Burkina Faso	55.0	-0.7	42.7	57.2	84.9	88.9	76.8	40	50	30	34	45.1
114	20	Benin	54.8	0.5	47.2	54.6	78.5	87.9	82.5	30	60	30	29	48.2
116	21	Ethiopia	54.4	1.1	59.4	53.0	84.8	83.0	69.9	50	20	30	22	72.3
117	22	Cameroon	54.4	0.3	41.0	50.0	79.7	86.5	77.4	50	60	30	22	47.6
118	23	Lesotho	54.1	-2.8	68.2	44.4	79.5	53.7	76.7	30	50	40	34	64.9
123	24	Mali	53.7	-0.4	37.1	58.6	79.5	84.6	78.4	50	40	30	29	49.7
124	25	Niger	53.5	-0.0	38.4	52.4	77.5	89.2	80.7	50	50	30	24	43.1
126	26	Mauritania	53.2	-2.3	37.5	61.4	83.7	60.4	73.9	60	50	30	30	45.5
128	27	Equatorial Guinea	53.2	3.0	44.7	47.6	82.1	81.8	79.3	30	60	30	19	57.4
129	28	Gabon	53.0	-2.0	52.1	46.4	74.2	71.0	81.3	40	40	40	29	55.7
130	29	Djibouti	52.6	-2.4	37.1	26.4	87.0	53.4	79.0	50	60	30	30	73.5
131	30	Nigeria	52.6	3.8	63.1	56.6	89.5	41.7	70.5	30	50	30	19	75.2
136	31	Rwanda	52.1	-2.2	50.8	60.6	82.6	80.3	70.2	30	40	30	21	55.9
137	32	Central African Rep.	50.3	-4.5	38.9	44.2	77.1	90.2	76.4	40	40	20	30	45.9
139	33	Togo	49.8	1.4	37.5	58.4	69.8	90.6	76.5	30	30	30	30	45.5
141	34	Sierra Leone	48.4	1.6	50.5	50.2	82.0	83.8	72.9	30	40	10	24	40.2
146	35	Burundi	46.8	-2.8	40.9	50.6	80.0	60.0	68.1	30	30	30	23	55.2
147	36	Chad	46.4	-3.0	25.1	54.2	57.7	81.9	77.7	40	50	20	17	40.2
148	37	Guinea-Bissau	45.7	-1.4	27.2	52.8	88.6	59.9	80.7	40	40	20	10	37.9
149	38	Angola	43.5	0.1	33.9	68.0	90.0	38.4	47.7	20	40	20	20	56.7
151	39	Congo, Republic of	43.0	-0.6	40.4	44.4	73.2	56.9	77.3	30	30	10	23	44.8
154	40	Zimbabwe	35.8	1.8	42.9	42.6	79.5	83.9	-	10	20	10	26	43.2

Source: Tim Kane, Kim R. Holmes, and Mary Anastasia O'Grady, 2007 Index of Economic Freedom (Washington, D.C.: The Heritage Foundation and Dow Jones & Company, Inc., 2007), at www.heritage.org/index.

On the other hand, eight of the 20 countries ranked "repressed" around the world are located in this region.

Sub-Saharan Africa is also ranked last in seven of the 10 economic freedom categories and performs especially poorly in terms of property rights, freedom from corruption, and business freedom. Chart E4 shows regional scores in each of the 10 economic freedom categories. Some of the gaps between sub-Saharan Africa's score and the world average score are especially striking: almost 10 points for business freedom, 10 for freedom from corruption, and six for property rights. The single factor on which the region rates higher than the world average is in terms of government expenditure. Ironically, however, it is worse in terms of taxation. Labor freedom is perversely restricted in the region, which is odd because heavy labor regulations are much more common among higher-income nations. It appears that the countries of sub-Saharan Africa have been saddled with the worst policies of their former European colonizers but none of the prosperity.

The signs of government failure are overwhelming in the heart of Africa and in some cases are so severe that the next few years will be inevitably bleak. Zimbabwe's rate of inflation, for example, is 350 percent, and unemployment runs at 80 percent. With political instability rampant in the region, it is unlikely that even the liberalizing tendencies of Mauritius or Botswana can have a significant enough statistical impact to lift Africa out of its last-place status.

Within the region, Botswana is freest in the most absolute categories, although Mauritius is freest overall. Namibia scores highest in business and trade freedom, showing a strong commitment to free trade and pro-business regulations. Angola, as an oil-exporting nation,

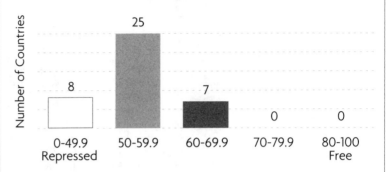

Chart E3: Distribution of Economic Freedom in Sub-Saharan Africa

Source: Tim Kane, Kim R. Holmes, and Mary Anastasia O'Grady, *2007 Index of Economic Freedom* (Washington, D.C.: The Heritage Foundation and Dow Jones & Company, Inc., 2007), at *www.heritage.org/index.*

Chart E4: Sub-Saharan Africa Ten Economic Freedoms

Source: Tim Kane, Kim R. Holmes, and Mary Anastasia O'Grady, *2007 Index of Economic Freedom* (Washington, D.C.: The Heritage Foundation and Dow Jones & Company, Inc., 2007), at *www.heritage.org/index.*

scores highest in fiscal freedom because of its low tax burden. Cape Verde has the lowest absolute inflation, giving it the highest score in monetary freedom, and Uganda has the highest labor freedom.

Chapter 5

The Countries

This chapter is a compilation of the 161 countries graded in the *Index of Economic Freedom*. Only 157 countries receive total scores, because grading has been suspended for four countries (the Democratic Republic of Congo, Iraq, Sudan, and Serbia–Montenegro). Each graded country is given a percent score ranging from 0 to 100 for all 10 factors of economic freedom, and these scores are then averaged (using equal weights) to get the country's final *Index of Economic Freedom* score.

In addition to these factor and overall scores, each summary includes a brief introduction that describes the country's economic strengths and weaknesses, as well as its political and economic background, and a statistical profile with the country's main economic indicators. These statistics and their sources are outlined in detail below.

Two charts are included on each country page. The first shows a time series of the overall economic freedom score for the country for each year, from 1995 through 2007, compared

Chart 1: Angola's Economic Freedom

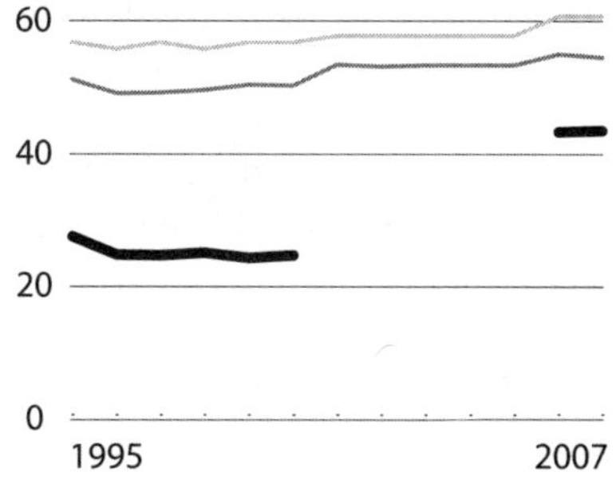

The economy is 43.5% free

Sub-Saharan Africa Average = 54.7
World Average = 60.6

Source: Tim Kane, Kim R. Holmes, and Mary Anastasia O'Grady, *2007 Index of Economic Freedom* (Washington, D.C.: The Heritage Foundation and Dow Jones & Company, Inc., 2007), at *www.heritage.org/index*.

Chart 2: Angola's 2007 Economic Freedom Scores

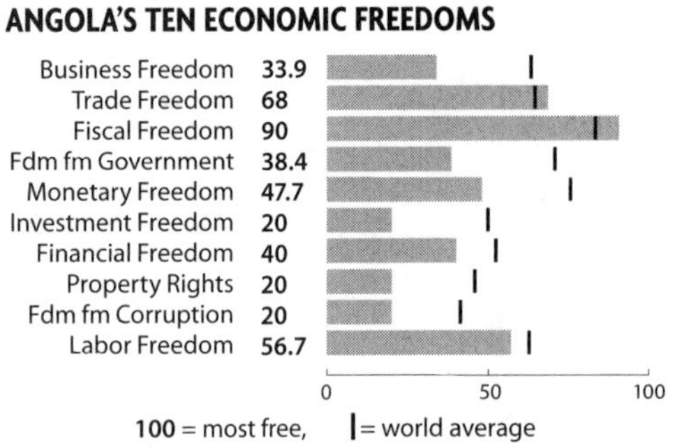

ANGOLA'S TEN ECONOMIC FREEDOMS

Business Freedom	33.9
Trade Freedom	68
Fiscal Freedom	90
Fdm fm Government	38.4
Monetary Freedom	47.7
Investment Freedom	20
Financial Freedom	40
Property Rights	20
Fdm fm Corruption	20
Labor Freedom	56.7

0   50   100

100 = most free, | = world average

Source: Tim Kane, Kim R. Holmes, and Mary Anastasia O'Grady, *2007 Index of Economic Freedom* (Washington, D.C.: The Heritage Foundation and Dow Jones & Company, Inc., 2007), at *www.heritage.org/index*.

to the world average and regional average. In many cases, a country is not graded continuously for all 13 years, often because grading did not begin until 1996 and frequently because of violence or natural disaster. This year, four countries are not graded, so their respective charts show a line that stops in 2005 or earlier. The second chart for each country graphs each of the 10 freedom scores for 2007 using horizontal bars. A hash mark is included to show the world average so that one can quickly identify the strengths and weaknesses of economic freedom in each country according to the 10 different component freedoms. The charts for Angola presented here are examples of what the reader will see on each country page.

To assure consistency and reliability for each of the 10 factors on which the countries are graded, every effort has been made to use the same source for each country; when data are unavailable from the primary source, secondary sources are used as explained in the chapter on methodology.

DEFINING THE "QUICK FACTS"

Each country page includes "Quick Facts" with 16 different categories of information: population size, macroeconomic data, official development assistance, and more. Unless otherwise indicated, the data in each country's profile are for 2004 (the year for which the most recent data are widely available) and in current 2004 U.S. dollars, also the latest available. The few cases in which no reliable statistical data were available are indicated by "n/a." Definitions and sources for each category of information are as follows.

Population: 2004 estimate from World Bank, *World Development Indicators Online*. Another major source is U.S. Central Intelligence Agency, *The World Factbook 2006*. For some countries, another source is the country's statistical agency and/or central bank.

GDP: Gross domestic product—total production of goods and services—expressed as purchasing power parity (PPP) in current 2004 U.S. dollars. The primary source for GDP data is World Bank, *World Development Indicators Online*. Other sources include U.S. Central Intelligence Agency, *The World Factbook 2006*; the country's statistical agency; and the country's central bank.

GDP growth rate: Annual percentage growth rate of real GDP derived from constant national currency units, based on country-specific years. Annual percent changes are year-on-year. The primary source is International Monetary Fund, *World Economic Outlook Database, 2006*, which has growth data from 2004. Secondary sources include World Bank, *World Development Indicators Online*; Economist Intelligence Unit, *Country Reports*, 2005 and 2006; the country's statistical agency; and the country's central bank.

GDP five-year compound annual growth: The geometric average growth rate measured over a specified period of time. The compound annual growth rate is measured using data from 2000 to 2004, based on the total percentage growth rate of real GDP expressed in constant national currency units, based on country-specific years. It is calculated by taking the nth root of the total percentage growth rate, where n is the number of years in the period being considered. The primary source for 2004 data is International Monetary Fund, *World Economic Outlook Database, 2006*.

GDP per capita: Gross domestic product expressed as PPP in current 2004 U.S. dollars divided by total population. The sources for these data are World Bank, *World Development Indicators Online*; U.S. Central Intelligence Agency, *The World Factbook 2006*; and the country's statistical agency or central bank.

Unemployment rate: A measure of the portion of the workforce that is not employed but is actively seeking work. The primary sources are Economist Intelligence Unit, *Country Reports*, 2005 and 2006, and *Country Profiles*, 2004–2005 and 2005–2006; U.S. Central Intelligence Agency, *The World Factbook 2006*; the country's statistical agency; and the country's labor ministry.

Inflation: The annual percent change in consumer prices as measured from 2003 to 2004. The primary source for 2004 data is International Monetary Fund, *World Economic Outlook Database, 2006*. The secondary sources are Economist Intelligence Unit, *Country Reports*, 2005 and 2006, and *Country Profiles*, 2004–2005 and 2005–2006; U.S. Central Intelligence Agency, *The World Factbook 2006*; the country's statistical agency; and the country's central bank.

Foreign direct investment (FDI): This series indicates total annual flow of *net* FDI, which is the sum of FDI inflows less the sum of FDI outflows in 2004. Data are in current 2004 U.S. dollars. FDI flows are defined as investments that acquire a lasting management interest (10 percent or more of voting stock) in a local enterprise by an investor operating in another country. Such investment is the sum of equity capital, reinvestment of earnings, other long-term capital, and short-term capital as shown in the balance of payments and both short-term and long-term international loans. Data are from United Nations Conference on Trade and Development, *World Investment Report 2005*; World Bank, *World Development Indicators Online*; the country's statistical agency; and the country's central bank.

Official development assistance (ODA): Grants or loans to developing countries and territories, as defined by part I of the Development Assistance Committee (DAC) list of aid recipients, that are undertaken either by the official sector, with promotion of economic development and welfare as the main objective, or on concessional financial terms (a loan

that has a grant element of at least 25 percent). Aid includes technical cooperation as well as financial flows. Grants, loans, and credits for military purposes are excluded. Transfer payments to private individuals (e.g., pensions, reparations, or insurance payouts) are usually not counted. Data are listed in current 2004 U.S. dollars. The primary source is Organisation for Economic Co-operation and Development, *Official Development Figures for 2004* (on-line).

- **Multilateral:** In DAC statistics, this includes international institutions with governmental membership that conduct all or a significant part of their activities in favor of development and aid recipient countries. They include multilateral development banks (e.g., the World Bank and regional development banks), United Nations agencies, and regional groupings. A contribution by a DAC member to such an agency is deemed multilateral if it is pooled with other contributions and disbursed at the discretion of the agency.
- **Bilateral:** Bilateral flows are provided directly by a donor country to an aid recipient country.

External Debt: Debt owed to non-residents that is repayable in foreign currency, goods, or services. It is the sum of public, publicly guaranteed, and private non-guaranteed long-term debt, use of International Monetary Fund credit, and short-term debt. Short-term debt includes all debt having an original or extended maturity of one year or less and interest in arrears on long-term debt. Long-term debt is debt that has an original or extended maturity of more than one year. It has three components: public, publicly guaranteed, and private non-guaranteed debt. Public and publicly guaranteed debt comprises the long-term external obligations of public debtors, including the national government and political subdivisions (or an agency of either) and autonomous public bodies, as well as the external obligations of private debtors that are guaranteed for repayment by a public entity. Private non-guaranteed debt consists of the long-term external obligations of private debtors that are not guaranteed for repayment by a public entity. The data for 2004 are listed in current 2004 U.S. dollars, calculated on an exchange rate basis rather than PPP terms. The primary source is World Bank, *World Development Indicators, 2006*. The data for 2005 are from U.S. Central Intelligence Agency, *The World Factbook 2006*.

Exports: The value of all goods and other market services, f.o.b. Included is the value of merchandise, freight, insurance, travel, and other non-factor services. Factor and property income, such as investment income, interest, and labor income, is excluded. Data are in current 2004 U.S. dollars. The primary source is World Bank, *World Development Indicators Online*. Other sources include Economist Intelligence Unit, *Country Reports*, 2005 and 2006, and *Country Profiles*, 2004–2005 and 2005–2006; U.S. Central Intelligence Agency, *The World Factbook 2006*; and the country's statistical agency.

Primary exports: The country's four to six principal export products. Data for major exports are from U.S. Central Intelligence Agency, *The World Factbook 2006*.

Imports: The value of all goods and other market services, f.o.b. Included is the value of merchandise, freight, insurance, travel, and other non-factor services. Factor and property income, such as investment income, interest, and labor income, is excluded. Data are in current 2004 U.S. dollars. The primary source is World Bank, *World Development Indicators Online*. Other sources include Economist Intelligence Unit, *Country Reports*, 2005 and 2006, and *Country Profiles*, 2004–2005 and 2005–2006; U.S. Central Intelligence Agency, *The World Factbook 2006*; and the country's statistical agency.

Primary imports: The country's six to eight principal import products. Data for major imports are from U.S. Central Intelligence Agency, *The World Factbook 2006*.

COMMONLY USED ACRONYMS

CIS: Commonwealth of Independent States, consisting of Azerbaijan, Armenia, Belarus, Georgia, Kazakhstan, the Kyrgyz Republic, Moldova, Russia, Tajikistan, Turkmenistan, Uzbekistan, and Ukraine.

EU: European Union, consisting of Austria, Belgium, Cyprus, the Czech Republic, Denmark, Estonia, Finland, France, Germany, Greece, Hungary, Ireland, Italy, Latvia, Lithuania, Luxembourg, Malta, the Netherlands, Poland, Portugal, Slovakia, Slovenia, Spain, Sweden, and the United Kingdom.

IMF: International Monetary Fund, established in 1945 to help stabilize countries during crises and now with 181 member countries.

MERCOSUR: Customs union that includes Brazil, Argentina, Uruguay, Paraguay, and Venezuela.

OECD: Organisation for Economic Co-operation and Development, an international organization of developed countries, founded in 1948, that now includes 30 member countries.

SACU: Southern African Customs Union, consisting of Botswana, Lesotho, Namibia, South Africa, and Swaziland.

VAT: Value-added tax.

WTO: World Trade Organization, founded in 1995 as the central organization dealing with the rules of trade between nations and based on signed agreements among 149 member countries.

ALBANIA

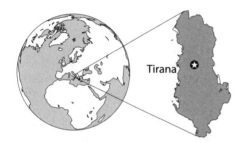

Tirana

Rank: 66

Regional Rank: 30 of 41

Albania's economy is 61.4 percent free, according to our 2007 assessment, which makes it the world's 66th freest economy. Albania is ranked 30th freest among the 41 countries in the European region. The level of economic freedom decreased by 0.6 percentage point during the past year, partially reflecting new methodological detail, leaving Albania below the regional average.

Comparatively, Albania's freedom level is on par with other developing Balkan states like Croatia and Macedonia but still higher than that of Greece, a member of the European Union. Fiscal freedom, freedom from government, and monetary freedom all rate highly, but the overall score is reduced by Albania's poor performance in property rights and freedom from corruption. The unimpressive score in property rights is largely a result of political interference in the judiciary, leading to erratic enforcement of the country's laws.

Albania's economic freedom ranks above the world average, and its score has risen over the past seven years, a noteworthy achievement in a region characterized by federal separatism and instability. If Albania maintains its impressively low tax levels while doing more to combat corruption, its score should continue to rise.

BACKGROUND: In 1992, Albania ended nearly 50 years of Communist rule. The 1990s were a period of transition, but economic growth and reform have advanced since then. In July 2006, Albania signed a Stabilization and Association Agreement with the European Union as the first step toward EU membership. The agricultural sector is the largest source of employment, but services and the increased production of chrome and chromium products have led to steady economic growth. In 2005, the Organisation for Economic Co-operation and Development reported that informal activity may exceed 50 percent of the economy.

How Do We Measure Economic Freedom? See Chapter 3 (page 37) for an explanation of the methodology or visit the *Index* Web site at *heritage.org/index*.

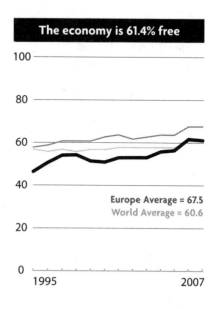

The economy is 61.4% free

Europe Average = 67.5
World Average = 60.6

1995   2007

QUICK FACTS

Population: 3.1 million

GDP (PPP): $15.5 billion
    5.9% growth in 2004
    5.7% 5-yr. comp. ann. growth
    $4,978 per capita

Unemployment: 14.4%

Inflation (CPI): 2.3%

FDI (net inflow): $426 million (gross)

Official Development Assistance:
Multilateral: $137 million
Bilateral: $250 million (16% from the U.S.)

External Debt: $1.6 billion

Exports: $1.2 billion
Primarily textiles and footwear, tobacco, vegetables, food, beverages, machinery

Imports: $2.6 billion
Primarily chemicals, machinery and equipment, minerals, fuels, electricity

ALBANIA'S TEN ECONOMIC FREEDOMS

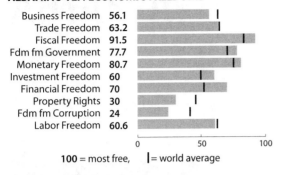

Business Freedom	56.1
Trade Freedom	63.2
Fiscal Freedom	91.5
Fdm fm Government	77.7
Monetary Freedom	80.7
Investment Freedom	60
Financial Freedom	70
Property Rights	30
Fdm fm Corruption	24
Labor Freedom	60.6

100 = most free, | = world average

BUSINESS FREEDOM — *56.1%*

Starting a business takes an average of 39 days, compared to the world average of 48 days. To maximize entrepreneurship and job creation, it should be easier to start a company. Obtaining a business license can be difficult because of regulations, and closing a business is very difficult. Regulations are sometimes inconsistent, causing unreliability of interpretation. Businesses have difficulty getting copies of laws and regulations. The overall freedom to start, operate, and close a business is limited by the national regulatory environment.

TRADE FREEDOM — *63.2%*

Albania's weighted average tariff rate in 2002 was 8.4 percent. There are no official non-tariff barriers, but administrative bureaucracy can delay trade and increase costs. Consequently, an additional 20 percent is deducted from Albania's trade freedom score.

FISCAL FREEDOM — *91.5%*

Albania enjoys low income tax rates, which enhance incentives for entrepreneurs and workers. The top income tax rate is 20 percent. In January 2006, the government reduced the flat corporate tax rate by 3 percentage points to 20 percent. Other taxes include a value-added tax (VAT), a property tax, and a vehicle tax. In the most recent year, overall tax revenue as a percentage of GDP was 21.7 percent.

FREEDOM FROM GOVERNMENT — *77.7%*

Total government expenditures, including consumption and transfer payments, are moderate. In the most recent year, government spending equaled 28.8 percent of GDP, and the government received 8.8 percent of its revenues from state-owned enterprises and government ownership of property.

MONETARY FREEDOM — *80.7%*

Inflation is relatively low, averaging 2.2 percent between 2003 and 2005. Relatively low and stable prices explain most of the monetary freedom score. An additional 10 percent is deducted from Albania's monetary freedom score to adjust for price control measures that distort domestic prices for water, railway transport, and electricity.

INVESTMENT FREEDOM — *60%*

Foreign and domestic firms are treated equally under the law, and nearly all sectors of the economy are open to foreign investment. Foreigners may lease agricultural land for up to 99 years but may not purchase it. Political instability, corruption, and a thriving informal market discourage foreign investment and undermine the implementation of reform. The International Monetary Fund reports that both residents and non-residents may hold foreign exchange accounts. The Bank of Albania, through licensed agencies, monitors and reviews the purchase of capital and money market instruments, outward direct investment, most credit operations, and residents' purchase of real estate abroad.

FINANCIAL FREEDOM — *70%*

Albania's financial sector is small and largely cash-based. Banking dominates the sector and is overseen by the central Bank of Albania. The government introduced deposit insurance in 2004. In December 2005, the government sold its stake in the last partially state-owned bank. There are 17 banks, of which 15 are foreign-owned. The non-bank financial sector is rudimentary, and government enforcement of financial regulations can be weak. The government has separated the Tirana Stock Exchange from the central bank, giving the country an independent stock exchange. In October 2003, the government sold a stake in the state-owned insurance company. The insurance sector remains underdeveloped.

PROPERTY RIGHTS — *30%*

Albania's judicial system enforces the law weakly. Judges are supposed to be independent, but several are corrupt, having been appointed strictly for political reasons. Organized crime is a strong deterrent to the administration of justice. Judges are subject to intimidation, pressure, and bribery, and the pace of judicial reform remains very slow.

FREEDOM FROM CORRUPTION — *24%*

Corruption is perceived as widespread. Albania ranks 126th out of 158 countries in Transparency International's Corruption Perceptions Index for 2005.

LABOR FREEDOM — *60.6%*

The labor market operates under inflexible employment regulations that hinder overall productivity growth. The non-salary cost of employing a worker is very high, and dismissing a redundant employee is relatively costly. The unemployment insurance system, funded primarily by employer contributions, provides for approximately 17 percent of an average worker's yearly salary.

ALGERIA

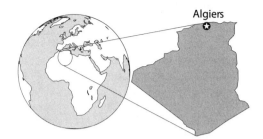

Algiers

Algeria's economy is 52.2 percent free, according to our 2007 assessment, which makes it the world's 134th freest economy. Its overall score is 1.1 percentage points lower than last year, partially reflecting new methodological detail. Algeria is ranked 14th out of 17 countries in the Middle East/North Africa region.

Algeria scores high in several of the 10 factors of economic freedom, such as business freedom, fiscal freedom, and monetary freedom. On average, it takes far less time to start a business in Algeria than it does elsewhere in the world. Algeria has a high income tax rate but, because of widespread poverty and substantial oil income, collects only a small proportion of GDP in taxes. Inflation is relatively low, and prices are relatively stable, although the government does subsidize various necessities.

In other areas, the outlook is not so positive. Algeria has significant problems with the overall size of government, banking restrictions, corruption, and political interference in the judiciary. The government has been slow to implement its privatization plan, and state-owned companies still dominate several critical industries, such as banking.

BACKGROUND: Algeria gained its independence from France in 1962 and imposed a socialist economic model that stifled economic growth and wasted its huge oil and gas wealth: Algeria is the world's second-largest exporter of natural gas and has the world's seventh-largest natural gas reserves and 14th-largest oil reserves. In 1992, Islamic radicals launched a brutal civil war that claimed more than 100,000 lives. President Abdelaziz Bouteflika negotiated a fragile peace accord and has delivered greater political stability. His government has made slow progress on liberalization, privatization, and attracting foreign investment, and the economy has benefited from high world energy prices.

The economy is 52.2% free

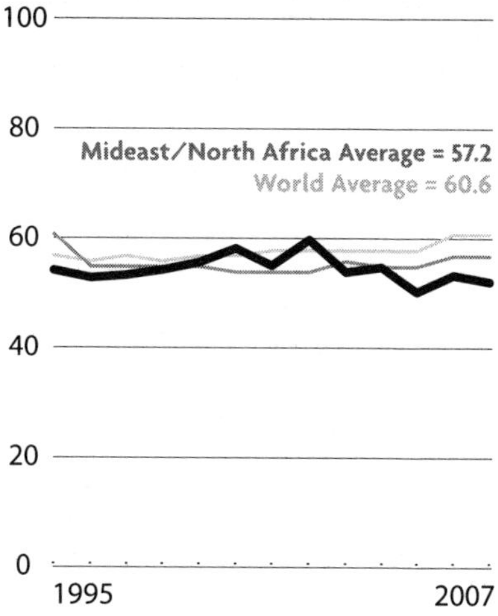

Mideast/North Africa Average = 57.2
World Average = 60.6

[line chart showing scores from 1995 to 2007 with y-axis from 0 to 100]

QUICK FACTS

Population: 32.4 million

GDP (PPP): $213.7 billion
5.2% growth in 2004
4.3% 5-yr. comp. ann. growth
$6,603 per capita

Unemployment: 20.9% (2003)

Inflation (CPI): 3.6%

FDI (net inflow): $624 million

Official Development Assistance:
Multilateral: $90 million
Bilateral: $299 million (1% from the U.S.)

External Debt: $22.0 billion

Exports: $32.2 billion
Primarily petroleum, natural gas, petroleum products

Imports: $18.0 billion
Primarily capital goods, food, consumer goods

How Do We Measure Economic Freedom? See Chapter 3 (page 37) for an explanation of the methodology or visit the *Index* Web site at *heritage.org/index*.

ALGERIA'S TEN ECONOMIC FREEDOMS

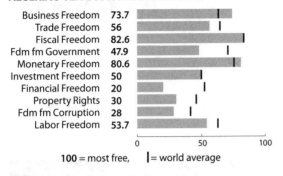

Business Freedom	73.7	
Trade Freedom	56	
Fiscal Freedom	82.6	
Fdm fm Government	47.9	
Monetary Freedom	80.6	
Investment Freedom	50	
Financial Freedom	20	
Property Rights	30	
Fdm fm Corruption	28	
Labor Freedom	53.7	

100 = most free, | = world average

BUSINESS FREEDOM — 73.7%

Starting a business takes an average of 24 days, compared to the world average of 48 days. To maximize entrepreneurship and job creation, it should be easier to start a company. Obtaining a business license can be difficult because of regulations, but closing a business is relatively easy. With more than 400 legislative and regulatory texts, however, business regulations can be complex and technical. The overall freedom to start, operate, and close a business is relatively well protected by the national regulatory environment.

TRADE FREEDOM — 56%

Algeria's weighted average tariff rate in 2003 was 12 percent. Non-tariff barriers include customs clearance procedures, some import and export controls, and regulatory restrictions that delay trade and increase costs. Consequently, an additional 20 percent is deducted from Algeria's trade freedom score.

FISCAL FREEDOM — 82.6%

Algeria has a high income tax rate and moderate corporate tax rate. The top income tax rate is 40 percent, and the top corporate tax rate is 30 percent. Other taxes include a value-added tax (VAT), a tax on professional activity, and an apprenticeship tax. In the most recent year, overall tax revenue as a percentage of GDP was 10.8 percent.

FREEDOM FROM GOVERNMENT — 47.9%

Total government expenditures, including consumption and transfer payments, are moderate. In the most recent year, government spending equaled 34.6 percent of GDP, and the government received 72.6 percent of its revenues from state-owned enterprises and government ownership of property.

MONETARY FREEDOM — 80.6%

Inflation is relatively low, averaging 2.2 percent between 2003 and 2005. Relatively low and stable prices explain most of the monetary freedom score. Government policies distort prices through subsidies and direct controls on some commodities, such as agricultural goods. Consequently, an additional 10 percent is deducted from Algeria's monetary freedom score to adjust for price control measures.

INVESTMENT FREEDOM — 50%

Foreign investors receive nondiscriminatory treatment. In August 2001, the National Investment Development Agency was created to simplify investment, but investors still face complex and burdensome procedures. Foreign ownership of pipelines is prohibited. Foreign exchange and capital transactions are subject to numerous restrictions. The International Monetary Fund reports that both residents and non-residents may hold foreign exchange accounts, subject to some restrictions. Payments and transfers are subject to various limits, approvals, surrender requirements, and restrictions. Purchase, sale, or issue of capital market securities is permitted through an authorized intermediary.

FINANCIAL FREEDOM — 20%

The government exerts heavy influence on the financial sector. There were 15 private banks in 2004, but six state-owned banks accounted for over 86 percent of total bank assets in 2003. While banking sector reform and privatization has ostensibly been a goal since 1999, progress has been slow. State dominance of banking has undermined private banks and led to several bankruptcies. The government intervenes in credit markets, including subsidizing credit for loss-making public enterprises. Governance of the financial sector is weak. The insurance sector is small and dominated by six state-owned firms, although private insurers are permitted and six private insurers were operational in 2004. The stock exchange is extremely small.

PROPERTY RIGHTS — 30%

The constitution provides for an independent judiciary, but the judicial environment is inefficient and, in fields like the adjudication of intellectual property disputes, suffers from a lack of trained magistrates. The judiciary is influenced by the executive branch and the Ministry of Interior.

FREEDOM FROM CORRUPTION — 28%

Corruption is perceived as widespread. Algeria ranks 97th out of 158 countries in Transparency International's Corruption Perceptions Index for 2005.

LABOR FREEDOM — 53.7%

The labor market operates under restrictive employment regulations that hinder employment and productivity growth. The non-salary cost of employing a worker is high, but dismissing a redundant employee is costless. Algeria's unemployment insurance system, funded by workers and their employers only, offers benefits equaling about 38 percent of an average worker's annual salary.

ANGOLA

Luanda

Rank: 149

Regional Rank: 38 of 40

Angola's economy is 43.5 percent free, according to our 2007 assessment, which makes it the world's 149th freest economy. Its overall score is 0.1 percentage point higher than last year, partially reflecting new methodological detail. Angola is also ranked 38th out of 40 countries in the sub-Saharan Africa region. Data are spotty for Angola because of a protracted civil war, but the country has attained a moderate degree of economic freedom despite a devastated infrastructure and a fledgling government.

Angola scores high in fiscal freedom and receives fairly positive scores in trade, but it receives overwhelmingly negative scores for most of its policies. The income tax rate is low, and overall tax revenues are low as a percentage of GDP. Trade freedom is progressing, but significant non-tariff barriers on imports are still imposed.

Angola faces serious economic problems in other areas. Inflation is high, regulation chokes business, investment is basically unwelcome, government size is excessive, corruption is crippling, and political influence mars the judiciary. Commercial regulations are a major hindrance to opening and closing a business, and inconsistent, confusing regulations make operating a successful company difficult.

BACKGROUND: Despite extensive oil and gas resources, diamonds, hydroelectric potential, and rich agricultural land, Angola remains poor. Since 2002, when the country's economically devastating 27-year civil war ended, the government has worked to repair and improve Angola's ravaged infrastructure and its weakened political and social institutions. High international oil prices and rising oil production have led to strong economic growth in recent years, but corruption and public-sector mismanagement remain common, particularly in the oil sector, which accounted for over 50 percent of gross domestic product and 78 percent of government revenues in 2005.

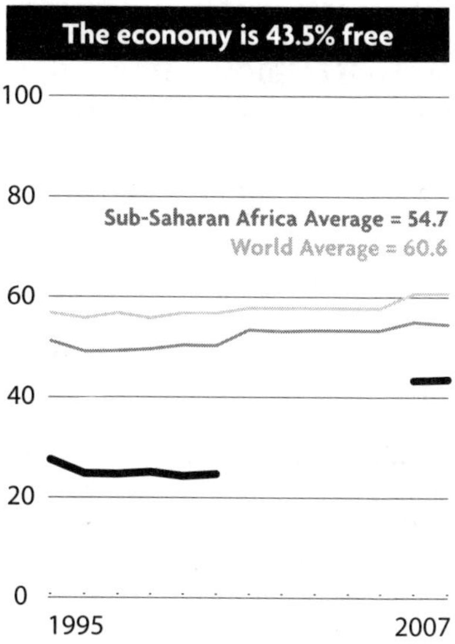

How Do We Measure Economic Freedom? See Chapter 3 (page 37) for an explanation of the methodology or visit the *Index* Web site at *heritage.org/index.*

The economy is 43.5% free

Sub-Saharan Africa Average = 54.7
World Average = 60.6

100
80
60
40
20
0

1995   2007

QUICK FACTS

Population: 15.5 million

GDP (PPP): $33.8 billion
11.1% growth in 2004
6.9% 5-yr. comp. ann. growth
$2,180 per capita

Unemployment: n/a

Inflation (CPI): 43.5%

FDI (net inflow): $2 billion

Official Development Assistance:
Multilateral: $138 million
Bilateral: $1 billion (12% from the U.S.)

External Debt: $9.5 billion

Exports: $13.8 billion
Primarily crude oil, petroleum, diamonds, petroleum products, coffee, fish

Imports: $10.6 billion
Primarily machinery and electrical equipment, vehicles, medicines, food, textiles

ANGOLA'S TEN ECONOMIC FREEDOMS

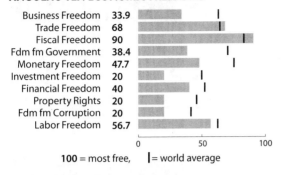

Business Freedom	33.9
Trade Freedom	68
Fiscal Freedom	90
Fdm fm Government	38.4
Monetary Freedom	47.7
Investment Freedom	20
Financial Freedom	40
Property Rights	20
Fdm fm Corruption	20
Labor Freedom	56.7

100 = most free, ▌= world average

BUSINESS FREEDOM — *33.9%*

Starting a business takes an average of 124 days, compared to the world average of 48 days. This makes entrepreneurship far too difficult to enable a dynamic official economy. Obtaining a business license can be very difficult because of regulations, and closing a business is also very difficult. Inconsistently enforced, the regulatory system has been vague and complicated. The overall freedom to start, operate, and close a business is seriously limited by the national regulatory environment.

TRADE FREEDOM — *68%*

Angola's weighted average tariff rate was 6 percent in 2005. While Angola has made solid progress in reforming its trade regime, non-tariff barriers still impose a cost on trade. Some non-tariff barriers include subsidies, import controls, customs barriers, some prohibitive regulations and standards, and issues involving the enforcement and protection of intellectual property rights. Consequently, an additional 20 percent is deducted from Angola's trade freedom score.

FISCAL FREEDOM — *90%*

Angola has a low income tax rate but a high corporate tax rate. The top income tax rate is 15 percent, and the top corporate tax rate is 35 percent. Other taxes include a fuel tax and a consumption tax. In the most recent year, overall tax revenue as a percentage of GDP was 6.9 percent.

FREEDOM FROM GOVERNMENT — *38.4%*

Total government expenditures, including consumption and transfer payments, are high. In the most recent year, government spending equaled 38.9 percent of GDP, and the government received 79 percent of its total revenues from state-owned enterprises and government ownership of property.

MONETARY FREEDOM — *47.7%*

Inflation in Angola is high and unstable, averaging 34.8 percent between 2003 and 2005. Relatively high and unstable prices explain most of the monetary freedom score. Government price controls are pervasive in many sectors of the economy, including fuel and electricity. Consequently, an additional 15 percent is deducted from Angola's monetary freedom score to adjust for the high economic cost of these price control measures.

INVESTMENT FREEDOM — *20%*

Angola's Law on Private Investment provides equal treatment to foreign investors, simplifies investment regulations, and lowers the required investment. However, procedures to register a foreign investment remain burdensome. Capital and money market transactions, capital repatriation, real estate transactions, and personal capital movements are subject to strict controls. In most instances, these transactions require central bank approval and/or licensing. Foreign investment in defense, internal public order, state security, certain banking activities, and the administration of ports and airports is not explicitly prohibited but is somewhat off-limits.

FINANCIAL FREEDOM — *40%*

Angola's financial system is small and underdeveloped but growing. The banking sector in 2003 consisted of seven commercial banks, of which three were foreign-owned. The two state-owned banks, which are slated for privatization, control approximately 45 percent of banking assets. Angola has been liberalizing the banking and insurance sectors in accordance with International Monetary Fund and World Bank advice, but financial governance remains poor. Available financial instruments are limited by the overall economic environment. The state remains heavily involved in the insurance sector. The government has formally constituted Angola's stock exchange with plans for it to be fully operational by the end of 2006.

PROPERTY RIGHTS — *20%*

The rule of law cannot be guaranteed through the local justice system, which suffers from political interference. Angola's legal and judicial system is not efficient in handling commercial disputes. Legal fees are high, and most businesses avoid taking disputes to court.

FREEDOM FROM CORRUPTION — *20%*

Corruption is perceived as widespread and hinders all other economic freedoms. Angola ranks 151st out of 158 countries in Transparency International's Corruption Perceptions Index for 2005.

LABOR FREEDOM — *56.7%*

The labor market operates under restrictive employment regulations that hinder employment and productivity growth. The non-salary cost of employing a worker is low, but dismissing a redundant employee is relatively costly. Angola has very rigid restrictions on increasing or contracting the number of working hours.

ARGENTINA

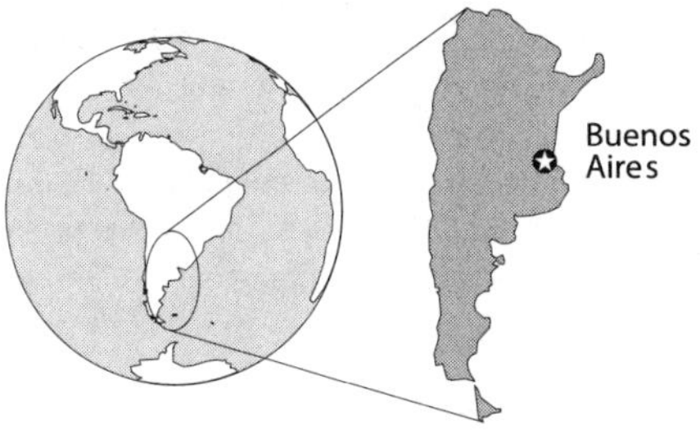

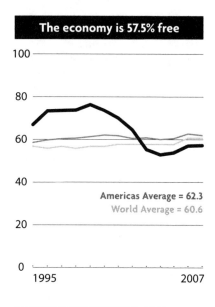

Buenos Aires

Rank: 95

Regional Rank: 21 of 29

Argentina's economy is 57.5 percent free, according to our 2007 assessment, which makes it the world's 95th freest economy. Its overall score is 0.2 percentage point higher than last year, partially reflecting new methodological detail. Argentina is ranked 21st out of 29 countries in the Americas, and its overall score is slightly below the regional average.

Argentina scores high in fiscal freedom, freedom from government, and monetary freedom. Top tax levels are comparable to those of the United States, as Argentina levies corporate and top income tax rates of 35 percent. While this is relatively high, government tax revenue as a percentage of GDP is low, and expenditure is correspondingly low as well. State ownership of businesses is also comparatively insignificant.

Property rights, labor freedom, and freedom from corruption are all problems for Argentina (labor freedom less so than the others). Political interference with an inefficient judiciary hinders greater foreign investment, and numerous popular and official obstructions of due process make international courts preferable to Argentine courts. Not surprisingly, corruption is also a problem. On the labor side, employing and dismissing employees is complicated, expensive, and a further hindrance to economic flexibility.

BACKGROUND: Under Néstor Kirchner, who became president in May 2003 following the fifth presidential election since Argentina's return to democracy in 1983, the state's role in the economy has expanded, primarily through price controls in some industries and the creation of state-owned enterprises. Argentina has abundant natural resources, and agriculture has always been important, but the principal industries are food processing and beverages, chemicals, petrochemicals, and motor vehicles. High GDP growth in the past few years is largely attributable to high commodity prices, a debt moratorium, and an economic recovery from the 2001 crisis rather than to sound government economic policies.

How Do We Measure Economic Freedom? See Chapter 3 (page 37) for an explanation of the methodology or visit the *Index* Web site at *heritage.org/index*.

The economy is 57.5% free

Americas Average = 62.3
World Average = 60.6

1995 — 2007

QUICK FACTS

Population: 38.4 million

GDP (PPP): $510.3 billion
9.0% growth in 2004
0.1% 5-yr. comp. ann. growth
$13,298 per capita

Unemployment: 13.6%

Inflation (CPI): 4.4%

FDI (net inflow): $3.9 billion

Official Development Assistance:
Multilateral: $27 million
Bilateral: $94 million (2% from the U.S.)

External Debt: $169.3 billion

Exports: $39.7 billion
Primarily edible oils, fuels and energy, cereals, feed, motor vehicles

Imports: $28.2 billion
Primarily machinery and equipment, vehicles, chemicals, metal manufactures, plastics

ARGENTINA'S TEN ECONOMIC FREEDOMS

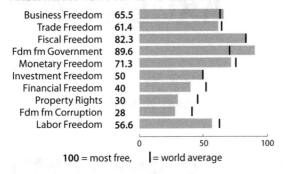

Business Freedom	65.5	
Trade Freedom	61.4	
Fiscal Freedom	82.3	
Fdm fm Government	89.6	
Monetary Freedom	71.3	
Investment Freedom	50	
Financial Freedom	40	
Property Rights	30	
Fdm fm Corruption	28	
Labor Freedom	56.6	

100 = most free, | = world average

BUSINESS FREEDOM — *65.5%*

Starting a business takes an average of 32 days, compared to the world average of 48 days. Entrepreneurship should be easier for maximum job creation. Both obtaining a business license and closing a business can be difficult because of regulations. Businesses still face difficulties involving inconsistent application of regulations. The overall freedom to start, operate, and close a business is relatively well protected by the national regulatory environment.

TRADE FREEDOM — *61.4%*

Argentina's weighted average tariff rate was 9.3 percent in 2004. Several non-tariff barriers are designed to constrain trade and protect domestic industries, including minimum import prices, import controls, quotas, restrictive sanitary rules, and issues involving the enforcement and protection of intellectual property rights. The customs process is burdensome and weakened by corruption. Consequently, an additional 20 percent is deducted from Argentina's trade freedom score to account for non-tariff barriers.

FISCAL FREEDOM — *82.3%*

Argentina has high tax rates. Both the top income tax rate and the top corporate tax rate are 35 percent. Other taxes include a value-added tax (VAT) and a wealth tax. In the most recent year, overall tax revenue as a percentage of GDP was 14.2 percent.

FREEDOM FROM GOVERNMENT — *89.6%*

Total government expenditures, including consumption and transfer payments, are low. In the most recent year, government spending equaled 20.9 percent of GDP, and the government received 0.8 percent of its revenues from state-owned enterprises and government ownership of property.

MONETARY FREEDOM — *71.3%*

Inflation is relatively volatile, averaging 8.7 percent between 2003 and 2005. Relatively high and unstable prices explain most of the monetary freedom score. The government imposes price controls on electricity, water, and gas distribution at the retail level, along with urban transport and local telephone services. Consequently, an additional 10 percent is deducted from Argentina's monetary freedom score to adjust for distortionary price controls.

INVESTMENT FREEDOM — *50%*

Registering a foreign business is fairly simple, and most local companies may be wholly owned by foreign investors. Foreign investment is prohibited in a few sectors, including shipbuilding, fishing, border-area real estate, and nuclear power generation, and is restricted in media and Internet companies. The most significant deterrent is legal uncertainty concerning creditor, contract, and property rights. The flow of capital is restricted, and repatriation is subject to some controls.

FINANCIAL FREEDOM — *40%*

Argentina's financial system was devastated by the 2001–2002 debt default and banking crisis. The sector is recovering and in some cases has returned to pre-crisis levels. Non-performing bank loans are down, but Argentines still hesitate to deposit funds in local banks. The government has not fully compensated banks for the conversion of dollar-denominated instruments to pesos. The largest bank is state-owned and serves as the sole financial institution in parts of the country. A number of foreign banks operate in Argentina. The government role in the financial sector increased after the crisis, and all financial services are subject to government regulation and supervision. The stock market is active, although market capitalization is dominated by a few firms.

PROPERTY RIGHTS — *30%*

The executive branch influences Argentina's judiciary, and independent surveys indicate that public confidence remains weak. Many foreign investors resort to international arbitration. An important violation of property rights is the "piquete," a form of protest in which protestors take over private business, causing extensive losses with no effective punishment by the police or the government. Argentine courts are notoriously slow, inefficient, secretive, and corrupt.

FREEDOM FROM CORRUPTION — *28%*

Corruption is perceived as widespread. Argentina ranks 97th out of 158 countries in Transparency International's Corruption Perceptions Index for 2005.

LABOR FREEDOM — *56.6%*

The labor market operates under restrictive employment regulations that hinder employment and productivity growth. The non-salary cost of employing a worker is very high, and dismissing a redundant employee is costly. Barriers to creating more jobs include severance costs, pension payments, mandatory contributions to a union-run health plan, mandatory holidays, and overtime. Argentina's labor market flexibility is one of the 20 lowest in the world.

ARMENIA

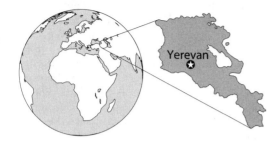

Yerevan

A rmenia's economy is 69.4 percent free, according to our 2007 assessment, which makes it the world's 32nd freest economy. Armenia is ranked 19th freest among the 41 countries in the European region. Armenia's score puts it above Europe's average—an impressive feat for an impoverished landlocked country. The overall score dropped sharply during the year by 5.1 percentage points, which partially reflects new methodological detail.

Armenia rates highly in many areas, such as fiscal freedom, freedom from government, monetary freedom, financial freedom, business freedom, and labor freedom. Low tax rates, low government expenditure, and low revenue from state-owned businesses contribute to its impressive fiscal and government freedom rankings. Armenia has low inflation, and its banking sector is both wholly private and well regulated. Commercial regulations are flexible and relatively simple. There are few restrictions on foreign investment, except for land ownership.

Armenia could still make some improvement in property rights and freedom from corruption. The judiciary is fairly weak and subject to political interference. For a post-Soviet country, however, Armenia shows an impressive amount of freedom.

BACKGROUND: Since 1988, Armenia, a former Soviet republic, has sparred with neighboring Azerbaijan, occupying Azerbaijan's Nagorno–Karabakh region and adjacent lands. President Robert Kocharyan, former president of the self-proclaimed Nagorno–Karabakh Republic, presides over a coalition government that is rife with fundamental policy differences. Despite these differences, however, the government has managed to achieve macroeconomic stabilization in recent years and maintains a positive relationship with various international financial institutions. Armenia's economy relies in nearly equal measure on manufacturing, services, and agriculture, including its famous cognac production.

How Do We Measure Economic Freedom? See Chapter 3 (page 37) for an explanation of the methodology or visit the *Index* Web site at *heritage.org/index*.

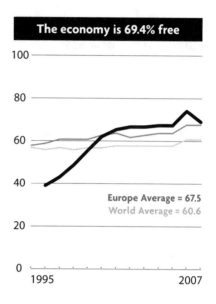

The economy is 69.4% free

Europe Average = 67.5
World Average = 60.6

QUICK FACTS

Population: 3 million

GDP (PPP): $12.4 billion
10.1% growth in 2004
10.5% 5-yr. comp. ann. growth
$4,101 per capita

Unemployment: 9.5%

Inflation (CPI): 8.1%

FDI (net inflow): $233 million

Official Development Assistance:
Multilateral: $146 million
Bilateral: $136 million (55% from the U.S.)

External Debt: $1.2 billion

Exports: $984.9 million
Primarily diamonds, mineral products, food, energy

Imports: $1.5 billion
Primarily natural gas, petroleum, tobacco products, food

ARMENIA'S TEN ECONOMIC FREEDOMS

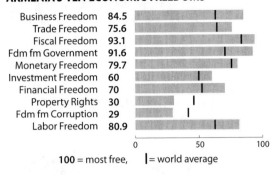

Business Freedom	84.5
Trade Freedom	75.6
Fiscal Freedom	93.1
Fdm fm Government	91.6
Monetary Freedom	79.7
Investment Freedom	60
Financial Freedom	70
Property Rights	30
Fdm fm Corruption	29
Labor Freedom	80.9

0   50   100

100 = most free, | = world average

BUSINESS FREEDOM — 84.5%

Starting a business takes an average of 24 days, compared to the world average of 48 days. Entrepreneurship should be easier for maximum job creation. Obtaining a business license can be relatively simple, and closing a business is easy. However, the business environment can be risky because of the poor implementation and application of business legislation. The overall freedom to start, operate, and close a business is relatively well protected by the national regulatory environment.

TRADE FREEDOM — 75.6%

Armenia's weighted average tariff rate in 2001 was a relatively low 2.2 percent. Improper implementation of the customs code is a significant barrier to trade, especially for importers. Consequently, an additional 20 percent is deducted from Armenia's trade freedom score.

FISCAL FREEDOM — 93.1%

Armenia has low tax rates. Both the top income tax rate and the top corporate tax rate are 20 percent. Other taxes include a value-added tax (VAT) and a vehicle tax. In the most recent year, overall tax revenue as a percentage of GDP was 15.3 percent.

FREEDOM FROM GOVERNMENT — 91.6%

Total government expenditures in Armenia, including consumption and transfer payments, are low. In the most recent year, government spending equaled 17.5 percent of GDP, and the government received 3.7 percent of its revenues from state-owned enterprises and government ownership of property.

MONETARY FREEDOM — 79.7%

Inflation in Armenia is relatively low, averaging 2.6 percent between 2003 and 2005. Relatively low and stable prices explain most of the monetary freedom score. Government policies distort prices through direct price controls in some sectors, such as public transportation, electricity, gas, and telecommunications. Consequently, an additional 10 percent is deducted from Armenia's monetary freedom score to adjust for price control measures.

INVESTMENT FREEDOM — 60%

Officially, foreign investors have the same right to establish businesses as native Armenians in nearly all sectors of the economy. Non-residents may not own land but are permitted to lease it. The major impediments to foreign investors are weak implementation of business legislation and corruption in the bureaucracy. The International Monetary Fund reports that there are no restrictions or controls on the holding of foreign exchange accounts, invisible transactions, or current transfers and no repatriation requirements.

FINANCIAL FREEDOM — 70%

Armenia's underdeveloped financial sector is dominated by banking. Following a banking crisis in the 1990s, the government embarked on a process of bank privatization and regulatory reform, including adopting International Accounting Standards and minimum capital requirements. Under the revised rules and standards, many banks have closed or merged; the number of banks fell from 31 in 2001 to 21 in March 2005. The state no longer has a stake in any bank, and all 21 commercial banks are privately owned. However, banks remain hindered by difficulty in debt recovery. All financial institutions are overseen by the central bank. The Ministry of Finance and Economy regulates the small insurance industry. Foreign insurance companies and banks are permitted. The active stock exchange includes 190 listed companies.

PROPERTY RIGHTS — 30%

The judiciary is influenced by the executive and is also underdeveloped and corrupt, substantially impeding the enforcement of contracts. In November 2005, the constitution was amended to increase judicial independence, but it remains to be seen how this translates into practice. A special Economic Court hears commercial disputes.

FREEDOM FROM CORRUPTION — 29%

Corruption is perceived as widespread. Armenia ranks 88th out of 158 countries in Transparency International's Corruption Perceptions Index for 2005.

LABOR FREEDOM — 80.9%

The labor market operates under flexible employment regulations that could be improved to enhance employment and productivity growth. The non-salary cost of employing a worker is moderate, and dismissing a redundant employee is relatively costless.

AUSTRALIA

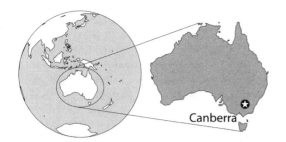

Canberra

Australia's economy is 82.7 percent free, according to our 2007 assessment, which makes it the world's 3rd freest economy. Its overall score is 1.2 percentage points higher than last year, partially reflecting new methodological detail. Australia is ranked 3rd out of 30 countries in the Asia–Pacific region, and its overall score is well above the regional average.

Australia rates highly in virtually all areas but is most impressive in financial freedom, property rights, business freedom, labor freedom, and freedom from corruption. Low inflation and low tariff rates buttress a globally competitive financial system based on market principles. As befits a Western democracy, a strong rule of law protects property rights and tolerates virtually no corruption. Foreign investment in Australia receives equal treatment with national investment, and both foreign and domestically owned businesses enjoy considerable flexibility in licensing, regulation, and employment practices.

The top income tax rate in Australia is high, as is government spending, but the overall effect is eclipsed by the impressive amount of economic freedom offered generally. Australia's economy is a global competitor and a regional leader in economic freedom.

BACKGROUND: In the 1980s, Australia deregulated its labor markets and reduced its trade barriers, transforming itself into an internationally competitive producer of services, technologies, and high-value-added manufactured goods. John Howard, the country's second longest-serving prime minister, has stepped up the privatization of state enterprises, including telecommunications. The government's policy agenda has been dominated in recent years by reforms of the taxation, welfare, public health, and higher education systems.

How Do We Measure Economic Freedom? See Chapter 3 (page 37) for an explanation of the methodology or visit the *Index* Web site at *heritage.org/index*.

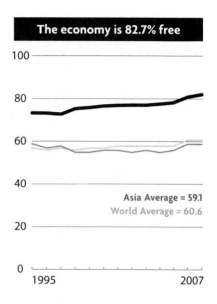

The economy is 82.7% free

Asia Average = 59.1
World Average = 60.6

QUICK FACTS

Population: 20.1 million

GDP (PPP): $610.0 billion
3.6% growth in 2004
3.3% 5-yr. comp. ann. growth
$30,331 per capita

Unemployment: 5.5%

Inflation (CPI): 2.3%

FDI (net inflow): $26.3 billion

Official Development Assistance:
Multilateral: None
Bilateral: None

External Debt: $287.8 billion

Exports: $112.5 billion
Primarily coal, gold, meat, wool, aluminum, iron ore, wheat, machinery

Imports: $131.4 billion
Primarily machinery, computers and office machines, telecommunications equipment, crude oil

AUSTRALIA'S TEN ECONOMIC FREEDOMS

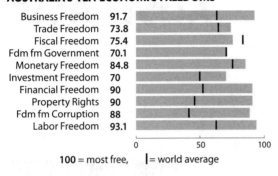

Business Freedom	91.7
Trade Freedom	73.8
Fiscal Freedom	75.4
Fdm fm Government	70.1
Monetary Freedom	84.8
Investment Freedom	70
Financial Freedom	90
Property Rights	90
Fdm fm Corruption	88
Labor Freedom	93.1

0   50   100

100 = most free, | = world average

BUSINESS FREEDOM — *91.7%*

Starting a business takes an average of two days, compared to the world average of 48 days. Ease of entrepreneurship promotes maximum job creation. Obtaining a business license is easy, and closing a business is very easy. In sectors dominated by small businesses, the government generally follows a hands-off approach. The overall freedom to start, operate, and close a business is strongly protected by the national regulatory environment.

TRADE FREEDOM — *73.8%*

Australia's weighted average tariff rate in 2004 was a relatively low 3.1 percent. However, the government implements a number of non-tariff barriers that impede and raise the cost of trade. These include stringent sanitary measures, support programs for agriculture and manufacturing products, and commodity boards. Consequently, an additional 20 percent is deducted from Australia's trade freedom score.

FISCAL FREEDOM — *75.4%*

Australia has a high income tax rate and a moderate corporate tax rate. The top income tax rate is 47 percent, and the top corporate tax rate is 30 percent. Other taxes include a value-added tax (VAT), a tax on insurance contracts, and a fuel tax. In the most recent year, overall tax revenue as a percentage of GDP was 24.1 percent.

FREEDOM FROM GOVERNMENT — *70.1%*

Total government expenditures in Australia, including consumption and transfer payments, are high. In the most recent year, government spending equaled 35.3 percent of GDP, and the government received 2.3 percent of its total revenues from state-owned enterprises and government ownership of property.

MONETARY FREEDOM — *84.8%*

Inflation is relatively low, averaging 2.6 percent between 2003 and 2005. Relatively low and stable prices explain most of the monetary freedom score. The government does not impose national price controls on goods, but states retain the power to impose price controls (although the range of goods actually subject to control is diminishing as competition reforms are implemented). Consequently, an additional 5 percent is deducted from Australia's monetary freedom score.

INVESTMENT FREEDOM — *70%*

Foreign investors receive national treatment. Proposals to start new businesses with an investment of A$10 million must receive prior authorization. The government accepts most of these proposals routinely, although it may reject them if the investment is determined not to be consistent with the "national interest." Foreign investment in media, banking, airlines, airports, shipping, urban and residential real estate, and telecommunications is subject to limitations. Residents and non-residents have access to foreign exchange and may conduct international payments and capital transactions. There are no capital repatriation controls.

FINANCIAL FREEDOM — *90%*

Australia's highly developed, competitive financial system includes advanced banking, insurance, and equity industries. The central bank has the authority to set lending policies and interest rates but has not exercised those powers since the deregulation of financial markets in the 1980s. Markets set interest rates. Government regulation of banks is minimal, and foreign banks may be licensed as branches or subsidiaries and may offer a full range of banking operations. Australia had 53 financial institutions holding banking licenses in 2005, including 14 Australian banks, 11 foreign subsidiaries, and 28 foreign bank branches, and numerous other non-bank financial institutions. There are no government-owned banks. Foreign insurance companies are permitted, and regulation of the sector is undemanding, focusing on capital adequacy, solvency, and prudential behavior. Australia's stock market is well developed and open to foreign listings.

PROPERTY RIGHTS — *90%*

Property rights are well protected. Contracts are secure, although subject to backlogs. Government expropriation is highly unusual.

FREEDOM FROM CORRUPTION — *88%*

Corruption is perceived as minimal. Australia ranks 9th out of 158 countries in Transparency International's Corruption Perceptions Index for 2005.

LABOR FREEDOM — *93.1%*

The labor market operates under highly flexible employment regulations that enhance employment and productivity growth. The non-salary cost of employing a worker can be high, but dismissing a redundant employee is costless. Australia's labor market flexibility is one of the 20 highest in the world.

AUSTRIA

Vienna ✪

Rank: 25

Regional Rank: 15 of 41

Austria's economy is 71.3 percent free, according to our 2007 assessment, which makes it the world's 25th freest economy. Austria is ranked 15th freest among the 41 countries in the European region, putting it well above the regional average. Austria's score declined by 0.1 percentage point this year, but it has been high since the inception of the *Index*, never deviating more than 5 points in either direction.

Austria rates well in trade, monetary, and business freedom, as well as property rights and freedom from corruption. As a member of the European Union, its tariff is standardized at the low 1.7 percent rate, property rights are strong, and inflation is relatively stable for the euro currency. Starting a business takes a relatively short time. Foreigners wishing to invest in Austria are not subject to particularly stringent requirements.

As a modern European social democracy, Austria maintains very high personal income tax rates to support a significant welfare state. Extensive commercial regulations have been reduced slightly, although rigid labor laws remain. Hiring and firing employees is difficult, as is true almost everywhere else in the EU, and inflexibility of the labor market hurts overall competitiveness.

BACKGROUND: Over the past decade, Austria's government has relinquished control of formerly nationalized oil, gas, steel, and engineering companies and has deregulated telecommunications and electricity; yet foreign investors still face regulatory rigidities and barriers to market entry. Parliamentary elections led to reconfiguration of the fragile governing coalition in February 2003, and People's Party Chancellor Wolfgang Schüssel has accelerated the pace of market reform. A major tax reform initiative simplifying both wage and income taxes was enacted in May 2004. Corporate tax rates were reduced by nearly a third to 25 percent, giving Austria one of the lowest rates in Western Europe.

How Do We Measure Economic Freedom? See Chapter 3 (page 37) for an explanation of the methodology or visit the *Index* Web site at *heritage.org/index*.

The economy is 71.3% free

100

80

60

40

Europe Average = 67.5
World Average = 60.6

20

0

1995   2007

QUICK FACTS

Population: 8.2 million

GDP (PPP): $263.8 billion
2.4% growth in 2004
1.8% 5-yr. comp. ann. growth
$32,276 per capita

Unemployment: 7.1%

Inflation (CPI): 2.1%

FDI (net inflow): −$2.3 billion

Official Development Assistance:
Multilateral: None
Bilateral: None

External Debt: $510.6 billion (2005 estimate)

Exports: $161.1 billion
Primarily machinery and equipment, motor vehicles and parts, paper and paperboard, metal goods, chemicals, iron and steel

Imports: $155.3 billion
Primarily machinery and equipment, motor vehicles, chemicals, metal goods, oil and oil products, food

AUSTRIA'S TEN ECONOMIC FREEDOMS

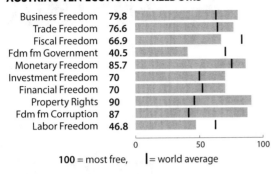

Business Freedom	79.8
Trade Freedom	76.6
Fiscal Freedom	66.9
Fdm fm Government	40.5
Monetary Freedom	85.7
Investment Freedom	70
Financial Freedom	70
Property Rights	90
Fdm fm Corruption	87
Labor Freedom	46.8

100 = most free, | = world average

BUSINESS FREEDOM — 79.8%

Starting a business takes an average of 29 days, compared to the world average of 48 days. Entrepreneurship should be easier for maximum job creation. Obtaining a business license is relatively simple, and closing a business is easy. In recent years, the government has moved to streamline its complex and time-consuming regulatory environment. The overall freedom to start, operate, and close a business is relatively well protected by the national regulatory environment.

TRADE FREEDOM — 76.6%

Austria's trade policy is the same as those of other members of the European Union. The common EU weighted average tariff rate was 1.7 percent in 2005. Non-tariff barriers reflected in EU and Austrian policy include agricultural and manufacturing subsidies, regulatory and licensing restrictions, and other market access restrictions. Consequently, an additional 20 percent is deducted from Austria's trade freedom score.

FISCAL FREEDOM — 66.9%

Austria has a very high income tax rate and a low corporate tax rate. The top income tax rate is 50 percent, and the top corporate tax rate is 25 percent. Other taxes include a value-added tax (VAT), an advertising tax, and a tax on insurance contracts. In the most recent year, overall tax revenue as a percentage of GDP remained very high at 42.9 percent.

FREEDOM FROM GOVERNMENT — 40.5%

Total government expenditures, including consumption and transfer payments, are very high. In 2004, government spending equaled 50.1 percent of GDP, and the government received 2.7 percent of its total revenues from state-owned enterprises and government ownership of property.

MONETARY FREEDOM — 85.7%

Austria is a member of the euro zone. From 2003 to 2005, its weighted average annual rate of inflation was 2.2 percent. Relatively low and stable prices explain most of the monetary freedom score. As a participant in the EU's Common Agricultural Policy, the government subsidizes agricultural production, distorting the prices of agricultural products. Consequently, an additional 5 percent is deducted from Austria's monetary freedom score to account for these policies.

INVESTMENT FREEDOM — 70%

There are no formal sectoral or geographic restrictions on foreign investment. Foreign investment is forbidden in arms, explosives, and industries in which the state has a monopoly (casinos, printing of banknotes, and minting of coins). Restrictions exist for non-residents in the auditing and legal professions, transportation, and electric power generation. There are no controls or requirements on current transfers, access to foreign exchange, or repatriation of profits. Real estate transactions are subject to approval by local authorities.

FINANCIAL FREEDOM — 70%

Austria's financial system is subject to limited government intervention. An independent supervisory body established in 2002 oversees retirement funds, insurance, securities, and banking (where oversight is performed by the central bank). Banks offer the full range of services, and the erosion of barriers has been leading to consolidation. Markets set interest rates, and foreign banks operate freely. The largest bank is a unit of Germany's HypoVereinsbank. In May 2005, the government and several private institutions announced a plan to support Austria's fourth-largest bank, Bawag PSK, after it almost collapsed from a speculation debacle. Tax incentives have been adopted to promote equity investment through pension funds. The stock exchange was privatized in 1999 and is modest in size, although financing from other European capital markets is readily available.

PROPERTY RIGHTS — 90%

Private property is very secure in Austria. Contractual agreements are secure, and the protection of private property and intellectual property is well established.

FREEDOM FROM CORRUPTION — 87%

Corruption is perceived as minimal. Austria ranks 10th out of 158 countries in Transparency International's Corruption Perceptions Index for 2005.

LABOR FREEDOM — 46.8%

The labor market operates under highly restrictive employment regulations that hinder employment and productivity growth. The non-salary cost of employing a worker is high, and dismissing a redundant employee is costly. The cost of fringe benefits per employee (one of the EU's highest) is equivalent to nearly 100 percent of base salary.

AZERBAIJAN

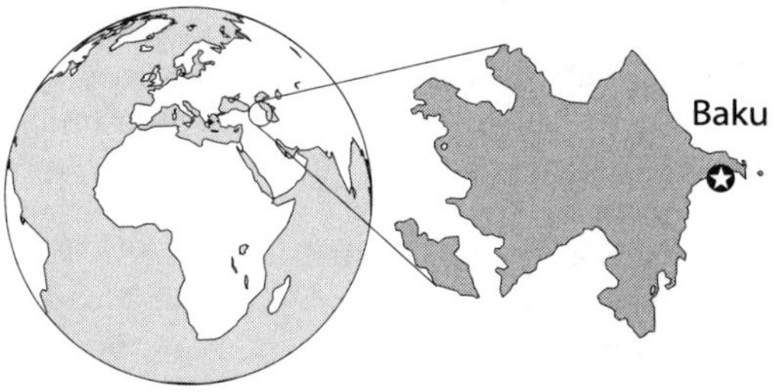

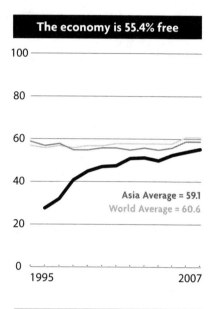

Baku

A zerbaijan's economy is 55.4 percent free, according to our 2007 assessment, which makes it the world's 107th freest economy. Its overall score is 1.4 percentage points higher than last year, partially reflecting new methodological detail. Azerbaijan is ranked 20th out of 30 countries in the Asia–Pacific region, and its overall score is just below the regional average.

Azerbaijan's level of monetary freedom is fairly high. Corporate tax rates enhance Azerbaijan's score, although the government also imposes other taxes. Most of the state-owned businesses have been privatized. That and limited government spending give Azerbaijan a high freedom from government score.

As a transforming Second World economy, Azerbaijan still faces substantial challenges. Financial freedom, investment freedom, property rights, and corruption remain problematic, and an underdeveloped judicial system engenders a debilitating lack of property rights. Major hurdles, both formal and informal, stand in the way of foreign investment, and wide sectors of the economy are off-limits to non-Azerbaijanis.

BACKGROUND: Azerbaijan regained its independence from the Soviet Union in 1991, but a long-running dispute with Armenia over the Nagorno–Karabakh region has cost Azerbaijan 16 percent of its territory. President Ilham Aliyev is placing loyalists in positions of power with a view to contesting the 2008 election. Large inflows of foreign direct investment continue to support the hydrocarbons sector. Surging exports of oil and gas are expected to raise GDP significantly in the years ahead.

How Do We Measure Economic Freedom? See Chapter 3 (page 37) for an explanation of the methodology or visit the *Index* Web site at *heritage.org/index*.

The economy is 55.4% free

Asia Average = 59.1
World Average = 60.6

1995 — 2007

QUICK FACTS

Population: 8.3 million

GDP (PPP): $34.5 billion
10.2% growth in 2004
8.3% 5-yr. comp. ann. growth
$4,153 per capita

Unemployment: 1.1%

Inflation (CPI): 6.7%

FDI (net inflow): $3.4 billion

Official Development Assistance:
Multilateral: $81 million
Bilateral: $122 million (39% from the U.S.)

External Debt: $2.0 billion

Exports: $4.2 billion
Primarily oil and petroleum, machinery, cotton, food

Imports: $6.3 billion
Primarily machinery and equipment, oil products, food, metals, chemicals

91

AZERBAIJAN'S TEN ECONOMIC FREEDOMS

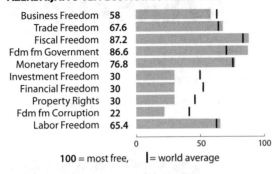

Business Freedom	58
Trade Freedom	67.6
Fiscal Freedom	87.2
Fdm fm Government	86.6
Monetary Freedom	76.8
Investment Freedom	30
Financial Freedom	30
Property Rights	30
Fdm fm Corruption	22
Labor Freedom	65.4

100 = most free, | = world average

BUSINESS FREEDOM — 58%

Starting a business takes an average of 53 days, compared to the world average of 48 days. Entrepreneurship should be easier for maximum job creation. Obtaining a business license can be very difficult, but closing a business is relatively easy. The lack of transparent and effective regulations to establish clear rules and foster competition are serious impediments to investment. The overall freedom to start, operate, and close a business is limited by the national regulatory environment.

TRADE FREEDOM — 67.6%

Azerbaijan's weighted average tariff rate was a relatively moderate 6.2 percent in 2002. Non-tariff barriers include a weak legal regime, arbitrary customs administration, conflicts of interest in regulatory matters, subsidies, and corruption. Consequently, an additional 20 percent is deducted from the trade freedom score.

FISCAL FREEDOM — 87.2%

Azerbaijan has a moderate income tax rate and a low corporate tax rate. The top income tax rate is 35 percent, and the top corporate tax rate is 22 percent (effective January 2006). Other taxes include a value-added tax (VAT) and a property tax. In the most recent year, overall tax revenue as a percentage of GDP was 14.4 percent.

FREEDOM FROM GOVERNMENT — 86.6%

Total government spending, including consumption and transfer payments, is low. In the most recent year, government spending equaled 17.9 percent of GDP, and the government received 17.7 percent of its total revenues from state-owned enterprises and government ownership of property. Structural reform has been very slow in many sectors. Privatization of small and medium-sized enterprises is almost complete, but only limited progress has been made in large-scale enterprises.

MONETARY FREEDOM — 76.8%

Inflation averaged 8.3 percent between 2003 and 2005. Relatively moderate and unstable prices explain most of the monetary freedom score. The government continues to impose artificially low prices on most energy products. Consequently, an additional 5 percent is deducted from Azerbaijan's monetary freedom score to adjust for distortionary price control measures.

INVESTMENT FREEDOM — 30%

Even though the government has issued some decrees to improve the business environment, the Ministry of Justice serves as a screening process, acting in a non-transparent, arbitrary manner. The government prohibits investments in national security and defense sectors and restricts investment in government-controlled sectors like energy, mobile telephony, and oil and gas. The Azerbaijan National Bank regulates most foreign exchange transactions and foreign exchange accounts. Payments and transfers are subject to restrictions, and the central bank must authorize most capital transactions. Direct investment abroad by residents, including real estate transactions, requires central bank approval.

FINANCIAL FREEDOM — 30%

Azerbaijan's financial system is underdeveloped and largely cash-based. The banking sector is weak and burdened by non-performing loans. The central bank has overseen a process of closures, consolidation, and privatization under which the number of banks has fallen from 210 in 1994 to 44 in 2006. The two state-owned banks together account for about 60 percent of banking sector assets and provide financing for most government departments and many of the state-owned enterprises, often at below-market rates. The central bank raised minimum capital requirements, but many commercial banks are undercapitalized. Foreign banks have a minimal presence. The government has imposed increased regulatory requirements and supervision on the insurance sector, which consisted of about 60 companies in 2005, including two state companies and eight foreign companies. The stock exchange is very small.

PROPERTY RIGHTS — 30%

The judiciary is the least developed branch of the government and suffers from corruption. Problems in the quality, reliability, and transparency of governance, as well as abuse of the regulatory system and poor contract enforcement, significantly impede the ability of many companies to do business. Politically connected business interests benefit from their control of lucrative sectors of the economy.

FREEDOM FROM CORRUPTION — 22%

Corruption is perceived as widespread. Azerbaijan ranks 137th out of 158 countries in Transparency International's Corruption Perceptions Index for 2005.

LABOR FREEDOM — 65.4%

The labor market operates under restrictive employment regulations that hinder employment and productivity growth. The non-salary cost of employing a worker is high, and dismissing a redundant employee is costly. Azerbaijan's unemployment insurance program pays out the equivalent of 70 percent of the average national salary, which is so generous that it diminishes the incentive to work.

THE BAHAMAS

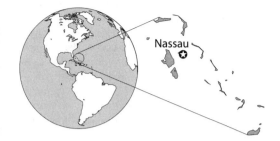

Nassau ✪

The Bahamian economy is 71.4 percent free, according to our 2007 assessment, which makes it the world's 24th freest economy. Its overall score is 1.2 percentage points lower than last year, partially reflecting new methodological detail. The Bahamas is ranked 5th out of 29 countries in the Americas, and its overall score is higher than the regional average.

The Bahamas enjoys high levels of business freedom, freedom from government, monetary freedom, fiscal freedom, property rights, and labor freedom. The government imposes no income or corporate tax. Regulations can be subject to official whim, but the environment remains generally business-friendly. The labor market is highly flexible, and severance packages are not overly onerous for employers. A focus on transparency represents the best traditions of English common law in protecting private property, which is nowhere more apparent than in the advanced financial system.

Despite a healthy respect for law and a relatively positive economic environment, the Bahamas levies significant tariffs on a wide array of trade goods, and non-tariff barriers further impede trade. Foreign investment is restricted and subject to numerous approvals by the civil service.

BACKGROUND: The Bahamas was settled by the British and became independent in 1973. Tourism employs about half of the working population, either directly or indirectly. Banking and international financial services also contribute heavily to the economy, which is the most prosperous in the Caribbean. The government is funded in part by high import tariffs that serve as a mercantilist barrier to higher prosperity as well as closer trade integration with island neighbors and the United States. The economy experiences periodic waves of Haitian and Cuban immigrants and is unable to stop the drug trafficking through the country's numerous cays and small islands.

How Do We Measure Economic Freedom? See Chapter 3 (page 37) for an explanation of the methodology or visit the *Index* Web site at *heritage.org/index*.

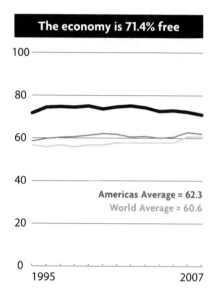

The economy is 71.4% free

Americas Average = 62.3
World Average = 60.6

1995 — 2007

QUICK FACTS

Population: 0.3 million

GDP (PPP): $6.98 billion (2005 estimate)
3.0% growth in 2004
1.8% 5-yr.comp. ann. growth
$20,200 per capita (2005 estimate)

Unemployment: 10.2%

Inflation (CPI): 0.5%

FDI (net inflow): $211.9 million

Official Development Assistance:
Multilateral: $2 million
Bilateral: $6 million (100% from the U.S.)

External Debt: $342.6 million (2004 estimate)

Exports: $2.7 billion
Primarily mineral products and salt, animal products, rum, chemicals

Imports: $3.0 billion
Primarily machinery and transport equipment, manufactures, chemicals, mineral fuels, food and live animals

THE BAHAMAS' TEN ECONOMIC FREEDOMS

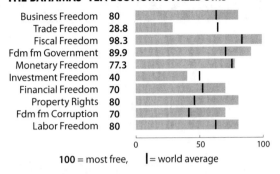

Business Freedom	80
Trade Freedom	28.8
Fiscal Freedom	98.3
Fdm fm Government	89.9
Monetary Freedom	77.3
Investment Freedom	40
Financial Freedom	70
Property Rights	80
Fdm fm Corruption	70
Labor Freedom	80

0   50   100

100 = most free, | **= world average**

BUSINESS FREEDOM — 80%

The Bahamian government generally follows a hands-off approach to business. However, starting, operating, and closing a business can be hindered by a burdensome regulatory environment.

TRADE FREEDOM — 28.8%

According to the World Bank, The Bahamas' weighted average tariff rate was a high 25.6 percent in 2002. The government imposes occasional import bans and implements import licensing procedures. The government imposes a 7 percent "stamp tax" on most imports, and higher stamp taxes are charged on some duty-free goods, including china, crystal, wristwatches, clocks, jewelry, table linens, leather goods, perfume, wine, and liquor. The government also uses import permits to restrict imports of some agricultural goods. Consequently, an additional 20 percent is deducted from the Bahamas' trade freedom score to account for non-tariff barriers.

FISCAL FREEDOM — 98.3%

The Bahamas' tax burden is one of the lowest in the world. There is no income tax, no corporate income tax, no capital gains tax, no inheritance tax, and no value-added tax. In the most recent year, overall tax revenue (mainly from import tariffs) as a percentage of GDP was 16 percent.

FREEDOM FROM GOVERNMENT — 89.9%

Total government spending, including consumption and transfer payments, is low. In the most recent year, government spending equaled 19.4 percent of GDP, and the government received 3.8 percent of its revenues from state-owned enterprises and government ownership of property. Privatization of state-owned business has been slow and limited.

MONETARY FREEDOM — 77.3%

Inflation is relatively low, averaging 1.5 percent between 2003 and 2005. Relatively stable prices explain most of the monetary freedom score. An additional 15 percent is deducted from the Bahamas' monetary freedom score to adjust for price control measures that distort domestic prices for such "breadbasket" items as drugs, gasoline, diesel oil, and petroleum gas.

INVESTMENT FREEDOM — 40%

Foreign investment is restricted in many sectors, including wholesale and retail operations, real estate, newspapers, advertising, nightclubs and some restaurants, security services, building supplies, construction, fishing, and public transportation. All outward capital transfers and inward transfers by non-residents require exchange control approval. Foreign direct investment must be approved by the central bank. To purchase real estate for commercial purposes or to purchase more than five acres, foreigners must obtain a permit from the Investments Board.

FINANCIAL FREEDOM — 70%

The Bahamian financial sector is an international financial hub and is open to foreigners. Yielding to international pressure, such as the listing in June 2000 by the Financial Action Task Force, the government passed regulations on international business companies, mutual funds, money laundering, and trusts in the 1990s and established a Financial Intelligence Unit, improved international legal cooperation, and tightened rules on reporting of suspicious transactions in 2000. The Bahamas was removed from the FATF list in 2001. These changes impose extra regulatory costs on the financial sector but do not constrain financial services, although stricter regulation and supervision did result in fewer licensed banks and companies. The government has adopted incentives to encourage foreign financial business and remains involved in the financial sector through ownership of the Bahamas Mortgage Corporation and the Bahamas Development Bank. The stock market is underdeveloped and small.

PROPERTY RIGHTS — 80%

The Bahamas has an efficient legal system based on English common law. The judiciary is independent and conducts generally fair public trials. However, the judicial process tends to be very slow, and some investors complain of malfeasance on the part of court officials.

FREEDOM FROM CORRUPTION — 70%

Piracy of software, music, and videos is a problem. Existing copyright laws are ignored. Illegal drug trafficking and money laundering are also significant.

LABOR FREEDOM — 80%

The labor market generally operates under flexible employment regulations that enhance overall productivity growth. Although labor laws can be burdensome, especially for domestic business, their cost is relatively low. Employment contracts are not mandatory but are often prepared. Legal entitlement to notice on termination is not required, but one pay period is the custom.

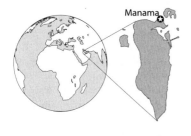
Manama

BAHRAIN

Bahrain's economy is 68.4 percent free, according to our 2007 assessment, which makes it the world's 39th freest economy. Its overall score is 2.6 percentage points lower than last year, partially due to new methodological detail. Bahrain is ranked 2nd out of 17 countries in the Middle East/North Africa region, and its economy is ideal in several respects, such as tax and banking freedom.

Bahrain's economy is very free for the Middle East, with high scores in several of the 10 factors of economic freedom. Business freedom, fiscal freedom, monetary freedom, and financial freedom all rate well but are tempered by a score of only 40 percent for labor freedom, based on government regulations mandating the hiring of Bahrainis. The complete absence of income or corporate taxes in all industries except oil gives Bahrain a competitive commercial advantage globally.

Despite some high scores, however, overall freedom has declined consistently since 1999. The main areas in which the country could improve are labor freedom and freedom from government. Specifically, the economy would do well if state-owned enterprises were not so dominant, generating three-quarters of government revenue.

BACKGROUND: Bahrain has become one of the Persian Gulf's most advanced economies and most progressive political systems since gaining its independence from Great Britain in 1971. Under a constitution promulgated by Sheikh Hamad bin Isa al-Khalifa, the country became a constitutional monarchy in 2002, and the government has sought to reduce dependence on declining oil reserves and encourage foreign investment by diversifying the economy. Because of its communications and transportation infrastructure, regulatory structure, and cosmopolitan outlook, Bahrain is home to many multinational firms that do business in the region. In 2005, the U.S. and Bahrain ratified a free trade agreement.

How Do We Measure Economic Freedom? See Chapter 3 (page 37) for an explanation of the methodology or visit the *Index* Web site at *heritage.org/index*.

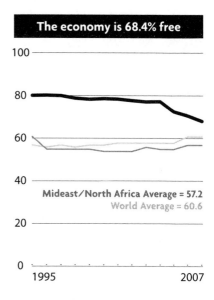

The economy is 68.4% free

Mideast/North Africa Average = 57.2
World Average = 60.6

1995 — 2007

QUICK FACTS

Population: 0.7 million

GDP (PPP): $14.9 billion
5.4% growth in 2004
5.6% 5-yr. comp. ann. growth
$20,758 per capita

Unemployment: 14.0% (2004 estimate)

Inflation (CPI): 2.3%

FDI (net inflow): −$170.3 million

Official Development Assistance:
Multilateral: $0.2 million
Bilateral: $111 million (0% from the U.S.)

External Debt: $6.1 billion (2004 estimate)

Exports: $9.2 billion
Primarily petroleum and petroleum products, aluminum, textiles

Imports: $7.1 billion
Primarily crude oil, machinery, chemicals

BAHRAIN'S TEN ECONOMIC FREEDOMS

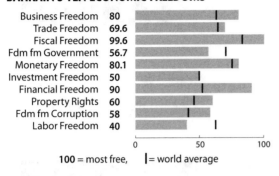

Business Freedom	80
Trade Freedom	69.6
Fiscal Freedom	99.6
Fdm fm Government	56.7
Monetary Freedom	80.1
Investment Freedom	50
Financial Freedom	90
Property Rights	60
Fdm fm Corruption	58
Labor Freedom	40

0   50   100

100 = most free, | = world average

BUSINESS FREEDOM — *80%*

Bahrain's commercial law system is relatively straightforward, but starting, operating, and closing a business can be hindered by a regulatory environment that lacks coordination. Obtaining a business license is difficult because of complicated bureaucratic procedures. In recent years, steps to streamline licensing and approval procedures have been taken.

TRADE FREEDOM — *69.6%*

Bahrain's simple average tariff rate was 5.2 percent in 2005. There are few non-tariff barriers, but a limited number of products are subject to import and export prohibitions and licenses, and discrepancies between legislation and practice reduce transparency and predictability and may increase the scope for administrative discretion, particularly at the border. Consequently, an additional 20 percent is deducted from Bahrain's trade freedom score to account for non-tariff barriers.

FISCAL FREEDOM — *99.6%*

Bahrain imposes no taxes on personal income. Most companies are not subject to corporate tax, but a 46 percent corporate tax rate is levied on oil companies. In the most recent year, overall tax revenue as a percentage of GDP was 7.6 percent.

FREEDOM FROM GOVERNMENT — *56.7%*

Total government expenditures, including consumption and transfer payments, are moderate. In the most recent year, government spending equaled 28.7 percent of GDP, and the government received 72.1 percent of its revenues from state-owned enterprises and government ownership of property.

MONETARY FREEDOM — *80.1%*

Inflation is relatively low, averaging 2.5 percent between 2003 and 2005. Relatively low and stable prices explain most of the monetary freedom score. An additional 10 percent is deducted from Bahrain's monetary freedom score to adjust for price control measures that distort domestic prices for electricity, water, and petroleum.

INVESTMENT FREEDOM — *50%*

The government welcomes foreign investment, except in cases that involve competition with established local enterprises or existing government-owned or parastatal companies. All significant investments, whether by Bahraini or foreign firms, are subject to a lengthy and complicated government approval process. Gulf Cooperation Council (GCC) nationals may own 100 percent of the shares of domestic enterprises, but non-GCC nationals are allowed only 49 percent ownership of most companies. The stock exchange restricts ownership by non-GCC firms and persons to 49 percent of listed companies. Bahrain has no restrictions on the repatriation of profits or capital, no exchange controls, and no restrictions on converting or transferring funds, whether associated with an investment or not.

FINANCIAL FREEDOM — *90%*

Bahrain aims to become a regional financial hub, and both foreign and local individuals and companies have access to credit on market terms. Of the 25 commercial banks operating in 2006, 15 were branches of foreign banks. Some 52 offshore banking units, which use Bahrain as a base from which to conduct banking operations in other countries, dominate the financial sector. The Arab Banking Corporation and the Gulf International Bank control 45 percent of total offshore banking unit assets. The International Monetary Fund has praised Bahrain's financial supervision as effective and its regulation as modern and comprehensive. The stock exchange is small but active. In March 2004, Bahrain lifted the requirement that foreign insurance brokers and loss adjusters have at least 51 percent Bahraini ownership. They may now operate with 100 percent foreign ownership.

PROPERTY RIGHTS — *60%*

Property is secure, and expropriation is unlikely. The judiciary is not fully independent, because the king has the right to appoint judges and amend the constitution. Nevertheless, the legal system is well regarded, and foreign firms have been able to resolve disputes satisfactorily through the local courts. There are no prohibitions on the use of international arbitration to safeguard contracts.

FREEDOM FROM CORRUPTION — *58%*

Corruption is perceived as present. Bahrain ranks 36th out of 158 countries in Transparency International's Corruption Perceptions Index for 2005.

LABOR FREEDOM — *40%*

The labor market operates under inflexible employment regulations that hinder overall productivity growth. Government regulations require businesses, by law, to employ Bahrainis, and this practice hinders job creation as the government tries to micromanage decisions by private businesses. Rigid regulations about dismissing a worker are also a burden to the private sector.

BANGLADESH

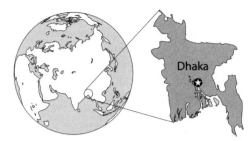

Dhaka

Rank: 143

Regional Rank: 27 of 30

Bangladesh's economy is 47.8 percent free, according to our 2007 assessment, which makes it the world's 143rd freest economy. Its overall score is 6.6 percentage points lower than last year, partially reflecting new methodological detail. Bangladesh is ranked 27th out of 30 countries in the Asia–Pacific region.

Bangladesh's fiscal freedom and freedom from government score well. Monetary freedom, labor freedom, and business freedom are also relatively positive. Government expenditures relative to GDP are low, and the top income and corporate tax rates are not excessive. Privatization continues to proceed slowly, and Bangladesh maintains fairly loose restrictions on starting new businesses and obtaining commercial licenses. Closing a business, however, is not quite as simple.

Bangladesh has extreme barriers to trade freedom. Tariffs are prohibitively high. It is also weak in investment freedom, property rights, and financial freedom. In addition, corruption is rampant. Chaotic regulations and restricted market sectors impede greater foreign investment, as does a haphazard and politicized approach to the rule of law. The banking sector is plagued by similar problems.

BACKGROUND: The People's Republic of Bangladesh is one of the world's poorest countries. The run-up to the establishment of a caretaker government preceding the October 2005 national elections was marked by a dangerous and violent political struggle. However, the current government has achieved some success in tackling environmental issues and the economy. Natural disasters, inadequate infrastructure, and poor management have hindered the economy, in which the service sector accounts for half of GDP, while the majority of the population is engaged in the agricultural sector.

The economy is 47.8% free

```
100

80

60

40        Asia Average = 59.1
          World Average = 60.6
20

0
   1995                    2007
```

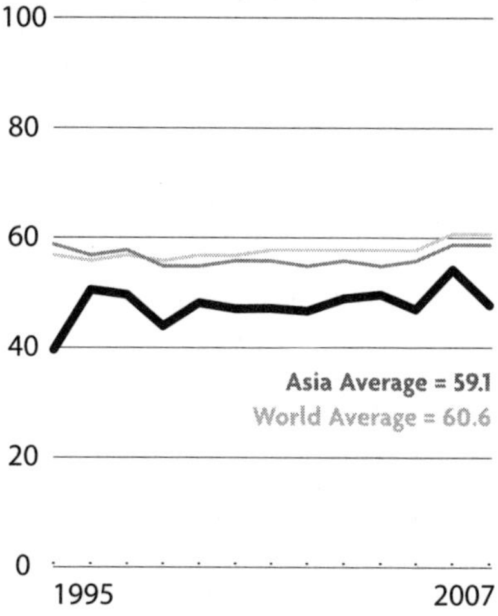

QUICK FACTS

Population: 139.2 million

GDP (PPP): $260.4 billion
5.9% growth in 2004
5.4% 5-yr. comp. ann. growth
$1,870 per capita

Unemployment: 2.5% (2004 estimate)

Inflation (CPI): 6.1%

FDI (net inflow): $456.1 million

Official Development Assistance:
Multilateral: $1.0 billion
Bilateral: $1.0 billion (9% from the U.S.)

External Debt: $20.3 billion

Exports: $9.2 billion
Primarily garments, jute and jute goods, leather, fish

Imports: $13.1 billion
Primarily machinery and equipment, chemicals, iron and steel, textiles, food, petroleum products, cement

How Do We Measure Economic Freedom? See Chapter 3 (page 37) for an explanation of the methodology or visit the *Index* Web site at *heritage.org/index.*

BANGLADESH'S TEN ECONOMIC FREEDOMS

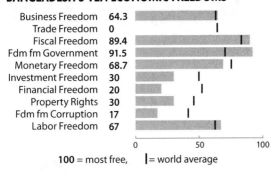

Business Freedom	64.3
Trade Freedom	0
Fiscal Freedom	89.4
Fdm fm Government	91.5
Monetary Freedom	68.7
Investment Freedom	30
Financial Freedom	20
Property Rights	30
Fdm fm Corruption	17
Labor Freedom	67

0   50   100

100 = most free, | = world average

BUSINESS FREEDOM — *64.3%*

Starting a business takes an average of 37 days, compared to the world average of 48 days. Entrepreneurship should be easier for maximum job creation. Obtaining a business license is relatively simple, but closing a business is difficult. Commercial regulations can be unclear and inconsistent, and the lack of transparency raises start-up and operational costs. The overall freedom to start, operate, and close a business is relatively well protected by the national regulatory environment.

TRADE FREEDOM — *0%*

Bangladesh's weighted average tariff rate was 55.8 percent in 2005. Barriers to trade include prohibitions and restrictions on imports, restrictive labeling requirements, and ineffectively operated customs procedures. Corruption serves as a non-tariff barrier. Consequently, an additional 20 percent is deducted from Bangladesh's trade freedom score to account for non-tariff barriers.

FISCAL FREEDOM — *89.4%*

Bangladesh has moderate tax rates. The top income tax rate is 25 percent, and the top corporate tax rate is 30 percent. Other taxes include a value-added tax (VAT), a property tax, and a tax on interest. In the most recent year, overall tax revenue as a percentage of GDP was 7.9 percent.

FREEDOM FROM GOVERNMENT — *91.5%*

Total government expenditures, including consumption and transfer payments, are low. In the most recent year, government spending equaled 14.2 percent of GDP, and the government received 11.4 percent of its total revenues from state-owned enterprises and government ownership of property. Privatization has been hindered by bureaucratic resistance and opposition from labor unions.

MONETARY FREEDOM — *68.7%*

Inflation averaged a moderate 6.6 percent between 2003 and 2005. Relatively moderate and unstable prices explain most of the monetary freedom score. An additional 15 percent is deducted from Bangladesh's monetary freedom score to adjust for price control measures that distort domestic prices for goods produced in state-owned enterprises, some pharmaceuticals, and petroleum products.

INVESTMENT FREEDOM — *30%*

Foreign investment is generally welcomed, but utilities and other critical sectors are not open to the private sector. Bureaucratic procedures, unnecessary licenses, corruption, and uncertainty about contract and regulatory enforcement constitute strong barriers to foreign investment. Most capital transactions are controlled or prohibited. Non-resident companies are subject to a higher corporate tax rate (37.5 percent) than are publicly traded companies (30 percent).

FINANCIAL FREEDOM — *20%*

Bangladesh has a small, underdeveloped financial services sector. The banking system consisted of four nationalized commercial banks, five state-owned specialized banks, 30 private domestic banks, and 10 foreign banks in 2005. Foreign banks are generally restricted to offshore and foreign trade business. The nationalized commercial banks dominate the system, controlling over half of banking assets. The government is both owner and major customer of the state-owned banks. The central bank is not independent. Financial supervision is weak, and fraudulent transactions, mismanagement, and political influence over lending are common. Non-performing loans are declining but still represented 10 percent of all loans in 2004. The extensive microfinance presence is largely unsupervised. There are 30 private insurance companies, including a foreign-owned firm, but the major portion of insurance activity is controlled by two state-owned companies. Capital markets are small and underdeveloped. Banks, insurance companies, and financial institutions are taxed at a higher rate (45 percent) than are other corporations (30 percent).

PROPERTY RIGHTS — *30%*

The constitution provides for an independent judiciary, although the lower courts are considered to be part of the executive branch. Contracts are weakly enforced. The lower courts suffer from corruption. Dispute settlement is also hampered by shortcomings in accounting practices and the registration of real property.

FREEDOM FROM CORRUPTION — *17%*

Corruption is perceived as widespread. Bangladesh ranks last in Transparency International's Corruption Perceptions Index for 2005. Given that corruption is cancerous to all other economic freedoms, this is the key area that needs improvement.

LABOR FREEDOM — *67%*

The labor market operates under restrictive employment regulations that hinder employment and productivity growth. The non-salary cost of employing a worker is low, but dismissing a redundant employee is costly. The labor laws specify wage levels, leave policies, and working hours. There are 49 labor regulations, and the government has taken initiatives to amend and codify 27 of them as a single version of the labor laws.

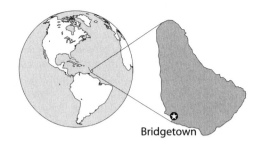

Bridgetown

BARBADOS

Barbados's economy is 70.5 percent free, according to our 2007 assessment, which makes it the world's 28th freest economy. Its overall score is 4.7 percentage points lower than last year, partially reflecting new methodological detail. Barbados is ranked 6th out of 29 countries in the Americas, and its overall score is well above the regional average.

Barbados's business freedom, property rights, and labor freedom all rate highly, as do financial and monetary freedoms, although to a lesser extent. Business regulations, clearly laid out in commercial laws and generally followed, are simple and not cumbersome. The labor market is highly flexible and open. A focus on transparency levels the playing field for domestic and foreign businesses alike, though certain restrictions on foreign investment and moderately high taxes exist. A strong legal system allows for the effective adjudication of business disputes, as well as a relatively low level of corruption and the protection of private property.

Despite a healthy respect for law and a relatively positive economic environment, Barbados does levy significant tariffs on non-CARICOM goods. Average tariff rates are similarly high, and non-tariff barriers are a hindrance to a more efficient flow of goods.

BACKGROUND: Barbados has a two-party parliamentary system, and the Barbados Labor Party, led by Owen Arthur, has been in power since 1994. Tourism is the most important economic sector. Barbados emphasizes economic and cultural cooperation within the Caribbean region and the development of a common trade policy position within the Caribbean Community and Common Market (CARICOM) trade bloc. The heavily subsidized sugar industry, although diminishing in importance, remains an important employer and exporter. The offshore financial sector is smaller than others in the Caribbean but makes a significant contribution to the economy and is generally well regulated.

How Do We Measure Economic Freedom? See Chapter 3 (page 37) for an explanation of the methodology or visit the *Index* Web site at *heritage.org/index*.

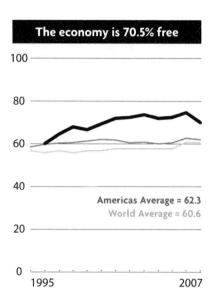

The economy is 70.5% free

Americas Average = 62.3
World Average = 60.6

1995 — 2007

QUICK FACTS

Population: 0.3 million

GDP (PPP): $4.6 billion
4.8% growth in 2004
1.4% 5-yr. comp. ann. growth
$16,825 per capita

Unemployment: 9.6%

Inflation (CPI): 1.4%

FDI (net inflow): $50 million (gross)

Official Development Assistance:
Multilateral: $33 million
Bilateral: $3 million (36% from the U.S.)

External Debt: $643.5 million

Exports: $1.5 billion
Primarily sugar and molasses, rum, food, beverages, chemicals, electrical components

Imports: $1.8 billion
Primarily consumer goods, machinery, food, construction materials, chemicals, fuel, electrical components

BARBADOS'S TEN ECONOMIC FREEDOMS

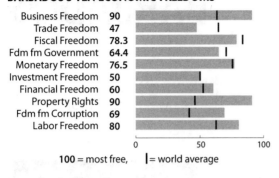

Business Freedom	90
Trade Freedom	47
Fiscal Freedom	78.3
Fdm fm Government	64.4
Monetary Freedom	76.5
Investment Freedom	50
Financial Freedom	60
Property Rights	90
Fdm fm Corruption	69
Labor Freedom	80

0   50   100

100 = most free, | = world average

BUSINESS FREEDOM — 90%

Starting, operating, and closing a business are easy and free from burdensome regulation. Transparent policies and effective laws enhance competition and establish clear rules for foreign and domestic investors. The Company Act ensures flexibility and simplicity for establishing and operating companies in Barbados.

TRADE FREEDOM — 47%

The simple average tariff rate in Barbados was 16.5 percent in 2003. The government requires permits, licenses, or permission prior to importation and maintains restrictive sanitary and phytosanitary policies. Consequently, an additional 20 percent is deducted from Barbados's trade freedom score to account for non-tariff barriers.

FISCAL FREEDOM — 78.3%

Barbados has a high income tax rate and a moderate corporate tax rate. The top income tax rate is 37.5 percent, and the top corporate income tax rate is 30 percent. Other taxes include a value-added tax (VAT) and a tax on interest. In the most recent year, overall tax revenue as a percentage of GDP was 30.9 percent.

FREEDOM FROM GOVERNMENT — 64.4%

Total government expenditures, including consumption and transfer payments, are high. In the most recent year, government spending equaled 38.1 percent of GDP, and the government received 5.1 percent of its total revenues from state-owned enterprises and government ownership of property.

MONETARY FREEDOM — 76.5%

Inflation is moderate, averaging 4.5 percent between 2003 and 2005. Relatively moderate but unstable prices explain most of the monetary freedom score. Although prices are generally set by the market, an additional 10 percent is deducted from Barbados's monetary freedom score to adjust for price control measures that distort domestic prices for basic food items and fuel.

INVESTMENT FREEDOM — 50%

Barbados permits 100 percent foreign ownership of enterprises and treats domestic and foreign firms equally, but the government is more likely to approve projects that it believes will create jobs and increase exports. Foreign investors can be subject to performance requirements. Central bank approval is required for both residents and non-residents to hold foreign exchange accounts. Foreign currency transactions and current transfers are restricted by quantitative limits. Exchange control approval is required for direct investment and real estate purchases, and the central bank must approve all credit operations.

FINANCIAL FREEDOM — 60%

Barbados has a smaller financial sector than other Caribbean financial hubs. Commercial banking is dominated by foreign banks, including Canadian, British, and Caribbean banks based in other countries. Citicorp Merchant Bank initiated operations in 2001. In recent years, the government has intervened in the domestic credit market to influence interest rates, restrict the volumes of funds, and borrow funds. Domestic financing is generally restricted to Barbadians or permanent residents. As of 2004, the offshore financial sector included over 4,500 international business companies, exempt insurance companies, and offshore banks. Legislation passed in 1998 tightened the controls against money laundering. The securities exchange is small, listing about two dozen local and foreign Caribbean companies in 2005. Sagicor, the largest local insurance company, controls 75 percent of the eastern Caribbean market.

PROPERTY RIGHTS — 90%

Private property is well protected. The legal tradition is based on British common law. The highest court of appeal is the new Caribbean Court of Justice. By Caribbean standards, the police and court systems are efficient and unbiased, and the government operates in an essentially transparent manner.

FREEDOM FROM CORRUPTION — 69%

Corruption is perceived as present. Barbados ranks 24th out of 158 countries in Transparency International's Corruption Perceptions Index for 2005.

LABOR FREEDOM — 80%

The labor market generally operates under flexible employment regulations that enhance overall productivity growth. Under the Trade Union Act of 1964, employers have no legal obligation to recognize unions. Employees are guaranteed a minimum of two weeks of annual leave and are covered by unemployment benefits and National Insurance legislation. Enhancing labor market flexibility has become one of the key areas for further reform.

BELARUS

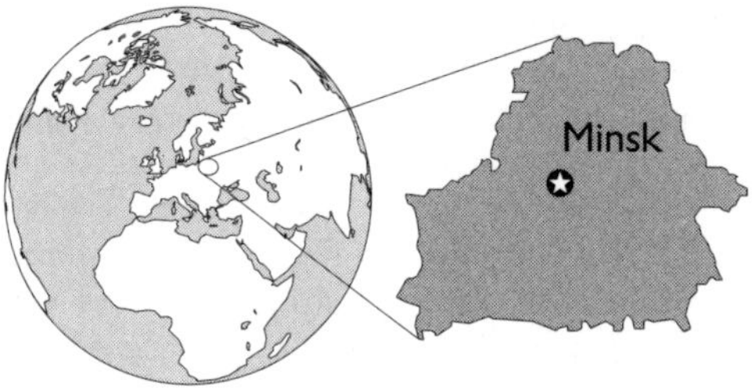

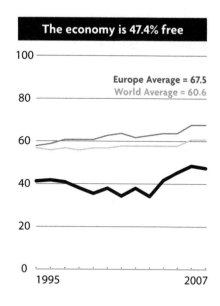

Minsk ✪

Rank: 145

Regional Rank: 41 of 41

Belarus's economy is 47.4 percent free, according to our 2007 assessment, which makes it the world's 145th freest economy. Belarus is ranked 41st among the 41 countries in the European region, and its overall score is below the regional average. Belarus's persistently low score has been blamed on the failure of post-Soviet reforms, and this year it experienced a 1.2 percentage point decrease overall.

Belarus's fiscal freedom scores highly. Others are simply in line with world averages, such as freedom from government, trade freedom, and monetary freedom. The top income and corporate tax rates are a moderate 30 percent, and although the government adds additional costs such as a value-added tax, revenue collected from taxes is relatively low. Belarus has a low average tariff rate, but non-tariff barriers lower its overall trade freedom score.

Belarus's economy has significant shortcomings. Financial freedom, investment freedom, property rights, and freedom from corruption are weak. The government dominates the banking sector, which is politically influenced. Foreign investment in all sectors faces hurdles, from outright restrictions to bureaucratic incompetence. Weak rule of law allows for significant corruption and insecure property rights.

BACKGROUND: Belarus won independence from the Soviet Union in 1991 but has retained close economic and political ties to Russia. President Alexander Lukashenko declared himself the winner of the March 2006 elections—a result that was challenged by internal democratic opposition and Western observers. The economy deteriorated after 1995, when Lukashenko vowed to guide his country toward a path of "market socialism." Belarus's continuing dependence on Russian gas to meet its energy needs could be a problem because Russian gas giant Gazprom has signaled its intention to increase gas prices in early 2007.

How Do We Measure Economic Freedom? See Chapter 3 (page 37) for an explanation of the methodology or visit the *Index* Web site at *heritage.org/index*.

The economy is 47.4% free

Europe Average = 67.5
World Average = 60.6

100

80

60

40

20

0

1995 — 2007

QUICK FACTS

Population: 9.8 million

GDP (PPP): $68.5 billion
11.4% growth in 2004
6.8% 5-yr. comp. ann. growth
$6,970 per capita

Unemployment: 1.9%

Inflation (CPI): 18.1%

FDI (net inflow): $170.7 million

Official Development Assistance:
Multilateral: $4 million
Bilateral: $46 million (12% from the U.S.)

External Debt: $3.7 billion

Exports: $15.7 billion
Primarily machinery and equipment, mineral products, chemicals, metals, textiles

Imports: $17.0 billion
Primarily mineral products, machinery and equipment, chemicals, food

BELARUS'S TEN ECONOMIC FREEDOMS

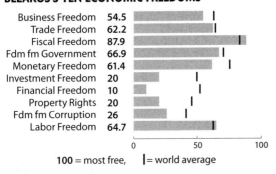

Business Freedom	54.5
Trade Freedom	62.2
Fiscal Freedom	87.9
Fdm fm Government	66.9
Monetary Freedom	61.4
Investment Freedom	20
Financial Freedom	10
Property Rights	20
Fdm fm Corruption	26
Labor Freedom	64.7

100 = most free, I = world average

BUSINESS FREEDOM — 54.5%

Starting a business takes an average of 69 days, compared to the world average of 48 days. Entrepreneurship should be easier for maximum job creation. Obtaining a business license is difficult, and closing a business is very difficult. Burdensome regulations discourage private enterprises, leading small and medium-sized private companies to concentrate in retail and catering, where relatively low sunk costs prevent excessively high losses. The overall freedom to start, operate, and close a business is limited by the national regulatory environment.

TRADE FREEDOM — 62.2%

The weighted average tariff rate in Belarus was 8.9 percent in 2002. The government maintains extensive import licensing and quotas. Consequently, an additional 20 percent is deducted from Belarus's trade freedom score to account for non-tariff barriers.

FISCAL FREEDOM — 87.9%

Belarus has moderate tax rates. The top income tax rate is 30 percent, and the top corporate income tax rate is 24 percent. Other taxes include a value-added tax (VAT), an ecological tax, and a turnover tax. In the most recent year, overall tax revenue as a percentage of GDP was 18.6 percent.

FREEDOM FROM GOVERNMENT — 66.9%

Total government expenditures, including consumption and transfer payments, are high. In the most recent year, government spending equaled 36.5 percent of GDP, and the government received 5.9 percent of its total revenues from state-owned enterprises and government ownership of property. Privatization is stalled.

MONETARY FREEDOM — 61.4%

Inflation is relatively high, averaging 13.9 percent between 2003 and 2005. Relatively high and unstable prices explain most of the monetary freedom score. The government subsidizes many basic goods and services, sets prices of products made by state-owned enterprises, and regulates prices in the retail sector. Consequently, an additional 15 percent is deducted from Belarus's monetary freedom score to adjust for price control measures that distort domestic prices.

INVESTMENT FREEDOM — 20%

There are significant restrictions on capital transactions. Foreign investment must be registered with the Minsk City Executive Committee. There are restrictions in the share of foreign investment in insurance organizations and banks. An inefficient bureaucracy, corruption, and concerted resistance to the private sector all serve to hinder foreign investment. In March 2004, the government extended the "golden share" rule to include companies in which the government has no claim at all. Foreigners may not own land. Capital transactions, resident and non-resident accounts, invisibles, and current transfers are subject to strict controls.

FINANCIAL FREEDOM — 10%

Belarus's financial system is very heavily influenced by the government. All but one of the 31 banks are owned or controlled by the state. A handful of commercial banks dominate the financial sector and account for about 85 percent of banking assets. Five of these banks are state-controlled. The central bank is fully controlled by the government. Banks are frequently pressured into making politically motivated loans, which comprised over half of all outstanding loans in 2004. Foreign banks face high barriers, and barriers to credit are high. The non-bank financial sector is small and inhibited by state intervention and irregular regulatory enforcement. Policies enacted in 2004 and 2005 curtailed competition in the insurance sector and led many companies to leave the market. The stock market is small and largely dormant.

PROPERTY RIGHTS — 20%

The legal system does not fully protect private property, and the inefficient court system does not enforce contracts consistently. The judiciary has proved neither independent nor objective by international standards. Independent lawyers were barred from practicing in 1997.

FREEDOM FROM CORRUPTION — 26%

Corruption is perceived as widespread. Belarus ranks 107th out of 158 countries in Transparency International's Corruption Perceptions Index for 2005.

LABOR FREEDOM — 64.7%

The labor market operates under relatively flexible employment regulations that hinder employment and productivity growth. The non-salary cost of employing a worker is very high, but dismissing a redundant employee is relatively costless. The unemployment insurance system, funded almost entirely by employers with some government assistance, offers benefits approximately equivalent to 30 percent of an average worker's annual salary.

BELGIUM

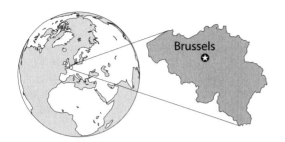
Brussels

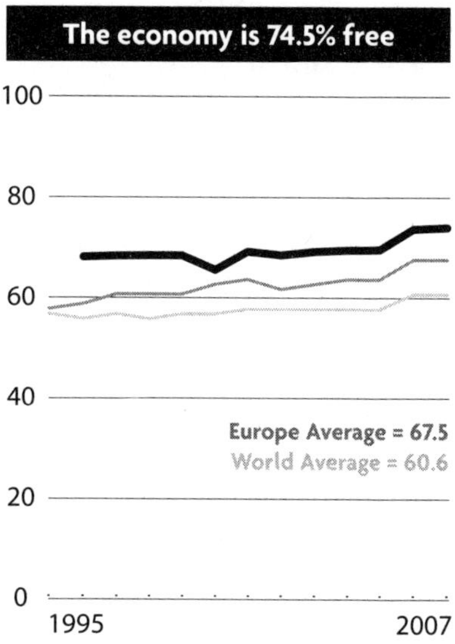

Belgium's economy is 74.5 percent free, according to our 2007 assessment, which makes it the world's 17th freest economy. This is a 0.3 percentage point increase, partially reflecting new methodological detail. Belgium is ranked 10th freest among the 41 countries in the European region, and its overall score is above the regional average. Over the past decade, it has almost always scored in the low 70s.

As a modern Western economy, Belgium scores highly in many areas. Investment freedom, property rights, monetary freedom, and business freedom are the strongest areas of the economy. As a member of the European Union, Belgium has a standardized monetary policy that yields relatively low inflation despite some government distortion in the agricultural sector. The protection of property by a transparent rule of law encourages confidence among foreign investors, who enjoy excellent market access.

As in many other European social democracies, government spending and income tax rates are exceptionally high in order to support an extensive welfare state. Additional taxes complement the income and corporate levies, bringing overall tax revenue to an uncommonly high 45.6 percent of GDP.

BACKGROUND: Belgium is a federal state consisting of three regions: Flanders, Wallonia, and the capital city of Brussels. Brussels also houses the headquarters of NATO and the European Union. Since his re-election in 2003, Prime Minister Guy Verhofstadt and his Socialist–Liberal coalition have sought to ease the income tax burden and balance the budget, yet sluggish growth persists. The services sector accounts for over three-quarters of GDP. Leading exports are electrical equipment, vehicles, diamonds, and chemicals.

How Do We Measure Economic Freedom? See Chapter 3 (page 37) for an explanation of the methodology or visit the *Index* Web site at *heritage.org/index*.

The economy is 74.5% free

100

80

60

40

Europe Average = 67.5
World Average = 60.6

20

0

1995   2007

QUICK FACTS

Population: 10.4 million

GDP (PPP): $324.1 billion
2.4% growth in 2004
1.9% 5-yr. comp. ann. growth
$31,096 per capita

Unemployment: 8.4%

Inflation (CPI): 2.1%

FDI (net inflow): $8.2 billion

Official Development Assistance:
Multilateral: None
Bilateral: None

External Debt: $980.1 billion (2005 estimate)

Exports: $298.0 billion
Primarily machinery and equipment, chemicals, diamonds, metals and metal products, food

Imports: $284.7 billion
Primarily machinery and equipment, chemicals, diamonds, pharmaceuticals, food, transportation equipment, oil products

BELGIUM'S TEN ECONOMIC FREEDOMS

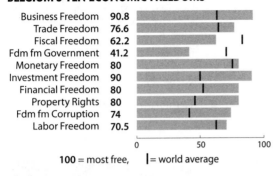

Business Freedom	90.8
Trade Freedom	76.6
Fiscal Freedom	62.2
Fdm fm Government	41.2
Monetary Freedom	80
Investment Freedom	90
Financial Freedom	80
Property Rights	80
Fdm fm Corruption	74
Labor Freedom	70.5

0   50   100

100 = most free, **|** = world average

BUSINESS FREEDOM — *90.8%*

Starting a business takes an average of 27 days, compared to the world average of 48 days. Entrepreneurship should be easier for maximum job creation. Obtaining a business license is relatively simple, and closing a business is very easy. Commercial regulations can hinder entrepreneurial activities, especially for small and medium-size enterprises. The overall freedom to start, operate, and close a business is strongly protected by the national regulatory environment.

TRADE FREEDOM — *76.6%*

Belgium's trade policy is the same as those of other members of the European Union. The common EU weighted average tariff rate was 1.7 percent in 2005. Non-tariff barriers reflected in EU and Belgian policy include agricultural and manufacturing subsidies, regulatory and licensing restrictions, and other market access restrictions. Consequently, an additional 20 percent is deducted from Belgium's trade freedom score.

FISCAL FREEDOM — *62.2%*

Belgium's income tax rate is one of the world's highest, but its corporate tax rate is moderate. The top income tax rate is 50 percent, and the top corporate tax rate is 34 percent (composed of a 33 percent tax rate and a 3 percent surcharge). Other taxes include a value-added tax (VAT), a transport tax, and a property tax. In the most recent year, overall tax revenue as a percentage of GDP was 45.6 percent.

FREEDOM FROM GOVERNMENT — *41.2%*

Total government expenditures, including consumption and transfer payments, are very high. In the most recent year, government spending equaled 49.6 percent of GDP, and the government received 4.3 percent of its total revenues from state-owned enterprises and government ownership of property.

MONETARY FREEDOM — *80%*

Belgium is a member of the euro zone. Between 2003 and 2005, its weighted average annual rate of inflation was 2.5 percent. Relatively low and stable prices explain most of the monetary freedom score. As a participant in the EU's Common Agricultural Policy, the government subsidizes agricultural production, distorting the prices of agricultural products. Price control policies affect water, electricity, and gas distribution; waste handling; medicines; automobiles; compulsory insurance; and petroleum products. Consequently, 10 percent is deducted from Belgium's monetary freedom score to account for these policies.

INVESTMENT FREEDOM — *90%*

Most restrictions on foreign investment also apply to domestic investment. Authorization is required for investment in Belgian flag vessels operated by shipping companies that do not have their main offices in Belgium. There are some restrictions on non–European Union investment in public works as required under EU regulations. There are no restrictions on the purchase of real estate, residents' and non-residents' accounts, repatriation of profit, or transfer of capital.

FINANCIAL FREEDOM — *80%*

Belgium has one of the world's most developed financial systems. The independent Banking, Finance and Insurance Commission supervises the financial sector. Belgium has over 100 banks, including over 70 foreign banks, and numerous financial service providers. Banks are required to provide a minimum set of services under a "universal service" law. Credit is allocated at market terms and is available to foreign and domestic investors without discrimination. Belgian law differentiates between EU and non-EU banks, financial institutions, and insurance companies, although firms from European Economic Area or World Trade Organization countries may be treated equally. Regional authorities may subsidize medium- and long-term borrowing. The world's first stock market was organized in Antwerp, and capital markets are sound and well-established.

PROPERTY RIGHTS — *80%*

Property is well protected, and contractual agreements are secure. Belgium's laws are codified, and the quality of the judiciary and civil service is high, although the process is often slow.

FREEDOM FROM CORRUPTION — *74%*

Corruption is perceived as minimal. Belgium ranks 19th out of 158 countries in Transparency International's Corruption Perceptions Index for 2005.

LABOR FREEDOM — *70.5%*

The labor market operates under relatively flexible employment regulations that hinder employment and productivity growth. The non-salary cost of employing a worker can be very high, and dismissing a redundant employee is relatively costly. Belgium's high labor costs are sustainable for high-value-added processes, but labor market rigidities remain a major barrier to employing a worker. The unemployment insurance system offers benefits that are worth approximately 50 percent of an average worker's annual salary.

2007 Index of Economic Freedom

BELIZE

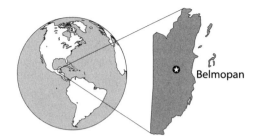

Belmopan

Belize's economy is 63.7 percent free, according to our 2007 assessment, which makes it the world's 56th freest economy. Its overall score is 1.8 percentage points lower than last year, partially reflecting new methodological detail. Belize is ranked 13th out of 29 countries in the Americas, and its overall score is equal to the regional average.

Belize rates highly in fiscal freedom, freedom from government, and labor freedom and somewhat highly in monetary freedom. Despite a high top income tax rate, corporate taxes are low, and government tax revenue is not particularly large as a percentage of GDP. Government expenditures are likewise fairly low, and the number of state-owned businesses is not significant. Flexible labor regulations contribute to an elastic employment market with no major regulatory distortions. Low inflation and stable prices contribute positively to the economic climate, but certain government price controls also exist.

Investment freedom, financial freedom, property rights, and corruption are less strong. Foreign investment is hampered in a wide array of sectors by special licensing requirements, and foreign exchange regulations are neither consistent nor transparent. A weak judicial system allows for political interference in the courts and significant corruption.

BACKGROUND: Belize is a parliamentary democracy and member of the British Commonwealth. Prime Minister Said Musa was re-elected in March 2003. Tourism is a major contributor to the economy, as is agriculture. Traditionally, sugar has been the principal export, but the government is fostering export diversification into other products, including shrimp, citrus, bananas, papayas, and soybeans. Crime is a serious problem, and Belize suffers from one of the highest murder rates in the Caribbean region. International relations are dominated by a territorial dispute with Guatemala.

How Do We Measure Economic Freedom? See Chapter 3 (page 37) for an explanation of the methodology or visit the *Index* Web site at *heritage.org/index*.

The economy is 63.7% free

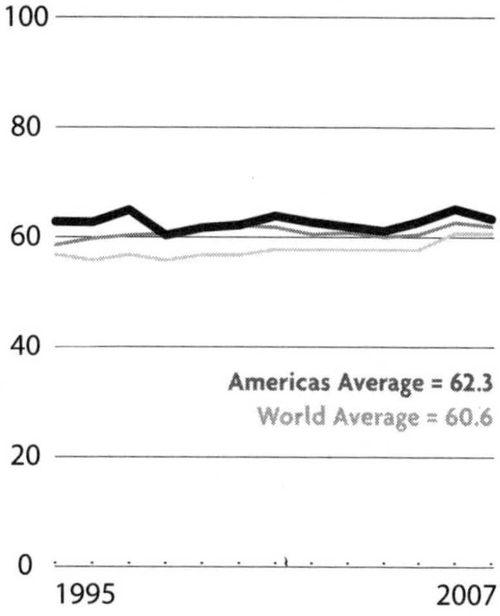

Americas Average = 62.3
World Average = 60.6

1995   2007

QUICK FACTS

Population: 0.3 million

GDP (PPP): $1.9 billion
4.6% growth in 2004
7.2% 5-yr. comp. ann. growth
$6,747 per capita

Unemployment: 11.6%

Inflation (CPI): 3.1%

FDI (net inflow): $169.9 million

Official Development Assistance:
Multilateral: $7 million
Bilateral: $8 million (26% from the U.S.)

External Debt: $1.4 billion (2004 estimate)

Exports: $506.1 million
Primarily sugar, bananas, citrus, clothing, fish products, molasses, wood

Imports: $626.4 million
Primarily machinery and transport equipment, manufactured goods, fuels, chemicals, pharmaceuticals

BELIZE'S TEN ECONOMIC FREEDOMS

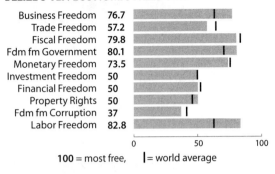

Business Freedom	76.7
Trade Freedom	57.2
Fiscal Freedom	79.8
Fdm fm Government	80.1
Monetary Freedom	73.5
Investment Freedom	50
Financial Freedom	50
Property Rights	50
Fdm fm Corruption	37
Labor Freedom	82.8

100 = most free, ▌ = world average

BUSINESS FREEDOM — *76.7%*

Starting a business takes an average of 45 days, three times longer than the world average of 48 days. Entrepreneurship should be easier for maximum job creation. Despite a lack of transparency in the administration of some laws and procedures, obtaining a business license is relatively simple, and closing a business is relatively easy. The overall freedom to start, operate, and close a business is relatively well protected by the national regulatory environment.

TRADE FREEDOM — *57.2%*

The weighted average tariff rate in Belize was 11.4 percent in 2003. Foreign exchange shortages, quotas, and restrictive import licensing rules add to the cost of trade. Consequently, an additional 20 percent is deducted from Belize's trade freedom score to account for non-tariff barriers.

FISCAL FREEDOM — *79.8%*

Belize has a high income tax rate and a moderate tax rate. The top income tax rate is 45 percent, and the top corporate tax rate is 25 percent. Other taxes include a value-added tax (VAT) and a stamp duty. In the most recent year, overall tax revenue as a percentage of GDP was 19.4 percent.

FREEDOM FROM GOVERNMENT — *80.1%*

Total government expenditures, including consumption and transfer payments, are very moderate. In the most recent year, government spending equaled 28.9 percent of GDP, and the government received 1.2 percent of its total revenues from state-owned enterprises and government ownership of property.

MONETARY FREEDOM — *73.5%*

Inflation is fairly low, averaging 3.3 percent between 2003 and 2005. Relatively low and stable prices explain most of the monetary freedom score. The government maintains the prices of some basic commodities, such as rice, flour, beans, sugar, bread, butane gas, and fuel, and controls the retail price of electricity. Consequently, an additional 15 percent is deducted from Belize's monetary freedom score to adjust for price control measures that distort domestic prices.

INVESTMENT FREEDOM — *50%*

Belize generally is open to foreign investment but requires special licenses in commercial fishing within the barrier reef, merchandising, sugarcane farming, real estate and insurance, transportation, tourism activities, accounting and legal services, entertainment, beauty salons, and restaurants and bars. Both residents and non-residents may hold foreign exchange accounts subject to government approval. The central bank rations its foreign exchange for invisible payments on an ad hoc basis, controls some payments, and requires that repatriation be made through an authorized dealer. All capital transactions must be approved by the central bank.

FINANCIAL FREEDOM — *50%*

Belize's financial system is dominated by the banking sector. There are five domestic commercial banks, seven international banks, three quasi-government banks, and some small credit unions. Subsidiaries of foreign banks are active and competitive, but approval is required to secure a foreign currency loan from outside Belize, and only authorized dealers are permitted to retain foreign currency. The government affects the allocation of credit through the quasi-government banks. Plans to sell the Development Finance Corporation (the state development bank) were shelved, and the government assumed its debts. The International Financial Services Act promotes offshore financial services, and the government offers extensive banking confidentiality.

PROPERTY RIGHTS — *50%*

The constitution provides for an independent judiciary, which is subject to political influence. There is a severe lack of trained personnel, and police officers often act as prosecutors in the magistrates' courts. The result is lengthy trial backlogs. Expropriation of personal property is possible.

FREEDOM FROM CORRUPTION — *37%*

Corruption is perceived as significant. Belize ranks 62nd out of 158 countries in Transparency International's Corruption Perceptions Index for 2005.

LABOR FREEDOM — *82.8%*

The labor market operates under flexible employment regulations that can enhance employment and productivity growth. The non-salary cost of employing a worker is low, and dismissing a redundant employee can be costless. Labor regulations do not distort efficient business activities to any considerable degree.

BENIN

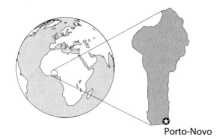

Porto-Novo

Rank: 114

Regional Rank: 20 of 40

Benin's economy is 54.8 percent free, according to our 2007 assessment, which makes it the world's 114th freest economy. Its overall score is 0.5 percentage point higher than last year, partially reflecting new methodological detail. Benin is ranked 20th out of 40 countries in the sub-Saharan African region, and its overall score is equal to the regional average.

Benin scores well on freedom from government and monetary freedom. Relatively high tax rates on income and corporations dampen the fiscal score, but tax revenue collected is fairly low as a percentage of GDP. Government expenditures are moderate, and state-owned businesses do not figure significantly into Benin's revenue. Benin has pegged its currency to the euro, resulting in admirable price stability.

Economic development has been hampered, however, by a serious lack of liberalization in many areas, such as investment freedom, labor freedom, property rights, and business freedom. Bureaucratic inefficiency and corruption hamper virtually all areas of the economy. Foreign investment is subject to government approval and regulations that require the hiring of native Beninese. Court enforcement of intrusive labor regulations and property rights is subject to pervasive political interference.

BACKGROUND: Benin became one of the first African countries to move peacefully from dictatorship to elected government when Mathieu Kérékou, who had seized power in 1972, accepted defeat in 1991. Kérékou won the presidency in 1996 and 2001, and Yayi Boni, former president of the regional development bank, was elected president in 2006. Economic reform has encouraged growth, but Benin remains underdeveloped. Corruption persists, and much of the population is engaged in agriculture. Cotton is the primary export and source of GDP, and both the port of Cotonou and trade with Nigeria are central to the economy.

How Do We Measure Economic Freedom? See Chapter 3 (page 37) for an explanation of the methodology or visit the *Index* Web site at *heritage.org/index*.

The economy is 54.8% free

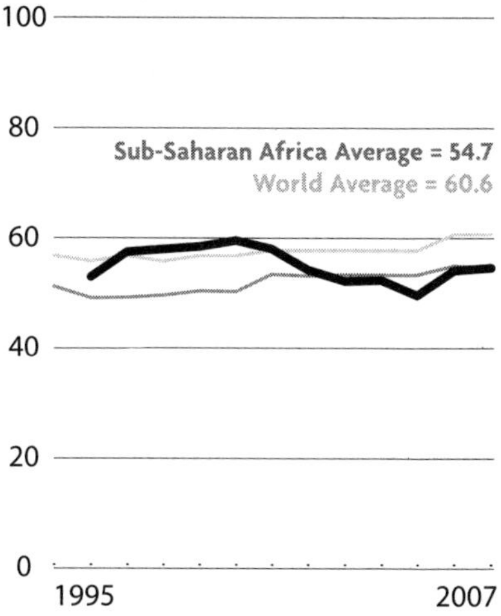

100

80 — Sub-Saharan Africa Average = 54.7
World Average = 60.6

60

40

20

0
1995   2007

QUICK FACTS

Population: 8.2 million

GDP (PPP): $8.9 billion
3.1% growth in 2004
4.5% 5-yr. comp. ann. growth
$1,091 per capita

Unemployment: n/a

Inflation (CPI): 0.9%

FDI (net inflow): $60 million (gross)

Official Development Assistance:
Multilateral: $203 million
Bilateral: $257 million (11% from the U.S.)

External Debt: $1.9 billion

Exports: $713.2 million
Primarily cotton, crude oil, palm products, cocoa

Imports: $1.1 billion
Primarily food, capital goods, petroleum products

BENIN'S TEN ECONOMIC FREEDOMS

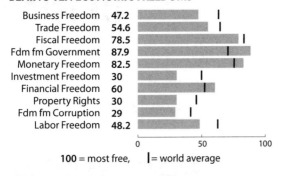

Business Freedom	47.2
Trade Freedom	54.6
Fiscal Freedom	78.5
Fdm fm Government	87.9
Monetary Freedom	82.5
Investment Freedom	30
Financial Freedom	60
Property Rights	30
Fdm fm Corruption	29
Labor Freedom	48.2

0   50   100

100 = most free, ▌**= world average**

BUSINESS FREEDOM — *47.2%*

Starting a business takes an average of 31 days, compared to the world average of 48 days. Entrepreneurship should be easier for maximum job creation. Both obtaining a business license and closing a business can be difficult. Bureaucratic procedures are not streamlined and are rarely transparent. The overall freedom to start, operate, and close a business is significantly limited by the national regulatory environment.

TRADE FREEDOM — *54.6%*

Benin's weighted average tariff rate was 12.7 percent in 2004. The customs process is inefficient and corrupt, and the government restricts some imports, applies selected import bans, and levies import taxes to protect "strategic products" such as rice and sugar against world price fluctuations. Consequently, an additional 20 percent is deducted from Benin's trade freedom score to account for these non-tariff barriers.

FISCAL FREEDOM — *78.5%*

Benin has high tax rates. The top income tax rate is 40 percent, and the top corporate tax rate is 38 percent. Other taxes include a value-added tax (VAT), a property tax, and a tax on insurance contracts. In the most recent year, overall tax revenue as a percentage of GDP was 13.2 percent.

FREEDOM FROM GOVERNMENT — *87.9%*

Total government expenditures, including consumption and transfer payments, are moderate. In the most recent year, government spending equaled 20.8 percent of GDP, and the government received 6.1 percent of its total revenues from state-owned enterprises and government ownership of property. Privatization of public enterprises has been slow.

MONETARY FREEDOM — *82.5%*

As a member of the West African Economic and Monetary Union, Benin uses the CFA franc, which is pegged to the euro. Inflation in Benin averaged a relatively low 3.9 percent between 2003 and 2005. Relatively low and stable prices explain most of the monetary freedom score. The cotton sector benefits from government subsidies and price supports. Consequently, an additional 5 percent is deducted from Benin's monetary freedom score to adjust for price control measures that distort domestic prices.

INVESTMENT FREEDOM — *30%*

Bureaucracy is inefficient and subject to corruption. The government requires part-Beninese ownership of any privatized company. Foreign exchange accounts must be authorized by the government and the Central Bank of West African States (BCEAO). Many capital transactions, including direct investment, are subject to reporting requirements and government and BCEAO approval. There are no controls on the purchase of land by non-residents, except for investments in enterprises, branches, or corporations.

FINANCIAL FREEDOM — *60%*

Benin's underdeveloped financial system is concentrated in banking. Enforcement of contracts, transparency in financial operations, and fraud prevention are weak. The Central Bank of West African States (BCEAO) governs Benin's financial institutions. The eight BCEAO member countries use the CFA franc, pegged to the euro. The banking sector is predominantly private, and foreign ownership in banking and insurance is prominent. Credit is allocated on market terms and is available without discrimination. Legal and regulatory requirements can be burdensome. Banks experience difficulty with non-performing loans and recovering collateral on those loans. There are many microcredit and savings and loan institutions.

PROPERTY RIGHTS — *30%*

Benin's justice system is weak and subject to corruption. There is no separate commercial court system, and backlogs of civil cases cause long delays. Widespread corruption in public administration clouds the business environment and is a major disincentive to investment.

FREEDOM FROM CORRUPTION — *29%*

Corruption is perceived as widespread. Benin ranks 88th out of 158 countries in Transparency International's Corruption Perceptions Index for 2005.

LABOR FREEDOM — *48.2%*

The labor market operates under highly restrictive employment regulations that hinder employment and productivity growth. The non-salary cost of employing a worker is high, but dismissing a redundant employee can be relatively costless. Restrictions on increasing or contracting the number of working hours are very rigid. Benin's labor market flexibility is one of the 20 lowest in the world.

BOLIVIA

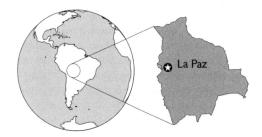

La Paz

Rank: 112

Regional Rank: 25 of 29

Bolivia's economy is 55 percent free, according to our 2007 assessment, which makes it the world's 112th freest economy. Its overall score is 4.1 percentage points lower than last year, partially reflecting new methodological detail. Bolivia is ranked 25th out of 29 countries in the Americas, and its overall score is well below the regional average.

Bolivia rates highly in fiscal freedom and solidly in freedom from government and monetary freedom. A very low income tax rate and moderately low corporate tax rate give it an enviable fiscal freedom score. Its freedom from government rating is also relatively positive despite a large amount of government spending. Inflation is not high, although prices are unstable and the government imposes *de facto* price controls on most utilities.

Bolivia suffers from low scores in investment freedom, property rights, labor freedom, and freedom from corruption. Pervasive corruption and significant regulation are major hurdles for foreign investment, as is possible nationalization of the energy sector. Rule of law is weak, and private property can be subject to bureaucratic interference, forced transactions, and even expropriation. Restrictive labor laws further cloud the business climate.

BACKGROUND: Bolivia's history has been characterized by much authoritarianism punctuated by periodic bouts of democracy. In the 1980s, democracy returned to the country, and from 1993 to 1997, the democratically elected government reduced the state's role through partial privatization and lowered taxes and tariffs. Following an economic downturn in 1999, social unrest compounded fiscal pressures. Unable to defend the rule of law, two successive constitutional presidents were removed from office by mob action in 2003 and 2005. In December 2005, Evo Morales was elected as the first indigenous Bolivian president on a platform of anti-globalization. Morales has partially nationalized Bolivia's hydrocarbon industry and declared his intention to redistribute private lands to indigenous supporters.

How Do We Measure Economic Freedom? See Chapter 3 (page 37) for an explanation of the methodology or visit the *Index* Web site at *heritage.org/index*.

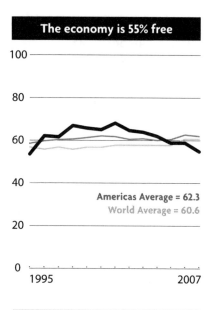

The economy is 55% free

Americas Average = 62.3
World Average = 60.6

1995   2007

QUICK FACTS

Population: 9 million

GDP (PPP): $24.5 billion
3.6% growth in 2004
2.6% 5-yr. comp. ann. growth
$2,720 per capita

Unemployment: 8.7%

Inflation (CPI): 4.4%

FDI (net inflow): $113.7 million

Official Development Assistance:
Multilateral: $285 million
Bilateral: $1.1 billion (13% from the U.S.)

External Debt: $6.1 billion

Exports: $2.5 billion
Primarily natural gas, soybeans and soy products, crude petroleum, zinc ore, tin

Imports: $2.3 billion
Primarily petroleum products, plastics, paper, aircraft and aircraft parts, food, automobiles, insecticides, soybeans

BOLIVIA'S TEN ECONOMIC FREEDOMS

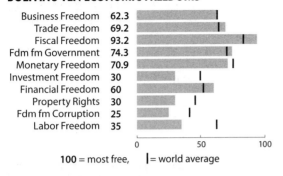

Business Freedom	62.3
Trade Freedom	69.2
Fiscal Freedom	93.2
Fdm fm Government	74.3
Monetary Freedom	70.9
Investment Freedom	30
Financial Freedom	60
Property Rights	30
Fdm fm Corruption	25
Labor Freedom	35

100 = most free,   **| = world average**

BUSINESS FREEDOM — *62.3%*

Starting a business takes an average of 50 days, compared to the world average of 48 days. Entrepreneurship should be easier for maximum job creation. Obtaining a business license is relatively simple, and closing a business is relatively easy. However, red tape and the lack of transparency still hinder entrepreneurial activities. The overall freedom to start, operate, and close a business is restricted by the national regulatory environment.

TRADE FREEDOM — *69.2%*

Bolivia's weighted average tariff rate was 5.4 percent in 2004. The government has made progress in lowering trade barriers and simplifying the trade regime, but import bans, restrictive sanitary and phytosanitary rules, export subsidies, and issues related to the enforcement and protection of intellectual property rights add to the costs of trade. Consequently, an additional 20 percent is deducted from Bolivia's trade freedom score to account for these non-tariff barriers.

FISCAL FREEDOM — *93.2%*

Bolivia has low tax rates. The top income tax rate is 13 percent, and the corporate tax rate is 25 percent. Other taxes include a value-added tax (VAT), a transaction tax, and a property tax. In the most recent year, overall tax revenue as a percentage of GDP was 15 percent.

FREEDOM FROM GOVERNMENT — *74.3%*

Bolivia's total government expenditures, including consumption and transfer payments, are moderate. In the most recent year, government spending equaled 33 percent of GDP, and the government received 0.9 percent of its total revenues from state-owned enterprises and government ownership of property.

MONETARY FREEDOM — *70.9%*

Inflation is moderate, averaging 5 percent between 2003 and 2005. Relatively moderate and unstable prices explain most of the monetary freedom score. Government regulations effectively control prices for hydrocarbons and most public utilities, and price controls are maintained for petroleum products, potable water, and garbage collection. Consequently, an additional 15 percent is deducted from Bolivia's monetary freedom score to adjust for price control measures that distort domestic prices.

INVESTMENT FREEDOM — *30%*

In general, foreign investment laws are simple, but public-sector corruption is a major challenge to foreigners who want to establish a business. The energy sector is heavily regulated. In early 2006, the government nationalized the natural gas industry, ordering companies to give up control of fields and accept much tougher operating terms or leave. A 2005 hydrocarbons law increased state control to 50 percent of production by raising taxes and royalties. Public officials sometimes ask for bribes to speed up bureaucratic procedures or not to initiate adverse actions. Both residents and non-residents may hold foreign exchange accounts. There are no restrictions or controls on payments, transactions, transfers, purchase of real estate, access to foreign exchange, or repatriation of profits.

FINANCIAL FREEDOM — *60%*

Bolivia's financial sector is concentrated in banking. Bolivia had 12 commercial banks in 2005, of which three were foreign-owned and others had some level of foreign ownership, and several microfinance institutions, savings and loans, and credit unions. Credit is allocated on market terms, although foreign borrowers may find it difficult to qualify for loans. Government-owned banks no longer exist. Financial sector regulations and accounting standards are somewhat burdensome and do not conform to international standards. The insurance sector is small. Capital markets are focused on trading in government bonds, although corporate debt and mutual funds have grown in recent years.

PROPERTY RIGHTS — *30%*

Legal protection of private property is weak. The legal process is time-consuming and subject to political influence and pervasive corruption. For that reason, the National Chamber of Commerce, with assistance from USAID, has established a local Arbitration Tribunal. The Investment Law provides that investors may submit their differences to arbitration in accordance with the constitution and international norms. Expropriation is very possible.

FREEDOM FROM CORRUPTION — *25%*

Corruption is perceived as widespread. Bolivia ranks 117th out of 158 countries in Transparency International's Corruption Perceptions Index for 2005.

LABOR FREEDOM — *35%*

The labor market operates under highly restrictive employment regulations that hinder employment and productivity growth. The non-salary cost of employing a worker is moderate, but dismissing a redundant employee can be very costly. The government has established the minimum wage for the public and private sectors. About 65 percent of the work force participates in the informal economy.

BOSNIA AND HERZEGOVINA

Sarajevo

The economy of Bosnia and Herzegovina (Bosnia) is 54.7 percent free, according to our 2007 assessment, which makes it the world's 115th freest economy. The overall score is 2.2 percentage points lower than last year, partially reflecting new methodological detail. Bosnia is ranked 38th freest among the 41 countries in the European region, and its overall score is well below the regional average. Its score has risen dramatically since 1998.

Bosnia scores highly in fiscal freedom and monetary freedom. The income tax rate is enviably low, and the corporate tax rate is moderate, although other taxes create a significant drag. Inflation is less than 2 percent, but government price controls in some sectors lower Bosnia's overall monetary score.

Bosnia faces many challenges associated with recovering from a decade-long civil war. Freedom from government, property rights, and freedom from corruption are problems, and the complex and irregularly enforced regulations affect almost everything. Commercial courts do not exist, and trade disputes must be handled among the claimants or out of the country. Government expenditure is high but does not result in a more efficient or streamlined bureaucracy.

BACKGROUND: The 1995 Dayton Agreement signaled Bosnia–Herzegovina's secession from the former Yugoslavia. Within its loose central government, two separate governing entities exist along ethnic lines: Republika Srpska and the Bosnian–Croat Federation. Rule of law is weak, and local courts are subject to substantial political interference and lack the resources to prosecute complex crimes. The state's overly large role, characterized by an intrusive bureaucracy and costly registration procedures, has yet to be fully addressed. The main exports are wood, paper, and metal, in addition to a large informal sector. The economy still relies heavily on agriculture.

How Do We Measure Economic Freedom? See Chapter 3 (page 37) for an explanation of the methodology or visit the *Index* Web site at *heritage.org/index*.

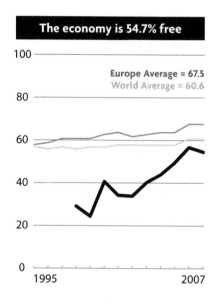

The economy is 54.7% free

Europe Average = 67.5
World Average = 60.6

100

80

60

40

20

0

1995   2007

QUICK FACTS

Population: 3.9 million

GDP (PPP): $27.5 billion
6.2% growth in 2004
5.1% 5-yr. comp. ann. growth
$7,032 per capita

Unemployment: 44.0% Bosnian–Croat Federation (2003); 37.0% Republika Srpska (2003)

Inflation (CPI): 0.3%

FDI (net inflow): $495.6 million

Official Development Assistance:
Multilateral: $351 million
Bilateral: $336 million (18% from the U.S.)

External Debt: $3.2 billion

Exports: $2.9 billion
Primarily metals, clothing, wood products

Imports: $7.1 billion
Primarily machinery and equipment, chemicals, fuels, food

111

BOSNIA & HERZEGOVINA'S TEN ECONOMIC FREEDOMS

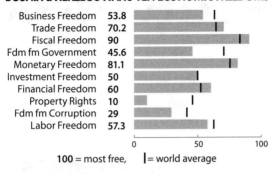

Business Freedom	53.8
Trade Freedom	70.2
Fiscal Freedom	90
Fdm fm Government	45.6
Monetary Freedom	81.1
Investment Freedom	50
Financial Freedom	60
Property Rights	10
Fdm fm Corruption	29
Labor Freedom	57.3

100 = most free, | = world average

BUSINESS FREEDOM — 53.8%

Starting a business takes an average of 54 days, compared to the world average of 48 days. Entrepreneurship should be easier for maximum job creation. Obtaining a business license is difficult, but closing a business can be relatively easy. Heavily bureaucratic systems that lack transparency remain a problem for investors and entrepreneurs. The overall freedom to start, operate, and close a business is limited by the national regulatory environment.

TRADE FREEDOM — 70.2%

The weighted average tariff rate in Bosnia and Herzegovina was 4.9 percent in 2001. The government maintains import and export restrictions, as well as restrictive import licensing rules, and customs procedures are inefficient. Consequently, an additional 20 percent is deducted from Bosnia and Herzegovina's trade freedom score to account for these non-tariff barriers.

FISCAL FREEDOM — 90%

Bosnia and Herzegovina has a very low income tax rate and a moderate corporate tax rate. The top income tax rate is 10 percent, and the top corporate income tax rate is 30 percent. Other taxes include a sales tax and a property tax. In the most recent year, overall tax revenue as a percentage of GDP was 22.4 percent.

FREEDOM FROM GOVERNMENT — 45.6%

Total government expenditures, including consumption and transfer payments, are high. In the most recent year, government spending equaled 46.6 percent of GDP, and the government received 11.3 percent of its total revenues from state-owned enterprises and government ownership of property.

MONETARY FREEDOM — 81.1%

Inflation is low, averaging 2 percent between 2003 and 2005. Relatively low and stable prices explain most of the monetary freedom score. Price controls apply to electricity, gas, and telecommunications services. Consequently, an additional 10 percent is deducted from Bosnia and Herzegovina's monetary freedom score to adjust for price control measures that distort domestic prices.

INVESTMENT FREEDOM — 50%

Foreign investment laws grant national treatment to foreign investors, protecting them from changes in legislation and against expropriation and nationalization of assets. Arms and media are the only sectors subject to restrictions. The main obstacles to foreign investment are a complex legal and regulatory framework, non-transparent business procedures, and weak judicial structures. There are few restrictions on capital transactions and foreign exchange accounts. A privatization law passed by the lower and upper houses of the Federation parliament would prohibit the sale of state-owned companies to foreign-owned companies unless they were majority-owned by the private sector.

FINANCIAL FREEDOM — 60%

The country's two autonomous government entities operate functionally independent financial systems. The inherited banking system was dominated by large state-owned banks, burdened with non-performing loans, and populated by numerous, undercapitalized private banks. Banking reform begun in 1997 led to consolidation and privatization. Most of Bosnia and Herzegovina's banks are now private, accounting for 86 percent of banking capital in 2004. The Republika Srpska had 10 privately owned banks in 2004, most of them foreign-owned. Long-term lending is hindered by insufficient enforcement of contracts. International accounting standards are in the process of being adopted. Each region has an underdeveloped non-bank financial sector and a small stock exchange.

PROPERTY RIGHTS — 10%

The judicial system does not cover commercial activities adequately. There are no commercial courts and no efficient ways to resolve commercial disputes. Contract and property rights are almost unenforceable. Judges typically request bribes and respond to pressure from public officials. Court decisions are difficult to enforce.

FREEDOM FROM CORRUPTION — 29%

Corruption is perceived as widespread. Bosnia and Herzegovina ranks 88th out of 158 countries in Transparency International's Corruption Perceptions Index for 2005.

LABOR FREEDOM — 57.3%

The labor market operates under restrictive employment regulations that hinder employment and productivity growth. The non-salary cost of employing a worker is very high, but dismissing a redundant employee is relatively costless. Rigidity in wage determination hinders job creation and worker mobility. Informal employment is estimated at about 30 percent of total employment.

BOTSWANA

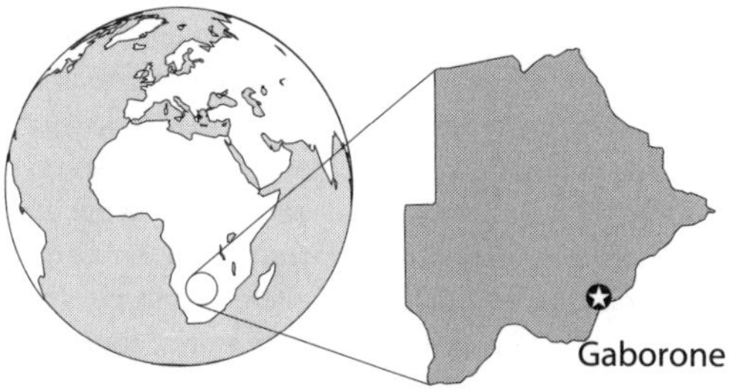

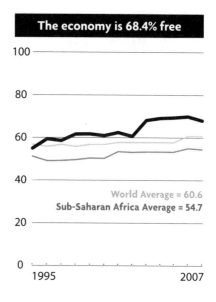

Gaborone

Botswana's economy is 68.4 percent free, according to our 2007 assessment, which makes it the world's 38th freest economy. Its overall score is 1.9 percentage points lower than last year, partially reflecting new methodological detail. Botswana is ranked 2nd out of 40 countries in the sub-Saharan Africa region, and its overall score is well above the regional average.

Botswana is an economic regional leader, scoring highly in property rights, investment freedom, financial freedom, and labor freedom. Labor freedom is strong, thanks to ease of hiring and firing employees. The financial sector is a regional leader, with an independent central bank and little government intervention. Businesses take a longer than average time to open, and licenses are sometimes subject to burdensome regulation. The overall business climate is superior for Africa but also is a model for the world.

Botswana's scores in freedom from government and trade freedom are somewhat lower. Privatization is moving forward, but government expenditures are high.

BACKGROUND: Botswana, a multi-party democracy since 1966, has a market-oriented economy that encourages private enterprise and is ranked as Africa's least corrupt. It also had one of the world's highest average growth rates during the past four decades and possesses Africa's highest sovereign credit rating. However, it still suffers from high unemployment and poverty; and despite efforts to diversify the economy, diamonds account for 80 percent of exports, over 40 percent of GDP, and about 50 percent of government revenue. Botswana has one of the world's highest HIV/AIDS infection rates, and political turmoil in neighboring Zimbabwe is an ongoing concern.

The economy is 68.4% free

World Average = 60.6
Sub-Saharan Africa Average = 54.7

1995   2007

QUICK FACTS

Population: 1.8 million

GDP (PPP): $17.6 billion
4.9% growth in 2004
5.8% 5-yr. comp. ann. growth
$9,945 per capita

Unemployment: 23.8%

Inflation (CPI): 6.9%

FDI (net inflow): −$227.3 million

Official Development Assistance:
Multilateral: $18 million
Bilateral: $37 million (59% from the U.S.)

External Debt: $524.0 million

Exports: $3.7 billion
Primarily diamonds, copper, nickel, soda ash, meat, textiles

Imports: $2.8 billion
Primarily food, machinery, electrical goods, transport equipment, textiles, fuel and petroleum products, wood and paper products

How Do We Measure Economic Freedom? See Chapter 3 (page 37) for an explanation of the methodology or visit the *Index* Web site at *heritage.org/index*.

BOTSWANA'S TEN ECONOMIC FREEDOMS

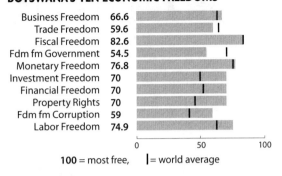

Business Freedom	66.6
Trade Freedom	59.6
Fiscal Freedom	82.6
Fdm fm Government	54.5
Monetary Freedom	76.8
Investment Freedom	70
Financial Freedom	70
Property Rights	70
Fdm fm Corruption	59
Labor Freedom	74.9

100 = most free, | = world average

BUSINESS FREEDOM — 66.6%

Starting a business takes an average of 108 days, compared to the world average of 48 days. Entrepreneurship should be easier for maximum job creation. Obtaining a business license can be difficult, but closing a business is easy. The government has created a one-stop shop for investors to avoid unnecessary bureaucratic steps to start a new business. The overall freedom to start, operate, and close a business is relatively well protected by the national regulatory environment.

TRADE FREEDOM — 59.6%

The weighted average tariff rate in Botswana was 10.2 percent in 2005. There are very few non-tariff barriers to trade, but the government maintains import bans and a restrictive standards regime. Consequently, an additional 20 percent is deducted from Botswana's trade freedom score to account for these non-tariff barriers.

FISCAL FREEDOM — 82.6%

Botswana has one of Southern Africa's lower tax burdens. Both the top income tax rate and the top corporate tax rate are 25 percent. Other taxes include a value-added tax (VAT), an additional company tax, and a fuel tax. In the most recent year, overall tax revenue as a percentage of GDP was 36.9 percent.

FREEDOM FROM GOVERNMENT — 54.5%

Total government expenditures, including consumption and transfer payments, are high. In the most recent year, government spending equaled 43.6 percent of GDP, and the government received 3.4 percent of its total revenues from state-owned enterprises and government ownership of property. Botswana has pursued plans for privatization and other initiatives to improve the performance of its remaining public-sector enterprises.

MONETARY FREEDOM — 76.8%

Inflation is relatively high, averaging 8.3 percent between 2003 and 2005. Relatively high and unstable prices explain most of the monetary freedom score. Most prices are set by the market, but the government maintains price policies for some agricultural and livestock goods. Consequently, an additional 5 percent is deducted from Botswana's monetary freedom score to adjust for price control measures that distort domestic prices.

INVESTMENT FREEDOM — 70%

The laws encourage foreign investment, particularly in the non-mining sector. The government has implemented reforms expediting the process of applications for business ventures. There are no restrictions on capital transactions or foreign exchange accounts, residents' and non-residents' accounts, or international transfers. The government restricts foreign investment in some areas reserved for Botswana citizens, including butchery and produce, gasoline filling stations, bars and liquor stores, supermarkets, and retail.

FINANCIAL FREEDOM — 70%

Botswana's banking system is competitive and one of the most advanced in Africa. The central bank is independent. There were five private commercial banks in 2004, all of them foreign-owned. The government is involved in the banking sector through state-owned financial institutions. Credit is allocated on market terms, although the government provides subsidized loans. The insurance sector and pension funds are active. The state owns the Botswana Motor Vehicle Insurance Fund, but private firms dominate the insurance sector. The stock market is small but growing. The government has introduced bonds of varying maturities to stimulate the domestic capital market. Botswana is trying to become a regional financial hub and offers incentives to financial institutions and facilitates the free flow of financial resources.

PROPERTY RIGHTS — 70%

The constitution provides for an independent judiciary, and the government respects this provision in practice. The legal system is sufficient to conduct secure commercial dealings. However, a serious and increasing backlog of cases prevents investors from having timely trials.

FREEDOM FROM CORRUPTION — 59%

Corruption is perceived as present. Botswana ranks 32nd out of 158 countries in Transparency International's Corruption Perceptions Index for 2005.

LABOR FREEDOM — 74.9%

The labor market operates under relatively flexible employment regulations that could be improved to enhance employment and productivity growth. The non-salary cost of employing a worker is very low, but dismissing a redundant employee can be costly. Labor laws do not mandate retraining or replacement before firing a worker.

BRAZIL

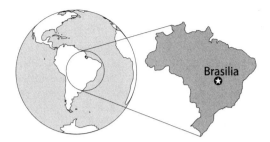

Brasilia

Rank: 70

Regional Rank: 17 of 29

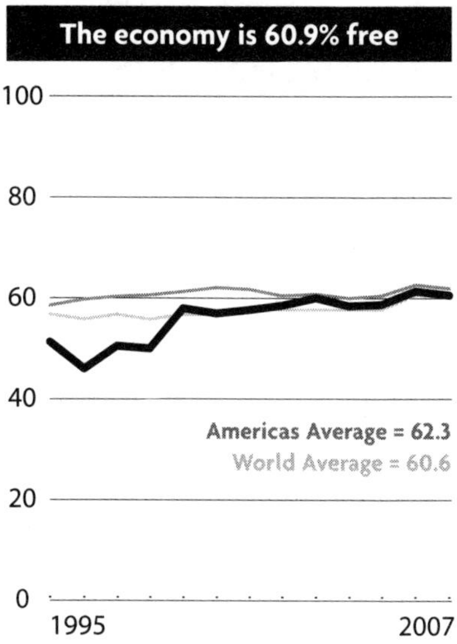

Brazil's economy is 60.9 percent free, according to our 2007 assessment, which makes it the world's 70th freest economy. Its overall score is 0.8 percentage point lower than last year, partially reflecting new methodological detail. Brazil is ranked 17th out of 29 countries in the Americas, and its overall score is slightly below the regional average.

Brazil is a regional economic power and receives high scores in fiscal freedom and freedom from government. It has moderate tax rates, both personal and corporate, and overall tax revenue is not high as a percentage of GDP relative to neighboring countries.

Brazil suffers from a highly inefficient and corrupt bureaucracy, which contributes to low scores in business freedom, investment freedom, financial freedom, and freedom from corruption. Because of serious regulatory inflexibility, starting a business takes more than three times the world average. Significant restrictions on foreign capital exist in a wide variety of sectors, and the government remains heavily involved in the banking and financial sectors. The judicial system is inefficient and subject to corruption, as are other areas of the public sector.

BACKGROUND: This vast democratic nation possesses abundant natural resources but is known for its high and persistent income inequality. Brazil suffers from serious obstacles to long-term investment and economic growth, including a convoluted tax system, barriers to foreign investment in some sectors, government management of most of the oil and electricity sectors and a significant part of the banking system, a weak judiciary, and a complicated regulatory system. Agriculture and industry account for 10 percent and 40 percent, respectively, of Brazil's gross domestic product.

How Do We Measure Economic Freedom? See Chapter 3 (page 37) for an explanation of the methodology or visit the *Index* Web site at *heritage.org/index*.

The economy is 60.9% free

Americas Average = 62.3
World Average = 60.6

1995   2007

QUICK FACTS

Population: 183.9 million

GDP (PPP): $1.5 trillion
4.9% growth in 2004
2.6% 5-yr. comp. ann. growth
$8,195 per capita

Unemployment: 11.5%

Inflation (CPI): 6.6%

FDI (net inflow): $8.7 billion

Official Development Assistance:
Multilateral: $173 million
Bilateral: $366 million (6% from the U.S.)

External Debt: $222.0 billion

Exports: $109.1 billion
Primarily transport equipment, iron ore, soybeans, footwear, coffee, automobiles

Imports: $80.1 billion
Primarily machinery, electrical and transport equipment, chemical products, oil

BRAZIL'S TEN ECONOMIC FREEDOMS

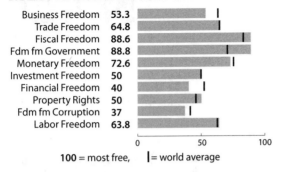

Business Freedom	53.3
Trade Freedom	64.8
Fiscal Freedom	88.6
Fdm fm Government	88.8
Monetary Freedom	72.6
Investment Freedom	50
Financial Freedom	40
Property Rights	50
Fdm fm Corruption	37
Labor Freedom	63.8

100 = most free, ▌= world average

BUSINESS FREEDOM — 53.3%

Starting a business takes an average of 152 days, compared to the world average of 48 days. Entrepreneurship should be easier for maximum job creation. Obtaining a business license is difficult, and closing a business is very difficult. The process for opening a business requires about 100 different documents. The overall freedom to start, operate, and close a business is limited by the national regulatory environment.

TRADE FREEDOM — 64.8%

The weighted average tariff rate in Brazil was 7.6 percent in 2004. The government continues to liberalize its trade regime, but export support programs, restrictive regulatory and licensing rules, quotas and import bans, and issues involving the enforcement and protection of intellectual property rights persist. Consequently, an additional 20 percent is deducted from Brazil's trade freedom score to account for these non-tariff barriers.

FISCAL FREEDOM — 88.6%

Brazil has moderate tax rates. The top income tax rate is 27.5 percent, and the top corporate tax rate is 25 percent (a 15 percent tax rate and 10 percentage point surcharge). Other taxes include a financial transactions tax and a tax on interest. In the most recent year, overall tax revenue as a percentage of GDP was 18 percent.

FREEDOM FROM GOVERNMENT — 88.8%

Total government expenditures, including consumption and transfer payments, are relatively high. In the most recent year, government spending equaled 20.9 percent of GDP, and the government received 3 percent of its total revenues from state-owned enterprises and government ownership of property.

MONETARY FREEDOM — 72.6%

Inflation averaged a relatively high 7.5 percent between 2003 and 2005. Relatively high and unstable prices explain most of the monetary freedom score. Although such public services as railways, telecommunications, and electricity have been privatized, the government oversees prices through regulatory agencies. The National Petroleum Agency fixes the wholesale price of fuel, and the government controls airfare prices. Consequently, an additional 10 percent is deducted from Brazil's monetary freedom score to adjust for price controls.

INVESTMENT FREEDOM — 50%

Foreign capital may enter freely and by law receives national treatment. However, setting up new companies is complex. Foreign investment is restricted in nuclear energy, health services, media, rural property, fishing, mail and telegraph, aviation, and aerospace. Foreign ownership of rural land and land adjacent to national borders is prohibited. There are limited restrictions on foreign exchange accounts, and legal restrictions prohibit foreign participation in certain economic activities. The central bank must approve outward direct investment in some cases, including transfers and remittances, where it has broad administrative discretion.

FINANCIAL FREEDOM — 40%

Brazil's financial system is South America's largest and one of the largest among all emerging markets. Despite state involvement, banking and capital markets are diversified, dynamic, and competitive. There are about 200 public and private commercial banks and many non-banking financial institutions. The top 10 domestic banks hold two-thirds of total assets, and the sector is dominated by two publicly controlled banks with half of all assets. The government maintains several specialized financial institutions. The growing insurance market remains dominated by a few large firms. The stock market is not a major source of corporate finance, but it is growing and trading is active.

PROPERTY RIGHTS — 50%

Contracts are generally considered secure, but it is important to specify the jurisdiction for any disputes. Brazil's judiciary is inefficient, subject to political and economic influence, and plagued by problems relating to lack of resources and training of officials. Decisions can take years, and decisions of the Supreme Federal Tribunal are not automatically binding on lower courts, causing more appeals than would otherwise occur.

FREEDOM FROM CORRUPTION — 37%

Corruption is perceived as significant. Brazil ranks 62nd out of 158 countries in Transparency International's Corruption Perceptions Index for 2005.

LABOR FREEDOM — 63.8%

The labor market operates under relatively flexible employment regulations that could be improved to enhance employment and productivity growth. The non-salary cost of employing a worker is high, and dismissing a redundant employee can be costly. Benefits mandated by the rigid labor legislation amplify the overall labor cost.

BULGARIA

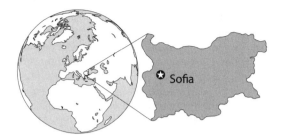

Sofia

Rank: 62

Regional Rank: 29 of 41

Bulgaria's economy is 62.2 percent free, according to our 2007 assessment, which makes it the world's 62nd freest economy. Its overall score is 2.1 percentage points lower than last year, partially reflecting new methodological detail. Bulgaria is ranked 29th freest among the 41 countries in the European region, and its overall score is near the regional average.

Bulgaria scores highly in fiscal freedom and receives positive marks in business freedom, monetary freedom, and financial freedom. An impressively low corporate tax rate of 15 percent complements a top income tax rate of 24 percent. Licensing, opening, and closing a business are all relatively efficient, providing a highly flexible commercial environment.

Bulgaria still needs to develop a more independent judicial system. Property rights and corruption are problems, and the inefficient bureaucracy bleeds over into other areas of economic freedom as well. Judicial corruption is an impediment to greater foreign investment, and property rights and business regulations are enforced in an arbitrary manner.

BACKGROUND: In 1990, Bulgaria held its first multi-party election since World War II, ending nearly 50 years of Communist rule. The country ratified its European Union accession treaty in 2005, with a planned entry date of January 2007; but with several member states inclined to oppose further enlargement, the EU could activate the treaty's safeguard clause and delay Bulgaria's entry until January 2008. Natural resources such as coal, copper, and zinc play an important role in the industrial sector, and the economy has benefited from significant economic policy reform since the fall of the socialist government in 1996.

How Do We Measure Economic Freedom? See Chapter 3 (page 37) for an explanation of the methodology or visit the *Index* Web site at *heritage.org/index*.

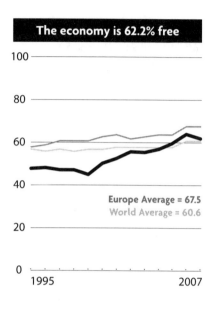

The economy is 62.2% free

Europe Average = 67.5
World Average = 60.6

QUICK FACTS

Population: 7.8 million

GDP (PPP): $62.7 billion
5.7% growth in 2004
4.9% 5-yr. comp. ann. growth
$8,078 per capita

Unemployment: 12.7%

Inflation (CPI): 6.3%

FDI (net inflow): $2.7 billion

Official Development Assistance:
Multilateral: $361 million
Bilateral: $265 million (15% from the U.S.)

External Debt: $15.7 billion

Exports: $14.0 billion
Primarily clothing, footwear, iron and steel, machinery and equipment, fuels

Imports: $16.5 billion
Primarily machinery and equipment, metals and ores, chemicals and plastics, fuels, minerals, and raw materials

BULGARIA'S TEN ECONOMIC FREEDOMS

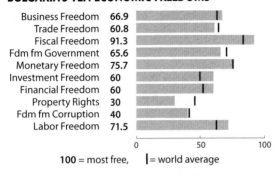

Business Freedom	66.9
Trade Freedom	60.8
Fiscal Freedom	91.3
Fdm fm Government	65.6
Monetary Freedom	75.7
Investment Freedom	60
Financial Freedom	60
Property Rights	30
Fdm fm Corruption	40
Labor Freedom	71.5

100 = most free, ▮ = world average

BUSINESS FREEDOM — 66.9%

Starting a business takes an average of 32 days, compared to the world average of 48 days. Entrepreneurship should be easier for maximum job creation. Obtaining a business license can be difficult, but closing a business is relatively easy. Arbitrary interpretation and enforcement of regulatory regimes by the bureaucracy are still seen as impediments to investment. However, the overall freedom to start, operate, and close a business is relatively well protected by the national regulatory environment.

TRADE FREEDOM — 60.8%

The weighted average tariff rate in Bulgaria was 9.6 percent in 2004. The main non-tariff barriers are issues involving the enforcement and protection of intellectual property rights and cumbersome, arbitrary, and inconsistent customs and regulatory policies. Consequently, an additional 20 percent is deducted from Bulgaria's trade freedom score to account for these non-tariff barriers.

FISCAL FREEDOM — 91.3%

Bulgaria has low tax rates. The top income tax rate is 24 percent, and the corporate tax rate is a flat 15 percent. Other taxes include a value-added tax (VAT), a road tax, and a vehicle tax. In the most recent year, overall tax revenue as a percentage of GDP was 22.3 percent.

FREEDOM FROM GOVERNMENT — 65.6%

Total government expenditures, including consumption and transfer payments, are high. In the most recent year, government spending equaled 37.5 percent of GDP, and the government received 4.8 percent of its total revenues from state-owned enterprises and government ownership of property.

MONETARY FREEDOM — 75.7%

Inflation is moderate, averaging 5.1 percent between 2003 and 2005. Relatively moderate and unstable prices explain most of the monetary freedom score. The market determines most prices, but the government oversees electricity, water, natural gas, and pharmaceutical prices through its regulatory regime. Consequently, an additional 10 percent is deducted from Bulgaria's monetary freedom score to adjust for price control measures that distort domestic prices.

INVESTMENT FREEDOM — 60%

The law mandates equal treatment for foreign and domestic investors. Bulgaria requires approval for majority foreign ownership in some sectors. Government bureaucracy, frequent changes in the legal framework, and corruption impede foreign investment. Residents may hold foreign exchange accounts subject to some restrictions; non-residents may hold foreign exchange accounts without restriction. Prior registration with the central bank is required for a few capital transactions. Foreign ownership of land is permitted if the owners are from European Union countries or countries with an international agreement permitting such purchases.

FINANCIAL FREEDOM — 60%

Bulgaria's financial system is dominated by the banking sector. The banking system has undergone major reform since its virtual collapse in 1996, influenced strongly by the 1997 introduction of the currency board and stronger supervision and tighter prudential rules for the banking sector. With the possibility of bailouts eliminated under the currency board, banks have had to focus on sound banking practices. There are 31 private banks and four public banks. Foreign banks hold over 70 percent of bank capital. The insurance market is fully private with the sale of two state-owned firms and has expanded rapidly since the adoption of the 1997 insurance law. Foreign insurers are strong participants. The well-maintained stock market is active but small. The government is active in capital markets through the auction of short-term treasury bills.

PROPERTY RIGHTS — 30%

Bulgaria's constitution provides for an independent judiciary, but ineffective rule of law limits investor confidence in the ability of the courts to enforce contracts, ownership and shareholders rights, and intellectual property rights. Judicial corruption is a serious problem.

FREEDOM FROM CORRUPTION — 40%

Corruption is perceived as significant. Bulgaria ranks 55th out of 158 countries in Transparency International's Corruption Perceptions Index for 2005.

LABOR FREEDOM — 71.5%

The labor market operates under relatively flexible employment regulations that could be improved to enhance employment and productivity growth. The non-salary cost of employing a worker is very high, but dismissing a redundant employee can be costless. Registration of labor contracts is compulsory. The unemployment insurance system offers benefits to the unemployed for four to 12 months, depending on the duration of employment.

BURKINA FASO

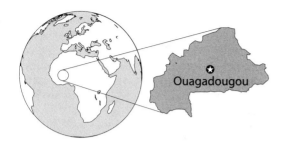

Ouagadougou

Burkina Faso's economy is 55 percent free, according to our 2007 assessment, which makes it the world's 113th freest economy. Its overall score is 0.7 percentage point lower than last year, partially reflecting new methodological detail. Burkina Faso is ranked 19th out of 40 countries in the sub-Saharan Africa region, and its overall score is slightly higher than the regional average.

Burkina Faso scores well in fiscal freedom, freedom from government, and monetary freedom. The top income and corporate tax rates are comparable to those in the United States, but overall tax revenue is quite low. Government expenditure is moderate, and state-owned businesses are not a primary source of revenue.

Business freedom, labor freedom, property rights, and corruption are problems for Burkina Faso. Extensive regulations prevent a flexible commercial environment, and licensing and bankruptcy procedures are costly. The lack of a universal judicial system enforced by the government means that property rights cannot be guaranteed or adjudicated effectively, as local villages often use traditional courts. As with most other nations in the region, Burkina Faso experiences significant corruption.

BACKGROUND: Blaise Compaore seized power in a 1987 coup, oversaw a transition to multi-party democracy, and won a third term as Burkina Faso's president in November 2005. (Under a constitutional amendment adopted in 2002, the president is limited to two terms starting in 2005.) Burkina Faso is a poor agrarian country beset by frequent drought, and over 80 percent of the population is engaged in subsistence agriculture. Many Burkinabé work abroad, and remittances are a substantial source of income. HIV/AIDS infections are high. Instability in the Ivory Coast disrupts trade and has led to hundreds of thousands of returning émigrés.

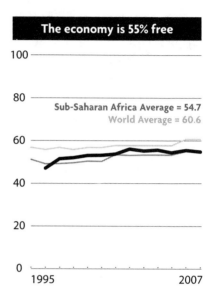

The economy is 55% free

Sub-Saharan Africa Average = 54.7
World Average = 60.6

QUICK FACTS

Population: 12.8 million

GDP (PPP): $15.0 billion
5.5% growth in 2004
5.7% 5-yr. comp. ann. growth
$1,169 per capita

Unemployment: n/a

Inflation (CPI): −0.4%

FDI (net inflow): $34.0 million

Official Development Assistance:
Multilateral: $325 million
Bilateral: $347 million (5% from the U.S.)

External Debt: $2.0 billion

Exports: $438.6 million
Primarily cotton, livestock, gold

Imports: $888.2 million
Primarily capital goods, food, petroleum

How Do We Measure Economic Freedom? See Chapter 3 (page 37) for an explanation of the methodology or visit the *Index* Web site at *heritage.org/index*.

BURKINA FASO'S TEN ECONOMIC FREEDOMS

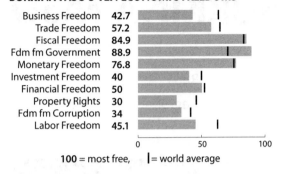

Business Freedom	42.7	
Trade Freedom	57.2	
Fiscal Freedom	84.9	
Fdm fm Government	88.9	
Monetary Freedom	76.8	
Investment Freedom	40	
Financial Freedom	50	
Property Rights	30	
Fdm fm Corruption	34	
Labor Freedom	45.1	

0   50   100

100 = most free, | = world average

BUSINESS FREEDOM — 42.7%

Starting a business takes an average of 34 days, compared to the world average of 48 days. Entrepreneurship should be easier for maximum job creation. The government has made an effort to implement a one-stop system for registering businesses in an attempt to reduce the bureaucracy in recent years. Nevertheless, obtaining a business license can be very difficult, and closing a business is difficult. The overall freedom to start, operate, and close a business remains highly limited.

TRADE FREEDOM — 57.2%

Burkina Faso's weighted average tariff rate in 2004 was a relatively high 11.4 percent. The government imposes supplementary taxes on imports, targeted import bans, restrictive licensing rules, and corruption is a growing problem. Consequently, an additional 20 percent is deducted from Burkina Faso's trade freedom score to account for these non-tariff barriers.

FISCAL FREEDOM — 84.9%

Burkina Faso has a moderate tax rate and a high corporate tax rate. The top income tax rate is 30 percent, and the top corporate tax rate is 35 percent. Other burdensome taxes include a value-added tax (VAT) and a tax on insurance contracts. In the most recent year, overall tax revenue as a percentage of GDP was 11.7 percent.

FREEDOM FROM GOVERNMENT — 88.9%

Burkina Faso's total government expenditures, including consumption and transfer payments, are moderate. In the most recent year, government spending equaled 21.2 percent of GDP. Many state-owned companies have been privatized, but progress has not been smooth due to managerial delays and the government's weakness.

MONETARY FREEDOM — 76.8%

Inflation in Burkina Faso is moderate, averaging 4.4 percent between 2003 and 2005. Relatively moderate and unstable prices explain most of the monetary freedom score. The market determines most prices, but the government maintains price supports for the cotton sector and influences prices through the public sector. Consequently, an additional 10 percent is deducted from Burkina Faso's monetary freedom score to adjust for price control measures that distort domestic prices.

INVESTMENT FREEDOM — 40%

The investment code guarantees equal treatment of foreign and domestic investors, but the Ministry of Industry, Commerce, and Mines must approve new investment. Foreign investors are also hindered by poor infrastructure, a weak legal system, and growing corruption. Residents may hold foreign exchange accounts with permission of the government and the Central Bank of West African States (BCEAO). Payments and transfers over a specified amount require supporting documents, and proceeds from non-WEAMU (West African Economic and Monetary Union) countries must be surrendered to an authorized dealer. All capital investments abroad by residents require government approval, as do most commercial and financial credits.

FINANCIAL FREEDOM — 50%

Burkina Faso's financial system is underdeveloped and concentrated in banking. The BCEAO governs Burkina Faso's banking and other financial institutions. The eight BCEAO member countries use the CFA franc, pegged to the euro. In 2004, the small financial system was composed primarily of eight commercial banks and a network of microfinance institutions and credit unions. The government has pursued privatization and restructuring in the banking sector since the 1990s and limits its participation in the banking sector to 25 percent. All major banks have some degree of foreign ownership, primarily from France or other West African countries. Burkina Faso participates in a regional stock exchange. The insurance sector is small.

PROPERTY RIGHTS — 30%

Burkina Faso's judicial system is weak. Villagers have their own customary or traditional courts. The executive has extensive appointment and other judicial powers. Systemic weaknesses in the justice system include removal of judges, outdated legal codes, an insufficient number of courts, a lack of financial and human resources, and excessive legal costs.

FREEDOM FROM CORRUPTION — 34%

Corruption is perceived as significant. Burkina Faso ranks 70th out of 158 countries in Transparency International's Corruption Perceptions Index for 2005.

LABOR FREEDOM — 45.1%

The labor market operates under highly restrictive employment regulations that hinder employment and productivity growth. The non-salary cost of employing a worker is high, but dismissing a redundant employee is relatively costless. Night and weekend work are not allowed, and the minimum wage is about 82 percent of the average value-added worker. Burkina Faso's labor market flexibility is one of the 20 lowest in the world.

BURMA (MYANMAR)

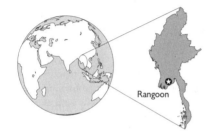

Rangoon

Burma's economy is 40.1 percent free, according to our 2007 assessment, which makes it the world's 153rd freest economy. Its overall score is 0.5 percentage point higher than last year, partially reflecting new methodological detail. Burma is ranked 29th out of 30 countries in the Asia–Pacific region, and its overall score is much lower than the regional average.

Burma scores well in fiscal freedom, freedom from government, and trade freedom. The top income and corporate tax rates are moderate, and government tax revenue amounts to less than 5 percent of GDP. Government expenditures are likewise low, amounting to less than 10 percent of GDP. State-owned businesses, however, contribute about 30 percent of the government's revenues.

As an autocratic state, Burma imposes severe restrictions on many areas of its economy. Investment freedom, financial freedom, property rights, and corruption are weak. The almost complete lack of a judicial system means that domestic and foreign companies must negotiate directly with the government to resolve disputes. Foreign investment is adjudicated in each instance, with no clear guidelines for investors. Heavy restrictions in the financial sector and labor market inflexibility are serious economic problems.

BACKGROUND: Burma is a repressive military dictatorship. The country gained its independence from Britain in 1948 and has been ruled by a military junta since 1962. The current political incarnation of martial rule is the State Peace and Development Council (SPDC). The SPDC offers its "roadmap for democracy" and National Convention to rewrite the constitution as examples of reform, but little real change has been forthcoming. Though Burma has significant national resources, restrictive economic policies and international sanctions have impeded economic development. In addition, foreign aid plummeted during the 1990s in response to the government's harsh anti-democratic repression.

How Do We Measure Economic Freedom? See Chapter 3 (page 37) for an explanation of the methodology or visit the *Index* Web site at *heritage.org/index.*

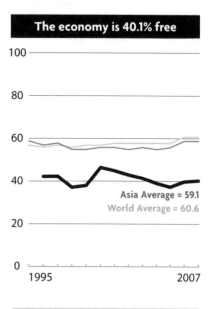

The economy is 40.1% free

Asia Average = 59.1
World Average = 60.6

QUICK FACTS

Population: 50 million

GDP (PPP): $78.7 billion (2005 estimate)
3.0% growth in 2004
10.7% 5-yr. comp. ann. growth
$1,700 per capita (2005 estimate)

Unemployment: 5.0% (2005 estimate)

Inflation (CPI): 4.2%

FDI (net inflow): $214 million (gross)

Official Development Assistance:
Multilateral: $40 million
Bilateral: $89 million (6% from the U.S.)

External Debt: $7.2 billion

Exports: $3.2 billion
Primarily clothing, gas, wood products, pulses, beans, fish, rice

Imports: $2.5 billion
Primarily fabric, petroleum products, plastics, machinery, transport equipment, construction materials, crude oil

BURMA'S TEN ECONOMIC FREEDOMS

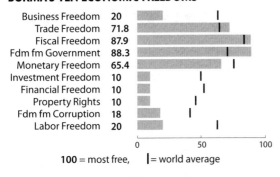

Business Freedom	20
Trade Freedom	71.8
Fiscal Freedom	87.9
Fdm fm Government	88.3
Monetary Freedom	65.4
Investment Freedom	10
Financial Freedom	10
Property Rights	10
Fdm fm Corruption	18
Labor Freedom	20

0   50   100

100 = most free, | = world average

BUSINESS FREEDOM — 20%

Burma's lack of legal and regulatory transparency virtually impedes creation of new businesses. Bureaucratic red tape often complicates the process for starting, operating, and closing a business. Policy changes tend to be inconsistent and unpredictable. The often arbitrary and unpublished regulatory changes are barriers to improving the investment climate.

TRADE FREEDOM — 71.8%

The weighted average tariff rate in Burma was 4.1 percent in 2004. Burma imposes restrictive trade policies designed to protect "crony" companies and state-owned enterprises. The government imposes high import taxes, restrictive permit and licensing rules, and import bans. Customs corruption is common. Consequently, an additional 20 percent is deducted from Burma's trade freedom score to account for these non-tariff barriers.

FISCAL FREEDOM — 87.9%

Burma has moderate tax rates. Both the top income tax rate and the top corporate tax rate are 30 percent. In the most recent year, overall tax revenue as a percentage of GDP was 3.3 percent.

FREEDOM FROM GOVERNMENT — 88.3%

Total government expenditures in Burma, including consumption and transfer payments, are low. In the most recent year, government spending equaled 8.1 percent of GDP, and the government received 30.6 percent of its total revenues from state-owned enterprises and government ownership of property. Given the lack of available data, Burma's economic statistics are questionable and need to be viewed with caution.

MONETARY FREEDOM — 65.4%

Inflation in Burma is high, averaging 15 percent between 2003 and 2005. Relatively high and unstable prices explain most of the monetary freedom score. The government attempts to control some prices for such staple products as gasoline, cooking oil, propane, and soap. However, the quantities of such products made available to customers are strictly rationed, so retailers often sell their stocks on the black market for a higher price. Consequently, an additional 10 percent is deducted from Burma's monetary freedom score to adjust for measures that distort domestic prices.

INVESTMENT FREEDOM — 10%

Foreign investment is approved by the Cabinet on a case-by-case basis. Once permission is granted, the foreign investor needs to get a business license to trade. The government restricts foreign exchange accounts and current transfers and controls all capital transactions. Multiple exchange rates make conversion and repatriation of foreign exchange very complex and ripe for corruption. Foreign firms are prohibited from owning land, but it may be leased from the government.

FINANCIAL FREEDOM — 10%

Burma's financial sector is subject to very heavy government intervention, and forced loans to government projects have almost frozen new deposits and smaller loans by private banks. The private banking sector crashed in February 2003. The government claims that no banks closed. Some private banks resumed full operation in 2004. There were five state-owned banks in 2005. Foreign banks are permitted to enter into joint ventures with domestic private banks, although none have done so. Only 16 of the original 49 authorized foreign banks remain. The state-owned insurer retains a near monopoly of that sector. Capital markets are largely absent.

PROPERTY RIGHTS — 10%

Private property is not protected in Burma. Private and foreign companies are at a disadvantage in disputes with governmental and quasi-governmental organizations. The military regime controls all the courts, so foreign investors who have had conflicts with the local government, or whose businesses have been illegally expropriated, have had little success getting compensation. Pervasive corruption further serves to undermine the impartiality of the justice system.

FREEDOM FROM CORRUPTION — 18%

Corruption is perceived as widespread. Burma ranks 155th out of 158 countries in Transparency International's Corruption Perceptions Index for 2005.

LABOR FREEDOM — 20%

The labor market is controlled and distorted by the state. Labor regulations regarding wage rates and maximum work hours are not uniformly observed. The government unilaterally sets public-sector wages and influences wage setting in the private sector. The state uses forced labor in constructing military buildings and commercial enterprises. Formal labor markets are not fully developed.

BURUNDI

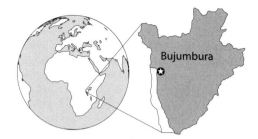

Bujumbura

Rank: 146

Regional Rank: 35 of 40

Burundi's economy is 46.8 percent free, according to our 2007 assessment, which makes it the world's 146th freest economy. Its overall score is 2.8 percentage points lower than last year, partially reflecting new methodological detail. Burundi is ranked 35th out of 40 countries in the sub-Saharan Africa region, and its overall score is much lower than the regional average.

Burundi does not have very strong economic freedom in any category. Fiscal freedom is moderately strong due to low overall tax revenues as a percentage of GDP, even though the top income and corporate tax rates are relatively high. The national inflation rate is also high but is not hyperinflationary.

As a developing economy recovering from years of civil strife, Burundi faces significant economic challenges. Its worst scores are for business freedom, investment freedom, financial freedom, property rights, and freedom from corruption. Rule of law is highly politicized, inefficient, and subject to erratic control over much of the country. Virtually all aspects of business are subject to intrusive regulation that inhibits business formation or survival, from obtaining licenses to firing inefficient workers.

BACKGROUND: Burundi gained its independence in 1962. In 1993, ethnic tensions sparked a civil war that resulted in an estimated 300,000 deaths and 1.2 million refugees. A transitional government oversaw the adoption of a new constitution and elections in 2005. Encouraged by growing stability and political progress, refugees have been returning. Corruption and economic mismanagement are common, however, and Burundi remains very poor. Agriculture accounts for nearly 50 percent of GDP, and a majority of the population is engaged in subsistence agriculture. The state remains heavily involved in the economy, and efforts to privatize publicly held enterprises have stalled.

How Do We Measure Economic Freedom? See Chapter 3 (page 37) for an explanation of the methodology or visit the *Index* Web site at *heritage.org/index*.

The economy is 46.8% free

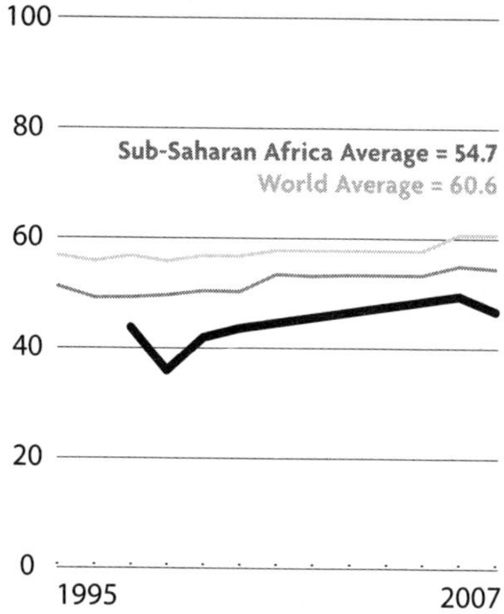

Sub-Saharan Africa Average = 54.7
World Average = 60.6

100

80

60

40

20

0

1995 — 2007

QUICK FACTS

Population: 7.3 million

GDP (PPP): $4.9 billion
4.8% growth in 2004
1.8% 5-yr. comp. ann. growth
$677 per capita

Unemployment: n/a

Inflation (CPI): 8.0%

FDI (net inflow): $3.0 million (gross)

Official Development Assistance:
Multilateral: $196 million
Bilateral: $217 million (20% from the U.S.)

External Debt: $1.4 billion (2004 estimate)

Exports: $43.1 million
Primarily coffee, tea, sugar, cotton, hides

Imports: $175.1 million
Primarily capital goods, petroleum products, food

BURUNDI'S TEN ECONOMIC FREEDOMS

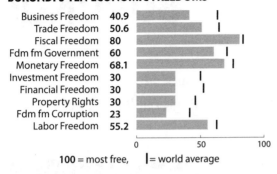

Business Freedom	40.9
Trade Freedom	50.6
Fiscal Freedom	80
Fdm fm Government	60
Monetary Freedom	68.1
Investment Freedom	30
Financial Freedom	30
Property Rights	30
Fdm fm Corruption	23
Labor Freedom	55.2

0   50   100

100 = most free,   I = world average

BUSINESS FREEDOM — 40.9%

Starting a business takes an average of 43 days, compared to the world average of 48 days. Entrepreneurship should be easier for maximum job creation. Both obtaining a business license and closing a business are very difficult. Burundi's continuing instability and massive, corrupt bureaucracy make it difficult to conduct entrepreneurial activities. The overall freedom to start, operate, and close a business is seriously limited by the national regulatory environment.

TRADE FREEDOM — 50.6%

Burundi's weighted average tariff rate was a high 14.7 percent In 2002. The government has removed most quantitative restrictions on imports but applies numerous fees and taxes on imports. Corruption in the customs and excise administration also adds to the cost of trade with Burundi. Consequently, an additional 20 percent is deducted from Burundi's trade freedom score to account for these non-tariff barriers.

FISCAL FREEDOM — 80%

Burundi has relatively high tax rates. Both the top income tax rate and the top corporate tax rate are 35 percent. Other taxes include a sales tax and a tax on interest. In the most recent year, overall tax revenue as a percentage of GDP was 23.3 percent.

FREEDOM FROM GOVERNMENT — 60%

Total government expenditures in Burundi, including consumption and transfer payments, are high. In the most recent year, government spending equaled 39.8 percent of GDP, and the government received 9.1 percent of its total revenues from state-owned enterprises and government ownership of property.

MONETARY FREEDOM — 68.1%

Inflation in Burundi is high, averaging 12 percent between 2003 and 2005. Relatively high and unstable prices explain most of the monetary freedom score. The government influences prices through state-owned enterprises, subsidies, and agriculture support programs. Consequently, an additional 10 percent is deducted from Burundi's monetary freedom score to adjust for measures that distort domestic prices.

INVESTMENT FREEDOM — 30%

The government welcomes, but political instability continues to hinder, foreign investment. The investment code reflects a policy of import substitution. Residents may hold foreign exchange accounts, but documentation must be submitted to the central bank, withdrawals over set limits require supporting documentation, and central bank approval is required to hold them abroad. Non-residents may hold foreign exchange accounts and withdraw funds up to a set limit upon presentation of documentation. Most capital transactions, including credit operations, direct investment, and personal capital movements, are subject to restrictions or authorization requirements.

FINANCIAL FREEDOM — 30%

Burundi has a very small, undeveloped financial sector that is dominated by banking. There are seven commercial banks. Government participation in the banking sector is strong. The government retains stakes in several banks, and the many loans made to the government and to state-owned enterprises have resulted in a large number of non-performing loans. Regulation of banking is largely bureaucratic and arduous. There were seven insurance firms in 2004.

PROPERTY RIGHTS — 30%

Private property is subject to government expropriation and armed banditry. Judges, who are appointed by the government, have generally proved to be strongly influenced by political pressure. The judiciary has proved especially ineffective in dealing with politically charged cases, such as the earlier coups and human rights abuses by members of the armed forces.

FREEDOM FROM CORRUPTION — 23%

Corruption is perceived as widespread. Burundi ranks 130th out of 158 countries in Transparency International's Corruption Perceptions Index for 2005.

LABOR FREEDOM — 55.2%

The labor market operates under restrictive employment regulations that hinder employment and productivity growth. The non-salary cost of employing a worker is low, but dismissing a redundant employee is relatively costly. There are very rigid restrictions on increasing or contracting the number of working hours.

CAMBODIA

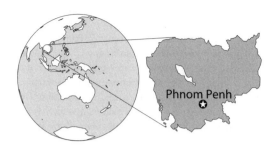

Phnom Penh

Cambodia's economy is 56.5 percent free, according to our 2007 assessment, which makes it the world's 102nd freest economy. Its overall score is 2.7 percentage points lower than last year, partially reflecting new methodological detail. Cambodia is ranked 18th out of 30 countries in the Asia–Pacific region, and its overall score is slightly lower than the regional average.

Cambodia scores well in fiscal freedom and freedom from government and moderately well in monetary freedom. Low income and corporate tax rates are complemented by a low level of government tax revenue, giving the country a high fiscal score despite some additional taxes. Government spending is also low, although the state receives a significant amount of its income from publicly owned businesses.

Cambodia is still shaking off the legacy of a disastrous Communist history and therefore has significant areas of economic freedom that could be improved. Business freedom, property rights, and freedom from corruption all receive low scores, and trade freedom is not much better. A highly restrictive labor market makes it difficult for businesses to fill seasonal employment needs, and widespread corruption makes even simple regulations inconsistent. Weak rule of law in many areas leads to unreliable resolution of commercial disputes.

BACKGROUND: Cambodia has experienced solid economic growth over the past three years without significant political liberalization. The country gained its independence in 1953 after nine decades of French colonial rule. Since the end of Cambodia's civil war and the Khmer Rouge regime in 1991, national strongman Hun Sen has held *de facto* power, and the government's repression of political opponents has damaged Cambodia's international reputation. To achieve its stated goal of 6 percent annual growth, Cambodia must foster a more transparent, rules-based economic system to encourage business development and expansion beyond the current base of textiles, tourism, and agriculture.

How Do We Measure Economic Freedom? See Chapter 3 (page 37) for an explanation of the methodology or visit the *Index* Web site at *heritage.org/index*.

The economy is 56.5% free

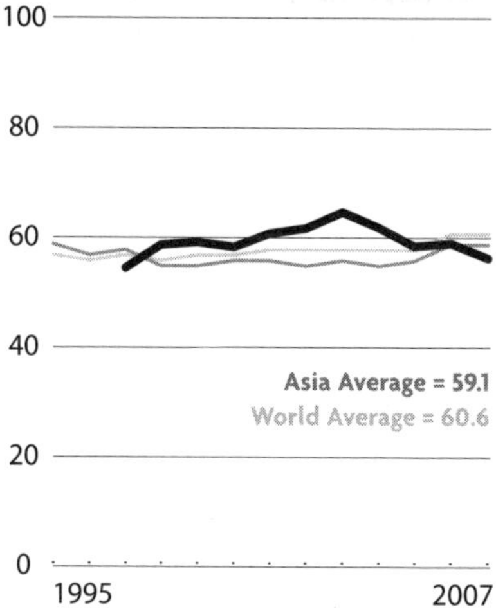

100

80

60

40

Asia Average = 59.1
World Average = 60.6

20

0

1995   2007

QUICK FACTS

Population: 13.8 million

GDP (PPP): $33.4 billion
7.7% growth in 2004
6.9% 5-yr. comp. ann. growth
$2,423 per capita

Unemployment: 2.5% (2000 estimate)

Inflation (CPI): 3.9%

FDI (net inflow): $121.2 million

Official Development Assistance:
Multilateral: $169 million
Bilateral: $324 million (15% from the U.S.)

External Debt: $3.4 billion

Exports: $3.2 billion
Primarily clothing, timber, rubber, rice, fish, tobacco, footwear

Imports: $3.7 billion
Primarily petroleum products, cigarettes, gold, construction materials, machinery, motor vehicles, pharmaceutical products

CAMBODIA'S TEN ECONOMIC FREEDOMS

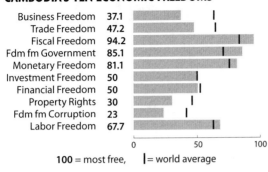

Business Freedom	37.1	
Trade Freedom	47.2	
Fiscal Freedom	94.2	
Fdm fm Government	85.1	
Monetary Freedom	81.1	
Investment Freedom	50	
Financial Freedom	50	
Property Rights	30	
Fdm fm Corruption	23	
Labor Freedom	67.7	

0   50   100

100 = most free,   ⏐= world average

BUSINESS FREEDOM — 37.1%

Starting a business takes an average of 86 days, compared to the world average of 48 days. Entrepreneurship should be easier for maximum job creation. Both obtaining a business license and closing a business are very difficult. Transparency in the regulatory regime is very poor, and bureaucratic delays are commonplace. The overall freedom to start, operate, and close a business is significantly limited by the national regulatory environment.

TRADE FREEDOM — 47.2%

Cambodia's weighted average tariff rate was a relatively high 16.4 percent in 2003. The government has eliminated most non-tariff barriers to trade. However, import licenses are required for firearms and pharmaceuticals; export licenses are required for antiquities, rubber, and timber; and customs and regulation of trade are burdensome. Consequently, an additional 20 percent is deducted from Cambodia's trade freedom score to account for these non-tariff barriers.

FISCAL FREEDOM — 94.2%

Cambodia has low tax rates. Both the top income tax rate and the top corporate tax rate are 20 percent. Other taxes include a value-added tax (VAT) and a tax on interest. In the most recent year, overall tax revenue as a percentage of GDP was 8 percent.

FREEDOM FROM GOVERNMENT — 85.1%

Total government expenditures in Cambodia, including consumption and transfer payments, are low. In the most recent year, government spending equaled 14.9 percent of GDP, and the government received 29.1 percent of its total revenues from state-owned enterprises and government ownership of property.

MONETARY FREEDOM — 81.1%

Inflation in Cambodia is moderate, averaging 4.8 percent between 2003 and 2005. Relatively moderate and unstable prices explain most of the monetary freedom score. The market determines most prices, but the government attempts to maintain stable retail prices for fuel through subsidies. Consequently, an additional 5 percent is deducted from Cambodia's monetary freedom score to adjust for measures that distort domestic prices.

INVESTMENT FREEDOM — 50%

The foreign investment regime is generally liberal, although certain sectors face restriction, including law, accountancy, and certain areas of transport, construction, and foreign trade, as well as publishing, printing, broadcasting, gemstone exploitation, brick making, rice mills, wood and stone carving manufacture, and silk weaving. Foreign-owned hospitals may not employ non-Cambodian doctors if the Ministry of Health considers that there is an adequate number of Cambodian practitioners. There are no restrictions or controls on the holding of foreign exchange accounts by either residents or non-residents. Non-residents may not own land, and the government still must approve foreign direct investment.

FINANCIAL FREEDOM — 50%

Cambodia's financial system is small, underdeveloped, and subject to government influence. The government has pursued privatization and consolidation since 2000. All 15 commercial banks are private except the Foreign Trade Bank of Cambodia and the Rural Development Bank. Much credit is in the informal sector. A state-owned firm dominates the insurance sector. There is no stock market. The National Bank of Cambodia, which used to operate as a commercial bank as well as the central bank, is now solely a regulatory and supervisory agency.

PROPERTY RIGHTS — 30%

Cambodia's legal system does not protect private property effectively and contains many gaps in company law, bankruptcy, and arbitration. The executive branch usually dominates the legislature and the judiciary. There are frequent problems with inconsistent judicial rulings as well as outright corruption. The land titling system is not fully functional; most property owners do not have documentation to prove their ownership.

FREEDOM FROM CORRUPTION — 23%

Corruption is perceived as widespread. Cambodia ranks 130th out of 158 countries in Transparency International's Corruption Perceptions Index for 2005.

LABOR FREEDOM — 67.7%

The labor market operates under relatively flexible employment regulations that could be improved to enhance employment and productivity growth. The non-salary cost of employing a worker is low, but dismissing a redundant employee is relatively costly. The formal labor market is not fully developed, and the rigid labor market runs the risk of creating an arbitrary dual labor market.

CAMEROON

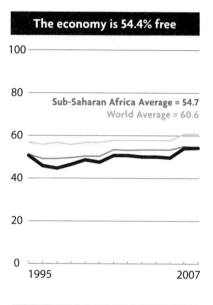

Yaoundé

Rank: 117

Regional Rank: 22 of 40

Cameroon's economy is 54.4 percent free, according to our 2007 assessment, which makes it the world's 117th freest economy. Its overall score is 0.3 percentage point higher than last year, partially reflecting new methodological detail. Cameroon is ranked 22nd out of 40 countries in the sub-Saharan Africa region, and its overall score is equal to the regional average.

Cameroon scores well in freedom from government and somewhat well in fiscal freedom. Both the top income tax rate and the top corporate tax rate are 38.5 percent, but total tax revenue is relatively small as a percentage of GDP. Government expenditures are also relatively low. Economic development has been spurred by privatization, which needs to proceed more extensively.

Cameroon faces problems similar to those faced by other developing African nations. Because corruption is extensive and the rule of law is weak, neither property rights nor justice in the courts can be guaranteed. Employment regulations are costly and restrictive, and firing a worker is difficult. Business licenses are difficult to obtain. Foreign investment remains heavily restricted, although the government has promised reforms.

BACKGROUND: Cameroon is a multi-party democracy under President Paul Biya, who has been in office since 1982. A majority of the population is rural, and agriculture accounts for over 40 percent of GDP. Government intervention in the economy, including state ownership of utilities and industries and onerous regulation, hinders foreign investment and economic growth. Per capita income is relatively high for sub-Saharan Africa but is supported by declining oil production and exports of commodities that are subject to volatile shifts in world prices. Ongoing problems include bureaucracy, an unreliable legal system, widespread corruption, and Cameroon's inadequate and poorly maintained infrastructure.

How Do We Measure Economic Freedom? See Chapter 3 (page 37) for an explanation of the methodology or visit the *Index* Web site at *heritage.org/index*.

The economy is 54.4% free

Sub-Saharan Africa Average = 54.7
World Average = 60.6

1995 — 2007

QUICK FACTS

Population: 16 million

GDP (PPP): $34.9 billion
3.6% growth in 2004
4.1% 5-yr. comp. ann. growth
$2,174 per capita

Unemployment: 17.0% (2006 estimate)

Inflation (CPI): 0.3%

FDI (net inflow): $0.3 million (gross)

Official Development Assistance:
Multilateral: $235 million
Bilateral: $717 million (2% from the U.S.)

External Debt: $9.5 billion

Exports: $2.7 billion (2004 estimate)
Primarily crude oil and petroleum products, lumber, cocoa beans, aluminum, coffee, cotton

Imports: $2.5 billion (2004 estimate)
Primarily machinery, electrical equipment, transport equipment, fuel, food

CAMEROON'S TEN ECONOMIC FREEDOMS

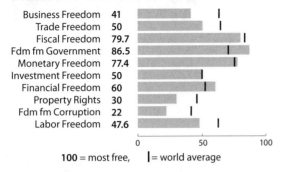

Business Freedom	41	
Trade Freedom	50	
Fiscal Freedom	79.7	
Fdm fm Government	86.5	
Monetary Freedom	77.4	
Investment Freedom	50	
Financial Freedom	60	
Property Rights	30	
Fdm fm Corruption	22	
Labor Freedom	47.6	

0   50   100

100 = most free, | = world average

BUSINESS FREEDOM — 41%

Starting a business takes an average of 37 days, compared to the world average of 48 days. Entrepreneurship should be easier for maximum job creation. Obtaining a business license can be very difficult, and closing a business is difficult. Regulations are applied unevenly and impose a substantial burden on businesses. Obtaining government approval after incorporation can involve a series of agencies. The overall freedom to start, operate, and close a business is seriously limited by the national regulatory environment.

TRADE FREEDOM — 50%

Cameroon's weighted average tariff rate was 15 percent in 2002. Non-tariff barriers include surcharges on certain imports, import bans, and issues involving the enforcement and protection of intellectual property rights. Customs fraud and protracted negotiations with customs officers over the value of imported goods are common. Consequently, an additional 20 percent is deducted from Cameroon's trade freedom score to account for these non-tariff barriers.

FISCAL FREEDOM — 79.7%

Cameroon has high tax rates. Both the top income tax rate and the top corporate tax rate are 38.5 percent. Other taxes include a value-added tax (VAT). In recent years, the government has expanded excise taxes, increased the property tax, and modified forestry taxation in an effort to reduce the potential for fraud. In the most recent year, overall tax revenue as a percentage of GDP was 9.3 percent.

FREEDOM FROM GOVERNMENT — 86.5%

Cameroon's total government expenditures, including consumption and transfer payments, are low. The most recent data show that government spending equaled 15.9 percent of GDP, and the government received 22.7 percent of its total revenues from state-owned enterprises and government ownership of property. Privatization has been one of the pillars of economic reform, but progress has been sluggish.

MONETARY FREEDOM — 77.4%

Inflation in Cameroon is low, averaging 1.5 percent between 2003 and 2005. Relatively low and stable prices explain most of the monetary freedom score. The market determines most prices, but the government controls prices for "strategic"

goods and services, including electricity, water, petroleum products, telecommunications, cooking gas, pharmaceuticals, and cotton. Consequently, an additional 15 percent is deducted from Cameroon's monetary freedom score to adjust for measures that distort domestic prices.

INVESTMENT FREEDOM — 50%

In March 2002, Cameroon passed an investment charter to improve its difficult investment environment. However, regulations to implement this charter will not be fully in place until 2007 because of delays in drafting them. Some capital transfers are subject to requirements, controls, and authorization. Residents may open foreign exchange accounts with prior approval of the central bank and the Ministry of Finance and Budget. Most capital transactions, including foreign borrowing, foreign direct investment, and foreign securities, are subject to controls and generally require approval of or declaration to the government.

FINANCIAL FREEDOM — 60%

Cameroon's financial sector is small and dominated by banking. Cameroon is a member of the Central African Economic and Monetary Community along with five other countries. These countries share a common central bank and a common currency pegged to the euro. The banking sector is private and consists of 10 commercial banks. It also is highly concentrated, with three banks controlling 60 percent of assets. Microfinance is increasing. The insurance sector is also concentrated, with four companies accounting for about 60 percent of the market. The first stock exchange was founded in 2003, but its first listing was not until 2006. Outdated bankruptcy laws favor debtors, discouraging lending. The government-owned Postal Savings Bank became insolvent in 2004 and is being reformed.

PROPERTY RIGHTS — 30%

Corruption and an uncertain legal environment can lead to confiscation of private property. Some foreign companies have alleged that judgments against them were obtained fraudulently or through frivolous lawsuits. The enforcement of judicial decisions is subject to administrative and legal bottlenecks. The Constitutional Council, established by the National Assembly in April 2004, should improve general governance and efforts to fight corruption.

FREEDOM FROM CORRUPTION — 22%

Corruption is perceived as widespread. Cameroon ranks 137th out of 158 countries in Transparency International's Corruption Perceptions Index for 2005.

LABOR FREEDOM — 47.6%

The labor market operates under highly restrictive employment regulations that hinder employment and productivity growth. The non-salary cost of employing a worker can be high, but dismissing a redundant employee is relatively costless. Labor legislation mandates retraining or replacement before firing a worker. Despite an overall legal framework for the emergence of an efficient labor market, such a market has not emerged.

CANADA

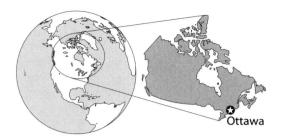
Ottawa

Canada's economy is 78.7 percent free, according to our 2007 assessment, which makes it the world's 10th freest economy. Its overall score is unchanged from last year. Canada is ranked 2nd out of 29 countries in the Americas, and its overall score is well above the regional average.

As a developed Western democracy, Canada scores well in business freedom, property rights, labor freedom, and fiscal freedom. Opening a business is fast and painless, and closing one is equally simple. A strong rule of law ensures property rights, a low level of corruption, and transparent application of the country's admittedly thorough commercial code. Inflation of consumer prices is low, as are the top commercial and income tax rates.

On the other hand, freedom from government scores comparatively poorly. As in many European democracies, government spending is high because Canada maintains elaborate social programs and a welfare state. Regulation of foreign investment discourages liquid capital transfers, and foreign investment in several areas of the economy is heavily restricted. The banking sector, however, is becoming more open to foreign capital as the government loosens restrictions.

BACKGROUND: Canada is one of the world's leading free-market democracies. It enjoys a large trade surplus, thanks to oil and mineral exports. Because of its bilateral trade relationship with the United States, its economy tends to track that of its larger southern neighbor. A protracted dispute with the United States over softwood lumber was settled in 2005. Despite maintaining one of the Organisation for Economic Co-operation and Development's most restrictive foreign ownership policies in telecommunications, publishing, broadcasting, aviation, mining, and fishing, macroeconomic fundamentals remain strong, and unemployment is at a 30-year low.

How Do We Measure Economic Freedom? See Chapter 3 (page 37) for an explanation of the methodology or visit the *Index* Web site at *heritage.org/index*.

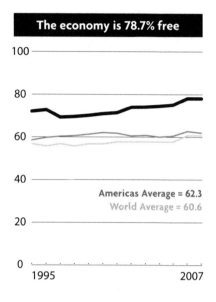

The economy is 78.7% free

Americas Average = 62.3
World Average = 60.6

QUICK FACTS

Population: 32 million

GDP (PPP): $999.6 billion
2.9% growth in 2004
3.0% 5-yr. comp. ann. growth
$31,263 per capita

Unemployment: 7.2%

Inflation (CPI): 1.8%

FDI (net inflow): −$41.2 billion

Official Development Assistance:
Multilateral: None
Bilateral: None

External Debt: $439.8 billion (2005)

Exports: $377.6 billion
Primarily motor vehicles and parts, industrial machinery, aircraft, telecommunications equipment, chemicals, plastics, fertilizers, wood pulp, timber

Imports: $336.7 billion
Primarily machinery and equipment, motor vehicles and parts, crude oil, chemicals, electricity, durable consumer goods

CANADA'S TEN ECONOMIC FREEDOMS

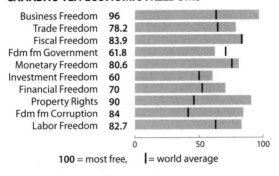

Business Freedom	96	
Trade Freedom	78.2	
Fiscal Freedom	83.9	
Fdm fm Government	61.8	
Monetary Freedom	80.6	
Investment Freedom	60	
Financial Freedom	70	
Property Rights	90	
Fdm fm Corruption	84	
Labor Freedom	82.7	

0   50   100

100 = most free,   ▌= world average

BUSINESS FREEDOM — *96%*

Starting a business takes an average of three days, compared to the world average of 48 days. Entrepreneurship should be easier for maximum job creation. Obtaining a business license is simple, and closing a business is very easy. The regulatory system is thorough but essentially transparent. The overall freedom to start, operate, and close a business is strongly protected by the national regulatory environment.

TRADE FREEDOM — *78.2%*

Canada's weighted average tariff rate was a low 0.9 percent in 2005. However, the government maintains some non-tariff barriers, at both the federal and provincial levels, that impede access to the Canadian market. Canada closely restricts imports of certain domestic "supply managed" agricultural products such as dairy products, eggs, and poultry and restricts access to the telecommunications and media sectors. Issues involving the enforcement and protection of intellectual property rights also contribute to the cost of trade. Consequently, an additional 20 percent is deducted from Canada's trade freedom score to account for these non-tariff barriers.

FISCAL FREEDOM — *83.9%*

Canada has a moderate income tax rate and a moderate corporate tax rate. The top income tax rate is 29 percent, and the top corporate tax rate is 22.1 percent. Other taxes include a value-added tax (VAT), a tax on insurance contracts, and a property tax. In the most recent year, overall tax revenue as a percentage of GDP was 33 percent.

FREEDOM FROM GOVERNMENT — *61.8%*

Total government expenditures, including consumption and transfer payments, are high. In the most recent year, government spending equaled 39.9 percent of GDP, and the government received 3.1 percent of its total revenues from state-owned enterprises and government ownership of property.

MONETARY FREEDOM — *80.6%*

Inflation in Canada is low, averaging 2.2 percent between 2003 and 2005. Relatively low and stable prices explain most of the monetary freedom score. The market determines most prices, but the government regulates the prices of some utilities and subsidizes and controls prices for some agricultural sectors. Consequently, an additional 10 percent is deducted from Canada's monetary freedom score to adjust for measures that distort domestic prices.

INVESTMENT FREEDOM — *60%*

The government regulates foreign investment. A federal agency, Investment Canada, must approve direct foreign investments, whether through a new venture or through an acquisition. Restricted sectors include broadcasting and telecommunications, newspapers, energy monopolies, book publishing, filmmaking and distribution, banking and insurance, and air transport. There are no restrictions on current transfers, repatriation of profits, purchase of real estate, or access to foreign exchange.

FINANCIAL FREEDOM — *70%*

Canada has a strong, sound financial system. The six large domestic banks that dominate the sector controlled over 90 percent of banking assets in 2005. The 50 foreign banks operating in Canada in 2006 accounted for a very small portion of sector assets. The government owns the Business Development Bank, which makes loans to the small and medium enterprise sector. The government has loosened restrictions on financial institutions, giving them more freedom to offer financial services. Mergers between large banks are restricted, and large banks are not permitted to buy large insurance companies. Banks are permitted to open their own insurance subsidiaries but may not sell policies in their bank branches. Securities markets are well developed.

PROPERTY RIGHTS — *90%*

Private property is well protected in Canada. The judiciary is independent. Judges and civil servants are generally honest, and bribery and other forms of corruption are rare.

FREEDOM FROM CORRUPTION — *84%*

Corruption is perceived as minimal. Canada ranks 14th out of 158 countries in Transparency International's Corruption Perceptions Index for 2005.

LABOR FREEDOM — *82.7%*

The labor market operates under flexible employment regulations that enhance employment and productivity growth. The non-salary cost of employing a worker is moderate, and dismissing a redundant employee is relatively costless. The labor law does not mandate retraining or replacement before firing a worker. Canada's labor market flexibility is one of the 20 highest in the world.

CAPE VERDE

Praia

Cape Verde's economy is 58.4 percent free, according to our 2007 assessment, which makes it the world's 88th freest economy. Its overall score is 1.8 percentage points lower than last year, partially reflecting new methodological detail. Cape Verde is ranked 10th out of 40 countries in the sub-Saharan Africa region, and its overall score is slightly higher than the regional average.

Cape Verde scores well in freedom from government, property rights, and monetary freedom. Inflation is low, although the government does subsidize some staples. The top income and corporate tax rates are high, but total tax revenue is relatively small as a percentage of GDP, and government expenditures are correspondingly moderate. Property rights are fairly well secured by the rule of law in comparison to the situation in neighboring countries.

Cape Verde faces serious challenges. Its trade freedom and freedom from corruption are particularly weak, and business and financial freedoms are not much better. Corruption inhibits economic development, and bureaucracy makes business operations difficult. Trade is hindered by a high average tariff rate and significant non-tariff barriers.

BACKGROUND: Cape Verde is a stable multi-party parliamentary democracy with few natural resources, frequent droughts, and serious water shortages. The economy is dominated by services, but manufacturing, agriculture, and fishing employ most of the work force. Cape Verde has close economic and political ties to the European Union and is seeking EU associate status. The currency is pegged to the euro. Many Cape Verdeans live abroad, and remittances contribute significantly to GDP. Economic growth through market liberalization, good governance, and judicious public investment has earned Cape Verde middle-income status, which is high by sub-Saharan African standards.

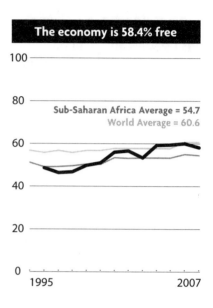

The economy is 58.4% free

Sub-Saharan Africa Average = 54.7
World Average = 60.6

QUICK FACTS

Population: 0.5 million

GDP (PPP): $2.8 billion
4.4% growth in 2004
5.5% 5-yr. comp. ann. growth
$5,727 per capita

Unemployment: 16% (2002 estimate)

Inflation (CPI): −1.9%

FDI (net inflow): $20.5 million (gross)

Official Development Assistance:
Multilateral: $54 million
Bilateral: $97 million (7% from the U.S.)

External Debt: $325.0 million (2002)

Exports: $276.9 million
Primarily fuel, shoes, garments, fish, hides

Imports: $547.2 million
Primarily food, industrial products, transport equipment, fuels

How Do We Measure Economic Freedom? See Chapter 3 (page 37) for an explanation of the methodology or visit the *Index* Web site at *heritage.org/index*.

CAPE VERDE'S TEN ECONOMIC FREEDOMS

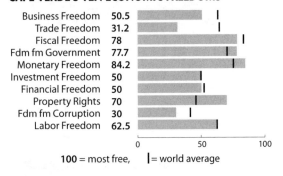

Business Freedom	50.5
Trade Freedom	31.2
Fiscal Freedom	78
Fdm fm Government	77.7
Monetary Freedom	84.2
Investment Freedom	50
Financial Freedom	50
Property Rights	70
Fdm fm Corruption	30
Labor Freedom	62.5

0   50   100

100 = most free, ❙ = world average

BUSINESS FREEDOM — 50.5%

Starting a business takes an average of 52 days, compared to the world average of 48 days. Entrepreneurship should be easier for maximum job creation. In recent years, government has made efforts to streamline the cumbersome bureaucracy and increase transparency, but obtaining a business license can still be still difficult, and closing a business is likewise difficult. The overall freedom to start, operate, and close a business is restrained by the national regulatory environment.

TRADE FREEDOM — 31.2%

Cape Verde's average tariff rate was a high 24.4 percent in 2003. Import taxes and sanitary and phytosanitary restrictions also increase the cost of trade. Consequently, an additional 20 percent is deducted from Cape Verde's trade freedom score to account for these non-tariff barriers.

FISCAL FREEDOM — 78%

Cape Verde has a high income tax rate and a moderate corporate tax rate. The top income tax rate is 45 percent, and the top corporate tax rate is 30 percent. Other taxes include a value-added tax (VAT) and a special consumption tax. In the most recent year, tax revenue as a percentage of GDP was 19.3 percent.

FREEDOM FROM GOVERNMENT — 77.7%

Total government expenditures in Cape Verde, including consumption and transfer payments, are moderate. In the most recent year, government spending equaled 30.6 percent of GDP, and the government received 1.4 percent of its total revenues from state-owned enterprises and government ownership of property.

MONETARY FREEDOM — 84.2%

The average rate of inflation in Cape Verde was –0.8 percent between 2003 and 2005. Relatively stable prices explain most of the monetary freedom score. The market determines most prices, but the government maintains price controls for water and electricity and regulates some other prices, including those for petroleum products and basic food items. Consequently, an additional 10 percent is deducted from Cape Verde's monetary freedom score.

INVESTMENT FREEDOM — 50%

The government encourages foreign investment, particularly in tourism, fishing, light manufacturing, communications, and transportation. It has simplified the registration process and has opened privatization to foreign investors, although shares are reserved for Cape Verdean investors. All sectors of the economy are now open. Both residents and non-residents may hold foreign exchange accounts, subject to government approval and regulations. Most payments and transfers are subject to controls. Real estate transactions require central bank approval. While most capital transactions are permitted, most are also subject to advance approval by the central bank.

FINANCIAL FREEDOM — 50%

Cape Verde has a small financial sector. Banking reform initiated in the 1990s led to privatization of the two largest commercial banks, Comercial do Atlântico and Caixa Económica de Cabo Verde, although the government retains a large minority stake in Caixa Económica de Cabo Verde. There has been a significant improvement in the non-performing loan ratio. In addition, Cape Verde has a Portuguese bank, a West African bank, and a private domestic bank with Portuguese participation. The sector remains highly concentrated, with the two largest banks controlling 89 percent of banking assets. The government remains active in the banking sector through financial institutions that handle public investment and international aid. There are two insurance companies and two state-run pension funds. The stock market, founded in 1999, has been largely inactive.

PROPERTY RIGHTS — 70%

Private property is fairly well protected in Cape Verde. The Constitution provides for an independent judiciary, and the government generally respects this provision. However, the judiciary is understaffed and inefficient. In general, due process is provided, although the right to an expeditious trial is constrained by a seriously overburdened and understaffed judicial system. A backlog of cases routinely leads to trial delays of six months or more.

FREEDOM FROM CORRUPTION — 30%

To overcome the lack of resources in Cape Verde, the poor turn to migration and the informal sector. In urban areas, informal activities are the only source of income for many families. It is estimated that informal employment accounts for about 40 percent of total employment.

LABOR FREEDOM — 62.5%

The labor market operates under restrictive employment regulations that could be improved to enhance employment and productivity growth. The non-salary cost of employing a worker is high, and dismissing a redundant employee is relatively costly. The labor laws were revised recently to make labor contracts more flexible. There is no private-sector minimum wage, but most private-sector wages are linked to those of equivalent civil servants.

CENTRAL AFRICAN REPUBLIC

❂ Bangui

Rank: 137

Regional Rank: 32 of 40

The Central African Republic's economy is 50.3 percent free, according to our 2007 assessment, which makes it the world's 137th freest economy. Its overall score is 4.5 percentage points lower than last year, partially reflecting new methodological detail. The Central African Republic is ranked 32nd out of 40 countries in the sub-Saharan Africa region, and its overall score is lower than the regional average.

The Central African Republic scores well in freedom from government and monetary freedom. Government expenditures are low, and state-owned businesses do not account for an exceptionally large amount of revenue. Tax revenue is not high as a percentage of GDP, but tax rates are high. Inflation is low, but the government interferes extensively with market prices.

Business freedom, trade freedom, financial freedom, property rights, and freedom from corruption are weak. Regulatory procedures are burdensome, and business operations tend to be significantly hampered by the government. Labor laws are restrictive, imposing exceptionally high costs on employers. The banking system is subject to political pressure, as is the rule of law. Property rights cannot be guaranteed, and corruption is rampant.

BACKGROUND: The Central African Republic is very poor and has been politically unstable ever since gaining its independence in 1960. A civilian government established in 1993 was overthrown in 2003 by General Francois Bozize. Despite pledging not to run, Bozize won the 2005 presidential election. The incidence of HIV/AIDS infection is high. Most of the population is engaged in subsistence farming, and agriculture comprises over half of GDP. Mineral resources, aside from diamonds, remain undeveloped. Infrastructure is poor, institutions are weak, and corruption is prevalent, although initial steps have been taken to standardize and simplify the labor and investment codes.

How Do We Measure Economic Freedom? See Chapter 3 (page 37) for an explanation of the methodology or visit the *Index* Web site at *heritage.org/index*.

The economy is 50.3% free

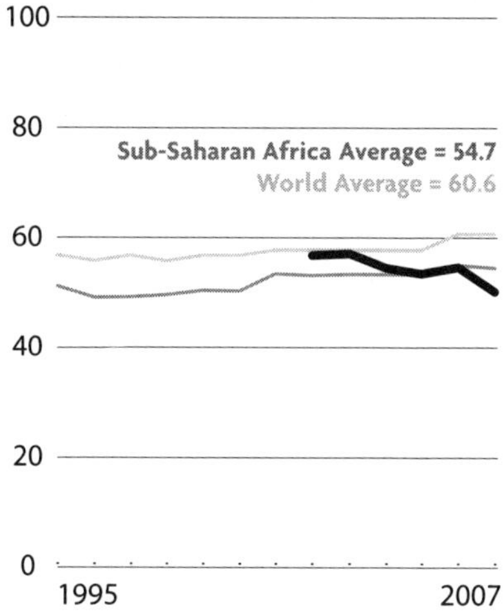

Sub-Saharan Africa Average = 54.7
World Average = 60.6

(Chart: vertical axis 0 to 100; horizontal axis from 1995 to 2007)

QUICK FACTS

Population: 4 million

GDP (PPP): $4.4 billion
1.3% growth in 2004
−1.0% 5-yr. comp. ann. growth
$1,094 per capita

Unemployment: 8.0% (2001 estimate)

Inflation (CPI): −2.2%

FDI (net inflow): −$12.7 million (gross)

Official Development Assistance:
Multilateral: $52 million
Bilateral: $61 million (20% from the U.S.)

External Debt: $1.1 billion

Exports: $100.4 million (2004 estimate)
Primarily diamonds, timber, cotton, coffee, tobacco

Imports: $158.2 million (2004 estimate)
Primarily food, textiles, petroleum products, machinery, electrical equipment, motor vehicles, chemicals, pharmaceuticals

CENT. AFRICAN REP.'S TEN ECONOMIC FREEDOMS

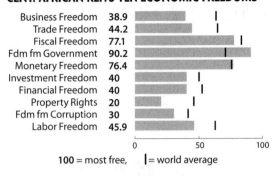

Business Freedom	38.9
Trade Freedom	44.2
Fiscal Freedom	77.1
Fdm fm Government	90.2
Monetary Freedom	76.4
Investment Freedom	40
Financial Freedom	40
Property Rights	20
Fdm fm Corruption	30
Labor Freedom	45.9

0   50   100

100 = most free, | = world average

BUSINESS FREEDOM — *38.9%*

Starting a business takes an average of 14 days, compared to the world average of 48 days. Entrepreneurship should be easier for maximum job creation. Obtaining a business license is difficult, and closing a business can be very difficult. The overall freedom to start, operate, and close a business is seriously limited by the national regulatory environment.

TRADE FREEDOM — *44.2%*

The Central African Republic's weighted average tariff rate was a high 17.9 percent in 2002. The government subjects imports from third countries to discriminatory treatment by attributing imported goods to categories for which a higher duty rate applies, and customs fraud and inefficiency is a major problem. Consequently, an additional 20 percent is deducted from the Central African Republic's trade freedom score to account for these non-tariff barriers.

FISCAL FREEDOM — *77.1%*

The Central African Republic has high tax rates. The top income tax rate is 50 percent, and the top corporate tax rate is 30 percent. Other taxes include a value-added tax (VAT) and a tax on check transactions. In the most recent year, overall tax revenue as a percentage of GDP was 6.5 percent.

FREEDOM FROM GOVERNMENT — *90.2%*

Total government expenditures in the Central African Republic, including consumption and transfer payments, are very low. In the most recent year, government spending equaled 13.7 percent of GDP, and the government received 16.3 percent of its total revenues from state-owned enterprises and government ownership of property.

MONETARY FREEDOM — *76.4%*

Inflation in the Central African Republic is low, averaging 1.9 percent between 2003 and 2005. Relatively stable prices explain most of the monetary freedom score. The government influences most prices through the large public sector, subsidies, and direct price controls. Consequently, an additional 15 percent is deducted from the Central African Republic's monetary freedom score to adjust for measures that distort domestic prices.

INVESTMENT FREEDOM — *40%*

Banditry and extortion are major obstacles to foreign investment. Foreign investment must be declared to the Ministry for the Economy, Finance, Planning and International Cooperation. Capital transfers and transactions are subject to exchange controls. Residents may hold foreign exchange accounts. All capital transactions, transfers, and payments to countries other than France, Monaco, members of the West African Economic and Monetary Union (WAEMU), members of the Central African Economic and Monetary Community (CEMAC), and Comoros are subject to government approval and some reporting requirements. Sale or issue of capital market securities and commercial credits requires government approval.

FINANCIAL FREEDOM — *40%*

The Central African Republic's financial sector is underdeveloped. CEMAC countries share a common central bank and a common currency pegged to the euro. In addition to a branch of the regional central bank, there are three commercial banks, a microfinance institution, and two postal financial institutions. The government has privatized the two largest commercial banks, Banque Internationale pour le Centrafrique and Commercial Bank Centrafrique, but still partially owns the Banque Populaire Marocco-Centrafricaine. The banking sector is used as a source of financing for government expenditures, and the accumulation of state debt has undermined the soundness of the banking system. There are two insurance companies. There is no stock market.

PROPERTY RIGHTS — *20%*

Protection of property rights is weak. The constitution has been suspended, and the judiciary is subject to executive interference. Judges are appointed by the president. The courts barely function because of inefficient administration, a shortage of trained personnel, growing salary arrears, and a lack of material resources. The police and the judiciary are among the most corrupt institutions in the country.

FREEDOM FROM CORRUPTION — *30%*

Informal market activity and smuggling, especially in the diamond industry, is extensive. The formal sector has contracted greatly because of extensive regulations and corruption. A significant part of the population works informally.

LABOR FREEDOM — *45.9%*

The labor market operates under highly restrictive employment regulations that hinder employment and productivity growth. The non-salary cost of employing a worker is high, and dismissing a redundant employee can be difficult. Regulations on increasing or contracting the number of work hours are rigid. The Central African Republic's labor freedom is one of the 20 lowest in the world.

CHAD

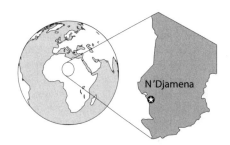

N'Djamena

Rank: 147

Regional Rank: 36 of 40

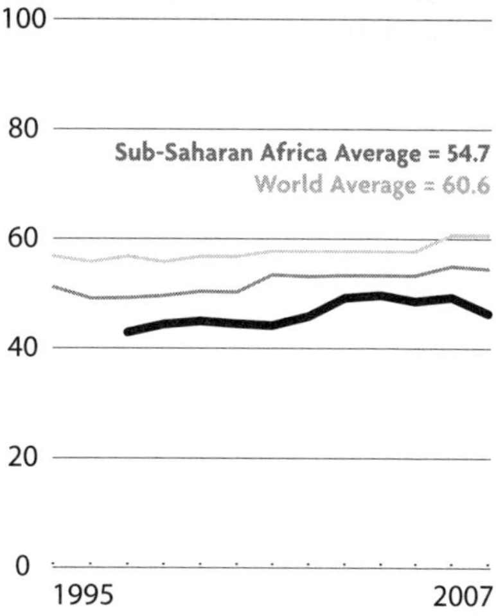

Chad's economy is 46.4 percent free, according to our 2007 assessment, which makes it the world's 147th freest economy. Its overall score is 3 percentage points lower than last year, partially reflecting new methodological detail. Chad is ranked 36th out of 40 countries in the sub-Saharan Africa region, and its overall score is lower than the regional average.

Chad scores moderately well in freedom from government and monetary freedom. Government spending as a percentage of GDP is relatively low, although the government receives substantial revenue from state-owned enterprises (mainly the oil sector). Inflation is low, but the government does intervene somewhat in the prices of certain goods.

Chad faces significant political and economic hurdles. It receives very low ratings in business freedom, fiscal freedom, property rights, freedom from corruption, and labor freedom. Starting a business takes over two months, and both licensing and closing a business are time-consuming and costly, reflecting a tedious regulatory environment. Nowhere is this more apparent than in employment, where inflexibility makes Chad one of the world's most restrictive labor markets. Weak rule of law means that property rights and regulations are rarely observed, and corruption is endemic.

BACKGROUND: Chad remains politically unstable and one of the world's 10 poorest countries. President Idriss Deby seized power in 1991 and won elections in 1996, 2001, and 2006. Eighty percent of the population is engaged in subsistence agriculture, herding, and fishing. Corruption, poor infrastructure, and lack of administrative and judicial reform undermine the business climate. Oil exports have increased growth in recent years, but violation of an agreement with the World Bank to set aside oil revenues for health, education, agriculture, and infrastructure led the Bank to suspend disbursement of loans, and negotiations are underway to resolve the dispute.

How Do We Measure Economic Freedom? See Chapter 3 (page 37) for an explanation of the methodology or visit the *Index* Web site at *heritage.org/index*.

The economy is 46.4% free

Sub-Saharan Africa Average = 54.7
World Average = 60.6

[Chart: vertical axis 0–100, horizontal axis 1995 to 2007]

QUICK FACTS

Population: 9.5 million

GDP (PPP): $19.7 billion
29.5% growth in 2004
12.1% 5-yr. comp. ann. growth
$2,090 per capita

Unemployment: n/a

Inflation (CPI): −5.4%

FDI (net inflow): $478.2 million (gross)

Official Development Assistance:
Multilateral: $181 million
Bilateral: $173 million (27% from the U.S.)

External Debt: $1.7 billion

Exports: $1.4 billion (2004 estimate)
Primarily cotton, cattle, gum arabic, oil

Imports: $933.4 million (2004 estimate)
Primarily machinery and transportation equipment, industrial goods, food, textiles

CHAD'S TEN ECONOMIC FREEDOMS

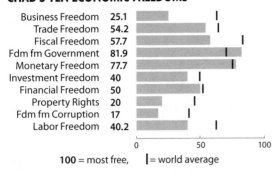

Business Freedom	25.1
Trade Freedom	54.2
Fiscal Freedom	57.7
Fdm fm Government	81.9
Monetary Freedom	77.7
Investment Freedom	40
Financial Freedom	50
Property Rights	20
Fdm fm Corruption	17
Labor Freedom	40.2

0   50   100

100 = most free, | = world average

BUSINESS FREEDOM — 25.1%

Starting a business takes an average of 75 days, compared to the world average of 48 days. Entrepreneurship should be easier for maximum job creation. Both obtaining a business license and closing a business are very difficult. Bureaucratic procedures are often burdensome and slow. Clear rules exist, but they are not always observed. The overall freedom to start, operate, and close a business is seriously limited by the national regulatory environment.

TRADE FREEDOM — 54.2%

Chad's weighted average tariff rate was 12.9 percent in 2002. Pervasive smuggling, corruption, bureaucracy, and red tape impede trade. Consequently, an additional 20 percent is deducted from Chad's trade freedom score to account for these non-tariff barriers.

FISCAL FREEDOM — 57.7%

Chad has very high tax rates. The top income tax rate is 65 percent, and the top corporate tax rate is 45 percent. Other taxes include a value-added tax (VAT) and an apprenticeship tax. In the most recent year, overall tax revenue as a percentage of GDP was 9.4 percent.

FREEDOM FROM GOVERNMENT — 81.9%

Total government expenditures in Chad, including consumption and transfer payments, are low. In the most recent year, government spending equaled 17.1 percent of GDP, and the government received 33.8 percent of its total revenues from state-owned enterprises and government ownership of property. Progress in privatization of the non-oil sector has been slow.

MONETARY FREEDOM — 77.7%

Inflation in Chad is moderate, averaging 3.8 percent between 2003 and 2005. Relatively moderate and unstable prices explain most of the monetary freedom score. Most prices are determined in the market, but the government influences the prices of important goods and services, such as cotton, telecommunications, and energy. Consequently, an additional 10 percent is deducted from Chad's monetary freedom score to adjust for measures that distort domestic prices.

INVESTMENT FREEDOM — 40%

Chad places no limits on foreign ownership and provides equal treatment to foreign investors, but they must satisfy several bureaucratic requirements, including a review and approval by the Ministry of Commerce. Foreign investments in cotton, electricity, and telecommunications are restricted to protect state-owned enterprises. The main constraints on investment are limited infrastructure, chronic energy shortages, high energy costs, a scarcity of skilled labor, a high tax burden, and corruption. Both residents and non-residents may hold foreign exchange accounts with government approval. Capital transactions, payments, and transfers to France, Monaco, members of the Central African Economic and Monetary Community (CEMAC), members of the West African Economic and Monetary Union, and Comoros are permitted freely and subject to controls to other countries.

FINANCIAL FREEDOM — 50%

Chad's financial sector is small, underdeveloped, and historically hindered by instability. Chad is a member of the Central African Economic and Monetary Community along with five other countries. These countries share a common central bank and a common currency pegged to the euro. Privatization of the banking sector was completed in the 1990s. There are seven banks. However, banking is weak, especially outside of the three main urban areas, and informal financial services are common. Supervision and regulation of the financial system is insufficient. The government has encouraged lending to CotonTchad to finance restructuring of the cotton sector. The insurance sector is small and dominated by the formerly state-owned Star Nationale. A French insurer entered the market after oil production began. There is no capital or money market, and sophisticated financial instruments are unavailable.

PROPERTY RIGHTS — 20%

Protection of private property is weak. There is a widespread perception that the courts should be avoided at all costs, so most disputes are settled privately. Chad's judiciary is easily influenced by the executive branch. Because magistrates are appointed by presidential decree with no legislative oversight, the careers of magistrates, judges, clerks, and other judicial agents depend on the presidency and the Ministry of Justice. Corruption is a serious problem.

FREEDOM FROM CORRUPTION — 17%

Corruption is perceived as widespread. Chad ranks last in Transparency International's Corruption Perceptions Index for 2005.

LABOR FREEDOM — 40.2%

The labor market operates under highly restrictive employment regulations that hinder employment and productivity growth. The non-salary cost of employing a worker is high, and dismissing a redundant employee is relatively costly. Restrictive labor laws and legal uncertainty discourage investment. Chad's labor market flexibility is one of the 20 lowest in the world.

CHILE

Santiago

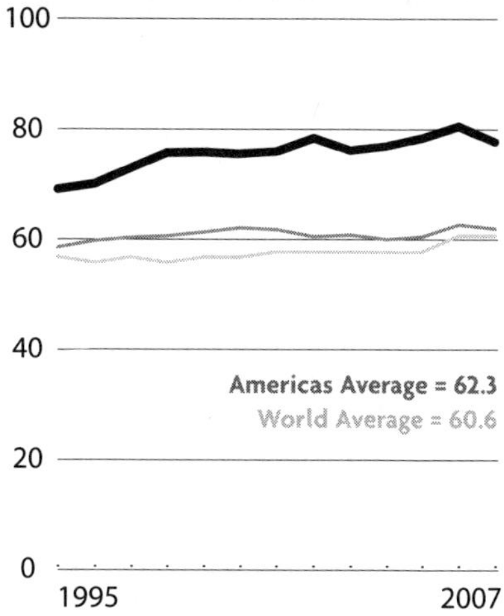

Chile's economy is 78.3 percent free, according to our 2007 assessment, which makes it the world's 11th freest economy. Its overall score is 2.9 percentage points lower than last year, partially reflecting new methodological detail. Chile is ranked 3rd out of 29 countries in the Americas and has been a regional leader for over a decade.

Chile is a regional economic power and receives good scores in virtually all areas of economic freedom. Scores in fiscal freedom, freedom from government, monetary freedom, property rights, and labor freedom are particularly high. Despite high income taxes, corporate tax rates are an extremely low 17 percent. Total government spending as a proportion of GDP is also moderate. Inflation is low, but the state maintains certain price controls. The rule of law is transparent and fair.

Though its overall record is impressive, Chile could improve in business freedom and trade freedom. Bankruptcy procedures can be cumbersome, although regulatory licensing is easy. Non-tariff barriers are also a problem, as the government restricts certain imports.

BACKGROUND: Chile is richly endowed with natural resources and is now the world's leading producer of copper. Tourism and a strong export sector have increasingly been the main engines of growth. Chile has been governed since 1990 by a center-left coalition. Michele Bachelet, a member of the Socialist Party—one of the governing coalition parties—won the presidential elections in January 2006. Her government remains committed to Chile's successful free-market institutions. As of this writing, a free trade agreement with China, signed in November 2005, awaits congressional ratification. Chile is also engaged in negotiations on possible trade agreements with India and Japan.

How Do We Measure Economic Freedom? See Chapter 3 (page 37) for an explanation of the methodology or visit the *Index* Web site at *heritage.org/index*.

The economy is 78.3% free

Americas Average = 62.3
World Average = 60.6

1995 — 2007

QUICK FACTS

Population: 16.1 million

GDP (PPP): $175.3 billion
6.1% growth in 2004
4.0% 5-yr. comp. ann. growth
$10,874 per capita

Unemployment: 8.8%

Inflation (CPI): 1.1%

FDI (net inflow): $6.7 billion

Official Development Assistance:
Multilateral: $25 million
Bilateral: $82 million (2% from the U.S.)

External Debt: $44.1 billion

Exports: $38.0 billion
Primarily machinery and transportation equipment, industrial goods, food, textiles

Imports: $29.5 billion
Primarily petroleum and petroleum products, chemicals, electrical and telecommunications equipment, industrial machinery, vehicles, natural gas

CHILE'S TEN ECONOMIC FREEDOMS

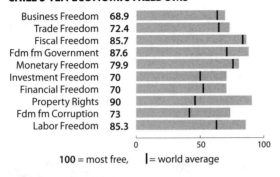

Business Freedom	68.9
Trade Freedom	72.4
Fiscal Freedom	85.7
Fdm fm Government	87.6
Monetary Freedom	79.9
Investment Freedom	70
Financial Freedom	70
Property Rights	90
Fdm fm Corruption	73
Labor Freedom	85.3

0   50   100

100 = most free,   **❙ = world average**

BUSINESS FREEDOM — *68.9%*

Starting a business takes an average of 27 days, compared to the world average of 48 days. Entrepreneurship should be easier for maximum job creation. Obtaining a business license is relatively simple, but closing a business can be difficult. The time and cost of going through bankruptcy can be burdensome. The overall freedom to start, operate, and close a business is relatively well protected by the national regulatory environment.

TRADE FREEDOM — *72.4%*

Chile's weighted average tariff rate was 3.8 percent in 2004. Chile generally has few non-tariff barriers to imports, but imports of agricultural products and processed food require approval, some imports are banned, and issues related to the enforcement and protection of intellectual property rights also contribute to the cost of trade. Consequently, an additional 20 percent is deducted from Chile's trade freedom score to account for these non-tariff barriers.

FISCAL FREEDOM — *85.7%*

Chile has a high income tax rate but a low corporate tax rate. The top income tax rate is 40 percent, and the top corporate tax rate is 17 percent. Other taxes include a value-added tax (VAT), a tax on check transactions, and a property tax. In the most recent year, overall tax revenue as a percentage of GDP was 15.9 percent.

FREEDOM FROM GOVERNMENT — *87.6%*

Total government expenditures in Chile, including consumption and transfer payments, are very moderate. In the most recent year, government spending equaled 20.4 percent of GDP, and the government received 8.2 percent of its total revenues from state-owned enterprises and government ownership of property.

MONETARY FREEDOM — *79.9%*

Inflation is relatively low, averaging 2.5 percent between 2003 and 2005. Relatively low and stable prices explain most of the monetary freedom score. Many prices are determined in the market, but the government maintains prices for utilities, including water, fixed-line telecommunications, and electricity, and prices for certain agriculture products are controlled within price bands. Consequently, an additional 10 percent is deducted from Chile's monetary freedom score to adjust for measures that distort domestic prices.

INVESTMENT FREEDOM — *70%*

Foreign and domestic investments receive equal treatment, and there are no restrictions on repatriation. Some restrictions apply for foreign ownership of local enterprises and joint ventures in the petroleum industry, uranium mining and other specialty mineral resources, communications, shipping, and fishing. In recent years, the authorities have lifted all remaining exchange controls, eliminated the minimum stay period on foreign investments, and eased procedures for placements in local capital markets. Both residents and non-residents may hold foreign exchange accounts. There are no controls on current transfers and capital transactions, but some restrictions apply.

FINANCIAL FREEDOM — *70%*

Chile's financial system is among the strongest and most developed among all emerging markets. The banking system is efficient and well supervised. There are strict limits on lending to a single debtor or group of related companies. There are 14 domestic banks and 12 foreign banks. Foreign banks controlled 39 percent of assets in 2005. The state-owned Banco Estado is the nation's third largest, accounting for about 13 percent of banking assets. A series of laws have substantially widened the range of operations in which banks and other financial services may engage and have streamlined and regularized the regulation of capital and credit markets. Chile's advanced private pension system has been a model for other countries and an important source of investment capital. Foreign banking and insurance companies are treated the same as domestic companies. The insurance sector is large and diverse, with over 50 insurance companies offering a variety of services. Chile's liberal capital market is the largest in Latin America as a proportion of GDP.

PROPERTY RIGHTS — *90%*

Private property is well protected. Contractual agreements are secure, and court administration is transparent and efficient at executing trials. Expropriation is highly unlikely and receives compensation. Judicial corruption is rare.

FREEDOM FROM CORRUPTION — *73%*

Corruption is perceived as minimal. Chile ranks 21st out of 158 countries in Transparency International's Corruption Perceptions Index for 2005.

LABOR FREEDOM — *85.3%*

The labor market operates under flexible employment regulations that enhance employment and productivity growth. The non-salary cost of employing a worker is very low, and dismissing a redundant employee is relatively costless. Chile's labor market flexibility is one of the 20 highest in the world.

CHINA, PEOPLE'S REPUBLIC OF

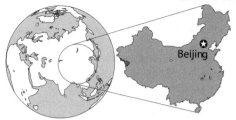

Beijing

Rank: 119

Regional Rank: 22 of 30

China's economy is 54 percent free, according to our 2007 assessment, which makes it the world's 119th freest economy. Its overall score is 1.4 percentage points lower than last year, partially reflecting new methodological detail. China is ranked 22nd out of 30 countries in the Asia–Pacific region, and its overall score is slightly lower than the regional average.

China scores well in the factors measuring government expenditures and freedom from government, and moderately well in monetary freedom and trade freedom. Total government expenditures equal less than 20 percent of GDP.

As an autocratic state, China imposes severe restrictions on many areas of its economy. Investment freedom, financial freedom, property rights, and corruption are particularly egregious. Foreign investment is highly controlled and regulated, the judicial system enforcing these regulations is highly politicized, and corruption is rampant. The state maintains a tight control over the financial sector, where the government owns all the banks directly or indirectly. Fiscally, the top income and corporate tax rates are fairly high at 45 percent and 33 percent, respectively.

BACKGROUND: China is the world's second largest economy in absolute terms but rather poor in terms of average income per person. Despite the government's efforts to cool double-digit economic growth through cutbacks of fixed asset investment and controls on bank lending, investment and a trade surplus continue to surge. Political repression persists with tight restraints on speech and expression, particularly via the Internet, and unrelenting persecution of religious and ethnic minorities. Violations of intellectual property rights also remain hurdles to improved trade relations with the United States. Industry makes up the vast majority of China's economic output, but rural areas have the highest population, driving a large urban migration.

How Do We Measure Economic Freedom? See Chapter 3 (page 37) for an explanation of the methodology or visit the *Index* Web site at *heritage.org/index*.

The economy is 54% free

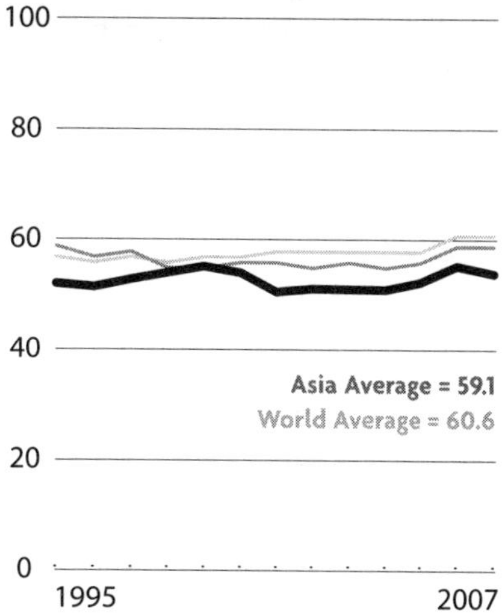

Asia Average = 59.1
World Average = 60.6

1995 — 2007

QUICK FACTS

Population: 1.3 billion

GDP (PPP): $7.6 trillion
10.1% growth in 2004
9.2% 5-yr. comp. ann. growth
$5,896 per capita

Unemployment: 9.9% (2004 estimate)

Inflation (CPI): 3.9%

FDI (net inflow): $58.8 billion

Official Development Assistance:
Multilateral: $231 million
Bilateral: $2.7 billion (0.8% from the U.S.)

External Debt: $248.9 billion

Exports: $655.8 billion
Primarily machinery and equipment, plastics, optical and medical equipment, iron and steel

Imports: $606.5 billion
Primarily machinery and equipment, oil and mineral fuels, plastics, optical and medical equipment, organic chemicals, iron and steel

CHINA'S TEN ECONOMIC FREEDOMS

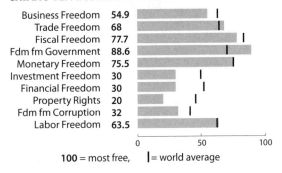

Business Freedom	54.9
Trade Freedom	68
Fiscal Freedom	77.7
Fdm fm Government	88.6
Monetary Freedom	75.5
Investment Freedom	30
Financial Freedom	30
Property Rights	20
Fdm fm Corruption	32
Labor Freedom	63.5

0   50   100

100 = most free, **❙** **= world average**

BUSINESS FREEDOM — *54.9%*

Starting a business takes an average of 35 days, compared to the world average of 48 days. Entrepreneurship should be easier for maximum job creation. Obtaining a business license can be difficult, and closing a business is difficult. China lacks legal and regulatory transparency, and its inconsistent enforcement of regulations is a barrier to entrepreneurial activities. The overall freedom to start, operate, and close a business is constrained by the national regulatory environment.

TRADE FREEDOM — *68%*

China's weighted average tariff rate was 6 percent in 2004. China has reduced its non-tariff barriers as a result of implementing its WTO protocol of accession, but the government continues to use quotas, import bans, burdensome licensing and regulatory rules, export taxes, and sanitary and phytosanitary restrictions to protect its economy. Issues involving the enforcement and protection of intellectual property rights also add to the cost of trade. Consequently, an additional 20 percent is deducted from China's trade freedom score to account for these non-tariff barriers.

FISCAL FREEDOM — *77.7%*

China has a high income tax rate and a moderate corporate tax rate. The top income tax rate is 45 percent, and the top corporate tax rate is 33 percent. Other taxes include a value-added tax (VAT) and a real estate tax. In the most recent year, overall tax revenue as a percentage of GDP was 15.1 percent.

FREEDOM FROM GOVERNMENT — *88.6%*

Total government expenditures in China, including consumption and transfer payments, are low. In the most recent year, government spending equaled 20.8 percent of GDP, and the government received 3.1 percent of its total revenues from state-owned enterprises and government ownership of property.

MONETARY FREEDOM — *75.5%*

Inflation in China is relatively low, averaging 2.3 percent between 2003 and 2005. Relatively low and stable prices explain most of the monetary freedom score. Roughly 90 percent of traded product prices are determined in the market, but the government maintains prices for petroleum, electricity, pharmaceuticals, coal, agricultural products, and other "essential" goods. Subsidies allow state-owned enterprises to produce and sell goods to wholesalers and retailers at artificially low prices. Consequently, an additional 15 percent is deducted from China's monetary freedom score to adjust for price controls.

INVESTMENT FREEDOM — *30%*

China's accession to the World Trade Organization has improved its operating environment, but weak rule of law, lack of transparency, and a complex approval process are major obstacles to foreign investors. The government allows foreign investment only in specific sectors. The central bank regulates the flow of foreign exchange into and out of the country, and the government controls investment in the stock market. There are extensive controls, government approval requirements, and quantitative limits on foreign exchange, current transfers, and capital transactions. Real estate transactions are subject to government approval.

FINANCIAL FREEDOM — *30%*

China's financial system is complex and tightly controlled by the government. Over 30,000 financial institutions were operating in 2005. The banking sector is the largest part of the financial system and is almost entirely state-owned. Four large state-owned banks account for over 53 percent of banking assets. Non-performing loans are estimated to be much higher than the official figure of 25 percent. The state directs the allocation of credit, and the big four state-owned banks lend primarily to state-owned enterprises. Numerous foreign banks have opened branches but face burdensome regulations. Capital markets are limited and plagued by poor governance and weak regulatory oversight. Foreign participation in capital markets is limited. The number of foreign insurers, who face looser restrictions, has grown rapidly.

PROPERTY RIGHTS — *20%*

China's judicial system is weak. Many companies resort to arbitration because of concerns about the speed and impartiality of the courts. The implementation of court rulings is inconsistent. Even when courts do attempt to enforce decisions, local officials often ignore them with impunity. Corruption is prevalent. New property legislation is on hold because of a strong ideological debate.

FREEDOM FROM CORRUPTION — *32%*

Corruption is perceived as significant. China ranks 78th out of 158 countries in Transparency International's Corruption Perceptions Index for 2005.

LABOR FREEDOM — *63.5%*

The labor market operates under restrictive employment regulations that hinder employment and productivity growth. The non-salary cost of employing a worker is very high, and dismissing a redundant employee can be relatively costly. In general, the capacity to end employment varies widely according to the location and the size of the enterprise. The labor code mandates retraining or replacement before firing a worker.

COLOMBIA

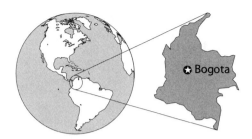

Bogota

Rank: 73

Regional Rank: 18 of 29

Colombia's economy is 60.5 percent free, according to our 2007 assessment, which makes it the world's 73rd freest economy. Its overall score is 2.4 percentage points lower than last year, partially reflecting new methodological detail. Colombia is ranked 18th out of 29 countries in the Americas, and its overall score is equal to the regional average.

Colombia scores moderately well in fiscal freedom and freedom from government and somewhat less well in several other factors. Income and corporate tax rates are high, but tax revenues are relatively low as a percentage of GDP. Government spending is also low, and the state does not receive significant income from government-owned businesses.

Colombia faces some economic challenges. It scores poorly in labor freedom, property rights, and freedom from corruption. Despite nominal openness to foreign investment, regulations are complex and uncertain, making it difficult to move capital into the country. Rule of law is uneven. Business contracts are generally respected, but judicial corruption and an ongoing civil war make an entirely transparent legal process difficult.

BACKGROUND: Colombia is one of South America's oldest continuous democracies. In the 1990s, however, leftist insurgents and paramilitary vigilante groups joined forces with drug traffickers, killing and marauding throughout 60 percent of the countryside. President Alvaro Uribe, who was elected in 2002, has begun to restore order and to demobilize these illegal rural armies. A safer environment for business has helped to cut unemployment by at least 4 percentage points in the past four years. Uribe's next challenge will be to stimulate growth in an economy that relies heavily on exporting petroleum, coffee, and cut flowers and to reduce the number of people living below the poverty line, which now stands at 55 percent.

How Do We Measure Economic Freedom? See Chapter 3 (page 37) for an explanation of the methodology or visit the *Index* Web site at *heritage.org/index.*

The economy is 60.5% free

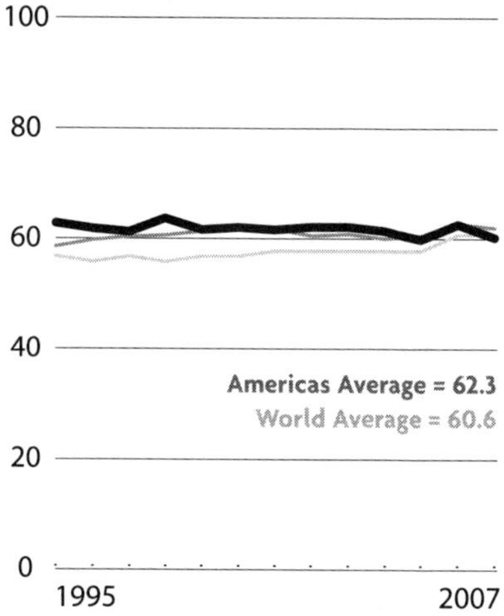

100

80

60

40

Americas Average = 62.3
World Average = 60.6

20

0

1995   2007

QUICK FACTS

Population: 44.9 million

GDP (PPP): $325.9 billion
4.8% growth in 2004
3.0% 5-yr. comp. ann. growth
$7,256 per capita

Unemployment: 13.6%

Inflation (CPI): 5.9%

FDI (net inflow): $2.6 billion

Official Development Assistance:
Multilateral: $62 million
Bilateral: $564 million (70% from the U.S.)

External Debt: $37.7 billion

Exports: $19.5 billion
Primarily petroleum, coffee, coal, apparel, bananas, cut flowers

Imports: $19.9 billion
Primarily industrial equipment, transportation equipment, consumer goods, chemicals, paper products, fuels, electricity

COLOMBIA'S TEN ECONOMIC FREEDOMS

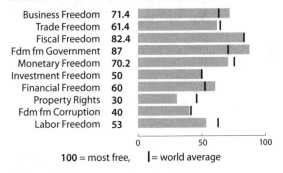

Business Freedom	71.4
Trade Freedom	61.4
Fiscal Freedom	82.4
Fdm fm Government	87
Monetary Freedom	70.2
Investment Freedom	50
Financial Freedom	60
Property Rights	30
Fdm fm Corruption	40
Labor Freedom	53

100 = most free, ❘ = world average

BUSINESS FREEDOM — 71.4%

Starting a business takes an average of 44 days, compared to the world average of 48 days. Entrepreneurship should be easier for maximum job creation. Obtaining a business license is difficult, but closing a business is relatively easy. Bureaucracy remains a barrier to entrepreneurial activities, but there has been some progress in simplifying procedures and eliminating red tape. The overall freedom to start, operate, and close a business is relatively well protected by the national regulatory environment.

TRADE FREEDOM — 61.4%

Colombia's weighted average tariff rate was 9.3 percent in 2004. Significant progress has been made in dismantling non-tariff barriers, but bureaucracy, lack of transparency, import bans and restrictions, price bands, issues involving the enforcement and protection of intellectual property rights, and corruption add to the cost of trade. Consequently, an additional 20 percent is deducted from Colombia's trade freedom score to account for these non-tariff barriers.

FISCAL FREEDOM — 82.4%

Colombia has high tax rates. Both the top income tax rate and the top corporate tax rate are 35 percent. Other taxes include a value-added tax (VAT) and a financial transactions tax. In the most recent year, overall tax revenue as a percentage of GDP was 13.8 percent.

FREEDOM FROM GOVERNMENT — 87%

Total government expenditures, including consumption and transfer payments, are low. In the most recent year, government spending equaled 20.9 percent of GDP, and the government received 8.3 percent of its total revenues from state-owned enterprises and government ownership of property.

MONETARY FREEDOM — 70.2%

Inflation is moderate, averaging 5.5 percent between 2003 and 2005. Relatively moderate and unstable prices explain most of the monetary freedom score. The government maintains prices for ground- and air-transport fares, some pharmaceutical products, petroleum derivatives, natural gas, some petrochemicals, public utility services, residential rents, schoolbooks, and school tuition. To avoid speculation, the Agriculture Ministry may intervene temporarily to freeze the prices of basic foodstuffs through agreements with regional wholesalers. Consequently, an additional 15 percent is deducted from Colombia's monetary freedom score to adjust for measures that distort domestic prices.

INVESTMENT FREEDOM — 50%

Most sectors of the economy are open to foreign investment, except for activities related to national security. Foreign investment in television network and programming companies is capped at 40 percent. The largest obstacles to foreign investment are excessive regulation and constantly changing business rules. Portfolio foreign investment must remain in the country for one year. Residents who work in certain internationally related companies may hold foreign exchange accounts. Payments and transfers must be registered with the central bank and may be subject to approval and quantitative limits. All foreign investment must be registered with the central bank.

FINANCIAL FREEDOM — 60%

Colombia's financial sector is relatively large and sophisticated. The banking sector has undergone significant consolidation and privatization since the 1998–1999 financial crisis. The government has strengthened regulations and seized some banks for falling below solvency requirements. All financial institutions nationalized during the crisis were privatized or liquidated by mid-2006 except for the state-owned Granbanco-Bancafé. A few conglomerates are emerging to take advantage of reforms that permit universal banking, and two groups accounted for 58 percent of financial sector assets in 2005. Foreign companies have a substantial presence in the insurance sector. An extensive informal credit market exists. Foreign investors face few restrictions in Colombia's small equity markets. There is a 4 percent tax on financial transactions through 2007.

PROPERTY RIGHTS — 30%

Corruption is present in the lowest levels of the judiciary and civil service, but contracts are generally respected. A reform approved in 2004 will shift the criminal system to a U.S.-style prosecutorial system. Arbitration is complex and dilatory, especially with regard to the enforcement of awards. Terrorism is a serious problem in some areas of the country.

FREEDOM FROM CORRUPTION — 40%

Corruption is perceived as significant. Colombia ranks 55th out of 158 countries in Transparency International's Corruption Perceptions Index for 2005.

LABOR FREEDOM — 53%

The labor market operates under restrictive employment regulations that hinder employment and productivity growth. The non-salary cost of employing a worker is high, but dismissing a redundant employee can be relatively costless. The unemployment insurance program consists of a mandatory individual severance account system. Individuals receive a month's worth of wages for each year of employment, with the option of making authorized withdrawals from one's account in certain situations.

CONGO, DEMOCRATIC REPUBLIC OF (FORMERLY ZAIRE)

Kinshasa

Rank: Not Ranked

Regional Rank: Not Ranked

The economic freedom of the Democratic Republic of Congo (DRC) cannot be graded because of the violence and chaos of recent years. The last time the DRC was graded was in 2000, when it received a score of 26.4 percent.

BACKGROUND: The Democratic Republic of Congo, despite a large population and abundant resources, is among the world's poorest countries, with most of the population engaged in subsistence agriculture. Aided by Rwandan and Ugandan troops, Laurent Kabila overthrew Mobutu Sese Seko's government in 1997. When those troops refused to leave and sought to oust Kabila, troops from Angola, Namibia, and Zimbabwe intervened. After Kabila's 2001 assassination, his son assumed power and set up a transitional government. The elections scheduled for July 2006 were the first in 40 years. Instability continues, corruption remains endemic, and the infrastructure is very poor.

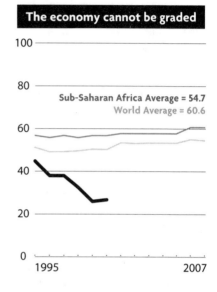

The economy cannot be graded

Sub-Saharan Africa Average = 54.7
World Average = 60.6

1995 — 2007

QUICK FACTS

Population: 55.9 million

GDP (PPP): $39.4 billion
6.9% growth in 2004
1.3% 5-yr. comp. ann. growth
$705 per capita

Unemployment: n/a

Inflation (CPI): 4.1%

FDI (net inflow): $900 million (gross)

Official Development Assistance:
Multilateral: $685 million
Bilateral: $1.2 billion (16% from the U.S.)

External Debt: $11.8 billion

Exports: $1.8 billion (2004 estimate)
Primarily diamonds, copper, crude oil, coffee, cobalt

Imports: $2.1 billion (2004 estimate)
Primarily food, mining and other machinery, transport equipment, fuels

How Do We Measure Economic Freedom? See Chapter 3 (page 37) for an explanation of the methodology or visit the *Index* Web site at *heritage.org/index*.

BUSINESS FREEDOM — NOT GRADED

Starting a business takes an average of 155 days, compared to the world average of 48 days. Entrepreneurship should be easier for maximum job creation. Obtaining a business license takes about 300 days and involves 16 different procedures. The overall freedom to start, operate, and close a business is restricted by the national regulatory environment.

TRADE FREEDOM — NOT GRADED

The Democratic Republic of Congo's weighted average tariff rate was 12.8 percent in 2003. Most of the country's trade barriers result from complex regulations, a multiplicity of administrative agencies, and a frequent lack of professionalism and control by officials who are responsible for their enforcement.

FISCAL FREEDOM — NOT GRADED

The Democratic Republic of Congo has high tax rates. The top income tax rate is 50 percent, and the top corporate tax rate is 40 percent. Other taxes include a sales tax and a tax on vehicles.

FREEDOM FROM GOVERNMENT — NOT GRADED

Total government expenditures in the Democratic Republic of Congo, including consumption and transfer payments, are low. In the most recent year, government spending equaled 15.3 percent of GDP.

MONETARY FREEDOM — NOT GRADED

Inflation in the Democratic Republic of Congo is high, averaging 16.3 percent between 2003 and 2005. Relatively unstable prices explain most of the monetary freedom score. While important structural measures have recently been implemented, including the liberalization of most prices, some prices are still controlled to some degree through the public sector.

INVESTMENT FREEDOM — NOT GRADED

War, economic and political instability, corruption, and anti-market policy decisions have deterred foreign investment. The execution of routine transactions through official bodies is fraught with difficulty. Political interference and the local cartels obstruct foreign investment. Nevertheless, foreign direct investment has increased in the years since the establishment of the transitional government, which has managed to make some progress in restoring peace. There are no restrictions on foreign exchange accounts for the credit or debit of international transactions for either residents or non-residents.

FINANCIAL FREEDOM — NOT GRADED

The banking system is unstable, and operations of the banks that continue to function have been hurt by war and political instability, frequent policy changes, unpredictable monetary policy and hyperinflation, and unrecoverable loans. Bank formation faces significant barriers, and the viability of the financial system depends on progress in establishing peace broadly through the country. Most banks act as financial agents for the government or extend credit to international institutions operating in the country. In 2005, there were 12 functioning commercial banks, half of which were undergoing extensive restructuring. Another nine banks are in process of liquidation. Larger banks are mostly subsidiaries of foreign banks. Supervision of banks is very poor, and most banks fail to meet basic prudential standards. Most credit is informal, although there is a growing network of microfinance and credit institutions. There is no stock exchange.

PROPERTY RIGHTS — NOT GRADED

Private property is not secure. Local conflicts are common, and fighting, banditry, and abuses of human rights threaten property rights and deter economic activity. Courts suffer from widespread corruption, the public administration is not reliable, and both expatriates and nationals are subject to selective application of a complex legal code. BBC News reports that the government has no control over large parts of the country.

FREEDOM FROM CORRUPTION — NOT GRADED

Corruption is perceived as widespread. The Democratic Republic of Congo ranks 144th out of 158 countries in Transparency International's Corruption Perceptions Index for 2005.

LABOR FREEDOM — NOT GRADED

The labor market operates under highly restrictive employment regulations that hinder employment and productivity growth. The non-salary cost of employing a worker is low, but dismissing a redundant employee is costly. Employment in the formal sector remains negligible as the informal sector dominates the economy.

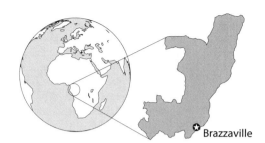

CONGO, REPUBLIC OF

Brazzaville

Rank: 151

Regional Rank: 39 of 40

The Republic of Congo's economy is 43 percent free, according to our 2007 assessment, which makes it the world's 151st freest economy. Its overall score is 0.6 percentage point lower than last year, partially reflecting new methodological detail but mostly reflecting reduced corruption. Congo is ranked 39th out of 40 countries in the sub-Saharan Africa region, and its overall score is lower than the regional average.

Congo does not rank strongly in any category, but it does score moderately well in monetary freedom and fiscal freedom. The top income tax rate is 50 percent, but the top corporate tax rate is a more moderate 38 percent, and overall tax revenue is relatively small as a percentage of GDP. Very low inflation and stable prices give Congo a positive monetary score; however, the government interferes extensively with market prices.

Congo is beset by substantial economic problems. Investment freedom, financial freedom, property rights, freedom from corruption, and labor freedom all score poorly. Significant restrictions on foreign investment combine with domestic regulations and an inflexible labor market to create a business-hostile climate. The weak rule of law jeopardizes the protection of property rights, and corruption is a problem.

BACKGROUND: Congo's parliament is controlled by allies of President Denis Sassou-Nguesso, who seized power in 1997 and won the 2002 election. Demobilization and disarmament efforts continue under the 2003 peace accord between the government and most rebel groups. Slow progress has been made toward a more market-oriented economy, but poor infrastructure, onerous regulation, and high labor, energy, and transportation costs discourage investment. Transparency has improved in the oil sector, and the government has promised to improve accountability and financial disclosure. Oil accounted for 55 percent of GDP, 95 percent of exports, and the preponderance of government revenue in 2004.

How Do We Measure Economic Freedom? See Chapter 3 (page 37) for an explanation of the methodology or visit the *Index* Web site at *heritage.org/index*.

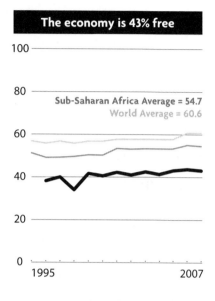

The economy is 43% free

Sub-Saharan Africa Average = 54.7
World Average = 60.6

QUICK FACTS

Population: 3.9 million

GDP (PPP): $3.8 billion
3.6% growth in 2004
4.2% 5-yr. comp. ann. growth
$978 per capita

Unemployment: n/a

Inflation (CPI): 1.7%

FDI (net inflow): $668 million (gross)

Official Development Assistance:
Multilateral: $84 million
Bilateral: $80 million (0.4% from the U.S.)

External Debt: $5.8 billion

Exports: $1.5 billion
Primarily petroleum, lumber, plywood, sugar, cocoa, coffee, diamonds

Imports: $994.8 million
Primarily capital equipment, construction materials, food

REPUBLIC OF CONGO'S TEN ECONOMIC FREEDOMS

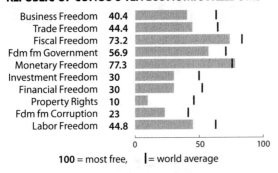

Business Freedom	40.4
Trade Freedom	44.4
Fiscal Freedom	73.2
Fdm fm Government	56.9
Monetary Freedom	77.3
Investment Freedom	30
Financial Freedom	30
Property Rights	10
Fdm fm Corruption	23
Labor Freedom	44.8

0   50   100

100 = most free, | = world average

BUSINESS FREEDOM — 40.4%

Starting a business takes an average of 71 days, compared to the world average of 48 days. Entrepreneurship should be easier for maximum job creation. Obtaining a business license is very difficult, but closing a business is relatively easy. The lack of legal and regulatory transparency impedes the creation of new businesses. The overall freedom to start, operate, and close a business is seriously limited by the national regulatory environment.

TRADE FREEDOM — 44.4%

Congo's weighted average tariff rate was 17.8 percent in 2002. The most significant non-tariff barriers include restrictive import licensing rules, red tape, an inefficient customs service, and corruption. Consequently, an additional 20 percent is deducted from Congo's trade freedom score to account for these non-tariff barriers.

FISCAL FREEDOM — 73.2%

Congo has a very high income tax rate and a high corporate tax rate. The top income tax rate is 50 percent, and the top corporate tax rate is 38 percent. Other taxes include a value-added tax (VAT), a tax on rental values, and an apprenticeship tax. In the most recent year, overall tax revenue as a percentage of GDP was 8.7 percent.

FREEDOM FROM GOVERNMENT — 56.9%

Total government expenditures in Congo, including consumption and transfer payments, are moderate. In the most recent year, government spending equaled 28.6 percent of GDP, and the government received 71.9 percent of its total revenues from state-owned enterprises and government ownership of property.

MONETARY FREEDOM — 77.3%

Inflation in Congo is relatively low, averaging 1.5 percent between 2003 and 2005. Relatively low and stable prices explain most of the monetary freedom score. The government maintains prices through ownership and subsidization of the large public sector, which affects rail transport, telecommunications, electricity, water, and other goods and services. Consequently, an additional 15 percent is deducted from Congo's monetary freedom score to adjust for measures that distort domestic prices.

INVESTMENT FREEDOM — 30%

In 2003, Congress approved a bill to attract foreign investors in the mining sector. Investments of over CFAF 100 million require the approval of the Ministry of Economy, Finance, and Budget within 30 days unless they involve the creation of a mixed public–private-ownership enterprise. Residents may not hold foreign exchange accounts, but companies can hold foreign exchange accounts with special approval. Non-residents may hold foreign exchange accounts subject to government approval. Payments and transfers to most countries are subject to documentation requirements. Capital transactions to most countries require exchange control approval and are restricted.

FINANCIAL FREEDOM — 30%

Congo's financial sector is small, underdeveloped, and hindered by instability. Congo is a member of the Central African Economic and Monetary Community along with five other countries. These countries share a common central bank, the Banque des Etats de l'Afrique Centrale, and a common currency pegged to the euro. A joint banking commission (Commission bancaire de l'Afrique Centrale) regulates Congo's commercial banks. The regulator considered only two of Congo's four banks to be in good condition, one to be in fragile condition, and the fourth to be critical at the end of 2004. The government has sold the healthy assets of three state banks to private investors. It has taken over the fourth bank but plans to reprivatize it after it has been recapitalized. The state is still dealing with non-performing loans accumulated by state-owned banks before privatization because of poor management and political interference.

PROPERTY RIGHTS — 10%

The war in the late 1990s reduced the country to chaos. The judiciary is corrupted, overburdened, underfinanced, and subject to political influence and bribery. Lack of resources continues to be a severe problem; the civil war left the country with almost no judicial records. Security of contracts and the enforcement of justice cannot be guaranteed through the slow-moving justice system.

FREEDOM FROM CORRUPTION — 23%

Corruption is perceived as widespread. The Republic of Congo ranks 130th out of 158 countries in Transparency International's Corruption Perceptions Index for 2005.

LABOR FREEDOM — 44.8%

The labor market operates under highly restrictive employment regulations that hinder employment and productivity growth. The non-salary cost of employing a worker is high, but dismissing a redundant employee can be relatively costless. There are very rigid restrictions on increasing or contracting the number of working hours. The Republic of Congo's labor flexibility is one of the lowest in the world.

COSTA RICA

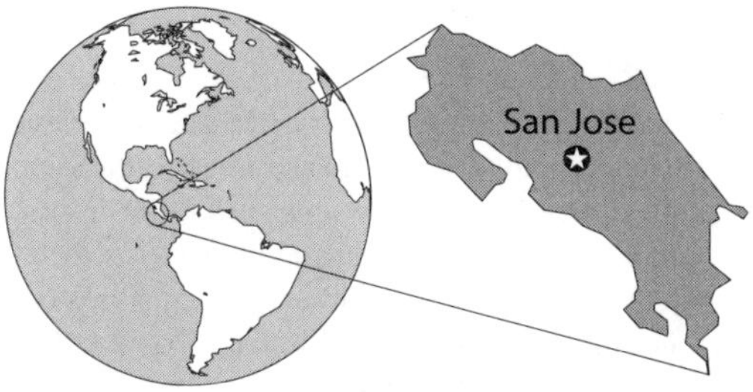

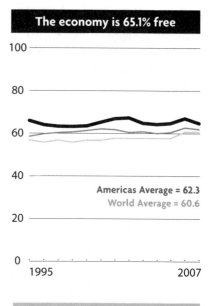

San Jose

Rank: 51

Regional Rank: 12 of 29

Costa Rica's economy is 65.1 percent free, according to our 2007 assessment, which makes it the world's 51st freest economy. Its overall score is 2.3 percentage points lower than last year, partially reflecting new methodological detail. Costa Rica is ranked 12th out of 29 countries in the Americas, and its overall score is higher than the regional average.

Costa Rica receives high scores in fiscal freedom and freedom from government. It has moderate personal and corporate tax rates, and tax revenue is fairly low as a percentage of GDP. Similarly, government expenditures are reasonable, and state-owned businesses are not a significant source of revenue. Costa Rica also receives moderate scores in other factors, such as trade freedom, where it boasts a low average tariff rate.

Although there are no glaring absences of freedom in the economy, Costa Rica could improve its monetary freedom, financial freedom, and property rights. Also, it takes far longer than the global average to start a business, and bankruptcy procedures are difficult. State-owned banks dominate the financial sector, over which there is significant government control. The court system, while transparent and not corrupt, is extremely time-consuming and complicated.

BACKGROUND: Costa Rica's democratic government is one of the few in Latin America to have a sound system of checks and balances, and its economy is generally business-friendly. However, Costa Rica also has a bloated public sector, including state monopolies in telecommunications, utilities, petroleum refining, banking, insurance, and social security pensions. President Oscar Arias, who narrowly won a second term in February 2006, has pledged to balance the budget and to guide Costa Rica's entrance into the Dominican Republic–Central America Free Trade Agreement (DR–CAFTA) with the United States.

How Do We Measure Economic Freedom? See Chapter 3 (page 37) for an explanation of the methodology or visit the *Index* Web site at *heritage.org/index*.

The economy is 65.1% free

100

80

60

40

Americas Average = 62.3
World Average = 60.6

20

0

1995   2007

QUICK FACTS

Population: 4.3 million

GDP (PPP): $40.3 billion
    4.1% growth in 2004
    3.2% 5-yr. comp. ann. growth
    $9,481 per capita

Unemployment: 6.6% (2005 estimate)

Inflation (CPI): 12.3%

FDI (net inflow): $555.8 million

Official Development Assistance:
Multilateral: $13 million
Bilateral: $64 million (6% from the U.S.)

External Debt: $5.7 billion

Exports: $8.6 billion
Primarily coffee, bananas, sugar, pineapples, textiles, electronic components, medical equipment

Imports: $9.1 billion
Primarily raw materials, consumer goods, capital equipment, petroleums

COSTA RICA'S TEN ECONOMIC FREEDOMS

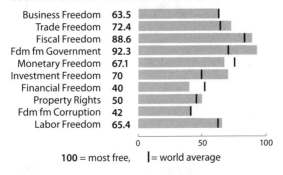

Business Freedom	63.5
Trade Freedom	72.4
Fiscal Freedom	88.6
Fdm fm Government	92.3
Monetary Freedom	67.1
Investment Freedom	70
Financial Freedom	40
Property Rights	50
Fdm fm Corruption	42
Labor Freedom	65.4

0   50   100

100 = most free, | = world average

BUSINESS FREEDOM — 63.5%
Starting a business takes an average of 77 days, compared to the world average of 48 days. Entrepreneurship should be easier for maximum job creation. Obtaining a business license is relatively simple, but closing a business is difficult. Commercial regulations and practices are generally transparent and foster competition. Bureaucratic procedures are often long and discourage entrepreneurial activities. The overall freedom to start, operate, and close a business is limited by the national regulatory environment.

TRADE FREEDOM — 72.4%
Costa Rica's weighted average tariff rate was 3.8 percent in 2004. An electronic "one-stop" import and export window and other recent improvements have significantly reduced the time required for customs processing, but customs procedures remain complex and bureaucratic. Sanitary and phytosanitary requirements, which can be cumbersome and lengthy, and issues involving the enforcement and protection of intellectual property rights add to the cost of trade. Consequently, an additional 20 percent is deducted from Costa Rica's trade freedom score to account for these non-tariff barriers.

FISCAL FREEDOM — 88.6%
Costa Rica has moderate tax rates. The top income tax rate is 25 percent, and the top corporate tax rate is 30 percent. Other taxes include a value-added tax (VAT) and a tax on interest. In the most recent year, overall tax revenue as a percentage of GDP was 13.4 percent.

FREEDOM FROM GOVERNMENT — 92.3%
Total government expenditures in Costa Rica, including consumption and transfer payments, are moderate. In the most recent year, government spending equaled 16.6 percent of GDP, and the government received 3.9 percent of its total revenues from state-owned enterprises and government ownership of property.

MONETARY FREEDOM — 67.1%
Inflation in Costa Rica is relatively high, averaging 13 percent between 2003 and 2005. Relatively high and unstable prices explain most of the monetary freedom score. The government applies price controls to all goods on a basic consumption list, including energy, petroleum, telecommunications, and water. Consequently, an additional 10 percent is deducted from Costa Rica's monetary freedom score to adjust for measures that distort domestic prices.

INVESTMENT FREEDOM — 70%
Costa Rica offers one of Central America's better investment climates, and foreign investors are treated the same as domestic investors. A few sectors, such as insurance, telecommunications, hydrocarbons, and radioactive materials, are reserved for state companies. There are no restrictions on land purchases, although the government has been known to expropriate land owned by foreign investors. There are no controls on capital flows, but reporting requirements are mandatory for some transactions. There are no restrictions or controls on the holding of foreign exchange accounts by either residents or non-residents.

FINANCIAL FREEDOM — 40%
Costa Rica's financial system is subject to extensive government influence. While private banks may operate freely, state-owned banks dominate the sector and account for over 58 percent of banking sector assets. About half of private banks are owned by foreign investors from Latin America or North America. Nearly all Costa Rican banks have significant offshore banking operations. The government retains considerable influence over lending. The insurance sector is monopolized by the state-owned Instituto Nacional de Seguros, although other institutions may sell policies underwritten by the INS. Foreign insurance companies are restricted in their ability to offer services. The government has partially privatized the pension system. Capital markets are small, and trading mostly involves short-term government debt.

PROPERTY RIGHTS — 50%
The judicial system can be slow and complicated. Contracts are generally upheld, and investments are secure, but a legal complaint filed over a contract takes an average of more than one and a half years to resolve. The process to resolve squatter cases through the courts can be especially cumbersome. The legal owner of land is at a disadvantage in a system that quickly recognizes rights acquired by squatters, especially when the disputed land is rural and not being worked actively.

FREEDOM FROM CORRUPTION — 42%
Corruption is perceived as present. Costa Rica ranks 51st out of 158 countries in Transparency International's Corruption Perceptions Index for 2005.

LABOR FREEDOM — 65.4%
The labor market operates under relatively flexible employment regulations that need to improve for employment and productivity growth. The non-salary cost of employing a worker is high, but dismissing a redundant employee is relatively costless. There are inflexible restrictions on increasing and contracting working hours.

CROATIA

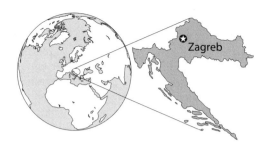

Zagreb

Rank: 109

Regional Rank: 37 of 41

Croatia's economy is 55.3 percent free, according to our 2007 assessment, which makes it the world's 109th freest economy. Its overall score is 0.9 percentage point lower than last year, partially reflecting new methodological detail. Croatia is ranked 37th out of 41 countries in the European region, and its overall score is below the regional average.

Croatia scores well in trade freedom and in monetary freedom. Although the top income tax rate is high, the corporate tax rate is low, and total tax revenue is not unreasonably high as a percentage of GDP. Inflation is low, and prices are fairly stable, but Croatia's monetary freedom score is hurt by lingering government price manipulations.

Croatia is recovering from a decade-long civil war. Freedom from government, investment freedom, property rights, and freedom from corruption are all low-scoring areas. Government expenditures are extremely high, and significant state regulation impedes the easy flow of commerce. The court system is prone to corruption, political interference, and inefficient bureaucracy, and some investors prefer to seek international arbitration. Significant unofficial restrictions on foreign investment, such as highly politicized decision-making, exist for those investors willing to brave Croatia's regulatory maze.

BACKGROUND: Croatia's hopes of beginning accession talks with the European Union have risen since the arraignment of Ante Gotovina, a Croatian general accused of war crimes, before the International Criminal Tribunal for the Former Yugoslavia. Recent efforts at economic reform have met with some success. Two-thirds of the economy is privatized, and banking assets are 90 percent privately owned. Organized crime is less prevalent in Croatia than in other Balkan countries, but other problems remain to be solved. The EU, for example, views the need for judicial reform as the central long-term obstacle to Croatia's possible membership.

How Do We Measure Economic Freedom? See Chapter 3 (page 37) for an explanation of the methodology or visit the *Index* Web site at *heritage.org/index*.

The economy is 55.3% free

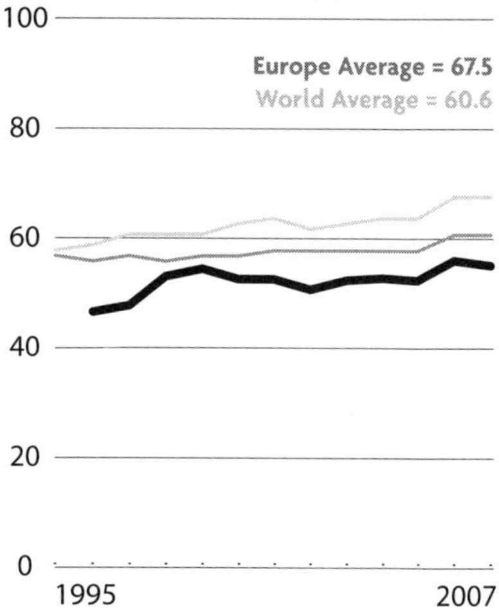

Europe Average = 67.5
World Average = 60.6

(Chart: economic freedom score from 1995 to 2007, y-axis 0 to 100)

QUICK FACTS

Population: 4.4 million

GDP (PPP): $54.2 billion
3.8% growth in 2004
4.1% 5-yr. comp. ann. growth
$12,191 per capita

Unemployment: 18.7%

Inflation (CPI): 2.1%

FDI (net inflow): $762.6 million

Official Development Assistance:
Multilateral: $32 million
Bilateral: $108 million (43% from the U.S.)

External Debt: $31.6 billion

Exports: $17.8 billion
Primarily transport equipment, textiles, chemicals, food, fuels

Imports: $20.2 billion
Primarily machinery, transport and electrical equipment, chemicals, fuels and lubricants, food

CROATIA'S TEN ECONOMIC FREEDOMS

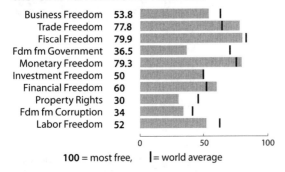

Business Freedom	53.8
Trade Freedom	77.8
Fiscal Freedom	79.9
Fdm fm Government	36.5
Monetary Freedom	79.3
Investment Freedom	50
Financial Freedom	60
Property Rights	30
Fdm fm Corruption	34
Labor Freedom	52

0   50   100

100 = most free, **|** = world average

BUSINESS FREEDOM — *53.8%*

Starting a business takes an average of 45 days, compared to the world average of 48 days. Entrepreneurship should be easier for maximum job creation. Obtaining a business license is very difficult, and closing a business is difficult. Bureaucratic obstacles remain onerous, as burdensome administrative regulations challenge new entrepreneurs. The overall freedom to start, operate, and close a business is restricted by the national regulatory environment.

TRADE FREEDOM — *77.8%*

Croatia's weighted average tariff rate was 1.1 percent in 2005. Non-tariff barriers include customs corruption and strict testing and certification requirements for some imports. Consequently, an additional 20 percent is deducted from Croatia's trade freedom score to account for these non-tariff barriers.

FISCAL FREEDOM — *79.9%*

Croatia has a high income tax rate but a low corporate tax rate. The top income tax rate is 45 percent, and the top corporate tax rate is 20 percent. The government also imposes a value-added tax (VAT). In the most recent year, overall tax revenue as a percentage of GDP was 24.2 percent.

FREEDOM FROM GOVERNMENT — *36.5%*

Total government expenditures in Croatia, including consumption and transfer payments, are very high. In the most recent year, government spending equaled 51.6 percent of GDP, and the government received 4.1 percent of its total revenues from state-owned enterprises and government ownership of property. Privatization has progressed slowly.

MONETARY FREEDOM — *79.3%*

Inflation in Croatia is relatively low, averaging 2.9 percent between 2003 and 2005. Relatively low and stable prices explain most of the monetary freedom score. Many price supports and subsidies have been eliminated, but price changes on some 30 products must be submitted for approval to the Ministry of Economy. For example, the Ministry must be notified two weeks in advance of price changes for milk and bread. Consequently, an additional 10 percent is deducted from Croatia's monetary freedom score.

INVESTMENT FREEDOM — *50%*

Foreign investors have the same rights and status as domestic investors and may invest in nearly every sector of the economy, but unofficial barriers persist. Because of a complex bureaucracy and lack of transparency, personal and political loyalty can trump economic merit when it comes to establishing a new investment. Foreigners may purchase real estate only with permission from the government. Both residents and non-residents are allowed to hold foreign exchange accounts, but numerous limitations exist, and government approval is required in certain instances. Some capital transactions, such as inward portfolio investment, are subject to limitations and conditions set by the Ministry of Finance.

FINANCIAL FREEDOM — *60%*

Croatia's financial system is stable and competitive. There were 34 commercial banks and four savings banks in 2005. Two national commercial banks (Zagrebacka Banka and Privredna Banka Zagreb) are majority foreign-owned and control over 40 percent of banking assets. The government owns over 98 percent of Hrvatska Poštanska Banka (the largest domestic bank) and the Croatian Bank for Reconstruction and Development. Many banking assets are foreign-owned, and newly adopted financial regulations harmonize with European Union standards. The insurance sector is small but highly competitive. The partially state-owned Croatia Osiguranje is the largest player in the insurance sector, accounting for over 40 percent of assets. The stock exchange has been growing rapidly, and securities markets are open to foreign investors.

PROPERTY RIGHTS — *30%*

The court system is cumbersome and inefficient. Very long case backlogs mean that business disputes can go unresolved for years; some investors have chosen to insist that contract arbitration take place outside of Croatia. The government of Croatia has made a commitment to reinvigorate its efforts to reform the judiciary, but much remains to be done. The judicial system is one of the areas that are most affected by corruption.

FREEDOM FROM CORRUPTION — *34%*

Corruption is perceived as significant. Croatia ranks 70th out of 158 countries in Transparency International's Corruption Perceptions Index for 2005.

LABOR FREEDOM — *52%*

The labor market operates under restrictive employment regulations that hinder employment and productivity growth. The non-salary cost of employing a worker is high, and dismissing a redundant employee is relatively costly. High wage costs and rigid labor laws impede business activities. The labor code mandates retraining or replacement before firing a worker.

CUBA

Havana

Rank: 156

Regional Rank: 29 of 29

Cuba's economy is 29.7 percent free, according to our 2007 assessment, which makes it the world's 156th freest economy. Its overall score is 2.5 percentage points lower than last year, partially reflecting new methodological detail. Cuba is ranked 29th out of 29 countries in the Americas, and its overall score is so low that it is less than half of the regional average.

As an avowedly Marxist state, Cuba scores relatively well in very few areas of economic freedom. Havana performs least egregiously in trade freedom and monetary freedom. Cuba has a moderate average tariff of 10 percent but very restrictive non-tariff barriers to trade. Inflation is moderate, but government efforts to control all kinds of prices are pervasive.

Business freedom, investment freedom, financial freedom, property rights, freedom from corruption, and labor freedom are all weak. In theory, Communist nations dictate central economic policy, and Cuba aims to fulfill this in practice. All aspects of business operations are tightly controlled and government-dominated, and the private sector is very small. There are no courts independent of political interference, and private property (particularly land) is strictly regulated by the state.

BACKGROUND: Cuba is a one-party Communist state with a command economy that depends heavily on external assistance and a captive labor force. The Castro government, in power since 1959, restricts basic human rights, such as freedom of expression, and has detained hundreds of political prisoners in harsh conditions. Little reliable, independent information on the economy is available, and official figures on per capita GDP may not reflect actual income. Venezuela supplies Cuba with up to 80,000 barrels of oil per day, and its assistance has enabled Cuba to retreat on limited reforms undertaken in the mid-1990s.

How Do We Measure Economic Freedom? See Chapter 3 (page 37) for an explanation of the methodology or visit the *Index* Web site at *heritage.org/index*.

The economy is 29.7% free

Americas Average = 62.3
World Average = 60.6

100
80
60
40
20
0

1995   2007

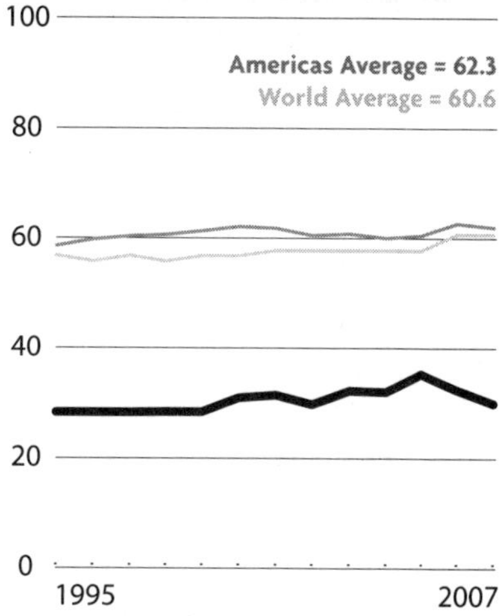

QUICK FACTS

Population: 11.2 million

GDP (PPP): $39.2 billion (2005 estimate)
n/a
n/a
$3,500 per capita (2005 estimate)

Unemployment: 1.9% (2004 estimate)

Inflation (CPI): 1.3%

FDI (net inflow): $2.0 million (gross)

Official Development Assistance:
Multilateral: $20 million
Bilateral: $73 million (14% from the U.S.)

External Debt: $12.0 billion (2004 estimate)

Exports: $2.2 billion
Primarily sugar, nickel, tobacco, fish, medical products, citrus, coffee

Imports: $5.6 billion
Primarily petroleum, food, machinery and equipment, chemicals

CUBA'S TEN ECONOMIC FREEDOMS

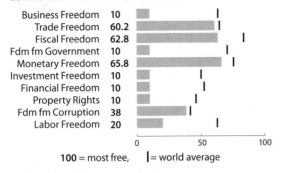

Business Freedom	10
Trade Freedom	60.2
Fiscal Freedom	62.8
Fdm fm Government	10
Monetary Freedom	65.8
Investment Freedom	10
Financial Freedom	10
Property Rights	10
Fdm fm Corruption	38
Labor Freedom	20

0   50   100

100 = most free, | = world average

BUSINESS FREEDOM — *10%*

Cuba's government controls and regulates the entire economy, and private entrepreneurship exists only on a very small scale. The inconsistent and non-transparent application of government regulations impedes the creation of new businesses. The overall freedom to start, operate, and close a business is seriously limited by the national regulatory environment.

TRADE FREEDOM — *60.2%*

Cuba's weighted average tariff rate was 9.9 percent in 2004. Procedures for the allocation of hard currency and centralizing of imports have resulted in delays and bottlenecks, and customs corruption is common. Consequently, an additional 20 percent is deducted from Cuba's trade freedom score to account for these non-tariff barriers.

FISCAL FREEDOM — *62.8%*

Cuba has a high income tax rate and a moderate corporate tax rate. The top income tax rate is 50 percent, and the top corporate tax rate is 35 percent.

FREEDOM FROM GOVERNMENT — *10%*

Total government expenditures in Cuba, including consumption and transfer payments, are very high. In the most recent year, government spending equaled 59.7 percent of GDP. The state produces most economic output and employs most of the labor force. The industrial and services sectors are largely dominated by the state. Revenues from state-owned enterprises are used to finance social spending and new public investment programs.

MONETARY FREEDOM — *65.8%*

Inflation in Cuba is moderate, averaging 5 percent between 2003 and 2005. Relatively moderate prices explain most of the monetary freedom score. The government determines prices for most goods and services and subsidizes much of the economy (although the retail sector has some private and black market activity that is not government-controlled). Consequently, an additional 20 percent is deducted from Cuba's monetary freedom score to adjust for measures that distort domestic prices.

INVESTMENT FREEDOM — *10%*

The government maintains exchange controls. All investments must be approved by the government, and licensing is required for all businesses. Cuba has recently backtracked on limited liberalization of foreign investment. The government has revised the terms for business licenses to include "social objectives" and has erected other deterrents to investment, such as delaying payments from Cuban enterprises, imposing onerous regulations, and increasing operating costs. Some restrictions have been loosened to permit investment commitments and credit lines from China and Venezuela.

FINANCIAL FREEDOM — *10%*

Cuba has increased freedom in the financial sector incrementally over the past decade, but the government remains firmly in control. The Cuban peso is used as the domestic currency, and a separate convertible peso is used as "hard" currency for foreign exchange and non-essential retail. A 2003 law requires that transactions between Cuban enterprises must be carried out in convertible pesos rather than U.S. dollars. Over a dozen foreign banks have opened representative offices but are not allowed to operate freely. The government established a central bank in 1997 and converted the Banco Nacional de Cuba into one of a new set of state banks. Central bank authority was enhanced in 2005 to more control the use of hard currency and convertible pesos more closely. Credit and insurance markets are heavily controlled by the central government.

PROPERTY RIGHTS — *10%*

Private ownership of land and productive capital by Cuban citizens is limited to farming and self-employment. The constitution explicitly subordinates the courts to the National Assembly of People's Power (NAPP) and the Council of State, which is headed by President Fidel Castro. The NAPP and its lower-level counterparts choose all judges. The law and trial practices do not meet international standards for fair public trials.

FREEDOM FROM CORRUPTION — *38%*

Corruption is perceived as significant. Cuba ranks 59th out of 158 countries in Transparency International's Corruption Perceptions Index for 2005.

LABOR FREEDOM — *20%*

The labor market operates under highly rigid employment regulations that hinder employment and productivity growth. The formal labor market is not fully developed, and the rigid labor market controlled by the government has contributed to creating a large informal economy that employs considerable labor.

CYPRUS (GREEK)

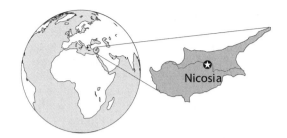

Nicosia

The economy of Cyprus is 73.1 percent free, according to our 2007 assessment, which makes it the world's 20th freest economy. Its overall score is 0.2 percentage point lower than last year, partially reflecting new methodological detail. Cyprus is ranked 12th out of 41 countries in the European region, and its overall score is higher than the regional average.

Cyprus scores highly in property rights, fiscal freedom, monetary freedom, trade freedom, labor freedom, business freedom, and financial freedom. The judiciary is independent of corruption or political influence from the executive. The labor market is relatively flexible, with moderate severance packages and unemployment benefits. The country's inflation and average tariff rates are low, although its monetary and trade freedom scores are muted by the government's adherence to the standard EU subsidies of agriculture. Starting, operating, and closing a business are all relatively easy. The Cypriot financial market is diverse, sound, and open to foreign competition.

Freedom from government and investment freedom could be improved. Total government expenditures are very high, amounting to more than two-fifths of the country's GDP. Foreign investment is deterred by government scrutiny, and certain sectors of the Cypriot economy are off-limits.

BACKGROUND: The Greek Cypriot economy is dominated by the service sector, especially tourism and financial services. The desire to meet EU requirements has helped to liberalize the economy. Since EU accession, Greek Cypriot fiscal policy has focused on consolidating the budget to prepare for entry into the Economic and Monetary Union, the central bank has sped the liberalization of capital flows, and government control of the economy has declined to around 25 percent. The government, however, enjoys significant trade union support and is unlikely to privatize remaining state-owned companies such as airports, power utilities, or the Cyprus Telecommunications Authority.

How Do We Measure Economic Freedom? See Chapter 3 (page 37) for an explanation of the methodology or visit the *Index* Web site at *heritage.org/index.*

The economy is 73.1% free

Europe Average = 67.5
World Average = 60.6

1995 — 2007

QUICK FACTS

Population: 0.8 million

GDP (PPP): $18.8 billion
3.9% growth in 2004
3.4% 5-yr. comp. ann. growth
$22,805 per capita

Unemployment: 3.7%

Inflation (CPI): 2.3%

FDI (net inflow): $516.4 million

Official Development Assistance:
Multilateral: $32 million
Bilateral: $33 million (46% from the U.S.)

External Debt: $10.5 billion (2005 estimate)

Exports: $7.4 billion
Primarily citrus, potatoes, pharmaceuticals, cement, clothing, cigarettes

Imports: $7.9 billion
Primarily consumer goods, petroleum and lubricants, intermediate goods, machinery, transport equipment

CYPRUS'S TEN ECONOMIC FREEDOMS

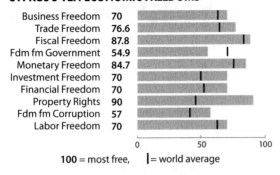

Business Freedom	70
Trade Freedom	76.6
Fiscal Freedom	87.8
Fdm fm Government	54.9
Monetary Freedom	84.7
Investment Freedom	70
Financial Freedom	70
Property Rights	90
Fdm fm Corruption	57
Labor Freedom	70

0   50   100

100 = most free, | = world average

BUSINESS FREEDOM — 70%

Establishing a business in Cyprus is relatively easy because regulations have been streamlined in recent years. Existing regulations affecting business are transparent and applied with consistency. Cyprus has been pursuing policies designed to maintain a favorable business environment and support private initiative. The overall freedom to start, operate, and close a business is relatively well protected by the national regulatory environment.

TRADE FREEDOM — 76.6%

Cyprus's trade policy is the same as those of other members of the European Union. The common EU weighted average tariff rate was 1.7 percent in 2005. Various non-tariff barriers are reflected in EU and Cypriot policy, including agricultural and manufacturing subsidies, regulatory and licensing restrictions, and other market access restrictions. Consequently, an additional 20 percent is deducted from Cyprus's trade freedom score to account for these non-tariff barriers.

FISCAL FREEDOM — 87.8%

Cyprus has a moderate income tax rate and a very low corporate tax rate. The top income tax rate is 30 percent, and the top corporate tax rate is 10 percent. Other taxes include a value-added tax (VAT) and a real estate tax. In the most recent year, tax revenue as a percentage of GDP was 28.7 percent.

FREEDOM FROM GOVERNMENT — 54.9%

Total government expenditures in Cyprus, including consumption and transfer payments, are high. In the most recent year, government spending equaled 41.5 percent of GDP, and the government received 14.6 percent of its total revenues from state-owned enterprises and government ownership of property.

MONETARY FREEDOM — 84.7%

Inflation in Cyprus is relatively low, averaging 2.6 percent between 2003 and 2005. Relatively stable prices explain most of the monetary freedom score. As a participant in the EU's Common Agricultural Policy, the government subsidizes agricultural production, distorting the prices of agricultural products. Consequently, 5 percent is deducted from Cyprus's monetary freedom score to account for these policies.

INVESTMENT FREEDOM — 70%

Residents of the European Union are permitted to own 100 percent of local companies and any company listed on the Cyprus Stock Exchange. The government has lifted most capital restrictions and limits on foreign equity participation and ownership, thereby granting national treatment to foreign investors. Non-EU investors may now invest freely in most sectors, either directly or indirectly. The only remaining exceptions involve the acquisition of property and investments in tertiary education and mass media. Non-resident purchase of real estate is subject to approval. Some payments, current transfers, and capital transactions are subject to central bank approval or restrictions.

FINANCIAL FREEDOM — 70%

Cyprus's financial sector is diverse and relatively sound. In compliance with EU requirements, the central bank is fully independent. There are 11 domestic banks, two foreign bank branches, and 27 international banking units, formerly known as offshore banks. Since the end of 2005, the international banking sector has had to comply with the same regulatory rules as local banks. There are also over 300 credit societies, co-operative savings banks, and other credit institutions that account for 32 percent of total deposits. The Cyprus Development Bank is 88 percent owned by the government, as is the Housing Finance Corporation, but these institutions are minor parts of the banking system. The government lifted exchange controls and abolished the interest rate ceiling in 2001. The Cyprus Stock Exchange continues to suffer from lack of trust following a speculative bubble that was encouraged by ineffective regulation.

PROPERTY RIGHTS — 90%

Contracts and property rights are enforced effectively. Under the constitution, the civil judiciary, including the Supreme Court (which carries out the functions of a constitutional court, a high court of appeal, and an administrative court), is independent from government interference. In practice, this is not always the case, but the judiciary has nevertheless caused the government to suffer several embarrassing defeats.

FREEDOM FROM CORRUPTION — 57%

Corruption is perceived as present. Cyprus ranks 37th out of 158 countries in Transparency International's Corruption Perceptions Index for 2005.

LABOR FREEDOM — 70%

The labor market operates under relatively flexible employment regulations that could be improved to enhance employment and productivity growth. Unemployment benefits last for only six months. This diminishes the incentive to enroll as unemployed after the end of the entitlement period, providing instead a strong incentive to find new work. A mandatory earnings-related social security scheme applies to both employed and self-employed individuals. The government mandates a minimum wage.

CZECH REPUBLIC

Prague

The Czech Republic's economy is 69.7 percent free, according to our 2007 assessment, which makes it the world's 31st freest economy. Its overall score is 0.3 percentage point lower than last year, partially reflecting new methodological detail. The Czech Republic is ranked 18th out of 41 countries in the European region, and its overall score is equal to the regional average.

The Czech Republic scores highly in financial freedom and monetary freedom and fairly high in fiscal freedom and labor freedom. Like many other Eastern European countries, the Czech Republic has relatively low top tax rates, both corporate and income. Inflation is very low, though the government does maintain a few price supports. The country has an extensive banking sector and highly developed financial services. There is extensive foreign ownership of banks, which operate under equal national rules, and minimal government involvement. Labor flexibility is fairly high, though hiring and firing workers can be costly.

As an emerging Eastern European country, the Czech Republic can improve in several areas, such as business freedom, freedom from government, and freedom from corruption. Licensing and bankruptcy procedures are extensive, characteristic of a perhaps overly intrusive regulatory environment. Government spending is high, and corruption exists as a minor irritant to commerce.

BACKGROUND: The Czech Republic separated from Slovakia and became an independent nation in 1993. The closely tied elections held in June 2006 led the ruling Czech Social Democratic Party to abandon planned structural reforms, and political deadlock is likely to continue. Economic growth over the past five years has relied heavily on exports to the European Union. Tourism also plays a central role in the country's economy. While this pattern is expected to continue in 2007 and subsequent years, internal reforms will need to replace mercantilism if real growth is to take place.

How Do We Measure Economic Freedom? See Chapter 3 (page 37) for an explanation of the methodology or visit the *Index* Web site at *heritage.org/index*.

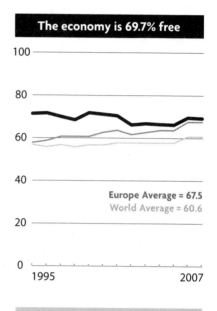

The economy is 69.7% free

Europe Average = 67.5
World Average = 60.6

QUICK FACTS

Population: 10.2 million

GDP (PPP): $198.3 billion
4.7% growth in 2004
3.2% 5-yr. comp. ann. growth
$19,408 per capita

Unemployment: 9.8%

Inflation (CPI): 2.8%

FDI (net inflow): $3.9 billion

Official Development Assistance:
Multilateral: $237 million
Bilateral: $43 million (2% from the U.S.)

External Debt: $45.6 billion

Exports: $76.6 billion
Primarily machinery and transport equipment, chemicals, raw materials and fuel

Imports: $77.0 billion
Primarily machinery and transport equipment, raw materials and fuels, chemicals

CZECH REPUBLIC'S TEN ECONOMIC FREEDOMS

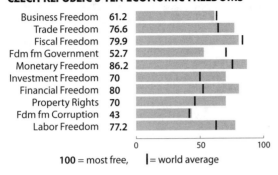

Business Freedom	61.2
Trade Freedom	76.6
Fiscal Freedom	79.9
Fdm fm Government	52.7
Monetary Freedom	86.2
Investment Freedom	70
Financial Freedom	80
Property Rights	70
Fdm fm Corruption	43
Labor Freedom	77.2

0   50   100

100 = most free, | = world average

BUSINESS FREEDOM — *61.2%*
Starting a business takes an average of 24 days, compared to the world average of 48 days. Entrepreneurship should be easier for maximum job creation. Obtaining a business license can be difficult, and closing a business is very difficult. General regulatory frameworks are consistent with a market economy, but bureaucracy and red tape are still problems. The overall freedom to start, operate, and close a business is limited by the national regulatory environment.

TRADE FREEDOM — *76.6%*
Trade policy in the Czech Republic is the same as the policies of other members of the European Union. The common EU weighted average tariff rate was 1.7 percent in 2005. Various non-tariff barriers are reflected in EU and Czech Republic policy, including agricultural and manufacturing subsidies, regulatory and licensing restrictions, and other market access restrictions. Consequently, an additional 20 percent is deducted from the Czech Republic's trade freedom score.

FISCAL FREEDOM — *79.9%*
The Czech Republic has a moderate income tax rate and a low corporate income tax rate. The top income tax rate is 32 percent, and the top corporate tax rate is 24 percent. Other taxes include a value-added tax (VAT), a property transfer tax, and a tax on dividends. In the most recent year, overall tax revenue as a percentage of GDP was 37.6 percent.

FREEDOM FROM GOVERNMENT — *52.7%*
Total government expenditures in the Czech Republic, including consumption and transfer payments, are high. In the most recent year, government spending equaled 44.3 percent of GDP, and the government received 4.5 percent of its total revenues from state-owned enterprises and government ownership of property.

MONETARY FREEDOM — *86.2%*
Inflation in the Czech Republic is low, averaging 1.9 percent between 2003 and 2005. As a participant in the EU's Common Agricultural Policy, the government subsidizes agricultural production, distorting the prices of agricultural products. Consequently, 5 percent is deducted from the Czech Republic's monetary freedom score to account for these policies.

INVESTMENT FREEDOM — *70%*
Foreign investors can freely establish new joint ventures and participate in existing enterprises, with as much as 100 percent foreign ownership in both cases. Foreign persons are not allowed to purchase land, but branches or offices of foreign companies may buy local real estate, with the exception of farmland or woodland. There are no restrictions on payments or current transfers, and both residents and non-residents may hold foreign exchange accounts. Prior authorization is required for issuance of debt securities and money market securities. A lack of transparency in the government procurement process is an obstacle to foreign tenders for government contracts.

FINANCIAL FREEDOM — *80%*
The Czech Republic's financial sector is one of the most advanced in Central and Eastern Europe. Following the 1990s banking crises and subsequent privatization, the government has had minimal direct involvement in the banking sector. There were 36 licensed commercial banks at the end of 2005, including 27 with some foreign ownership. Foreign-controlled banks accounted for 90 percent of assets in 2005 and are treated the same as domestic banks. Non-banking financial institutions are less developed than the banking sector. Insurance companies and pension funds are numerous and competitive, with significant foreign participation. Capital markets are small and lack transparency.

PROPERTY RIGHTS — *70%*
Private property is well protected, and contracts are generally secure. The judiciary is independent, although decisions may vary from court to court. Commercial disputes, particularly those related to bankruptcy proceedings, can take years to resolve. Registration of companies is in the hands of the courts and is sometimes slow and overly complicated.

FREEDOM FROM CORRUPTION — *43%*
Corruption is perceived as significant. The Czech Republic ranks 47th out of 158 countries in Transparency International's Corruption Perceptions Index for 2005.

LABOR FREEDOM — *77.2%*
The labor market operates under relatively flexible employment regulations that hinder employment and productivity growth. The non-salary cost of employing a worker can be high, and dismissing a redundant employee is relatively costly. Improving labor market flexibility has been a policy priority, as the Czech Republic's labor market is characterized by its rigidity and low labor force mobility.

DENMARK

Copenhagen

Rank: 13

Regional Rank: 6 of 41

Denmark's economy is 77.6 percent free, according to our 2007 assessment, which makes it the world's 13th freest economy. Its overall score is 1.4 percentage points higher than last year, partially reflecting new methodological detail. Denmark is ranked 6th freest among the 41 countries in the European region, and its overall score is well above the regional average.

Denmark scores highly in business freedom, financial freedom, monetary freedom, property rights, and freedom from corruption. Starting a business takes only five days, compared to the global average of 48 days, and the overall freedom of business operation (licensing, flexibility, etc.) is very high. Inflation is low, but Denmark's monetary score is lowered somewhat by distortionary EU agricultural subsidies. The financial markets are transparent, highly developed, and open to foreign capital and competition. As a modern Western democracy, Denmark has an efficient, independent judiciary that protects property rights effectively, and the level of corruption is low.

Denmark could do somewhat better in fiscal freedom and freedom from government, however. The top personal income tax rate is very high, as it is in many social democracies in the European Union, and tax revenue collected is correspondingly high. Government spending equals well over 50 percent of GDP, although state-owned businesses are few.

BACKGROUND: Denmark's economy depends heavily on foreign trade, and its private sector is characterized by many small and medium-sized companies. The country's large welfare state provides free public education, lifelong health care coverage, and subsidized care for children and the elderly; about 23 percent of working-age Danes rely on some kind of government transfer payment. In addition to restraining taxes and reducing immigration, addressing the costs and benefits of Denmark's social welfare system is a major part of the national political agenda.

How Do We Measure Economic Freedom? See Chapter 3 (page 37) for an explanation of the methodology or visit the *Index* Web site at *heritage.org/index*.

The economy is 77.6% free

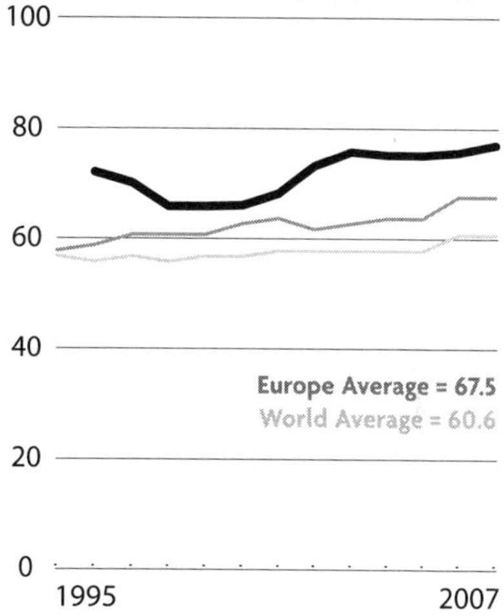

100

80

60

40

20

0

1995   2007

Europe Average = 67.5
World Average = 60.6

QUICK FACTS

Population: 5.4 million

GDP (PPP): $172.5 billion
1.9% growth in 2004
1.4% 5-yr. comp. ann. growth
$31,914 per capita

Unemployment: 6.4%

Inflation (CPI): 1.2%

FDI (net inflow): −$358.53 million

Official Development Assistance:
Multilateral: None
Bilateral: None

External Debt: $352.9 billion (2005)

Exports: $111.4 billion
Primarily machinery and instruments, meat and meat products, dairy products, fish, chemicals, furniture, ships, windmills

Imports: $98.9 billion
Primarily machinery and equipment, raw materials and semi-manufactures for industry, chemicals, grain and food, consumer goods

DENMARK'S TEN ECONOMIC FREEDOMS

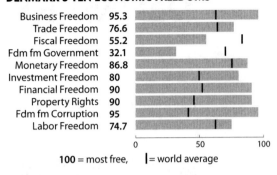

Business Freedom	95.3
Trade Freedom	76.6
Fiscal Freedom	55.2
Fdm fm Government	32.1
Monetary Freedom	86.8
Investment Freedom	80
Financial Freedom	90
Property Rights	90
Fdm fm Corruption	95
Labor Freedom	74.7

0   50   100

100 = most free, | = world average

BUSINESS FREEDOM — 95.3%

Starting a business takes an average of five days, compared to the world average of 48 days. Obtaining a business license is very simple, and closing a business is easy. Transparent regulations are applied evenly and efficiently in most cases. The overall freedom to start, operate, and close a business is strongly protected by the national regulatory environment, giving the nation a powerful competitive advantage.

TRADE FREEDOM — 76.6%

Denmark's trade policy is the same as the policies of other members of the European Union. The common EU weighted average tariff rate was 1.7 percent in 2005. Various non-tariff barriers are reflected in EU and Danish policy, including agricultural and manufacturing subsidies, regulatory and licensing restrictions, and other market access restrictions. Consequently, an additional 20 percent is deducted from Denmark's trade freedom score.

FISCAL FREEDOM — 55.2%

Denmark has a very high income tax rate and a moderate corporate tax rate. The top income tax rate is 59 percent, and the top corporate tax rate is 28 percent. Other taxes include a value-added tax (VAT) and an excise tax. In the most recent year, overall tax revenue as a percentage of GDP was 49.6 percent.

FREEDOM FROM GOVERNMENT — 32.1%

Total government expenditures in Denmark, including consumption and transfer payments, are very high. In the most recent year, government spending equaled 54.8 percent of GDP, and the government received 3.7 percent of its total revenues from state-owned enterprises and government ownership of property.

MONETARY FREEDOM — 86.8%

Inflation in Denmark is low, averaging 1.7 percent between 2003 and 2005. As a participant in the EU's Common Agricultural Policy, the government subsidizes agricultural production, distorting the prices of agricultural products. Consequently, 5 percent is deducted from Denmark's monetary freedom score to account for these distortionary policies.

INVESTMENT FREEDOM — 80%

Foreign investors are subject to the same laws as domestic investors. As a general rule, foreign direct investment in Denmark may take place without restrictions or pre-screening. Ownership restrictions apply to only a few sectors. A non-resident may not purchase real estate unless the person formerly resided in Denmark for at least five years, is an EU national working in Denmark, or is a non-EU national with a valid residence or business permit. There are no restrictions on capital transfers.

FINANCIAL FREEDOM — 90%

Denmark's well-developed financial system is open to foreign competition, and credit is allocated on market terms and freely available. The banking system is sound if somewhat concentrated, with the two largest banks accounting for over 70 percent of banking system assets in 2004. The Danish banking sector consists of 176 banks. There are also 18 foreign banks and four Faroese banks operating in Denmark, with other foreign banks possessing representative offices. The national payment system is jointly owned by Danish banks, which can make it difficult for foreign banks to gain access. Banks may provide services in a wide variety of areas. Supervision and regulation are based on EU legislation. Denmark has a mature, competitive insurance industry with over 200 companies and 30 pension funds. The stock market, which participates in a regional integrated network of exchanges that covers all Nordic and most Baltic countries, is highly developed and efficient. The bond market is well developed and one of the world's largest.

PROPERTY RIGHTS — 90%

The judiciary is independent and, in general, both fair and efficient. The legal system is independent of the government and is based on a centuries-old legal tradition. It includes written and consistently applied commercial and bankruptcy laws, and secured interests in property are recognized and enforced.

FREEDOM FROM CORRUPTION — 95%

Corruption is perceived as almost nonexistent. Denmark ranks 4th out of 158 countries in Transparency International's Corruption Perceptions Index for 2005.

LABOR FREEDOM — 74.7%

The labor market operates under relatively flexible employment regulations that could be improved to enhance employment and productivity growth. The non-salary cost of employing a worker is low, and dismissing a redundant employee is relatively costless. The country's efficient unemployment insurance system is not financed by employers.

DJIBOUTI

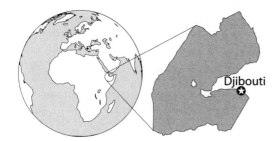

Djibouti

Rank: 130

Regional Rank: 29 of 40

Djibouti's economy is 52.6 percent free, according to our 2007 assessment, which makes it the world's 130th freest economy. Its overall score is 2.4 percentage points lower than last year, partially reflecting new methodological detail. Djibouti is ranked 29th out of 40 countries in the sub-Saharan Africa region, and its overall score is slightly lower than the regional average.

Djibouti has high levels of fiscal freedom, labor freedom, and monetary freedom. The top income taxes on individuals and corporations are moderate. Employment restrictions are moderate, resulting in a flexible labor market. Inflation is low, but the government does try to control some consumer prices.

Economic development has been hampered by weak business freedom, trade freedom, freedom from government, property rights, and freedom from corruption. Business regulations are extensive, even when enforced efficiently. Bureaucratic inefficiency and corruption hamper virtually all areas of the economy. Court enforcement of intrusive labor regulations and property rights is clouded by political interference and rampant corruption.

BACKGROUND: President Ismael Omar Guelleh was first elected in 1999 and re-elected in 2005, and his party controls all levels of government. Two-thirds of Djibouti's population lives in the capital city (also called Djibouti). Most of those who live outside the capital city are engaged in nomadic subsistence and were severely affected by drought and famine in 2006. Djibouti has few natural resources and a tremendously high unemployment rate. Its service-based economy is centered on port facilities, the railway, and foreign military bases. Ethiopia is responsible for some 88 percent of goods moving through the port.

How Do We Measure Economic Freedom? See Chapter 3 (page 37) for an explanation of the methodology or visit the *Index* Web site at *heritage.org/index*.

The economy is 52.6% free

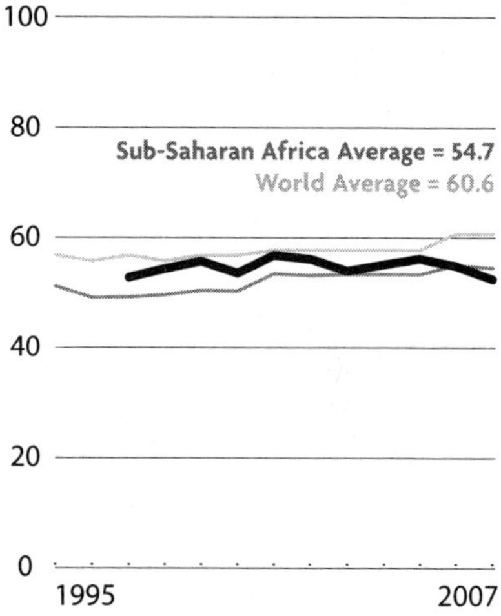

Sub-Saharan Africa Average = 54.7
World Average = 60.6

(Line chart showing economic freedom from 1995 to 2007, ranging between approximately 50 and 60)

QUICK FACTS

Population: 0.8 million

GDP (PPP): $1.6 billion
3% growth in 2004
2.2% 5-yr. comp. ann. growth
$1,993 per capita

Unemployment: 50% (2004 estimate)

Inflation (CPI): 3.1%

FDI (net inflow): $33 million (gross)

Official Development Assistance:
Multilateral: $31 million
Bilateral: $42.4 million (15% from the U.S.)

External Debt: $366.0 million (2002 estimate)

Exports: $90.0 million (2004 estimate)
Primarily re-exports, hides and skins, coffee (in transit)

Imports: $373.0 million (2004 estimate)
Primarily foods, beverages, transport equipment, chemicals, petroleum products

DJIBOUTI'S TEN ECONOMIC FREEDOMS

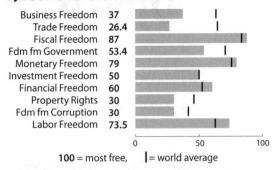

Business Freedom	37
Trade Freedom	26.4
Fiscal Freedom	87
Fdm fm Government	53.4
Monetary Freedom	79
Investment Freedom	50
Financial Freedom	60
Property Rights	30
Fdm fm Corruption	30
Labor Freedom	73.5

0   50   100

100 = most free, | = world average

BUSINESS FREEDOM — 37%

Starting a business takes an average of 37 days, compared to the world average of 48 days, but entrepreneurship is hindered in other ways. Both obtaining a business license and closing a business can be very difficult. A lack of transparency and the inconsistent application of the commercial code discourage entrepreneurial activities. The overall freedom to start, operate, and close a business is seriously limited by the national regulatory environment.

TRADE FREEDOM — 26.4%

Djibouti's average tariff rate was 26.8 percent in 2002. Much of Djibouti's trade with neighboring countries is informal. Non-tariff barriers include import and export bans, higher import taxes for some products, and market access restrictions in the services sector. Consequently, an additional 20 percent is deducted from Djibouti's trade freedom score to account for these non-tariff barriers.

FISCAL FREEDOM — 87%

Djibouti has moderate tax rates. The top income tax rate is 30 percent, and the top corporate tax rate is 25 percent. Other taxes include a property tax and an excise tax. In the most recent year, overall tax revenue as a percentage of GDP was 20.6 percent.

FREEDOM FROM GOVERNMENT — 53.4%

Total government expenditures in Djibouti, including consumption and transfer payments, are high. In the most recent year, government spending equaled 36.5 percent of GDP. Much of Djibouti's GDP is produced by the state. The government owns principal public utilities and infrastructures including water, electricity, telecommunications, the railway, and the port.

MONETARY FREEDOM — 79%

Inflation in Djibouti is moderate, averaging 3 percent between 2003 and 2005. Relatively stable prices explain most of the monetary freedom score. Goods and services such as medicines, "common bread," water, electricity, telecommunications, postal services, and urban transport are subject to price controls. The government also influences prices through the regulation of state-owned enterprises. Consequently, an additional 10 percent is deducted from Djibouti's monetary freedom score.

INVESTMENT FREEDOM — 50%

Djibouti has no major laws that discourage incoming foreign investment, but certain sectors, most notably public utilities, are state-owned and not currently open to investors. Bureaucratic procedures are complicated. The Finance Ministry will issue a license only if an investor possesses an approved investor visa, and the Interior Ministry will issue an investor visa only to a licensed business. Both residents and non-residents may hold foreign exchange accounts, and there are no restrictions on payments or transfers. The government imposes controls on all credit transactions between residents and non-residents.

FINANCIAL FREEDOM —60%

Djibouti's financial sector consists primarily of a small banking system. Two majority-owned or fully owned French banks account for 95 percent of deposits and 85 percent of credit. The government has a 49 percent minority stake in Banque pour le Commerce et l'Industrie-Mer Rouge. There is also an Ethiopian bank, but it focuses on international transactions for Ethiopian customers. Commercial banks generally provide only short-term financing and lending. A Development Fund for Djibouti was authorized by the government in 2001 but is still not operational. The pension system consists of three funds, two of which are dedicated to civil servants and the military. A law against money laundering was adopted in 2002. There are no capital markets, and little formal economic activity occurs outside of the capital city of Djibouti.

PROPERTY RIGHTS — 30%

Protection of private property rights is weak. The courts are frequently overburdened, and the enforcement of contracts can be time-consuming and cumbersome. Political manipulation undermines the credibility of the judicial system. Djibouti has written commercial and bankruptcy laws, but they are not applied consistently. Corruption is a problem in trials and judicial proceedings.

FREEDOM FROM CORRUPTION — 30%

Most economic activity still occurs informally. It is estimated that more than 80 percent of enterprises are within the informal and semi-informal sector, including a large number of informal microenterprises that play a key role in the economy.

LABOR FREEDOM — 73.5%

The labor market operates under relatively inflexible employment regulations that hinder employment and productivity growth. The non-salary cost of employing a worker is moderate, but dismissing a redundant employee can be relatively costly. Regulations on increasing or contracting the number of work hours can be rigid.

DOMINICAN REPUBLIC

Santo
Domingo

Rank: 100

Regional Rank: 23 of 29

The Dominican Republic's economy is 56.7 percent free, according to our 2007 assessment, which makes it the world's 100th freest economy. Its overall score is 0.1 percentage point higher than last year, partially reflecting new methodological detail. The Dominican Republic is ranked 23rd out of 29 countries in the Americas, and its overall score is slightly lower than the regional average.

The Dominican Republic receives high scores in fiscal freedom and freedom from government. Personal and corporate tax rates are moderate, and overall tax revenue is not particularly high as a percentage of GDP. Government expenditures are likewise moderate, and revenue from state-owned businesses is not large.

The Dominican Republic scores poorly in financial freedom, property rights, and freedom from corruption and somewhat low in business freedom and labor freedom. Starting a business takes far longer than the international average, and closing a business is costly and difficult. Over-regulation hampers business and labor market flexibility, and public administration is inefficient and corrupt. Failure to recover from scandals in the financial sector reflects the rudimentary level of banking operations. The weak application of commercial law means that private property is subject to adjudication based on political interference and corruption.

BACKGROUND: The Dominican Republic has been undemocratic for much of its history as an independent country, although regular competitive elections have taken place since 1996. President Leonel Fernández, elected in 2004, pushed for his country's entrance into the Dominican Republic–Central America Free Trade Agreement (DR–CAFTA), under which greater trade and economic freedom will benefit the population. Growth has surged, and niche-market producers have begun to appear. However, the country suffers from an inefficient legal system that lacks resources and personnel and from deteriorated infrastructure, including frequent electrical outages.

How Do We Measure Economic Freedom? See Chapter 3 (page 37) for an explanation of the methodology or visit the *Index* Web site at *heritage.org/index*.

The economy is 56.7% free

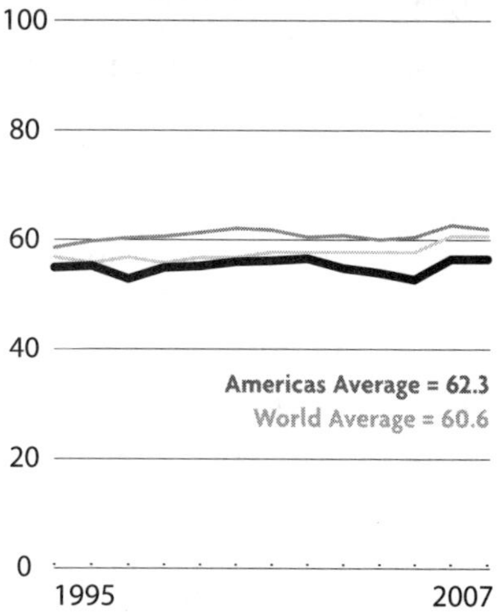

100

80

60

40

Americas Average = 62.3
World Average = 60.6

20

0

1995   2007

QUICK FACTS

Population: 8.8 million

GDP (PPP): $65.3 billion
2.0% growth in 2004
3.2% 5-yr. comp. ann. growth
$7,449 per capita

Unemployment: 17.5% (2004 estimate)

Inflation (CPI): 51.5%

FDI (net inflow): $645.1 million (gross)

Official Development Assistance:
Multilateral: $33 million
Bilateral: $127 million (23% from the U.S.)

External Debt: $7.0 billion

Exports: $9.3 billion
Primarily ferronickel, sugar, gold, silver, coffee, cocoa, tobacco, meats, consumer goods

Imports: $9.0 billion
Primarily food, petroleum, cotton and fabrics, chemicals, pharmaceuticals

DOMINICAN REPUBLIC'S TEN ECONOMIC FREEDOMS

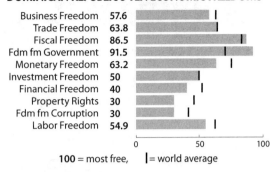

Business Freedom	57.6
Trade Freedom	63.8
Fiscal Freedom	86.5
Fdm fm Government	91.5
Monetary Freedom	63.2
Investment Freedom	50
Financial Freedom	40
Property Rights	30
Fdm fm Corruption	30
Labor Freedom	54.9

0   50   100

100 = most free, | **= world average**

BUSINESS FREEDOM — *57.6%*

Starting a business takes an average of 73 days, compared to the world average of 48 days. Entrepreneurship should be easier for maximum job creation. Obtaining a business license is relatively simple, but closing a business can be very difficult. Regulations are still burdensome and unstable, as interpretation of the commercial code is often arbitrary. The overall freedom to start, operate, and close a business is limited by the national regulatory environment.

TRADE FREEDOM — *63.8%*

The Dominican Republic's weighted average tariff rate was 8.1 percent in 2004. Customs implementation is burdensome and lacks transparency, especially for importers. Standards can be cumbersome, and discretionary import licenses are required for most agricultural products. Corruption and a lack of transparency characterize most of the trade process. Problems involving the enforcement and protection of intellectual property rights add to the cost of trade. Consequently, an additional 20 percent is deducted from the Dominican Republic's trade freedom score to account for these non-tariff barriers.

FISCAL FREEDOM — *86.5%*

The Dominican Republic has moderate tax rates. Both the top income tax rate and the top corporate tax rate are 30 percent. Other taxes include a value-added tax (VAT) and a tax on dividends. In the most recent year, overall tax revenue as a percentage of GDP was 15.1 percent.

FREEDOM FROM GOVERNMENT — *91.5%*

Total government expenditures in the Dominican Republic, including consumption and transfer payments, are low. In the most recent year, government spending equaled 18.1 percent of GDP, and the government received 2.6 percent of its total revenues from state-owned enterprises and government ownership of property.

MONETARY FREEDOM — *63.2%*

Although inflation in the Dominican Republic fell significantly between 2004 and 2005, it was relatively high between 2003 and 2005, averaging 17.9 percent per year. Relatively high and unstable prices explain most of the monetary freedom score. The government applies price controls to electricity and fuel and provides subsidies for some agricultural products and electricity generation. Consequently, an additional 10 percent is deducted from the Dominican Republic's monetary freedom score.

INVESTMENT FREEDOM — *50%*

Foreign investment is generally welcomed, but some laws discriminate between domestic and foreign investments. There is no screening of foreign investment, but investments must be registered with the Central Bank of the Dominican Republic. Foreign direct investment is permitted in all sectors except the disposal and storage of toxic, hazardous, or radioactive waste; activities that affect public health or the environment; and activities related to defense and security. Residents and non-residents may hold foreign exchange accounts. Payments and transfers are subject to documentation requirements. Some capital transactions are subject to approval, documentation, or reporting requirements.

FINANCIAL FREEDOM — *40%*

The Dominican Republic's small financial sector is poorly supervised and regulated. Confidence has been shaky since the crisis spurred by the 2003 collapse of Banco Intercontinental (Baninter), the country's second largest bank. Public skepticism was affirmed by a 2005 revelation that the head of the board of directors of the fifth largest bank had misappropriated funds. Financial sector assets are largely controlled by the 12 multiple service banks, including three foreign-owned banks, and five state-owned banks. Offshore banking activities are growing. The insurance sector included 23 companies in 2004. Ten companies control 85 percent of the markets. Capital markets are small and underdeveloped, and trading is slight.

PROPERTY RIGHTS — *30%*

The court system is inefficient, and bureaucratic red tape is common. The government can expropriate property arbitrarily. Despite recent judicial reforms, Dominican and foreign business leaders have complained that judicial and administrative corruption affects the settlement of business disputes.

FREEDOM FROM CORRUPTION — *30%*

Corruption is perceived as significant. The Dominican Republic ranks 85th out of 158 countries in Transparency International's Corruption Perceptions Index for 2005.

LABOR FREEDOM — *54.9%*

The labor market operates under restrictive employment regulations that hinder employment and productivity growth. The non-salary cost of employing a worker is moderate, but dismissing a redundant employee is costly. There are rigid restrictions on increasing and contracting working hours.

ECUADOR

Quito

Ecuador's economy is 55.3 percent free, according to our 2007 assessment, which makes it the world's 108th freest economy. Its overall score is 0.3 percentage point lower than last year, partially reflecting new methodological detail. Ecuador is ranked 24th out of 29 countries in the Americas, and its overall score is much lower than the regional average.

Ecuador receives high scores for fiscal freedom and freedom from government. It has moderate personal and corporate tax rates (although there are other taxes), and overall tax revenue is not excessively high as a percentage of GDP. Government expenditures are less than 25 percent of GDP, and the percentage of revenue from state-owned businesses is relatively low.

Ecuador scores particularly poorly in its investment freedom, property rights, labor freedom, freedom from corruption, and business freedom. Starting a business and closing a business can be difficult. Heavy regulation hurts business and labor flexibility. The rule of law is politically influenced and inefficient, and outright expropriation of private property is a constant concern. The judiciary often makes erratic judgments and is subject to corruption.

BACKGROUND: Ecuador has ample petroleum reserves and is the world's largest banana exporter. Feuding political factions have made consensus in the national legislature elusive and have contributed to the ouster of three presidents in the past decade. The dollarization of Ecuador's economy imposed some order, but other problems, including thousands of conflicting laws that result in an uncertain application of justice, have deterred foreign investment. Mismanagement and corruption plague the government-run oil industry, and production is dwindling. As of August 2006, negotiations for a free trade agreement with the United States had been suspended.

How Do We Measure Economic Freedom? See Chapter 3 (page 37) for an explanation of the methodology or visit the *Index* Web site at *heritage.org/index*.

The economy is 55.3% free

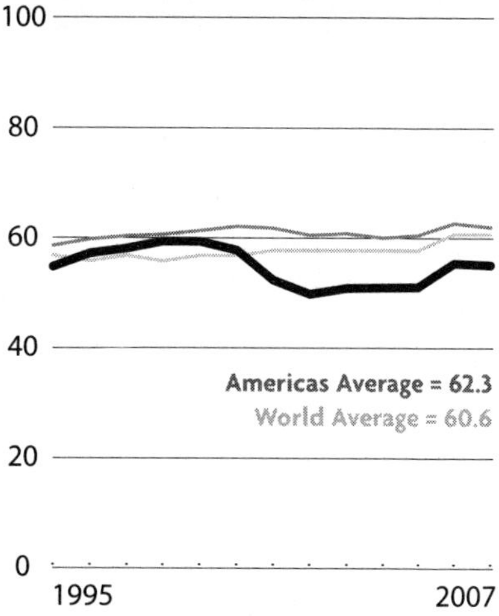

Americas Average = 62.3
World Average = 60.6

QUICK FACTS

Population: 13 million

GDP (PPP): $51.7 billion
6.9% growth in 2004
4.2% 5-yr. comp. ann. growth
$3,963 per capita

Unemployment: 11%

Inflation (CPI): 2.7%

FDI (net inflow): $1.2 billion (gross)

Official Development Assistance:
Multilateral: $33 million
Bilateral: $247 million (33% from the U.S.)

External Debt: $16.9 billion

Exports: $8.7 billion
Primarily petroleum, bananas, cut flowers, shrimp

Imports: $9.3 billion
Primarily vehicles, medicinal products, telecommunications equipment, electricity

163

ECUADOR'S TEN ECONOMIC FREEDOMS

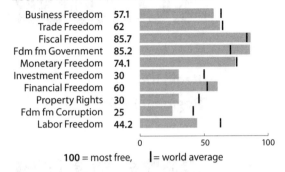

Business Freedom	57.1
Trade Freedom	62
Fiscal Freedom	85.7
Fdm fm Government	85.2
Monetary Freedom	74.1
Investment Freedom	30
Financial Freedom	60
Property Rights	30
Fdm fm Corruption	25
Labor Freedom	44.2

0   50   100

100 = most free, I = world average

BUSINESS FREEDOM — 57.1%

Starting a business takes an average of 65 days, compared to the world average of 48 days. Entrepreneurship should be easier for maximum job creation. Obtaining a business license is relatively simple, but closing a business can be very difficult. Businesses are subject to complex bureaucratic rules and the inconsistent application of commercial laws. The overall freedom to start, operate, and close a business is restricted by the national regulatory environment.

TRADE FREEDOM — 62%

Ecuador's weighted average tariff rate was 9 percent in 2004. Non-tariff barriers include restrictive requirements for import licensing, the requirement that firms receive prior authorization from various government agencies before importing most commodities, import bans, issues involving the enforcement and protection of intellectual property rights, and arbitrary and cumbersome regulations and customs procedures. Consequently, an additional 20 percent is deducted from Ecuador's trade freedom score to account for these non-tariff barriers.

FISCAL FREEDOM — 85.7%

Ecuador has moderate tax rates. Both the top income tax rate and the top corporate tax rate are 25 percent. Other taxes include a value-added tax (VAT) and a capital gains tax. In the most recent year, overall tax revenue as a percentage of GDP was 29.8 percent.

FREEDOM FROM GOVERNMENT — 85.2%

Total government expenditures in Ecuador, including consumption and transfer payments, are low. In the most recent year, government spending equaled 24.7 percent of GDP, and the government received 1.7 percent of its total revenues from state-owned enterprises and government ownership of property.

MONETARY FREEDOM — 74.1%

Ecuador uses the U.S. dollar as its legal tender. Inflation is relatively low, averaging 3 percent between 2003 and 2005, which explains most of the monetary freedom score. The government applies price bands for some agricultural products; controls the prices of electricity, telecommunications services, and pharmaceuticals; and implements subsidies for public transportation and cooking gas. Consequently, an additional 15 percent is deducted from Ecua-

dor's monetary freedom score to adjust for measures that distort domestic prices.

INVESTMENT FREEDOM — 30%

Ecuadorian foreign investment law grants foreign firms national treatment, but cumbersome labor laws and a lack of contract enforcement severely hamper both foreign and domestic investment. Many government officials use regulatory schemes and questionable legal interpretations to solicit bribes from and otherwise take advantage of foreign investors. The government maintains restrictions in the petroleum exploration and development, mining, domestic fishing, electricity, telecommunications, broadcast media, coastal and border real estate, and national security sectors. There are no restrictions on foreign exchange accounts, direct investment, or current transfers.

FINANCIAL FREEDOM — 60%

Ecuador's financial system is still recovering from a late 1990s banking crisis that spurred government default on foreign bonds and the takeover of many banks. Because the U.S. dollar is the official currency, the central bank is no longer the lender of last resort. In 2005, 25 commercial banks (one of them state-run) were operating, down from 40 in 1998. The state controlled 11 percent of bank assets in 2005. In addition, there are 11 finance companies, 36 co-operatives, and five mutual finance companies. The government has increased financial sector regulations in the wake of the crisis. The insurance sector consists of 43 companies, and the eight largest control a majority of policies. There are two stock markets. Most trading involves government debt. Foreign takeovers of limited partnership banks and insurance companies are restricted.

PROPERTY RIGHTS — 30%

Weak rule of law is a significant problem for entrepreneurs in Ecuador. Processing delays are significant, judgments are unpredictable, rulings are inconsistent, and the courts are subject to corruption. Expropriation is possible. A number of foreign and local investors have experienced agricultural land seizures by squatters over the years.

FREEDOM FROM CORRUPTION — 25%

Corruption is perceived as widespread. Ecuador ranks 117th out of 158 countries in Transparency International's Corruption Perceptions Index for 2005.

LABOR FREEDOM — 44.2%

The labor market operates under highly restrictive employment regulations that hinder employment and productivity growth. The non-salary cost of employing a worker is moderate, but dismissing a redundant employee can be very costly. Many employers often resort to short-term outsourcing contracts because job tenure regulations make it hard to terminate employment. Ecuador's labor market flexibility is one of the lowest 20 in the world.

EGYPT

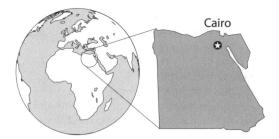

Cairo

Egypt's economy is 53.2 percent free, according to our 2007 assessment, which makes it the world's 127th freest economy. Its overall score is 1 percentage point higher than last year, partially reflecting new methodological detail. Egypt country is ranked 13th out of 17 countries in the Middle East/North Africa region, and its overall score is slightly lower than the regional average.

Egypt's economy scores well in a few of the 10 factors of economic freedom. Fiscal freedom is rated highly, and its freedom from government and monetary freedom also score reasonably well. The top income and corporate tax rates are impressively low, and government tax revenue relative to GDP is not high. Total government expenditures are moderately low, although Egypt receives a significant part of its income from state-owned businesses.

Egypt could improve in several areas, however. Business freedom, financial freedom, property rights, and corruption are all serious problems. Licensing, operating, or closing a business is difficult and heavily regulated by an intrusive bureaucracy. Fairly high tariff rates and nontariff barriers impede trade and foreign investment alike. Corruption is rampant, and the fair adjudication of property rights cannot be guaranteed.

BACKGROUND: Egypt is the most populous Arab country and a major force in Middle Eastern affairs. Although President Hosni Mubarak's government has undertaken incremental reforms to liberalize the socialist economic system that has hampered economic growth since the 1950s, the government until recently has emphasized such social policies as maintaining the payment of subsidies on food, energy, and other key commodities. Economic reform has become a higher priority under Prime Minister Ahmed Nazif, a technocrat who has placed liberal reformers in key positions. In 2005, the government reduced personal and corporate tax rates, cut energy subsidies, and privatized several enterprises.

How Do We Measure Economic Freedom? See Chapter 3 (page 37) for an explanation of the methodology or visit the *Index* Web site at *heritage.org/index.*

The economy is 53.2% free

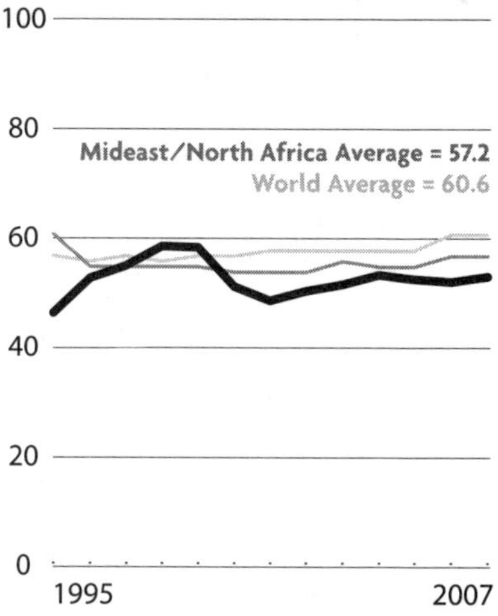

Mideast/North Africa Average = 57.2
World Average = 60.6

QUICK FACTS

Population: 72.6 million

GDP (PPP): $305.9 billion
4.1% growth in 2004
3.9% 5-yr. comp. ann. growth
$4,211 per capita

Unemployment: 10.0%

Inflation (CPI): 11.3%

FDI (net inflow): $1.1 billion

Official Development Assistance:
Multilateral: $349 million
Bilateral: $1.6 billion (58% from the U.S.)

External Debt: $30.3 billion

Exports: $26.5 billion
Primarily crude oil and petroleum products, cotton, textiles, metal products, chemicals

Imports: $26.9 billion
Primarily machinery and equipment, food, chemicals, wood products, fuels

165

EGYPT'S TEN ECONOMIC FREEDOMS

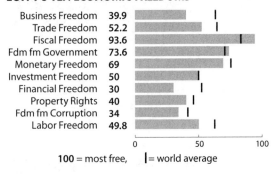

Business Freedom	39.9
Trade Freedom	52.2
Fiscal Freedom	93.6
Fdm fm Government	73.6
Monetary Freedom	69
Investment Freedom	50
Financial Freedom	30
Property Rights	40
Fdm fm Corruption	34
Labor Freedom	49.8

0   50   100

100 = most free, | = world average

BUSINESS FREEDOM — *39.9%*

Starting a business takes an average of 19 days, compared to the world average of 48 days. Entrepreneurship should be easier for maximum job creation. Both obtaining a business license and closing a business are very difficult. The government has established a "one-stop-shop" for investment procedures and has moved to revamp the regulatory environment in recent years, but bureaucracy still remains meddlesome. The overall freedom to start, operate, and close a business is seriously limited by the national regulatory environment.

TRADE FREEDOM — *52.2%*

Egypt's weighted average tariff rate was 13.9 percent in 2002. Non-tariff barriers include import restrictions and import bans, burdensome and non-transparent sanitary and phytosanitary measures, and cumbersome regulatory and customs procedures. Customs corruption also adds to the cost of trade. Consequently, an additional 20 percent is deducted from Egypt's trade freedom score to account for these non-tariff barriers.

FISCAL FREEDOM — *93.6%*

Egypt has implemented cuts in personal income and corporate tax rates since June 2005. Both the top income tax rate and the top corporate tax rate are 20 percent. Other taxes include a value-added tax (VAT) and a property tax. In the most recent year, overall tax revenue as a percentage of GDP was 12.8 percent.

FREEDOM FROM GOVERNMENT — *73.6%*

Total government expenditures in Egypt, including consumption and transfer payments, are moderate. In the most recent year, government spending equaled 26.7 percent of GDP, and the government received 29.4 percent of its total revenues from state-owned enterprises and government ownership of property. The government has been pushing forward the sale of non-strategic and smaller companies.

MONETARY FREEDOM — *69%*

Inflation in Egypt is relatively high, averaging 6.4 percent between 2003 and 2005. Relatively high and unstable prices explain most of the monetary freedom score. The government controls prices for some basic foods, energy (including fuel), transport, and medicine. It also implements subsidies for basic food items, sugar and pharmaceuticals,

and public transportation. In general, the massive size of the public sector limits the private sector's ability to set market prices. Consequently, an additional 15 percent is deducted from Egypt's monetary freedom score to adjust for measures that distort domestic prices.

INVESTMENT FREEDOM — *50%*

In theory, automatic approval should be granted to most investment projects; in practice, all projects must pass through a review process to gain legal status and qualify for incentives. Foreign investment in Sinai, military products, and tobacco requires approval from the relevant ministries. Foreign ownership of areas designated as agricultural lands (in the Nile Valley, Delta, and Oases), except for desert reclamation projects, is prohibited. Both residents and non-residents may hold foreign exchange accounts. There are no restrictions on payments and transfers. The Capital Market Authority must approve bond issues.

FINANCIAL FREEDOM — *30%*

Egypt's financial sector is characterized by a strong state presence. In 2005, 52 banks were licensed, including 41 Egyptian financial institutions and 11 foreign banks. The four large state-owned banks controlled about 50 percent of banking sector assets in 2004. The smallest state bank was approved for sale in 2006, and the government has sold its shares in some private banks. Non-performing loans are a significant problem, and new banks face significant constraints. There were 21 insurance companies in 2004, including four state-owned firms that dominate the sector and another state-owned reinsurance company. Foreign ownership of insurance companies and banks is permitted. Capital markets are large for the region.

PROPERTY RIGHTS — *40%*

The government sometimes circumvents the independence of the judiciary by using fast-track military courts. On average, it takes six years to decide commercial cases, and appeal procedures can extend court cases beyond 15 years. Nevertheless, local contractual arrangements are generally secure. Islamic law (Sharia) is officially the main inspiration for legislation, but the Napoleonic Code exerts a significant influence. Judicial procedures tend to be protracted, costly, and subject to political pressure.

FREEDOM FROM CORRUPTION — *34%*

Corruption is perceived as significant. Egypt ranks 70th out of 158 countries in Transparency International's Corruption Perceptions Index for 2005.

LABOR FREEDOM — *49.8%*

The government has made gradual progress toward a more competitive and flexible labor market, adopting a new labor code in recent years. However, the labor market still operates under restrictive employment regulations that hinder employment and productivity growth. The non-salary cost of employing a worker can be high, and dismissing a redundant employee is costly. There are rigid restrictions on increasing or contracting working hours.

EL SALVADOR

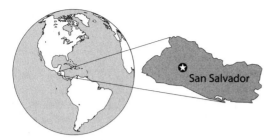
San Salvador

El Salvador's economy is 70.3 percent free, according to our 2007 assessment, which makes it the world's 29th freest economy. Its overall score is 0.7 percentage point lower than last year, partially reflecting new methodological detail. El Salvador is ranked 7th out of 29 countries in the Americas, and its overall score is notably higher than the regional average.

El Salvador receives high scores for fiscal freedom, freedom from government, labor freedom, and monetary freedom. Personal and corporate tax rates are low, and overall tax revenue is not high as a percentage of GDP. Government expenditures are less than 15 percent of GDP, and state-owned businesses account for less than 1 percent of total revenues. The labor market is fairly flexible, though firing an employee can be costly. Inflation is also low thanks to a currency pegged to the U.S. dollar, but the government does distort prices on certain staples through price controls.

Other freedoms are merely average, including business freedom, property rights, and freedom from corruption. Excessive regulation hampers business operations. The country's inefficient judiciary is a major deterrent to foreign investors, as it can often neither enforce its rulings nor rule in a consistently impartial manner. Corruption is also prevalent.

BACKGROUND: Since the signing of a 1992 peace accord between the government and guerrillas, El Salvador's political parties have moderated their positions to cooperate on political and economic reforms. President Elias "Tony" Saca, with three years left in his five-year term, continues to pursue the free-market policies of his National Republican Alliance party, though with slightly less vigor. Reform will be aided by El Salvador's participation in the Dominican Republic–Central America Free Trade Agreement (DR–CAFTA) with the United States. However, the country still suffers from a weak justice system, poor education, and rising violence associated with transnational youth gangs.

How Do We Measure Economic Freedom? See Chapter 3 (page 37) for an explanation of the methodology or visit the *Index* Web site at *heritage.org/index*.

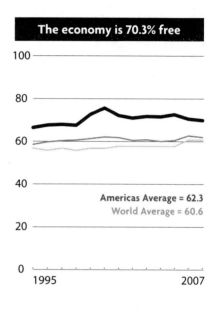

The economy is 70.3% free

Americas Average = 62.3
World Average = 60.6

1995 — 2007

QUICK FACTS

Population: 6.8 million

GDP (PPP): $34.1 billion
1.5% growth in 2004
1.9% 5-yr. comp. ann. growth
$5,041 per capita

Unemployment: 6.5% (2005 estimate)

Inflation (CPI): 4.5%

FDI (net inflow): $458.5 million

Official Development Assistance:
Multilateral: $38 million
Bilateral: $228 million (55% from the U.S.)

External Debt: $7.3 billion

Exports: $4.3 billion
Primarily offshore assembly exports, coffee, sugar, shrimp, textiles, chemicals, electricity

Imports: $7.0 billion
Primarily raw materials, consumer goods, capital goods, fuels, food, petroleum, electricity

EL SALVADOR'S TEN ECONOMIC FREEDOMS

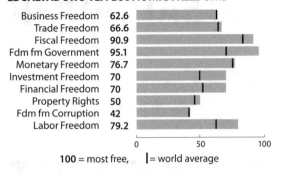

Business Freedom	62.6
Trade Freedom	66.6
Fiscal Freedom	90.9
Fdm fm Government	95.1
Monetary Freedom	76.7
Investment Freedom	70
Financial Freedom	70
Property Rights	50
Fdm fm Corruption	42
Labor Freedom	79.2

0   50   100

100 = most free, | = world average

BUSINESS FREEDOM — 62.6%

Starting a business takes an average of 26 days, compared to the world average of 48 days. Entrepreneurship should be easier for maximum job creation. Although El Salvador has made significant progress in reducing onerous regulations in recent years, both obtaining a business license and closing a business can be difficult. The overall freedom to start, operate, and close a business is restricted by the national regulatory environment.

TRADE FREEDOM — 66.6%

El Salvador's weighted average tariff rate was 6.7 percent in 2005. Non-tariff barriers include import quota systems on rice and pork, discriminatory sanitary practices on poultry, export subsidies, and a few other discriminatory applications of standards. Consequently, an additional 20 percent is deducted from El Salvador's trade freedom score to account for these non-tariff barriers.

FISCAL FREEDOM — 90.9%

El Salvador has relatively low tax rates. Both the top income tax rate and the top corporate tax rate are 25 percent. Other taxes include a value-added tax (VAT) and a tax on insurance contracts. In the most recent year, overall tax revenue as a percentage of GDP was 11 percent.

FREEDOM FROM GOVERNMENT — 95.1%

Total government expenditures in El Salvador, including consumption and transfer payments, are low. In the most recent year, government spending equaled 14.3 percent of GDP, and the government received 0.5 percent of its total revenues from state-owned enterprises and government ownership of property.

MONETARY FREEDOM — 76.7%

Inflation in El Salvador is moderate, averaging 4.4 percent between 2003 and 2005. Relatively moderate prices explain most of the monetary freedom score. The government controls the prices of some goods, including electricity, and implements subsidies for diesel, petroleum, and liquid propane gas. Consequently, an additional 10 percent is deducted from El Salvador's monetary freedom score to adjust for measures that distort domestic prices.

INVESTMENT FREEDOM — 70%

El Salvador maintains an open foreign investment climate, and foreign investors receive equal treatment. Foreign investors may obtain credit in the local financial market under the same conditions as local investors. The government limits foreign direct investment in commerce, industry, certain services, and fishing. Investments in railroads, piers, and canals require government approval. There are no controls or requirements on current transfers, access to foreign exchange, or most capital transactions. There are some restrictions on land ownership; foreign persons may purchase land, up to 245 hectares, only if there is a reciprocal arrangement with their home country.

FINANCIAL FREEDOM — 70%

The Salvadoran financial sector has experienced significant liberalization since the 1990s and is home to some of the region's largest banks. In 2005, there were nine private commercial banks, two state-owned banks, and two foreign bank branches. Private banks controlled nearly 96 percent of bank assets in August 2005. Banks are allowed to offer a wide range of financial services. Interest rates are set by the market. Regulations on banks are open and transparent. Non-bank financial institutions are limited. There were 18 insurance companies in 2004, two of which were foreign-owned. Foreign banks and insurance companies receive national treatment. The stock exchange participates in a regional association of stock exchanges.

PROPERTY RIGHTS — 50%

Property rights are moderately well protected in El Salvador. Lawsuits move very slowly and can be costly and unproductive. The course of some cases has shown that the legal system is subject to manipulation by private interests, and final rulings are sometimes not enforced. The inefficiency of the judiciary, along with crime, is cited as one of the main constraints on doing business.

FREEDOM FROM CORRUPTION — 42%

Corruption is perceived as significant. El Salvador ranks 51st out of 158 countries in Transparency International's Corruption Perceptions Index for 2005.

LABOR FREEDOM — 79.2%

The labor market operates under relatively flexible employment regulations that could be improved to enhance employment and productivity growth. The non-salary cost of employing a worker is low, but dismissing a redundant employee is relatively costly. There are rigid restrictions on increasing or contracting the number of working hours.

EQUATORIAL GUINEA

Malabo

Equatorial Guinea's economy is 53.2 percent free, according to our 2007 assessment, which makes it the world's 128th freest economy. Its overall score is 3 percentage points higher than last year, partially reflecting new methodological detail. Equatorial Guinea is ranked 27th out of 40 countries in the sub-Saharan Africa region, and its overall score is equal to the regional average.

Equatorial Guinea does not rank strongly in any category. Both the top income tax rate and the top corporate tax rate are a high 35 percent, and tax revenue is not large as a percentage of GDP. Government expenditures rely heavily on income from state-owned businesses (mainly oil). Inflation is relatively low because the currency is pegged to the euro.

Equatorial Guinea is beset by serious, self-imposed economic barriers. Business freedom, trade freedom, investment freedom, property rights, and freedom from corruption are weak. Regulations are burdensome, and business operations are significantly hampered by red tape. The average tariff rate is high, and the inefficient and corrupt bureaucracy makes the customs process difficult. Property rights are not secured by an independent judiciary, and corruption is rampant.

BACKGROUND: Since seizing power in 1979, Teodoro Obiang Nguema Mbasogo has been elected president in 1982 and re-elected to a fourth seven-year term in 2002. Obiang and his advisers maintain tight control of the military and the government. Oil and gas dominate the economy, and income has risen sharply as a result of increased crude oil production, but most of the population is still engaged in subsistence farming, hunting, and fishing. Government management of oil wealth lacks transparency. Despite laws providing for an open investment and trade regime, ongoing problems include a dysfunctional judiciary, unclear regulation, and corruption.

How Do We Measure Economic Freedom? See Chapter 3 (page 37) for an explanation of the methodology or visit the *Index* Web site at *heritage.org/index*.

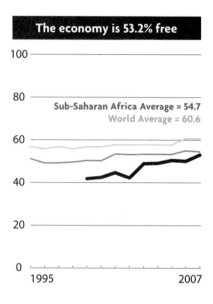

The economy is 53.2% free

Sub-Saharan Africa Average = 54.7
World Average = 60.6

QUICK FACTS

Population: 0.5 million

GDP (PPP): $25.7 billion (2005 estimate)
32.4% growth in 2004
30.1% 5-yr. comp. ann. growth
$50,200 per capita (2005 estimate)

Unemployment: 30% (1998 estimate)

Inflation (CPI): 3.8%

FDI (net inflow): $1.7 billion (gross)

Official Development Assistance:
Multilateral: $9 million
Bilateral: $42 million (0.1% from the U.S.)

External Debt: $353.0 million (2005 estimate)

Exports: $4.6 billion (2004 estimate)
Primarily petroleum, methanol, timber, cocoa

Imports: $1.5 billion (2004 estimate)
Primarily petroleum sector equipment, other equipment

EQUATORIAL GUINEA'S TEN ECONOMIC FREEDOMS

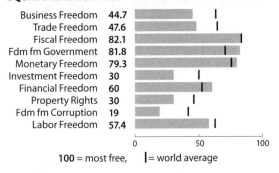

Business Freedom	44.7
Trade Freedom	47.6
Fiscal Freedom	82.1
Fdm fm Government	81.8
Monetary Freedom	79.3
Investment Freedom	30
Financial Freedom	60
Property Rights	30
Fdm fm Corruption	19
Labor Freedom	57.4

0   50   100

100 = most free, | = world average

BUSINESS FREEDOM — *44.7%*

Starting a business takes an average of 136 days—almost three times longer than the world average of 48 days. Entrepreneurship should be easier for maximum job creation. Obtaining a business license is difficult, and closing a business is very difficult. Lack of transparency and uneven application of commercial regulations are still major problems. The overall freedom to start, operate, and close a business is seriously restricted by the national regulatory environment.

TRADE FREEDOM — *47.6%*

Equatorial Guinea's weighted average tariff rate was 16.2 percent in 2005. A burdensome and corrupt customs process remains an important non-tariff barrier to trade, and the government provides export subsidies for cocoa. Consequently, an additional 20 percent is deducted from Equatorial Guinea's trade freedom score to account for these non-tariff barriers.

FISCAL FREEDOM — *82.1%*

Equatorial Guinea has high tax rates. Both the top income tax rate and the top corporate tax rate are 35 percent. In the most recent year, overall tax revenue as a percentage of GDP was 15.4 percent.

FREEDOM FROM GOVERNMENT — *81.8%*

Total government expenditures in Equatorial Guinea, including consumption and transfer payments, are moderate. In the most recent year, government spending equaled 23 percent of GDP, and the government received 17.6 percent of its total revenues from state-owned enterprises and government ownership of property.

MONETARY FREEDOM — *79.3%*

As a member of the Central African Economic and Monetary Community (CEMAC), Equatorial Guinea uses the CFA franc, pegged to the euro. Inflation in Equatorial Guinea is relatively high, averaging 6.2 percent between 2003 and 2005. Relatively unstable prices explain most of the monetary freedom score. The government sets the price of electricity and subsidizes both electricity and cocoa production. Consequently, an additional 5 percent is deducted from Equatorial Guinea's monetary freedom score to adjust for measures that distort domestic prices.

INVESTMENT FREEDOM — *30%*

The investment code, while liberal in intent, is extremely bureaucratic in practice and open to manipulation. Corruption and lax enforcement of investment law are serious impediments to investment. Foreign investors are required to obtain a local partner. Residents and non-residents may hold foreign exchange accounts, but approval is required for resident accounts held domestically. Capital transactions, payments, and transfers to countries other than France, Monaco, members of the CEMAC, members of the West African Economic and Monetary Union, and Comoros are subject to restrictions.

FINANCIAL FREEDOM — *60%*

Equatorial Guinea's financial system is small and under-developed. The Commission Bancaire de L'Afrique Centrale (COBAC) has acted as Equatorial Guinea's central bank since the country joined the franc zone in 1985. The banking sector consists of three main banks, all of which are primarily foreign-owned. The government maintains minority ownership in two banks. A fourth bank had its license approved in 2004 and began operation in 2005. Compliance with banking regulations is mixed, and the number of non-performing loans has increased in recent years. The insurance sector is very small, consisting of three insurance companies and one reinsurance company. Equatorial Guinea has no stock exchange or securities market.

PROPERTY RIGHTS — *30%*

Senior government officials sometimes extort money from foreign companies, threatening to take away concessions. The judicial system is open to political influence. Equatorial Guinea is a member of OHADA (Organisation pour l'Harmonisation en Afrique du Droit des Affaires), a regional organization that trains judges and lawyers in commercial law to help reform the enforcement of contracts.

FREEDOM FROM CORRUPTION — *19%*

Corruption is perceived as widespread. Equatorial Guinea ranks 152nd out of 158 countries in Transparency International's Corruption Perceptions Index for 2005.

LABOR FREEDOM — *57.4%*

The labor market operates under restrictive employment regulations that hinder employment and productivity growth. The non-salary cost of employing a worker is high, and dismissing a redundant employee is costly. There are rigid restriction on increasing and contracting the number of working hours.

ESTONIA

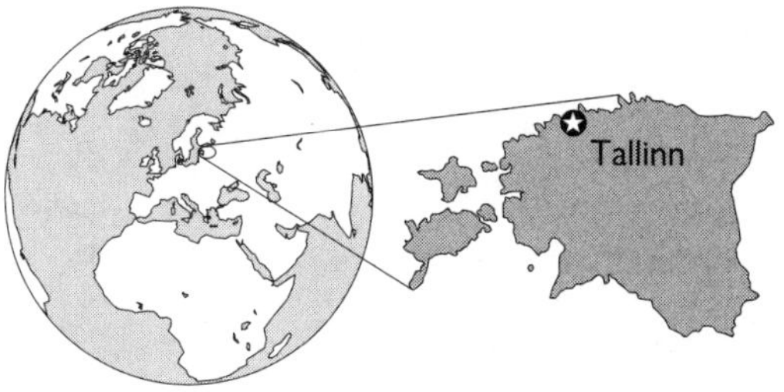

Estonia's economy is 78.1 percent free, according to our 2007 assessment, which makes it the world's 12th freest economy. Its overall score is 2.2 percentage points higher than last year, partially reflecting new methodological detail. Estonia is ranked 5th out of 41 countries in the European region, and its overall score is much higher than the regional average.

Estonia scores highly in investment freedom, fiscal freedom, financial freedom, property rights, business freedom, and monetary freedom. The top income and corporate tax rates are low, and business regulation is efficient. Inflation is fairly low, but Estonia's monetary freedom score is hurt by the European Union's agricultural subsidies. Investment is easy but subject to government licensing in some areas of the economy. Estonia's financial sector is the most developed among the Baltic States and, because of its transparency, should be a model for developing nations. The judiciary, independent of politics and free of corruption, protects property rights effectively.

Estonia could do slightly better in freedom from government and labor freedom. Total government spending is high (although in line with other EU economies), and the labor market is unnecessarily rigid.

BACKGROUND: Since the fall of the Soviet Union, Estonia has been one of the most radical reformers among the former Soviet nations and has transformed itself into one the world's most dynamic and modern economies. It is expected that the current ruling coalition, which includes the liberal Reform Party, the Center Party, and the Estonian People's Union, will remain in office until the 2007 elections. Estonia has strong trade ties to Finland, Sweden, and Germany, and its services and manufacturing sectors are thriving. The country aims to join the European Economic and Monetary Union in January 2007.

How Do We Measure Economic Freedom? See Chapter 3 (page 37) for an explanation of the methodology or visit the *Index* Web site at *heritage.org/index*.

The economy is 78.1% free

Europe Average = 67.5
World Average = 60.6

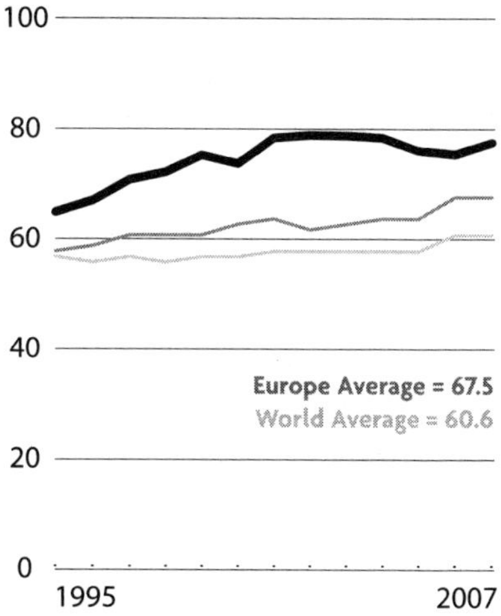

QUICK FACTS

Population: 1.4 million

GDP (PPP): $19.6 billion
7.8% growth in 2004
7.2% 5-yr. comp. ann. growth
$14,555 per capita

Unemployment: 9.7%

Inflation (CPI): 3.0%

FDI (net inflow): $668.6 million

Official Development Assistance:
Multilateral: $109 million
Bilateral: $27 million (11% from the U.S.)

External Debt: $10.0 billion

Exports: $8.8 billion
Primarily machinery and equipment, wood and paper, textiles, food products, furniture, metals, chemical products

Imports: $9.7 billion
Primarily machinery and equipment, chemical products, textiles, food, transportation equipment

ESTONIA'S TEN ECONOMIC FREEDOMS

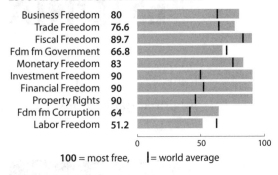

Business Freedom	80
Trade Freedom	76.6
Fiscal Freedom	89.7
Fdm fm Government	66.8
Monetary Freedom	83
Investment Freedom	90
Financial Freedom	90
Property Rights	90
Fdm fm Corruption	64
Labor Freedom	51.2

100 = most free, **|** = world average

BUSINESS FREEDOM — 80%

Starting a business takes an average of 35 days, compared to the world average of 48 days. The sound business climate has allowed entrepreneurship to flourish, ensuring high levels of job creation. Obtaining a business license is simple, and closing a business is relatively easy. Regulations are transparent and evenly applied. The overall freedom to start, operate, and close a business is relatively well protected by the national regulatory environment.

TRADE FREEDOM — 76.6%

Estonia's trade policy is the same as those of other members of the European Union. The common EU weighted average tariff rate was 1.7 percent in 2005. Various non-tariff barriers are reflected in EU and Estonian government policy, including agricultural and manufacturing subsidies, regulatory and licensing restrictions, and other market access restrictions. Consequently, an additional 20 percent is deducted from Estonia's trade freedom score.

FISCAL FREEDOM — 89.7%

Estonia has low tax rates. The income tax rate is a flat 23 percent, which the government intends to reduce to 20 percent by 2009. Only distributed profits are subject to the 23 percent corporate tax rate; undistributed profits of corporations are not subject to taxation regardless of whether they are invested or merely retained. Other taxes include a value-added tax (VAT) and an excise tax. In the most recent year, overall tax revenue as a percentage of GDP was 31.9 percent.

FREEDOM FROM GOVERNMENT — 66.8%

Total government expenditures in Estonia, including consumption and transfer payments, are high. In the most recent year, government spending equaled 37.5 percent of GDP, and the government received 1.1 percent of its total revenues from state-owned enterprises and government ownership of property. Privatization is nearly complete with the exceptions of the ports and the main power plants.

MONETARY FREEDOM — 83%

Inflation in Estonia is moderate, averaging 3.6 percent between 2003 and 2005. Relatively moderate and unstable prices explain most of the monetary freedom score. As a participant in the EU's Common Agricultural Policy, the government subsidizes agricultural production, distorting the prices of agricultural products. Consequently, 5 percent is deducted from Estonia's monetary freedom score to account for these policies.

INVESTMENT FREEDOM — 90%

The foreign investment code is transparent and equivalent to domestic rules. Foreigners may invest in all sectors and own real estate. The government requires licenses for investment in banking, mining, gas and water supply or related structures, railroads and transport, energy, and communications networks. Residents and non-residents may hold foreign exchange accounts, and payments, transfers, and most capital transactions are not subject to controls. Foreign direct investment rules regarding real estate, aviation, maritime transport, and security service enterprises were harmonized with EU regulations in 2004.

FINANCIAL FREEDOM — 90%

Estonia's financial sector is the strongest and most developed in the Baltic States. Before its accession to the EU, Estonia dramatically reformed its financial system. The central bank may not lend to the public sector, and the government has no stake in any bank. Estonia's universal banking model places no limits on what may be offered by financial institutions; for instance, banks may offer insurance, leasing, and brokerage services. Foreign financial institutions are welcome, and the insurance sector is dominated by foreign firms. The two largest banks are foreign and account for 60 percent of financial sector assets. Credit is allocated on market terms, and foreign investors may obtain credit freely. The stock exchange is small but active.

PROPERTY RIGHTS — 90%

Estonia's judiciary is independent and insulated from government influence. Property rights and contracts are enforced by the courts, and the commercial code is applied consistently. As part of its ongoing effort to strengthen its judicial procedures since gaining EU membership, Estonia adopted a new code of criminal procedure in 2004.

FREEDOM FROM CORRUPTION — 64%

Corruption is perceived as somewhat present. Estonia ranks 27th out of 158 countries in Transparency International's Corruption Perceptions Index for 2005.

LABOR FREEDOM — 51.2%

The labor market operates under rigid employment regulations that are barriers to continuing employment and productivity growth. The non-salary cost of employing a worker can be high, and dismissing a redundant employee is relatively costly. Unemployment insurance amounts to about 40 percent to 50 percent of the worker's previous wage, depending on the length of the unemployment period. There are rigid restrictions on increasing and contracting the number of work hours.

ETHIOPIA

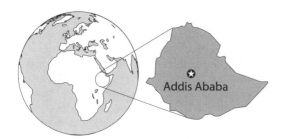

Addis Ababa

Rank: 116

Regional Rank: 21 of 40

Ethiopia's economy is 54.4 percent free, according to our 2007 assessment, which makes it the world's 116th freest economy. Its overall score is 1.1 percentage points higher than last year, partially reflecting new methodological detail. Ethiopia is ranked 21st out of 40 countries in the sub-Saharan Africa region, and its overall score is equal to the regional average.

Ethiopia does not rank strongly in any category but does score moderately well in fiscal freedom, freedom from government, and monetary freedom. The top income and corporate tax rates are moderate, and overall tax revenue is not large as a percentage of GDP. Government expenditures are not high, and the government receives only a small amount of its total revenues from state-owned businesses.

As a developing nation, Ethiopia faces typical and difficult challenges. It does not score well in trade freedom, investment freedom, financial freedom, property rights, and freedom from corruption. Commercial regulation and bureaucracy are burdensome, and business operations (except for closing a business) are significantly hampered by the government. Ethiopia's average tariff rate is high, and there are significant non-tariff barriers as well. The banking system is subject to strong political pressure, as is the rule of law. Property rights cannot be guaranteed.

BACKGROUND: Ethiopia is the second most populous country in sub-Saharan Africa and also one of the poorest. It is moving toward multi-party democracy, but obstacles to progress remain to be overcome, as demonstrated by the 2005 post-election crackdown on protestors. Over three-quarters of the population in rural areas is engaged in agriculture, and periodic drought can have severe consequences. The government remains involved in key sectors of the economy and reserves other sectors for Ethiopians. Landlocked Ethiopia has depended heavily on Djibouti for access to foreign goods ever since a border war with Eritrea.

How Do We Measure Economic Freedom? See Chapter 3 (page 37) for an explanation of the methodology or visit the *Index* Web site at *heritage.org/index*.

The economy is 54.4% free

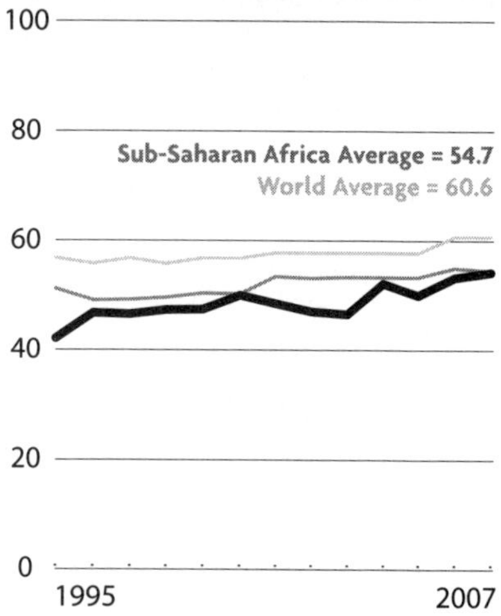

Sub-Saharan Africa Average = 54.7
World Average = 60.6

(Line chart showing scores from 1995 to 2007, y-axis from 0 to 100)

QUICK FACTS

Population: 70 million

GDP (PPP): $52.9 billion
12.3% growth in 2004
4.4% 5-yr. comp. ann. growth
$756 per capita

Unemployment: n/a

Inflation (CPI): 3.3%

FDI (net inflow): $545.1 million (gross)

Official Development Assistance:
Multilateral: $834 million
Bilateral: $1.1 billion (38% from the U.S.)

External Debt: $6.6 billion

Exports: $1.7 billion
Primarily coffee, qat, gold, leather products, live animals, oilseeds

Imports: $3.8 billion
Primarily food, live animals, petroleum and petroleum products, chemicals, machinery, motor vehicles, cereals, textiles

ETHIOPIA'S TEN ECONOMIC FREEDOMS

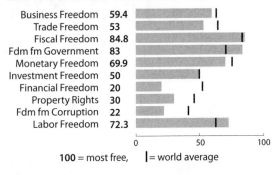

Business Freedom	59.4	
Trade Freedom	53	
Fiscal Freedom	84.8	
Fdm fm Government	83	
Monetary Freedom	69.9	
Investment Freedom	50	
Financial Freedom	20	
Property Rights	30	
Fdm fm Corruption	22	
Labor Freedom	72.3	

100 = most free, **I** = world average

BUSINESS FREEDOM — *59.4%*

Starting a business takes an average of 16 days, compared to the world average of 48 days. Entrepreneurship should be easier for maximum job creation. Obtaining a business license is difficult, but closing a business is relatively easy. The regulatory system is generally considered to be fair but not always transparent. Cumbersome bureaucracy deters entrepreneurial activities. The overall freedom to start, operate, and close a business is restricted by the national regulatory environment.

TRADE FREEDOM — *53%*

Ethiopia's weighted average tariff rate was 13.5 percent in 2002. Non-tariff barriers include foreign exchange controls, burdensome trade-related regulations and bureaucracy, and some import restrictions. Consequently, an additional 20 percent is deducted from Ethiopia's trade freedom score to account for these non-tariff barriers.

FISCAL FREEDOM — *84.8%*

Ethiopia has moderate tax rates. The top income tax rate is 35 percent, and the top corporate tax rate is 30 percent. Other taxes include a value-added tax (VAT) and a capital gains tax. In the most recent year, overall tax revenue as a percentage of GDP was 12.5 percent.

FREEDOM FROM GOVERNMENT — *83%*

Total government expenditures in Ethiopia, including consumption and transfer payments, are low. In the most recent year, government spending equaled 25 percent of GDP, and the government received 7.2 percent of its total revenues from state-owned enterprises and government ownership of property. State ownership and management still guides many sectors of the economy.

MONETARY FREEDOM — *69.9%*

Inflation in Ethiopia is relatively high, averaging 10.1 percent between 2003 and 2005. Relatively high and unstable prices explain most of the monetary freedom score. The government influences prices through the regulation of state-owned enterprises and utilities and provides subsidies and price controls for petroleum products. Consequently, an additional 10 percent is deducted from Ethiopia's monetary freedom score to adjust for measures that distort domestic prices.

INVESTMENT FREEDOM — *50%*

Ethiopia has taken several steps to liberalize its foreign investment laws and streamline the registration process, but official and unofficial barriers still deter foreign investment. Certain sectors remain off-limits. The government has lowered the minimum capital investment for wholly and partially owned foreign investments. The Ethiopian Investment Commission, the main contact point for foreign investors, provides a highly expedited one-stop service that significantly cuts the cost of obtaining investment and business licenses. Foreign exchange accounts, payments, and current transfers are subject to controls and restrictions. There are significant controls on capital transactions. All investments must be approved and certified by the government.

FINANCIAL FREEDOM — *20%*

Ethiopia's small financial sector is subject to strong government influence. The central bank is not independent, and the government retains a strong influence over lending, including controlling interest rates and owning the country's largest bank (Commercial Bank of Ethiopia), which accounts for three-quarters of total banking assets. However, the private banks have increased their share of total deposits, loans, and credit in recent years. Non-performing loans are a lower percentage of the total but still account for over 25 percent of all loans. Microfinance is well established. Foreign firms are prohibited from investing in the banking and insurance sectors. The insurance sector is small and composed of nine companies, including one state-owned company. Ethiopia does not have a stock market, but the private sale of shares is common.

PROPERTY RIGHTS — *30%*

The judicial system enforces property rights weakly. The system is underdeveloped, poorly staffed, and inexperienced, although efforts are underway to strengthen its capacity. Property and contractual rights are recognized, and there are written commercial and bankruptcy laws, but judges lack an understanding of commercial matters. There is no guarantee that the decision of an international arbitration body will be fully accepted and implemented by Ethiopian authorities.

FREEDOM FROM CORRUPTION — *22%*

Corruption is perceived as widespread. Ethiopia ranks 137th out of 158 countries in Transparency International's Corruption Perceptions Index for 2005.

LABOR FREEDOM — *72.3%*

The labor market operates under relatively flexible employment regulations that hinder employment and productivity growth. The non-salary cost of employing a worker is very low, but dismissing a redundant employee is relatively costly. There are rigid restrictions on increasing and contracting the number of working hours.

FIJI

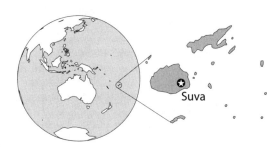

Suva

Fiji's economy is 59.8 percent free, according to our 2007 assessment, which makes it the world's 80th freest economy. Its overall score is 2.8 percentage points higher than last year, partially reflecting new methodological detail. Fiji is ranked 13th out of 30 countries in the Asia–Pacific region, and its overall score is slightly above the regional average.

Fiji scores well in business freedom, fiscal freedom, and labor freedom. Opening a business in Fiji is a routine procedure, and commercial licensing presents no problems. Closing an enterprise, however, can be costly. Fiji has moderate top tax rates, and overall tax revenue is not high as a percentage of GDP. The labor market operates under highly flexible conditions that make hiring and firing workers very easy. Inflation is fairly low, but Fiji's monetary freedom score is hurt by government price controls.

Fiji is weak in investment freedom, property rights, and freedom from corruption. Foreign investment is highly controlled and regulated, and the judicial system enforcing these regulations is erratic and clogged by a significant backlog of cases.

BACKGROUND: Fiji, a Pacific Island parliamentary democracy, is a developing economy in which agriculture and fishing account for around 15 percent of GDP. Tourism, which has expanded rapidly for two decades, remains a pillar of the economy and a major source of foreign exchange earnings. The sugar and clothing industries are direct sources of jobs for more than 10 percent of Fiji's labor force but need adjustments to remain viable and competitive. The government has tried to make the economy more business-friendly and diversified, but it still needs to deal with serious obstacles like the weak protection of property rights.

How Do We Measure Economic Freedom? See Chapter 3 (page 37) for an explanation of the methodology or visit the *Index* Web site at *heritage.org/index*.

The economy is 59.8% free

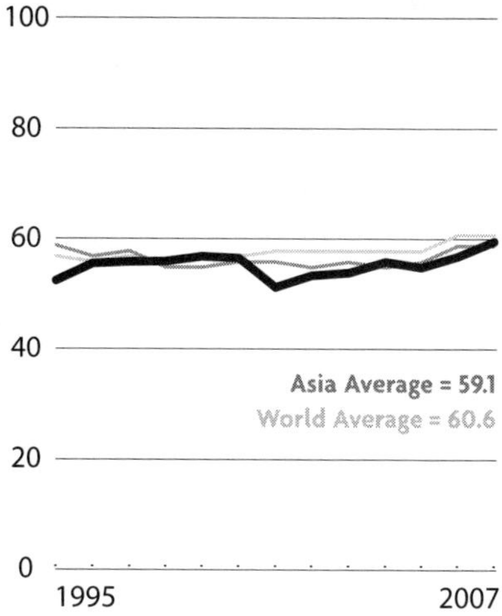

Asia Average = 59.1
World Average = 60.6

1995 — 2007

QUICK FACTS

Population: 0.8 million

GDP (PPP): $5.1 billion
4.1% growth in 2004
2.2% 5-yr. comp. ann. growth
$6,066 per capita

Unemployment: 7.6% (1999 estimate)

Inflation (CPI): 2.8%

FDI (net inflow): −$9.2 million

Official Development Assistance:
Multilateral: $27 million
Bilateral: $37 million (4.4% from the U.S.)

External Debt: $267 million

Exports: $678 million
Primarily sugar, garments, gold, timber, fish, molasses, coconut oil

Imports: $1.3 billion
Primarily manufactured goods, machinery, transport equipment, petroleum products, food, chemicals

FIJI'S TEN ECONOMIC FREEDOMS

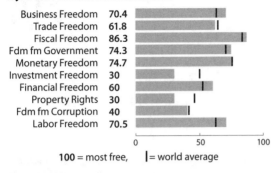

Business Freedom	70.4
Trade Freedom	61.8
Fiscal Freedom	86.3
Fdm fm Government	74.3
Monetary Freedom	74.7
Investment Freedom	30
Financial Freedom	60
Property Rights	30
Fdm fm Corruption	40
Labor Freedom	70.5

100 = most free, ▮ = world average

BUSINESS FREEDOM — *70.4%*

Starting a business takes an average of 46 days, compared to the world average of 48 days. Entrepreneurship should be easier for maximum job creation. Obtaining a business license is simple, but closing a business can be difficult. The lack of transparency still impedes entrepreneurial activities. The overall freedom to start, operate, and close a business is relatively well protected by the national regulatory environment.

TRADE FREEDOM — *61.8%*

Fiji's average tariff rate was 9.1 percent in 2004. The government also implements import licensing restrictions and quotas. Consequently, an additional 20 percent is deducted from Fiji's trade freedom score to account for these non-tariff barriers.

FISCAL FREEDOM — *86.3%*

Fiji has moderate tax rates. Both the top income tax rate and the top corporate tax rate are 31 percent. Other taxes include a value-added tax (VAT) and a property tax. In the most recent year, overall tax revenue as a percentage of GDP was 11.5 percent.

FREEDOM FROM GOVERNMENT — *74.3%*

Total government expenditures in Fiji, including consumption and transfer payments, are moderate. In the most recent year, government spending equaled 31.6 percent of GDP, and the government received 6.9 percent of its total revenues from state-owned enterprises and government ownership of property.

MONETARY FREEDOM — *74.7%*

Inflation in Fiji is relatively low, averaging 2.6 percent between 2003 and 2005. Relatively stable prices explain most of the monetary freedom score. The government influences prices through state-owned utilities; controls the prices of various products, including food; and is authorized to impose price controls on commodities to correct for "market inequities" for both consumers and producers. Consequently, an additional 15 percent is deducted from Fiji's monetary freedom score to adjust for measures that distort domestic prices.

INVESTMENT FREEDOM — *30%*

Fiji places a number of restrictions on foreign investment but also offers various tax incentives to investors in preferred activities. The government requires foreign investors to undergo several bureaucratic procedures to register and also must approve all foreign investments, exercising too much discretion according to unclear criteria. Residents may hold foreign exchange accounts subject to approval by the government. Non-residents may hold foreign exchange accounts subject to certain regulations. Most payments and transfers are subject to government approval and limitations on amounts. Capital transfers in excess of specified amounts require approval by the central bank, the South Pacific Stock Exchange, or commercial banks.

FINANCIAL FREEDOM — *60%*

Fiji's financial system is relatively well developed and is characterized by a significant degree of foreign participation. The banking system accounts for 35 percent of financial system assets and is largely private. The state-owned Fiji Development Bank provides business development loans and offers commercial banking services. The government sold its minority stake in the Colonial National Bank in January 2006. The two largest banks are Australian and account for 80 percent of the banking market, and three other foreign banks operate freely. The insurance sector consists of 10 companies and is dominated by foreign firms. Fiji has a small stock exchange. The national pension system accounts for 45 percent of financial sector assets.

PROPERTY RIGHTS — *30%*

Protection of property is highly uncertain in Fiji. The backlog of cases in the courts is significant, and processing is slowed by a shortage of prosecutors. The purported abrogation of the constitution and other events, including abolition of the Supreme Court, have undermined the independence of the judiciary. The many difficulties involved in obtaining land titles are serious obstacles to investment and growth.

FREEDOM FROM CORRUPTION — *40%*

Corruption is perceived as significant. Fiji ranks 55th out of 158 countries in Transparency International's Corruption Perceptions Index for 2005.

LABOR FREEDOM — *70.5%*

The labor market operates under relatively flexible employment regulations that could be improved to enhance employment and productivity growth. The non-salary cost of employing a worker is low, and dismissing a redundant employee is costless. There are rigid restrictions on increasing or contracting the number of working hours.

FINLAND

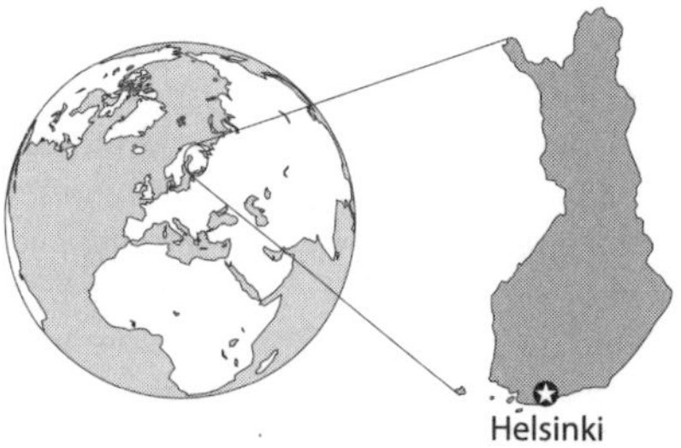

Helsinki

Rank: 16

Regional Rank: 9 of 41

Finland's economy is 76.5 percent free, according to our 2007 assessment, which makes it the world's 16th freest economy. Its overall score is 0.9 percentage point higher than last year, partially reflecting new methodological detail. Finland is ranked 9th out of 41 countries in the European region, and its overall score is well above the regional average.

Finland has high levels of investment freedom, property rights, financial freedom, monetary freedom, and business freedom. A business-friendly environment with minimal regulation is enabling the rapid growth of private enterprise. Property is protected by a transparent rule of law, and foreign investors enjoy excellent market access. There is virtually no corruption, and business operations are not hampered by the bureaucracy. As a member of the euro zone, Finland has a standardized monetary policy that yields low inflation, despite some government distortion in the agricultural sector.

Finland could improve its labor freedom and freedom from government. As in many other European social democracies, high government spending supports an extensive welfare state: Government spending equals half of Finland's GDP. The labor market operates under fairly restrictive regulations, such as a limited number of working hours allowed per week and very high unemployment benefits.

BACKGROUND: Finland ranks among the world's most competitive and transparent economies. Both the information and communications technology sectors make significant contributions to the economy. The government has given priority to reducing its labor market rigidities. Finland took its turn at the European Union presidency during the second half of 2006. Because Finland's contributions to the EU budget are expected to grow, however, the government faces the challenge of maintaining popular domestic support for EU policy.

How Do We Measure Economic Freedom? See Chapter 3 (page 37) for an explanation of the methodology or visit the *Index* Web site at *heritage.org/index*.

The economy is 76.5% free

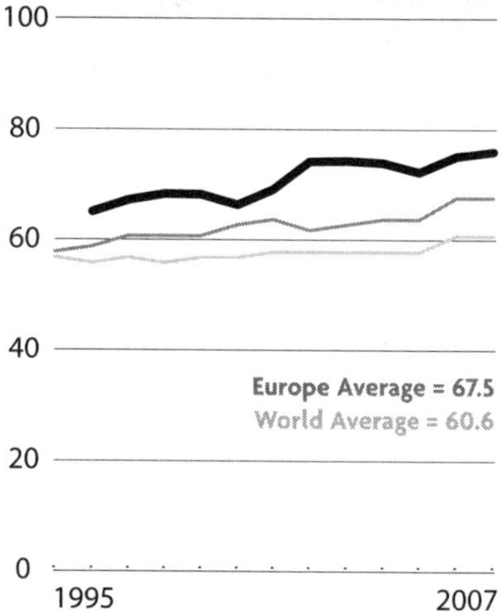

Europe Average = 67.5
World Average = 60.6

QUICK FACTS

Population: 5.2 million

GDP (PPP): $156.6 billion
3.6% growth in 2004
2.8% 5-yr. comp. ann. growth
$29,951 per capita

Unemployment: 8.8% (2004 estimate)

Inflation (CPI): 0.2%

FDI (net inflow): $5.7 billion

Official Development Assistance:
Multilateral: None
Bilateral: None

External Debt: $211.7 billion (2005)

Exports: $71.1 billion
Primarily machinery and equipment, chemicals, metals, timber, paper, pulp

Imports: $60.6 billion
Primarily food, petroleum and petroleum products, chemicals, transport equipment, iron and steel, machinery, textile yarn and fabrics, grains

FINLAND'S TEN ECONOMIC FREEDOMS

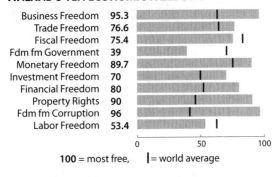

Business Freedom	95.3
Trade Freedom	76.6
Fiscal Freedom	75.4
Fdm fm Government	39
Monetary Freedom	89.7
Investment Freedom	70
Financial Freedom	80
Property Rights	90
Fdm fm Corruption	96
Labor Freedom	53.4

0   50   100

100 = most free, | = world average

BUSINESS FREEDOM — 95.3%

Starting a business takes an average of 14 days, compared to the world average of 48 days. The sound business environment allows entrepreneurship to flourish in Finland. Obtaining a business license is relatively simple, and closing a business is very easy. The overall freedom to start, operate, and close a business is strongly protected by the national regulatory environment.

TRADE FREEDOM — 76.6%

Finland's trade policy is the same as those of other members of the European Union. The common EU weighted average tariff rate was 1.7 percent in 2005. Various non-tariff barriers are reflected in EU and Finland government policy, including agricultural and manufacturing subsidies, regulatory and licensing restrictions, and other market access restrictions in sectors such as pharmaceuticals and services. Consequently, an additional 20 percent is deducted from Finland's trade freedom score.

FISCAL FREEDOM — 75.4%

Finland has moderate tax rates. The top income tax rate is 32.5 percent, and the top corporate tax rate is 26 percent. Other taxes include a value-added tax (VAT) and a real estate tax. The national wealth tax was abolished effective January 2006. In the most recent year, overall tax revenue as a percentage of GDP was 44.3 percent.

FREEDOM FROM GOVERNMENT — 39%

Total government expenditures in Finland, including consumption and transfer payments, are very high. In the most recent year, government spending equaled 50.7 percent of GDP, and the government received 3.1 percent of its total revenues from state-owned enterprises and government ownership of property.

MONETARY FREEDOM — 89.7%

Finland uses the euro as its currency. Between 2003 and 2005, Finland's weighted average annual rate of inflation was 0.7 percent. Stable prices explain most of the monetary freedom score. However, as a participant in the EU's Common Agricultural Policy, the government subsidizes agricultural production, distorting the prices of agricultural products. The government also imposes artificially low prices on pharmaceutical products. Consequently, an additional 5 percent is deducted from Finland's monetary freedom score to account for these policies.

INVESTMENT FREEDOM — 70%

Finland welcomes foreign investment and imposes few restrictions. Foreign investments do not require prior approval, but acquisitions of large Finnish companies may require follow-up clearance from the Ministry of Trade and Industry. Non–European Economic Area investors must apply for a license to invest in many sectors, including security, banking, insurance, mining, travel agencies, and restaurants. Restrictions on the purchase of land apply only to non-residents purchasing land in the Aaland Islands. There are no exchange controls and no restrictions on current transfers or repatriation of profits, and both residents and non-residents may hold foreign exchange accounts.

FINANCIAL FREEDOM — 80%

Finland's banking system is modern and sophisticated. Deregulation in the 1980s and a banking and financial crisis in the 1990s led to consolidation in the banking sector. There were 344 domestic banks operating at the end of 2004, but the banking system is dominated by three major bank groups (Nordea, OKO Bank, and the Sampo Group), which together account for over 80 percent of the banking market. The government owns about 14 percent of the Sampo Group, which is majority foreign-owned. The banking industry is totally open to foreign competition. Capital markets determine interest rates. The stock exchange is part of OMX Exchanges, a regional integrated network of exchanges.

PROPERTY RIGHTS — 90%

Property rights are well protected, and contractual agreements are strictly honored. The quality of Finland's judiciary and civil service is generally high. Expropriation is unlikely.

FREEDOM FROM CORRUPTION — 96%

Corruption is perceived as almost nonexistent. Finland ranks 2nd out of 158 countries in Transparency International's Corruption Perceptions Index for 2005.

LABOR FREEDOM — 53.4%

The labor market operates under restrictive employment regulations that hamper employment and productivity growth. The non-salary cost of employing a worker is high, and dismissing a redundant employee is relatively costly. Finland's unemployment insurance system provides both a government-funded basic unemployment benefit and the option of participating in an unemployment fund. Involuntarily unemployed individuals automatically receive benefits up to 500 working days.

FRANCE

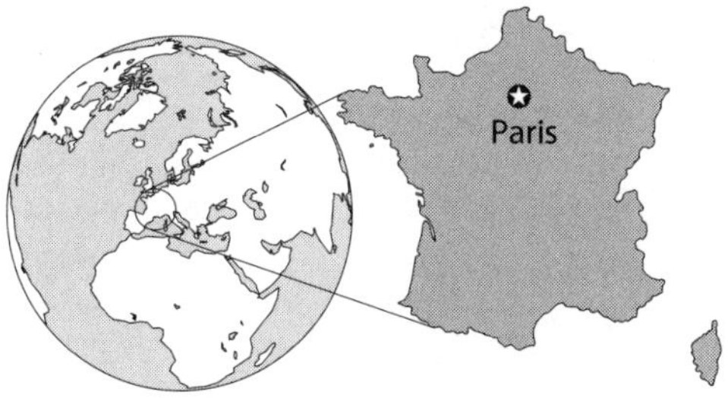

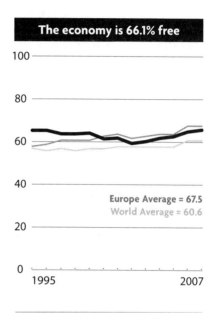

Paris

Rank: 45

Regional Rank: 26 of 41

France's economy is 66.1 percent free, according to our 2007 assessment, which makes it the world's 45th freest economy. Its overall score is 0.9 percentage point higher than last year, partially reflecting new methodological detail. France is ranked 26th out of 41 countries in the European region, and its overall score is lower than the regional average.

France scores well in business freedom, property rights, freedom from corruption, and monetary freedom. As a member of the European Union, France has a standard-ized monetary policy that yields relatively low inflation, despite agricultural distortions. Property is protected by transparent rule of law. Starting a business takes only eight days—far below the world average—and closing a business is fairly easy.

Fiscal freedom, freedom from government, and invest-ment freedom are weak. As in many other European social democracies, government spending and tax rates are exceptionally high in order to support an extensive welfare state. Foreign investment is also hurt by the intru-sive regulatory system. Excessive labor protections have generated widespread youth unemployment and under-employment but have proven resistant to reform.

BACKGROUND: Because France is a founding member of the EU, its rejection of the European Constitution in May 2005 was a major political crisis. Prime Minister Domi-nique de Villepin's capitulation to labor union elements with regard to new labor legislation demonstrates the strength of reactionary elements in France, but the gov-ernment has continued to open the telecommunications sector to more competition and recently announced its intentions to privatize the state-owned Gaz de France energy corporation. Services account for the largest por-tion of the economy. Agricultural products, particularly wine and cheese, are politically protected exports.

How Do We Measure Economic Freedom? See Chapter 3 (page 37) for an explanation of the methodology or visit the *Index* Web site at *heritage.org/index.*

The economy is 66.1% free

100

80

60

40

Europe Average = 67.5
World Average = 60.6

20

0

1995   2007

QUICK FACTS

Population: 60.4 million

GDP (PPP): $1.8 trillion
2.1% growth in 2004
2.1% 5-yr. comp. ann. growth
$29,300 per capita

Unemployment: 10%

Inflation (CPI): 2.1%

FDI (net inflow): −$23.5 billion

Official Development Assistance:
Multilateral: None
Bilateral: None

External Debt: $2.8 trillion (2005)

Exports: $531.5 billion
Primarily machinery and transportation equipment, aircraft, plastics, chemicals, pharmaceutical products, iron and steel, beverages

Imports: $526.6 billion
Primarily machinery and equipment, vehicles, crude oil, aircraft, plastics, chemicals

FRANCE'S TEN ECONOMIC FREEDOMS

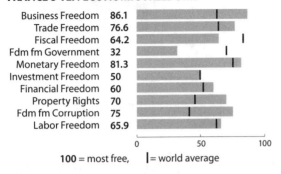

Business Freedom	86.1	
Trade Freedom	76.6	
Fiscal Freedom	64.2	
Fdm fm Government	32	
Monetary Freedom	81.3	
Investment Freedom	50	
Financial Freedom	60	
Property Rights	70	
Fdm fm Corruption	75	
Labor Freedom	65.9	

0   50   100

100 = most free, | = world average

BUSINESS FREEDOM — 86.1%

Starting a business takes an average of eight days, compared to the world average of 48 days. Obtaining a business license is simple, and closing a business is relatively easy. Although bureaucracy still remains pervasive, the government has made some progress in improving the transparency of the regulatory system. The overall freedom to start, operate, and close a business is protected by the national regulatory environment.

TRADE FREEDOM — 76.6%

France's trade policy is the same as those of other members of the European Union. The common EU weighted average tariff rate is 1.7 percent. Various non-tariff barriers are reflected in EU and French government policy, including agricultural and manufacturing subsidies, regulatory and licensing restrictions, and other market access restrictions. The government also applies additional standards, quotas, or regulations on some items. Consequently, an additional 20 percent is deducted from France's trade freedom score.

FISCAL FREEDOM — 64.2%

France has high tax rates. The top income tax rate is 48.1 percent, and the top corporate tax rate is 33.8 percent (a 33.3 percent corporate tax rate plus a surcharge of 1.5 percent). Other taxes include a value-added tax (VAT) and a business tax. In the most recent year, overall tax revenue as a percentage of GDP was 43.7 percent.

FREEDOM FROM GOVERNMENT — 32%

Total government expenditures in France, including consumption and transfer payments, are very high. In the most recent year, government spending equaled 53.7 percent of GDP, and the government received 3.9 percent of its total revenues from state-owned enterprises and government ownership of property.

MONETARY FREEDOM — 81.3%

France is a member of the euro zone. Between 2003 and 2005, France's weighted average annual rate of inflation was 1.9 percent. Relatively low and stable prices explain most of the monetary freedom score. As a participant in the EU's Common Agricultural Policy, the government subsidizes agricultural production, distorting the prices of agricultural products. The government has powers under the Commerce Code to impose price controls but uses them lightly. Prices

are regulated for pharmaceuticals, books, electricity, gas, and rail transportation. Consequently, an additional 10 percent is deducted from France's monetary policy score.

INVESTMENT FREEDOM — 50%

Foreign investment regulations are fairly simple, and many financial incentives are available. Foreign companies complain of high payroll and income taxes, pervasive regulation of labor and products markets, and negative attitudes toward foreign investors as disincentives. Foreign investment is restricted in agriculture, aircraft production, air transport, audiovisual, banking and financial and accounting services, insurance, maritime transport, publishing, radio and television media, road transportation, telecommunications, and tourism. Both residents and non-residents may hold foreign exchange accounts. There are no restrictions or controls on payments, transfers, or repatriation of profits, and non-residents may purchase real estate.

FINANCIAL FREEDOM — 60%

France has a large and sophisticated financial market. The financial, legal, regulatory, and accounting systems are somewhat burdensome but consistent with international norms. Holders of banking licenses may engage in any banking activity. Most loans are provided at market terms. The government has sold its majority stake in most banks and insurance companies but retains ownership of the Caisse des Depots et Consignations and a minority stake in several financial institutions. The postal service has its own bank and holds 10 percent of the financial services market. France is the world's fourth-largest insurance market, and foreign companies held 21.5 percent of the market in 2004. The government owns stakes in several insurance companies, including the country's largest. Capital markets are well developed, and foreign investors participate freely.

PROPERTY RIGHTS — 70%

Contractual agreements are secure, and both the judiciary and the civil service are highly professional. The bureaucracy is competent, though entanglements are common and can be time-consuming. The constitution states that any company defined as a national public service or natural monopoly must pass into state ownership.

FREEDOM FROM CORRUPTION — 75%

Corruption is perceived as minimal. France ranks 18th out of 158 countries in Transparency International's Corruption Perceptions Index for 2005.

LABOR FREEDOM — 65.9%

The labor market operates under regulated employment rules that could be improved to enhance employment and productivity growth. The non-salary cost of employing a worker is very high, and dismissing a redundant employee can be costly. There are rigid restrictions on increasing or expanding the number of working hours. Due partly to complicated and pervasive labor regulations, the unemployment rate is high. A recent effort to reform the regulated labor market met fierce resistance.

GABON

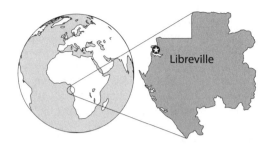

Libreville

Rank: 129

Regional Rank: 28 of 40

Gabon's economy is 53 percent free, according to our 2007 assessment, which makes it the world's 129th freest economy. Its overall score is 2 percentage points lower than last year, partially reflecting new methodological detail. Gabon is ranked 28th out of 40 countries in the sub-Saharan Africa region, and its overall score is almost equal to the regional average.

Gabon enjoys high levels of fiscal freedom, business freedom, and monetary freedom. Though taxes are high, overall revenue is relatively small as a percentage of GDP. National business licensing procedures are simple, but some other regulations are difficult and inefficient. Inflation is exceptionally low, but the government distorts market prices through a variety of price controls on certain goods.

Gabon faces many challenges, including weak trade freedom, investment freedom, financial freedom, property rights, and freedom from corruption. The average tariff rate is extremely high and is supplemented by extensive non-tariff barriers. Though the government agreed with the International Monetary Fund in 2005 to liberalize foreign investment rules, little progress has been made. Gabon's financial system is small and subject to substantial political interference. The judicial system is protective of private property but is also influenced by politics. Corruption is present in the civil service, although not as extensively as in other developing countries in the region.

BACKGROUND: Gabon's economy is driven by oil, forestry, and minerals. Oil accounts for over 40 percent of gross domestic product, 65 percent of government revenues, and over 80 percent of exports; but production is declining, and the government is trying to diversify the economy. Economic growth has barely exceeded 1 percent over the past decade. President Omar Bongo Ondimba has ruled Gabon since 1967. Ongoing problems include mismanagement and a lack of transparency in government finances, corruption, and outdated infrastructure. The government has privatized or dissolved over half of Gabon's state-owned firms.

How Do We Measure Economic Freedom? See Chapter 3 (page 37) for an explanation of the methodology or visit the *Index* Web site at *heritage.org/index*.

The economy is 53% free

Sub-Saharan Africa Average = 54.7
World Average = 60.6

1995   2007

QUICK FACTS

Population: 1.4 million

GDP (PPP): $9.0 billion
1.4% growth in 2004
0.7% 5-yr. comp. ann. growth
$6,623 per capita

Unemployment: 20.0% (Jan. 2004)

Inflation (CPI): 0.4%

FDI (net inflow): $317.7 million

Official Development Assistance:
Multilateral: $21 million
Bilateral: $74 million (4% from the U.S.)

External Debt: $4.2 billion

Exports: $3.4 billion
Primarily crude oil, timber, manganese, uranium

Imports: $1.9 billion
Primarily machinery and equipment, food, chemicals, construction materials

GABON'S TEN ECONOMIC FREEDOMS

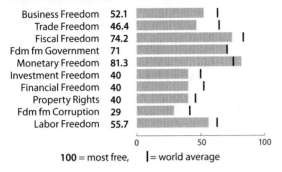

Business Freedom	52.1
Trade Freedom	46.4
Fiscal Freedom	74.2
Fdm fm Government	71
Monetary Freedom	81.3
Investment Freedom	40
Financial Freedom	40
Property Rights	40
Fdm fm Corruption	29
Labor Freedom	55.7

0   50   100

100 = most free, | = world average

BUSINESS FREEDOM — 52.1%

Starting a business takes an average of 60 days, compared to the world average of 48 days. Entrepreneurship should be easier for maximum job creation. Obtaining a business license is relatively simple, but closing a business is difficult. Complex regulations and bureaucratic delays are ongoing problems. The overall freedom to start, operate, and close a business is restricted by the national regulatory environment.

TRADE FREEDOM — 46.4%

Gabon's weighted average tariff rate was 16.8 percent in 2005. Import controls, high import taxes, and export quotas and subsidies add to the cost of trade. Consequently, an additional 20 percent is deducted from Gabon's trade freedom score to account for these non-tariff barriers.

FISCAL FREEDOM — 74.2%

Gabon has high tax rates. The top income tax rate is 50 percent, and the top corporate tax rate is 35 percent. The government also imposes a value-added tax (VAT). In the most recent year, overall tax revenue as a percentage of GDP was 11.9 percent.

FREEDOM FROM GOVERNMENT — 71%

Total government expenditures in Gabon, including consumption and transfer payments, are moderate. In the most recent year, government spending equaled 21.7 percent of GDP, and the government received 54 percent of its total revenues from state-owned enterprises and government ownership of property. Privatization of state-owned companies has been limited in recent years.

MONETARY FREEDOM — 81.3%

Inflation in Gabon is low, averaging 0.3 percent between 2003 and 2005. Such stable prices explain most of the monetary freedom score. The government influences prices through subsidies to state-owned enterprises and price controls on various products including fuel, pharmaceuticals, and medical equipment. Consequently, an additional 15 percent is deducted from Gabon's monetary freedom score to adjust for measures that distort domestic prices.

INVESTMENT FREEDOM — 40%

Foreign investment and domestic capital are not treated equally. Under an agreement signed with the IMF in July 2005, Gabon is committed to economic liberalization, but not much has been done in this regard. Residents may hold foreign exchange accounts subject to some restrictions. Non-residents may hold foreign exchange accounts but must report them to the government. The government must approve most transfers and payments to most countries. Capital transactions are subject to various reporting requirements, controls, and official authorization. All real estate transactions must be reported.

FINANCIAL FREEDOM — 40%

Gabon's financial system is small and subject to extensive government influence. Overall, government ownership shares account for about 25 percent of total financial sector assets. Gabon is a member of the Central African Economic and Monetary Community along with five other countries. These countries share a common central bank, the Central Bank of West African States (BCEAO), and a common currency. The banking system includes a development bank and five commercial banks and is open to foreign competition. Three banks are affiliated with French banks, and another is entirely foreign-owned. However, most banks are at least partially owned by the state. Domestic credit is limited and expensive but available to foreign investors without discrimination, although such loans require prior authorization. There are four major insurance companies and a small regional stock exchange headquartered in Gabon.

PROPERTY RIGHTS — 40%

Private property is moderately well protected in Gabon. The president influences the judiciary and both chambers of parliament, and other countries doing business in Gabon do not always treat giving or accepting a bribe as a criminal act. Expropriation is unlikely.

FREEDOM FROM CORRUPTION — 29%

Corruption is perceived as widespread. Gabon ranks 88th out of 158 countries in Transparency International's Corruption Perceptions Index for 2005.

LABOR FREEDOM — 55.7%

The labor market operates under restrictive employment regulations that hinder employment and productivity growth. The non-salary cost of employing a worker is high, and dismissing a redundant employee is relatively costly. Regulations related to increasing or contracting the number of work hours are rigid.

THE GAMBIA

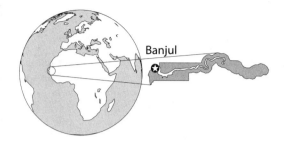

Banjul

The Gambia's economy is 57.6 percent free, according to our 2007 assessment, which makes it the world's 93rd freest economy. Its overall score is 0.3 percentage point lower than last year, partially reflecting new methodological detail. The Gambia is ranked 13th out of 40 countries in the sub-Saharan Africa region, and its overall score is slightly higher than the regional average.

The Gambia ranks moderately well in fiscal freedom, freedom from government, and labor freedom. Both the top income tax rate and the top corporate tax rate are 35 percent, which is comparable to the U.S., and overall tax revenue is not overly large as a percentage of GDP. Government expenditures are not excessive, and the level of income from state-owned businesses is relatively low. The labor market is highly flexible, and dismissing a redundant employee is easy.

As a developing nation, The Gambia faces significant challenges. Trade freedom, investment freedom, property rights, and freedom from corruption all score relatively poorly. The average tariff rate is fairly high, and an inefficient and corrupt bureaucracy has a negative impact on most aspects of commercial life. Property rights are not secured by an independent judiciary, and the judiciary is subject to political interference.

BACKGROUND: The Gambia is Africa's smallest country. President Yahya Jammeh, who led a successful military coup in 1994, was re-elected in 2001 and, as of this writing, was expected to win a third term in September 2006. Most of the population lives in rural villages and is engaged in subsistence agriculture. The agricultural sector accounts for about 30 percent of GDP. Corruption remains a problem, and many parts of the government are poorly managed, lacking in transparency, and inefficient. The government has announced its commitment to improving infrastructure, advancing privatization, and removing regulatory impediments to business.

How Do We Measure Economic Freedom? See Chapter 3 (page 37) for an explanation of the methodology or visit the *Index* Web site at *heritage.org/index*.

The economy is 57.6% free

Sub-Saharan Africa Average = 54.7
World Average = 60.6

100
80
60
40
20
0

1995   2007

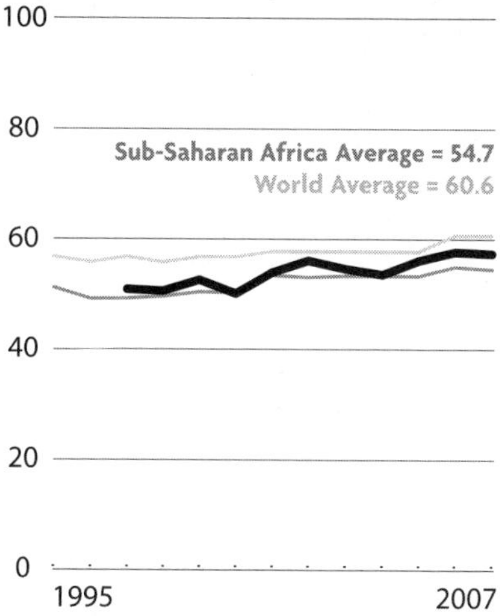

QUICK FACTS

Population: 1.5 million

GDP (PPP): $2.9 billion
5.1% growth in 2004
4.1% 5-yr. comp. ann. growth
$1,991 per capita

Unemployment: n/a

Inflation (CPI): 14.2%

FDI (net inflow): $59 million

Official Development Assistance:
Multilateral: $70 million
Bilateral: $15 million (21% from the U.S.)

External Debt: $674.0 million

Exports: $126.8 million (2004 estimate)
Primarily peanut products, fish, cotton lint, palm kernels, re-exports

Imports: $234.4 million (2004 estimate)
Primarily food, manufactures, fuel, machinery, transport equipment

THE GAMBIA'S TEN ECONOMIC FREEDOMS

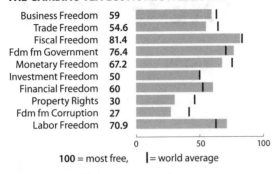

Business Freedom	59
Trade Freedom	54.6
Fiscal Freedom	81.4
Fdm fm Government	76.4
Monetary Freedom	67.2
Investment Freedom	50
Financial Freedom	60
Property Rights	30
Fdm fm Corruption	27
Labor Freedom	70.9

0   50   100

100 = most free, | = world average

BUSINESS FREEDOM — 59%

Starting a business takes an average of 27 days, compared to the world average of 48 days. This benefits entrepreneurship and helps to maximize job creation. Obtaining a business license is relatively simple, but closing a business is difficult. Bureaucratic inefficiency and lack of transparency remain problems. The overall freedom to start, operate, and close a business is restricted by the national regulatory environment.

TRADE FREEDOM — 54.6%

The Gambia's simple average tariff rate was 12.7 percent in 2003. Non-tariff barriers to trade include an inefficient and sometimes corrupt customs process, restrictive licensing arrangements, and sanitary and phytosanitary prohibitions on a few products. Consequently, an additional 20 percent is deducted from The Gambia's trade freedom score to account for these non-tariff barriers.

FISCAL FREEDOM — 81.4%

The Gambia has moderately high tax rates. Both the top income tax rate and the top corporate tax rate are 35 percent. Other taxes include a capital gains tax, a sales tax, and a road tax. In the most recent year, overall tax revenue as a percentage of GDP was 18.6 percent.

FREEDOM FROM GOVERNMENT — 76.4%

Total government expenditures in The Gambia, including consumption and transfer payments, are moderate. In the most recent year, government spending equaled 31.2 percent of GDP, and the government received 2.6 percent of its total revenues from state-owned enterprises and government ownership of property. Most leading companies are still under government control, and privatization has proceeded slowly.

MONETARY FREEDOM — 67.2%

Inflation in The Gambia is relatively high, averaging 7.9 percent between 2003 and 2005. Relatively high and unstable prices explain most of the monetary freedom score. The government influences prices through a large public sector, and most leading companies, including those in agriculture, water, electricity, maritime services, public transportation, and telecommunications, remain in government hands. Consequently, an additional 15 percent is deducted

from The Gambia's monetary freedom score to adjust for measures that distort domestic prices.

INVESTMENT FREEDOM — 50%

Foreign and domestic investment receive equal treatment. There are no limits on foreign ownership or control of businesses in all sectors except television broadcasting and defense-related activities. Repatriation of profits is permitted, and foreign investors may invest without a local partner, although the government does state its intent to encourage joint ventures. Regulatory barriers—including the absence of a transparent competition law—need to be addressed in order to attract the foreign capital needed to jump-start sustainable growth. Residents and non-residents may hold foreign exchange accounts. There are no restrictions on payments and transfers. Some capital transactions are controlled.

FINANCIAL FREEDOM — 60%

The Gambia's financial system is small and dominated by banking. The Gambia is a member of the Economic Community of West African States (ECOWAS), which promotes regional trade and economic integration. Plans to establish a West African Monetary Zone (WAMZ) with four other countries based on a second West African common currency, the eco, and possessing a joint central bank have been delayed. The largest commercial bank is a locally incorporated subsidiary of the U.K.-based Standard Chartered, which is 25 percent owned by Gambian shareholders. There are four other commercial banks and a development bank that opened in 1998. Microfinance is growing in importance. The insurance sector and the stock market remain small. Supervision and regulation of the financial system remain deficient because of weak institutional capacity, and the central bank is subject to government influence.

PROPERTY RIGHTS — 30%

The judiciary, especially at the lower levels, is sometimes subject to pressure from the executive branch. Intimidation of lawyers, a lack of independence, and a lack of technical support for the legal profession severely undermine the administration of justice. Lack of judicial security is one of the main deterrents to doing business. The Supreme Court is in disarray and has not functioned since 2003.

FREEDOM FROM CORRUPTION — 27%

Corruption is perceived as widespread. The Gambia ranks 103rd out of 158 countries in Transparency International's Corruption Perceptions Index for 2005.

LABOR FREEDOM — 70.9%

The labor market operates under relatively flexible employment regulations that could be improved to enhance employment and productivity growth. The non-salary cost of employing a worker is moderate, and dismissing a redundant employee is relatively costless.

GEORGIA

Tbilisi

Georgia's economy is 68.7 percent free, according to our 2007 assessment, which makes it the world's 35th freest economy. Its overall score is 3.9 percentage points higher than last year, partially reflecting new methodological detail but mostly as a result of an increase in labor freedom. Georgia is ranked 20th out of 41 countries in the European region, and its overall score is equal to the regional average.

Georgia scores highly in business freedom, fiscal freedom, freedom from government, and labor freedom. Business operations are simple and not hampered by red tape. A very low top income tax rate complements the low corporate tax rate, and government tax revenue is fairly low as a percentage of GDP. Government expenditures are also low, and government-owned businesses are a negligible source of revenue. Georgia's labor market is highly flexible and far freer than those of most advanced economies.

As a transforming post-Communist economy, Georgia has much to improve. Trade freedom, property rights, and freedom from corruption remain problems, and an inefficient bureaucracy burdens many commercial sectors. Non-tariff trade barriers are correspondingly high, and property rights cannot be guaranteed by the courts because of inefficiency and persistent corruption.

BACKGROUND: Georgia became independent with the collapse of the Soviet Union in 1991, but its survival was later threatened by civil wars and secessionist movements. President Mikheil Saakashvili has remained politically dominant since February 2005. On May 2, 2006, Saakashvili announced that Georgia will re-examine its membership in the Commonwealth of Independent States, a Russian-dominated bloc of former Soviet republics. The government has undertaken several privatizations and structural reforms, such as streamlining trade tariffs and taxes. Georgia has benefited from completion of the Baku–Tbilisi–Ceyhan oil pipeline from Azerbaijan to Turkey, which provides oil transit revenue.

How Do We Measure Economic Freedom? See Chapter 3 (page 37) for an explanation of the methodology or visit the *Index* Web site at *heritage.org/index*.

The economy is 68.7% free

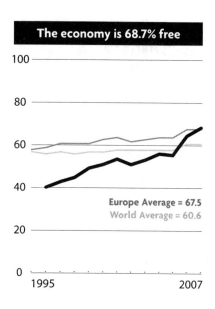

Europe Average = 67.5
World Average = 60.6

QUICK FACTS

Population: 4.5 million

GDP (PPP): $12.8 billion
6.2% growth in 2004
5.8% 5-yr. comp. ann. growth
$2,844 per capita

Unemployment: 15.3%

Inflation (CPI): 5.7%

FDI (net inflow): $489.5 million

Official Development Assistance:
Multilateral: $137 million
Bilateral: $221 million (42% from the U.S.)

External Debt: $2.1 billion

Exports: $1.6 billion
Primarily scrap metal, machinery, chemicals, fuel re-exports, citrus fruits, tea, wine

Imports: $2.5 billion
Primarily fuels, machinery and parts, transport equipment, grain and other foods, pharmaceuticals

GEORGIA'S TEN ECONOMIC FREEDOMS

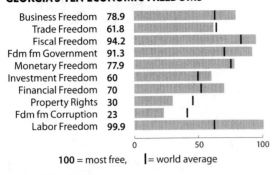

Business Freedom	78.9
Trade Freedom	61.8
Fiscal Freedom	94.2
Fdm fm Government	91.3
Monetary Freedom	77.9
Investment Freedom	60
Financial Freedom	70
Property Rights	30
Fdm fm Corruption	23
Labor Freedom	99.9

0   50   100

100 = most free, | = world average

BUSINESS FREEDOM — 78.9%

Starting a business takes an average of 16 days, compared to the world average of 48 days. This benefits entrepreneurship and helps to maximize job creation. Obtaining a business license and closing a business are relatively simple. The overall freedom to start, operate, and close a business is relatively well protected by the national regulatory environment.

TRADE FREEDOM — 61.8%

Georgia's weighted average tariff rate was 9.1 percent in 2004. While Georgia has made progress toward liberalizing its trade regime, certain non-tariff barriers, including agriculture subsidies and an inefficient and corrupt customs process, continue to add to the cost of trade. Consequently, an additional 20 percent is deducted from Georgia's trade freedom score to account for these non-tariff barriers.

FISCAL FREEDOM — 94.2%

Georgia has low tax rates. The top income tax rate is a flat 12 percent, and the top corporate tax rate is 20 percent. Other taxes include a value-added tax (VAT), a tax on interest, and a tax on dividends. In the most recent year, overall tax revenue as a percentage of GDP was 18.2 percent.

FREEDOM FROM GOVERNMENT — 91.3%

Total government expenditures in Georgia, including consumption and transfer payments, are low. In the most recent year, government spending equaled 19.1 percent of GDP, and the government received 0.7 percent of its total revenues from state-owned enterprises and government ownership of property.

MONETARY FREEDOM — 77.9%

Inflation in Georgia is relatively high, averaging 7.3 percent between 2003 and 2005. Relatively unstable prices explain most of the monetary freedom score. Prices are generally set in the market, but the government may impose control over prices through regulation of state-owned enterprises. The government also provides subsidies for agricultural products. Consequently, an additional 5 percent is deducted from Georgia's monetary freedom score.

INVESTMENT FREEDOM — 60%

Georgia has undergone a major structural reform to create a business-friendly environment. Foreign investment receives equal treatment. There are no restrictions on purchases of or investment in domestic companies, stocks, bonds, or any other property, and local participation in businesses or investments is not required. Both domestic and foreign investors can use a one-stop-window system to obtain a business license in 24 hours. Foreign firms are allowed to participate freely in privatizations. Residents and non-residents may hold foreign exchange accounts. There are limits and tests for payments and current transfers. Capital transactions are not restricted but must be registered. Judicial inefficiency and corruption are the only major impediments to foreign investors.

FINANCIAL FREEDOM — 70%

Georgia's small financial sector has undergone substantial liberalization since the 1990s. The central bank assumed a supervisory role and imposed stringent reporting and capital requirements that led to the closure or merging of a number of banks. There were 20 banks as of April 2005, down from 247 in 1995. The top six banks account for about 87 percent of banking assets. Non-performing loans are a problem for some banks. Foreign bank branches are welcome, and foreign investors are majority owners of several banks. The government does not have a stake in any bank. Despite consolidation, the banking sector remains weak, and banks remain risk-averse. The insurance sector includes significant foreign participation. The stock exchange is small and underdeveloped.

PROPERTY RIGHTS — 30%

Judicial corruption is still a problem despite the government's substantial improvement in trying to raise the level of efficiency and fairness in the courts. Under its anti-corruption program, the government has fired thousands of civil servants and police and has prosecuted several bureaucrats. Both foreigners and Georgians continue to doubt the judicial system's ability to protect private property and contracts.

FREEDOM FROM CORRUPTION — 23%

Corruption is perceived as widespread. Georgia ranks 130th out of 158 countries in Transparency International's Corruption Perceptions Index for 2005.

LABOR FREEDOM — 99.9%

The labor market operates under highly flexible employment regulations that enhance employment and productivity growth. The non-salary cost of employing a worker can be high, but dismissing a redundant employee is costless. Rules on increasing or contracting the number of work hours are very flexible. Georgia leads the world in labor market freedom.

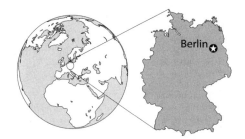

Berlin ★

GERMANY

Germany's economy is 73.5 percent free, according to our 2007 assessment, which makes it the world's 19th freest economy. Its overall score is 0.5 percentage point lower than last year, partially reflecting new methodological detail. Germany is ranked 11th out of 41 countries in the European region, and its overall score is higher than the regional average.

Germany enjoys strong business freedom, property rights, freedom from corruption, and investment freedom. Business regulations are clear and efficient, enforced by the rule of law, and free of political interference. The government imposes few restrictions on foreign capital, which is subject to the same regulations as domestic investment. There is almost no corruption.

Freedom from government, financial freedom, and labor freedom are weaker. As in many other European social democracies, government spending and tax rates are exceptionally high in order to support an extensive welfare state. The labor market operates under restrictive conditions, although Germany has made a serious effort to lower its labor protectionism.

BACKGROUND: Germany is the European Union's largest economy. Even though it is home to many world-class companies and rates as the world's largest exporter, the economy has performed poorly in recent years. Over 5 million Germans were unemployed in 2005 when the unemployment rate surged over 10 percent to highs not seen in seven decades, where it remained in 2006. Overall growth is weak, and a fiscal budget deficit in 2005 again violated the EU's Stability and Growth Pact. Per capita income is now below nine other EU countries. The fact that Germany's non-wage labor costs are among the world's highest indicates an area in need of fundamental reform.

How Do We Measure Economic Freedom? See Chapter 3 (page 37) for an explanation of the methodology or visit the *Index* Web site at *heritage.org/index*.

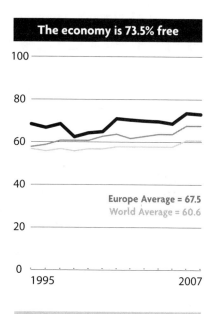

The economy is 73.5% free

Europe Average = 67.5
World Average = 60.6

QUICK FACTS

Population: 82.5 million

GDP (PPP): $2.3 trillion
1.6% growth in 2004
1.2% 5-yr. comp. ann. growth
$28,303 per capita

Unemployment: 10.6% (4th quarter 2004)

Inflation (CPI): 1.7%

FDI (net inflow): −$31.3 billion

Official Development Assistance:
Multilateral: None
Bilateral: None

External Debt: $3.6 trillion (2005)

Exports: $1.1 trillion
Primarily machinery, vehicles, chemicals, metals and manufactures, food, textiles

Imports: $912.6 billion
Primarily machinery, vehicles, chemicals, food, textiles, metals

GERMANY'S TEN ECONOMIC FREEDOMS

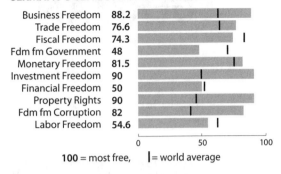

Business Freedom	88.2
Trade Freedom	76.6
Fiscal Freedom	74.3
Fdm fm Government	48
Monetary Freedom	81.5
Investment Freedom	90
Financial Freedom	50
Property Rights	90
Fdm fm Corruption	82
Labor Freedom	54.6

0   50   100

100 = most free, | = world average

BUSINESS FREEDOM — 88.2%

Starting a business takes an average of 24 days, compared to the world average of 48 days. Obtaining a business license is simple, and closing a business is easy. Germany's regulatory system is transparent and consistent, but some bureaucratic obstacles persist. The overall freedom to start, operate, and close a business is protected by the national regulatory environment.

TRADE FREEDOM — 76.6%

Germany's trade policy is the same as those of other members of the European Union. The common EU weighted average tariff rate was 1.7 percent in 2005. Various non-tariff barriers are reflected in EU and German government policy, including agricultural and manufacturing subsidies, regulatory and licensing restrictions, and other market access restrictions. The government also applies standards, quotas, or regulations beyond EU standards on selected items, and regulations and bureaucratic procedures can be difficult. Consequently, an additional 20 percent is deducted from Germany's trade freedom score.

FISCAL FREEDOM — 74.3%

Germany has a high income tax rate and a moderate corporate income tax rate. The top income tax rate is 44.3 percent (a reduced top income tax rate of 42 percent plus a 5.5 percent surcharge), and the top corporate tax rate is 25 percent (raised to 26.4 percent by an additional 5.5 percent solidarity tax). Other taxes include a value-added tax (VAT) and a trade tax that varies from 13 percent to 20 percent. In the most recent year, overall tax revenue as a percentage of GDP was 34.6 percent.

FREEDOM FROM GOVERNMENT — 48%

Total government expenditures in Germany, including consumption and transfer payments, are very high. In the most recent year, government spending equaled 47 percent of GDP, and the government received 1.4 percent of its total revenues from state-owned enterprises and government ownership of property.

MONETARY FREEDOM — 81.5%

Germany is a member of the euro zone. Between 2003 and 2005, Germany's weighted average annual rate of inflation was 1.8 percent. Relatively stable prices explain most of the monetary freedom score. As a participant in the EU's Common Agricultural Policy, the government subsidizes agricultural production, distorting the prices of agricultural products. It also regulates prices for pharmaceuticals, electricity, telecommunications, and other public services. Consequently, an additional 10 percent is deducted from Germany's monetary freedom score.

INVESTMENT FREEDOM — 90%

Foreign and domestic investors receive equal treatment. There are no restrictions on capital transactions or current transfers, real estate purchases, repatriation of profits, or access to foreign exchange. There are no serious limitations on new projects, except for requiring permission for the sale of defense companies to foreign investors, and no permanent currency controls on foreign investments. The government is somewhat skeptical of takeovers of key German companies by foreign groups. Some businesses, including certain financial institutions, passenger transport businesses, and real estate agencies, require licenses.

FINANCIAL FREEDOM — 50%

Germany's financial system is open and modern. Regulations are generally transparent and consistent with international norms. The banking sector is dominated by public-sector financial institutions. Private banks account for less than 30 percent of the market, and publicly owned banks linked to state and local governments account for nearly 50 percent. The government has stopped providing state guarantees and subsidies to public banks. Interest rates are market-determined, and foreign investors may access credit freely. Non-European banks need a license to open a branch or subsidiary. The 120 banks with foreign ownership comprise a modest element of banking sector activity. The insurance sector and capital markets are sophisticated, deep, and open to foreign participation.

PROPERTY RIGHTS — 90%

Property is well protected in Germany. The judiciary is independent and efficient. Contractual agreements are secure, and the judiciary and civil service are highly professional. There are separate supreme courts to deal with cases on commercial, tax, labor, and constitutional issues.

FREEDOM FROM CORRUPTION — 82%

Corruption is perceived as minimal. Germany ranks 16th out of 158 countries in Transparency International's Corruption Perceptions Index for 2005.

LABOR FREEDOM — 54.6%

The labor market operates under restrictive employment regulations that seriously hinder employment and productivity growth. The non-salary cost of employing a worker is high, and dismissing a redundant employee is costly. Reforms implemented in recent years focus on reducing welfare benefits for the unemployed. However, Germany's wages and fringe benefits remain among the world's highest, and the ability of businesses to fire workers is subject to rigid conditions, all of which serves as a disincentive to invest and create jobs.

GHANA

Accra

Rank: 91

Regional Rank: 11 of 40

Ghana's economy is 58.1 percent free, according to our 2007 assessment, which makes it the world's 91st freest economy. Its overall score is 1.5 percentage points higher than last year, partially reflecting new methodological detail. Ghana is ranked 11th out of 40 countries in the sub-Saharan Africa region, and its overall score is slightly higher than the regional average.

Ghana has good scores for fiscal freedom, freedom from government, and monetary freedom. The top income and corporate tax rates are fairly low, and overall tax revenue is not excessive as a percentage of GDP. The amount of revenue from government-owned businesses is likewise relatively small. Inflation is fairly high, but Ghana has made progress in reducing price subsidies and state distortions of the market.

Ghana could make significant progress in several other areas such as investment freedom, financial freedom, property rights, labor freedom, and freedom from corruption. Commercial regulations are extensive, and the labor market is inflexible. Ghana restricts foreign investment in several sectors, and the weak rule of law means that consistent judicial adjudication cannot be guaranteed. This inconsistency is due more to an inefficient public sector than to outright corruption.

BACKGROUND: Ghana was the first colony in sub-Saharan Africa to gain independence. Political discourse is deepening with the development of private radio and mobile telephony. Agriculture accounts for over half of employment, almost half of gross domestic product, and about one-third of total exports (predominantly cocoa and timber). The government has made improving the infrastructure a priority and has generally followed through on economic reform. Over 300 state-owned enterprises (of about 350) have been privatized. Regulatory barriers can be onerous, however, and corruption, while lower than in other African countries, remains a problem.

How Do We Measure Economic Freedom? See Chapter 3 (page 37) for an explanation of the methodology or visit the *Index* Web site at *heritage.org/index.*

The economy is 58.1% free

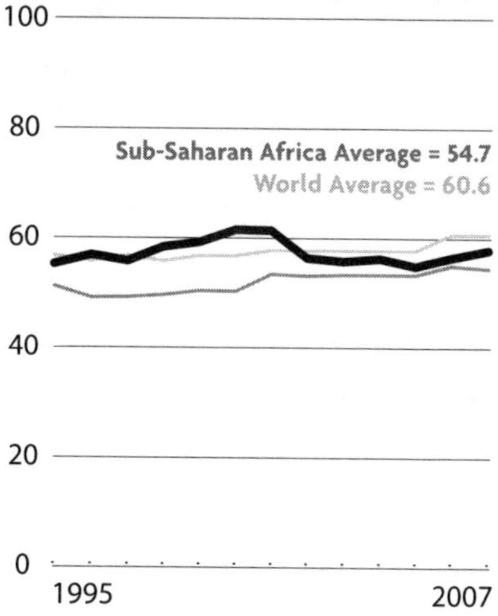

Sub-Saharan Africa Average = 54.7
World Average = 60.6

(chart showing values from 1995 to 2007, vertical axis 0 to 100)

QUICK FACTS

Population: 21.7 million

GDP (PPP): $48.5 billion
5.8% growth in 2004
4.7% 5-yr. comp. ann. growth
$2,240 per capita

Unemployment: 10% (1997 estimate)

Inflation (CPI): 12.6%

FDI (net inflow): $139.3 million (gross)

Official Development Assistance:
Multilateral: $571 million
Bilateral: $1.8 billion (4% from the U.S.)

External Debt: $7.0 billion

Exports: $3.5 billion
Primarily gold, cocoa, timber, tuna, bauxite, aluminum, manganese ore, diamonds

Imports: $5.4 billion
Primarily capital equipment, petroleum, food

GHANA'S TEN ECONOMIC FREEDOMS

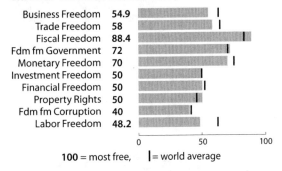

Business Freedom	54.9
Trade Freedom	58
Fiscal Freedom	88.4
Fdm fm Government	72
Monetary Freedom	70
Investment Freedom	50
Financial Freedom	50
Property Rights	50
Fdm fm Corruption	40
Labor Freedom	48.2

100 = most free, | = world average

BUSINESS FREEDOM — *54.9%*

Starting a business takes an average of 81 days, compared to the world average of 48 days. Entrepreneurship should be easier for maximum job creation. Obtaining a business license and closing a business are difficult. Although the government has focused on streamlining regulations as part of its strategy of empowering the private sector, bureaucratic processes remain slow. The overall freedom to start, operate, and close a business is limited by the national regulatory environment.

TRADE FREEDOM — *58%*

Ghana's weighted average tariff rate was 11 percent in 2004. Non-tariff barriers include special import fees and taxes, cumbersome and non-transparent regulations, and import bans and restrictions. The government also supports domestic private enterprise with financial incentives and tax holidays as part of its export promotion policies. Consequently, an additional 20 percent is deducted from Ghana's trade freedom score to account for these non-tariff barriers.

FISCAL FREEDOM — *88.4%*

Ghana has moderate tax rates. Both the top income tax rate and the top corporate tax rate are 25 percent. Other taxes include a value-added tax (VAT) and a capital gains tax. In the most recent year, overall tax revenue as a percentage of GDP was 22.3 percent.

FREEDOM FROM GOVERNMENT — *72%*

Total government expenditures in Ghana, including consumption and transfer payments, are moderate. In the most recent year, government spending equaled 33.3 percent of GDP, and the government received 6.3 percent of its total revenues from state-owned enterprises and government ownership of property. Privatization has been slow in recent years, and many state owned enterprises perform poorly.

MONETARY FREEDOM — *70%*

Inflation in Ghana is relatively high, averaging 15.6 percent between 2003 and 2005. Relatively unstable prices explain most of the monetary freedom score. Although the government has made significant progress toward privatizing the public sector, it influences prices through the regulation of state-owned utilities and controls prices for petro-

leum products. Consequently, an additional 5 percent is deducted from Ghana's trade freedom score to adjust for measures that distort domestic prices.

INVESTMENT FREEDOM — *50%*

The foreign investment code eliminates screening of foreign investment, guarantees capital repatriation, and does not discriminate against foreign investors. The laws restrict petty trading, taxi services, gambling and lotteries, beauty salons, and barbershops to Ghanaians. The process to set up a business requires compliance with regulations and procedures of at least five government agencies. Residents may hold foreign exchange accounts, and non-residents may hold them subject to restrictions. Payments and current transfers are subject to restrictions. The Bank of Ghana must approve most capital transactions, and foreign direct investment faces a minimum capital requirement.

FINANCIAL FREEDOM — *50%*

Ghana's financial system is small and dominated by banking. Ghana is a member of the Economic Community of West African States (ECOWAS), which promotes regional trade and economic integration. Plans to establish a West African Monetary Zone (WAMZ) with four other countries based on a second West African common currency have been delayed. There were 18 banks as of 2005: 10 commercial banks, five merchant banks, and three development banks. Five commercial banks are foreign-owned and play a leading role in the sector. The government owns over 34 percent of the Ghana Commercial Bank (the largest domestic bank) and owns two other banks. There were 19 insurance companies in 2004, including two state-owned companies that dominate the sector. The stock exchange is small, and foreign investors face some restrictions.

PROPERTY RIGHTS — *50%*

Ghana's judicial system suffers from corruption, albeit less so than those of some other African countries, and the judiciary is subject to political influence. The courts are slow in disposing of cases and at times face challenges in enforcing decisions, largely because of resource constraints and institutional inefficiencies.

FREEDOM FROM CORRUPTION — *40%*

Corruption is perceived as significant. Ghana ranks 65th out of 158 countries in Transparency International's Corruption Perceptions Index for 2005.

LABOR FREEDOM — *48.2%*

The labor market operates under highly restrictive employment regulations that hinder employment and productivity growth. The non-salary cost of employing a worker can be high, and dismissing a redundant employee is costly and difficult. Daily minimum wages, which were raised in recent years, are set by a tripartite commission composed of representatives of government, labor, and employers.

GREECE

Rank: 94

Regional Rank: 36 of 41

Greece's economy is 57.6 percent free, according to our 2007 assessment, which makes it the world's 94th freest economy. Its overall score is 0.5 percentage point lower than last year, partially reflecting new methodological detail. Greece is ranked 36th out of 41 countries in the European region, and its overall score is much lower than the regional average.

As a developed nation, Greece scores highly in surprisingly few areas. Trade freedom and monetary freedom are the best parts of the economy, and fiscal freedom also scores well. The average tariff rate is low, but trade suffers from numerous non-tariff barriers. As a member of the European Union, Greece has a standardized monetary policy that yields relatively low inflation, but government distortions in the agricultural sector persist. Greece has a high top income tax rate but is moving to reduce its relatively low corporate tax rate to 25 percent.

Freedom from government, financial freedom, and labor freedom could be improved. As in many other European welfare states, government spending is exceptionally high. A highly restrictive labor market is another problem, as firing employees is difficult and keeping them on the payroll is costly.

BACKGROUND: Since the abolition of the monarchy in 1974, Greece has been governed by a parliamentary democracy. The modernization of infrastructure and increased tourism associated with the 2004 Olympic Games led to strong economic growth in recent years, but the sharp decline in financial assistance from the EU that is scheduled for 2007 makes implementation of the economic reforms promised by Prime Minister Costas Karamanlis and his New Democracy Party a matter of some urgency. Corruption within state enterprises and the country's inefficient bureaucracy continues to deter foreign investors. Although exports of textiles and foodstuffs have increased, Greece still relies heavily on its services sector, particularly tourism.

How Do We Measure Economic Freedom? See Chapter 3 (page 37) for an explanation of the methodology or visit the *Index* Web site at *heritage.org/index*.

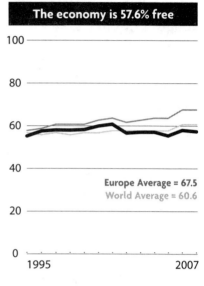

The economy is 57.6% free

Europe Average = 67.5
World Average = 60.6

1995   2007

QUICK FACTS

Population: 11.1 million

GDP (PPP): $245.5 billion
4.7% growth in 2004
4.4% 5-yr. comp. ann. growth
$22,205 per capita

Unemployment: 10.5% (2004 estimate)

Inflation (CPI): 2.9%

FDI (net inflow): $744.5 million

Official Development Assistance:
Multilateral: None
Bilateral: None

External Debt: $75.2 billion (2005 estimate)

Exports: $48.8 billion
Primarily food and beverages, manufactured goods, petroleum products, chemicals, textiles

Imports: $61.4 billion
Primarily machinery, transport equipment, fuels, chemicals

191

GREECE'S TEN ECONOMIC FREEDOMS

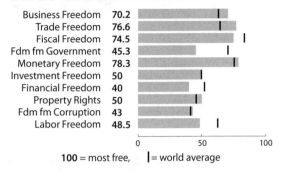

Business Freedom	70.2
Trade Freedom	76.6
Fiscal Freedom	74.5
Fdm fm Government	45.3
Monetary Freedom	78.3
Investment Freedom	50
Financial Freedom	40
Property Rights	50
Fdm fm Corruption	43
Labor Freedom	48.5

100 = most free, | = world average

BUSINESS FREEDOM — *70.2%*

Starting a business takes an average of 38 days, compared to the world average of 48 days. Entrepreneurship should be easier for maximum job creation. Obtaining a business license and closing a business are relatively simple. Bureaucratic obstacles and slowness are still obstacles to business. The overall freedom to start, operate, and close a business is relatively well protected by the national regulatory environment.

TRADE FREEDOM — *76.6%*

Greece's trade policy is the same as those of other members of the European Union. The common EU weighted average tariff rate was 1.7 percent in 2005. Various non-tariff barriers are reflected in EU and Greek government policy, including agricultural and manufacturing subsidies, regulatory and licensing restrictions, and other market access restrictions. Regulations and bureaucratic procedures can be difficult, and corruption raises the cost of trade. Consequently, an additional 20 percent is deducted from Greece's trade freedom score.

FISCAL FREEDOM — *74.5%*

Greece has a high income tax rate and a moderate corporate tax rate. The top income tax rate is 40 percent, and the top corporate tax rate is 29 percent effective January 2006. The corporate tax rate will be lowered to 25 percent within the next three years. Other taxes include a value-added tax (VAT) and a tax on interest. In the most recent year, overall tax revenue as a percentage of GDP was 37.3 percent.

FREEDOM FROM GOVERNMENT — *45.3%*

Total government expenditures in Greece, including consumption and transfer payments, are very high. In the most recent year, government spending equaled 48.3 percent of GDP, and the government received 0.8 percent of its total revenues from state-owned enterprises and government ownership of property.

MONETARY FREEDOM — *78.3%*

Greece is a member of the euro zone. Between 2003 and 2005, Greece's weighted average annual rate of inflation was 3.4 percent. Relatively moderate prices explain most of the monetary freedom score. As a participant in the EU's Common Agricultural Policy, the government subsidizes agricultural production, distorting the prices of agricul-

tural products. The government also regulates prices for pharmaceuticals and transportation and retains the right to set a ceiling on retail petroleum prices. Consequently, an additional 10 percent is deducted from Greece's monetary freedom score to account for these policies.

INVESTMENT FREEDOM — *50%*

Greece officially welcomes foreign investment, but the government restricts both foreign and domestic investment in utilities, and non-EU investors receive less advantageous treatment than other investors in the banking, mining, broadcasting, maritime, and air transport sectors. An inefficient bureaucracy is one of the strongest impediments to foreign investment. Both residents and non-residents may hold foreign exchange accounts. There are no restrictions or controls on payments, real estate transactions, transfers, or repatriation of profits. Investments in border regions are restricted to EU residents.

FINANCIAL FREEDOM — *40%*

Greece has a relatively efficient and well-developed financial system. At the end of 2004, there were 62 domestic and foreign banks and special credit institutions. The state dominated the banking system in the 1990s, but privatization and mergers have reduced the level of state influence. Six large commercial groups that operate as private universal banks now dominate the system, although the state still directly controls one bank and indirectly controls two other large banks that account for a large percentage of banking assets. State-controlled banks are highly exposed to state-owned enterprises that are financially unhealthy. The insurance sector is small, and capital markets are well established.

PROPERTY RIGHTS — *50%*

Enforcing property and contractual rights through the court system is time-consuming and often problematic. The judiciary is supposed to be nonpartisan but tends to reflect the political sensibilities of the government in power. Seeking legal advice and assistance before entering into a lawsuit is critical. Expropriation of property is unlikely.

FREEDOM FROM CORRUPTION — *43%*

Corruption is perceived as significant. Greece ranks 47th out of 158 countries in Transparency International's Corruption Perceptions Index for 2005.

LABOR FREEDOM — *48.5%*

The labor market operates under highly restrictive employment regulations that hinder employment and productivity growth. The non-salary cost of employing a worker is high, and dismissing a redundant employee can be difficult. Penalizing overtime, labor codes limit working hours and part-time employment. A new labor law passed in 2005 aims at providing greater flexibilities to employers.

GUATEMALA

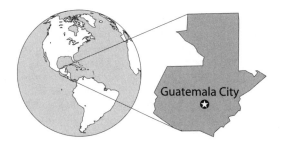

Guatemala City

Guatemala's economy is 61.2 percent free, according to our 2007 assessment, which makes it the world's 68th freest economy. Its overall score is 0.6 percentage point higher than last year, partially reflecting new methodological detail. Guatemala is ranked 16th out of 29 countries in the Americas, and its overall score is slightly lower than the regional average.

Guatemala receives high scores in fiscal freedom, freedom from government, labor freedom, and monetary freedom. Personal and corporate tax rates are moderate, and overall tax revenue is relatively low as a percentage of GDP. Government expenditures are very low (almost 10 percent of GDP), and income from state-owned businesses is negligible. The labor market is fairly flexible, although firing an employee can be costly. Despite inflationary problems, the government has wisely avoided direct price controls.

Guatemala scores poorly in business freedom, investment freedom, and financial freedom. The scores for property rights and corruption are lowest of all, and both areas need to be improved to nurture investment. Closing a business is difficult, and licensing procedures are burdensome. Many sectors of the economy are off-limits to foreign investors, and an inefficient bureaucracy further repels foreign capital. The judiciary is not an effective arbiter of cases, and corruption is extensive.

BACKGROUND: Guatemala is Central America's most populous country. The government has withdrawn from ownership of services and energy utilities, and the Dominican Republic–Central America Free Trade Agreement (DR–CAFTA), ratified in 2005, should boost trade and employment prospects in the formal sector. About 75 percent of the population lives below the poverty line, less than one-third of all age-appropriate youth are enrolled in secondary school, and 50 percent of the labor force works in agriculture. High crime rates and rising youth gang membership challenge Guatemala's police, and a weak judiciary remains plagued by corruption.

How Do We Measure Economic Freedom? See Chapter 3 (page 37) for an explanation of the methodology or visit the *Index* Web site at *heritage.org/index*.

The economy is 61.2% free

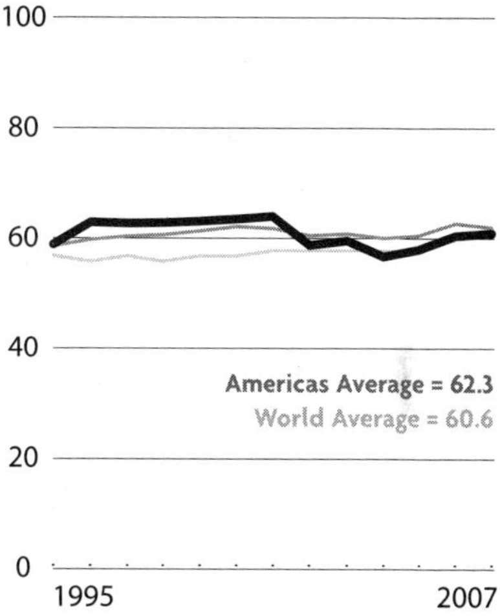

100

80

60

40

Americas Average = 62.3
World Average = 60.6

20

0

1995   2007

QUICK FACTS

Population: 12.3 million

GDP (PPP): $53.0 billion
2.7% growth in 2004
2.6% 5-yr. comp. ann. growth
$4,313 per capita

Unemployment: 7.5% (2003 estimate)

Inflation (CPI): 7.4%

FDI (net inflow): $154.7 million (gross)

Official Development Assistance:
Multilateral: $37 million
Bilateral: $241 million (33% from the U.S.)

External Debt: $5.5 billion

Exports: $4.6 billion
Primarily coffee, sugar, petroleum, apparel, bananas, fruits and vegetables, cardamom

Imports: $8.5 billion
Primarily fuels, machinery and transport equipment, construction materials, grain, fertilizers, electricity

GUATEMALA'S TEN ECONOMIC FREEDOMS

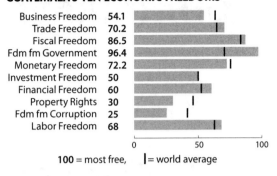

Business Freedom	54.1
Trade Freedom	70.2
Fiscal Freedom	86.5
Fdm fm Government	96.4
Monetary Freedom	72.2
Investment Freedom	50
Financial Freedom	60
Property Rights	30
Fdm fm Corruption	25
Labor Freedom	68

0   50   100

100 = most free, | = world average

BUSINESS FREEDOM — 54.1%

Starting a business takes an average of 30 days, compared to the world average of 48 days. Entrepreneurship should be easier for maximum job creation. Obtaining a business license can be very difficult, and closing a business is difficult. Bureaucratic impediments and slowness are persistent problems. The overall freedom to start, operate, and close a business is restricted by the national regulatory environment.

TRADE FREEDOM — 70.2%

Guatemala's weighted average tariff rate was 4.9 percent in 2004. Non-tariff barriers to trade include regulatory restrictions, some limitations on market access in the services sector, and a burdensome and corrupt customs process. Consequently, an additional 20 percent is deducted from Guatemala's trade freedom score to account for these non-tariff barriers.

FISCAL FREEDOM — 86.5%

Guatemala has moderate tax rates. Both the top income tax rate and the top corporate tax rate are 31 percent. Other taxes include a value-added tax (VAT), a capital gains tax, and a tax on interest. In the most recent year, overall tax revenue as a percentage of GDP was 10.1 percent.

FREEDOM FROM GOVERNMENT — 96.4%

Total government expenditures in Guatemala, including consumption and transfer payments, are low. In the most recent year, government spending equaled 11.4 percent of GDP, and the government received 1.8 percent of its total revenues from state-owned enterprises and government ownership of property. The pace of privatization has been slowed by the government's indecisiveness.

MONETARY FREEDOM — 72.2%

Inflation in Guatemala is relatively high, averaging 7.9 percent between 2003 and 2005. Relatively high and unstable prices explain most of the monetary freedom score. The government maintains few price controls, but it does subsidize numerous economic activities and products, such as fuel and housing construction. Consequently, an additional 10 percent is deducted from Guatemala's monetary freedom score to adjust for measures that distort domestic prices.

INVESTMENT FREEDOM — 50%

Guatemala grants foreign investors national treatment and allows the full repatriation of profits. Licenses to foreign investors to provide professional services are restricted, as is foreign ownership of domestic airlines, newspapers and commercial radio stations, mining and forestry operations, petroleum operations, and real estate. Time-consuming administrative procedures, arbitrary bureaucratic impediments and judicial decisions, a high crime rate, and corruption impede investment. Minerals, petroleum, and natural resources are considered the property of the state. Residents and non-residents may hold foreign exchange accounts. There are no restrictions or controls on payments, transactions, and transfers.

FINANCIAL FREEDOM — 60%

Guatemala's financial system is small and dominated by bank-centered financial conglomerates. As of November 2005, 24 domestic banks and one foreign bank were operating. The third and tenth largest banks are partially or fully owned by the government and together account for about 14 percent of banking assets. There are also 20 private finance companies (two of them inactive) and 11 authorized offshore banks. Foreign borrowers are able to secure domestic credit. Bank supervision and transparency have been strengthened under a legal and regulatory framework adopted in 2002, which also makes it easier for the government to intervene in troubled banks. Capital markets are small and involved primarily in trading government debt. The government permits foreign currency to be used as legal tender for accounts, salaries, and monetary instruments.

PROPERTY RIGHTS — 30%

Dispute resolution through Guatemala's judicial system is time-consuming and often unreliable. Civil cases can take as long as a decade to resolve. Judicial corruption is not uncommon. Land invasions by squatters are increasingly common in rural areas, and squatters can be difficult to evict.

FREEDOM FROM CORRUPTION — 25%

Corruption is perceived as widespread. Guatemala ranks 117th out of 158 countries in Transparency International's Corruption Perceptions Index for 2005.

LABOR FREEDOM — 68%

The labor market operates under relatively flexible employment regulations that could be improved to enhance employment and productivity growth. The non-salary cost of employing a worker is moderate, but dismissing a redundant employee is relatively costly. There are some restrictions on increasing or contracting the number of work hours.

GUINEA

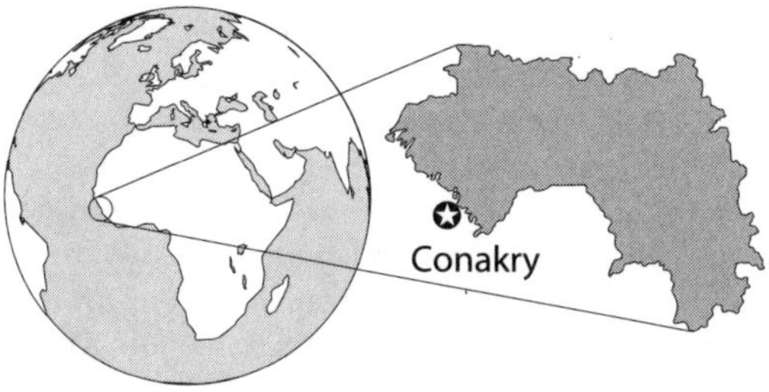

Conakry

Rank: 111

Regional Rank: 18 of 40

Guinea's economy is 55.1 percent free, according to our 2007 assessment, which makes it the world's 111th freest economy. Its overall score is 1.4 percentage points higher than last year, partially reflecting new methodological detail. Guinea is ranked 18th out of 40 countries in the sub-Saharan Africa region, and its overall score is equal to the regional average.

Guinea scores well in fiscal freedom, freedom from government, and labor freedom. Relatively high tax rates on income and corporations dampen its overall fiscal score, but tax revenue is low as a percentage of GDP. Government expenditures are also low, and state-owned businesses do not account for a significant portion of total revenues. The labor market is highly flexible, although the non-salary cost of employing a worker is high.

As a developing sub-Saharan African country, Guinea faces challenges in such areas as investment freedom, monetary freedom, property rights, and business freedom. Bureaucratic inefficiency and corruption affect virtually all areas of the economy. Foreign investment is subject to an opaque process of government approval, and the lack of basic infrastructure exacerbates the corruption and inefficiency of the bureaucracy. The judiciary is subject to pervasive political interference and corruption at all levels, despite nominal government efforts to improve.

BACKGROUND: President Lansana Conté has ruled Guinea since seizing power in 1984. He won his first presidential election in 1993 and a third term in 2003. Most opposition parties are not represented because they boycott the elections. Instability in the Ivory Coast and Liberia affects the social, political, and economic situation. The government is marked by corruption and lack of transparency. Electricity and water shortages are common. More than three-quarters of the population is engaged in subsistence agriculture. Guinea possesses half of the world's bauxite reserves, and the mining of aluminum, gold, and diamonds is important to the economy.

How Do We Measure Economic Freedom? See Chapter 3 (page 37) for an explanation of the methodology or visit the *Index* Web site at *heritage.org/index*.

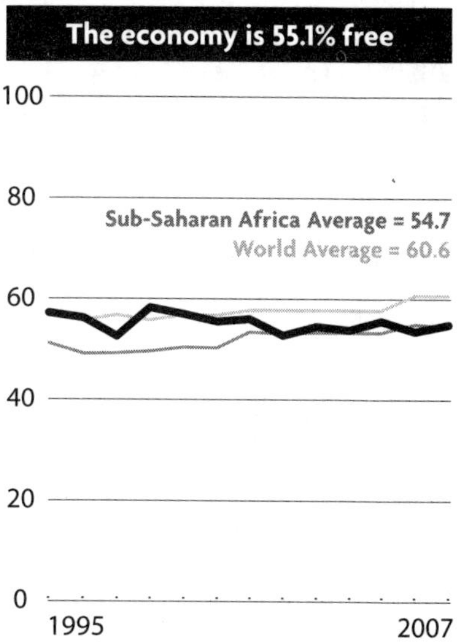

The economy is 55.1% free

Sub-Saharan Africa Average = 54.7
World Average = 60.6

QUICK FACTS

Population: 9.2 million

GDP (PPP): $20.1 billion
2.7% growth in 2004
2.8% 5-yr. comp. ann. growth
$2,180 per capita

Unemployment: n/a

Inflation (CPI): 17.5%

FDI (net inflow): $100 million (gross)

Official Development Assistance:
Multilateral: $157 million
Bilateral: $202 million (24% from the U.S.)

External Debt: $3.5 billion

Exports: $810.9 million
Primarily bauxite, alumina, gold, diamonds, coffee, fish, agricultural products

Imports: $963.6 million
Primarily petroleum products, metals, machinery, transport equipment, textiles, grain and other food

GUINEA'S TEN ECONOMIC FREEDOMS

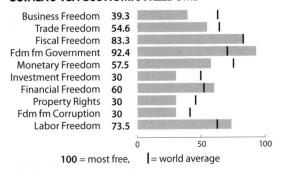

Business Freedom	39.3
Trade Freedom	54.6
Fiscal Freedom	83.3
Fdm fm Government	92.4
Monetary Freedom	57.5
Investment Freedom	30
Financial Freedom	60
Property Rights	30
Fdm fm Corruption	30
Labor Freedom	73.5

100 = most free, | = world average

BUSINESS FREEDOM — *39.3%*

Starting a business takes an average of 49 days, compared to the world average of 48 days. Entrepreneurship should be easier for maximum job creation. Obtaining a business license is very difficult, and closing a business is difficult. The application of commercial law lacks both transparency and consistency. The overall freedom to start, operate, and close a business is seriously restricted by the national regulatory environment.

TRADE FREEDOM — *54.6%*

Guinea's average tariff rate was 12.7 percent in 2005. Non-tariff barriers include a lack of foreign currency for transacting formal trade, import taxes, state-owned import and export monopolies, regulatory controls, subsidies, and corruption in the customs process. Consequently, an additional 20 percent is deducted from Guinea's trade freedom score to account for these non-tariff barriers.

FISCAL FREEDOM — *83.3%*

Guinea has high tax rates. Both the top income tax rate and the top corporate tax rate are 35 percent. Other taxes include a value-added tax (VAT), a tax on insurance contracts, and an apprenticeship tax. In the most recent year, overall tax revenue as a percentage of GDP was 7.9 percent.

FREEDOM FROM GOVERNMENT — *92.4%*

Total government expenditures in Guinea, including consumption and transfer payments, are low. In the most recent year, government spending equaled 16.5 percent of GDP, and the government received 3.9 percent of its total revenues from state-owned enterprises and government ownership of property.

MONETARY FREEDOM — *57.5%*

Inflation in Guinea is high, averaging 26.3 percent between 2003 and 2005. Relatively high and unstable prices explain most of the monetary freedom score. The government influences prices through the regulation of state-owned enterprises and administrative price controls for cement, petroleum products, water, and electricity. It also provides subsidies for rice importers. Consequently, an additional 10 percent is deducted from Guinea's monetary freedom score to adjust for measures that distort domestic prices.

INVESTMENT FREEDOM — *30%*

Investment is deterred by bureaucratic inefficiency, a lack of basic services infrastructure, and opaque application procedures that allow for significant corruption. Foreign investors are restricted from majority ownership in radio, television, and newspapers. Both residents and non-residents may hold foreign exchange accounts, but residents may hold such accounts abroad only with central bank approval. Payments and transfers are subject to government approval in some cases, and repatriation is controlled. All capital transfers through the official exchange market and many capital transactions, including all real estate transactions and all outward direct investment, must be authorized by the central bank.

FINANCIAL FREEDOM — *60%*

Guinea's financial system is small and dominated by banking. Guinea is a member of the Economic Community of West African States (ECOWAS), which promotes regional trade and economic integration. Regulation can be somewhat burdensome, and supervision is weak. The financial sector consists of six deposit-taking banks, four insurance companies, a social security institution, two cooperative banks, and a number of foreign exchange bureaus and microfinance institutions. There are few restrictions on banks, and foreign banks dominate the sector. Microfinance institutions, although growing in number and importance, account for only about 3 percent of sector assets. Overall, Guinea's banking system remains fragile, risk-averse, and unable to meet the private sector's development needs. There is no stock market.

PROPERTY RIGHTS — *30%*

Property is weakly protected in Guinea. Entrepreneurs complain that poorly trained magistrates, high levels of corruption, and nepotism plague the administration of justice. The government intends to reform the judiciary with the help of international donor agencies. To that end, it established an arbitration court in 1999, but much remains to be done.

FREEDOM FROM CORRUPTION — *30%*

The difficulties involved in registering a business have resulted in the existence of a very large informal economy. Much of the population finds the informal sector the only place in which to obtain income.

LABOR FREEDOM — *73.5%*

The labor market operates under relatively flexible employment regulations that do not hinder employment or productivity growth. The non-salary cost of employing a worker is high, but dismissing a redundant employee is costless. Regulations on increasing or contracting the number of work hours are rigid.

GUINEA–BISSAU

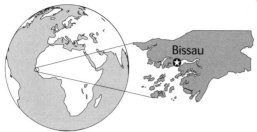

Bissau

Guinea–Bissau's economy is 45.7 percent free, according to our 2007 assessment, which makes it the world's 148th freest economy. Its overall score is 1.4 percentage points lower than last year, partially reflecting new methodological detail. Guinea–Bissau is ranked 37th out of 40 countries in the sub-Saharan Africa region, and its overall score is lower than the regional average.

Guinea–Bissau scores well in fiscal freedom, and somewhat well in monetary freedom. The top income tax is a low 20 percent, but the top corporate rate is higher. Taxes are not excessive as a percentage of GDP. Inflation is low, and the government directly distorts prices in only one area (cashew nuts), although it does influence the market slightly through state-owned enterprises.

Guinea–Bissau's business freedom, investment freedom, financial freedom, property rights, labor freedom, and freedom from corruption all score poorly. Normal business operations are intensely difficult. Significant restrictions on foreign investment combine with domestic regulations and an inflexible labor market to create a business-hostile climate. Partially as a consequence, Guinea–Bissau has the West African Economic and Monetary Union's weakest financial system. Weak rule of law jeopardizes the protection of property rights. Corruption is so rampant that the informal market (mainly diamonds) dwarfs the legitimate market.

BACKGROUND: Guinea–Bissau is one of the world's poorest countries and has a history of instability. A September 2003 military intervention forced President Kumba Yala to resign. The military appointed a civilian transitional government, and legislative elections were held in March 2004. In August 2005, former President João Bernardo Vieira was declared the winner of the presidential election. Agriculture, forestry, and fishing account for the bulk of GDP and employ most people. Cashew nuts are the primary export. Instability has greatly hindered economic growth, the infrastructure is dilapidated, and corruption is substantial.

How Do We Measure Economic Freedom? See Chapter 3 (page 37) for an explanation of the methodology or visit the *Index* Web site at *heritage.org/index*.

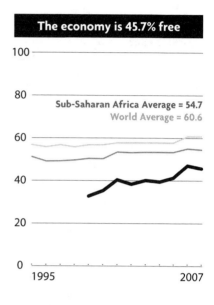

The economy is 45.7% free

Sub-Saharan Africa Average = 54.7
World Average = 60.6

QUICK FACTS

Population: 1.5 million

GDP (PPP): $1.1 billion
2.2% growth in 2004
0.3% 5-yr. comp. ann. growth
$722 per capita

Unemployment: n/a

Inflation (CPI): 0.8%

FDI (net inflow): $4.5 million

Official Development Assistance:
Multilateral: $59 million
Bilateral: $29 million (0.4% from the U.S.)

External Debt: $765 million

Exports: $71 million (2003 estimate)
Primarily cashew nuts, shrimp, peanuts, palm kernels, sawn lumber

Imports: $101.5 million (2003 estimate)
Primarily food, machinery and transport equipment, petroleum products

GUINEA-BISSAU'S TEN ECONOMIC FREEDOMS

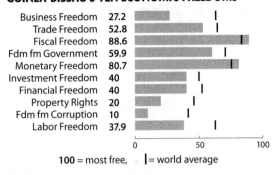

Business Freedom	27.2
Trade Freedom	52.8
Fiscal Freedom	88.6
Fdm fm Government	59.9
Monetary Freedom	80.7
Investment Freedom	40
Financial Freedom	40
Property Rights	20
Fdm fm Corruption	10
Labor Freedom	37.9

100 = most free, I = world average

BUSINESS FREEDOM — 27.2%

Starting a business takes an average of 233 days, compared to the world average of 48 days. Entrepreneurship should be easier for maximum job creation. Despite government efforts to streamline the registration process and reduce bureaucracy, obtaining a business license is difficult, and closing a business is very difficult. The overall freedom to start, operate, and close a business is seriously limited by the national regulatory environment.

TRADE FREEDOM — 52.8%

Guinea–Bissau's weighted average tariff rate was 13.6 percent in 2004. Abuses in customs, including irregularities in the valuation of imports and difficulty tracking and monitoring goods, add to the cost of trade. Consequently, an additional 20 percent is deducted from Guinea–Bissau's trade freedom score to account for these non-tariff barriers.

FISCAL FREEDOM — 88.6%

Guinea–Bissau has a low income tax rate but a high corporate tax rate. The top income tax rate is 20 percent, and the top corporate tax rate is 35 percent. In the most recent year, overall tax revenue as a percentage of GDP was 9.1 percent.

FREEDOM FROM GOVERNMENT — 59.9%

Total government expenditures in Guinea–Bissau, including consumption and transfer payments, are high. In the most recent year, government spending equaled 40.4 percent of GDP, and the government received 5.9 percent of its total revenues from state-owned enterprises and government ownership of property.

MONETARY FREEDOM — 80.7%

Inflation in Guinea–Bissau is relatively low, averaging 2.1 percent between 2003 and 2005. Relatively low and stable prices explain most of the monetary freedom score. The government influences prices through the regulation of state-owned utilities and controls prices for cashew nuts, the country's primary export. Consequently, an additional 10 percent is deducted from Guinea–Bissau's monetary freedom score to adjust for measures that distort domestic prices.

INVESTMENT FREEDOM — 40%

Political and economic instability, a weak infrastructure, and an unskilled workforce discourage foreign investment in Guinea–Bissau. The investment code provides for investment incentives and guarantees against nationalization and expropriation. Non-residents may hold foreign exchange accounts with permission of the Central Bank of West African States (BCEAO), and residents may hold them with permission of the Ministry of Finance and the BCEAO. Capital transfers to most foreign countries are restricted. The government must approve most personal capital movements between residents and non-residents, such as personal loans, gifts or inheritances, or transfers of assets.

FINANCIAL FREEDOM — 40%

Guinea–Bissau has the weakest, least developed financial sector among the eight members of the West African Economic and Monetary Union (WAEMU). The BCEAO governs banking and other financial institutions. The eight BCEAO member countries use the CFA franc, pegged to the euro. Three banks were operating in the first half of 2006, including the country's first microfinance institution (a subsidiary of a regional development bank) that began operations at the end of 2005 and the new Banco da União that opened in early 2006 with the government, a regional development bank, and the WAEMU as shareholders. A fourth bank is expected to open in late 2006. The government, regional government institutions, and foreign investors participate in the banking sector. There is a regional development bank as well as a regional stock exchange based in the Ivory Coast.

PROPERTY RIGHTS — 20%

Protection of property in Guinea–Bissau is extremely weak. The judiciary is subject to executive influence and control. Judges are poorly trained, poorly paid, and subject to corruption. Traditional practices still prevail in most rural areas, and persons who live in urban areas often bring judicial disputes to traditional counselors to avoid the costs and bureaucratic impediments of the official system. The police often resolve disputes.

FREEDOM FROM CORRUPTION — 10%

Guinea–Bissau's informal market is so large that it eclipses the legal market. Trade in smuggled diamonds is very large, as is trade in food and fishing products. There is a substantial level of corruption.

LABOR FREEDOM — 37.9%

The labor market operates under highly restrictive employment regulations that hinder employment and productivity growth. The non-salary cost of employing a worker is high, and dismissing a redundant employee is relatively costly. Guinea–Bissau's labor freedom is one of the 20 lowest in the world.

GUYANA

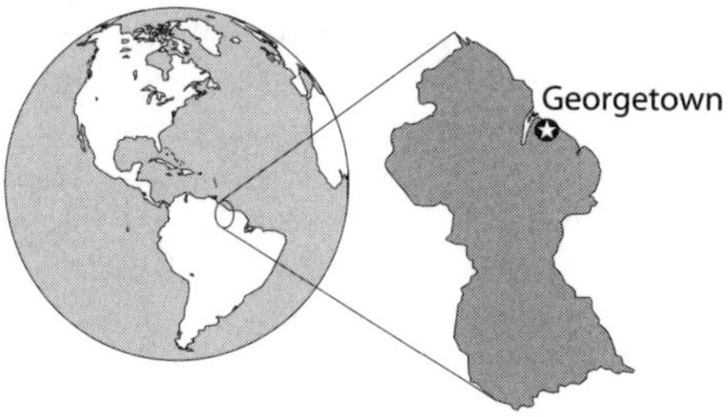

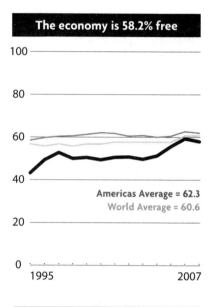

Georgetown

Rank: 90

Regional Rank: 20 of 29

Guyana's economy is 58.2 percent free, according to our 2007 assessment, which makes it the world's 90th freest economy. Its overall score is 1.4 percentage points lower than last year, partially reflecting new methodological detail and partly reflecting a sharp drop in labor freedom. Guyana is ranked 20th out of 29 countries in the Americas, and its overall score is slightly lower than the regional average.

Guyana does not rank strongly in any category but scores best in monetary freedom, labor freedom, and fiscal freedom. The top income and corporate tax rates are high but not excessive, and overall tax revenue is moderate as a percentage of GDP. Inflation is below 10 percent, and Guyana benefits from a highly flexible labor market. Firing a worker can be difficult, but employing labor is relatively easy.

As a developing nation, Guyana faces substantial economic challenges. Investment freedom, business freedom, property rights, and freedom from corruption all score poorly. Significant restrictions on foreign investment are slowly being addressed, and these restrictions, combined with an inefficient bureaucracy, substantially limit Guyana's economic freedom. The substandard rule of law means that property rights are protected only erratically, and corruption is a problem in all areas of government.

BACKGROUND: Colonized by the Dutch and later by the British, Guyana gained its independence in 1966. Support for the two major political parties is highly polarized by ethnic tensions, and any attempts at reform have been made only under framework agreements with international organizations. Guyana's economy depends mainly on agriculture and mining. Parliamentary and presidential elections originally scheduled for August 4, 2006, were delayed because of problems with voter registration. Recent high-profile killings have highlighted a growing crime problem and threaten public order: Minister of Agriculture Satyadeo Sawh, for example, was assassinated in April 2006.

The economy is 58.2% free

100

80

60

40

Americas Average = 62.3
World Average = 60.6

20

0

1995   2007

QUICK FACTS

Population: 0.8 million

GDP (PPP): $3.3 billion
1.6% growth in 2004
0.6% 5-yr. comp. ann. growth
$4,439 per capita

Unemployment: 9.1% (2000)

Inflation (CPI): 4.7%

FDI (net inflow): $48.4 million (gross)

Official Development Assistance:
Multilateral: $95 million
Bilateral: $81 million (24% from the U.S.)

External Debt: $1.2 billion (2002)

Exports: $748.0 million
Primarily sugar, gold, bauxite, alumina, rice, shrimp, molasses, rum, timber

Imports: $782.4 million
Primarily manufactures, machinery, petroleum, food

How Do We Measure Economic Freedom? See Chapter 3 (page 37) for an explanation of the methodology or visit the *Index* Web site at *heritage.org/index*.

GUYANA'S TEN ECONOMIC FREEDOMS

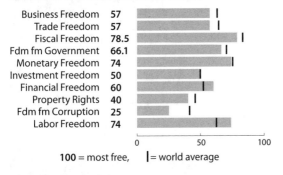

Business Freedom	57
Trade Freedom	57
Fiscal Freedom	78.5
Fdm fm Government	66.1
Monetary Freedom	74
Investment Freedom	50
Financial Freedom	60
Property Rights	40
Fdm fm Corruption	25
Labor Freedom	74

100 = most free, | = world average

BUSINESS FREEDOM — 57%

Starting a business takes an average of 46 days, roughly equal to the world average of 48 days. Obtaining a business license is relatively simple, but closing a business can be very difficult. Bureaucratic procedures are burdensome and time-consuming. The overall freedom to start, operate, and close a business is restricted by the national regulatory environment.

TRADE FREEDOM — 57%

Guyana's weighted average tariff rate was 11.5 percent in 2003. Non-tariff barriers include import-licensing requirements for a relatively large number of products, delays, customs corruption, import taxes, import restrictions, and burdensome standards and regulations. Consequently, an additional 20 percent is deducted from Guyana's trade freedom score to account for these non-tariff barriers.

FISCAL FREEDOM — 78.5%

Guyana has high tax rates. The top income tax rate is 33.3 percent, and the top corporate tax rate is 35 percent. Other taxes include a fuel tax and a sales tax. In the most recent year, overall tax revenue as a percentage of GDP was 29.9 percent.

FREEDOM FROM GOVERNMENT — 66.1%

Total government expenditures in Guyana, including consumption and transfer payments, are high. In the most recent year, government spending equaled 35.9 percent of GDP, and the government received 11.5 percent of its total revenues from state-owned enterprises and government ownership of property.

MONETARY FREEDOM — 74%

Inflation in Guyana is relatively high, averaging 6.4 percent between 2003 and 2005. Relatively high and unstable prices explain most of the monetary freedom score. Guyana has made progress in removing most price controls and privatizing the large public sector, but the government still influences prices through the regulation of state-owned utilities and enterprises. Consequently, an additional 10 percent is deducted from Guyana's monetary freedom score to adjust for measures that distort domestic prices.

INVESTMENT FREEDOM — 50%

Guyana has been moving toward a more welcoming environment for foreign investors, although the government remains cautious about approving new foreign investment and encourages joint ventures with the government. The approval process can be bureaucratic and non-transparent. Residents involved in exporting activities (which are subject to approval) and non-residents are allowed to hold foreign exchange accounts. Payments and transfers are not restricted. Most capital transactions are unrestricted, but all credit operations are controlled. Guyana's constitution guarantees the right of foreigners to own property or land.

FINANCIAL FREEDOM — 60%

Guyana's financial system is small and underdeveloped. The banking sector dominates the financial system. Legislation implemented in 1997 introduced more effective bank regulation and supervision, but weaknesses remain. Non-performing loans are relatively high at 14 percent, down from 25 percent during the mid-1990s. There are six commercial banks, the two largest of which—the Bank of Nova Scotia and Republic Bank (Guyana)—are foreign-owned. There are approximately two dozen credit unions. The last state-owned bank, the Guyana National Co-Operative Bank (GNCB), was sold in 2003. There are some restrictions on financial activities with non-residents. Guyana also has six insurance companies and a small stock exchange.

PROPERTY RIGHTS — 40%

Guyana's judicial system is often slow, inefficient, and subject to corruption. Law enforcement officials and prominent lawyers question the independence of the judiciary and accuse the government of intervening in some cases. A shortage of trained court personnel and magistrates, poor resources, and persistent bribery prolong the resolution of court cases unreasonably.

FREEDOM FROM CORRUPTION — 25%

Corruption is perceived as widespread. Guyana ranks 117th out of 158 countries in Transparency International's Corruption Perceptions Index for 2005.

LABOR FREEDOM — 74%

The labor market operates under relatively flexible employment regulations that could be improved to enhance employment and productivity growth. The non-salary cost of employing a worker is low, but dismissing a redundant employee is relatively costly.

HAITI

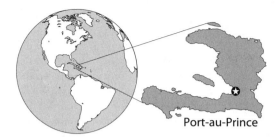

Port-au-Prince

Haiti's economy is 52.2 percent free, according to our 2007 assessment, which makes it the world's 135th freest economy. Its overall score is 2.4 percentage points higher than last year, partially reflecting new methodological detail. Haiti is ranked 27th out of 29 countries in the Americas, and its overall score is lower than the regional average.

Haiti has high levels of freedom from government, labor freedom, and trade freedom. The top income and corporate tax rates are somewhat high, but overall tax revenue is low as a percentage of GDP. Government expenditures are also low. Overall labor flexibility is impressively high.

Major weaknesses are found in business freedom, investment freedom, property rights, and freedom from corruption. Starting a business takes four times longer than the world average, and regulation is intrusive. There are significant restrictions on foreign capital, and investment decisions are often subject to the arbitrary will of the bureaucracy. Rule of law is weak as a result of prolonged political instability. Haiti's judicial system is affected by the crippling corruption in most areas of the public sector.

BACKGROUND: Haiti is the Western Hemisphere's poorest country. Government policies sustain a dominant tradition of subsistence farming that contributes to the depletion of forests and vegetation. Since gaining its independence from France, Haiti has been ruled by a series of despotic governments, although a model democratic constitution was adopted in 1987. President Jean-Bertrand Aristide resigned in February 2004 when his regime collapsed, and presidential and parliamentary elections were conducted (with outside help) in 2006. Current President René Préval has named a diverse cabinet.

How Do We Measure Economic Freedom? See Chapter 3 (page 37) for an explanation of the methodology or visit the *Index* Web site at *heritage.org/index*.

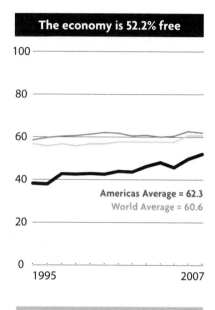

The economy is 52.2% free

Americas Average = 62.3
World Average = 60.6

1995 — 2007

QUICK FACTS

Population: 8.4 million

GDP (PPP): $14.15 billion (2005 estimate)
−3.8% growth in 2004
−0.8% 5-yr. comp. ann. growth
$1,700 per capita (2005 estimate)

Unemployment: n/a

Inflation (CPI): 22.8%

FDI (net inflow): $6.5 million (gross)

Official Development Assistance:
Multilateral: $93 million
Bilateral: $210 million (44% from the U.S.)

External Debt: $1.2 billion

Exports: $469.2 million
Primarily manufactures, coffee, oils, cocoa, mangoes

Imports: $1.4 billion
Primarily food, manufactured goods, machinery and transport equipment, fuels, raw materials

HAITI'S TEN ECONOMIC FREEDOMS

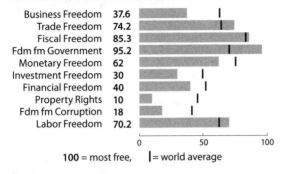

Business Freedom	37.6	
Trade Freedom	74.2	
Fiscal Freedom	85.3	
Fdm fm Government	95.2	
Monetary Freedom	62	
Investment Freedom	30	
Financial Freedom	40	
Property Rights	10	
Fdm fm Corruption	18	
Labor Freedom	70.2	

100 = most free, ┃ = world average

BUSINESS FREEDOM — 37.6%

Starting a business takes an average of 203 days, compared to the world average of 48 days, stifling entrepreneurship and job creation. Obtaining a business license is difficult, and closing a business is very difficult. The application of commercial laws is characterized by inconsistency and lack of transparency. The overall freedom to start, operate, and close a business is seriously restricted by the national regulatory environment.

TRADE FREEDOM — 74.2%

Haiti's simple average tariff rate was 2.9 percent in 2003. Non-tariff barriers include the high cost of shipping goods through inefficient state-owned international seaports, customs corruption, import controls, import quotas on some food products, and import licensing requirements for agricultural products, chemicals, and pharmaceuticals. Consequently, an additional 20 percent is deducted from Haiti's trade freedom score to account for these non-tariff barriers.

FISCAL FREEDOM — 85.3%

Haiti has a moderate income tax rate and a high corporate tax rate. The top income tax rate is 30 percent, and the top corporate tax rate is 35 percent. Other taxes include a value-added tax (VAT) and a capital gains tax. In the most recent year, overall tax revenue as a percentage of GDP was 8.9 percent.

FREEDOM FROM GOVERNMENT — 95.2%

Total government expenditures in Haiti, including consumption and transfer payments, are low. In the most recent year, government spending equaled 12.7 percent of GDP, and the government received 3.2 percent of its total revenues from state-owned enterprises and government ownership of property. Restructuring of the inefficient state enterprises to reduce their burden on government finances is an important objective, but the process has been slow.

MONETARY FREEDOM — 62%

Inflation in Haiti is high, averaging 19.6 percent between 2003 and 2005. Unstable prices explain most of the monetary freedom score. Prices are generally determined by the market, but the government imposes restrictions on the mark-up of some products. For example, retailers are prohibited from marking up pharmaceutical products by

more than 40 percent, and prices of petroleum products are strictly controlled. Consequently, an additional 10 percent is deducted from Haiti's monetary freedom score to adjust for measures that distort domestic prices.

INVESTMENT FREEDOM — 30%

Special government authorization is required for some foreign investments, particularly in electricity, water, public health, and telecommunications. There are restrictions on foreign ownership of land. Unofficial barriers to investment include judicial inadequacies, lack of transparency, corruption, bureaucratic inefficiency, and political instability. Residents may hold foreign exchange accounts only for specified purposes, and non-residents may hold them without restriction. There are no restrictions on payments, transfers, or capital transactions.

FINANCIAL FREEDOM — 40%

Haiti's financial sector is very small and prone to crisis. Supervision and regulation of the financial system is poor, and domestic standards do not comply with internationally recognized accounting standards. The banking sector, consisting of 11 banks overall, remains undeveloped. There are two state-owned banks, which accounted for about 10 percent of banking assets in 2004. Two foreign-owned banks accounted for a similar level of bank assets. The sector also includes a development finance institution and two mortgage banks. Credit is available on market terms, foreigners have access to domestic credit, and banks may offer a full range of banking services. There is no stock market.

PROPERTY RIGHTS — 10%

The protection and guarantees that Haitian law extends to investors are severely compromised by weak enforcement mechanisms, a lack of updated laws to handle modern commercial practices, and a dysfunctional, resource-poor legal system. Business litigants are often frustrated with the legal process, and most commercial disputes are settled out of court. Widespread corruption has allowed disputing parties to purchase favorable outcomes.

FREEDOM FROM CORRUPTION — 18%

Corruption is perceived as widespread. Haiti ranks 155th out of 158 countries in Transparency International's Corruption Perceptions Index for 2005.

LABOR FREEDOM — 70.2%

The labor market operates under relatively flexible employment regulations that could be improved to enhance employment and productivity growth. The non-salary cost of employing a worker is moderate, but dismissing a redundant employee is relatively costly. There are restrictions on increasing or contracting the number of working hours.

HONDURAS

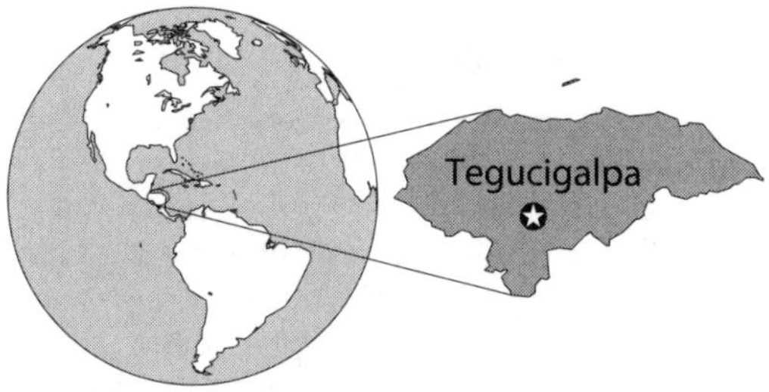

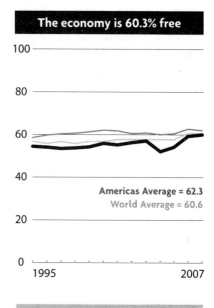

Tegucigalpa

The economy of Honduras is 60.3 percent free, according to our 2007 assessment, which makes it the world's 76th freest economy. Its overall score is 0.7 percentage point higher than last year, partially reflecting new methodological detail. Honduras is ranked 19th out of 29 countries in the Americas, and its overall score is slightly lower than the regional average.

Honduras receives high scores for fiscal freedom, freedom from government, and financial freedom. Personal and corporate income tax rates are fairly low, and overall tax revenue is just 17 percent of GDP. Government expenditures are similarly moderate, although the level of revenue from state-owned businesses is significant. Honduran financial freedom is boosted by the developing banking sector, which has been instituting stronger rules and better, more transparent oversight.

Honduras suffers from weak property rights, freedom from corruption, investment freedom, and business freedom. Starting a business takes about as long as the international average, but closing a business and obtaining commercial licenses are difficult. Public administration is inefficient and widely corrupt. The rule of law is undermined by weak basic security.

BACKGROUND: Honduras is one of Central America's poorest nations, and three-quarters of the population lives below the poverty line. Approximately 34 percent of the labor force works in agriculture, and the estimated unemployment rate is 28 percent. However, peaceful democratic elections have been held regularly since 1981, and an economy that once subsisted on coffee and banana exports has been diversified to include shrimp, melons, tourism, and a growing clothing-assembly industry. The government has met targeted macroeconomic objectives and is reducing debt under World Bank and International Monetary Fund initiatives. Ongoing problems include drug trafficking, youth gangs, and violent crime.

How Do We Measure Economic Freedom? See Chapter 3 (page 37) for an explanation of the methodology or visit the *Index* Web site at *heritage.org/index*.

The economy is 60.3% free

Americas Average = 62.3
World Average = 60.6

1995 — 2007

QUICK FACTS

Population: 7.0 million

GDP (PPP): $20.3 billion
4.6% growth in 2004
3.8% 5-yr. comp. ann. growth
$2,876 per capita

Unemployment: 28% (2005 estimate)

Inflation (CPI): 8.1%

FDI (net inflow): $293 million (gross)

Official Development Assistance:
Multilateral: $363 million
Bilateral: $337 million (33% from the U.S.)

External Debt: $6.3 billion

Exports: $3.1 billion
Primarily coffee, shrimp, bananas, gold, palm oil, fruit, lobster, lumber

Imports: $4.4 billion
Primarily machinery and transport equipment, industrial raw materials, chemical products, fuels, food

HONDURAS'S TEN ECONOMIC FREEDOMS

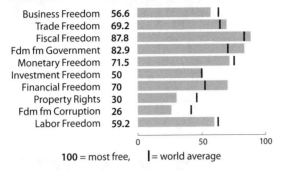

Business Freedom	56.6
Trade Freedom	69.2
Fiscal Freedom	87.8
Fdm fm Government	82.9
Monetary Freedom	71.5
Investment Freedom	50
Financial Freedom	70
Property Rights	30
Fdm fm Corruption	26
Labor Freedom	59.2

100 = most free, | = world average

BUSINESS FREEDOM — 56.6%

Starting a business takes an average of 44 days, compared to the world average of 48 days. Entrepreneurship should be easier for maximum job creation. Obtaining a business license and closing a business are difficult. The government does not always publish regulations before they enter into force, and obtaining government approval for investment activities commonly involves procedural red tape. The overall freedom to start, operate, and close a business is restricted by the national regulatory environment.

TRADE FREEDOM — 69.2%

The weighted average tariff rate in Honduras was 5.4 percent in 2004. Non-tariff barriers include differential import taxes, customs corruption, some limitations on market access in the services sector, subsidies, coffee export fees, and restrictive sanitary and phytosanitary rules. Consequently, an additional 20 percent is deducted from Honduras's trade freedom score to account for these non-tariff barriers.

FISCAL FREEDOM — 87.8%

Honduras has moderate tax rates. Both the top income tax rate and the top corporate tax rate are 30 percent (a 25 percent corporate tax rate plus a 5 percent temporary social contribution tax). Other taxes include a value-added tax (VAT) and a capital gains tax. In the most recent year, overall tax revenue as a percentage of GDP was 17.3 percent.

FREEDOM FROM GOVERNMENT — 82.9%

Total government expenditures in Honduras, including consumption and transfer payments, are low. In the most recent year, government spending equaled 24.1 percent of GDP, and the government received 10.8 percent of its total revenues from state-owned enterprises and government ownership of property.

MONETARY FREEDOM — 71.5%

Inflation in Honduras is relatively high, averaging 8.5 percent between 2003 and 2005. Relatively high and unstable prices explain most of the monetary freedom score. The government regulates the price of petroleum products, steel, pharmaceuticals, and services from state-owned utilities and reserves the right to impose price controls across other goods and services as needed. Consequently, an additional 10 percent is deducted from Honduras's monetary freedom score to adjust for measures that distort domestic prices.

INVESTMENT FREEDOM — 50%

Honduras welcomes foreign investment, which is generally accorded the same rights as domestic investment. The investment climate is hampered by high levels of crime, a weak judicial system, and high levels of corruption. Government authorization is required for foreign investment in basic health services, telecommunications, electricity, air transport, fishing and hunting, exploration and exploitation of minerals, forestry, agriculture, insurance and financial services, and private education. Foreign ownership of land near the coast or along borders is generally prohibited but may be allowed in some cases with government permission. Both residents and non-residents may hold foreign exchange accounts. Payments and transfers are not restricted, and few capital transactions require approval.

FINANCIAL FREEDOM — 70%

The Honduran financial sector is developing. The banking sector has undergone consolidation through mergers and closures in recent years. The collapse of several banks has led to stronger capital-adequacy rules, clarification of the role of the central bank, and greater oversight. There were 16 private commercial banks (several with foreign ownership), two state-owned banks, and about a dozen other small financial institutions operating in 2005. Foreign investors face few formal restrictions on accessing domestic credit, but informal constraints can be significant. The insurance sector is very small, accounting for only 4 percent of financial sector assets, and consisted of nine domestic and two foreign insurance companies as of October 2004. There are two small stock exchanges.

PROPERTY RIGHTS — 30%

Protection of property is weak. The lack of judicial security, a deteriorating security environment, and endemic corruption pose real risks, making business disputes difficult to resolve. Expropriation of property is possible, but compensation, when awarded, is in 20-year government bonds.

FREEDOM FROM CORRUPTION — 26%

Corruption is perceived as widespread. Honduras ranks 107th out of 158 countries in Transparency International's Corruption Perceptions Index for 2005.

LABOR FREEDOM — 59.2%

The labor market operates under restrictive employment regulations that impede employment and productivity growth. The non-salary cost of employing a worker can be low, but dismissing a redundant employee is costly. Restrictions on contracting or increasing the number of work hours are rigid.

HONG KONG

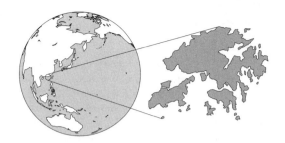

Hong Kong's economy is 89.3 percent free, according to our 2007 assessment, which makes it the world's freest economy. Its overall score is 1.6 percentage points lower than last year, partially reflecting new methodological detail. Hong Kong is ranked 1st out of 30 countries in the Asia–Pacific region, and its overall score is well above the regional average.

Hong Kong scores exceptionally well in almost all areas of economic freedom. Income and corporate tax rates are extremely low, and overall taxation is relatively small as a percentage of GDP. Business regulation is simple, and the labor market is highly flexible. Inflation is low, although the government distorts the prices of several staples. Investment in Hong Kong is wide open, with virtually no restrictions on foreign capital. The island is also one of the world's leading financial centers, with an extensive banking and services industry that is regulated non-intrusively and transparent. The judiciary, independent of politics and virtually free of corruption, has an exemplary ability to protect property rights.

Hong Kong could do slightly better in trade freedom, however. Enforcing intellectual property rights is a problem, though the country's zero percent average tariff rate is impressively open.

BACKGROUND: Hong Kong is part of the People's Republic of China, although it remains a separate economic system. It was a British colony for 130 years until the 1997 transfer of sovereignty to China. A major gateway to the Chinese economy, Hong Kong maintains the rule of law, simple procedures for enterprises, free entry of foreign capital and repatriation of earnings, and transparency. The vast bulk of Hong Kong's economy is built on the service sector. Governance of Hong Kong is run as a Special Administrative Region (SAR), headed by a Chief Executive. The current Chief Executive is Donald Tsang, who took power after Tung Chee-hwa resigned in the wake of massive pro-democracy demonstrations.

How Do We Measure Economic Freedom? See Chapter 3 (page 37) for an explanation of the methodology or visit the *Index* Web site at *heritage.org/index*.

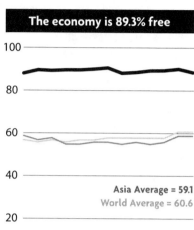

The economy is 89.3% free

Asia Average = 59.1
World Average = 60.6

1995 — 2007

QUICK FACTS

Population: 6.9 million

GDP (PPP): $212.1 billion
8.6% growth in 2004
4.8% 5-yr. comp. ann. growth
$30,822 per capita

Unemployment: 6.8%

Inflation (CPI): −0.4%

FDI (net inflow): −$5.7 billion

Official Development Assistance:
Multilateral: None
Bilateral: $7 million (3% from the U.S.)

External Debt: $72.0 billion (2005 estimate)

Exports: $314.4 billion
Primarily electrical machinery and appliances, textiles, apparel, footwear, watches and clocks, toys, plastics, precious stones, printed material

Imports: $299.6 billion
Primarily raw materials and semi-manufactures, consumer goods, capital goods, food, fuel

HONG KONG'S TEN ECONOMIC FREEDOMS

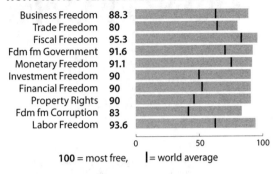

Business Freedom	88.3
Trade Freedom	80
Fiscal Freedom	95.3
Fdm fm Government	91.6
Monetary Freedom	91.1
Investment Freedom	90
Financial Freedom	90
Property Rights	90
Fdm fm Corruption	83
Labor Freedom	93.6

100 = most free, | = world average

BUSINESS FREEDOM — 88.3%

Starting a business takes an average of 11 days, compared to the world average of 48 days. The sound business environment allows entrepreneurship to flourish. Obtaining a business license is relatively simple, and closing a business is very easy. Business regulations are streamlined and applied uniformly. The overall freedom to start, operate, and close a business is protected by the national regulatory environment.

TRADE FREEDOM — 80%

Hong Kong's weighted average tariff rate was zero percent in 2003. With the exception of four categories of goods—liquors, tobacco, hydrocarbon oil, and methyl alcohol—trade is essentially duty-free. Non-tariff barriers include restrictive regulation of pharmaceuticals, market access restrictions for legal services, and issues involving the enforcement and protection of intellectual property rights. Consequently, an additional 20 percent is deducted from Hong Kong's trade freedom score to account for these non-tariff barriers.

FISCAL FREEDOM — 95.3%

Hong Kong's tax rates are among the lowest in the world. Under a dual income tax system, individuals are taxed either progressively, between 2 percent and 19 percent, on income adjusted for deductions and allowances or at a flat rate of 16 percent on their gross income, depending on which liability is lower. The top income tax rate is 17.5 percent. The estate (inheritance) tax was abolished effective February 11, 2006. In the most recent year, overall tax revenue as a percentage of GDP was 11.7 percent.

FREEDOM FROM GOVERNMENT — 91.6%

Total government expenditures in Hong Kong, including consumption and transfer payments, are low. In the most recent year, government spending equaled 18.3 percent of GDP, and the government received 1.9 percent of its total revenues from state-owned enterprises and government ownership of property.

MONETARY FREEDOM — 91.1%

Inflation in Hong Kong is low, averaging 0.4 percent between 2003 and 2005. Stable prices explain most of the monetary freedom score. The government regulates the price of public transport, electricity, and some residential rents. Consequently, an additional 5 percent is deducted from Hong Kong's monetary freedom score to adjust for measures that distort domestic prices.

INVESTMENT FREEDOM — 90%

Foreign investment is strongly encouraged. There are no limits to foreign ownership and no screening or special approval procedures to set up a foreign firm. The only exception is broadcasting, where foreign entities may own no more than 49 percent of the local stations. The Hong Kong dollar is freely convertible. There are no controls or requirements on current transfers, purchase of real estate, access to foreign exchange, or repatriation of profits.

FINANCIAL FREEDOM — 90%

Hong Kong is a global financial center with an innovative and efficient financial system. The regulatory and legal environment is non-intrusive, focused on prudent minimum standards and transparency. Banks are overseen by the independent Hong Kong Monetary Authority. Credit is allocated on market terms to all investors. There are no restrictions on foreign banks, which are treated the same as domestic institutions. The stock exchange ranks ninth in the world in terms of capitalization. In April 1998, the government intervened in the stock market by purchasing $15.2 billion in private stocks, but it has since largely divested itself of all but $410 million of these holdings.

PROPERTY RIGHTS — 90%

Contracts are strongly protected. Hong Kong has a transparent legal system based on common law, and its constitution strongly supports private property and freedom of exchange. These protections do not seem to be in danger. The government controls all land and grants renewable land leases through public auctions. The leases are valid up to 2047 for all land in the SAR, and it is uncertain what the government's land policy will be after 2047 vis-à-vis China's land policy.

FREEDOM FROM CORRUPTION — 83%

Corruption is perceived as minimal. Hong Kong ranks 15th out of 158 countries in Transparency International's Corruption Perceptions Index for 2005.

LABOR FREEDOM — 93.6%

The labor market operates under highly flexible employment regulations that enhance employment and productivity growth. The non-salary cost of employing a worker is low, but dismissing a redundant employee can be relatively costly. Regulations on expanding or contracting the number of working hours are very flexible. The labor code is strictly enforced but does not impede business activities.

HUNGARY

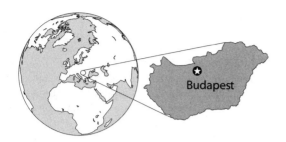

Budapest

Rank: 44

Regional Rank: 25 of 41

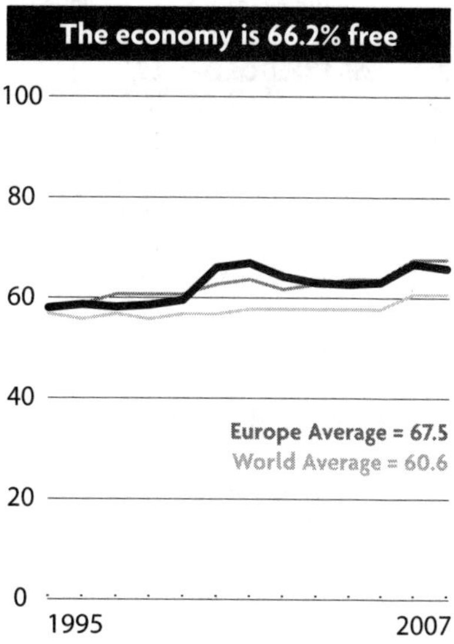

Hungary's economy is 66.2 percent free, according to our 2007 assessment, which makes it the world's 44th freest economy. Its overall score is 0.9 percentage point lower than last year, partially reflecting new methodological detail. Hungary is ranked 25th out of 41 countries in the European region, and its overall score is slightly lower than the regional average.

Hungary enjoys strong trade freedom, fiscal freedom, monetary freedom, property rights, investment freedom, business freedom, and labor freedom. The top income tax rate is fairly high, but corporate taxes are low. Inflation is low, but Hungary's monetary score is hurt by the EU's agricultural subsidies. Investment in Hungary is easy, although it is subject to government licensing in security-sensitive areas. Foreign capital enjoys virtually the same protections and privileges as domestic capital. The rule of law is strong, a professional judiciary protects property rights, and the level of corruption is low.

Hungary's freedom from government is weak. Total government spending is high, and many state-owned enterprises have not been privatized. Business licensing is also a problem, as regulations are not applied consistently.

BACKGROUND: Hungary held its first multi-party elections in 1990, following nearly 50 years of Communist rule, and has succeeded in transforming its centrally planned economy into a market economy. Both foreign ownership of and foreign investment in Hungarian firms are widespread. The governing coalition, comprising the Hungarian Socialist Party and the liberal Alliance of Free Democrats, prevailed in the April 2006 general election. Hungary needs to reduce government spending and further reform its economy in order to meet the 2010 target date for accession to the euro zone.

The economy is 66.2% free

[Line chart showing economic freedom scores from 1995 to 2007, with values mostly between 60 and 67. Y-axis marked at 0, 20, 40, 60, 80, 100. X-axis from 1995 to 2007.]

Europe Average = 67.5
World Average = 60.6

QUICK FACTS

Population: 10.1 million

GDP (PPP): $169.9 billion
4.6% growth in 2004
4.3% 5-yr. comp. ann. growth
$16,814 per capita

Unemployment: 6.1%

Inflation (CPI): 6.8%

FDI (net inflow): $3.6 billion

Official Development Assistance:
Multilateral: $241 million
Bilateral: $63 million (2% from the U.S.)

External Debt: $63.2 billion

Exports: $66.4 billion
Primarily machinery and equipment, other manufactures, food products, raw materials, fuels and electricity

Imports: $69.4 billion
Primarily machinery and equipment, other manufactures, fuels and electricity, food products, raw materials

How Do We Measure Economic Freedom? See Chapter 3 (page 37) for an explanation of the methodology or visit the *Index* Web site at *heritage.org/index*.

207

HUNGARY'S TEN ECONOMIC FREEDOMS

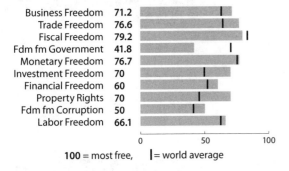

Business Freedom	71.2
Trade Freedom	76.6
Fiscal Freedom	79.2
Fdm fm Government	41.8
Monetary Freedom	76.7
Investment Freedom	70
Financial Freedom	60
Property Rights	70
Fdm fm Corruption	50
Labor Freedom	66.1

100 = most free, ❙ = world average

BUSINESS FREEDOM — 71.2%

Starting a business takes an average of 38 days, compared to the world average of 48 days. Entrepreneurship should be easier for maximum job creation. Obtaining a business license is difficult, but closing a business is relatively easy. Regulations are not always applied transparently or evenly. The overall freedom to start, operate, and close a business is relatively well protected by the national regulatory environment.

TRADE FREEDOM — 76.6%

Hungary's trade policy is the same as those of other members of the European Union. The common EU weighted average tariff rate was 1.7 percent in 2005. Various non-tariff barriers are reflected in EU and Hungarian government policy, including agricultural and manufacturing subsidies, regulatory and licensing restrictions, and other market access restrictions. The government also implements restrictive biotechnology regulations for food and feed products. Consequently, an additional 20 percent is deducted from Hungary's trade freedom score.

FISCAL FREEDOM — 79.2%

Hungary has a high income tax rate but a low corporate tax rate. The top income tax rate is 38 percent, and the top corporate tax rate is 16 percent. Other taxes include a value-added tax (VAT), a property tax, and a community tax. In the most recent year, overall tax revenue as a percentage of GDP was 37.7 percent.

FREEDOM FROM GOVERNMENT — 41.8%

Total government expenditures in Hungary, including consumption and transfer payments, are extremely high. In the most recent year, government spending equaled 49.4 percent of GDP, and the government received 3.9 percent of its total revenues from state-owned enterprises and government ownership of property. The sale of remaining state-owned enterprises has been accelerated.

MONETARY FREEDOM — 76.7%

Inflation in Hungary is moderate, averaging 4.4 percent between 2003 and 2005. Relatively unstable prices explain most of the monetary freedom score. As a participant in the EU's Common Agricultural Policy, the government subsidizes agricultural production, distorting the prices of agricultural products. It also regulates prices for energy,

telecommunications services, and subsidized pharmaceutical products, among others. Consequently, an additional 10 percent is deducted from Hungary's monetary freedom score to account for these policies.

INVESTMENT FREEDOM — 70%

Foreign companies account for a large share of manufacturing, telecommunications, and energy activity. The government allows 100 percent foreign ownership in almost all sectors, with the exception of some defense-related industries, some types of land, airlines, and broadcasting. The law provides for equal treatment of foreign and domestic capital. Both residents and non-residents may hold foreign exchange accounts. There are no restrictions or controls on payments for invisible transactions, current transfers, or repatriation of profits and no restrictions on issues or sales of capital market instruments, although there are some reporting requirements.

FINANCIAL FREEDOM — 60%

To prepare for accession to the European Union, Hungary undertook significant reform of its financial system, particularly financial regulation, permitting greater foreign participation. The law still restricts financial institutions from offering a full range of services. Although most large financial institutions are subsidiaries of foreign financial groups, EU institutions have easier access than others. The banking industry is competitive. Foreign investors account for over 80 percent of banking capital. Two major banks and the FHB Land Credit and Mortgage Bank are partially state-owned and together account for over 7.5 percent of bank assets. The state also has a very small stake and a "golden share" in the largest domestic bank, OTP Bank. There were 28 insurance companies and 34 insurance co-operatives in 2004, and the top three insurers were foreign companies. Capital markets are well developed, and foreign investors participate freely.

PROPERTY RIGHTS — 70%

The constitution provides for an independent judiciary, and the government respects this provision in practice. The threat of expropriation is low. The court system is slow and severely overburdened, and it often takes more than a year to obtain a final ruling on a contract dispute.

FREEDOM FROM CORRUPTION — 50%

Corruption is perceived as present. Hungary ranks 40th out of 158 countries in Transparency International's Corruption Perceptions Index for 2005.

LABOR FREEDOM — 66.1%

The labor market operates under relatively flexible employment regulations that could be improved to enhance employment and productivity growth. The non-salary cost of employing a worker can be high, and dismissing a redundant employee is relatively costly. The unemployment insurance system offers benefits for up to 270 calendar days to the involuntarily unemployed, with an average worker receiving about 65 percent of his or her salary in benefits.

ICELAND

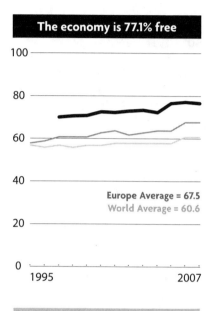

Reykjavik

Rank: 15

Regional Rank: 8 of 41

Iceland's economy is 77.1 percent free, according to our 2007 assessment, which makes it the world's 15th freest economy. Its overall score is 0.6 percentage point lower than last year, partially reflecting new methodological detail. Iceland is ranked 8th out of 41 countries in the European region, and its overall score is higher than the regional average.

Iceland enjoys high levels of freedom from corruption, investment freedom, trade freedom, financial freedom, property rights, business freedom, fiscal freedom, and monetary freedom. A point of pride is that Iceland is rated as the world's least corrupt economy. The average tariff rate is low (though non-tariff barriers such as phytosanitary and agricultural restrictions are extensive), and business regulation is efficient. Virtually all commercial operations are simple and transparent. Inflation is fairly low, and foreign investment is permitted without government approval, although capital is subject to restrictions in some areas of the economy. Iceland's financial sector is highly modern. The judiciary, independent of politics and free of corruption, has an exemplary ability to protect property rights.

Iceland is relatively weaker in terms of labor freedom, investment freedom, and especially freedom from government. Total government spending equals almost 50 percent of GDP.

BACKGROUND: The Republic of Iceland is a North Atlantic island with a centuries-old democratic tradition. In per capita terms, it is one of the world's wealthiest economies. Recent market liberalization and a considerable reduction in government ownership have strengthened entrepreneurial dynamism and increased productivity in many sectors of the economy. Iceland has never applied for EU membership, which is unpopular among the country's citizens. Although the marine sector accounts for the majority of exports, its share of the economy has declined over the years. The service sector employs more than 60 percent of the working population.

How Do We Measure Economic Freedom? See Chapter 3 (page 37) for an explanation of the methodology or visit the *Index* Web site at *heritage.org/index*.

The economy is 77.1% free

Europe Average = 67.5
World Average = 60.6

1995 — 2007

QUICK FACTS

Population: 0.3 million

GDP (PPP): $9.7 billion
8.2% growth in 2004
3.6% 5-yr. comp. ann. growth
$33,051 per capita

Unemployment: 3.1%

Inflation (CPI): 2.8%

FDI (net inflow): −$2.3 billion

Official Development Assistance:
Multilateral: None
Bilateral: None

External Debt: $3.1 billion (2002)

Exports: $4.5 billion
Primarily fish, fish products, aluminum, animal products, ferrosilicon, diatomite

Imports: $5.3 billion
Primarily machinery and equipment, petroleum products, food, textiles

ICELAND'S TEN ECONOMIC FREEDOMS

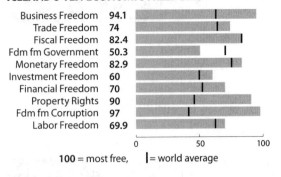

Business Freedom	94.1
Trade Freedom	74
Fiscal Freedom	82.4
Fdm fm Government	50.3
Monetary Freedom	82.9
Investment Freedom	60
Financial Freedom	70
Property Rights	90
Fdm fm Corruption	97
Labor Freedom	69.9

100 = most free, **|** = world average

BUSINESS FREEDOM — 94.1%

Starting a business takes an average of five days, compared to the world average of 48 days. The business environment has allowed entrepreneurship to flourish. Obtaining a business license is simple, and closing a business is very easy. In recent years, the government has made progress in streamlining its complex and time-consuming regulatory environment. The overall freedom to start, operate, and close a business is strongly protected by the national regulatory environment.

TRADE FREEDOM — 74%

Iceland's weighted average tariff rate was 3 percent in 2003. Strict phytosanitary regulations, import taxes, import bans, import and export restrictions, prohibitively high agriculture tariffs, burdensome regulations, and a government agricultural policy that includes a price equalization mechanism to support agricultural exports add to the cost of trade. Consequently, an additional 20 percent is deducted from Iceland's trade freedom score to account for these non-tariff barriers.

FISCAL FREEDOM — 82.4%

Iceland has a moderate income tax rate and a low corporate tax rate. The top income tax rate is 23.8 percent, and the top corporate tax rate is 18 percent. Other taxes include a value-added tax (VAT) and a net wealth tax. In the most recent year, overall tax revenue as a percentage of GDP was 41.9 percent.

FREEDOM FROM GOVERNMENT — 50.3%

Total government expenditures in Iceland, including consumption and transfer payments, are high. In the most recent year, government spending equaled 45.5 percent of GDP, and the government received 4.2 percent of its total revenues from state-owned enterprises and government ownership of property.

MONETARY FREEDOM — 82.9%

Inflation in Iceland is moderate, averaging 3.6 percent between 2003 and 2005. Relatively unstable prices explain most of the monetary freedom score. The government subsidizes agricultural production, distorting the prices of agriculture products. Milk is subject to production-linked direct payments, production quotas, and administered prices, and sheep farmers receive direct payments based on support targets and quality-dependent payments. Consequently, an additional 5 percent is deducted from Iceland's monetary freedom score to account for these policies.

INVESTMENT FREEDOM — 60%

Iceland generally welcomes foreign investment, although the government maintains restrictions in some key areas. Foreign ownership in the fishing industry, which constitutes a major portion of the economy, is limited to 25 percent, and individuals must live in Iceland to purchase real estate. Residents and non-residents may own foreign exchange accounts, subject to reporting requirements. There are no controls or requirements on payments or current transfers, access to foreign exchange, or repatriation of profits.

FINANCIAL FREEDOM — 70%

Iceland's financial sector is modern and provides a full range of financial services. Since joining the European Economic Area, Iceland has liberalized and deregulated its financial markets, allowing Icelandic financial institutions to operate on a cross-border basis in the EEA and vice versa. The government sold its stakes in two partially state-owned banks in 2003 and no longer has a presence in the commercial banking sector. The state-owned Housing Financing Fund (HFF), which enjoys public guarantees from the government and is exempt from tax liability according to the European Banking Federation, now faces competition from Icelandic banks in residential housing mortgages. The HFF holds approximately 80 percent of the individual home loan market and about 50 percent of the individual credit loan market. There were 13 domestic insurance companies and a number of foreign insurance companies operating in June 2005. The stock market has expanded rapidly and is part of a regional integrated network of exchanges in Nordic and some Baltic countries.

PROPERTY RIGHTS — 90%

Private property is well protected in Iceland. The constitution provides for an independent judiciary, and the government generally respects this provision in practice. With just a few exceptions, trials are public and conducted fairly, with no official intimidation.

FREEDOM FROM CORRUPTION — 97%

Corruption is perceived as almost nonexistent. Iceland ranks first out of 158 countries in Transparency International's Corruption Perceptions Index for 2005.

LABOR FREEDOM — 69.9%

The labor market operates under relatively flexible employment regulations that could be improved to enhance employment and productivity growth. The non-salary cost of employing a worker is moderate, and dismissing a redundant employee is not difficult. Regulations on increasing or contracting the number of work hours are rigid.

INDIA

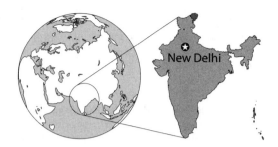

New Delhi

Rank: 104

Regional Rank: 19 of 30

India's economy is 55.6 percent free, according to our 2007 assessment, which makes it the world's 104th freest economy. Its overall score is 3.3 percentage points higher than last year, partially reflecting new methodological detail. India is ranked 19th out of 30 countries in the Asia–Pacific region, and its overall score is lower than the regional average.

India enjoys strong fiscal freedom, freedom from government, and monetary freedom. The top individual and corporate income tax rates are moderate, and overall tax revenue is not excessive as a percentage of GDP. Government expenditure is relatively low as well, although a significant amount of total tax revenue comes from state-owned businesses. Inflation is fairly low, but government price controls hinder market forces.

India could improve in several areas, including business freedom, trade freedom, financial freedom, investment freedom, and freedom from corruption. The average tariff rate is high, and the government imposes severe non-tariff barriers. Foreign investment is overly regulated, and the judicial system is erratic and clogged by a significant backlog of cases. Though the country has a large financial sector, the government interferes extensively with foreign capital.

BACKGROUND: India is the world's most populous democracy. Though one of the oldest civilizations in existence, it has been a nation only since the end of British colonial rule in 1947. India's fast-growing population of 1.1 billion people offers a potential human capital advantage, but a tradition of protectionism and a large public sector are heavy burdens. Nevertheless, the private sector is vibrant and diversified, and 2006 saw strong economic growth, mostly due to residual benefits earned from past reforms. Historically, services and manufacturing have driven economic gains, but the majority of Indians still work in agriculture.

How Do We Measure Economic Freedom? See Chapter 3 (page 37) for an explanation of the methodology or visit the *Index* Web site at *heritage.org/index.*

The economy is 55.6% free

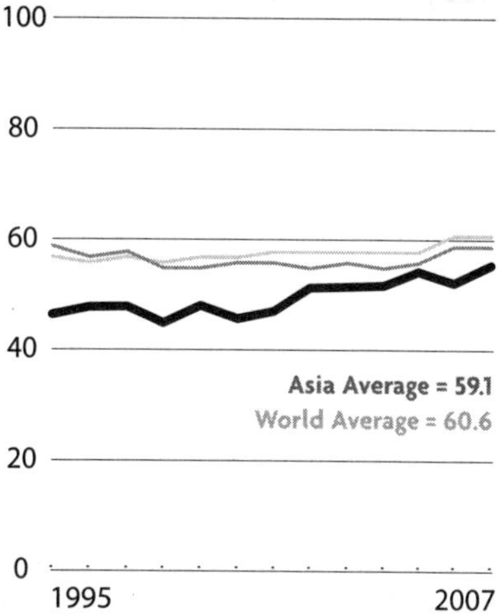

100

80

60

40

Asia Average = 59.1
World Average = 60.6

20

0

1995   2007

QUICK FACTS

Population: 1.1 billion

GDP (PPP): $3.4 trillion
8.1% growth in 2004
5.8% 5-yr. comp. ann. growth
$3,139 per capita

Unemployment: 9.1% (2004 estimate)

Inflation (CPI): 3.8%

FDI (net inflow): $3.1 billion

Official Development Assistance:
Multilateral: $1.3 billion
Bilateral: $1.8 billion (9% from the U.S.)

External Debt: $122.7 billion

Exports: $82.7 billion
Primarily textile goods, gems and jewelry, engineering goods, chemicals, leather manufactures

Imports: $93.9 billion
Primarily crude oil, machinery, gems, fertilizer, chemicals

INDIA'S TEN ECONOMIC FREEDOMS

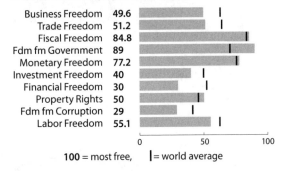

Business Freedom	49.6
Trade Freedom	51.2
Fiscal Freedom	84.8
Fdm fm Government	89
Monetary Freedom	77.2
Investment Freedom	40
Financial Freedom	30
Property Rights	50
Fdm fm Corruption	29
Labor Freedom	55.1

0   50   100

100 = most free,   ┃ = world average

BUSINESS FREEDOM — 49.6%

Starting a business takes an average of 35 days, compared to the world average of 48 days. Obtaining a business license and closing a business can be very difficult. All businesses must contend with extensive federal and state regulation as well as an infamously slow bureaucracy. The overall freedom to start, operate, and close a business is significantly restricted by the national regulatory environment.

TRADE FREEDOM — 51.2%

India's weighted average tariff rate was 14.4 percent in 2005. Non-tariff barriers include excessive bureaucracy, restrictive licensing requirements, export subsidies, import taxes, onerous standards and certifications on many goods, discriminatory sanitary and phytosanitary measures, problematic enforcement of intellectual property rights, and a negative import list that bans or restricts many goods. Consequently, an additional 20 percent is deducted from India's trade freedom score to account for these extensive non-tariff barriers.

FISCAL FREEDOM — 84.8%

India's tax rates are moderate. Both the top income tax rate and the top corporate tax rate are 33 percent (a top rate of 30 percent plus a 10 percent surcharge). Other taxes include a dividend tax, a property tax, and a tax on insurance contracts. In the most recent year, overall tax revenue as a percentage of GDP was 10.2 percent.

FREEDOM FROM GOVERNMENT — 89%

Total government expenditures in India, including consumption and transfer payments, are low. In the most recent year, government spending equaled 16.3 percent of GDP, and the government received 14.3 percent of its total revenues from state-owned enterprises and government ownership of property—an extraordinarily high percentage relative to other countries.

MONETARY FREEDOM — 77.2%

Inflation in India is moderate, averaging 4.1 percent between 2003 and 2005. Relatively unstable prices explain most of the monetary freedom score. The government subsidizes agricultural, gas, and kerosene production and (under the Essential Commodities Act of 1955) applies price controls at three levels (factory, wholesale, and retail) on "essential" commodities, electricity, some petroleum products and certain types of coal, and pharmaceuticals. Consequently, an additional 10 percent is deducted from India's monetary freedom score to account for these policies.

INVESTMENT FREEDOM — 40%

India controls foreign investment with limits on equity and voting rights and mandatory government approvals. Highly complex rules and laws limit FDI and, in some sectors, even prohibit it. Rules established in 2005 maintain restrictions on most existing joint ventures but allow new ones to negotiate their own terms on a commercial basis. Central bank approval is required for residents to open foreign currency accounts, either domestically or abroad, which are subject to significant restrictions. Non-residents may hold conditional foreign exchange and domestic currency accounts. Capital transactions and some credit operations are subject to certain restrictions and requirements.

FINANCIAL FREEDOM — 30%

India's financial system, the largest in South Asia, is characterized by heavy government involvement. India's 27 state-owned banks control about 70 percent of banking loans and deposits. In addition, the government owns nearly all of approximately 600 rural and cooperative banks; many national, state, and local development banks; financial institutions; and even venture capital funds. Banks are required to extend a specified percent of their loans to "priority" borrowers. Foreign investors face restrictions on ownership of Indian banks and insurance companies. While the insurance sector has been partially liberalized, the five state-owned insurers dominate the market. Capital markets are widespread, but foreign participation faces some restrictions.

PROPERTY RIGHTS — 50%

Protection of property rights is applied unevenly in India. Because of large backlogs, it takes several years for the courts to reach decisions. Foreign corporations often resort to international arbitration to bypass the court system. Protection of property for local investors, particularly the smallest ones, is weak.

FREEDOM FROM CORRUPTION — 29%

Corruption is perceived as widespread. India ranks 88th out of 158 countries in Transparency International's Corruption Perceptions Index for 2005.

LABOR FREEDOM — 55.1%

The labor market operates under restrictive employment regulations that hinder employment and productivity growth. The non-salary cost of employing a worker is moderate, but dismissing a redundant employee is costly. The rigid labor code impedes job creation and keeps the majority of the work force in the informal economy, which is estimated to employ about 90 percent of workers.

INDONESIA

Jakarta

Indonesia's economy is 55.1 percent free, according to our 2007 assessment, which makes it the world's 110th freest economy. Its overall score is 1 percentage point higher than last year, partially reflecting new methodological detail. Indonesia is ranked 21st out of 30 countries in the Asia–Pacific region, and its overall score is lower than the regional average.

Indonesia scores well in fiscal freedom, freedom from government, and labor freedom. The top income tax rate is high, but corporate tax rates are moderate. Government expenditures are fairly low, and state-owned businesses do not account for a significant portion of total revenues. The labor market operates under somewhat flexible conditions, but employing and firing workers can be costly.

Indonesia is weak in business freedom, investment freedom, financial freedom, property rights, and freedom from corruption. Starting a business takes twice as long as the world average, and regulations are onerous. Foreign investment is restricted, and judicial enforcement is both erratic and non-transparent in its treatment of foreigners. Because corruption is rampant, impartial adjudication of cases is not guaranteed.

BACKGROUND: Indonesia, the world's largest Muslim country and third largest democracy, straddles strategically important shipping lanes and has the largest economy in Southeast Asia. In his second term, President Susilo Bambang Yudhoyono has successfully negotiated a peace deal in Aceh and substantial reductions in fuel subsidies. Currently, the government is hard-pressed to deliver on its campaign promises to fight corruption and provide jobs. The economy is helped by development in industry and services, but the agriculture sector is the dominant employer.

The economy is 55.1% free

Asia Average = 59.1
World Average = 60.6

1995 — 2007

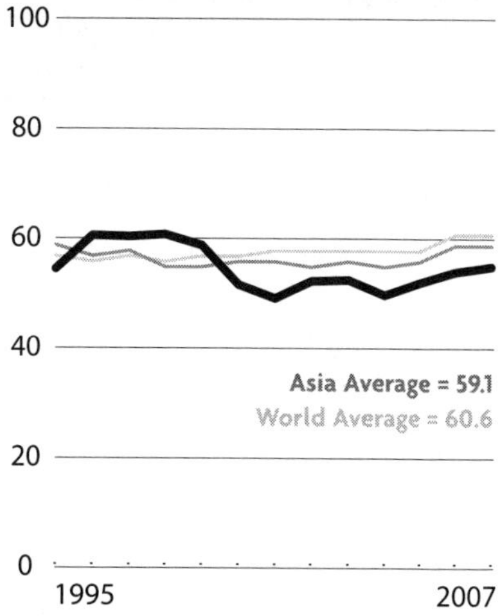

QUICK FACTS

Population: 217.6 million

GDP (PPP): $785.2 billion
5.1% growth in 2004
4.7% 5-yr. comp. ann. growth
$3,609 per capita

Unemployment: 10.9% (2004 estimate)

Inflation (CPI): 6.2%

FDI (net inflow): $915.8 million

Official Development Assistance:
Multilateral: $262 million
Bilateral: $1.3 billion (13% from the U.S.)

External Debt: $140.7 billion

Exports: $89.8 billion
Primarily oil and gas, electrical appliances, plywood, textiles, rubber

Imports: $79.1 billion
Primarily machinery and equipment, chemicals, fuels, food

How Do We Measure Economic Freedom? See Chapter 3 (page 37) for an explanation of the methodology or visit the *Index* Web site at *heritage.org/index.*

INDONESIA'S TEN ECONOMIC FREEDOMS

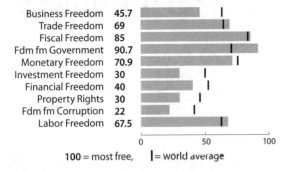

Business Freedom	45.7
Trade Freedom	69
Fiscal Freedom	85
Fdm fm Government	90.7
Monetary Freedom	70.9
Investment Freedom	30
Financial Freedom	40
Property Rights	30
Fdm fm Corruption	22
Labor Freedom	67.5

0   50   100

100 = most free, | = world average

BUSINESS FREEDOM — 45.7%

Starting a business takes an average of 97 days, compared to the world average of 48 days. Entrepreneurship should be easier for maximum job creation. Obtaining a business license is difficult, and closing a business is very difficult. Despite recent deregulation, bureaucracy and lack of transparency are persistent problems. The overall freedom to start, operate, and close a business is significantly restricted by the national regulatory environment.

TRADE FREEDOM — 69%

Indonesia's weighted average tariff rate was 5.5 percent in 2004. Non-tariff barriers include import and export restrictions, customs corruption, import bans, nontransparent regulations, quotas, and weak enforcement of intellectual property rights. Consequently, an additional 20 percent is deducted from Indonesia's trade freedom score.

FISCAL FREEDOM — 85%

Indonesia has a high income tax rate and a moderate corporate tax rate. The top income tax rate is 35 percent, and the top corporate tax rate is 30 percent. Implementation of a tax reform package that includes reduction of the corporate tax rate has been delayed. Other taxes include a value-added tax (VAT) and a tax on interest. In the most recent year, overall tax revenue as a percentage of GDP was 11.2 percent.

FREEDOM FROM GOVERNMENT — 90.7%

Total government expenditures in Indonesia, including consumption and transfer payments, are low. In the most recent year, government spending equaled 19.1 percent of GDP, and the government received 2.3 percent of its total revenues from state-owned enterprises and government ownership of property. State-owned enterprises still dominate many sectors, including oil and gas, retail distribution, and electric power generation and transmission.

MONETARY FREEDOM — 70.9%

Inflation is relatively high, averaging 9.1 percent between 2003 and 2005. Relatively high and unstable prices explain most of the monetary freedom score. Fuel, housing, and health care are subsidized, and prices for goods and services, including gasoline, electricity, liquefied petroleum gas, rice, cigarettes, cement, hospital services, potable piped water, city transport, air transport, telephone charges, trains, salt, toll-road tariffs, and postage, are administered. Consequent-

ly, an additional 10 percent is deducted from Indonesia's monetary freedom score to account for these policies.

INVESTMENT FREEDOM — 30%

Rampant corruption, lack of security, and taxation and labor issues are among the greatest obstacles to foreign investment. Foreign investors complain that corruption makes it very difficult to negotiate and enforce contracts and leads to unequal treatment of foreign investors. In 2000, the government closed 11 business sectors to foreign and domestic investment and closed eight others to foreign investment. Subject to restrictions, residents and non-residents may hold foreign exchange accounts. Most capital transactions are restricted. Non-residents may not purchase real estate but may purchase the right to use real estate. Several investments require domestic partners.

FINANCIAL FREEDOM — 40%

After the Asian financial crisis of 1997–1998, the number of banks fell from 238 in 1997 to 131 at the end of 2005. All banks taken over by the Indonesian Bank Restructuring Agency (IBRA) in the wake of the crisis have been privatized, but the state remains a considerable presence in the banking sector. At the end of 2005, the 41 foreign-owned or foreign-controlled banks accounted for over 45 percent of banking assets, and government-controlled banks accounted for 38 percent. Provincial governments also own and operate development banks. Supervision of financial institutions remains insufficient, and regulations are somewhat burdensome. State-owned banks are estimated to have a non-performing loan ratio of about 15 percent. Several insurers and foreign insurers rank among the top 10 companies. Capital markets are developing, and two small stock exchanges were operating in 2005. Foreign investors are permitted to invest in Indonesian banks, insurance companies, and capital markets.

PROPERTY RIGHTS — 30%

Court rulings can be arbitrary and inconsistent, and judicial corruption is substantial. Businesses find the judicial process unpredictable and the actions of local officials arbitrary. Judges have been known to rule against foreigners in commercial disputes, ignoring the facts of the case and the contracts between the parties. It is also difficult to get the courts to enforce international arbitration awards.

FREEDOM FROM CORRUPTION — 22%

Corruption is perceived as widespread. Indonesia ranks 137th out of 158 countries in Transparency International's Corruption Perceptions Index for 2005.

LABOR FREEDOM — 67.5%

The labor market operates under relatively flexible employment regulations that could be improved to enhance employment and productivity growth. The non-salary cost of employing a worker can be high, and dismissing a redundant employee is relatively costly. Although the government has vowed to improve labor market flexibility in recent years, significant changes have not been made.

IRAN

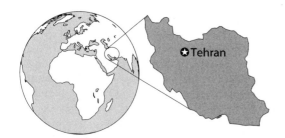

Tehran

Iran's economy is 43.1 percent free, according to our 2007 assessment, which makes it the world's 150th freest economy. Its overall score is 0.2 percentage point lower than last year, partially reflecting new methodological detail. Iran is ranked 16th out of 17 countries in the Middle East/North Africa region, and its overall score is extremely low—almost one-third below the regional average.

Iran's economy scores well in only one of the 10 factors measured: fiscal freedom. The top income tax rate is high, and the top corporate tax is moderate at 25 percent. Overall tax revenue as a percentage of GDP, however, is significant.

Iran's economy is unfree in many ways. Business freedom, trade freedom, investment freedom, financial freedom, property rights, and freedom from corruption are all weak. Business licensing and closing are regulated heavily by an intrusive and highly inefficient bureaucracy. High tariff rates and non-tariff barriers impede trade and foreign investment alike. Corruption is rampant, and the fair adjudication of property rights in a court of law cannot be guaranteed.

BACKGROUND: Iran's economy, once one of the most advanced in the Middle East, was crippled by the 1979 Islamic revolution, the Iran–Iraq war, and attendant economic mismanagement. The June 2005 presidential election elevated Mahmoud Ahmadinejad to power and halted tentative efforts to reform the state-dominated economy; instead, Ahmadinejad has promised the poor a greater share of Iran's oil wealth, greater subsidies, and greater state control. High world oil prices have raised export revenues and helped to service Iran's large foreign debt, but the economy remains burdened by high unemployment, inflation, corruption, expensive subsidies, and a bloated and inefficient public sector.

How Do We Measure Economic Freedom? See Chapter 3 (page 37) for an explanation of the methodology or visit the *Index* Web site at *heritage.org/index*.

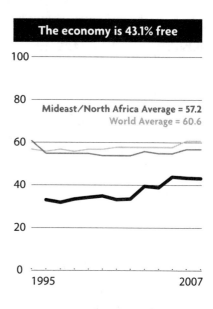

The economy is 43.1% free

Mideast/North Africa Average = 57.2
World Average = 60.6

QUICK FACTS

Population: 67 million

GDP (PPP): $504.2 billion
5.6% growth in 2004
5.7% 5-yr. comp. ann. growth
$7,525 per capita

Unemployment: 11.2%

Inflation (CPI): 14.8%

FDI (net inflow): $614.1 million

Official Development Assistance:
Multilateral: $35 million
Bilateral: $173 million (3% from the U.S.)

External Debt: $13.6 billion

Exports: $18.2 billion (2004 estimate)
Primarily petroleum, chemical and petrochemical products, fruits and nuts, carpets

Imports: $14.9 billion (2004 estimate)
Primarily industrial raw materials and intermediate goods, capital goods, food and other consumer goods, technical services, military supplies

IRAN'S TEN ECONOMIC FREEDOMS

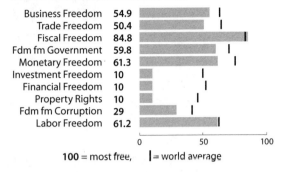

Business Freedom	54.9
Trade Freedom	50.4
Fiscal Freedom	84.8
Fdm fm Government	59.8
Monetary Freedom	61.3
Investment Freedom	10
Financial Freedom	10
Property Rights	10
Fdm fm Corruption	29
Labor Freedom	61.2

100 = most free, | = world average

BUSINESS FREEDOM — *54.9%*

Starting a business takes an average of 47 days, compared to the world average of 48 days. Entrepreneurship should be easier for maximum job creation. Obtaining a business license can be very difficult, and closing a business is difficult. Bureaucratic hurdles and slowness are persistent problems. The overall freedom to start, operate, and close a business is restricted by the national regulatory environment.

TRADE FREEDOM — *50.4%*

Iran's weighted average tariff rate was 14.8 percent in 2004. The government imposes restrictive sanitary and phytosanitary regulations, burdensome customs procedures, and import bans. Consequently, an additional 20 percent is deducted from Iran's trade freedom score to account for these non-tariff barriers.

FISCAL FREEDOM — *84.8%*

Iran has a high income tax rate and a moderate corporate tax rate. The top income tax rate is 35 percent, and the top corporate tax rate is 25 percent. Other taxes include a tax on check transactions and a tax of property transfers. In the most recent year, overall tax revenue as a percentage of GDP was 20.9 percent.

FREEDOM FROM GOVERNMENT — *59.8%*

Total government expenditures in Iran, including consumption and transfer payments, are moderate. In the most recent year, government spending equaled 31.4 percent of GDP, and the government received 51.5 percent of its total revenues from state-owned enterprises and government ownership of property. Privatization has proceeded slowly.

MONETARY FREEDOM — *61.3%*

Inflation in Iran is high, averaging 14 percent between 2003 and 2005. Relatively unstable prices explain most of the monetary freedom score. The government controls the prices of goods, including petroleum products, electricity, water, and wheat for the production of bread. It also provides economic subsidies and influences prices through the regulation of Iran's many state-owned enterprises. Consequently, an additional 15 percent is deducted from Iran's monetary freedom score to adjust for measures that distort domestic prices.

INVESTMENT FREEDOM — *10%*

Foreign investment is restricted in banking, telecommunications, transport, and border control. The government allows the sale of 65 percent of the shares of state-owned enterprises, except for defense and security-related industries and the National Iranian Oil Company. Iran's constitution forbids foreigners to own any concessions, operate projects, or participate in production-sharing agreements in the oil and gas sector. The parliament has the power to veto projects in which foreign investors have a majority stake and has blocked two proposed investments. Most payments, transfers, credit operations, and capital transactions are subject to limitations, quantitative limits, or approval requirements.

FINANCIAL FREEDOM — *10%*

Iran's financial sector is subject to very heavy government influence. All banks were nationalized following the 1979 revolution. Iran's laws require that the banking sector be run according to Islamic law, which prohibits interest payments. There are six state-owned commercial banks, four state-owned specialized banks, and a state-owned postal bank. State banks account for 98 percent of banking assets. Six small private banks have been established recently. Foreign banks are legally permitted to operate in free trade zones. The government directs credit allocation. All insurance companies were nationalized during the revolution, and the sector remains dominated by five state-owned companies. There were also five small private domestic companies and one foreign insurance company in 2005. Iran has a small stock exchange. Supervision of the financial sector is weak, and regulations on private banks are very restrictive.

PROPERTY RIGHTS — *10%*

Resort to Iranian courts is often counterproductive and rarely leads to a fast resolution of disputes. Most foreign firms have bad experiences when disputing a contract. Written agreements offer very little protection for the contracting party. Finding an influential local business partner who also enjoys substantial political patronage is the more effective way to protect contracts.

FREEDOM FROM CORRUPTION — *29%*

Corruption is perceived as widespread. Iran ranks 88th out of 158 countries in Transparency International's Corruption Perceptions Index for 2005.

LABOR FREEDOM — *61.2%*

The labor market operates under restrictive employment regulations that hinder employment and productivity growth. The non-salary cost of employing a worker is high, and dismissing a redundant employee is costly. Regulations on increasing or contracting the number of work hours are very inflexible. Firing a worker requires approval of the Islamic Labor Council or the Labor Discretionary Board.

IRAQ

Baghdad

Rank: Not ranked

Regional Rank: Not ranked

The economic freedom of Iraq cannot be scored in our 2007 assessment because sufficient reliable data for the country are not available. In the years since the invasion by U.S. military forces in 2003, the Iraq economy has slowly recovered. However, the country is still unstable and faces continuing violence among different ethnic and religious factions. Iraq was last graded in 2002, when it received a score of 0 percent.

The Iraqi economy should benefit from many excellent reforms and institutions that have been put in place since 2003, including tax policies, simple and low tariffs, new investment laws, and a significantly liberalized and modernized banking system; but these reforms and institutions cannot be fully effective as long as they have to depend on a foundation of weak physical security and persistent corruption.

BACKGROUND: Iraq gained its independence from Britain in 1932 and was a constitutional monarchy until a 1958 military coup led to a series of dictatorships. Saddam Hussein's regime was ousted in 2003, and an elected government led by Prime Minister Nuri al-Maliki took office in May 2006. Iraq's oil industry provides more than 90 percent of hard-currency earnings but has been hurt by pipeline sabotage, electricity outages, and years of neglect and postponed maintenance. Economic recovery, though helped by high oil prices and economic aid from the United States and other foreign donors, is hampered by continued insurgency and instability.

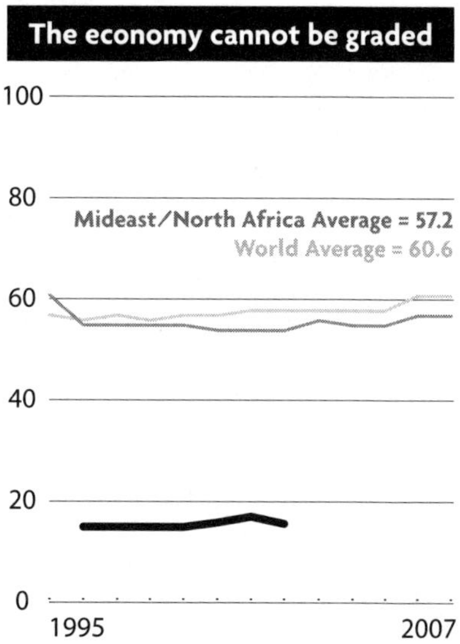

The economy cannot be graded

Mideast/North Africa Average = 57.2
World Average = 60.6

100

80

60

40

20

0

1995   2007

QUICK FACTS

Population: 26.8 million (2006 estimate)

GDP (PPP): $94.1 billion (2005 estimate)
n/a
n/a
$3,400 per capita (2005 estimate)

Unemployment: 25%–30% (2005 estimate)

Inflation (CPI): 31.7%

FDI (net inflow): $300 million (gross)

Official Development Assistance:
Multilateral: $151 million
Bilateral: $4.5 billion (67% from the U.S.)

External Debt: $102.2 billion

Exports: $16.9 billion
Primarily crude oil, crude materials excluding fuels, food, live animals

Imports: $21.3 billion
Primarily food, medicine, manufactures

How Do We Measure Economic Freedom? See Chapter 3 (page 37) for an explanation of the methodology or visit the *Index* Web site at *heritage.org/index*.

BUSINESS FREEDOM — NOT GRADED

Iraq's old commercial code has been significantly amended in recent years. The changes have aimed at liberalizing the investment and business environment in order to enhance job creation and economic growth. Despite some progress in establishing an investment-friendly business environment, significant problems remain to be addressed as Iraq tries to deal with challenges to its security and stability.

TRADE FREEDOM — NOT GRADED

Iraq is in the process of rebuilding its economy. According to the U.S. Department of Commerce, Iraq applied a flat tariff rate of 5 percent in 2004. Non-tariff barriers include significant delays in trade through customs as well as some import and export bans.

FISCAL FREEDOM — NOT GRADED

The suspension of personal and corporate income taxes ended after May 2004. Both individual and corporate income tax rates are capped at 15 percent. Workers must pay 5 percent of their salary as a mandatory contribution to the social security system; the employer's contribution is 12 percent of the same salary base. There is a flat sales tax of 10 percent. Data on overall tax revenue are not available.

FREEDOM FROM GOVERNMENT — NOT GRADED

Total government expenditures in Iraq, including consumption and transfer payments, are very high. It is estimated that government spending equals about 90 percent of GDP. The oil sector accounts for over 95 percent of exports and government revenue.

MONETARY FREEDOM — NOT GRADED

Inflation in Iraq is high, averaging 33 percent between 2003 and 2005. Such unstable prices are harmful to savings and therefore to investment. The government maintains a large public sector and provides a number of subsidies and price controls to consumers and businesses. As it implements steps to create a social security safety net, the government may be able to move closer to its target of reducing overall subsidies by 25 percent and, specifically, price subsidies by some 13 percent as it makes progress in restoring overall stability.

INVESTMENT FREEDOM — NOT GRADED

The Foreign Investment Law of 2003 allows foreign companies to own up to 100 percent of Iraqi companies, but it specifically excludes the energy sector. Under this legislation, foreign companies are treated the same as Iraqi companies, and foreign investors may acquire 40-year leases on—but not ownership of—real estate. Iraq continues to face substantial difficulties in attracting investment, largely as a result of the security situation.

FINANCIAL FREEDOM — NOT GRADED

The Coalition Provisional Authority and the new Iraqi government have introduced many changes to Iraq's financial system. A new banking law significantly liberalized and modernized the banking system. Although there were 17 private banks in 2004, the two largest state-owned banks—Rafidain and Rasheed—accounted for 85 percent of banking sector assets. In addition, there were four specialized state-owned banks serving the agricultural, industrial, real estate, and social sectors. It is planned that these banks will be merged with the two state-owned commercial banks and sold. Three foreign banks have been granted licenses. The central bank is now independent, and interest rates on loans, deposits, and securities were fully liberalized in March 2004. The insurance sector is very small and included three state-owned companies in 2004. The new stock exchange is small. Iraqi banks have been the most actively traded shares.

PROPERTY RIGHTS — NOT GRADED

There is no protection of property in Iraq. The aftermath of the war resulted in high insecurity, rioting, and looting, discouraging any kind of investment. The absence of an enforceable legal system means that foreigners are further disadvantaged in terms of dispute resolution, although this affects local investors to a large degree as well. U.S. forces are trying to help Iraqis feel safer, but that remains a daunting task.

FREEDOM FROM CORRUPTION — NOT GRADED

Corruption is perceived as widespread. Iraq ranks 137th out of 158 countries in Transparency International's Corruption Perceptions Index for 2005.

LABOR FREEDOM — NOT GRADED

Iraq's formal labor market is not yet fully developed. Most jobs in the private sector are informal. It is estimated that unemployment and underemployment combined are around 50 percent.

IRELAND

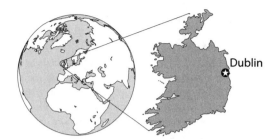

Dublin

Rank: 7

Regional Rank: 2 of 41

Ireland's economy is 81.3 percent free, according to our 2007 assessment, which makes it the world's 7th freest economy. Its overall score is 0.1 percentage point higher than last year, partially reflecting new methodological detail. Ireland is ranked 2nd out of 41 countries in the European region, and its overall score is much higher than the regional average.

Ireland has high levels of business freedom, investment freedom, financial freedom, monetary freedom, property rights, and freedom from corruption. Entrepreneurship is made easy by the light regulatory hand of government. Inflation is low, but Ireland's monetary score suffers somewhat from distortionary EU agricultural subsidies. Foreign investment is welcome and restricted only in a few sectors. Financial markets are transparent and open to foreign competition. Property rights are well protected by an efficient, independent judiciary.

Ireland's weakest area is labor freedom. As in many other European nations, generous labor laws mean that employment is not as flexible as it should be for maximum job creation and sectoral dynamics. Government spending as a proportion of GDP is also a disincentive. Even though tariffs are low, non-trade barriers reduce Ireland's trade freedom score.

BACKGROUND: Ireland's modern, highly industrialized economy performed well throughout the 1990s. The country has one of the world's most business-friendly environments, especially for investment. In January 2003, the government lowered the corporate tax rate to 12.5 percent—far below the EU average. Ireland receives nearly one-third of total U.S. investment going to the EU. Due largely to its close trading ties with the United States, Ireland is the world's largest exporter per capita. However, it also is saddled with an underperforming health service whose costs have tripled in seven years with only limited gains in output.

How Do We Measure Economic Freedom? See Chapter 3 (page 37) for an explanation of the methodology or visit the *Index* Web site at *heritage.org/index*.

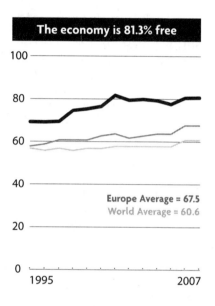

The economy is 81.3% free

100

80

60

40

Europe Average = 67.5
World Average = 60.6

20

0

1995   2007

QUICK FACTS

Population: 4.1 million

GDP (PPP): $158.0 billion
4.5% growth in 2004
6.1% 5-yr. comp. ann. growth
$38,827 per capita

Unemployment: 4.5%

Inflation (CPI): 2.2%

FDI (net inflow): $16.5 billion

Official Development Assistance:
Multilateral: None
Bilateral: None

External Debt: $1.1 trillion (2005 estimate)

Exports: $152.2 billion
Primarily machinery and equipment, computers, chemicals, pharmaceuticals, live animals, animal products

Imports: $124.7 billion
Primarily data processing equipment, other machinery and equipment, chemicals, petroleum and petroleum products, textiles, clothing

219

IRELAND'S TEN ECONOMIC FREEDOMS

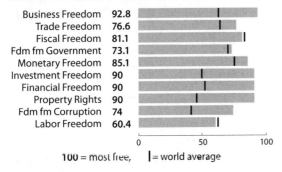

Business Freedom	92.8
Trade Freedom	76.6
Fiscal Freedom	81.1
Fdm fm Government	73.1
Monetary Freedom	85.1
Investment Freedom	90
Financial Freedom	90
Property Rights	90
Fdm fm Corruption	74
Labor Freedom	60.4

100 = most free, I = world average

BUSINESS FREEDOM — 92.8%

Starting a business takes an average of 19 days, compared to the world average of 48 days. The business environment has allowed entrepreneurship to flourish in Ireland. Obtaining a business license is simple, and closing a business is very easy. Bureaucratic procedures generally are transparent and efficient. The overall freedom to start, operate, and close a business is strongly protected by the national regulatory environment.

TRADE FREEDOM — 76.6%

Ireland's trade policy is the same as those of other members of the European Union. The common EU weighted average tariff rate was 1.7 percent in 2005. Various non-tariff barriers are reflected in EU and Irish government policy, including agricultural and manufacturing subsidies, regulatory and licensing restrictions, and other market access restrictions. The government also implements restrictive procurement rules. Consequently, an additional 20 percent is deducted from Ireland's trade freedom score to account for non-tariff barriers.

FISCAL FREEDOM — 81.1%

Ireland has a high income tax rate but a low corporate tax rate. The top income tax rate is 42 percent, and the top corporate tax rate is 12.5 percent. Other taxes include a value-added tax (VAT) and a tax on interest. In the most recent year, overall tax revenue as a percentage of GDP was 30.2 percent.

FREEDOM FROM GOVERNMENT — 73.1%

Total government expenditures in Ireland, including consumption and transfer payments, are high. In the most recent year, government spending equaled 33.7 percent of GDP, and the government received 1.2 percent of its total revenues from state-owned enterprises and government ownership of property.

MONETARY FREEDOM — 85.1%

Ireland is a member of the euro zone. Inflation in Ireland is relatively low, averaging 2.5 percent between 2003 and 2005. Relatively low and stable prices explain most of the monetary freedom score. As a participant in the EU's Common Agricultural Policy, the government subsidizes agricultural production, distorting the prices of agricultural products. The government also influences prices through state-owned enterprises. Consequently, an additional 5 percent is deducted from Ireland's monetary freedom score to account for these policies.

INVESTMENT FREEDOM — 90%

Ireland welcomes foreign investment. All domestic and foreign firms that are incorporated in Ireland receive equal treatment. The only restrictions apply to ownership of airlines by non-EU residents and the purchase of agricultural lands. Foreign investors may participate in the sale of Irish state-owned companies. There is no approval process for foreign investment or capital inflows unless the company is applying for incentives. There are no restrictions or barriers with respect to current transfers, repatriation of profits, or access to foreign exchange.

FINANCIAL FREEDOM — 90%

Ireland's banking and financial system is advanced and competitive. Some 115 banks and other credit institutions, a majority of which were foreign, were authorized to conduct business in 2004. There is substantial offshore banking. Domestic banking is dominated by two Irish banks that together account for about 75 percent of deposits. The government sold its shares in the last state-owned financial institution, the ACC Bank, in 2002. Ireland is increasingly an international hub for insurance, fund management, and venture capital. About 190 insurance companies and subsidiaries, including over half of the world's top 20 insurance companies, were operating in 2004. The stock exchange is independent but small, trading mostly in Irish equities and government bonds.

PROPERTY RIGHTS — 90%

Expropriation is highly unlikely. Property is well protected by the court system, and contracts are secured. Both the judiciary and the civil service are of high quality.

FREEDOM FROM CORRUPTION — 74%

Corruption is perceived as minimal. Ireland ranks 19th out of 158 countries in Transparency International's Corruption Perceptions Index for 2005.

LABOR FREEDOM — 60.4%

The labor market operates under somewhat restrictive employment regulations that could be improved to enhance employment and productivity growth. The non-salary cost of employing a worker is moderate, but dismissing a redundant employee can be costly. The unemployment insurance system offers benefits for up to 15 months to the involuntarily unemployed, and an average worker receives about 15 percent of his or her salary in benefits.

ISRAEL

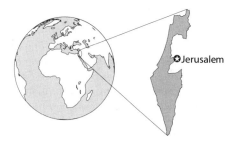

●Jerusalem

Israel's economy is 68.4 percent free, according to our 2007 assessment, which makes it the world's 37th freest economy. Its overall score is 1.7 percentage points higher than last year, partially reflecting new methodological detail. Israel is ranked 1st out of 17 countries in the Middle East/North Africa region, and its overall score is much higher than the regional average.

Israel enjoys high levels of trade freedom, monetary freedom, investment freedom, and labor freedom. The economy is open to foreign investment in almost all sectors except defense. Tariff rates are low. Inflation is very low, although the government interferes with the market by subsidizing certain basic goods. The labor market is highly flexible.

Israel is weak in business freedom and freedom from government. Complicated and inefficient bureaucracy makes closing a business difficult. Government spending is high, constituting over 40 percent of GDP, although revenue generated by state-owned businesses is not large. Though advanced for the region, Israel's financial sector is still subject to government intervention and control.

BACKGROUND: Israel gained its independence from Britain in 1948 and fought a series of wars against its Arab neighbors that imposed a high defense burden on the state-dominated economy. Despite few natural resources, Israel has developed a modern market economy with a thriving technology sector. The collapse of the 1993 Oslo peace agreement with the Palestinians and the onset of the Intifada in September 2000 depressed tourism, discouraged foreign investment, and contributed to economic recession. A recovery in 2003–2004 was due to increased tourism, foreign investment, and greater demand for Israeli exports, especially high-tech goods and services. The conflict in Lebanon in 2006 casts a cloud of uncertainty over the current economy.

How Do We Measure Economic Freedom? See Chapter 3 (page 37) for an explanation of the methodology or visit the *Index* Web site at *heritage.org/index*.

The economy is 68.4% free

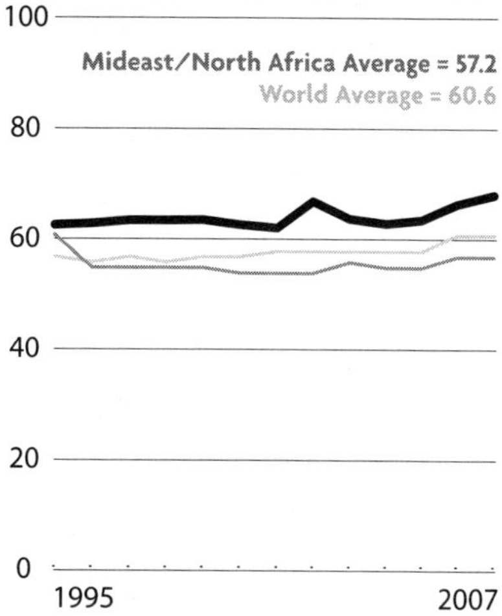

Mideast/North Africa Average = 57.2
World Average = 60.6

[Line chart showing economic freedom from 1995 to 2007, with y-axis from 0 to 100]

QUICK FACTS

Population: 6.8 million

GDP (PPP): $165.7 billion
4.4% growth in 2004
2.4% 5-yr. comp. ann. growth
$24,382 per capita

Unemployment: 10.4%

Inflation (CPI): −0.4%

FDI (net inflow): −$1.4 billion

Official Development Assistance:
Multilateral: $2 million
Bilateral: $588 million (93% from the U.S.)

External Debt: $75.6 billion (2005 estimate)

Exports: $51.4 billion
Primarily machinery and equipment, software, cut diamonds, agricultural products, chemicals, textiles, apparel

Imports: $52.0 billion
Primarily raw materials, military equipment, investment goods, rough diamonds, fuels, grain, consumer goods

ISRAEL'S TEN ECONOMIC FREEDOMS

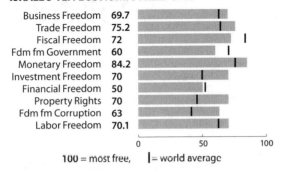

Business Freedom	69.7	
Trade Freedom	75.2	
Fiscal Freedom	72	
Fdm fm Government	60	
Monetary Freedom	84.2	
Investment Freedom	70	
Financial Freedom	50	
Property Rights	70	
Fdm fm Corruption	63	
Labor Freedom	70.1	

0   50   100

100 = most free, | = world average

BUSINESS FREEDOM — 69.7%

Starting a business takes an average of 34 days, compared to the world average of 48 days. Entrepreneurship should be easier for maximum job creation. Obtaining a business license is relatively simple, but closing a business can be difficult. Although Israel has been moving toward deregulation, bureaucratic hurdles persist. The overall freedom to start, operate, and close a business is relatively well protected by the national regulatory environment.

TRADE FREEDOM — 75.2%

Israel's weighted average tariff rate was 2.4 percent in 2005. The government has made progress in liberalizing its trade regime but still maintains import restrictions, import bans, a non-transparent tariff rate quota system, burdensome regulations and standards, import fees, government procurement rules, and export subsidies. Consequently, an additional 20 percent is deducted from Israel's trade freedom score to account for these non-tariff barriers.

FISCAL FREEDOM — 72%

Israel has a very high income tax rate but a moderate corporate tax rate. The top income tax rate is 49 percent, and the top corporate tax rate is 31 percent (scheduled to be reduced to 25 percent by 2010). Other taxes include a value-added tax (VAT) and a capital gains tax. In the most recent year, overall tax revenue as a percentage of GDP was 28.9 percent.

FREEDOM FROM GOVERNMENT — 60%

Total government expenditures in Israel, including consumption and transfer payments, are high. In the most recent year, government spending equaled 40.8 percent of GDP, and the government received 3.5 percent of its total revenues from state-owned enterprises and government ownership of property. Privatization has accelerated in recent years.

MONETARY FREEDOM — 84.2%

Inflation is low, averaging less than 1 percent between 2003 and 2005. Stable prices explain most of the monetary freedom score. The government influences prices through the public sector and provides some subsidies, especially for agriculture production. The energy sector remains largely state-owned and heavily regulated, and the government has authority to impose price controls on vital goods and services. Consequently, an additional 10 percent is deducted from Israel's monetary freedom score to account for these policies.

INVESTMENT FREEDOM — 70%

Foreign investment is restricted is some sectors, including the defense industry. Foreign investment is not screened, and the same regulations regarding acquisitions, mergers, and takeovers apply to both foreign and domestic investors. Investments in regulated industries, such as banking, require prior government approval. Both residents and non-residents may hold foreign exchange accounts, and there are no controls or restrictions on current transfers, repatriation of profits, or other transactions. The bureaucracy can be difficult to navigate. The government has equalized the tax applied to foreign and domestically traded securities.

FINANCIAL FREEDOM — 50%

Israel's financial sector is modern and sophisticated. Credit is available on market terms, and financial institutions offer a wide array of credit instruments. Supervision is prudent, and regulations conform to international norms. Five main groups (Bank Hapoalim, Bank Leumi, Israel Discount Bank, United Mizrahi Bank, and First International Bank) dominate the banking sector with over 90 percent of banking assets. As of late 2005, the government owned over 14 percent of Bank Leumi and over 30 percent of Israel Discount Bank. There are restrictions on bank ownership of insurance companies and vice versa, and the 2005 Bachar Reform bars commercial banks from owning holdings in mutual funds. The Postal Bank provides bill payment and a few other services but no credit. Foreign investments in the banking and insurance sector require prior government approval, and there are two foreign bank branches.

PROPERTY RIGHTS — 70%

Contractual arrangements in Israel are generally secure. The legal system is perceived as independent, fair, and honest. Commercial law is clearly written and consistently applied. Expropriation is possible, particularly for Palestinians, but reportedly occurs only if the property is linked to a terrorist threat and expropriation is deemed to be in the interest of national security.

FREEDOM FROM CORRUPTION — 63%

Corruption is perceived as present. Israel ranks 28th out of 158 countries in Transparency International's Corruption Perceptions Index for 2005.

LABOR FREEDOM — 70.1%

The labor market operates under relatively flexible employment regulations that could be improved to enhance employment and productivity growth. The non-salary cost of employing a worker is low, but dismissing a redundant employee is relatively costly. There are rigid regulations on increasing or contracting the number of work hours.

ITALY

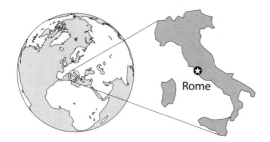

Rome

Italy's economy is 63.4 percent free, according to our 2007 assessment, which makes it the world's 60th freest economy. Its overall score is 0.7 percentage point higher than last year, partially reflecting new methodological detail. Italy is ranked 28th out of 41 countries in the European region, and its overall score is equal to the regional average.

Italy scores highly in business freedom, trade freedom, investment freedom, and monetary freedom. Starting a business takes about 13 days, which is far below the world average. The tariff rate is low, although the country's inefficient bureaucracy implements some non-trade barriers that also deter foreign investment. As an EU member, Italy has a standardized monetary policy that yields relatively low inflation, despite government distortion in the agricultural sector.

Freedom from government, property rights, and freedom from corruption are relatively weak. As in many other European social democracies, government spending and tax rates are exceptionally high in order to support an extensive welfare state. Corruption is not severe relative to some other nations, but it is high for an advanced economy. Enforcement of government regulations and judicial decisions are further impeded by an inefficient civil service.

BACKGROUND: Since World War II, Italy has been a central force in European integration and the military structure of NATO. Italy faces some serious economic challenges, however. The state's large pension liabilities, labor market rigidities, and bureaucratic burdens remain unaddressed, and it remains to be seen whether the limited reforms made by former Prime Minister Silvio Berlusconi will be repealed or augmented by his successor, Romano Prodi. Despite strong international competition, small and medium-sized enterprises continue to thrive in manufacturing and high design, particularly in the northern regions. Tourism and services are among the most important sectors.

How Do We Measure Economic Freedom? See Chapter 3 (page 37) for an explanation of the methodology or visit the *Index* Web site at *heritage.org/index*.

The economy is 63.4% free

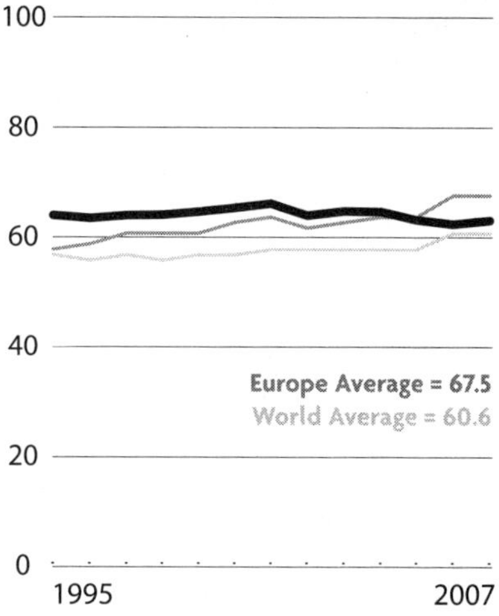

100

80

60

40

Europe Average = 67.5
World Average = 60.6

20

0

1995   2007

QUICK FACTS

Population: 57.6 million

GDP (PPP): $1.6 trillion
0.9% growth in 2004
1.2% 5-yr. comp. ann. growth
$28,180 per capita

Unemployment: 8.0%

Inflation (CPI): 2.2%

FDI (net inflow): –$2.5 billion

Official Development Assistance:
Multilateral: None
Bilateral: None

External Debt: $922.5 billion (2005 estimate)

Exports: $435.9 billion
Primarily engineering products, textiles and clothing, machinery, vehicles, transport equipment, chemicals, food

Imports: $423.2 billion
Primarily engineering products, chemicals, transport equipment, energy products, minerals, nonferrous metals, textiles, clothing, food, beverages, tobacco

ITALY'S TEN ECONOMIC FREEDOMS

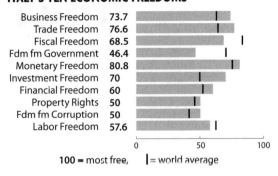

Business Freedom	73.7
Trade Freedom	76.6
Fiscal Freedom	68.5
Fdm fm Government	46.4
Monetary Freedom	80.8
Investment Freedom	70
Financial Freedom	60
Property Rights	50
Fdm fm Corruption	50
Labor Freedom	57.6

100 = most free, | = world average

BUSINESS FREEDOM — 73.7%

Starting a business takes an average of 13 days, compared to the world average of 48 days. Entrepreneurship should be easier for maximum job creation and economic growth. Obtaining a business license and closing a business are relatively simple. The overall freedom to start, operate, and close a business is relatively well protected by the national regulatory environment.

TRADE FREEDOM — 76.6%

Italy's trade policy is the same as those of other members of the European Union. The common EU weighted average tariff rate was 1.7 percent in 2005. Various non-tariff barriers are reflected in EU and Italian government policy, including agricultural and manufacturing subsidies, regulatory and licensing restrictions, and other market access restrictions. The government implements restrictive pharmaceutical and biotechnology regulations, and enforcement of intellectual property is weak. Consequently, an additional 20 percent is deducted from Italy's trade freedom score to account for non-tariff barriers.

FISCAL FREEDOM — 68.5%

Italy has high tax rates. The top income tax rate is 43 percent, and the top corporate tax rate is 33 percent. Other taxes include a value-added tax (VAT), a tax on interest, and an advertising tax. In the most recent year, overall tax revenue as a percentage of GDP was 42.2 percent.

FREEDOM FROM GOVERNMENT — 46.4%

Total government expenditures in Italy, including consumption and transfer payments, are very high. In the most recent year, government spending equaled 47.8 percent of GDP, and the government received 0.9 percent of its total revenues from state-owned enterprises and government ownership of property.

MONETARY FREEDOM — 80.8%

Italy is a member of the euro zone. Inflation in Italy is relatively low, averaging 2.1 percent between 2003 and 2005. Relatively stable prices explain most of the monetary freedom score. As a participant in the EU's Common Agricultural Policy, the government subsidizes agricultural production, distorting agricultural prices. The government also retains the power to introduce price controls. Items subject to rate setting at the national level include drinking water, electricity, gas, highway tolls, prescription drugs, telecommunications, and domestic travel. Consequently, an additional 10 percent is deducted from Italy's monetary freedom score to account for these policies.

INVESTMENT FREEDOM — 70%

Italy welcomes foreign investment, although the government can veto acquisitions involving foreign investors. The government does not block foreign investment, and the tax code does not discriminate against foreign investments. Foreign investment is closely regulated in the defense, aircraft manufacturing, domestic airline, and shipping sectors. Investors cite excessive bureaucracy, inadequate infrastructure, and a rigid labor market as major disincentives. Foreigners may not buy land along the Italian border. There are no barriers to repatriation of profits, transfers, payments, or current transfers.

FINANCIAL FREEDOM — 60%

In Italy's modern financial sector, credit is allocated on market terms, and foreign participation is welcome. Italy's banking sector was dominated by the state until a recent series of privatizations and consolidations. Government ownership of banks has fallen sharply, and only two major financial institutions (Cassa Depositi e Prestiti and Bancoposta) remain state-controlled. The six largest banks account for over 54.6 percent of total assets. Regulations and prohibitions can be burdensome, and approval is required to gain control of a financial institution. Italy has the EU's fourth-largest insurance market. The government has adopted reforms, including privatization of the stock exchange, that are intended to revitalize Italy's underdeveloped capital markets.

PROPERTY RIGHTS — 50%

Property rights and contracts are secure, but the delivery of justice is extremely slow, and many companies choose to settle out of court. Corruption is more common than in other European countries, and many judges are politically oriented.

FREEDOM FROM CORRUPTION — 50%

Corruption is perceived as present. Italy ranks 40th out of 158 countries in Transparency International's Corruption Perceptions Index for 2005.

LABOR FREEDOM — 57.6%

The labor market operates under restrictive employment regulations that hinder employment and productivity growth. The non-salary cost of employing a worker is very high, and dismissing a redundant employee can be costly. Rules on expanding or contracting the number of work hours are rigid. Unemployed individuals receive benefits for up to 180 days (270 days if over 50 years of age), and an average worker receives about 40 percent of his or her salary in benefits.

IVORY COAST

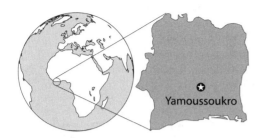

Yamoussoukro

Rank: 105

Regional Rank: 16 of 40

Ivory Coast's economy is 55.5 percent free, according to our 2007 assessment, which makes it the world's 105th freest economy. Its overall score is 1.3 percentage points lower than last year, partially reflecting new methodological detail. Ivory Coast's current score is based on the government's data and policies that, because of ongoing civil unrest, may not be applicable to areas that the government does not control. If the current situation fails to improve, grading of economic freedom will be suspended next year.

Ivory Coast has relatively high levels of freedom from government and monetary freedom. It would also score well in financial freedom if it were not for civil unrest. Government expenditures are low, and the level of income from state-owned businesses is relatively low. Inflation is also low, but the government subsidizes basic goods like petroleum.

As a nation in the middle of civil unrest, Ivory Coast faces significant challenges. Business freedom, trade freedom, investment freedom (if it were graded), property rights, and corruption all score poorly. Commercial regulation and bureaucratic red tape are burdensome. The average tariff rate is high, and imports are subject to substantial non-tariff barriers. The political atmosphere makes it difficult to invest in Ivory Coast even though the state nominally welcomes capital. Property rights are not secured by an independent judiciary, and corruption is debilitating.

BACKGROUND: General Robert Guei seized power in a 1999 coup and later was forced to flee after refusing to accede to President Laurent Gbagbo's victory in the 2000 election. Civil war erupted in 2002 after a failed coup. A tenuous peace was facilitated, and as of this writing, legislative elections originally set for October 2005 have been rescheduled for October 2006. Instability undermines economic growth and discourages investment, and the government and judiciary are subject to corruption and lack of accountability. The economy relies on cash crops, and the agricultural sector employs more than 60 percent of the population.

How Do We Measure Economic Freedom? See Chapter 3 (page 37) for an explanation of the methodology or visit the *Index* Web site at *heritage.org/index*.

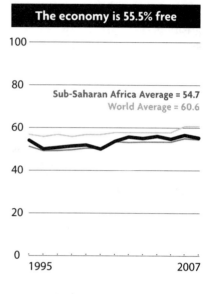

The economy is 55.5% free

Sub-Saharan Africa Average = 54.7
World Average = 60.6

100

80

60

40

20

0

1995   2007

QUICK FACTS

Population: 17.9 million

GDP (PPP): $27.7 billion
1.8% growth in 2004
−0.9% 5-yr. comp. ann. growth
$1,551 per capita

Unemployment: 13% (1998 estimate)

Inflation (CPI): 1.4%

FDI (net inflow): $360 million (gross)

Official Development Assistance:
Multilateral: $93 million
Bilateral: $252 million (13% from the U.S.)

External Debt: $11.7 billion

Exports: $7.7 billion
Primarily cocoa, coffee, timber, petroleum, cotton, bananas, pineapples, palm oil, fish

Imports: $6.2 billion
Primarily fuel, capital equipment, food

IVORY COAST'S TEN ECONOMIC FREEDOMS

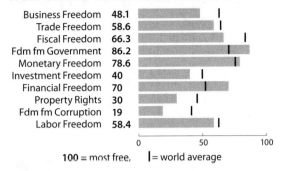

Business Freedom	48.1
Trade Freedom	58.6
Fiscal Freedom	66.3
Fdm fm Government	86.2
Monetary Freedom	78.6
Investment Freedom	40
Financial Freedom	70
Property Rights	30
Fdm fm Corruption	19
Labor Freedom	58.4

100 = most free, **I** = world average

BUSINESS FREEDOM — 48.1%

Starting a business takes an average of 45 days, compared to the world average of 48 days. Entrepreneurship should be easier for maximum job creation. Obtaining a business license is difficult, but closing a business can be relatively easy. Although the government has made some efforts to increase regulatory transparency, red tape and bureaucracy still impede entrepreneurial activities. The overall freedom to start, operate, and close a business is seriously restricted by the national regulatory environment.

TRADE FREEDOM — 58.6%

Ivory Coast's weighted average tariff rate was 10.7 percent in 2004. Non-tariff barriers include import fees and taxes, import price floors, import prohibitions and restrictions, corruption in customs and government procurement, weak protection of intellectual property rights, and import authorization requirements for various goods including petroleum products, animal products, live plants, seeds, plastic bags, distilling equipment, and saccharin. Consequently, an additional 20 percent is deducted from Ivory Coast's trade freedom score.

FISCAL FREEDOM — 66.3%

Ivory Coast has high tax rates. The top income tax rate is 60 percent, and the top corporate tax rate is 35 percent. Other taxes include a value-added tax (VAT) and a tax on interest. In the most recent year, overall tax revenue as a percentage of GDP was 15.2 percent.

FREEDOM FROM GOVERNMENT — 86.2%

Total government expenditures in Ivory Coast, including consumption and transfer payments, are low. In the most recent year, government spending equaled 20.2 percent of GDP, and the government received 12.7 percent of its total revenues from state-owned enterprises and government ownership of property. Privatization remains stalled.

MONETARY FREEDOM — 78.6%

Inflation in Ivory Coast is moderate, averaging 3.2 percent between 2003 and 2005. Relatively moderate and unstable prices explain most of the monetary freedom score. The government regulates the prices of pharmaceuticals, petroleum products, and public-sector goods and services. Cocoa prices and quotas are maintained as part of a government cocoa price stabilization program. Consequently, an additional 10 percent is deducted from Ivory Coast's monetary freedom score to account for these policies.

INVESTMENT FREEDOM — 40%

The government welcomes foreign investment, but the ongoing political crisis and corruption pose significant disincentives. Residents may hold foreign exchange accounts with the approval of the government and the Central Bank of West African States (BCEAO), and non-residents may hold them with BCEAO approval. Transfers to countries other than France, Monaco, members of the West African Economic and Monetary Union (WAEMU), members of the Central African Economic and Monetary Community (CEMAC), and Comoros must be approved by the government. Other transfers are subject to numerous requirements, controls, and authorization, depending on the transaction. Capital transactions are subject to government authorization in many cases.

FINANCIAL FREEDOM — 70%

Ivory Coast's financial sector is affected by the ongoing political crisis. The BCEAO governs banking and other financial institutions. The eight BCEAO member countries use the CFA franc, pegged to the euro. The banking sector accounts for 80 percent of financial sector assets. There were 17 commercial banks in 2005. Although the financial system remains functional, commercial banks in rebel-controlled areas have been closed since the start of the civil war. The government retains small stakes in several banks and owns two specialized financial institutions. The two largest banks are majority-owned by French banks. The insurance sector consists of about 30 companies and is part of a larger regional insurance system involving 14 African countries. Ivory Coast is home to the WAEMU's capital markets. Trading on the stock market is minimal despite over 40 listings.

PROPERTY RIGHTS — 30%

The judiciary, although constitutionally independent, is slow, inefficient, and subject to executive branch, military, and other outside influence. Judges serve at the discretion of the executive, and there are credible reports that they submit to political pressure and financial influence.

FREEDOM FROM CORRUPTION — 19%

Corruption is perceived as widespread. Ivory Coast ranks 152nd out of 158 countries in Transparency International's Corruption Perceptions Index for 2005.

LABOR FREEDOM — 58.4%

The labor market operates under restrictive employment regulations that hinder employment and productivity growth. The non-salary cost of employing a worker is high, and dismissing a redundant employee is costly. Regulations on increasing or contracting the number of work hours are rigid.

JAMAICA

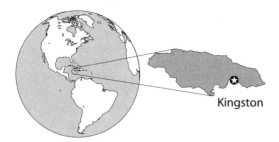

Kingston

Jamaica's economy is 66.1 percent free, according to our 2007 assessment, which makes it the world's 46th freest economy. Its overall score is 1.6 percentage points lower than last year, partially reflecting new methodological detail. Jamaica is ranked 9th out of 29 countries in the Americas, and its overall score is higher than the regional average.

Jamaica enjoys high fiscal freedom, investment freedom, labor freedom, and business freedom. Starting and closing a business are simple, although an inefficient bureaucracy hinders business activity. The labor market is highly flexible and open. The top corporate tax rate is relatively low (though personal income rates are higher), and tax revenue is not particularly large as a percentage of GDP. Jamaica welcomes foreign investment in almost all areas of its economy, including the purchase of privatized state enterprises.

Jamaica has weak property rights, freedom from corruption, trade freedom, and freedom from government. Despite a positive economic environment, average tariff rates are high. The court system is rooted in English common law traditions but suffers from a significant case backlog and some corruption. An understaffed police force is also a problem. Government expenditure is high as a percentage of GDP and up to the level of some EU social welfare states.

BACKGROUND: A former British colony, Jamaica was once a major sugar producer. Today, it gets most of its foreign exchange from remittances, tourism, and bauxite. Its economy is diverse, but industries lack investment and modernization. In recent years, factory closures have contributed to rising unemployment, largely as a result of growing industrial competition from Mexico, Central America, and Asia. Sworn in as prime minister in March 2006, Portia Simpson-Miller faces major challenges from crime, corruption, money laundering, and drug-related violence. The growing use of ethanol blends in gasoline throughout the hemisphere could lead to a revival of Jamaica's sugar industry.

How Do We Measure Economic Freedom? See Chapter 3 (page 37) for an explanation of the methodology or visit the *Index* Web site at *heritage.org/index*.

The economy is 66.1% free

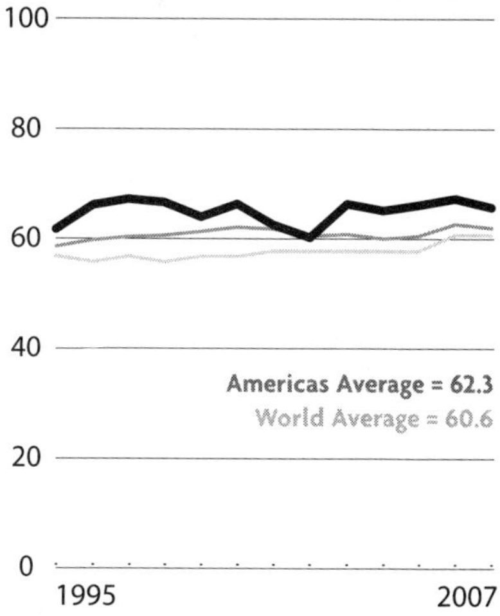

Americas Average = 62.3
World Average = 60.6

1995 — 2007

QUICK FACTS

Population: 2.6 million

GDP (PPP): $11.0 billion
2.5% growth in 2004
1.6% 5-yr. comp. ann. growth
$4,163 per capita

Unemployment: 11.7%

Inflation (CPI): 13.6%

FDI (net inflow): $560 million

Official Development Assistance:
Multilateral: $86 million
Bilateral: $81 million (41% from the U.S.)

External Debt: $6.4 billion

Exports: $3.9 billion
Primarily alumina, bauxite, sugar, bananas, rum, coffee, yams, beverages, chemicals, wearing apparel, mineral fuels

Imports: $5.3 billion
Primarily food, other consumer goods, industrial supplies, fuel, capital goods parts and accessories, machinery, transport equipment, construction materials

JAMAICA'S TEN ECONOMIC FREEDOMS

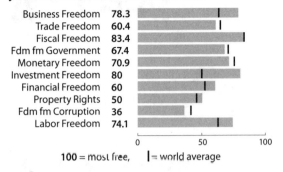

Business Freedom	78.3
Trade Freedom	60.4
Fiscal Freedom	83.4
Fdm fm Government	67.4
Monetary Freedom	70.9
Investment Freedom	80
Financial Freedom	60
Property Rights	50
Fdm fm Corruption	36
Labor Freedom	74.1

100 = most free, ❙ = world average

BUSINESS FREEDOM — 78.3%

Starting a business takes an average of 8 days, compared to the world average of 48 days. Obtaining a business license can be difficult, but closing a business is relatively easy. Cumbersome bureaucracy is a major problem for business. The overall freedom to start, operate, and close a business is relatively well protected by the national regulatory environment.

TRADE FREEDOM — 60.4%

Jamaica's weighted average tariff rate was 9.8 percent in 2003. While non-tariff barriers remain fairly low, restrictive import and export licensing rules, import fees, import and export bans, and export subsidies add to the cost of trade and restrict competition. Consequently, an additional 20 percent is deducted from Jamaica's trade freedom score to account for these non-tariff barriers.

FISCAL FREEDOM — 83.4%

Jamaica has moderate tax rates. The top income tax rate is 25 percent, and the top corporate tax rate is 33.3 percent. Other taxes include a value-added tax (VAT) and a property transfer tax. In the most recent year, overall tax revenue as a percentage of GDP was 27.5 percent.

FREEDOM FROM GOVERNMENT — 67.4%

Total government expenditures in Jamaica, including consumption and transfer payments, are moderate. In the most recent year, government spending equaled 35.7 percent of GDP, and the government received 8.6 percent of its total revenues from state-owned enterprises and government ownership of property.

MONETARY FREEDOM — 70.9%

Inflation in Jamaica is high, averaging 14.4 percent between 2003 and 2005. Unstable prices explain most of the monetary freedom score. Most prices are set in the market, but the government regulates utility services including electricity, water, and bus fares. While there are no official policies on price regulation or control, the government does monitor the pricing of consumer items. Consequently, an additional 5 percent is deducted from Jamaica's monetary freedom score to account for these policies.

INVESTMENT FREEDOM — 80%

Jamaica encourages foreign investment in all sectors. Foreign investors and domestic interests receive equal treatment, and foreign investors are not excluded from acquiring privatized state-owned enterprises. There is no screening of foreign investments, but projects that affect national security, have a negative impact on the environment, or involve sectors such as life insurance, media, or mining are subject to some restrictions. Residents and non-residents may hold foreign exchange accounts. There are no restrictions on transactions, transfers, or repatriation of funds, and non-residents may purchase real estate.

FINANCIAL FREEDOM — 60%

Jamaica's financial markets are underdeveloped and emerging from a mid-1990s financial crisis. In 1997, the government started to rehabilitate the banking and insurance sectors and strengthened supervision and regulation. After restructuring and consolidation, 15 financial institutions were operational in 2005 including six commercial banks, five merchant banks, four building societies, and several credit unions. The three largest commercial banks account for 85 percent of commercial bank assets, and five of the commercial banks are foreign-owned. The government no longer has any stake in any commercial bank. The government continues to provide concessionary financing through five development banks. There were 21 insurance companies in 2004. Capital markets are small and centered on the stock exchange. There are no specific restrictions on foreign participation in capital markets.

PROPERTY RIGHTS — 50%

Jamaica's legal system is based on English common law principles. However, the judiciary lacks adequate resources, and trials are sometimes delayed for years. An inadequate police force further weakens the security of property rights, and crime poses a great threat to foreign investment.

FREEDOM FROM CORRUPTION — 36%

Corruption is perceived as significant. Jamaica ranks 64th out of 158 countries in Transparency International's Corruption Perceptions Index for 2005.

LABOR FREEDOM — 74.1%

The labor market operates under relatively flexible employment regulations that could be improved to enhance employment and productivity growth. The non-salary cost of employing a worker is moderate, but dismissing a redundant employee is costly. Regulations on increasing or contracting the number of work hours are flexible.

JAPAN

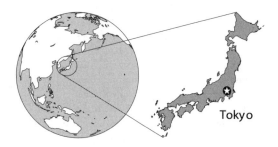

Tokyo

Japan's economy is 73.6 percent free, according to our 2007 assessment, which makes it the world's 18th freest economy. Its overall score is 1 percentage point lower than last year, partially reflecting new methodological detail. Japan is ranked 5th out of 30 countries in the Asia–Pacific region, and its overall score is much higher than the regional average.

Japan enjoys high levels of trade freedom, property rights, business freedom, freedom from corruption, fiscal freedom, labor freedom, and monetary freedom. The average tariff rate is low, and business regulation is efficient. Virtually all commercial operations are simple and transparent. A very modest, stable deflation in prices has been occurring. Taxes are fairly high, and overall tax revenue is moderate as a percentage of GDP. Contracts in Japan are often imprecise, which can impede smooth judicial handling of commercial disputes. Despite the confusion, contract agreements are highly respected by the judiciary. There is very little corruption in the civil service.

Japan is weaker in freedom from government and financial freedom. Total government spending equals more than a third of GDP. The financial sector is wholly modern and developed, but it is also subject to strong government influence and host to a variety of legal restrictions on capital.

BACKGROUND: Japan is one of the world's most developed countries. After World War II, it achieved rapid economic growth by pursuing an aggressive export-oriented economic policy, but high levels of protectionism left the country vulnerable. The economy experienced a severe recession in the early 1990s and stagnated for the rest of the decade. Long-term challenges include an immense government debt equaling 170 percent of GDP, a rapidly aging population combined with low birth rates, and the economic dominance of large corporations. Prime Minister Junichiro Koizumi initiated structural reforms, such as privatization of the postal system and banking and financial reforms, but results remain largely unrealized.

How Do We Measure Economic Freedom? See Chapter 3 (page 37) for an explanation of the methodology or visit the *Index* Web site at *heritage.org/index*.

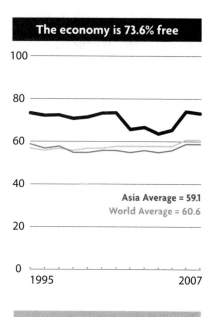

The economy is 73.6% free

100

80

60

40

Asia Average = 59.1
World Average = 60.6

20

0

1995   2007

QUICK FACTS

Population: 127.8 million

GDP (PPP): $3.7 trillion
2.3% growth in 2004
1.5% 5-yr. comp. ann. growth
$29,251 per capita

Unemployment: 4.7%

Inflation (CPI): 0%

FDI (net inflow): −$23.1 billion

Official Development Assistance:
Multilateral: None
Bilateral: None

External Debt: $1.6 trillion

Exports: $636.6 billion
Primarily transport equipment, motor vehicles, semiconductors, electrical machinery, chemicals

Imports: $542.4 billion
Primarily machinery and equipment, fuels, food, chemicals, textiles, raw materials

JAPAN'S TEN ECONOMIC FREEDOMS

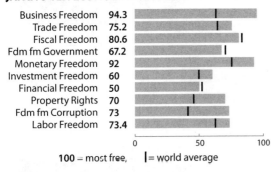

Business Freedom	94.3
Trade Freedom	75.2
Fiscal Freedom	80.6
Fdm fm Government	67.2
Monetary Freedom	92
Investment Freedom	60
Financial Freedom	50
Property Rights	70
Fdm fm Corruption	73
Labor Freedom	73.4

100 = most free, | = world average

BUSINESS FREEDOM — 94.3%

Starting a business takes an average of 23 days, compared to the world average of 48 days. Obtaining a business license is relatively simple, and closing a business is easy. The government has undertaken much-needed reform measures to ensure greater regulatory transparency. The overall freedom to start, operate, and close a business is strongly protected by the national regulatory environment.

TRADE FREEDOM — 75.2%

Japan's weighted average tariff rate was 2.4 percent in 2004. Non-transparent regulations, import restrictions, import bans, restrictive sanitary and phytosanitary rules, services and agricultural market access barriers, agriculture and other subsidies, a non-transparent tariff rate quota system, and an inefficient customs process add to the cost of trade. Consequently, an additional 20 percent is deducted from Japan's trade freedom score to account for these non-tariff barriers.

FISCAL FREEDOM — 80.6%

Japan has a high income tax rate and a burdensome corporate tax rate. The top income tax rate is 37 percent, and the top corporate tax rate is 30 percent. Other taxes include a value-added tax (VAT), a tax on interest, and an inhabitants' tax. In the most recent year, overall tax revenue as a percentage of GDP was 25.3 percent.

FREEDOM FROM GOVERNMENT — 67.2%

Total government expenditures in Japan, including consumption and transfer payments, are high. In the most recent year, government spending equaled 37.3 percent of GDP, and the government received 1 percent of its total revenues from state-owned enterprises and government ownership of property.

MONETARY FREEDOM — 92%

Japan experienced a –0.2 percent average rate of deflation between 2003 and 2005. Such stable prices explain most of the monetary freedom score. The only formal price controls apply to rice, but indirect regulation influences prices on a variety of products. For decades, major producers, backed by regulators ostensibly concerned with price stability, have been able to dictate retail as well as wholesale prices. Consequently, an additional 5 percent is deducted from Japan's monetary freedom score to account for these policies.

INVESTMENT FREEDOM — 60%

Foreign acquisition of Japanese firms is inhibited by insufficient financial disclosure practices, cross-holding of shares among companies belonging to the same business grouping (keiretsu), and public attitudes about foreign takeovers. Exclusive buyer-supplier networks and alliances are still maintained by some keiretsu, limiting competition from foreign firms and domestic newcomers. Foreign investors must notify and obtain approval from the government for investments in agriculture, forestry, petroleum, electricity, gas, water, aerospace, telecommunications, and leather manufacturing. There are no controls on the holding of foreign exchange accounts or on transactions, current transfers, repatriation of profits, or real estate transactions by residents or non-residents.

FINANCIAL FREEDOM — 50%

Japan's financial system is competitive but remains subject to considerable government influence. Financial transparency is insufficient. Deregulation and international competition have changed Japanese banking and led to consolidation. Japanese corporations and banks maintain tight relationships, and banks are often shareholders in companies with which they conduct business. Both domestic and foreign investors have free access to a wide array of credit instruments at market rates. The government affects the supply of credit through state-run financial institutions. The government-owned postal savings system, which does not pay taxes and offers higher than market rate interest on deposits, is the world's largest single pool of savings and accounts for a third of Japan's deposits. Japan's insurance industry is the world's second largest, and 26 foreign firms account for 25 percent of the insurance market. Capital markets are well developed.

PROPERTY RIGHTS — 70%

Property rights are generally secure in Japan. The courts do not discriminate against foreign investors but are not well suited to litigation of investment and business disputes. Japanese businesses tend to write their contracts in general terms, but despite this lack of precision, contracts are highly respected.

FREEDOM FROM CORRUPTION — 73%

Corruption is perceived as minimal. Japan ranks 21st out of 158 countries in Transparency International's Corruption Perceptions Index for 2005.

LABOR FREEDOM — 73.4%

The labor market operates under relatively flexible employment regulations that could be improved to enhance employment and productivity growth. The non-salary cost of employing a worker is moderate, and dismissing a redundant employee is not costly. Regulations related to increasing or contracting the number of work hours are not flexible.

JORDAN

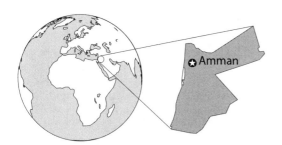

● Amman

Jordan's economy is 64 percent free, according to our 2007 assessment, which makes it the world's 53rd freest economy. Its overall score is 0.2 percentage point higher than last year, partially reflecting new methodological detail. Jordan is ranked 3rd out of 17 countries in the Middle East/North Africa region, and its overall score is higher than the regional average.

Jordan enjoys relatively high levels of monetary freedom, fiscal freedom, financial freedom, freedom from corruption, and labor freedom. Inflation is low, and the government has succeeded in phasing out direct subsidies of goods. Personal and corporate income tax rates are low, and overall tax revenue represents about one-fifth of GDP. The labor market is fairly flexible, though firing workers remains overly complicated. Developed and increasingly modern, Jordan's financial sector is making serious efforts to meet international standards. Corruption is extremely low, particularly for the Middle East.

Jordan is weaker in terms of trade freedom, freedom from government, property rights, and investment freedom. The government maintains regulatory obstacles to trade and an opaque bureaucracy. A variety of restrictions have limited the opportunities for foreign investment in Jordan. The judiciary is not corrupt, but it is subject to royal influence.

BACKGROUND: Jordan gained its independence from Britain in 1946 and is a constitutional monarchy with relatively few natural resources and an economy supported by foreign loans, aid, and remittances from expatriate workers, many of whom work in the Persian Gulf oil kingdoms. King Abdullah II has undertaken political, economic, and regulatory reforms since coming to power in 1999. Jordan joined the World Trade Organization and signed a free trade agreement with the United States in 2000 and signed an association agreement with the European Union in 2001. Jordan suffers from high unemployment, heavy debt, and the high cost of oil imports.

How Do We Measure Economic Freedom? See Chapter 3 (page 37) for an explanation of the methodology or visit the *Index* Web site at *heritage.org/index*.

The economy is 64% free

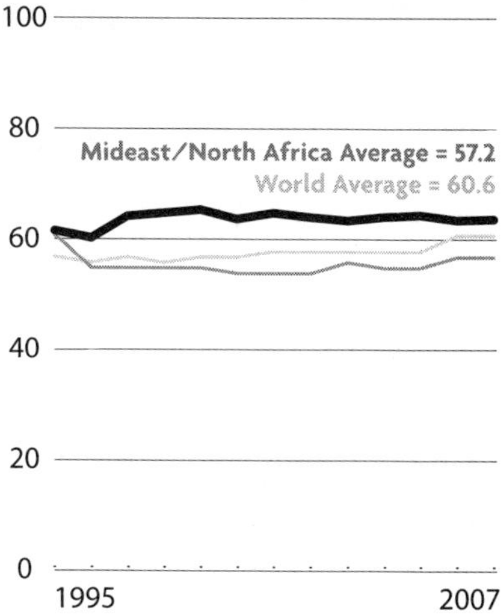

100

80

Mideast/North Africa Average = 57.2
World Average = 60.6

60

40

20

0

1995   2007

QUICK FACTS

Population: 5.4 million

GDP (PPP): $25.5 billion
7.7% growth in 2004
5.4% 5-yr. comp. ann. growth
$4,688 per capita

Unemployment: 14.5% (2003 estimate)

Inflation (CPI): 3.4%

FDI (net inflow): $620.3 million

Official Development Assistance:
Multilateral: $166 million
Bilateral: $527 million (72% from the U.S.)

External Debt: $8.2 billion

Exports: $6.0 billion
Primarily clothing, phosphates, fertilizers, potash, vegetables, manufactures, pharmaceuticals

Imports: $9.4 billion
Primarily crude oil, textile fabrics, machinery, transport equipment, manufactured goods

JORDAN'S TEN ECONOMIC FREEDOMS

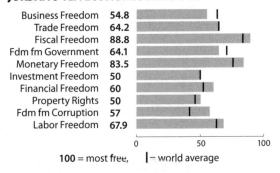

Business Freedom	54.8
Trade Freedom	64.2
Fiscal Freedom	88.8
Fdm fm Government	64.1
Monetary Freedom	83.5
Investment Freedom	50
Financial Freedom	60
Property Rights	50
Fdm fm Corruption	57
Labor Freedom	67.9

0   50   100

100 = most free, | = world average

BUSINESS FREEDOM — *54.8%*

Starting a business takes an average of 18 days, compared to the world average of 48 days. Obtaining a business license is relatively simple, but closing a business is difficult. In recent years, the government has made efforts to reform its complex regulatory environment, but bureaucratic obstacles and delays remain persistent problems. The overall freedom to start, operate, and close a business is restricted by the national regulatory environment.

TRADE FREEDOM — *64.2%*

Jordan's weighted average tariff rate was 7.9 percent in 2005. The government has made progress in liberalizing the trade regime, but import restrictions, import bans, import taxes and fees, red tape and delays in customs, and import licensing requirements continue to add to the cost of trade. Consequently, an additional 20 percent is deducted from Jordan's trade freedom score to account for these non-tariff barriers.

FISCAL FREEDOM — *88.8%*

Jordan has low tax rates. Both the top income tax rate and the top corporate tax rate are 25 percent. Other taxes include a value-added tax (VAT), a tax on interest, and a property transfer tax. In the most recent year, overall tax revenue as a percentage of GDP was 20.8 percent.

FREEDOM FROM GOVERNMENT — *64.1%*

Total government expenditures in Jordan, including consumption and transfer payments, are high. In the most recent year, government spending equaled 36.9 percent of GDP, and the government received 12.5 percent of its total revenues from state-owned enterprises and government ownership of property. Despite modest progress in privatization, the state still dominates many sectors of the economy.

MONETARY FREEDOM — *83.5%*

Inflation in Jordan is moderate, averaging 3.3 percent between 2003 and 2005. Relatively unstable prices explain most of the monetary freedom score. While most price controls and subsidies have been eliminated, the government influences the prices of fuel products through subsidies and sets prices for electricity, telecommunications, and water. Consequently, an additional 5 percent is deducted

from Jordan's monetary freedom score to account for these policies.

INVESTMENT FREEDOM — *50%*

The government promotes foreign investment. There is no formal screening process, but foreign investors face minimum capital requirements. Residents and non-residents may hold foreign exchange accounts. There are no restrictions or controls on payments, transactions, transfers, or repatriation of profits. Real estate purchases require approval. Foreign investments may not exceed 50 percent in construction, wholesale and retail trade, transport, wastewater treatment, food services, travel agent services, import and export services, and advertising. Foreigners are prohibited from investing in investigative and security services, sports clubs, stone quarrying, custom clearance services, and land transportation.

FINANCIAL FREEDOM — *60%*

Jordan's financial sector, dominated by banking, is fairly well developed, and reforms are being implemented to bring supervision and regulation in line with international standards. There are nine domestic commercial banks, two Islamic banks, five investment banks, and eight foreign banks. The Arab Bank dominates the sector, accounting for about 60 percent of total banking assets. The government does not own any commercial banks, but it does own five specialized credit institutions focused on agricultural credit, housing, rural and urban development, and industry. The government guarantees loans to Jordanian small and medium-size industries through the Jordan Loan Guarantee Corporation. The insurance sector has 26 companies, and a foreign insurer dominates the life insurance market. Capital markets are small, but the stock exchange is robust by regional standards.

PROPERTY RIGHTS — *50%*

The judiciary is generally independent, but the king is the country's ultimate authority. Despite a law passed in 2001 to limit its influence, the Ministry of Justice still wields significant influence over judges' careers. Expropriation is unlikely.

FREEDOM FROM CORRUPTION — *57%*

Corruption is perceived as present. Jordan ranks 37th out of 158 countries in Transparency International's Corruption Perceptions Index for 2005.

LABOR FREEDOM — *67.9%*

The labor market operates under relatively flexible employment regulations that could be improved to enhance employment and productivity growth. The non-salary cost of employing a worker is moderate, but dismissing a redundant employee is not easy.

KAZAKHSTAN

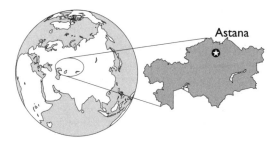

Astana

Kazakhstan's economy is 60.4 percent free, according to our 2007 assessment, which makes it the world's 75th freest economy. Its overall score is 0.8 percentage point lower than last year, partially reflecting new methodological detail. Kazakhstan is ranked 10th out of 30 countries in the Asia–Pacific region, and its overall score is just above the regional average.

Kazakhstan scores highly in fiscal freedom, freedom from government, and labor freedom. The top income and corporate tax rates are a moderate 20 percent and 30 percent, respectively. The government also imposes additional taxes, however, and overall tax revenue is somewhat high as a percentage of GDP. Government expenditure is also somewhat high, although the government has gradually been privatizing businesses. Kazakhstan has a highly flexible labor system.

Kazakhstan's economy has significant shortcomings. Investment freedom, property rights, and freedom from corruption are weak. Foreign investment in virtually all sectors is restricted by exclusive barriers and bureaucratic incompetence. Government policy actively favors domestic businesses, and the weak rule of law allows for significant corruption and insecure property rights.

BACKGROUND: Kazakhstan became an independent nation in 1991, following the collapse of the Soviet Union. Although Nursultan Nazarbayev prevailed in the December 2005 presidential election, political infighting continues within the ruling class. The energy sector has driven economic growth, thanks to an energy boom that began in 2000. China has invested billions in oil companies and pipelines to access Kazakhstan's hydrocarbon resources, and output is projected to grow from 1.2 million barrels a day in 2006 to 3.5 million barrels a day in 2020. Kazakhstan has also begun to develop financial services and light industry sectors.

How Do We Measure Economic Freedom? See Chapter 3 (page 37) for an explanation of the methodology or visit the *Index* Web site at *heritage.org/index*.

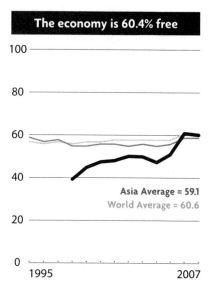

The economy is 60.4% free

Asia Average = 59.1
World Average = 60.6

QUICK FACTS

Population: 15 million

GDP (PPP): $111.6 billion
9.6% growth in 2004
10.4% 5-yr. comp. ann. growth
$7,440 per capita

Unemployment: 8.4%

Inflation (CPI): 6.9%

FDI (net inflow): $5.6 billion

Official Development Assistance:
Multilateral: $19 million
Bilateral: $262 million (22% from the U.S.)

External Debt: $32.3 billion

Exports: $22.6 billion
Primarily oil and oil products, ferrous metals, chemicals, machinery, grain

Imports: $18.8 billion
Primarily machinery and equipment, metal products, food

KAZAKHSTAN'S TEN ECONOMIC FREEDOMS

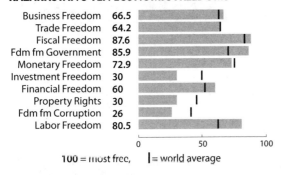

Business Freedom	66.5
Trade Freedom	64.2
Fiscal Freedom	87.6
Fdm fm Government	85.9
Monetary Freedom	72.9
Investment Freedom	30
Financial Freedom	60
Property Rights	30
Fdm fm Corruption	26
Labor Freedom	80.5

0   50   100

100 = most free,   ▌= world average

BUSINESS FREEDOM — 66.5%

Starting a business takes an average of 20 days, compared to the world average of 48 days. Obtaining a business license and closing a business can be difficult. Lack of transparency and inconsistent application of commercial laws remain obstacles to business. The overall freedom to start, operate, and close a business is relatively well protected by the national regulatory environment.

TRADE FREEDOM — 64.2%

Kazakhstan's average tariff rate was 7.9 percent in 2005. The government has made progress toward a more liberal trade regime, but non-transparent and burdensome regulations and standards, service market access barriers, opaque government procurement procedures, and customs corruption continue to add to the cost of trade. Consequently, an additional 20 percent is deducted from Kazakhstan's trade freedom score to account for these non-tariff barriers.

FISCAL FREEDOM — 87.6%

Kazakhstan has a low income tax rate and a moderate corporate tax rate. The top income tax rate is 20 percent, and the top corporate tax rate is 30 percent. Other taxes include a value-added tax (VAT) and a vehicle tax. In the most recent year, overall tax revenue as a percentage of GDP was 23.6 percent.

FREEDOM FROM GOVERNMENT — 85.9%

Total government expenditures in Kazakhstan, including consumption and transfer payments, are low. In the most recent year, government spending equaled 23.3 percent of GDP, and the government received 4.2 percent of its total revenues from state-owned enterprises and government ownership of property. Privatization has been gradual but successful, although the transactions involved have lacked transparency.

MONETARY FREEDOM — 72.9%

Inflation in Kazakhstan is relatively high, averaging 7.3 percent between 2003 and 2005. Relatively high and unstable prices explain most of the monetary freedom score. The market sets most prices, but the government retains the right to control prices when necessary. The government also influences prices through numerous state-owned enterprises and manufacturing subsidies, and little progress has been made in promoting competition in agricul-

ture. Consequently, an additional 10 percent is deducted from Kazakhstan's monetary freedom score to account for these policies.

INVESTMENT FREEDOM — 30%

The government constantly challenges contractual rights and legislates to favor domestic investors over foreign ones, all of which significantly deters foreign investment. No sector of the economy is closed to investment, but the government imposes a 25 percent cap on foreign capital in the banking system and a 20 percent ceiling on foreign ownership in media companies. It also screens foreign investment proposals in a process that is often non-transparent, arbitrary, and slow. Subject to restrictions, foreign exchange accounts may be held by residents and non-residents. Most capital transactions, payments, and transfers are subject to government approval, quantitative limits, and strict documentary requirements.

FINANCIAL FREEDOM — 60%

Kazakhstan's banking system is the most developed in Central Asia. All banks are now required to meet international banking standards, including a risk-weighted 8 percent capital-adequacy ratio. As a result, the number of banks has fallen from 130 banks operating at the end of 1995 to 34 with licenses in January 2006. Foreign banks may not have branches but may establish subsidiaries, joint ventures, and representative offices. The government must approve ownership of over 25 percent of a bank. At the end of 2005, 14 banks had foreign participation, and 18 foreign banks had representative offices. There are three state-owned banks (a development bank, an export–import bank, and a housing finance bank) and two development funds, as well as a number of microfinance institutions. The insurance sector is small but has 34 licensed companies. Foreign insurance companies are limited to joint ventures with local companies. Capital markets are underdeveloped.

PROPERTY RIGHTS — 30%

Kazakhstan's legal system does not provide sufficient protection for private property. Most legal disputes arise from contract breaches or non-payment on the part of the government. Corruption remains widespread, and the judiciary views itself more as an arm of the executive than as an enforcer of contracts or guardian of property rights.

FREEDOM FROM CORRUPTION — 26%

Corruption is perceived as widespread. Kazakhstan ranks 107th out of 158 countries in Transparency International's Corruption Perceptions Index for 2005.

LABOR FREEDOM — 80.5%

The labor market operates under flexible employment regulations that enhance employment and productivity growth. The non-salary cost of employing a worker can be high, but dismissing a redundant employee is costless. Regulations regarding firing a worker are flexible and straightforward.

KENYA

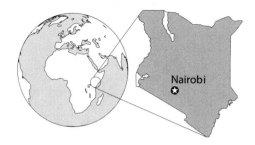

Nairobi

Kenya's economy is 59.4 percent free, according to our 2007 assessment, which makes it the world's 82nd freest economy. Its overall score is 0.6 percentage point lower than last year, partially reflecting new methodological detail. Kenya is ranked 8th out of 40 countries in the sub-Saharan Africa region, and its overall score is higher than the regional average.

Kenya scores well in fiscal freedom, freedom from government, and labor freedom. Personal income and corporate taxes are moderate, and overall tax revenue as a percentage of GDP is low. Government expenditures are about one-fourth of GDP, and state-owned businesses produce a small amount of revenue. The labor market is flexible, and dismissing redundant employees is almost costless.

Property rights, freedom from corruption, financial freedom, monetary freedom, and investment freedom are all weak. Corruption is extremely high, giving Kenya one of the world's lowest freedom from corruption scores. Non-transparent trade regulations and an inefficient customs service hurt trade. Kenya has a well-developed financial sector, particularly for the region, but it is vulnerable to government influence. As in many other sub-Saharan African nations, Kenya's judiciary is underdeveloped and subject to the political whims of the executive.

BACKGROUND: Kenya, transportation and financial hub of East Africa, experienced high economic growth in the years following independence in 1963. During the past two decades, government mismanagement and corruption have hindered economic growth, although growth has improved under the current National Rainbow Coalition (NARC) government. Despite government steps to combat corruption, officials have been implicated in corruption in recent years, and fractures in the coalition have stalled progress on economic reform. Bureaucracy is extensive, and civil service reform has been slow. Agriculture accounts for about 25 percent of GDP and employs about 70 percent of the population. Much of the infrastructure is in poor condition.

How Do We Measure Economic Freedom? See Chapter 3 (page 37) for an explanation of the methodology or visit the *Index* Web site at *heritage.org/index*.

The economy is 59.4% free

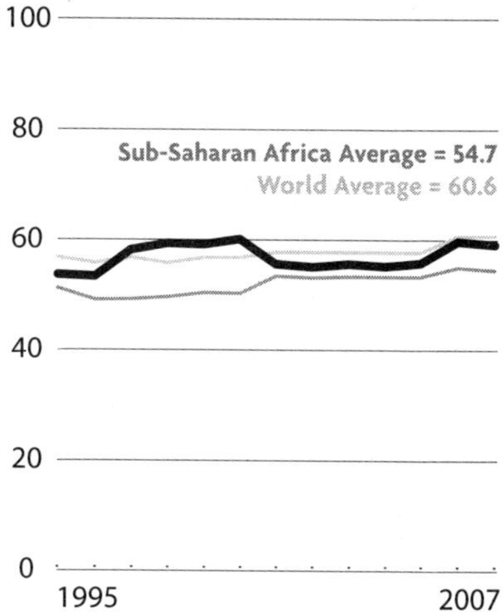

Sub-Saharan Africa Average = 54.7
World Average = 60.6

100

80

60

40

20

0

1995   2007

QUICK FACTS

Population: 33.5 million

GDP (PPP): $38.1 billion
4.3% growth in 2004
2.5% 5-yr. comp. ann. growth
$1,140 per capita

Unemployment: 40% (2001 estimate)

Inflation (CPI): 11.6%

FDI (net inflow): −$2.6 million

Official Development Assistance:
Multilateral: $259 million
Bilateral: $521 million (27% from the U.S.)

External Debt: $6.8 billion

Exports: $4.2 billion
Primarily tea, horticultural products, coffee, petroleum products, fish, cement

Imports: $5.1 billion
Primarily machinery, transportation equipment, petroleum products, motor vehicles, iron, steel, resins, plastics

KENYA'S TEN ECONOMIC FREEDOMS

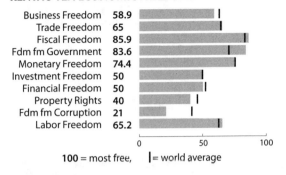

Business Freedom	58.9
Trade Freedom	65
Fiscal Freedom	85.9
Fdm fm Government	83.6
Monetary Freedom	74.4
Investment Freedom	50
Financial Freedom	50
Property Rights	40
Fdm fm Corruption	21
Labor Freedom	65.2

100 = most free, I = world average

BUSINESS FREEDOM — 58.9%

Starting a business takes an average of 54 days, compared to the world average of 48 days. Entrepreneurship should be easier for maximum job creation. Obtaining a business license is difficult, but closing a business is relatively easy. Lack of transparency and inconsistent application of commercial codes are persistent problems. The overall freedom to start, operate, and close a business is restricted by the national regulatory environment.

TRADE FREEDOM — 65%

Kenya's weighted average tariff rate was 7.5 percent in 2005. Non-transparent and restrictive regulations, sanitary and phytosanitary rules and standards, opaque government procurement procedures, import restrictions, manipulation of import taxes to protect strategic sectors, weak enforcement of intellectual property rights, and customs corruption add to the cost of trade. Consequently, an additional 20 percent is deducted from Kenya's trade freedom score to account for these non-tariff barriers.

FISCAL FREEDOM — 85.9%

Kenya has moderate income and corporate tax rates. Both the top income tax and top corporate tax rates are 30 percent. Other taxes include a value-added tax (VAT) and an apprentice tax. In the most recent year, overall tax revenue as a percentage of GDP was 17.7 percent.

FREEDOM FROM GOVERNMENT — 83.6%

Total government expenditures in Kenya, including consumption and transfer payments, are low. In the most recent year, government spending equaled 24.4 percent of GDP, and the government received 7.5 percent of its revenues from the earnings of state-owned enterprises. Privatization of state-owned enterprises has been stagnant. Legislation on privatization was passed by Parliament in August 2005 but does not specify an exact timetable.

MONETARY FREEDOM — 74.4%

Inflation in Kenya is relatively high, averaging 10.6 percent between 2003 and 2005. Relatively high and unstable prices explain most of the monetary freedom score. Price controls were officially dismantled in 1994, but the government reserves the right to set maximum prices in certain cases and influences prices through agricultural marketing boards and state-owned utilities and enterprises. Conse-

quently, an additional 5 percent is deducted from Kenya's monetary freedom score to account for these policies.

INVESTMENT FREEDOM — 50%

Kenya's government has relaxed its screening standards and has established the Investment Promotion Center for investment approval. Foreigners face ownership restrictions in only a few industries, including infrastructure, insurance, and the media. Work permits are required for all foreigners and are hard to obtain. Both residents and non-residents may hold foreign exchange accounts. There are no controls or requirements on payments and transfers. Most capital transactions are permitted, but government approval is required for the sale or issue of most capital and money market instruments and for the purchase of real estate by non-residents.

FINANCIAL FREEDOM — 50%

Kenya's financial system is one of the most developed in sub-Saharan Africa but is subject to considerable government influence and inadequate supervision. At the end of 2005, the banking sector included two mortgage financial companies, two building societies, a large number of savings and credit cooperatives, and 41 commercial banks. The six largest banks, including two majority state-owned banks and two foreign banks, control about two-thirds of banking assets. The government also owns or owns shares in several other domestic financial institutions and influences the allocation of credit. Non-performing loans, particularly from state-owned banks to state-owned enterprises, remain a problem. There were 39 insurance companies in 2005, but the sector was highly concentrated with four companies accounting for 75 percent of premiums. Capital markets are relatively small and focused on the stock exchange. Foreign investors may acquire shares in the stock market, subject to specified limits.

PROPERTY RIGHTS — 40%

Kenya's judicial system is modeled after the British system. Commercial courts were established in 2000 to deal with commercial cases. Property and contractual rights are enforceable but subject to very long delays. The government has taken some steps to address judicial corruption.

FREEDOM FROM CORRUPTION — 21%

Corruption is perceived as widespread. Kenya ranks 144th out of 158 countries in Transparency International's Corruption Perceptions Index for 2005.

LABOR FREEDOM — 65.2%

The labor market operates under relatively flexible employment regulations that could be improved to enhance employment and productivity growth. The non-salary cost of employing a worker is low, and dismissing a redundant employee is relatively costless.

KOREA, DEMOCRATIC PEOPLE'S REPUBLIC OF (NORTH KOREA)

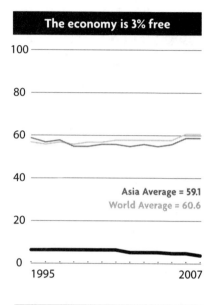

Pyongyang

Rank: 157

Regional Rank: 30 of 30

N orth Korea's economy is 3 percent free, according to our 2007 assessment, which makes it the world's least free economy, or 157th out of 157 countries. North Korea is ranked 30th out of 30 countries in the Asia–Pacific region, and its overall score is the lowest in the world.

North Korea does not score well in a single area of economic freedom, although it does score 10 percent in investment freedom and property rights. The opening of the Kaesong industrial venture in cooperation with South Korea has been a start in foreign investment.

Business freedom, investment freedom, trade freedom, financial freedom, freedom from corruption, and labor freedom are nonexistent. All aspects of business operations are totally controlled and dominated by the government. Normal foreign trade is almost zero. No courts are independent of political interference, and private property (particularly land) is strictly regulated by the state. Corruption is virtually immeasurable and, in the case of North Korea, hard to distinguish from necessity. Much of North Korea's economy cannot be measured, and world bodies like the International Monetary Fund and World Bank are not permitted to gather information. Our policy is to give countries low marks for specific freedoms when it is country policy to restrict measurement of those freedoms.

BACKGROUND: The Democratic People's Republic of Korea has maintained its Communist system since its founding in 1948. A serious economic decline began in the early 1990s with the end of economic support from the Soviet Union and other Communist-bloc countries, including China. Floods and droughts all but destroyed the agricultural infrastructure and led to severe famine and dislocation of the population during the 1990s. South Korean and Chinese investments in the economy have alleviated dire conditions. The government continues to rely on counterfeiting foreign currency and sales of missiles for money. That and the nuclear ambitions and isolationism of Kim Jong Il reinforce North Korea's status as the hermit kingdom.

How Do We Measure Economic Freedom? See Chapter 3 (page 37) for an explanation of the methodology or visit the *Index* Web site at *heritage.org/index*.

The economy is 3% free

100	
80	
60	
40	Asia Average = 59.1
	World Average = 60.6
20	
0	
1995	2007

QUICK FACTS

Population: 22.4 million

GDP (PPP): n/a
n/a
n/a
n/a

Unemployment: n/a

Inflation (CPI): n/a

FDI (net inflow): $40 million (gross)

Official Development Assistance:
Multilateral: $49 million
Bilateral: $152 million (37% from U.S.)

External Debt: $12 billion (1996 estimate)

Exports: $1.3 billion
Primarily minerals, metallurgical products, manufactures (including armaments), textiles, fishery products

Imports: $2.3 billion
Primarily petroleum, coking coal, machinery and equipment, textiles, grain

NORTH KOREA'S TEN ECONOMIC FREEDOMS

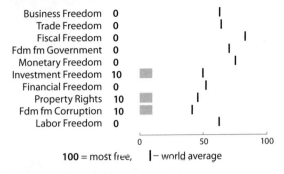

Business Freedom	0
Trade Freedom	0
Fiscal Freedom	0
Fdm fm Government	0
Monetary Freedom	0
Investment Freedom	10
Financial Freedom	0
Property Rights	10
Fdm fm Corruption	10
Labor Freedom	0

100 = most free, | – world average

BUSINESS FREEDOM — *0%*

The state regulates the economy heavily through central planning. The economic reforms implemented in 2002 allegedly brought some changes at the enterprise and industrial level, but government regulations make the creation of any entrepreneurial activities virtually impossible. The overall freedom to start, operate, and close a business is extremely restricted by the national regulatory environment.

TRADE FREEDOM — *0%*

The government controls all imports and exports, and formal trade is minimal. Data on North Korean trade are limited and compiled from trading partners' statistics. Most North Korean trade is de facto aid, mainly from North Korea's two main trading partners, China and South Korea. Non-tariff barriers are significant. Inter-Korean trade remains constrained in scope by North Korea's difficulties with implementing needed reform. Given the lack of necessary tariff data, a score of zero is assigned.

FISCAL FREEDOM — *0%*

No data on income or corporate tax rates are available. Given the absence of published official macroeconomic data, such figures as are available with respect to North Korea's government expenditures are highly suspect and outdated.

FREEDOM FROM GOVERNMENT — *0%*

The government owns all property and sets production levels for most products, and state-owned industries account for nearly all GDP. The state directs all significant economic activity. The government implemented limited economic reforms, such as changes in foreign investment codes and restructuring in industry and management, in 2002.

MONETARY FREEDOM — *0%*

In July 2002, North Korea introduced price and wage reforms that consisted of reducing government subsidies and telling producers to charge prices that more closely reflect costs. However, without matching supply-side measures to boost output, the result of these measures has been rampant inflation for many staple goods. With the ongoing crisis in agriculture, the government has banned sales of grain at markets and returned to a rationing system.

Given the lack of necessary inflation data, a score of zero is assigned.

INVESTMENT FREEDOM — *10%*

North Korea does not welcome foreign investment. One attempt to open the economy to foreigners was its first special economic zone, located at Rajin-Sonbong in the northeast. However, Rajin-Sonbong is remote and still lacks basic infrastructure. Wage rates in the special zone are unrealistically high, as the state controls the labor supply and insists on taking its share. More recent special zones at Mt. Kumgang and Kaesong are more enticing. Aside from these few economic zones where investment is approved on a case-by-case basis, foreign investment is prohibited.

FINANCIAL FREEDOM — *0%*

North Korea is a Communist command economy and lacks a private financial sector. The central bank also serves as a commercial bank with a network of local branches. The government provides most funding for industries and takes a percentage from enterprises. There is an increasing preference for foreign currency. Foreign aid agencies have set up microcredit schemes to lend to farmers and small businesses. A rumored overhaul of the financial system to permit firms to borrow from banks has not materialized. Because of debts dating back to the 1970s, most foreign banks will not consider entering North Korea. A South Korean bank has opened a branch in the Kaesong zone. The state holds a monopoly on insurance, and there are no equity markets.

PROPERTY RIGHTS — *10%*

Property rights are not guaranteed in North Korea. Almost all property belongs to the state, and the judiciary is not independent.

FREEDOM FROM CORRUPTION — *10%*

North Korea's informal market is immense, especially in agricultural goods, as a result of famines and oppressive government policies. There is also an active informal market in currency and in trade with China.

LABOR FREEDOM — *0%*

The government controls and determines all wages. Since the 2002 economic reforms, factory managers have had more autonomy to set wages and offer incentives, but the labor market still operates under highly restrictive employment regulations that seriously hinder employment and productivity growth.

KOREA, REPUBLIC OF (SOUTH KOREA)

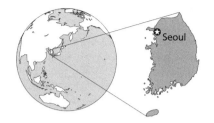
Seoul

South Korea's economy is 68.6 percent free, according to our 2007 assessment, which makes it the world's 36th freest economy. Its overall score is 0.6 percentage point higher than last year, partially reflecting new methodological detail. South Korea is ranked 7th out of 30 countries in the Asia–Pacific region, and its overall score is higher than the regional average.

South Korea has high levels of business freedom, fiscal freedom, freedom from government, investment freedom, monetary freedom, and property rights. The corporate tax rate is low. Both total government expenditures relative to GDP and inflation are fairly low as well, but South Korea's monetary score is hurt by government subsidies of several sectors. Investment in South Korea is easy, as the government has made several efforts over the past decade to open the economy to foreign capital. The rule of law is strong, and property rights are protected in a transparent manner.

South Korea's trade freedom, financial freedom, and labor freedom are weak. Non-tariff barriers are common. The financial system is advanced, but it remains partially dominated by the government. The labor market remains rigid despite the government's efforts to enhance market flexibility in recent years.

BACKGROUND: South Korea is one of Asia's most vibrant democracies. After several decades of rapid industrialization and modernization, a 1997 economic financial crisis revealed structural deficiencies that have been largely corrected. Although the government did much to liberalize the financial and economic sectors in the aftermath of the crisis, the economy continues to be dominated by the chaebols (large conglomerates). South Korea's greatest challenge, both economically and politically, is managing its increasing interaction with North Korea in light of ongoing tensions resulting from the North's nuclear programs and deteriorating relations with major powers in the region.

How Do We Measure Economic Freedom? See Chapter 3 (page 37) for an explanation of the methodology or visit the *Index* Web site at *heritage.org/index*.

The economy is 68.6% free

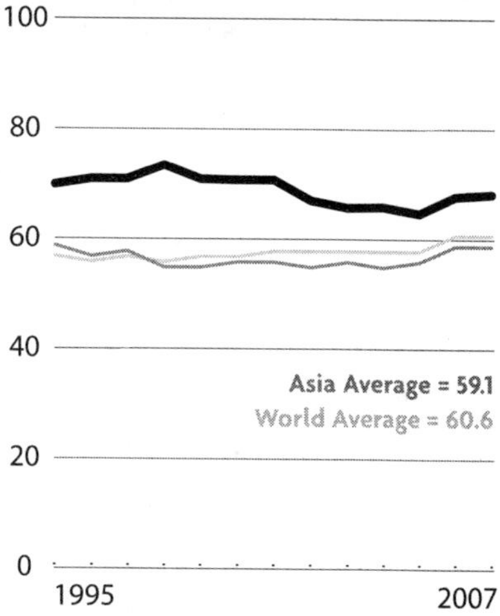

Asia Average = 59.1
World Average = 60.6

1995 — 2007

QUICK FACTS

Population: 48.1 million

GDP (PPP): $985.6 billion
4.6% growth in 2004
5.4% 5-yr. comp. ann. growth
$20,499 per capita

Unemployment: 3.7%

Inflation (CPI): 3.6%

FDI (net inflow): $2.9 billion

Official Development Assistance:
Multilateral: $1 million
Bilateral: $109 million (0% from the U.S.)

External Debt: $153.9 billion (2005 estimate)

Exports: $299.2 billion
Primarily semiconductors, wireless telecommunications equipment, motor vehicles, computers, steel, ships, petrochemicals

Imports: $269.8 billion
Primarily machinery, electronics, electronic equipment, oil, steel, transport equipment, organic chemicals, plastics

239

SOUTH KOREA'S TEN ECONOMIC FREEDOMS

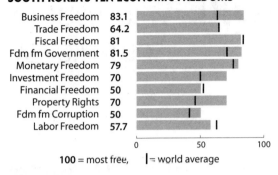

Business Freedom	83.1
Trade Freedom	64.2
Fiscal Freedom	81
Fdm fm Government	81.5
Monetary Freedom	79
Investment Freedom	70
Financial Freedom	50
Property Rights	70
Fdm fm Corruption	50
Labor Freedom	57.7

0   50   100

100 = most free, | = world average

BUSINESS FREEDOM — *83.1%*

Starting a business takes an average of 22 days, compared to the world average of 48 days. Obtaining a business license is simple, and closing a business is easy. The regulatory process has improved over the years, but bureaucracy and lack of transparency can still hinder entrepreneurial activities. The overall freedom to start, operate, and close a business is protected by the national regulatory environment.

TRADE FREEDOM — *64.2%*

South Korea's weighted average tariff rate was 7.9 percent in 2005. Prohibitive tariffs, non-transparent and restrictive regulations and standards, import restrictions, import taxes, weak enforcement of intellectual property rights, export subsidies, and services market access barriers add to the cost of trade. Consequently, an additional 20 percent is deducted from South Korea's trade freedom score to account for these non-tariff barriers.

FISCAL FREEDOM — *81%*

South Korea has a high income tax rate but a moderate corporate tax rate. The top income tax rate is 38.5 percent (a 35 percent income tax rate plus a 10 percent resident surcharge), and the top corporate tax rate is 27.5 percent (a 25 percent income tax rate plus a 10 percent resident surcharge). Other taxes include a value-added tax (VAT), a special excise tax, and a property tax. In the most recent year, overall tax revenue as a percentage of GDP was 24.6 percent.

FREEDOM FROM GOVERNMENT — *81.5%*

Total government expenditures in South Korea, including consumption and transfer payments, are modest. In the most recent year, government spending equaled 28.1 percent of GDP, and the government received 0.19 percent of its total revenues from state-owned enterprises and government ownership of property. There were 32 state-owned enterprises as of January 2006.

MONETARY FREEDOM — *79%*

Inflation in South Korea is moderate, averaging 3 percent between 2003 and 2005. Relatively unstable prices explain most of the monetary freedom score. The government regulates or controls prices in certain sectors, including agriculture, telecommunications, and other utilities; pharmaceuticals and medical services; and some energy prod-

ucts. Consequently, an additional 10 percent is deducted from South Korea's monetary freedom score to account for these policies.

INVESTMENT FREEDOM — *70%*

The Foreign Investment Promotion Act of November 1998 and other reforms substantially opened South Korea's economy to foreign investment, but media, electric power, and certain agricultural sectors remain partially closed. The government has removed restrictions on foreign investors that acquire companies through mergers and acquisitions. In August 2005, the government eased regulations and expanded tax incentives. Both residents and non-residents may hold foreign exchange accounts. Payments, transactions, transfers, or repatriation of profits are subject to reporting requirements or restrictions on amounts permitted for specified periods.

FINANCIAL FREEDOM — *50%*

South Korea has one of the most advanced and sophisticated financial systems among the world's fast-growing economies. Foreign banks own majority stakes in four of the eight major commercial banks and account for roughly one-third of banking assets. The government has been selling its shares in private banks but retains some ownership positions, including a majority of the second largest domestic bank. The post office network offers some banking services and personal insurance products and is a major participant in both sectors. The government still owns the Korea Development Bank, Export–Import Bank of Korea, Industrial Bank of Korea, Industrial Bank of Korea, National Agricultural Co-operative Federation, and National Federation of Fisheries Co-operatives. Supervision and transparency remain insufficient. There are numerous restrictions on ownership of financial institutions. The insurance sector is large and well developed, and foreign insurers are prominent. Capital markets are deep and sophisticated.

PROPERTY RIGHTS — *70%*

Private property is secure, and expropriation is highly unlikely. However, the justice system can be inefficient and slow. Contracts are often considered as a matter of consensus that allows for flexibility. Strict adherence to contract terms is difficult.

FREEDOM FROM CORRUPTION — *50%*

Corruption is perceived as present. South Korea ranks 40th out of 158 countries in Transparency International's Corruption Perceptions Index for 2005.

LABOR FREEDOM — *57.7%*

The labor market operates under restrictive employment regulations that hinder employment and productivity growth. The non-salary cost of employing a worker is high, and dismissing a redundant employee is relatively costly. Regulations related to increasing or contracting the number of work hours are not flexible.

KUWAIT

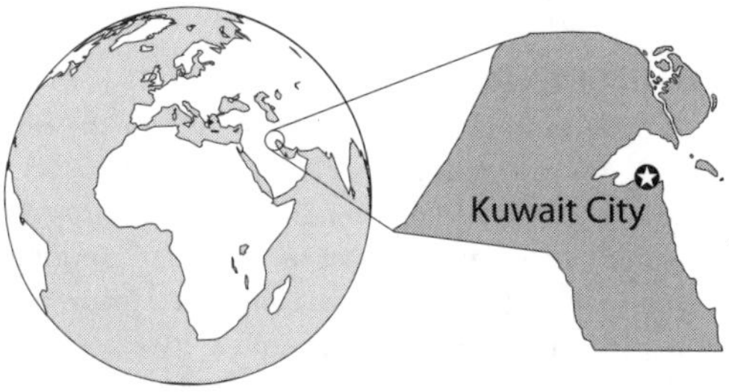

Kuwait City

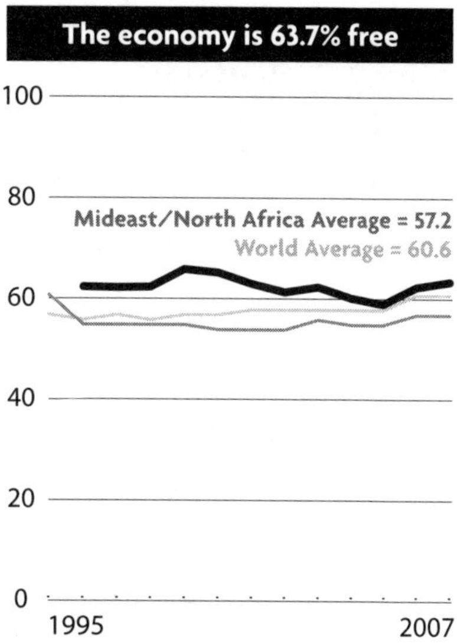

K uwait's economy is 63.7 percent free, according to our 2007 assessment, which makes it the world's 57th freest economy. Its overall score is 1.1 percentage points higher than last year, partially reflecting new methodological detail. Kuwait is ranked 5th out of 17 countries in the Middle East/North Africa region, and its overall score is much higher than the regional average.

Kuwait scores highly in fiscal freedom, labor freedom, and monetary freedom. There is no income tax, but corporate tax rates on foreign businesses can be high. Kuwait is a major energy producer, and overall tax revenue relative to GDP is not high. Low inflation boosts its monetary freedom score. The labor market is fairly flexible.

Economic freedom is weak in several areas, including freedom from government, property rights, and freedom from corruption. Government spending is relatively high, and a significant amount of revenue is received from state-owned businesses. Corruption is a problem, though less so than in many other developing nations. Property rights cannot be guaranteed because the courts are heavily influenced by the government and reportedly favor Kuwaiti nationals over foreigners.

BACKGROUND: Kuwait, an Arab constitutional monarchy that gained its independence from Britain in 1961, is endowed with billions of barrels of oil reserves—roughly 10 percent of the world's oil supply. Oil accounts for nearly 50 percent of GDP and 95 percent of export revenues. The Al-Sabah dynasty has used state-owned oil revenues to build a modern infrastructure and cradle-to-grave welfare system for Kuwait's small population. Former Prime Minister Sabah al-Ahmad al-Jabr al-Sabah was chosen as amir in January 2006 and remains committed to cautious economic reforms, but he faces opposition from Islamist and populist members of parliament.

How Do We Measure Economic Freedom? See Chapter 3 (page 37) for an explanation of the methodology or visit the *Index* Web site at *heritage.org/index*.

The economy is 63.7% free

100

80

Mideast/North Africa Average = 57.2
World Average = 60.6

60

40

20

0

1995   2007

QUICK FACTS

Population: 2.5 million

GDP (PPP): $47.7 billion
6.2% growth in 2004
5.9% 5-yr. comp. ann. growth
$19,384 per capita

Unemployment: 3.4% (2003 Kuwaiti nationals)

Inflation (CPI): 1.2%

FDI (net inflow): $1.9 billion

Official Development Assistance:
Multilateral: $0.4 million
Bilateral: $2 million (0% from the U.S.)

External Debt: $16.1 billion (2005 estimate)

Exports: $33.5 billion
Primarily oil and refined products, fertilizers

Imports: $18.5 billion
Primarily food, construction materials, vehicles and parts, clothing

KUWAIT'S TEN ECONOMIC FREEDOMS

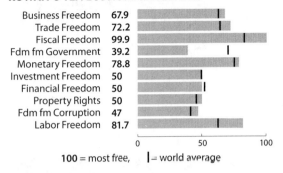

Business Freedom	67.9
Trade Freedom	72.2
Fiscal Freedom	99.9
Fdm fm Government	39.2
Monetary Freedom	78.8
Investment Freedom	50
Financial Freedom	50
Property Rights	50
Fdm fm Corruption	47
Labor Freedom	81.7

0   50   100

100 = most free, | = world average

BUSINESS FREEDOM — 67.9%

Starting a business takes an average of 35 days, compared to the world average of 48 days. Entrepreneurship should be easier for maximum job creation. Obtaining a business license and closing a business can be relatively simple. Bureaucracy and lack of transparency are persistent problems. The overall freedom to start, operate, and close a business is relatively well protected by the national regulatory environment.

TRADE FREEDOM — 72.2%

Kuwait's weighted average tariff rate was 3.9 percent in 2002. Prohibitive tariffs, import bans, inefficient customs implementation, restrictive and burdensome regulations and standards, service market access barriers, and weak enforcement of intellectual property rights all add to the cost of trade. Consequently, an additional 20 percent is deducted from Kuwait's trade freedom score to account for these non-tariff barriers.

FISCAL FREEDOM — 99.9%

Kuwait does not levy a tax on individual income or domestic business income. Foreign-owned firms and joint ventures are the only businesses subject to corporate income tax, which can be as high as 55 percent. The National Assembly recently rejected a proposal to cut the corporate tax rate to 15 percent, but other proposals to reform the tax code are still being considered. In the most recent year, overall tax revenue (mainly from customs duties and taxes on transfers of property) was 1.6 percent of GDP.

FREEDOM FROM GOVERNMENT — 39.2%

Total government expenditures in Kuwait, including consumption and transfer payments, are high. In the most recent year, government spending equaled 35.2 percent of GDP, and the government received 95.6 percent of its total revenues from state-owned enterprises and government ownership of property.

MONETARY FREEDOM — 78.8%

Inflation in Kuwait is moderate, averaging 3.1 percent between 2003 and 2005. Relatively moderate prices explain most of the monetary freedom score. The government provides some subsidies and controls prices through state-owned utilities and enterprises, including telecommunications, ports, and transportation. Consequently, an additional 10 percent is deducted from Kuwait's monetary freedom score to account for these policies.

INVESTMENT FREEDOM — 50%

Kuwait is open to some types of foreign investment, but there are significant restrictions. Foreign investors may own 100 percent of investments in infrastructure projects such as water, power, waste water treatment, or communications; investment and exchange companies; insurance companies; information technology and software development; hospitals and pharmaceuticals; air, land, and sea freight; tourism, hotels, and entertainment; and housing projects and urban development. Kuwait still restricts foreign investment in the upstream petroleum sector. Residents and non-residents may hold foreign exchange accounts, and there are no restrictions or controls on payments, transactions, transfers, or repatriation of profits.

FINANCIAL FREEDOM — 50%

Kuwait has a well-developed financial system by regional standards. Seven commercial banks, including one operating on Islamic banking principles, were operating in 2005. The government retains stakes in a number of these commercial banks, acquired after the 1982 stock market crash, but maintains its intent to divest these assets. Kuwait also has three government-owned specialized banks that provide medium- and long-term financing. Foreign investors are permitted to own 100 percent of Kuwaiti banks, subject to approval. The government has permitted foreign banks to open branches under 2004 banking legislation, but strict restrictions still apply. Capital markets are relatively well developed, and stock market trading is vigorous.

PROPERTY RIGHTS — 50%

The constitution provides for an independent judiciary, but the amir appoints all judges. The majority of the judges are non-citizens, and renewal of their appointments is subject to government approval. Foreign residents involved in legal disputes with citizens frequently claim that the courts demonstrate a bias in favor of citizens. Trials are lengthy.

FREEDOM FROM CORRUPTION — 47%

Corruption is perceived as significant. Kuwait ranks 45th out of 158 countries in Transparency International's Corruption Perceptions Index for 2005.

LABOR FREEDOM — 81.7%

The labor market operates under flexible employment regulations that can enhance employment and productivity growth. The non-salary cost of employing a worker is moderate, but dismissing a redundant employee can be costly. The labor force dominates Kuwait's public sector. Different labor codes define working conditions in the public and private sectors. For example, there is no minimum wage in the private sector, but there is one in the public sector.

2007 Index of Economic Freedom

KYRGYZ REPUBLIC

Bishkek

The Kyrgyz Republic's economy is 59.9 percent free, according to our 2007 assessment, which makes it the world's 79th freest economy. Its overall score is 3 percentage points lower than last year, partially reflecting new methodological detail. The Kyrgyz Republic is ranked 12th out of 30 countries in the Asia–Pacific region, and its overall score is equal to the regional average.

Fiscal freedom and labor freedom in the Kyrgyz Republic score highly, while monetary freedom, trade freedom, and freedom from government somewhat less highly. The labor system is very flexible; despite some remaining restrictions, the implementation of a new labor code has helped to tailor employment to free-market conditions. The top income and corporate tax rates are low, although the government imposes other taxes as well. Government expenditure is also moderate.

The Kyrgyz Republic's investment freedom, property rights, and freedom from corruption are weak. Foreign investment in virtually all sectors faces hurdles, not so much from outright restrictions as from bureaucratic incompetence and opaque regulatory enforcement. The weak rule of law allows for significant corruption and insecure property rights.

BACKGROUND: The Kyrgyz Republic was once part of the U.S.S.R. The popular, autocratic President Askar Akayev ruled the nation from 1990 until 2005. In March 2005, violent protests over fraudulent parliamentary elections brought Kurmanbek Bakiyev to power. His presidency was cemented by a June 2005 election and a power-sharing agreement with rival Feliks Kulov, now the prime minister. The government has made significant progress in market reforms, including privatization and trade liberalization, but political turmoil is worsening. The country is landlocked, with underdeveloped agricultural and industrial sectors, and has had difficulty attracting significant foreign investment. GDP growth in the past two years has been strong, but the Kyrgyz Republic remains saddled with a large external debt and heavy dependence on foreign aid.

How Do We Measure Economic Freedom? See Chapter 3 (page 37) for an explanation of the methodology or visit the *Index* Web site at *heritage.org/index*.

The economy is 59.9% free

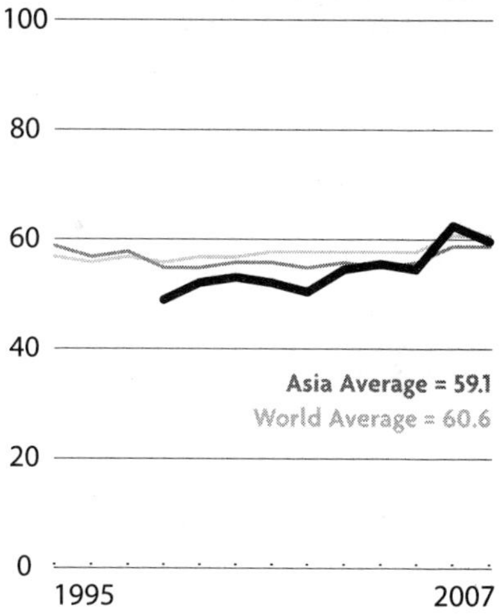

Asia Average = 59.1
World Average = 60.6

1995 — 2007

QUICK FACTS

Population: 5.1 million

GDP (PPP): $9.9 billion
7.0% growth in 2004
4.9% 5-yr. comp. ann. growth
$1,935 per capita

Unemployment: 10.4%

Inflation (CPI): 4.1%

FDI (net inflow): $250.3 million

Official Development Assistance:
Multilateral: $149 million
Bilateral: $147 million (27% from the U.S.)

External Debt: $2.1 billion

Exports: $942.1 million
Primarily cotton, wool, meat, tobacco, gold, mercury, uranium, natural gas, hydropower, machinery, shoes

Imports: $1.1 billion
Primarily oil and gas, machinery and equipment, chemicals, food

KYRGYZ REPUBLIC'S TEN ECONOMIC FREEDOMS

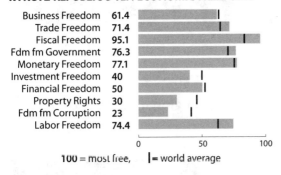

Business Freedom	61.4
Trade Freedom	71.4
Fiscal Freedom	95.1
Fdm fm Government	76.3
Monetary Freedom	77.1
Investment Freedom	40
Financial Freedom	50
Property Rights	30
Fdm fm Corruption	23
Labor Freedom	74.4

100 = most free, | = world average

BUSINESS FREEDOM — 61.4%

Starting a business takes an average of 21 days, compared to the world average of 48 days. Obtaining a business license is not always easy, and closing a business can be difficult. Lack of transparency and inconsistent application of commercial codes plague the business environment. The overall freedom to start, operate, and close a business is only partially protected by the national regulatory environment.

TRADE FREEDOM — 71.4%

The Kyrgyz Republic's weighted average tariff rate was 4.3 percent in 2003. Import taxes, burdensome regulations, restrictive licensing and sanitary and phytosanitary rules, and a customs process that is inefficiently implemented and corrupt all add to the cost of trade. Consequently, an additional 20 percent is deducted from the Kyrgyz Republic's trade freedom score to account for these non-tariff barriers.

FISCAL FREEDOM — 95.1%

The Kyrgyz Republic implemented tax reductions in 2006. Both the income tax rate and the corporate tax rate are a flat 10 percent, down from 20 percent. Other taxes include a value-added tax (VAT) and a land tax. In the most recent year, overall tax revenue as a percentage of GDP was 23.1 percent.

FREEDOM FROM GOVERNMENT — 76.3%

Total government expenditures in the Kyrgyz Republic, including consumption and transfer payments, are moderate. In the most recent year, government spending equaled 27.6 percent of GDP, and the government received 17.9 percent of its total revenues from state-owned enterprises and government ownership of property.

MONETARY FREEDOM — 77.1%

Inflation in the Kyrgyz Republic is moderate, averaging 4.2 percent between 2003 and 2005. Relatively moderate and unstable prices explain most of the monetary freedom score. Most price controls and subsidies have been eliminated, but the government regulates or influences prices through state-owned industries, including electricity, agriculture, telecommunications, water, and energy. Consequently, an additional 5 percent is deducted from the Kyrgyz Republic's monetary freedom score to account for these policies.

INVESTMENT FREEDOM — 40%

The Kyrgyz Republic has opened most of its economy to foreign investment, has adopted guarantees against expropriation or nationalization, and permits investors to bid on privatized firms. Licensing and approval procedures are not transparent, and contracts are not enforced effectively. Foreign corporations may not purchase land. Residents and non-residents may hold foreign exchange accounts. There are no restrictions on payments and transfers, but most capital transactions must be registered with the relevant government authority or are subject to controls.

FINANCIAL FREEDOM — 50%

The Kyrgyz Republic's financial system is improving, but it remains underdeveloped. There are 18 commercial banks and a settlement-saving company, all but three of them private, and a large number of credit unions. Government officials may not own or control over 5 percent of any bank. There are 66 microcredit institutions that provide most of the credit used by small and medium enterprises. There are no limits on foreign ownership of banks and microcredit institutions. Eleven banks have foreign participation, including two fully foreign-owned banks. Foreign-controlled banks account for about half of banking assets. The nominally independent central bank has improved supervision and established minimum capital requirements for banks. Although the state dominates the insurance sector, several companies provide private insurance services. Capital markets are limited and centered on the small stock exchange.

PROPERTY RIGHTS — 30%

The legal system does not protect private property sufficiently. Contracts are not fully enforced. Individual investors have become involved in disputes over licensing, registration, and enforcement of contracts. Corruption is a serious problem.

FREEDOM FROM CORRUPTION — 23%

Corruption is perceived as widespread. The Kyrgyz Republic ranks 130th out of 158 countries in Transparency International's Corruption Perceptions Index for 2005.

LABOR FREEDOM — 74.4%

The labor market operates under relatively flexible employment regulations that could be improved to enhance employment and productivity growth. The non-salary cost of employing a worker is high, but dismissing a redundant employee is not difficult. The labor code reform adopted in 2004 has been recognized as a key step toward increasing labor market flexibility.

LAOS

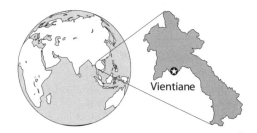

Vientiane

The Laotian economy is 49.1 percent free, according to our 2007 assessment, which makes it the world's 140th freest economy. Its overall score is 2.4 percentage points higher than last year, partially reflecting new methodological detail. Laos is ranked 26th out of 30 countries in the Asia–Pacific region, and its overall score is much lower than the regional average.

Laos scores well in freedom from government and fiscal freedom. Income and corporate tax rates are high, but overall tax revenue is relatively small as a percentage of GDP. Government spending is also fairly low, and the government does not receive a large amount of its income from state-owned businesses.

As an avowedly Communist nation, Laos could improve in most areas of economic freedom. Business freedom, investment freedom, financial freedom, property rights, and freedom from corruption all receive low scores. Business regulations hinder entrepreneurship, and enforcement is in the hands of an opaque bureaucracy. Rule of law does not operate independently of political influence, and corruption is rampant. The average tariff rate is high, and there are substantial non-tariff barriers.

BACKGROUND: Laos is one of the world's few remaining Communist nations but has slowly been adopting some market reforms. The borders of modern Laos were set by a treaty between France and Thailand in 1907, though the Laotian monarchy was established five centuries earlier. The current Communist government came to power in 1975 and immediately imposed a rigid socialist economic program. Change began in 1986 with the loosening of restrictions on private enterprise. Laos has experienced high economic growth since 1988 but continues to be hampered by a poor national infrastructure. As a final affront to Communist orthodoxy, Laos has recently begun formal negotiations to join the World Trade Organization.

How Do We Measure Economic Freedom? See Chapter 3 (page 37) for an explanation of the methodology or visit the *Index* Web site at *heritage.org/index*.

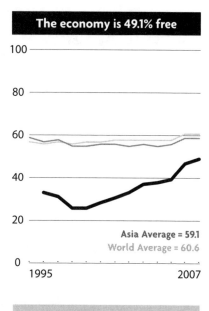

The economy is 49.1% free

Asia Average = 59.1
World Average = 60.6

QUICK FACTS

Population: 5.8 million

GDP (PPP): $11.3 billion
6.4% growth in 2004
6.0% 5-yr. comp. ann. growth
$1,954 per capita

Unemployment: 2.4% (2005 estimate)

Inflation (CPI): 10.5%

FDI (net inflow): $17 million (gross)

Official Development Assistance:
Multilateral: $116 million
Bilateral: $182 million (2% from the U.S.)

External Debt: $2.1 billion

Exports: $361.0 million
Primarily garments, wood products, coffee, electricity, tin

Imports: $506.0 million
Primarily machinery and equipment, vehicles, fuel, consumer goods

LAOS'S TEN ECONOMIC FREEDOMS

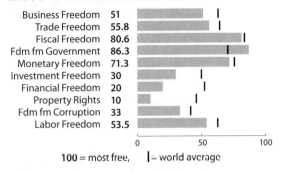

Business Freedom	51
Trade Freedom	55.8
Fiscal Freedom	80.6
Fdm fm Government	86.3
Monetary Freedom	71.3
Investment Freedom	30
Financial Freedom	20
Property Rights	10
Fdm fm Corruption	33
Labor Freedom	53.5

100 = most free, I = world average

BUSINESS FREEDOM — 51%

Starting a business takes an average of 163 days, compared to the world average of 48 days. Entrepreneurship should be easier for maximum job creation. Obtaining a business license is relatively simple, but closing a business can be very difficult. Lack of transparency and inconsistent interpretation of commercial laws are still problems for investors. The overall freedom to start, operate, and close a business is restricted by the national regulatory environment.

TRADE FREEDOM — 55.8%

Laos's weighted average tariff rate was 12.1 percent in 2004. The government has made progress in liberalizing the trade regime and improving customs procedures, but a corrupt customs process, prohibitive tariffs, import bans, import restrictions, import taxes, and weak enforcement of intellectual property rights still add to the cost of trade. Consequently, an additional 20 percent is deducted from Laos's trade freedom score to account for these non-tariff barriers.

FISCAL FREEDOM — 80.6%

Laos has high tax rates. The top income tax rate is 40 percent, and the top corporate tax rate is 35 percent. Other taxes include a vehicle tax and a tax on insurance contracts. In the most recent year, overall tax revenue as a percentage of GDP was 9.6 percent.

FREEDOM FROM GOVERNMENT — 86.3%

Total government expenditures in Laos, including consumption and transfer payments, are low. In the most recent year, government spending equaled 19 percent of GDP, and the government received 15.8 percent of its total revenues from state-owned enterprises and government ownership of property. Laos has been making progress on reforming state-owned enterprises, but remaining government enterprises take a large share of the non-performing loans.

MONETARY FREEDOM — 71.3%

Inflation in Laos is high, averaging 8.8 percent between 2003 and 2005. Relatively high and unstable prices explain most of the monetary freedom score. There are no formal laws governing the pricing of products or services, but the government influences many prices through state-owned

enterprises and utilities and sets the price of fuel products. Consequently, an additional 10 percent is deducted from Laos's monetary freedom score to account for these policies.

INVESTMENT FREEDOM — 30%

Laos's foreign investment law guarantees foreign investors that their investments will be protected, that their property will not be confiscated without compensation, that their operations will be free from government interference, and that they have the right to lease land and repatriate earnings. However, foreign investment is threatened by the country's macroeconomic instability, particularly the tendency for the currency to weaken, and the potential for deterioration in security. Both residents and non-residents may hold foreign exchange accounts, subject to certain restrictions and government approval. Some payments and transfers face quantitative restrictions. All capital transactions require central bank approval.

FINANCIAL FREEDOM — 20%

The Laotian financial system is small and subject to heavy government involvement. Supervision and regulation of financial services are weak. The banking sector is the most important part of the financial system. Three state-owned banks dominate the banking sector, accounting for about 70 percent of assets. There are 10 private and foreign banks, but their activities are limited. The government extensively directs credit. The banking sector is hindered by non-performing loans, predominantly from state-owned banks to state-owned enterprises. Microfinance has a small presence. Capital markets are primitive.

PROPERTY RIGHTS — 10%

The judiciary is not independent. Foreign investors are generally advised to seek arbitration outside of Laos, since the domestic arbitration authority lacks the ability to enforce its decisions. Corruption is a serious problem, and judges can be bribed.

FREEDOM FROM CORRUPTION — 33%

Corruption is perceived as significant. Laos ranks 77th out of 158 countries in Transparency International's Corruption Perceptions Index for 2005.

LABOR FREEDOM — 53.5%

The labor market operates under restrictive employment regulations that hinder employment and productivity growth. The non-salary cost of employing a worker is low, but dismissing a redundant employee can be both costly and difficult. Increasing or modifying the number of work hours can be burdensome. The government raised the official minimum wage in 2005.

LATVIA

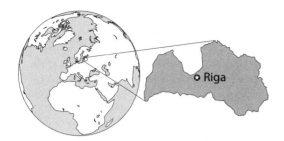

○ Riga

Latvia's economy is 68.2 percent free, according to our 2007 assessment, which makes it the world's 41st freest economy. Its overall score is 1 percentage point lower than last year, partially reflecting new methodological detail. Latvia is ranked 22nd out of 41 countries in the European region, and its overall score is equal to the regional average.

Latvia scores well in most areas of economic freedom, including business freedom, trade freedom, fiscal freedom, investment freedom, and financial freedom. Top income and corporate tax rates are low, and business regulation is relatively light. In accordance with the European Union standard, the average tariff is low. Investment in Latvia is welcome, with a few restrictions. The financial sector is modern and subject to few intrusive regulations.

Latvia can improve its freedom from government, property rights, and freedom from corruption. Total government spending is high, although not as high as in other EU states. The judiciary is somewhat inefficient, with a significant backlog of cases, but this is due more to slow jurisprudence than to corruption.

BACKGROUND: Latvia regained its independence when the Soviet Union collapsed in 1991, and it joined the EU in 2004. Its economy, including financial and transportation services, banking, electronic manufacturing, and dairy, is developing quickly, and GDP has grown rapidly as a result. However, political leaders have objected strongly to the construction of a North European Gas Pipeline, being planned by Germany and Russia, which would bypass Latvia and other Baltic states. Latvia's May 2005 admission to the European Exchange Rate Mechanism has further aligned its economy with that of the euro zone.

How Do We Measure Economic Freedom? See Chapter 3 (page 37) for an explanation of the methodology or visit the *Index* Web site at *heritage.org/index*.

The economy is 68.2% free

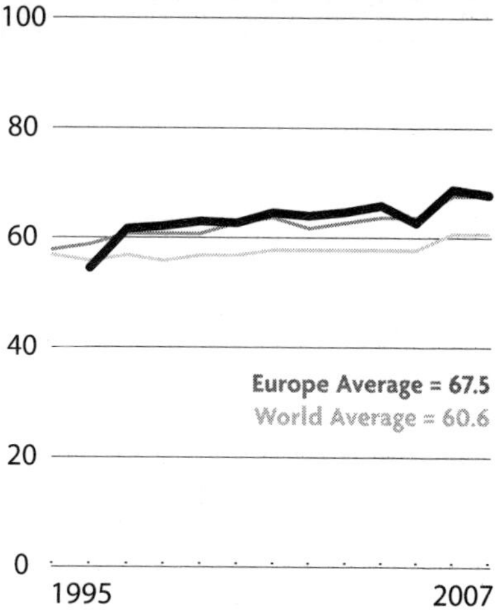

Europe Average = 67.5
World Average = 60.6

QUICK FACTS

Population: 2.3 million

GDP (PPP): $27.0 billion
8.5% growth in 2004
7.7% 5-yr. comp. ann. growth
$11,653 per capita

Unemployment: 8.5%

Inflation (CPI): 6.2%

FDI (net inflow): $538 million

Official Development Assistance:
Multilateral: $135 million
Bilateral: $29 million (11% from the U.S.)

External Debt: $12.7 billion

Exports: $6.0 billion
Primarily wood and wood products, machinery and equipment, metals, textiles, food

Imports: $8.2 billion
Primarily machinery and equipment, chemicals, fuels, vehicles

LATVIA'S TEN ECONOMIC FREEDOMS

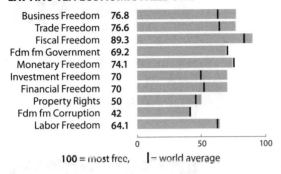

Business Freedom	76.8
Trade Freedom	76.6
Fiscal Freedom	89.3
Fdm fm Government	69.2
Monetary Freedom	74.1
Investment Freedom	70
Financial Freedom	70
Property Rights	50
Fdm fm Corruption	42
Labor Freedom	64.1

0   50   100

100 = most free, **|** = world average

BUSINESS FREEDOM — *76.8%*

Starting a business takes an average of 16 days, compared to the world average of 48 days. Entrepreneurship is easy and encourages maximum job creation. Obtaining a business license is relatively simple, but closing a business can be difficult. The overall freedom to start, operate, and close a business is relatively well protected by the national regulatory environment.

TRADE FREEDOM — *76.6%*

Latvia's trade policy is the same as those of other members of the European Union. The common EU weighted average tariff rate was 1.7 percent in 2005. Various non-tariff barriers are reflected in EU and Latvian government policy, including agricultural and manufacturing subsidies, regulatory and licensing restrictions, and other market access restrictions. Consequently, an additional 20 percent is deducted from Latvia's trade freedom score to account for these non-tariff barriers.

FISCAL FREEDOM — *89.3%*

Latvia has a moderate income tax rate and a low corporate tax rate. The income tax rate is a flat 25 percent, and the corporate tax rate is 15 percent. Other taxes include a value-added tax (VAT) and a real estate tax. In the most recent year, overall tax revenue as a percentage of GDP was 27.5 percent.

FREEDOM FROM GOVERNMENT — *69.2%*

Total government expenditures in Latvia, including consumption and transfer payments, are high. In the most recent year, government spending equaled 35.9 percent of GDP, and the government received 2.2 percent of its total revenues from state-owned enterprises and government ownership of property.

MONETARY FREEDOM — *74.1%*

Inflation in Latvia is relatively high, averaging 6.3 percent between 2003 and 2005. Relatively unstable prices explain most of the monetary freedom score. As a participant in the EU's Common Agricultural Policy, the government subsidizes agricultural production, distorting the prices of agricultural products. The government also regulates rents, utility rates, transportation, and energy prices and influences prices through state-owned enterprises. Con-

sequently, 10 percent is deducted from Latvia's monetary freedom score to account for these policies.

INVESTMENT FREEDOM — *70%*

Latvia welcomes foreign investment, and foreigners receive equal treatment. The government has no screening process. Bureaucratic obstacles include poor availability of information on government procedures and the insufficient professionalism of many civil servants. Foreign investors may not hold controlling shares in companies involved in security services, air transport, or raffles and gambling interests. Foreign investors may own land for agricultural or forestry purposes but only subject to prerequisites. Both residents and non-residents may hold foreign exchange accounts. There are no restrictions or controls on payments, transactions, transfers, or repatriation of profits.

FINANCIAL FREEDOM — *70%*

Latvia has a modern financial sector with substantial foreign participation. Supervision is prudent, and regulations are transparent, straightforward, and focused on minimum accounting and financial standards, minimum capital requirements, restrictions on exposure, and open foreign exchange positions. There were 23 commercial banks operating in 2004. The top 10 banks accounted for about 80 percent of banking assets. Approximately half of banking assets was controlled by foreign-owned banks. Foreign banks receive domestic treatment, and bank formation faces few barriers. The government owns one bank that accounts for over 4 percent of bank assets. The insurance sector is small and was composed of about 20 companies in 2004. The largest insurer is majority foreign-owned. Capital markets are small, but the stock exchange is part of a regional network of exchanges that includes Nordic and most Baltic countries.

PROPERTY RIGHTS — *50%*

Latvia's constitution provides for an independent judiciary, which in practice is inefficient. There are long delays in court hearings and enforcement of decisions. Some judges are not well trained.

FREEDOM FROM CORRUPTION — *42%*

Corruption is perceived as significant. Latvia ranks 51st out of 158 countries in Transparency International's Corruption Perceptions Index for 2005.

LABOR FREEDOM — *64.1%*

The labor market operates under relatively flexible employment regulations that could be improved to enhance employment and productivity growth. The non-salary cost of employing a worker is high, but dismissing a redundant employee is costless. There are rigid regulations on increasing or modifying the number of work hours.

LEBANON

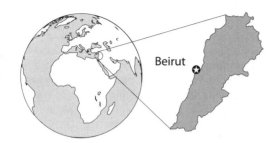

Beirut

Rank: 77

Regional Rank: 9 of 17

Lebanon's economy is 60.3 percent free, according to our 2007 assessment, which makes it the world's 77th freest economy. Its overall score is 1.8 percentage points higher than last year, partially reflecting new methodological detail. Lebanon is ranked 9th out of 17 countries in the Middle East/North Africa region, and its overall score is slightly higher than the regional average.

Lebanon's economy has strong fiscal freedom, monetary freedom, financial freedom, and labor freedom. The top income and corporate tax rates are low, and inflation is very low. The financial sector is well developed for the region, with an array of private banks and services. The labor market is highly flexible.

Business freedom, investment freedom, property rights, and freedom from corruption are all areas in which Lebanon could improve. Intrusive bureaucracy makes closing a business difficult, and the generally chaotic regulatory regime deters foreign capital. Corruption is rampant, and fair adjudication of property rights cannot be guaranteed because the courts are subject to singificant influence from the security services and the police.

BACKGROUND: Lebanon gained its independence from France in 1943 and developed one of the Middle East's most advanced economies. As a trading and international banking center, it was known as "the Switzerland of the Middle East" until the disastrous 1975–1990 civil war. Syria intervened with a stranglehold on Lebanese politics that continued until it was forced to withdraw in 2005 after being implicated in the February assassination of former Prime Minister Rafiq Hariri. Prime Minister Fuad Siniora has pledged to carry out economic reforms, but the Hezbollah-instigated conflict with Israel in 2006 will undoubtedly haunt the economy for years to come. Lebanon's huge $26 billion foreign debt will pose an obstacle to reconstruction as well.

How Do We Measure Economic Freedom? See Chapter 3 (page 37) for an explanation of the methodology or visit the *Index* Web site at *heritage.org/index*.

The economy is 60.3% free

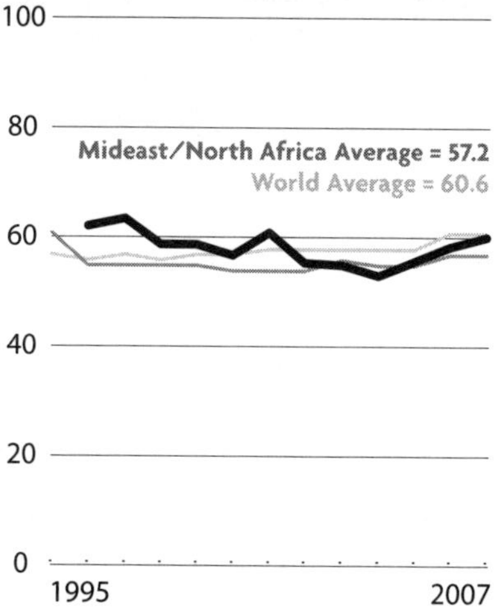

Mideast/North Africa Average = 57.2
World Average = 60.6

(Graph showing values from 1995 to 2007, y-axis 0 to 100)

QUICK FACTS

Population: 3.5 million

GDP (PPP): $20.7 billion
6.0% growth in 2004
3.8% 5-yr. comp. ann. growth
$5,837 per capita

Unemployment: 20% (2000 estimate)

Inflation (CPI): 3.0%

FDI (net inflow): $242.7 million

Official Development Assistance:
Multilateral: $146 million
Bilateral: $153 million (19% from the U.S.)

External Debt: $22.2 billion

Exports: $1.8 billion
Primarily jewelry, inorganic chemicals, consumer goods, fruit, tobacco, construction minerals, electric power machinery and switchgear, textile fibers

Imports: $9.1 billion
Primarily petroleum products, cars, medicinal products, clothing, meat, live animals, consumer goods, paper, textile fabrics, tobacco

LEBANON'S TEN ECONOMIC FREEDOMS

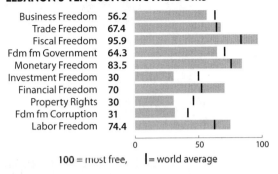

Business Freedom	56.2
Trade Freedom	67.4
Fiscal Freedom	95.9
Fdm fm Government	64.3
Monetary Freedom	83.5
Investment Freedom	30
Financial Freedom	70
Property Rights	30
Fdm fm Corruption	31
Labor Freedom	74.4

0   50   100

100 = most free, | = world average

BUSINESS FREEDOM — 56.2%

Starting a business takes an average of 46 days, compared to the world average of 48 days. Entrepreneurship should be easier for maximum job creation. Obtaining a business license is relatively simple, but closing a business is very difficult. Bureaucracy and lack of transparency are persistent problems. The overall freedom to start, operate, and close a business is restricted by the national regulatory environment.

TRADE FREEDOM — 67.4%

Lebanon's weighted average tariff rate was 6.3 percent in 2002. The government maintains import bans, restrictive licensing rules, quotas, and burdensome sanitary and phytosanitary regulations that add to the cost of trade, as does corruption. Consequently, an additional 20 percent is deducted from Lebanon's trade freedom score to account for these non-tariff barriers.

FISCAL FREEDOM — 95.9%

Lebanon has low tax rates. The top income tax rate is 20 percent, and the top corporate tax rate is 15 percent. Other taxes include a value-added tax (VAT) and a capital gains tax. In the most recent year, tax revenue as a percentage of GDP was 16.9 percent.

FREEDOM FROM GOVERNMENT — 64.3%

Total government expenditures in Lebanon, including consumption and transfer payments, are moderate. In the most recent year, government spending equaled 34.5 percent of GDP, and the government received 23.8 percent of its total revenues from state-owned enterprises and government ownership of property. Privatization has been stalled since 2000.

MONETARY FREEDOM — 83.5%

Inflation in Lebanon is low, averaging 1.1 percent between 2003 and 2005. Relatively low and stable prices explain most of the monetary freedom score. The government influences prices through state-owned enterprises and subsidies and controls the prices of bread, petroleum derivatives, pharmaceuticals, and electricity. Consequently, an additional 10 percent is deducted from Lebanon's monetary freedom score to account for these policies.

INVESTMENT FREEDOM — 30%

Lebanon welcomes foreign investment, although with some restrictions, particularly in real estate, insurance, media companies, and banks. Red tape and corruption, arbitrary licensing decisions, archaic legislation, and an ineffectual judicial system are serious impediments to foreign investment. Residents and non-residents may hold foreign exchange accounts, but central bank approval is required to purchase treasury securities, money market instruments, and derivatives, and some credit operations are prohibited. All foreigners must obtain a license from the government to acquire real estate. There are no restrictions on payments and transfers.

FINANCIAL FREEDOM — 70%

Lebanon's financial sector is one of the region's most liberal and sophisticated. There are few restrictions on domestic bank formation and few barriers to foreign banks. Financial regulations are transparent, and credit is allocated to all investors on market terms. The five largest commercial banks accounted for over 60 percent of total banking assets in 2004. Non-performing loans were estimated to exceed 25 percent at the end of September 2004. Private-sector borrowers complain about being crowded out of the market because much bank credit goes to the government. There are more than 70 insurance firms, and regulations have been passed to tighten supervision and establish minimum capital requirements to address a problem with small, undercapitalized firms that charge low premiums but rarely pay claims.

PROPERTY RIGHTS — 30%

The judiciary is significantly influenced by the security services and the police. The government-appointed prosecuting magistrate exerts considerable influence over judges by, for example, recommending verdicts and sentences. Trials, particularly commercial cases, drag for years.

FREEDOM FROM CORRUPTION — 31%

Corruption is perceived as significant. Lebanon ranks 83rd out of 158 countries in Transparency International's Corruption Perceptions Index for 2005.

LABOR FREEDOM — 74.4%

The labor market operates under restrictive employment regulations that could be improved to enhance employment and productivity growth. The non-salary cost of employing a worker can be high, and dismissing a redundant employee is relatively costly. Regulations on increasing or contracting the number of work hours are flexible.

LESOTHO

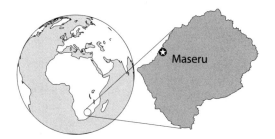

Maseru

Rank: 118

Regional Rank: 23 of 40

Lesotho's economy is 54.1 percent free, according to our 2007 assessment, which makes it the world's 118th freest economy. Its overall score is 2.8 percentage points lower than last year, partially reflecting new methodological detail. Lesotho is ranked 23rd out of 40 countries in the sub-Saharan Africa region, and its overall score is equal to the regional average.

Lesotho does not rank strongly in any category, but it does enjoy moderate levels of business freedom, monetary freedom, and labor freedom. High top income tax and top corporate tax rates are supplemented by additional taxes. Inflation is moderate, although the government intervenes in the price structure of certain goods. The labor market is flexible.

Lesotho faces substantial economic challenges that are common among poor African countries. Its trade freedom, freedom from government, investment freedom, property rights, and freedom from corruption are all weak. The country's average tariff rate is high, and non-tariff barriers to trade are significant. Regulation is oppressive, and business operations are significantly impeded by red tape. Government spending is also far too high. Property rights are not secured by an independent judiciary, and corruption is a problem.

BACKGROUND: Lesotho sells water and electricity to South Africa, and over half of all households depend on agriculture or migrant labor, primarily miners that work in South Africa. King Letsie III is head of state but has no executive authority. Prime Minister Pakalitha Mosisili and his party control a significant parliamentary majority. The government supports privatization and an improved business environment. Under the African Growth and Opportunity Act, Lesotho has become the largest African exporter of garments to the United States, but expiration of the Multi-Fiber Arrangement will hurt the textile sector. HIV/AIDS is a serious concern.

How Do We Measure Economic Freedom? See Chapter 3 (page 37) for an explanation of the methodology or visit the *Index* Web site at *heritage.org/index*.

The economy is 54.1% free

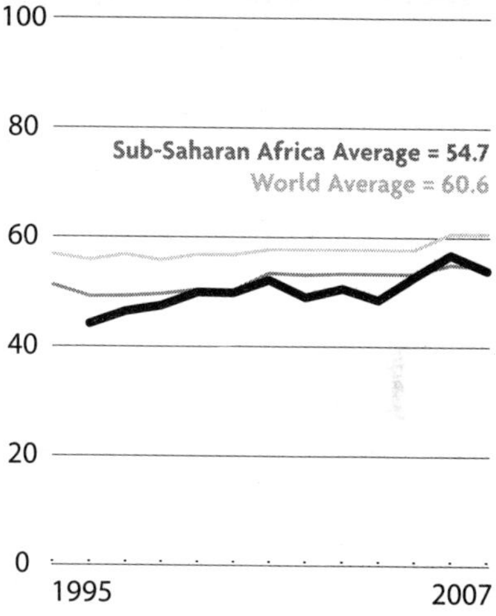

Sub-Saharan Africa Average = 54.7
World Average = 60.6

(Chart: vertical axis 0 to 100; horizontal axis 1995 to 2007)

QUICK FACTS

Population: 1.8 million

GDP (PPP): $4.7 billion
2.0% growth in 2004
2.6% 5-yr. comp. ann. growth
$2,619 per capita

Unemployment: 30% (2002 estimate)

Inflation (CPI): 5.2%

FDI (net inflow): $51.7 million

Official Development Assistance:
Multilateral: $79 million
Bilateral: $36 million (11 % from the U.S.)

External Debt: $764.0 million

Exports: $771.2 million
Primarily clothing, footwear, road vehicles, wool, mohair, food, live animals

Imports: $1.4 billion
Primarily food, building materials, vehicles, machinery, medicines, petroleum products

LESOTHO'S TEN ECONOMIC FREEDOMS

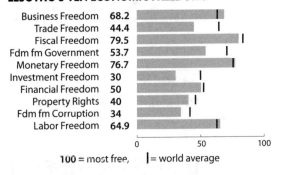

Business Freedom	68.2
Trade Freedom	44.4
Fiscal Freedom	79.5
Fdm fm Government	53.7
Monetary Freedom	76.7
Investment Freedom	30
Financial Freedom	50
Property Rights	40
Fdm fm Corruption	34
Labor Freedom	64.9

0   50   100

100 = most free, | = world average

BUSINESS FREEDOM — 68.2%

Starting a business takes an average of 73 days, compared to the world average of 48 days. Entrepreneurship should be easier for maximum job creation. Both obtaining a business license and closing a business are relatively simple. Although the regulatory framework generally lacks transparency, the overall freedom to start, operate, and close a business is relatively well protected by the national regulatory environment.

TRADE FREEDOM — 44.4%

Lesotho's weighted average tariff rate was 17.8 percent in 2001. Burdensome regulations, non-transparent and arbitrary import licensing, import bans, and import restrictions add to the cost of trade. Consequently, an additional 20 percent is deducted from Lesotho's trade freedom score to account for these non-tariff barriers.

FISCAL FREEDOM — 79.5%

Lesotho has high tax rates. The top income tax rate is 35 percent, and the top corporate tax rate for all companies other than manufacturing is 25 percent (a reduced rate of 10 percent is applicable to all manufacturing companies). Other taxes include a value-added tax (VAT) and a tax on dividends. In the most recent year, overall tax revenue as a percentage of GDP was 35 percent.

FREEDOM FROM GOVERNMENT — 53.7%

Total government expenditures in Lesotho, including consumption and transfer payments, are high. In the most recent year, government spending equaled 43.1 percent of GDP, and the government received 9 percent of its total revenues from state-owned enterprises and government ownership of property.

MONETARY FREEDOM — 76.7%

Inflation in Lesotho is moderate, averaging 4.4 percent between 2003 and 2005. Relatively moderate and unstable prices explain most of the monetary freedom score. Although many prices are freely determined in the market, the government influences prices through state-owned enterprises and utilities, especially in agriculture. Lesotho's tradition of direct government involvement has limited private-sector development in the economy, and the program for privatizing agricultural parastatals has made little headway. Consequently, an additional 10 percent is deducted from Lesotho's monetary freedom score to account for these policies.

INVESTMENT FREEDOM — 30%

Foreign investors have participated in the country's privatization program without discrimination. However, political instability and a lack of transparency discourage foreign investment. Local unrest often leads to the destruction of property owned by foreign businesses. Residents and non-residents no longer require government permission to hold foreign exchange accounts, but quantitative restrictions apply. Some payments and transfers are subject to prior government approval and limitations. Many capital transactions face restrictions or quantitative limits, and real estate purchases abroad require government approval.

FINANCIAL FREEDOM — 50%

Lesotho's small, underdeveloped financial system is closely tied to South Africa through the Common Monetary Area that also includes Namibia and Swaziland. The banking sector has four commercial banks, three of which are foreign-owned. The government privatized the Lesotho Bank in 1999 but still owns two development banks. The central bank established a Rural Credit Guarantee Fund in 2003 to encourage rural lending and established the Lesotho Post-Bank in 2005 to provide banking services to the poor and in rural areas. Non-performing loans are a legacy problem linked to historical exploitation of Lesotho Bank by politicians and lending to state-owned enterprises. Financial supervision remains insufficient. There are four insurance companies, the largest of which is 50 percent government-owned. Capital markets are marginal.

PROPERTY RIGHTS — 40%

Private property is guaranteed, and expropriation is unlikely. The judiciary is independent and has generally been allowed to carry out its role effectively, even during the years of military rule. However, draconian internal security legislation gives considerable power to the police and restricts the right of assembly and some forms of industrial action.

FREEDOM FROM CORRUPTION — 34%

Corruption is perceived as significant. Lesotho ranks 70th out of 158 countries in Transparency International's Corruption Perceptions Index for 2005.

LABOR FREEDOM — 64.9%

The labor market operates under relatively flexible employment regulations that could be improved to enhance employment and productivity growth. The non-salary cost of employing a worker is low, and dismissing a redundant employee is relatively costless. In recent years, the government has vowed to increase labor market flexibility.

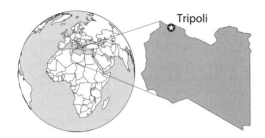
Tripoli

LIBYA

Libya's economy is 34.5 percent free, according to our 2007 assessment, which makes it the world's 155th freest economy, or third most repressed. Its overall score is 0.2 percentage point higher than last year, partially reflecting new methodological detail. Libya is ranked 17th out of 17 countries in the Middle East/North Africa region, and its overall score is much lower than the regional average.

Libya's fiscal freedom and monetary freedom are its strengths. The top income and corporate tax rates are moderate, but various surtaxes can be extremely high. Government tax revenue relative to GDP is low, perhaps because of the country's oil revenues. Inflation in Libya is also low, though price controls distort the market.

Libya has extremely low freedom in many areas. Business freedom, trade freedom, freedom from government, investment freedom, financial freedom, property rights, labor freedom, and freedom from corruption are all serious problems. Oil dominates the economy, and the government dominates the oil sector. Forming, operating, or closing a business is difficult and heavily regulated by an avowedly socialist state, which also manages the labor market inflexibly. Fairly high tariff rates and non-tariff barriers impede trade and foreign investment. Corruption is rampant, and fair adjudication of property rights is unlikely.

BACKGROUND: Oil revenues generate almost all export earnings in Libya's state-dominated economy. Despite one of Africa's highest per capita incomes, Libya has suffered from more than 30 years of socialist economic policies and international sanctions due to its role in the 1989 Lockerbie bombing. The United Nations lifted its sanctions in 2003 after Libya agreed to pay compensation to victims' families, and the U.S. lifted most of its sanctions in 2004 after Libyan leader Muammar Qadhafi abandoned his efforts to build weapons of mass destruction. The Department of State removed Libya from its list of state sponsors of terrorism in 2006.

How Do We Measure Economic Freedom? See Chapter 3 (page 37) for an explanation of the methodology or visit the *Index* Web site at *heritage.org/index*.

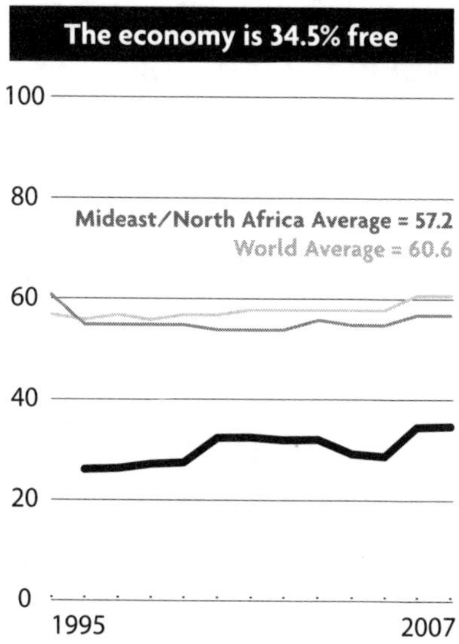

The economy is 34.5% free

Mideast/North Africa Average = 57.2
World Average = 60.6

100

80

60

40

20

0

1995   2007

QUICK FACTS

Population: 5.7 million

GDP (PPP): $65.8 billion (2005 estimate)
4.6% growth in 2004
4.5% 5-yr. comp. ann. growth
$11,400 per capita (2005 estimate)

Unemployment: 30% (2004 estimate)

Inflation (CPI): −2.2%

FDI (net inflow): $69.1 million

Official Development Assistance:
Multilateral: $7 million
Bilateral: $11 million (0.4% from the U.S.)

External Debt: $4.3 billion (2005 estimate)

Exports: $17.9 billion
Primarily crude oil, refined petroleum products, natural gas

Imports: $10.5 billion
Primarily machinery, transport equipment, semi-finished goods, food, consumer products

LIBYA'S TEN ECONOMIC FREEDOMS

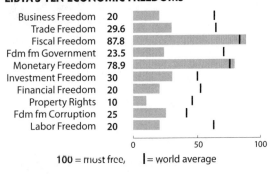

Business Freedom	20	
Trade Freedom	29.6	
Fiscal Freedom	87.8	
Fdm fm Government	23.5	
Monetary Freedom	78.9	
Investment Freedom	30	
Financial Freedom	20	
Property Rights	10	
Fdm fm Corruption	25	
Labor Freedom	20	

100 = most free, | = world average

BUSINESS FREEDOM — 20%

Libya still has a planned economy, although the private sector has been developing in recent years. A one-stop window has been established to simplify the business application process, and approval can now be obtained within 30 days. However, government regulations are applied randomly and still significantly impede the creation of new businesses. The freedom to start, operate, and close a business is significantly restricted by the national regulatory environment.

TRADE FREEDOM — 29.6%

Libya's weighted average tariff rate was 25.2 percent in 2002. Import restrictions, burdensome and non-transparent regulation, and customs corruption add to the cost of trade. Consequently, an additional 20 percent is deducted from Libya's trade freedom score to account for these non-tariff barriers.

FISCAL FREEDOM — 87.8%

Libya levies a top income tax rate of 15 percent on individual income from labor and any service or function, whether permanent or temporary. A jihad tax is also applied to all taxable income. For incomes over 200,000 Libyan dinars, other taxes (such as those on commercial and industrial profits) can raise the top rate to 90 percent. The top corporate tax rate is 40 percent. Oil companies are subject to special provisions. Libya has no value-added tax (VAT) or inheritance tax. In the most recent year, overall tax revenue as a percentage of GDP was 2.4 percent.

FREEDOM FROM GOVERNMENT — 23.5%

Total government expenditures in Libya, including consumption and transfer payments, are very high. In the most recent year, government spending equaled 44.2 percent of GDP, and the government received 92.9 percent of its total revenues from state-owned enterprises and government ownership of property. Privatization programs have been broadened, but results are not yet evident.

MONETARY FREEDOM — 78.9%

Inflation in Libya is low, averaging 0.9 percent between 2003 and 2005. Stable prices explain most of the monetary freedom score. Most prices are determined by the government through price controls and state-owned enterprises and utilities. Consequently, an additional 15 percent is deducted from Libya's monetary freedom score to account for these policies.

INVESTMENT FREEDOM — 30%

Almost all foreign direct investment is in the hydrocarbons sector. The government has partially liberalized rules on foreign investment, permitting it in limited sectors, but the regulatory and bureaucratic environment remains complex. Both residents and non-residents may hold foreign currency accounts with prior approval. Payments for authorized imports are not restricted; other payments require government approval or are subject to quantitative limits. Repatriation and most capital transactions, including transactions involving capital and money market instruments, credit operations, direct investment, and real estate, are subject to controls, including approval requirements.

FINANCIAL FREEDOM — 20%

Libya's financial system is primitive and highly centralized. The government nationalized all banks in 1970 and maintains tight control. Private ownership of financial institutions was permitted in 1993, and the first private bank since 1969 opened in 1996. An active central bank and eight other government-owned financial institutions dominate the sector. There is no coherent plan to privatize state banks, although the government has mentioned it as a goal. Legislation passed in 2005 permits foreign banks to open branches, and three foreign banks had representative offices as of June 2006. Regulation is bureaucratic and antiquated. Transparency and supervision of state banks is very weak. There is no capital market, although the government adopted a law to establish a stock market in June 2006.

PROPERTY RIGHTS — 10%

The judiciary is not independent. The private practice of law is illegal, and all lawyers must be members of the Secretariat of Justice. There is little land ownership, and the government may re-nationalize the little private property that is granted, especially to foreign companies.

FREEDOM FROM CORRUPTION — 25%

Corruption is perceived as widespread. Libya ranks 117th out of 158 countries in Transparency International's Corruption Perceptions Index for 2005.

LABOR FREEDOM — 20%

The labor market operates under highly restrictive employment regulations that hinder employment and productivity growth. Regulations make employing and dismissing a worker difficult and costly. The government sets most wages because it employs about 70 percent of the labor force. Unemployment is a major policy issue as the pace of privatization gradually increases.

LITHUANIA

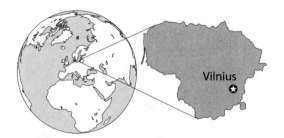

Vilnius

Lithuania's economy is 72 percent free, according to our 2007 assessment, which makes it the world's 22nd freest economy. Its overall score is 1 percentage point lower than last year, partially reflecting new methodological detail. Lithuania is ranked 14th out of 41 countries in the European region, and its overall score is higher than the regional average.

Lithuania scores well in most areas of economic freedom, including business freedom, trade freedom, fiscal freedom, monetary freedom, investment freedom, and financial freedom. Top income and corporate tax rates are low. Business regulation is simple. Investment in Lithuania is welcome, and foreign capital is subject to the same rules as domestic capital. The financial sector is advanced, regionally integrated, and subject to few intrusive regulations.

Lithuania could improve its labor freedom, property rights, and freedom from corruption. Labor restrictions are inflexible, and despite the fact that foreign investment is generally welcome, complicated regulations are a deterrent. The judiciary has a significant backlog of cases because of slow jurisprudence.

BACKGROUND: In 1993, Russian troops withdrew from Lithuania, and the country won its independence, followed by membership in the European Union and NATO. In May 2006, the four-party ruling coalition that had come to power in the October 2004 election collapsed following the decision of the Labor Party to withdraw its support. With more than 80 percent of its enterprises now privatized, Lithuania continues to navigate the transition from a command economy to a market economy successfully.

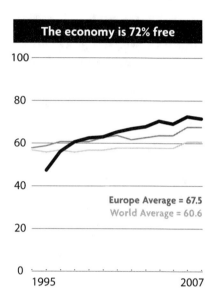

The economy is 72% free

Europe Average = 67.5
World Average = 60.6

1995 — 2007

QUICK FACTS

Population: 3.4 million

GDP (PPP): $45.0 billion
7.0% growth in 2004
7.1% 5-yr. comp. ann. growth
$13,107 per capita

Unemployment: 6.8%

Inflation (CPI): 1.2%

FDI (net inflow): $510.4 million

Official Development Assistance:
Multilateral: $219 million
Bilateral: $43 million (12% from the U.S.)

External Debt: $9.5 billion

Exports: $11.8 billion
Primarily mineral products, textiles, clothing, machinery and equipment, chemicals, wood, wood products, food

Imports: $13.3 billion
Primarily mineral products, machinery and equipment, transport equipment, chemicals, textiles, clothing, metals

How Do We Measure Economic Freedom? See Chapter 3 (page 37) for an explanation of the methodology or visit the *Index* Web site at *heritage.org/index*.

LITHUANIA'S TEN ECONOMIC FREEDOMS

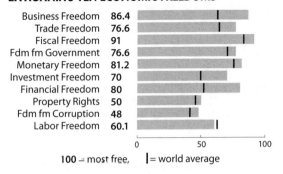

Business Freedom	86.4
Trade Freedom	76.6
Fiscal Freedom	91
Fdm fm Government	76.6
Monetary Freedom	81.2
Investment Freedom	70
Financial Freedom	80
Property Rights	50
Fdm fm Corruption	48
Labor Freedom	60.1

0   50   100

100 = most free, | = world average

BUSINESS FREEDOM — 86.4%

Starting a business takes an average of 26 days, compared to the world average of 48 days. The relatively sound business environment has encouraged entrepreneurial activities. Obtaining a business license is relatively simple, and closing a business is easy. The overall freedom to start, operate, and close a business is protected by the national regulatory environment.

TRADE FREEDOM — 76.6%

Lithuania's trade policy is the same as those of other members of the European Union. The common EU weighted average tariff rate was 1.7 percent in 2005. Various non-tariff barriers are reflected in EU and Lithuanian government policy, including agricultural and manufacturing subsidies, regulatory and licensing restrictions, and other market access restrictions. The government implements restrictive pharmaceutical and biotechnology regulations, as well as burdensome procurement rules, and the enforcement of intellectual property rights is weak. Consequently, an additional 20 percent is deducted from Lithuania's trade freedom score to account for these non-tariff barriers.

FISCAL FREEDOM — 91%

Lithuania has a moderate income tax rate and a low corporate tax rate. The income tax rate is a flat 27 percent (scheduled to be reduced to 24 percent effective January 2008), and the corporate tax rate is 15 percent. Other taxes include a value-added tax (VAT), a land tax, and a road tax. In the most recent year, overall tax revenue as a percentage of GDP was 19.8 percent.

FREEDOM FROM GOVERNMENT — 76.6%

Total government expenditures in Lithuania, including consumption and transfer payments, are moderate. In the most recent year, government spending equaled 31.2 percent of GDP, and the government received 2 percent of its total revenues from state-owned enterprises and government ownership of property.

MONETARY FREEDOM — 81.2%

Inflation in Lithuania is low, averaging 2 percent between 2003 and 2005. Relatively stable prices explain most of the monetary freedom score. As a participant in the EU's Common Agricultural Policy, the government subsidizes agricultural production, distorting the prices of agricul-

tural products. The government also regulates rents, electricity rates, and some energy prices and influences prices through state-owned enterprises. Consequently, 10 percent is deducted from Lithuania's monetary freedom score to account for these policies.

INVESTMENT FREEDOM — 70%

Foreign companies are accorded the same treatment as domestic firms. All sectors of the economy are open to foreign investment, with the exception of the security and defense sectors. Activities involving increased danger to human life, health, environment, manufacturing, or trade in weapons require permission or a license. Complex regulations and procedures are continuing problems for investors. Residents may hold foreign exchange accounts. There are no controls or restrictions on repatriation of profits, current transfers, or payments. Some capital transactions must be registered with the central bank, and there are limits on open foreign exchange positions by banks.

FINANCIAL FREEDOM — 80%

Lithuania's financial system is advanced and tightly intertwined with those of its Scandinavian neighbors. The banking system is stable and regulated according to European Union standards. Non-EU banks must be approved by the central bank. Restrictions on financial transactions are minimal under a universal banking model. Credit is allocated on market terms. The three largest banks account for over 70 percent of banking assets. Most commercial banks are foreign-owned, and foreign-owned banks accounted for over 90 percent of banking capital in 2004. Privatization of the last remaining state-owned bank was completed in 2002, and the state held less than 1 percent of banking assets at the end of 2005. The insurance sector is also dominated by foreign firms. Capital markets are well developed but small. The stock exchange is part of a regional network of exchanges that includes Nordic and most Baltic countries.

PROPERTY RIGHTS — 50%

Accession to the EU has played a major role in encouraging reforms in Lithuania's judicial system, including strengthening its independence and streamlining proceedings to clear up the backlog of criminal cases. Investors still complain that judicial enforcement of contracts is weak.

FREEDOM FROM CORRUPTION — 48%

Corruption is perceived as significant. Lithuania ranks 44th out of 158 countries in Transparency International's Corruption Perceptions Index for 2005.

LABOR FREEDOM — 60.1%

The labor market operates under restrictive employment regulations that hinder employment and productivity growth. The non-salary cost of employing a worker can be very high, but dismissing a redundant employee is relatively costless. Restrictions on increasing or modifying the number of work hours are rigid.

LUXEMBOURG

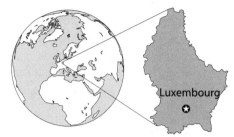

Luxembourg

Luxembourg's economy is 79.3 percent free, according to our 2007 assessment, which makes it the world's 8th freest economy. Its overall score is 1 percentage point lower than last year, partially reflecting new methodological detail. Luxembourg is ranked 3rd out of 41 countries in the European region, and its overall score is much higher than the regional average.

Luxembourg has high levels of investment freedom, trade freedom, financial freedom, property rights, business freedom, and monetary freedom. The average tariff rate is low (though non-tariff barriers include EU subsidies), and business regulation is efficient. Virtually all commercial operations are simple and transparent. The government has instituted a streamlined registration for all new businesses. Inflation is fairly low. Foreign investment in Luxembourg is welcome, although subject to government licensing in some sectors. The financial sector is highly developed and is regarded as a global financial hub that maintains depositor secrecy. The judiciary, independent of politics and free of corruption, has an exemplary ability to protect property rights.

Luxembourg could do slightly better in freedom from government. Total government spending equals more than two-fifths of GDP but is still lower than that of some other EU member countries.

BACKGROUND: Luxembourg is a founding member of the European Union and, despite a deceleration in per capita GDP in recent years, maintains one of the world's highest income levels. During the 20th century, it evolved into a manufacturing and services economy. With a financial services industry that accounts for about one-third of GDP, Luxembourg is Europe's principal center for mutual funds and a major force in the banking and insurance industries. It possesses a skilled workforce and well-developed infrastructure. There are no restrictions that apply specifically to foreign investors, and the regulatory structure is liberal and transparent.

How Do We Measure Economic Freedom? See Chapter 3 (page 37) for an explanation of the methodology or visit the *Index* Web site at *heritage.org/index*.

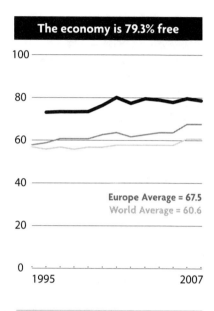

The economy is 79.3% free

Europe Average = 67.5
World Average = 60.6

QUICK FACTS

Population: 0.5 million

GDP (PPP): $31.7 billion
4.5% growth in 2004
4.1% 5-yr. comp. ann. growth
$69,961 per capita

Unemployment: 4.3% (2004 estimate)

Inflation (CPI): 2.2%

FDI (net inflow): −$2.0 billion

Official Development Assistance:
Multilateral: None
Bilateral: None

External Debt: n/a

Exports: $46.9 billion
Primarily machinery and equipment, steel products, chemicals, rubber products, glass

Imports: $37.9 billion
Primarily minerals, metals, food, quality consumer goods

257

LUXEMBOURG'S TEN ECONOMIC FREEDOMS

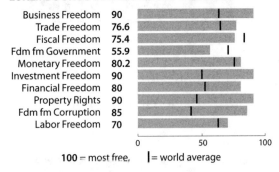

Business Freedom	90
Trade Freedom	76.6
Fiscal Freedom	75.4
Fdm fm Government	55.9
Monetary Freedom	80.2
Investment Freedom	90
Financial Freedom	80
Property Rights	90
Fdm fm Corruption	85
Labor Freedom	70

100 = most free, | = world average

BUSINESS FREEDOM — 90%

The process for establishing a business in Luxembourg is simple and straightforward. The government's one-stop-shopping system for business registration applies to foreign and domestic enterprises alike. Regulations are fair, transparent, and applied evenly in most cases. The overall freedom to start, operate, and close a business is well protected by the national regulatory environment.

TRADE FREEDOM — 76.6%

Luxembourg's trade policy is the same as those of other members of the European Union. The common EU weighted average tariff rate was 1.7 percent in 2005. Various non-tariff barriers are reflected in EU and Luxembourg government policy, including agricultural and manufacturing subsidies, regulatory and licensing restrictions, and other market access restrictions. Consequently, an additional 20 percent is deducted from Luxembourg's trade freedom score to account for these non-tariff barriers.

FISCAL FREEDOM — 75.4%

Luxembourg has a high income tax rate but a low corporate tax rate. The top income tax rate is 38.95 percent (38 percent plus a 2.5 percent surcharge), and the top corporate tax rate is 22.9 percent (including a 4 percent employment fund contribution). Municipal business tax rates vary. Other taxes include a value-added tax (VAT) and a wealth tax. In the most recent year, overall tax revenue as a percentage of GDP was 40.6 percent.

FREEDOM FROM GOVERNMENT — 55.9%

Total government expenditures in Luxembourg, including consumption and transfer payments, are high. In the most recent year, government spending equaled 43.2 percent of GDP, and the government received 1.7 percent of its total revenues from state-owned enterprises and government ownership of property.

MONETARY FREEDOM — 80.2%

Luxembourg is a member of the euro zone. Inflation in Luxembourg is low, averaging 2.4 percent between 2003 and 2005. Relatively stable prices explain most of the monetary freedom score. As a participant in the EU's Common Agricultural Policy, the government subsidizes agricultural production, distorting the prices of agricultural products. The government also regulates electricity rates and some fuel prices and influences prices through state-owned enterprises. Consequently, 10 percent is deducted from Luxembourg's monetary freedom score to account for these policies.

INVESTMENT FREEDOM — 90%

Luxembourg has a very open foreign investment regime. Foreign and domestic businesses receive equal treatment, and there are no local content requirements. Non–European Economic Area banks need a license from the Commission de Surveillance du Secteur Financier to set up a branch or subsidiary. The government restricts investments that directly affect national security. Both residents and non-residents may hold foreign exchange accounts. There are no restrictions or barriers with respect to capital transactions or current transfers, repatriation of profits, purchase of real estate, or access to foreign exchange.

FINANCIAL FREEDOM — 80%

Luxembourg has a sophisticated and well-developed financial sector that serves as a global financial hub. Supervision is strong, and regulations are transparent and undemanding. Banking is one of Luxembourg's largest industries, and the banking system is highly competitive. Banking secrecy is legally enforced. At the end of January 2006, Luxembourg had 155 banks from over 20 different countries. Of the world's 50 leading banks, 30 have subsidiaries in Luxembourg. Banks operate as universal banks, offering an unrestricted range of activities. The one state-owned bank, Société Nationale de Crédit et d'Investissement (SNCI), offers medium- and long-term financing of investments made by Luxembourg-based companies. Credit is allocated on market terms. Foreign investors may freely access credit domestically. There has been a withholding tax on interest from bank accounts held by non residents since July 2005.

PROPERTY RIGHTS — 90%

Private property is well protected in Luxembourg. Contractual agreements are strongly secured, and the judiciary is of high quality.

FREEDOM FROM CORRUPTION — 85%

Corruption is perceived as minimal. Luxembourg ranks 13th out of 158 countries in Transparency International's Corruption Perceptions Index for 2005.

LABOR FREEDOM — 70%

The labor market operates under somewhat flexible employment regulations that could be improved to enhance employment and productivity growth. Structural unemployment has been increasing in recent years. Generous unemployment benefits, which are almost twice as high as those in neighboring countries, pose a challenge to labor market flexibility. Luxembourg's minimum wage is the highest in the EU.

MACEDONIA

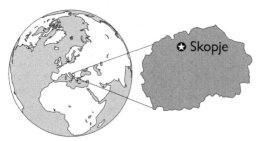

● Skopje

Rank: 71

Regional Rank: 32 of 41

Macedonia's economy is 60.8 percent free, according to our 2007 assessment, which makes it the world's 71st freest economy. Its overall score is 0.2 percentage point higher than last year, partially reflecting new methodological detail. Macedonia is ranked 32nd out of 41 countries in the European region, and its overall score is lower than the regional average.

Macedonia has high levels of fiscal freedom and monetary freedom. Personal and corporate income tax rates are very low, but total tax revenue is somewhat high as a percentage of GDP. Inflation is low. The government is pushing forward efforts to reduce its influence on the price of market goods, although some (like electricity) are distorted by state-owned businesses.

Macedonia faces many challenges, including weak freedom from government, investment freedom, property rights, and freedom from corruption. Government expenditures are high, although state-owned businesses do not account for a significant portion of total revenue. The court system is prone to corruption, political interference, and inefficiency, partially as a result of the country's political turmoil.

BACKGROUND: Since gaining its independence from the former Yugoslavia in 1991, Macedonia has faced a troublesome political and economic transition. Following civil strife in 2001, the Ohrid Agreement prevented an all-out civil war by giving greater recognition to the Albanian minority within a unitary state. Under the guidance of Prime Minister Vlado Buckovski, Macedonia has made great strides toward gaining membership in both the European Union and NATO. The principal exports include clothing, iron, and steel, but the high level of informal economic activity remains a concern.

How Do We Measure Economic Freedom? See Chapter 3 (page 37) for an explanation of the methodology or visit the *Index* Web site at *heritage.org/index*.

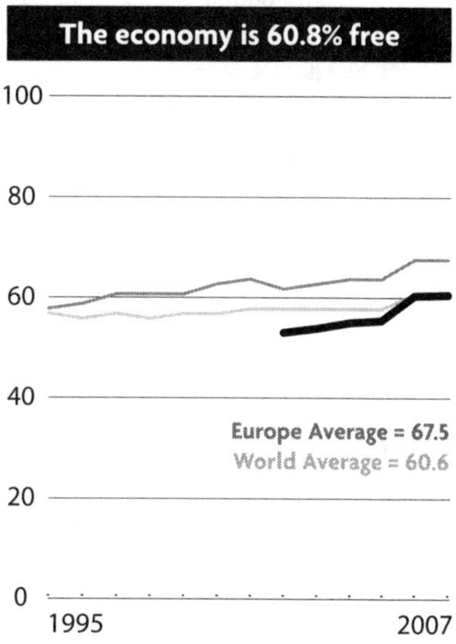

The economy is 60.8% free

Europe Average = 67.5
World Average = 60.6

1995 — 2007

QUICK FACTS

Population: 2 million

GDP (PPP): $13.4 billion
4.1% growth in 2004
1.5% 5-yr. comp. ann. growth
$6,610 per capita

Unemployment: 37.2% (end 2004)

Inflation (CPI): 1.0%

FDI (net inflow): $150.1 million

Official Development Assistance:
Multilateral: $96 million
Bilateral: $173 million (31% from the U.S.)

External Debt: $2.0 billion

Exports: $2.1 billion
Primarily food, beverages, tobacco, miscellaneous manufactures, iron and steel

Imports: $3.2 billion
Primarily machinery and equipment, automobiles, chemicals, fuels, food products

MACEDONIA'S TEN ECONOMIC FREEDOMS

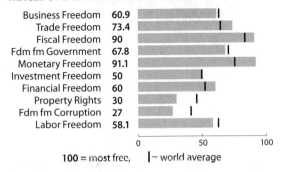

Business Freedom	60.9
Trade Freedom	73.4
Fiscal Freedom	90
Fdm fm Government	67.8
Monetary Freedom	91.1
Investment Freedom	50
Financial Freedom	60
Property Rights	30
Fdm fm Corruption	27
Labor Freedom	58.1

0   50   100

100 = most free, | = world average

BUSINESS FREEDOM — 60.9%

Starting a business takes an average of 18 days, compared to the world average of 48 days, encouraging entrepreneurship. Obtaining a business license is relatively simple, but closing a business can be very difficult. Although the government has made some effort to establish a regulatory system to promote competitiveness, poor and inconsistent enforcement of commercial legislation remains a problem. The overall freedom to start, operate, and close a business is restricted by the national regulatory environment.

TRADE FREEDOM — 73.4%

Macedonia's weighted average tariff rate was 3.3 percent in 2005. Import taxes, import and export quotas, import restrictions, non-transparent regulations and standards, and corruption in the customs process all add to the cost of trade. Consequently, an additional 20 percent is deducted from Macedonia's trade freedom score to account for these non-tariff barriers.

FISCAL FREEDOM — 90%

Macedonia enjoys low tax rates. The top income tax rate is 18 percent, and the top corporate tax rate is 15 percent. Other taxes include a value-added tax (VAT) and a property transfer tax. In the most recent year, overall tax revenue as a percentage of GDP was 30.8 percent.

FREEDOM FROM GOVERNMENT — 67.8%

Total government expenditures in Macedonia, including consumption and transfer payments, are high. In the most recent year, government spending equaled 36.1 percent of GDP, and the government received 5.5 percent of its total revenues from state-owned enterprises and government ownership of property. The government has almost completed the privatization of small and medium-sized enterprises, but this has not resulted in considerable progress toward sound corporate governance.

MONETARY FREEDOM — 91.1%

Inflation in Macedonia is extraordinarily low, averaging 0.4 percent between 2003 and 2005. Such stable prices explain most of the monetary freedom score. Most prices are determined in the market, and the government is continuing to privatize state-owned firms, but the government still retains an influence on certain prices through state-owned enterprises and utilities, such as electricity. Consequently,

an additional 5 percent is deducted from Macedonia's monetary freedom score to account for these policies.

INVESTMENT FREEDOM — 50%

Macedonia grants foreign and domestic investors equal treatment and permits non-residents to invest in domestic firms, except in arms manufacturing. Foreign investors may also acquire state-owned firms that are slated for privatization. Political instability, however, weakens the business environment. Residents may hold foreign exchange accounts with approval from the central bank, and non-residents may hold foreign exchange accounts subject to some restrictions. Payments and transfers face few controls and restrictions. Most capital and money market activities require the approval of or must be registered with the government. Residents are generally not permitted to buy real estate abroad.

FINANCIAL FREEDOM — 60%

Although Macedonia has adopted reforms aimed at strengthening the financial sector, it remains relatively weak. Supervision and regulation are insufficient. The financial system is dominated by the banking sector. Macedonia has 20 banks, 15 savings houses, and one state-owned bank. Savings banks are restricted and may not offer banking operations to companies. The private sector controls about 90 percent of banking assets. Foreign-owned banks may establish branches or representative offices and control over half of banking assets. The banking sector is highly concentrated, with three banks accounting for about 70 percent of assets. The insurance industry is small and included seven companies in 2004, the largest being the former state-owned insurer. The stock exchange is small.

PROPERTY RIGHTS — 30%

Protection of property in Macedonia is weak. The executive improperly influences the judiciary. The country is slowly trying to harmonize its judicial standards with those of the EU. The lack of an effective rule of law is a crucial impediment to economic development.

FREEDOM FROM CORRUPTION — 27%

Corruption is perceived as widespread. Macedonia ranks 103rd out of 158 countries in Transparency International's Corruption Perceptions Index for 2005.

LABOR FREEDOM — 58.1%

The labor market operates under restrictive employment regulations that hinder employment and productivity growth. The non-salary cost of employing a worker is very high, but dismissing a redundant employee can be easy. Regulations related to increasing or contracting the number of work hours are rigid. In an effort to increase labor market flexibility, Macedonia's parliament passed new legislation on labor relations in 2005.

MADAGASCAR

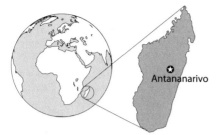
Antananarivo

M adagascar's economy is 61.4 percent free, according to our 2007 assessment, which makes it the world's 65th freest economy. Its overall score is 1.6 percentage points lower than last year, partially reflecting new methodological detail. Madagascar is ranked 7th out of 40 countries in the sub-Saharan Africa region, and its overall score is well above the regional average.

Madagascar enjoys high levels of fiscal freedom, freedom from government, trade freedom, property rights, and investment freedom. Personal income and corporate income tax rates are moderate, and overall tax revenue is fairly low as a percentage of GDP. Foreign investment in Madagascar is welcome. Despite some regulatory burdens, foreigners may own 100 percent of many businesses. Government expenditures are moderate, and state-owned businesses account for virtually no tax revenue.

Economic development in Madagascar is hurt by a lack of freedom in several areas. Labor freedom and freedom from corruption are weak, as are financial freedom and business freedom. As in many other sub-Saharan African nations, Madagascar's judiciary is underdeveloped and subject to the political whims of the executive. In addition, businesses are subject to an inefficient bureaucracy that is prone to corruption.

BACKGROUND: Madagascar has recovered from its 2001–2002 political crisis, in which both opposition candidate Marc Ravalomanana and former military dictator and president Didier Ratsiraka claimed victory. (Ratsiraka eventually fled to exile in France.) Madagascar is a poor nation with a history of anti-market economic policies, but economic growth has been strong in recent years as the government has begun to implement economic reforms. Poor weather continues to threaten the livelihood of the three-quarters of the population engaged in agriculture. Corruption, poor infrastructure, and onerous bureaucracy remain problems. The expiration the Multi-Fiber Arrangement has affected Madagascar's textile industry.

How Do We Measure Economic Freedom? See Chapter 3 (page 37) for an explanation of the methodology or visit the *Index* Web site at *heritage.org/index*.

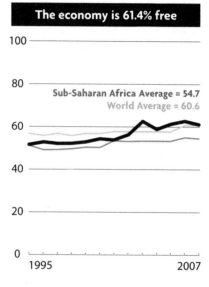

The economy is 61.4% free

Sub-Saharan Africa Average = 54.7
World Average = 60.6

QUICK FACTS

Population: 18.1 million

GDP (PPP): $15.5 billion
5.3% growth in 2004
2.3% 5-yr. comp. ann. growth
$857 per capita

Unemployment: n/a

Inflation (CPI): 13.8%

FDI (net inflow): $45 million (gross)

Official Development Assistance:
Multilateral: $599 million
Bilateral: $698 million (6% from the U.S.)

External Debt: $3.5 billion

Exports: $1.1 billion
Primarily coffee, vanilla, shellfish, sugar, cotton cloth, chromite, petroleum products

Imports: $1.7 billion
Primarily capital goods, petroleum, consumer goods, food

MADAGASCAR'S TEN ECONOMIC FREEDOMS

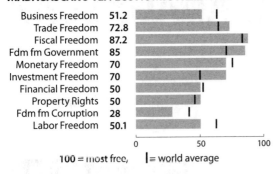

Business Freedom	51.2
Trade Freedom	72.8
Fiscal Freedom	87.2
Fdm fm Government	85
Monetary Freedom	70
Investment Freedom	70
Financial Freedom	50
Property Rights	50
Fdm fm Corruption	28
Labor Freedom	50.1

0   50   100

100 = most free, | = world average

BUSINESS FREEDOM — 51.2%

Starting a business takes an average of 21 days, compared to the world average of 48 days. Entrepreneurship should be easier for maximum job creation. Both obtaining a business license and closing a business can be very difficult. Despite the government's efforts to streamline the regulatory process, red tape and a lack of transparency remain problems. The overall freedom to start, operate, and close a business is restricted by the national regulatory environment.

TRADE FREEDOM — 72.8%

Madagascar's weighted average tariff rate was 3.6 percent in 2001. Import restrictions, import bans, sanitary and phytosanitary regulations, and a customs process that lacks transparency and is susceptible to corruption add to the cost of trade. Consequently, an additional 20 percent is deducted from Madagascar's trade freedom score to account for these non-tariff barriers.

FISCAL FREEDOM — 87.2%

Madagascar has moderate tax rates. Both the top income tax rate and the top corporate tax rate are 30 percent. Other taxes include a value-added tax (VAT) and a capital gains tax. In the most recent year, overall tax revenue as a percentage of GDP was 10.9 percent.

FREEDOM FROM GOVERNMENT — 85%

Total government expenditures in Madagascar, including consumption and transfer payments, are low. In the most recent year, government spending equaled 25.1 percent of GDP, and the government received 0.8 percent of its total revenues from state-owned enterprises and government ownership of property.

MONETARY FREEDOM — 70%

Inflation in Madagascar is high, averaging 15.6 percent between 2003 and 2005. Relatively high and unstable prices explain most of the monetary freedom score. Most prices are determined in the market, but the government retains an influence on certain prices through state-owned enterprises and utilities, such as electricity (although this influence is diminishing as the government pushes ahead with privatization). Consequently, an additional 5 percent is deducted from Madagascar's monetary freedom score to

account for these policies.

INVESTMENT FREEDOM — 70%

Foreign investors face a heavy bureaucratic burden, but the government has taken measures to improve the investment climate, such as a one-stop shop for approvals. Foreigners can also own land now. Most sectors of the economy are open to 100 percent foreign ownership. Both residents and non-residents may open foreign exchange accounts, subject to certain restrictions and government approval. There are no restrictions on payments or transfers, although profits must be repatriated within 30 days. Most capital movements with other nations require government authorization.

FINANCIAL FREEDOM — 50%

Madagascar has a small financial system that is dominated by the banking sector. The government has been pursuing banking reform, and the major banks are now partially privatized. Two new banks recently entered the sector: The locally based Compagnie Malgache de Banque was licensed in 2005, and an existing savings institution (Caisse d'Epargne de Madagascar) converted to a commercial bank. The central bank controls a third of financial sector assets. There is also an extensive network of savings and loans associations. Non-performing loans remain a problem. Six insurance companies, including two state-owned insurers and several foreign-owned companies, were operating in 2005. Capital markets are insignificant, and there is no stock market.

PROPERTY RIGHTS — 50%

The judiciary is influenced by the executive and subject to corruption. Investors face a legal and judicial environment in which neither the security of private property nor the enforcement of contracts can be guaranteed. The land titling process is very bureaucratic.

FREEDOM FROM CORRUPTION — 28%

Corruption is perceived as widespread. Madagascar ranks 97th out of 158 countries in Transparency International's Corruption Perceptions Index for 2005.

LABOR FREEDOM — 50.1%

The labor market operates under highly restrictive employment regulations that hinder employment and productivity growth. The non-salary cost of employing a worker is high, but dismissing a redundant employee can be easy. Regulations related to increasing or modifying the number of work hours are rigid.

MALAWI

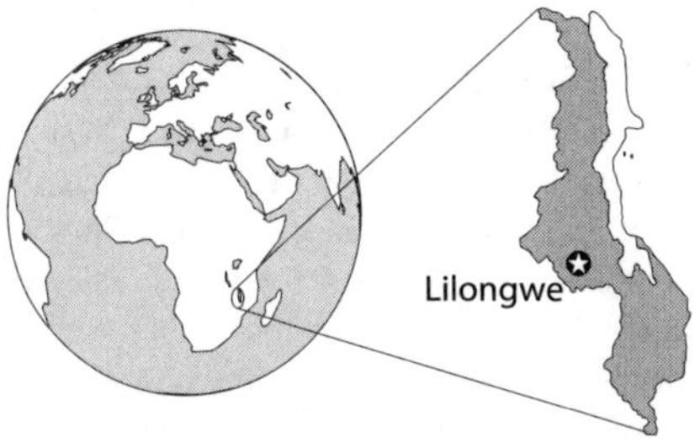

Lilongwe

Malawi's economy is 55.5 percent free, according to our 2007 assessment, which makes it the world's 106th freest economy. Its overall score is 2.4 percentage points lower than last year, partially reflecting new methodological detail. Malawi is ranked 17th out of 40 countries in the sub-Saharan Africa region, and its overall score is slightly higher than the regional average.

Malawi has a high level of labor freedom and moderate levels of investment freedom, financial freedom, and fiscal freedom. The top income tax and corporate tax rates are fairly high, but overall tax revenue is not large as a percentage of GDP. The labor market is surprisingly flexible, and employment is not heavily regulated in ways that impede job creation.

Malawi is beset by substantial economic problems that are characteristic of the region. Monetary freedom, freedom from corruption, freedom from government, and property rights are weak. Inflation in Malawi is very high, although government subsidies are not widespread. Government spending is over two fifths of GDP. A weak rule of law jeopardizes the protection of property rights, and corruption is a major problem.

BACKGROUND: Malawi is one of Africa's most densely populated countries. Its economy is hindered by bureaucracy, burdensome regulation, corruption, inadequate infrastructure, and state-owned enterprises and utilities. More than 85 percent of the population is engaged in subsistence agriculture, and recurring drought can create food shortages. Agriculture accounts for about 45 percent of gross domestic product and 90 percent of export earnings. Tobacco, tea, cotton, coffee, and sugar are the primary exports. Industrial activity is a small part of the economy, and Malawi possesses few natural resources. An estimated 15 percent of the population is infected with HIV/AIDS.

How Do We Measure Economic Freedom? See Chapter 3 (page 37) for an explanation of the methodology or visit the *Index* Web site at *heritage.org/index*.

The economy is 55.5% free

Sub-Saharan Africa Average = 54.7
World Average = 60.6

1995   2007

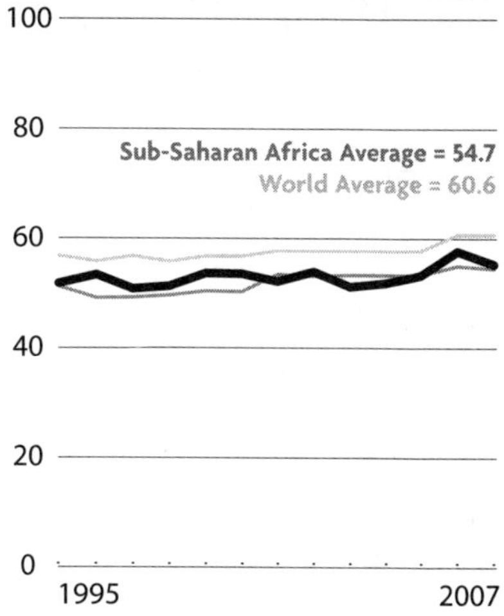

QUICK FACTS

Population: 12.6 million

GDP (PPP): $8.2 billion
5.1% growth in 2004
1.5% 5-yr. comp. ann. growth
$646 per capita

Unemployment: n/a

Inflation (CPI): 11.4%

FDI (net inflow): $16 million (gross)

Official Development Assistance:
Multilateral: $222 million
Bilateral: $332 million (17% from the U.S.)

External Debt: $3.4 billion

Exports: $483.3 million (2004 estimate)
Primarily tobacco, tea, sugar, cotton, coffee, peanuts, wood products, apparel

Imports: $613 million (2004 estimate)
Primarily food, petroleum products, semimanufactures, consumer goods, transportation equipment

MALAWI'S TEN ECONOMIC FREEDOMS

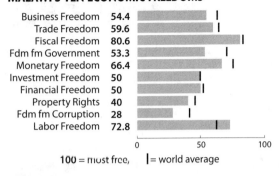

Business Freedom	54.4
Trade Freedom	59.6
Fiscal Freedom	80.6
Fdm fm Government	53.3
Monetary Freedom	66.4
Investment Freedom	50
Financial Freedom	50
Property Rights	40
Fdm fm Corruption	28
Labor Freedom	72.8

0   50   100

100 = most free, |= world average

BUSINESS FREEDOM — 54.4%

Starting a business takes an average of 37 days, compared to the world average of 48 days. Entrepreneurship should be easier for maximum job creation. Obtaining a business license is relatively simple, but closing a business can be very difficult. Red tape and bureaucratic delays are persistent problems. The overall freedom to start, operate, and close a business is restricted by the national regulatory environment.

TRADE FREEDOM — 59.6%

Malawi's weighted average tariff rate was 10.2 percent in 2001. The government has been working to liberalize the trade regime, but subsidies, export controls on maize, import and export licensing requirements, import taxes, burdensome regulations, and a customs process that can be non-transparent and corrupt add to the cost of trade. Consequently, an additional 20 percent is deducted from Malawi's trade freedom score to account for these non-tariff barriers.

FISCAL FREEDOM — 80.6%

Malawi has high tax rates. The top income tax rate is 40 percent, and the top corporate tax rate is 30 percent. Other taxes include a value-added tax (VAT) and a property tax. In the most recent year, overall tax revenue as a percentage of GDP was 20.1 percent.

FREEDOM FROM GOVERNMENT — 53.3%

Total government expenditures in Malawi, including consumption and transfer payments, are high. In the most recent year, government spending equaled 42.7 percent of GDP, and the government received 12.3 percent of its total revenues from state-owned enterprises and government ownership of property.

MONETARY FREEDOM — 66.4%

Inflation in Malawi is high, averaging 13.9 percent between 2003 and 2005. Such unstable prices explain most of the monetary freedom score. Although most prices are determined in the market, the government retains an influence on certain prices through state-owned enterprises and utilities, such as electricity, transportation, water and telecommunications; controls the prices of petroleum products and sugar; and uses subsidies to stabilize maize and fertilizer prices. Consequently, an additional 10 percent is deducted

from Malawi's monetary freedom score to account for these policies.

INVESTMENT FREEDOM — 50%

The government welcomes foreign investment. A short list of products require a license for both domestic and foreign investors, but this is not seen as an obstacle. Restrictions based on environmental, health, and national security concerns affect investment in weapons, explosives, and manufacturing that involves the treatment or disposal of hazardous waste or radioactive material. Residents may not hold foreign exchange accounts abroad. Non-residents may hold foreign exchange accounts, subject to restrictions and government approval in some cases. Some payments and transfers face quantitative limits. Most capital transactions by residents—including outward direct investment—require approval.

FINANCIAL FREEDOM — 50%

Malawi's financial sector is developing but remains unsophisticated, dominated by banking. Financial institutions offer a variety of credit instruments, generally allocated on market terms. Much bank lending goes to the government or state-owned enterprises. There were 10 full-service commercial banks and several other non-bank financial institutions in 2006. The two largest banks are the domestic National Bank of Malawi (NBM), which is half owned by the government, and Stanbic Bank (formerly known as Commercial Bank of Malawi), a subsidiary of a South African bank. The state also owns the Malawi Development Corporation, which services industry. There are 12 insurance companies, including one foreign insurer and one re-insurer. Capital markets are very small, and the stock exchange lists only 10 companies. Foreign investors are active participants in the stock market.

PROPERTY RIGHTS — 40%

Malawi's laws protect all rights to property, including real property and intellectual property. There are some reports of government intervention in some cases and frequent allegations of bribery in civil and criminal cases. Administration of the courts is weak, and due process can be very slow.

FREEDOM FROM CORRUPTION — 28%

Corruption is perceived as widespread. Malawi ranks 97th out of 158 countries in Transparency International's Corruption Perceptions Index for 2005.

LABOR FREEDOM — 72.8%

The labor market operates under relatively flexible employment regulations that could be improved to enhance employment and productivity growth. The non-salary cost of employing a worker is very low, but dismissing a redundant employee can be relatively costly. Regulations related to increasing or contracting the number of work hours are flexible.

MALAYSIA

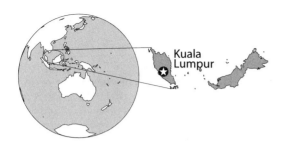

Kuala Lumpur

Malaysia's economy is 65.8 percent free, according to our 2007 assessment, which makes it the world's 48th freest economy. Its overall score is 2.1 percentage points higher than last year, partially reflecting new methodological detail. Malaysia is ranked 8th freest out of 30 countries in the Asia–Pacific region, and its overall score is higher than the regional average.

Malaysia enjoys high levels of fiscal freedom, monetary freedom, trade freedom, and labor freedom. Both the top income tax rate and the top corporate tax rate are moderate, and overall tax revenue is relatively low as a percentage of GDP. Inflation is minor, and the government does not widely distort market prices with direct subsidies. The tariff rate is fairly low, and the government has been working to eliminate some of the non-tariff barriers that impede trade. A highly flexible labor sector with simple employment procedures and no minimum wage helps businesses to stay competitive.

Malaysia suffers from weak investment freedom and weak financial freedom. Despite efforts to liberalize procedures, foreign investment is deterred by such impediments as limited voting shares in companies, enforced hiring of ethnic Malays, and case-by-case government preinvestment approval. Malaysia's financial sector is fairly well developed, but it is also subject to significant government interference and some restrictions on foreign involvement.

BACKGROUND: Malaysia's ruling political party, the United Malays National Organization, has held power in a 14-party coalition called Barisan National since 1957. Prime Minister Abdullah Badawi is expected to remain in power until the next election in 2009. Services and industry are the mainstays of the economy and provide the vast majority of employment opportunities. The Office of the U.S. Trade Representative announced on March 8, 2006, that it would initiate negotiations with Malaysia for a free trade agreement. Negotiating a comprehensive agreement is expected to be challenging for both sides.

How Do We Measure Economic Freedom? See Chapter 3 (page 37) for an explanation of the methodology or visit the *Index* Web site at *heritage.org/index*.

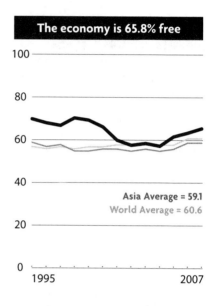

The economy is 65.8% free

Asia Average = 59.1
World Average = 60.6

QUICK FACTS

Population: 24.9 million

GDP (PPP): $255.8 billion
7.1% growth in 2004
5.2% 5-yr. comp. ann. growth
$10,276 per capita

Unemployment: 3.6%

Inflation (CPI): 1.5%

FDI (net inflow): $2.6 billion

Official Development Assistance:
Multilateral: $4 million
Bilateral: $447 million (0.2% from the U.S.)

External Debt: $52.1 billion

Exports: $118.6 billion
Primarily electronic equipment, petroleum, liquefied natural gas, wood, wood products, palm oil, rubber, textiles, chemicals

Imports: $96.8 billion
Primarily electronics, machinery, petroleum products, plastics, vehicles, iron and steel products, chemicals

MALAYSIA'S TEN ECONOMIC FREEDOMS

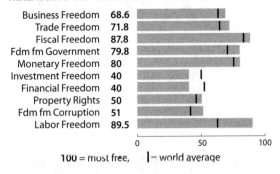

Business Freedom	68.6
Trade Freedom	71.8
Fiscal Freedom	87.8
Fdm fm Government	79.8
Monetary Freedom	80
Investment Freedom	40
Financial Freedom	40
Property Rights	50
Fdm fm Corruption	51
Labor Freedom	89.5

0   50   100

100 = most free, | = world average

BUSINESS FREEDOM — 68.6%

Starting a business takes an average of 30 days, compared to the world average of 48 days. Entrepreneurship should be easier for maximum job creation. Obtaining a business license can be difficult, but closing a business is relatively easy. The overall freedom to start, operate, and close a business is relatively well protected by the national regulatory environment.

TRADE FREEDOM — 71.8%

Malaysia's weighted average tariff rate was 4.1 percent in 2003. The government has made progress in liberalizing the trade regime, but non-automatic import licensing, import bans, burdensome regulations and standards, export licensing, non-transparent import tax rules, export subsidies, weak protection of intellectual property rights, restrictive government procurement rules, and services market access barriers add to the cost of trade. Consequently, an additional 20 percent is deducted from Malaysia's trade freedom score to account for these non-tariff barriers.

FISCAL FREEDOM — 87.8%

Malaysia has moderate tax rates. Both the top income tax rate and the top corporate tax rate are 28 percent. The government has announced that it will reduce individual and corporate tax rates when introducing a value-added tax (VAT). Other taxes include a capital gains tax and a vehicle tax. In the most recent year, overall tax revenue as a percentage of GDP was 16 percent.

FREEDOM FROM GOVERNMENT — 79.8%

Total government expenditures in Malaysia, including consumption and transfer payments, are moderate. In the most recent year, government spending equaled 26.5 percent of GDP, and the government received 11.5 percent of its revenues from state-owned enterprises and government ownership of property.

MONETARY FREEDOM — 80%

Inflation in Malaysia is relatively low, averaging 2.5 percent between 2003 and 2005. Relatively low and stable prices explain most of the monetary freedom score. Most prices are determined in the market, but the government influences certain prices through state-owned enterprises; controls the prices of petroleum products, steel, cement, wheat flour, sugar, milk, bread, and chicken meat; and

usually sets ceiling prices for an extended list of essential foods during major holidays. Consequently, an additional 10 percent is deducted from Malaysia's monetary freedom score to account for these policies.

INVESTMENT FREEDOM — 40%

Foreign investment rules have been eased over the years, but foreign investors still face such restrictions as limited voting shares, prior approval, and mandatory hiring of ethnic Malays. In September 2005, the government eased restrictions for domestic residents to buy foreign-listed securities and for foreigners to sell shares in the domestic market. Residents and non-residents may hold foreign exchange accounts, but government approval is required in many cases. Nearly all capital transactions are prohibited, are subject to restrictions, or require government approval.

FINANCIAL FREEDOM — 40%

Malaysia's financial sector is relatively well developed but subject to extensive government intervention. Of the 29 commercial banks operating as of September 2005, 10 were domestically owned and 13 were foreign-owned. Six Islamic banks (five domestic and one foreign) account for over 10 percent of baking assets. The government owns a majority of Malaysia's two largest local commercial banks. Foreign equity in banks is restricted, with participation in commercial banking limited to a maximum of 30 percent. The government influences the allocation of credit. There are several offshore banks, insurance companies, and other financial institutions. Numerous restrictions apply to the insurance industry, including restrictions on expatriate employment and foreign equity. Foreigners may trade in securities and derivatives, but foreign participation in stockbrokerages and trust management companies is restricted.

PROPERTY RIGHTS — 50%

Private property is protected in Malaysia, but the judiciary is subject to political influence. Corporate lawsuits take over a year to file. Cases are generally handled in a satisfactory manner, although many firms include a mandatory arbitration clause in their contracts.

FREEDOM FROM CORRUPTION — 51%

Corruption is perceived as present. Malaysia ranks 39th out of 158 countries in Transparency International's Corruption Perceptions Index for 2005.

LABOR FREEDOM — 89.5%

The labor market operates under flexible employment regulations that enhance employment and productivity growth. The non-salary cost of employing a worker is moderate, and dismissing a redundant employee is not difficult. The government restricts the number of expatriates that foreign and domestic firms may hire. Malaysia does not have a national minimum wage.

MALI

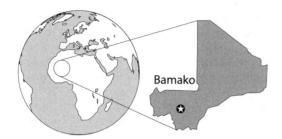

Mali's economy is 53.7 percent free, according to our 2007 assessment, which makes it the world's 123rd freest economy. Its overall score is 0.4 percentage point lower than last year, partially reflecting new methodological detail. Mali is ranked 24th out of 40 countries in the sub-Saharan Africa region, and its overall score is equal to the regional average.

Mali enjoys high levels of freedom from government and monetary freedom. Both the top income tax rate and the top corporate tax rate are high, though at a level comparable to the U.S., and government revenue from taxes is not huge compared to GDP. Government expenditures are moderately low, and there is very little income from state-owned businesses. The state controls prices on some staples, such as fuel, but on the whole does not significantly influence prices, and inflation is fairly low.

Mali has weak business freedom, financial freedom, property rights, labor freedom, and freedom from corruption. Business operations are difficult and inconsistently regulated; the country's inefficient and corrupt bureaucracy negatively affects most aspects of commercial life. Property rights are not secured by the judiciary, which is subject to political interference. The labor market is highly inflexible.

BACKGROUND: Most of the labor force in landlocked, drought-prone Mali works in agriculture and herding. Bolstered by a decade of enhanced political and social stability, including the first successful democratic transfer of power in 2002, the government has implemented policies to liberalize the economy and strengthen the investment climate. While Mali remains one of the world's poorest countries, economic growth over the past 10 years has averaged about 5 percent. Instability in the Ivory Coast affects the many Malians that live or work there. Other ongoing problems include desertification, deforestation, illiteracy, inadequate infrastructure, an inefficient judiciary, and corruption.

How Do We Measure Economic Freedom? See Chapter 3 (page 37) for an explanation of the methodology or visit the *Index* Web site at *heritage.org/index*.

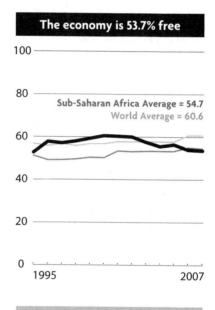

The economy is 53.7% free

Sub-Saharan Africa Average = 54.7
World Average = 60.6

QUICK FACTS

Population: 12.1 million

GDP (PPP): $13.1 billion
2.3% growth in 2004
4.4% 5-yr. comp. ann. growth
$998 per capita

Unemployment: 14.6% (2001 estimate)

Inflation (CPI): −3.1%

FDI (net inflow): $179.0 million

Official Development Assistance:
Multilateral: $311 million
Bilateral: $430 million (11% from the U.S.)

External Debt: $3.3 billion

Exports: $1.2 billion
Primarily mineral products, salt, animal products, rum, chemicals, fruit, vegetables

Imports: $1.5 billion
Primarily machinery, transport equipment, manufactures, chemicals, mineral fuels, food, live animals

MALI'S TEN ECONOMIC FREEDOMS

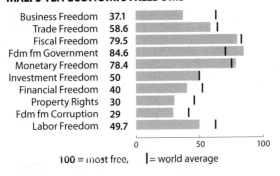

Business Freedom	37.1
Trade Freedom	58.6
Fiscal Freedom	79.5
Fdm fm Government	84.6
Monetary Freedom	78.4
Investment Freedom	50
Financial Freedom	40
Property Rights	30
Fdm fm Corruption	29
Labor Freedom	49.7

0   50   100

100 = most free, | = world average

BUSINESS FREEDOM — 37.1%

Starting a business takes an average of 42 days, compared to the world average of 48 days. Entrepreneurship should be easier for maximum job creation. Obtaining a business license is very difficult, and closing a business is difficult. Despite government efforts to improve the regulatory structure, businesses still have to deal with inconsistent application of regulations and bureaucratic delays. The overall freedom to start, operate, and close a business is significantly restricted by the national regulatory environment.

TRADE FREEDOM — 58.6%

Mali's weighted average tariff rate was 10.7 percent in 2004. Import restrictions, import bans, weak customs implementation, import licensing restrictions, and import taxes add to the cost of trade. Consequently, an additional 20 percent is deducted from Mali's trade freedom score to account for these non-tariff barriers.

FISCAL FREEDOM — 79.5%

Mali has high tax rates. The top income tax rate is 40 percent, and the top corporate tax rate is 35 percent. Other taxes include a value-added tax (VAT) and an insurance tax. In the most recent year, overall tax revenue as a percentage of GDP was 15.7 percent.

FREEDOM FROM GOVERNMENT — 84.6%

Total government expenditures in Mali, including consumption and transfer payments, are low. In the most recent year, government spending equaled 25 percent of GDP, and the government received 2.6 percent of its total revenues from state-owned enterprises and government ownership of property.

MONETARY FREEDOM — 78.4%

Inflation in Mali is moderate, averaging 3.4 percent between 2003 and 2005. Relatively moderate and unstable prices explain most of the monetary freedom score. Although most prices are determined in the market, the government retains an influence on certain prices through state-owned enterprises and utilities, such as telecommunications, and controls the price of fuel and cotton, which is one of the most important sectors of the economy. Consequently, an additional 10 percent is deducted from Mali's monetary freedom score to account for these policies.

INVESTMENT FREEDOM — 50%

The government allows for 100 percent foreign ownership of any new business. Corruption is a serious problem in procurement, where lower-rank civil workers request bribes to speed up the approval process. Residents and non-residents must obtain permission to hold foreign exchange accounts. Payments and transfers to some countries require government approval. Credit and loan operations, and issues and purchases of securities, derivatives, and other instruments, are subject to various requirements, controls, and authorization depending on the transaction. The purchase of real estate requires prior authorization from the Ministry of Finance.

FINANCIAL FREEDOM — 40%

Mali's financial sector is small, and the country participates in the West African Economic and Monetary Union (WAEMU) along with seven other countries. The Central Bank of West African States (BCEAO), a central bank common to the eight members of WAEMU, governs banking and other financial institutions. There were nine commercial banks as of mid-2004, including a development bank, an agricultural bank, and a housing bank. Only three commercial banks are fully private. The government has a minority stake in the three main banks (including 20 percent in the largest bank, Banque de développement du Mali) and a majority share in Banque Internationale du Mali, which is the process of being privatized. There is an extensive microfinance industry of over 300 institutions that primarily serves rural areas. There were five insurance firms and two pension funds in 2003. There is a relatively small regional stock exchange based in the Ivory Coast.

PROPERTY RIGHTS — 30%

The constitution provides for an independent judiciary, which in practice is corrupt and subject to political influence. Mali's judicial system is described as notoriously inefficient and corrupt, with frequent bribery and influence-peddling in the courts.

FREEDOM FROM CORRUPTION — 29%

Corruption is perceived as widespread. Mali ranks 88th out of 158 countries in Transparency International's Corruption Perceptions Index for 2005.

LABOR FREEDOM — 49.7%

The labor market operates under highly restrictive employment regulations that hinder employment and productivity growth. The non-salary cost of employing a worker is high, but dismissing a redundant employee can be relatively costless. Regulations on increasing or contracting the number of work hours are not flexible.

MALTA

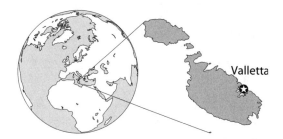

Valletta

Rank: 42

Regional Rank: 23 of 41

M alta's economy is 67.8 percent free, according to our 2007 assessment, which makes it the world's 42nd freest economy. Its overall score is 1.6 percentage points lower than last year, partially reflecting new methodological detail. Malta is ranked 23rd out of 41 countries in the European region, and its overall score is slightly higher than the regional average.

Malta scores highly in property rights, trade freedom, monetary freedom, business freedom, and financial freedom. The country's judiciary is independent and not tainted by political influence. In accordance with European Union standards, the average tariff rate is low, although Malta's trade freedom score is hurt by the standard EU subsidies of agricultural and other goods. All aspects of business formation are efficient, providing a highly flexible commercial environment. Malta's financial market is small but sound and is open to foreign competition.

Freedom from government, fiscal freedom, and labor freedom are relatively weak. Total government expenditures in Malta are high, equaling nearly half of the country's GDP. The labor market is inflexible, with restrictive rules and certain obsolete employment regulations. Foreign investment is deterred somewhat by government scrutiny, as decisions on foreign capital are made individually to judge the likely impact on domestic businesses.

BACKGROUND: The economy of Malta, which gained its independence from Great Britain in 1964, depends on tourism, foreign trade, and manufacturing. The country's well-trained workers, low labor costs, and proximity to the EU market attract foreign companies. But Malta also maintains a sprawling socialist market economy, with the majority of spending allocated to housing, education, and health care. As a member of the EU, Malta hopes to adopt the euro, which means that it must introduce more reforms. Both fiscal consolidation and job creation remain major economic policy challenges.

How Do We Measure Economic Freedom? See Chapter 3 (page 37) for an explanation of the methodology or visit the *Index* Web site at *heritage.org/index*.

The economy is 67.8% free

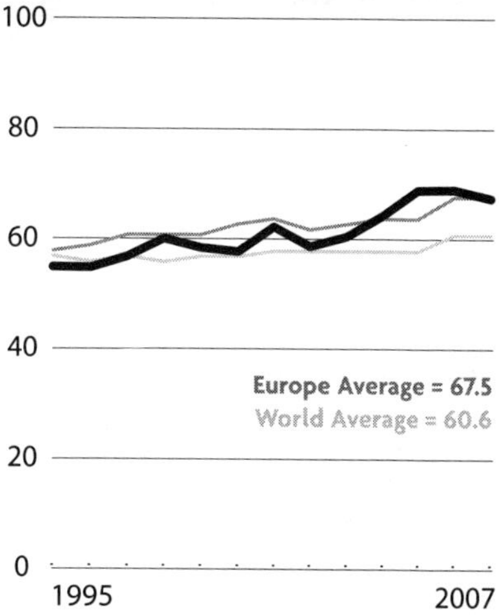

100

80

60

40

Europe Average = 67.5
World Average = 60.6

20

0

1995   2007

QUICK FACTS

Population: 0.4 million

GDP (PPP): $7.6 billion
1.0% growth in 2004
1.8% 5-yr. comp. ann. growth
$18,879 per capita

Unemployment: 7.2%

Inflation (CPI): 2.7%

FDI (net inflow): $412.2 million

Official Development Assistance:
Multilateral: $7 million
Bilateral: $2 million (29% from the U.S.)

External Debt: $188.8 million (2005)

Exports: $4.0 billion
Primarily machinery, transport equipment, manufactures

Imports: $4.4 billion
Primarily machinery, transport equipment, manufactured and semimanufactured goods, food, drink, tobacco

MALTA'S TEN ECONOMIC FREEDOMS

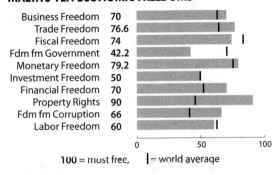

Business Freedom	70
Trade Freedom	76.6
Fiscal Freedom	74
Fdm fm Government	42.2
Monetary Freedom	79.2
Investment Freedom	50
Financial Freedom	70
Property Rights	90
Fdm fm Corruption	66
Labor Freedom	60

100 = most free, | = world average

BUSINESS FREEDOM — 70%

Malta has adopted transparent and effective policies and regulations to foster competition. It is striving to eliminate unnecessary bureaucratic procedure. Although they can be sometimes burdensome, existing regulations are relatively straightforward and applied uniformly most of the time. The overall freedom to start, operate, and close a business is relatively well protected by the national regulatory environment.

TRADE FREEDOM — 76.6%

Malta's trade policy is the same as those of other members of the European Union. The common EU weighted average tariff rate was 1.7 percent in 2005. Various non-tariff barriers are reflected in EU policy, including agricultural and manufacturing subsidies, regulatory and licensing restrictions, and other market access restrictions. Consequently, an additional 20 percent is deducted from Malta's trade freedom score.

FISCAL FREEDOM — 74%

Malta has burdensome tax rates. Both the top income tax rate and the top corporate tax rate are 35 percent. Other taxes include a value-added tax (VAT) and a capital gains tax. In the most recent year, overall tax revenue as a percentage of GDP was 38 percent.

FREEDOM FROM GOVERNMENT — 42.2%

Total government expenditures in Malta, including consumption and transfer payments, are very high. In the most recent year, government spending equaled 49.1 percent of GDP, and the government received 4.5 percent of its total revenues from state-owned enterprises and government ownership of property. In recent years, Malta has strengthened competition by reducing government aid to industry.

MONETARY FREEDOM — 79.2%

Inflation in Malta is relatively low, averaging 2.9 percent between 2003 and 2005. Relatively low and stable prices explain most of the monetary freedom score. As a participant in the EU's Common Agricultural Policy, the government subsidizes agricultural production, distorting the prices of agricultural products. The government also influences prices through state-owned enterprises, controls the prices of bread and milk, and heavily subsidizes energy.

Consequently, 10 percent is deducted from Malta's monetary freedom score to account for these policies.

INVESTMENT FREEDOM — 50%

Malta welcomes foreign investment, except in real estate, wholesale retail trade, and public utilities, and restricts foreign ownership in information technology. The government considers proposals on a case-by-case basis and carefully screens foreign proposals that are in direct competition with local business. Both residents and non-residents may hold foreign exchange accounts, subject to maximum amounts for residents and restricted to income earned in Malta for non-residents, and some capital transactions, including selected capital and money market transactions and real estate purchases by non-residents, require government approval.

FINANCIAL FREEDOM — 70%

Malta's financial sector is small but competitive. Supervision and regulation of the financial system are transparent and consistent with international norms. Formerly state-owned banks are now largely privatized, and foreign banks have a significant presence. HSBC (Malta) Ltd., which purchased the government's stake in Malta's largest bank in 1999, and the Bank of Valletta dominate the banking market. The government continues to hold a 25 percent stake in the Bank of Valletta but has announced its intention to sell its remaining interest. Foreign companies enjoy free access to domestic credit. Commercial banks may offer all forms of commercial banking services. There were over 30 licensed insurers as of mid-2006, including a number of foreign insurers. Malta's stock exchange is small but active.

PROPERTY RIGHTS — 90%

Malta's judiciary is independent, both under the constitution and in practice. Property rights are protected, and expropriation is unlikely.

FREEDOM FROM CORRUPTION — 66%

Corruption is perceived as present. Malta ranks 25th out of 158 countries in Transparency International's Corruption Perceptions Index for 2005.

LABOR FREEDOM — 60%

The labor market operates under restrictive employment regulations that could be improved to enhance employment and productivity growth. Labor relationships can be confrontational, and outdated and inefficient practices are persistent problems. The government mandates a minimum wage.

MAURITANIA

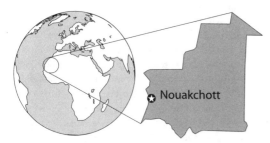

Nouakchott

Rank: 126

Regional Rank: 26 of 40

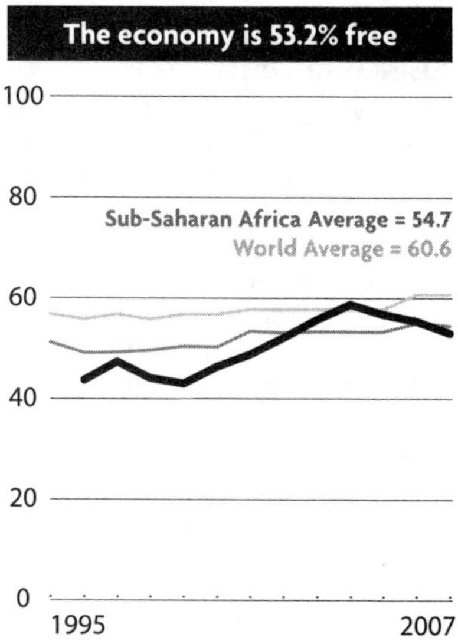

Mauritania's economy is 53.2 percent free, according to our 2007 assessment, which makes it the world's 126th freest economy. Its overall score is 2.3 percentage points lower than last year, partially reflecting new methodological detail. Mauritania is ranked 26th out of 40 countries in the sub-Saharan Africa region, and its overall score is lower than the regional average.

Mauritania scores well in fiscal freedom, monetary freedom, and investment freedom. Relatively high tax rates on income are balanced by the beneficial effects of low corporate tax rates, and overall tax revenue is fairly low as a percentage of GDP. Inflation is high, but the government does not intervene actively in market prices. Foreign investment is welcome in almost all sectors of the economy, except for a few specialized niches like fishing boats.

Economic development has been hampered by a serious lack of freedom in several other areas, such as business freedom, labor freedom, freedom from corruption, and property rights. Opening a business takes nearly twice the world average, and licensing and operational procedures are grueling. Bureaucratic inefficiency and corruption burden virtually all areas of the economy. Court enforcement of property rights and intrusive labor regulations is subject to pervasive political interference.

BACKGROUND: Mauritania is predominantly desert and beset by frequent drought, poor harvests, and unemployment. Mining and fishing dominate the economy, and efforts to diversify the economy have met with little success. Oil production from offshore fields discovered in 2001 began in 2006 and will boost gross domestic product. Mauritania has a fragile political climate, having experienced three failed coup attempts in 2003 and 2004 and a successful bloodless coup in 2005. The leaders of the coup dissolved the legislature, established a military council to rule the country, and announced that elections would be held in 2007.

How Do We Measure Economic Freedom? See Chapter 3 (page 37) for an explanation of the methodology or visit the *Index* Web site at *heritage.org/index*.

The economy is 53.2% free

Sub-Saharan Africa Average = 54.7
World Average = 60.6

[Line chart showing economic freedom from 1995 to 2007, with vertical axis from 0 to 100]

QUICK FACTS

Population: 3 million

GDP (PPP): $5.8 billion
6.2% growth in 2004
5.0% 5-yr. comp. ann. growth
$1,940 per capita

Unemployment: 20% (2004 estimate)

Inflation (CPI): 10.4%

FDI (net inflow): $300 million (gross)

Official Development Assistance:
Multilateral: $133 million
Bilateral: $173 million (6% from the U.S.)

External Debt: $2.3 billion

Exports: $409 million (2004 estimate)
Primarily iron ore, fish and fish products, gold

Imports: $925 million (2004 estimate)
Primarily machinery and equipment, petroleum products, capital goods, food, consumer goods

MAURITANIA'S TEN ECONOMIC FREEDOMS

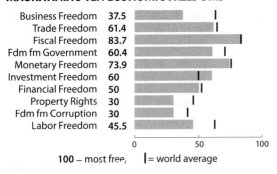

Business Freedom	37.5	
Trade Freedom	61.4	
Fiscal Freedom	83.7	
Fdm fm Government	60.4	
Monetary Freedom	73.9	
Investment Freedom	60	
Financial Freedom	50	
Property Rights	30	
Fdm fm Corruption	30	
Labor Freedom	45.5	

0   50   100

100 – most free, | = world average

BUSINESS FREEDOM — 37.5%

Starting a business takes an average of 82 days, compared to the world average of 48 days. Entrepreneurship should be easier for maximum job creation. Obtaining a business license is difficult, and closing a business is very difficult. Despite the government's effort to streamline its complex and time-consuming regulatory environment, bureaucratic obstacles and delays are persistent problems. The overall freedom to start, operate, and close a business is seriously restricted by the national regulatory environment.

TRADE FREEDOM — 61.4%

Mauritania's weighted average tariff rate was 9.3 percent in 2001. Import restrictions, import bans, weak enforcement of intellectual property rights, and a complexity and lack of transparency in the customs implementation that promote corruption and delays in processing shipments all add to the cost of trade. Consequently, an additional 20 percent is deducted from Mauritania's trade freedom score to account for these non-tariff barriers.

FISCAL FREEDOM — 83.7%

Mauritania has a high income tax rate and a low corporate tax rate. The top income tax rate is 40 percent, and the top corporate tax rate is 25 percent. Other taxes include a value-added tax (VAT) and a tax on insurance contracts. In the most recent year, overall tax revenue as a percentage of GDP was 14.9 percent.

FREEDOM FROM GOVERNMENT — 60.4%

Total government expenditures in Mauritania, including consumption and transfer payments, are high. In the most recent year, government spending equaled 37.7 percent of GDP, and the government received 19.3 percent of its total revenues from state-owned enterprises and government ownership of property.

MONETARY FREEDOM — 73.9%

Inflation in Mauritania is relatively high, averaging 11.1 percent between 2003 and 2005. Relatively high and unstable prices explain most of the monetary freedom score. Most prices are determined in the market, but the government retains an influence on certain prices through state-owned enterprises and utilities, such as electricity. Consequently, an additional 5 percent is deducted from Mauritania's monetary freedom score to account for these policies.

INVESTMENT FREEDOM — 60%

Almost all sectors of Mauritania's economy welcome foreign investment, except fishing boats, where foreign investment is limited to a 49 percent share. The 2002 investment code encourages foreign investors but does not cover the two most important sectors: mining and fisheries. Both residents and non-residents may hold foreign exchange accounts, but non-resident accounts are subject to some restrictions. Capital movements are subject to exchange controls, and payments and transfers are subject to quantitative limits, *bona fide* tests, and prior approval in some cases. Procurement, fishing licenses, bank loans, and land distribution are subject to serious corruption.

FINANCIAL FREEDOM — 50%

Mauritania's financial sector is small, underdeveloped, and dominated by the banking sector. Supervision and enforcement of financial sector regulation is insufficient. The banking sector has been undermined by non-performing loans. There were seven commercial banks as of mid-2004. The government owns 50 percent of one commercial bank. Most bank lending is focused on large companies. Government funds comprise a substantial portion of bank deposits. The financial sector also includes a government-owned development bank and a growing number of microfinance institutions. Six private insurance companies competed with the state-owned insurer in 2004. Capital markets are virtually nonexistent, and there is no stock market.

PROPERTY RIGHTS — 30%

Mauritania's judicial system is chaotic and corrupt. The judiciary is subject to influence from the executive. Poorly trained judges are intimidated by social, financial, tribal, and personal pressures.

FREEDOM FROM CORRUPTION — 30%

Mauritania's informal market includes consumer goods, agricultural products, and entertainment products. There is also a large black market for foreign currency. The informal sector represents about 30 percent of the economy.

LABOR FREEDOM — 45.5%

The labor market operates under highly restrictive employment regulations that hinder employment and productivity growth. The non-salary cost of employing a worker is moderate, but dismissing a redundant employee is difficult. Regulations on increasing or contracting the number of work hours are rigid. Mauritania's labor freedom is one of the 20 lowest in the world.

MAURITIUS

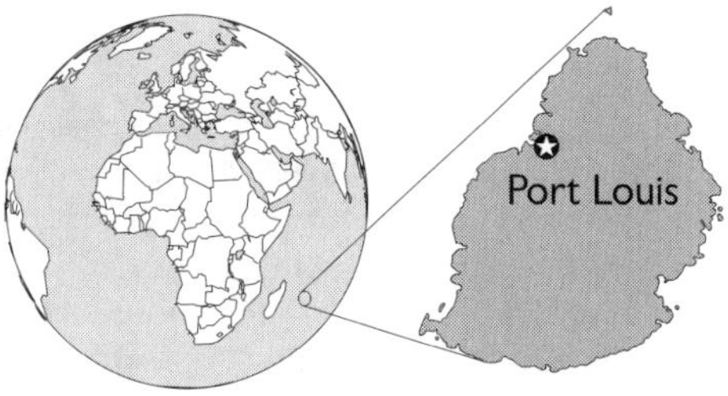

Rank: 34

Regional Rank: 1 of 40

The economy of Mauritius is 69 percent free, according to our 2007 assessment, which makes it the world's 34th freest economy. Its overall score is 2.5 percentage points higher than last year, partially reflecting new methodological detail. Mauritius is ranked the freest out of 40 countries in the sub-Saharan Africa region, and its overall score is well above the regional average.

Mauritius enjoys high levels of investment freedom, property rights, business freedom, trade freedom, labor freedom, fiscal freedom, and freedom from government. The environment is business-friendly, and licensing procedures are simple. Virtually all commercial operations are efficient and transparent. Foreign investment is actively promoted, although land ownership is restricted to arbitration on a case-by-case basis. The top income and corporate tax rates are moderate, and government expenditures are moderate as a percentage of GDP. The judiciary, independent of politics and relatively free of corruption, is able to protect property rights exceptionally well.

Mauritius has slightly weaker levels of monetary freedom and freedom from corruption. Inflation is moderate, but the government distorts prices of certain goods through direct subsidies. Although the government has been making an effort to liberalize foreign trade, it still imposes, through special permits, a variety of import and export restrictions.

BACKGROUND: With a well-developed legal and commercial infrastructure and a long tradition of entrepreneurship and representative government, Mauritius has one of Africa's strongest economies. Sugar and textiles, the traditional economic mainstays, are facing stronger international competition and the erosion of trade preferences, which has undermined growth in recent years and led to increased unemployment. The government is addressing this problem through business-friendly policies, training, and attempting to diversify the economy by promoting information and communication technology, financial and business services, seafood processing and exports, and free trade zones.

How Do We Measure Economic Freedom? See Chapter 3 (page 37) for an explanation of the methodology or visit the *Index* Web site at *heritage.org/index*.

The economy is 69% free

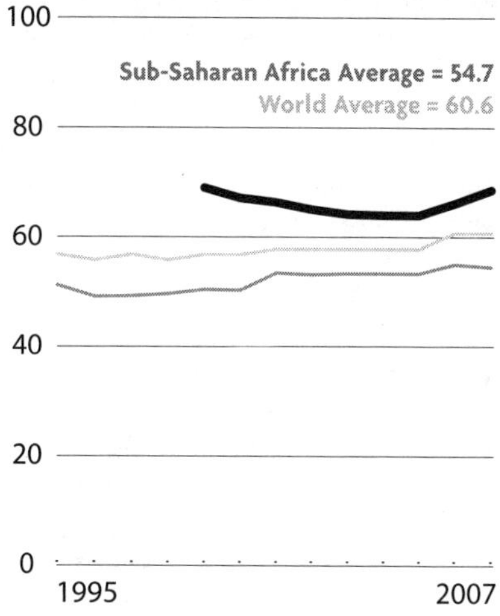

Sub-Saharan Africa Average = 54.7
World Average = 60.6

QUICK FACTS

Population: 1.2 million

GDP (PPP): $14.8 billion
4.2% growth in 2004
4.3% 5-yr. comp. ann. growth
$12,027 per capita

Unemployment: 8.5%

Inflation (CPI): 4.7%

FDI (net inflow): $32.3 million

Official Development Assistance:
Multilateral: $36 million
Bilateral: $35 million (1% from the U.S.)

External Debt: $2.3 billion

Exports: $3.5 billion
Primarily clothing and textiles, sugar, cut flowers, molasses

Imports: $3.6 billion
Primarily manufactured goods, capital equipment, food, petroleum products, chemicals

273

MAURITIUS'S TEN ECONOMIC FREEDOMS

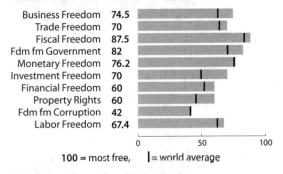

Business Freedom	74.5
Trade Freedom	70
Fiscal Freedom	87.5
Fdm fm Government	82
Monetary Freedom	76.2
Investment Freedom	70
Financial Freedom	60
Property Rights	60
Fdm fm Corruption	42
Labor Freedom	67.4

100 = most free, | = world average

BUSINESS FREEDOM — 74.5%

Starting a business takes an average of 46 days, compared to the world average of 48 days. Entrepreneurship should be easier for maximum job creation. Obtaining a business license and closing a business are relatively simple, but bureaucratic obstacles and delays are ongoing problems. The overall freedom to start, operate, and close a business is relatively well protected by the national regulatory environment.

TRADE FREEDOM — 70%

Mauritius's weighted average tariff rate was 5 percent in 2005. The government has made progress in liberalizing the trade regime, but subsidies, some quotas, import bans, weak enforcement of intellectual property rights, and controls on imports and exports of certain goods by means of special permit requirements all add to the cost of trade. Consequently, an additional 20 percent is deducted from Mauritius's trade freedom score to account for these non-tariff barriers.

FISCAL FREEDOM — 87.5%

Mauritius has moderate tax rates. The top income tax rate is 30 percent, and the top corporate tax rate is 25 percent. Other taxes include a value-added tax (VAT) and a transfer tax. In the most recent year, overall tax revenue as a percentage of GDP was 18.7 percent.

FREEDOM FROM GOVERNMENT — 82%

Total government expenditures in Mauritius, including consumption and transfer payments, are moderate. In the most recent year, government spending equaled 26 percent of GDP, and the government received 6.7 percent of its total revenues from state-owned enterprises and government ownership of property.

MONETARY FREEDOM — 76.2%

Inflation in Mauritius is moderate, averaging 4.8 percent between 2003 and 2005. Relatively unstable prices explain most of the monetary freedom score. The government controls prices for a number of goods, including flour, sugar, milk, bread, rice, petroleum products, steel, cement, fertilizers, and pharmaceuticals; is able to influence prices through state-owned enterprises and utilities; and subsidizes some agriculture and industry. Consequently, an additional 10 percent is deducted from Mauritius's monetary freedom score to account for these policies.

INVESTMENT FREEDOM — 70%

Mauritius generally welcomes foreign investment and has a transparent and well-defined foreign investment code. Foreigners may not own land without prior permission from the Prime Minister and the Minister of Internal Affairs. The only restrictions on foreign ownership of businesses apply to casinos and public utilities. Both residents and non-residents may hold foreign exchange accounts. There are no controls on payments or transfers and few controls on capital transactions.

FINANCIAL FREEDOM — 60%

Mauritius has an open, efficient, and competitive financial system. The 2004 Banking Act eliminated distinctions between onshore and offshore banks, and only one license is now offered. The two largest domestic banks are the Mauritius Commercial Bank and the State Bank of Mauritius, which is minority state-owned. The government also wholly owns both the Development Bank of Mauritius Ltd. and Mauritius Post and Cooperative Bank Ltd. and owns a majority of First City Bank. Banks that are entirely or partially state-owned constitute 12.4 percent of aggregated total assets. The two largest foreign banks account for 22 percent. Banks are free to conduct business in all currencies. The three largest insurance firms account for approximately 75 percent of the market. Capital markets are growing, and the Stock Exchange of Mauritius has links to regional exchange networks in Africa and Asia. A second stock exchange, focusing on smaller companies, is scheduled to open in 2006.

PROPERTY RIGHTS — 60%

The judiciary is independent and provides citizens with a fair trial. The domestic legal system is generally non-discriminatory and transparent. The highest court of appeal is the judicial committee of the Privy Council of England. Corruption exists but is much less than elsewhere in Africa. Expropriation of property is unlikely.

FREEDOM FROM CORRUPTION — 42%

Corruption is perceived as significant. Mauritius ranks 51st out of 158 countries in Transparency International's Corruption Perceptions Index for 2005.

LABOR FREEDOM — 67.4%

The labor market operates under relatively flexible employment regulations that could be improved to enhance employment and productivity growth. The non-salary cost of employing a worker is low, but dismissing a redundant employee can be relatively costly. Regulations related to increasing or modifying the number of work hours are somewhat rigid.

MEXICO

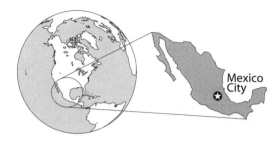

Mexico City

Mexico's economy is 65.8 percent free, according to our 2007 assessment, which makes it the world's 49th freest economy. Its overall score is 1.2 percentage points higher than last year, partially reflecting new methodological detail. Mexico is ranked 11th out of 29 countries in the Americas, and its overall score is slightly higher than the regional average.

Mexico enjoys high levels of business freedom, fiscal freedom, trade freedom, freedom from government, property rights, monetary freedom, and labor freedom. The business climate is positive and improving; commercial operations are becoming more streamlined, and business formation is efficient. Income and corporate tax rates are moderate, and overall tax revenue is low as a percentage of GDP. Government expenditures are likewise fairly low. Flexible labor regulations contribute to an elastic employment market with no major regulatory distortions.

Freedom from corruption is weak and is the only factor worse than the world average. Foreign investment in many sectors is deterred by special licensing requirements, although the government is working to make commercial regulations more investment-friendly. A weak judicial system produces slow resolution of cases and is subject to fairly significant corruption.

BACKGROUND: Mexico is a member of the North American Free Trade Agreement with Canada and the United States. In 2000, Vicente Fox became the first opposition-party president in 71 years. Despite a divided Congress, some reforms were adopted that helped Mexico to recover from an economic contraction following the 2001 terrorist attacks on the United States. Mexico still needs more private-sector job creation for new entrants into the workforce, and that means it must tackle the problem of monopolies in energy, telecommunications, and transportation to boost competitiveness. Felipe Calderón of the center-right National Action Party was elected president in July 2006.

How Do We Measure Economic Freedom? See Chapter 3 (page 37) for an explanation of the methodology or visit the *Index* Web site at *heritage.org/index*.

The economy is 65.8% free

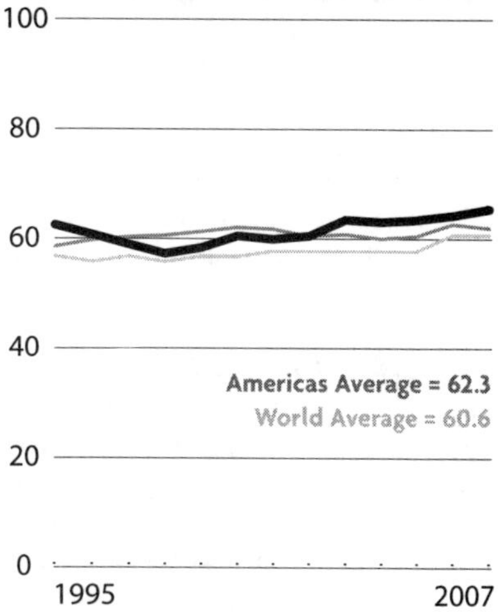

Americas Average = 62.3
World Average = 60.6

1995   2007

QUICK FACTS

Population: 103.8 million

GDP (PPP): $1.0 trillion
4.2% growth in 2004
2.6% 5-yr. comp. ann. growth
$9,803 per capita

Unemployment: 3.9%

Inflation (CPI): 4.7%

FDI (net inflow): $14.4 billion

Official Development Assistance:
Multilateral: $44 million
Bilateral: $176 million (24% from the U.S.)

External Debt: $138.7 billion

Exports: $202.0 billion
Primarily manufactured goods, oil and oil products, silver, fruits, vegetables, coffee, cotton

Imports: $216.6 billion
Primarily metalworking machines, steel mill products, agricultural machinery, electrical equipment, car parts for assembly, repair parts for motor vehicles, aircraft, aircraft parts

MEXICO'S TEN ECONOMIC FREEDOMS

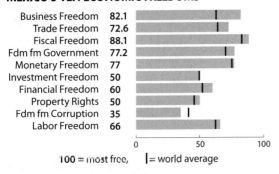

Business Freedom	82.1
Trade Freedom	72.6
Fiscal Freedom	88.1
Fdm fm Government	77.2
Monetary Freedom	77
Investment Freedom	50
Financial Freedom	60
Property Rights	50
Fdm fm Corruption	35
Labor Freedom	66

100 = most free, | = world average

BUSINESS FREEDOM — 82.1%

Starting a business takes an average of 27 days, compared to the world average of 48 days. Entrepreneurship should be easier for maximum job creation. Obtaining a business license is simple, and closing a business is relatively easy. In recent years, the government has made progress in streamlining its time-consuming regulatory environment. The overall freedom to start, operate, and close a business is protected by the national regulatory environment.

TRADE FREEDOM — 72.6%

Mexico's weighted average tariff rate was 3.7 percent in 2004. Sanitary and phytosanitary regulations, non-transparent and complex customs administration and valuation procedures, import licensing for sensitive products, import taxes, restrictive standards and labeling rules, service market access barriers, import restrictions, minimum import price requirements, import bans, customs corruption, and weak enforcement of intellectual property rights add to the cost of trade. Consequently, an additional 20 percent is deducted from Mexico's trade freedom score to account for these non-tariff barriers.

FISCAL FREEDOM — 88.1%

Mexico has been lowering its tax rates. Both the top income tax rate and the top corporate tax rate are 29 percent and are scheduled to be reduced to 28 percent by 2007. Other taxes include a value-added tax (VAT), a property tax, and a vehicle tax. In the most recent year, overall tax revenue as a percentage of GDP was 10.1 percent.

FREEDOM FROM GOVERNMENT — 77.2%

Total government expenditures in Mexico, including consumption and transfer payments, are low. In the most recent year, government spending equaled 23.5 percent of GDP, and the government received 29.7 percent of its total revenues from state-owned enterprises and government ownership of property. The energy and electricity industries remain under government control.

MONETARY FREEDOM — 77%

Inflation in Mexico is moderate, averaging 4.2 percent between 2003 and 2005. Relatively unstable prices explain most of the monetary freedom score. Although most prices are determined in the market, the government maintains suggested retail prices for medicines; influences prices

through state-owned enterprises and utilities, including electricity and energy; and implements minimum prices for a broad range of imports, including textiles, tools, and bicycles. Consequently, an additional 10 percent is deducted from Mexico's monetary freedom score to account for these policies.

INVESTMENT FREEDOM — 50%

Foreign investors are barred from important sectors of the economy, such as petroleum and electricity. Foreigners may invest in real estate subject to certain restrictions. Improvements introduced in recent years include less legal and administrative red tape, higher ceilings on foreign equity, fewer local content requirements, better intellectual property legislation, and the elimination of most import license requirements. Residents and non-residents may hold foreign exchange accounts. Most payments, transactions, and transfers are permissible. Some capital transactions, including capital and money market instruments and derivatives, are subject to government permission and controls.

FINANCIAL FREEDOM — 60%

Mexico's increasingly competitive financial sector is one of the most developed in Latin America. The government has significantly reduced its holdings in commercial banking, and foreign participation has grown rapidly since the lifting of restrictions on foreign ownership in 1998. The government has improved financial transparency and supervision by adopting U.S. accounting standards. There were 32 commercial banks in 2005. Foreign-controlled banks account for 85 percent of banking assets. Banks offer a wide range of services. The government owns six development banks that provide financing to specific areas of the economy, such as small and medium-size enterprises, through which the government influences credit. The insurance sector is well developed but highly concentrated, with five firms accounting for 65 percent of all policies. Although capital markets are fairly well developed, the stock exchange is relatively small, and most large Mexican companies are traded on U.S. exchanges.

PROPERTY RIGHTS — 50%

The threat of expropriation is low. Contractual agreements are generally upheld, but the courts are slow to resolve disputes and allegedly subject to corruption.

FREEDOM FROM CORRUPTION — 35%

Corruption is perceived as significant. Mexico ranks 65th out of 158 countries in Transparency International's Corruption Perceptions Index for 2005.

LABOR FREEDOM — 66%

The labor market operates under relatively flexible employment regulations that could be improved to enhance employment and productivity growth. The non-salary cost of employing a worker can be high, and dismissing a redundant employee is relatively costly. Labor reform remains stalled, with only limited progress in reducing rigidities in employment legislation.

MOLDOVA

Chişinău

Moldova's economy is 59.5 percent free, according to our 2007 assessment, which makes it the world's 81st freest economy. Its overall score is 0.1 percentage point lower than last year, partially reflecting new methodological detail. Moldova is ranked 33rd out of 41 countries in the European region, and its overall score is lower than the regional average.

Moldova's trade freedom, business freedom, and fiscal freedom are strong. The top income and corporate tax rates are 18 percent and 15 percent, respectively. Additional taxes are imposed by the government, and overall tax revenue is fairly high as a percentage of GDP. The average tariff rate is low, but the government maintains non-tariff barriers that include burdensome regulations and restrictive customs.

As the poorest country in Europe, Moldova has an economy with significant shortcomings. Monetary freedom, investment freedom, and freedom from corruption are weak. Inflation is high, although the government has been phasing out its price supports on certain goods. Foreign investment in virtually all sectors faces hurdles, from outright restrictions to bureaucratic inefficiency. There is also significant corruption in most areas of the bureaucracy, and although the government has been reforming its judiciary, public institutions are weak overall.

BACKGROUND: Moldova has struggled since becoming independent after the collapse of the Soviet Union in 1991. It is now trying to deal with problems created by a secessionist enclave in Transnistria. The March 2005 elections gave the Communist Party of Moldova a majority of seats, which is expected to reinforce commitment to European integration. Agriculture remains central to the economy, with foodstuffs and animal and vegetable products as the main exports. A Russian embargo on Moldovan wine imports has severely hurt the overall health of the economy.

How Do We Measure Economic Freedom? See Chapter 3 (page 37) for an explanation of the methodology or visit the *Index* Web site at *heritage.org/index*.

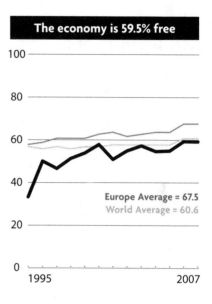

The economy is 59.5% free

Europe Average = 67.5
World Average = 60.6

QUICK FACTS

Population: 4.2 million

GDP (PPP): $7.3 billion
7.3% growth in 2004
6.0% 5-yr. comp. ann. growth
$1,729 per capita

Unemployment: 8%

Inflation (CPI): 12.5%

FDI (net inflow): $300 million (gross)

Official Development Assistance:
Multilateral: $35 million
Bilateral: $83 million (40% from the U.S.)

External Debt: $1.9 billion

Exports: $1.3 billion
Primarily food, textiles, machinery

Imports: $2.1 billion
Primarily mineral products and fuel, machinery and equipment, chemicals, textiles

MOLDOVA'S TEN ECONOMIC FREEDOMS

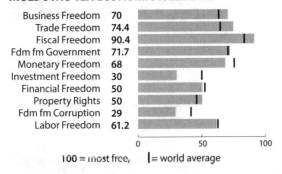

Business Freedom	70
Trade Freedom	74.4
Fiscal Freedom	90.4
Fdm fm Government	71.7
Monetary Freedom	68
Investment Freedom	30
Financial Freedom	50
Property Rights	50
Fdm fm Corruption	29
Labor Freedom	61.2

100 = most free, | = world average

BUSINESS FREEDOM — 70%

Starting a business takes an average of 30 days, compared to the world average of 48 days. Entrepreneurship should be easier for maximum job creation. Obtaining a business license and closing a business are relatively simple, but bureaucratic procedures are not always transparent, and red tape can make processing unnecessarily long. The overall freedom to start, operate, and close a business is relatively well protected by the national regulatory environment.

TRADE FREEDOM — 74.4%

Moldova's weighted average tariff rate was 2.8 percent in 2001. Cumbersome and restrictive customs procedures, corruption, burdensome regulations, and export restrictions add to the cost of trade. Consequently, an additional 20 percent is deducted from Moldova's trade freedom score to account for these non-tariff barriers.

FISCAL FREEDOM — 90.4%

Moldova enjoys low tax rates that have been gradually reduced over the years. The top income tax rate is 18 percent, and the top corporate tax rate is 15 percent. Other taxes include a value-added tax (VAT), an advertising tax, and a vehicle tax. In the most recent year, overall tax revenue as a percentage of GDP was 29.8 percent.

FREEDOM FROM GOVERNMENT — 71.7%

Total government expenditures in Moldova, including consumption and transfer payments, are moderate. In the most recent year, government spending equaled 34.6 percent of GDP, and the government received 1 percent of its total revenues from state-owned enterprises and government ownership of property.

MONETARY FREEDOM — 68%

Inflation in Moldova is relatively high, averaging 12.1 percent between 2003 and 2005. Relatively high and unstable prices explain most of the monetary freedom score. The government has phased out most price controls and many subsidies, but it still influences prices through numerous state-owned enterprises and utilities, including electricity and energy. Consequently, an additional 10 percent is deducted from Moldova's monetary freedom score to account for these policies.

INVESTMENT FREEDOM — 30%

Foreign investment is welcome as long as it does not conflict with national security interests, anti-monopoly legislation, environmental protection norms, public health, and public order. The business environment is overwhelmed with informal obstacles such as corruption and weak governance. Foreign investors may not purchase agricultural or forest land. Both residents and non-residents may hold foreign exchange accounts, but approval is required in some cases. Payments and transfers require supporting documentation and approval by the National Bank of Moldova if they exceed specified amounts. Nearly all capital transactions require approval by or registration with the National Bank of Moldova.

FINANCIAL FREEDOM — 50%

Moldova's small financial system was wholly controlled by the state as recently as the 1990s and has been undergoing restructuring and consolidation. Supervision and regulation fall short of international standards. There are 16 commercial banks, including two foreign bank branches. The sector is highly concentrated, with the top five banks controlling over 70 percent of bank assets. The government, which holds shares in two banks, has announced its intention to sell its majority stake in Banca de Economii, one of the country's largest banks. The insurance market was opened to foreign competition in mid-1999 and consisted of 33 insurance operators in March 2006. The formerly state-owned insurance company Asito, which dominates the market, is now majority foreign-owned. Capital markets are immature, and the stock market is very small.

PROPERTY RIGHTS — 50%

The judiciary has been improved in recent years but is still subject to executive influence. Delays in salary payments also make it difficult for judges to remain independent from outside influences and free from corruption.

FREEDOM FROM CORRUPTION — 29%

Corruption is perceived as widespread. Moldova ranks 88th out of 158 countries in Transparency International's Corruption Perceptions Index for 2005.

LABOR FREEDOM — 61.2%

The labor market operates under highly restrictive employment regulations that could be improved to enhance employment and productivity growth. The non-salary cost of employing a worker is high, but dismissing a redundant employee is relatively costless. There are rigid regulations on increasing or contracting the number of work hours.

MONGOLIA

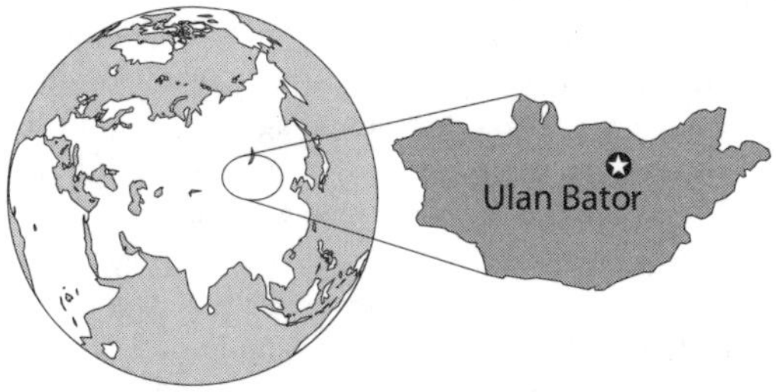

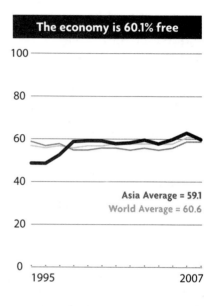

Ulan Bator

M ongolia's economy is 60.1 percent free, according to our 2007 assessment, which makes it the world's 78th freest economy. Its overall score is 3.1 percentage points lower than last year, partially reflecting new methodological detail. Mongolia is ranked 11th out of 30 countries in the Asia–Pacific region, and its overall score is slightly higher than the regional average.

Mongolia enjoys high levels of fiscal freedom, financial freedom, business freedom, investment freedom, and trade freedom. The top income and corporate tax rates are moderate. The average tariff rate is also moderate, although non-tariff barriers (such as customs corruption) have undermined the government's policy of liberalization. Commercial registration and licensing are efficient, though closing a business takes longer than it should. Inflation is fairly high, but the government has eliminated almost all of its price supports and market distortions.

Mongolia could do better in property rights, freedom from government, and freedom from corruption. The judicial protection of property rights is still weak, and judges often do not validate previously agreed contracts. The judiciary is further hampered by corruption. Total government expenditures are high.

BACKGROUND: Mongolia's efforts at political liberalization and economic reform have progressed unevenly but gradually since 1990. The new government, which came to power following the abrupt dissolution of the 17-month-old coalition government in January 2006, continues to face increasing public discontent with the ruling Mongolian People's Revolutionary Party (MPRP) and the MPRP-dominated cabinet over such issues as corruption, transparency, and economic development. Livestock herding employs a majority of the population, but copper mines are one of the leading destinations for foreign direct investment.

How Do We Measure Economic Freedom? See Chapter 3 (page 37) for an explanation of the methodology or visit the *Index* Web site at *heritage.org/index*.

The economy is 60.1% free

100

80

60

40

Asia Average = 59.1
World Average = 60.6

20

0

1995   2007

QUICK FACTS

Population: 2.5 million

GDP (PPP): $5.2 billion
10.7% growth in 2004
4.4% 5-yr. comp. ann. growth
$2,056 per capita

Unemployment: 6.7% (2003 estimate)

Inflation (CPI): 8.2%

FDI (net inflow): $147.5 million (gross)

Official Development Assistance:
Multilateral: $106 million
Bilateral: $175 million (15% from the U.S.)

External Debt: $1.5 billion

Exports: $1.2 billion
Primarily copper, apparel, livestock, animal products, cashmere, wool, hides, fluorspar, other nonferrous metals

Imports: $1.4 billion
Primarily machinery and equipment, fuel, cars, food products, industrial consumer goods, chemicals, building materials, sugar, tea

279

MONGOLIA'S TEN ECONOMIC FREEDOMS

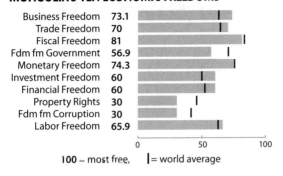

Business Freedom	73.1
Trade Freedom	70
Fiscal Freedom	81
Fdm fm Government	56.9
Monetary Freedom	74.3
Investment Freedom	60
Financial Freedom	60
Property Rights	30
Fdm fm Corruption	30
Labor Freedom	65.9

0   50   100

100 – most free, | = world average

BUSINESS FREEDOM — 73.1%

Starting a business takes an average of 20 days, compared to the world average of 48 days. Entrepreneurship should be easier for maximum job creation. Obtaining a business license is simple, but closing a business can be difficult. Bureaucratic bottlenecks and delays are persistent problems. The overall freedom to start, operate, and close a business is relatively well protected by the national regulatory environment.

TRADE FREEDOM — 70%

Mongolia's average tariff rate was 5 percent in 2004. The government has made progress liberalizing the trade regime, but import restrictions, import and export bans, import and export taxes, restrictive import licensing requirements, and inefficient and corrupt customs implementation add to the cost of trade. Consequently, an additional 20 percent is deducted from Mongolia's trade freedom score to account for these non-tariff barriers.

FISCAL FREEDOM — 81%

Mongolia has moderate tax rates. Both the top income tax rate and the top corporate tax rate are 30 percent. Other taxes include a value-added tax (VAT), a property tax, and a dividend tax. In the most recent year, overall tax revenue as a percentage of GDP was 32.3 percent.

FREEDOM FROM GOVERNMENT — 56.9%

Total government expenditures in Mongolia, including consumption and transfer payments, are high. In the most recent year, government spending equaled 41.7 percent of GDP, and the government received 7.4 percent of its total revenues from state-owned enterprises and government ownership of property.

MONETARY FREEDOM — 74.3%

Inflation in Mongolia is relatively high, averaging 10.6 percent between 2003 and 2005. Relatively high and unstable prices explain most of the monetary freedom score. Although most price controls and many subsidies have been phased out, the government influences prices through the public sector or through regulation; sometimes intervenes in the market to stabilize commodity prices; and still controls air fares and fuel prices. Consequently, an additional 5 percent is deducted from Mongolia's monetary freedom score to account for these policies.

INVESTMENT FREEDOM — 60%

Mongolia's laws support foreign direct investment in all sectors and businesses at whatever levels investors want. The government provides equal treatment and a non-screening process. Individual agencies often use their power to hinder investments in some sectors. Both domestic and foreign investors report similar abuses of inspections, permits, and licenses by regulatory agencies. Foreigners may own land but must register it. Residents may hold foreign exchange accounts in authorized banks; non-residents may hold foreign exchange accounts but must register them with the government. There are no restrictions on payments and transfers. Most credit and loan operations must be registered with the central bank.

FINANCIAL FREEDOM — 60%

Mongolia's financial system is small and dominated by banking. The government imposes very few restraints on the flow of capital in any of its markets, and foreign investors may freely tap domestic capital markets. There were 16 commercial banks in 2006. Two banks were foreign-owned. One bank was wholly state-owned, and another was partly state-owned. Supervision is insufficient, and regulation is poorly enforced. Non-performing loans are a problem, and several banks are believed to be insolvent. The four largest banks control over 60 percent of bank assets. There are also about six dozen smaller, largely unregulated non-bank lending institutions. The insurance sector included 16 companies in 2006. The largest insurance company was privatized in 2002. Capital markets are small and limited. The stock market was originally set up to facilitate privatization of state-owned enterprises but now functions as a regular exchange.

PROPERTY RIGHTS — 30%

The enforcement of laws protecting private property is weak. Judges in general do not understand such commercial principles as the sanctity of contracts and regularly ignore the terms of contracts in their decisions. Corruption is a serious obstacle to business.

FREEDOM FROM CORRUPTION — 30%

Corruption is perceived as significant. Mongolia ranks 85th out of 158 countries in Transparency International's Corruption Perceptions Index for 2005.

LABOR FREEDOM — 65.9%

The labor market operates under relatively flexible employment regulations that could be improved to enhance employment and productivity growth. The non-salary cost of employing a worker can be high, but dismissing a redundant employee is costless. Regulations related to increasing or contracting the number of work hours are not flexible.

MOROCCO

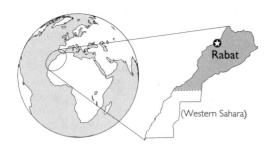

Rabat

(Western Sahara)

Morocco's economy is 57.4 percent free, according to our 2007 assessment, which makes it the world's 96th freest economy. Its overall score is 4.4 percentage points higher than last year, partially reflecting new methodological detail. Morocco is ranked 11th out of 17 countries in the Middle East/North Africa region, and its overall score is slightly higher than the regional average.

Morocco's economy is very free for the Middle East, with high scores in several of the 10 factors of economic freedom. Business freedom, monetary freedom, freedom from government, and investment freedom all score well. Inflation is low, but the kingdom still uses price supports for some goods. Despite regulatory obstacles, business formation is generally efficient. Foreign investment receives national treatment, but Morocco's bureaucracy provides its own *de facto* deterrent to foreign capital.

Morocco suffers from weak trade freedom, fiscal freedom, financial freedom, labor freedom, property rights, and freedom from corruption. The average tariff rate is high, and bureaucratic practices are opaque. The judiciary and the financial sector are inefficient and subject to substantial corruption (at least in the courts) and significant political interference from the king. The labor market is highly restrictive and one of the 20 least free in the world.

BACKGROUND: An Arab constitutional monarchy, Morocco gained its independence from France in 1956 and became a close ally of the United States. King Mohammed VI has encouraged political and economic reform, the expansion of civil rights, and the elimination of corruption. Morocco has rich resources, including the world's largest phosphate reserves, a large tourist industry, and a growing manufacturing sector; but agriculture still accounts for about 20 percent of GDP and employs roughly 40 percent of the labor force. A free trade agreement between Morocco and the United States that had been signed in 2004 took effect in January 2006.

How Do We Measure Economic Freedom? See Chapter 3 (page 37) for an explanation of the methodology or visit the *Index* Web site at *heritage.org/index*.

The economy is 57.4% free

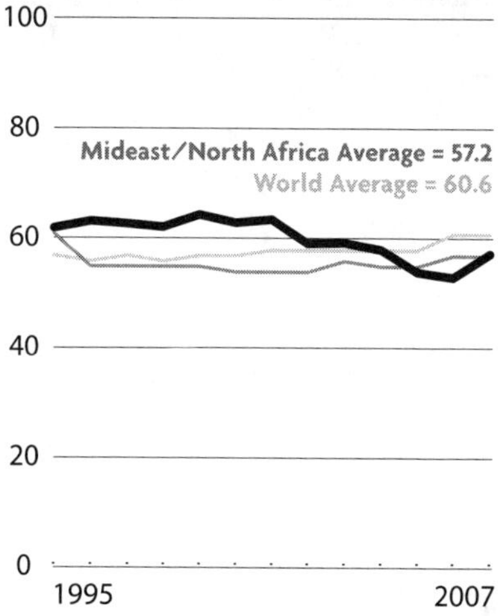

Mideast/North Africa Average = 57.2
World Average = 60.6

1995   2007

QUICK FACTS

Population: 29.8 million

GDP (PPP): $128.5 billion
4.2% growth in 2004
4.0% 5-yr. comp. ann. growth
$4,309 per capita

Unemployment: 10.8%

Inflation (CPI): 1.5%

FDI (net inflow): $822.2 million

Official Development Assistance:
Multilateral: $253 million
Bilateral: $773 million (3% from the U.S.)

External Debt: $17.7 billion

Exports: $16.6 billion
Primarily clothing, fish, inorganic chemicals, transistors, crude minerals, fertilizers, petroleum products, fruits, vegetables

Imports: $19.9 billion
Primarily crude petroleum, textile fabric, telecommunications equipment, wheat, gas and electricity, transistors, plastics

MOROCCO'S TEN ECONOMIC FREEDOMS

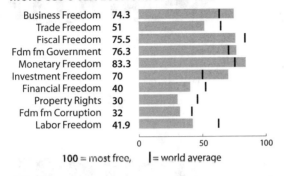

Business Freedom	74.3	
Trade Freedom	51	
Fiscal Freedom	75.5	
Fdm fm Government	76.3	
Monetary Freedom	83.3	
Investment Freedom	70	
Financial Freedom	40	
Property Rights	30	
Fdm fm Corruption	32	
Labor Freedom	41.9	

100 = most free, | = world average

BUSINESS FREEDOM — 74.3%

Starting a business takes an average of 12 days, compared to the world average of 48 days. Entrepreneurship should be easier for maximum job creation. Obtaining a business license is difficult, but closing a business is relatively easy. Despite attempts at reform, bureaucratic obstacles and delays remain problems. The overall freedom to start, operate, and close a business is relatively well protected by the national regulatory environment.

TRADE FREEDOM — 51%

Morocco's weighted average tariff rate was 14.5 percent in 2005. Prohibitive tariffs, import taxes, inconsistent and opaque government procurement procedures, non-transparent regulations and standards, import restrictions, and import bans add to the cost of trade. Consequently, an additional 20 percent is deducted from Morocco's trade freedom score to account for these non-tariff barriers.

FISCAL FREEDOM — 75.5%

Morocco has high tax rates. The top income tax rate is 44 percent, and the top corporate tax rate is 35 percent. Other taxes include a value-added tax (VAT) and a property tax. In the most recent year, overall tax revenue as a percentage of GDP was 22.7 percent.

FREEDOM FROM GOVERNMENT — 76.3%

Total government expenditures in Morocco, including consumption and transfer payments, are moderate. In the most recent year, government spending equaled 30.8 percent of GDP, and the government received 4.7 percent of its total revenues from state-owned enterprises and government ownership of property.

MONETARY FREEDOM — 83.3%

Inflation in Morocco is low, averaging 1.1 percent between 2003 and 2005. Relatively low and stable prices explain most of the monetary freedom score. Although price controls and subsidies are slowly being phased out, the government influences prices through state-owned enterprises and utilities, including electricity; subsidizes fuel, health products, and educational supplies; and sets prices for staple commodities, including vegetable oil, sugar, flour, bread, and cereals. Consequently, an additional 10 percent is deducted from Morocco's monetary freedom score to account for these policies.

INVESTMENT FREEDOM — 70%

Morocco treats foreign and locally owned investments equally and permits 100 percent foreign ownership in most sectors. There is no screening requirement, but foreign investment in some sectors is restricted. Morocco's unwieldy bureaucracy remains a major constraint on competitiveness and deters investors. The government has set up regional investment centers to decentralize and accelerate investment-related bureaucratic procedures. Residents and non-residents may hold foreign exchange accounts, subject to restrictions and requirements. Personal payments, transfer of interest, and travel payments are subject to limits, documentation requirements, and approval in some cases. Some capital transactions, including many capital and money market transactions and credit operations, require government approval.

FINANCIAL FREEDOM — 40%

Morocco's financial system is fairly well developed but subject to considerable government influence. Institutional weaknesses, poor supervision, and underdeveloped infrastructure are primary weaknesses. Most private banks are partially owned by European banks, but foreign investment in commercial banks and financial institutions is restricted by law. The state continues to possess large holdings in several banks. There are a number of state-owned specialized banks that together account for 43 percent of banking sector assets. Foreign investors have access to domestic credit. The government still uses the banking system to influence domestic savings and finance government debt. Non-performing loans are a serious problem, particularly at publicly owned banks. Capital markets are relatively developed, and the Casablanca Stock Exchange (Africa's third oldest exchange) does not restrict foreign participation.

PROPERTY RIGHTS — 30%

The judiciary is influenced by the king and is slow to deal with cases, bankruptcy protection, and liquidation procedures, as well as to enforce contracts. Corruption in the legal system is regarded as one of the main impediments to doing business.

FREEDOM FROM CORRUPTION — 32%

Corruption is perceived as significant. Morocco ranks 78th out of 158 countries in Transparency International's Corruption Perceptions Index for 2005.

LABOR FREEDOM — 41.9%

The labor market operates under highly restrictive employment regulations that hinder employment and productivity growth. The non-salary cost of employing a worker is high, and dismissing a redundant employee is costly. To increase labor flexibility, a new labor code came into effect in mid-2004, but it has not been fully implemented. Morocco's labor freedom is one of the 20 lowest in the world.

2007 Index of Economic Freedom

MOZAMBIQUE

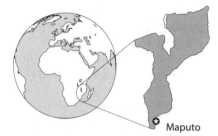

Maputo

Mozambique's economy is 56.6 percent free, according to our 2007 assessment, which makes it the world's 101st freest economy. Its overall score is 1.4 percentage points higher than last year, partially reflecting new methodological detail. Mozambique is ranked 14th out of 40 countries in the sub-Saharan Africa region, and its overall score is slightly higher than the regional average.

Mozambique ranks highly in fiscal freedom, freedom from government, investment freedom, and monetary freedom. Both the top income tax rate and the top corporate tax rate are moderate, and overall tax revenue is low as a percentage of GDP. Government expenditures are not high, and state-owned businesses account for a negligible portion of total tax revenues. Inflation is fairly high, but the government does not generally distort market prices with subsidies.

Economic development has been hampered by weak labor freedom, property rights, freedom from corruption, financial freedom, and business freedom. Opening a business takes about two and a half times the world average, and the overall regulatory environment is a burden on business formation. Most aspects of the labor market are inflexible, from the number of allowable hours in the workweek to employee severance. Judicial enforcement is weakened by corruption and subject to the political whims of the executive.

BACKGROUND: Mozambique's 16-year civil war ended in 1992. Since then, it has been a model for economic development and post-war recovery through liberalization, privatization, and stability. Economic growth averaged over 8 percent from 1992 to 2004. Mozambique remains very poor, however, and needs significant reform, including civil service reform and streamlining of the regulatory and administrative barriers to business. President Armando Guebuza has announced plans to address judicial inadequacies and corruption. Over three-quarters of the population is engaged in small-scale agriculture. Infrastructure is poor, and HIV/AIDS is a serious problem.

How Do We Measure Economic Freedom? See Chapter 3 (page 37) for an explanation of the methodology or visit the *Index* Web site at *heritage.org/index*.

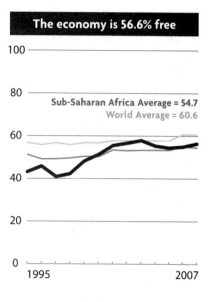

The economy is 56.6% free

Sub-Saharan Africa Average = 54.7
World Average = 60.6

QUICK FACTS

Population: 19.4 million

GDP (PPP): $24 billion
7.5% growth in 2004
7.7% 5-yr. comp. ann. growth
$1,237 per capita

Unemployment: 21% (1997 estimate)

Inflation (CPI): 12.6%

FDI (net inflow): $131.9 million

Official Development Assistance:
Multilateral: $544 million
Bilateral: $748 million (15% from the U.S.)

External Debt: $4.7 billion

Exports: $1.8 billion
Primarily aluminum, prawns, cashews, cotton, sugar, citrus, timber, bulk electricity

Imports: $2.4 billion
Primarily machinery and equipment, vehicles, fuel, chemicals, metal products, food, textiles

MOZAMBIQUE'S TEN ECONOMIC FREEDOMS

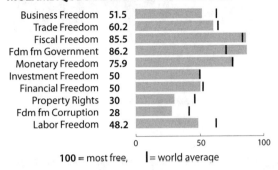

Business Freedom	51.5
Trade Freedom	60.2
Fiscal Freedom	85.5
Fdm fm Government	86.2
Monetary Freedom	75.9
Investment Freedom	50
Financial Freedom	50
Property Rights	30
Fdm fm Corruption	28
Labor Freedom	48.2

100 = most free, | = world average

BUSINESS FREEDOM — 51.5%

Starting a business takes an average of 113 days, compared to the world average of 48 days. Entrepreneurship should be easier for maximum job creation. Obtaining a business license is relatively simple, but closing a business is difficult. Implementation of regulatory reforms has been behind schedule due to the complexity of the process. Businesses still have to deal with extensive and opaque regulations. The overall freedom to start, operate, and close a business is restricted by the national regulatory environment.

TRADE FREEDOM — 60.2%

Mozambique's weighted average tariff rate was 9.9 percent in 2003. The government has made progress in liberalizing the trade regime, but time-consuming and bureaucratic customs clearance procedures, import restrictions, import bans, and corruption still add to the cost of trade. Consequently, an additional 20 percent is deducted from Mozambique's trade freedom score to account for these non-tariff barriers.

FISCAL FREEDOM — 85.5%

Mozambique has moderate tax rates. Both the top income tax rate and the top corporate tax rate are 32 percent. Other taxes include a value-added tax (VAT) and a tax on interest. In the most recent year, overall tax revenue as a percentage of GDP was 11.4 percent.

FREEDOM FROM GOVERNMENT — 86.2%

Total government expenditures in Mozambique, including consumption and transfer payments, are moderate. In the most recent year, government spending equaled 24 percent of GDP, and the government received 1 percent of its total revenues from state-owned enterprises and government ownership of property. Privatization has transformed a state-dominated economy into one that is driven by the private sector.

MONETARY FREEDOM — 75.9%

Inflation in Mozambique is relatively high, averaging 9.1 percent between 2003 and 2005. Relatively high and unstable prices explain most of the monetary freedom score. The government influences prices through state-owned utilities, including electricity, telecommunications, ports, and transportation, and subsidizes passenger rail services. Consequently, an additional 5 percent is deducted from Mozambique's monetary freedom score to account for these policies.

INVESTMENT FREEDOM — 50%

Most sectors of Mozambique's economy are open to foreign investment, but some restrictions remain in effect. Outright private ownership of land, for example, is prohibited, and mining and management contracts are subject to specific performance requirements. Lengthy registration procedures can be problematic. Foreign investors have participated in Mozambique's privatization program, subject to some impediments. Mozambique allows 100 percent repatriation of profits and retention of earned foreign exchange in domestic accounts. Both residents and non-residents may hold foreign exchange accounts. Payments and transfers are subject to maximum amounts, above which they must be approved by the central bank. Capital transactions, money market instruments, and derivatives are subject to controls.

FINANCIAL FREEDOM — 50%

Mozambique's financial system has undergone substantial reform and liberalization but remains small and dominated by banking. Supervision is insufficient. Non-performing loans led to a banking crisis in 2000–2001 and remain a problem. The banking sector had eight commercial banks in 2003, all of which were majority foreign-owned. Banco Internacional de Moçambique, majority-owned by a Portuguese bank, is Mozambique's largest bank and controls a majority of total banking assets. The state retains shares in two large banks. Most banks concentrate their lending to large companies, but microfinance is expanding. The small insurance sector is dominated by the state-owned insurance firm. Capital markets are very small, and the stock market mostly trades government debt.

PROPERTY RIGHTS — 30%

Property rights are weakly protected, and the judiciary is corrupt. There is a severe shortage of qualified legal personnel, and the backlog of cases is substantial. Enforcement of contracts and legal redress through the court system cannot be assured. Most commercial disputes are settled privately because of the judicial system's inefficiency.

FREEDOM FROM CORRUPTION — 28%

Corruption is perceived as widespread. Mozambique ranks 97th out of 158 countries in Transparency International's Corruption Perceptions Index for 2005.

LABOR FREEDOM — 48.2%

The labor market operates under highly restrictive employment regulations that hinder employment and productivity growth. The non-salary cost of employing a worker can be low, but dismissing a redundant employee is costly. There are rigid regulations on increasing or contracting the number of work hours.

NAMIBIA

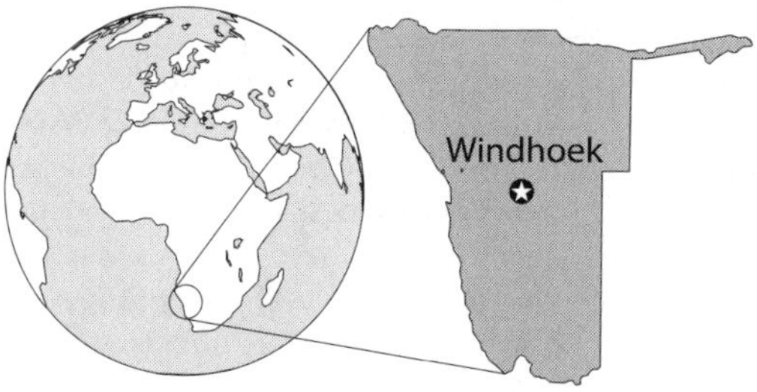

Rank: 55

Regional Rank: 4 of 40

Namibia's economy is 63.8 percent free, according to our 2007 assessment, which makes it the world's 55th freest economy. Its overall score is 2.9 percentage points higher than last year, partially reflecting new methodological detail. Namibia is ranked 4th out of 40 countries in the sub-Saharan Africa region, and its overall score is much higher than the regional average.

Namibia enjoys high levels of business freedom, trade freedom, labor freedom, financial freedom, and monetary freedom. Although starting a business takes longer than the world average, other commercial operations, such as licensing and bankruptcy, are simple. The average tariff rate is less than 1 percent. The labor market is highly flexible and one of the freest in the world. Namibia's financial sector is small but developed for the region, and much of the banking industry is intertwined with that of South Africa.

Namibia has low levels of investment freedom and property rights. The state policy of appropriating white-owned farms is a terrible signal to foreign investors. Although foreign investment is officially welcomed, the government strongly encourages investors to form partnerships with local companies. Corruption is present, but not to the degree found in the rest of the region.

BACKGROUND: Namibia is rich in minerals, including uranium, diamonds, lead, silver, tin, tungsten, and zinc. The economy is dependent on mining, fishing, and livestock, but a majority of Namibians are employed in subsistence agriculture and herding. President Hifikepunye Pohamba is committed to a "willing seller, willing buyer" effort to redistribute land, but commercial farmers are under increasing pressure to cooperate. Pohamba has pledged to clamp down on corruption. The government opposes privatization of state-owned enterprises, and its Black Economic Empowerment (BEE) policy forces foreign investors to partner with local BEE firms or trusts. Poverty, HIV/AIDS, and unemployment remain problems.

How Do We Measure Economic Freedom? See Chapter 3 (page 37) for an explanation of the methodology or visit the *Index* Web site at *heritage.org/index*.

The economy is 63.8% free

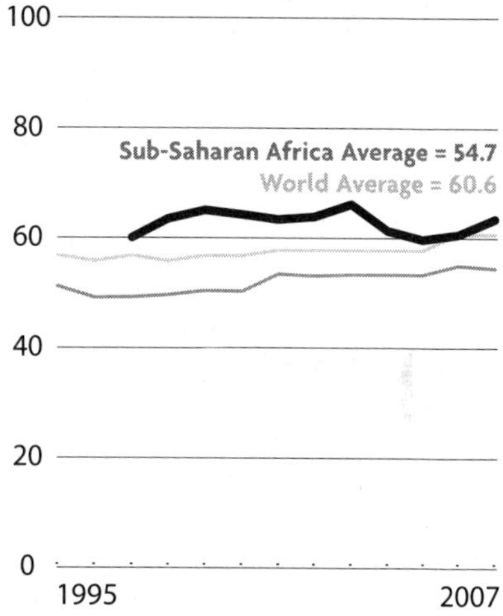

Sub-Saharan Africa Average = 54.7
World Average = 60.6

QUICK FACTS

Population: 2 million

GDP (PPP): $14.9 billion
5.9% growth in 2004
4.4% 5-yr. comp. ann. growth
$7,418 per capita

Unemployment: 34% (July 2004 estimate)

Inflation (CPI): 4.1%

FDI (net inflow): $307 million

Official Development Assistance:
Multilateral: $43 million
Bilateral: $141 million (24% from the U.S.)

External Debt: $712.9 million (2005 estimate)

Exports: $2.3 billion
Primarily diamonds, copper, gold, zinc, lead, uranium, cattle, processed fish, karakul skins

Imports: $2.5 billion
Primarily food, petroleum products and fuel, machinery and equipment, chemicals

NAMIBIA'S TEN ECONOMIC FREEDOMS

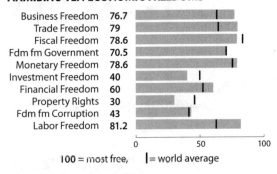

Business Freedom	76.7
Trade Freedom	79
Fiscal Freedom	78.6
Fdm fm Government	70.5
Monetary Freedom	78.6
Investment Freedom	40
Financial Freedom	60
Property Rights	30
Fdm fm Corruption	43
Labor Freedom	81.2

100 = most free, I = world average

BUSINESS FREEDOM — 76.7%

Starting a business takes an average of 95 days, compared to the world average of 48 days. Entrepreneurship should be easier for maximum job creation. Obtaining a business license is very simple, and closing a business is relatively easy. The overall freedom to start, operate, and close a business is relatively well protected by the national regulatory environment.

TRADE FREEDOM — 79%

Namibia's weighted average tariff rate was 0.5 percent in 2001. The government maintains a relatively open trade regime, but non-automatic import licensing regulations, import restrictions, and weak enforcement of intellectual property rights add to the cost of trade. Consequently, an additional 20 percent is deducted from Namibia's trade freedom score to account for these non-tariff barriers.

FISCAL FREEDOM — 78.6%

Namibia has burdensome tax rates. Both the top income tax rate and the top corporate tax rate are 35 percent. Other taxes include a value-added tax (VAT), a property transfer tax, and a vehicle tax. In the most recent year, overall tax revenue as a percentage of GDP was 27.7 percent.

FREEDOM FROM GOVERNMENT — 70.5%

Total government expenditures in Namibia, including consumption and transfer payments, are moderate. In the most recent year, government spending equaled 34.5 percent of GDP, and the government received 5.3 percent of its total revenues from state-owned enterprises and government ownership of property.

MONETARY FREEDOM — 78.6%

Inflation in Namibia is moderate, averaging 3.3 percent between 2003 and 2005. Relatively stable prices explain most of the monetary freedom score. The government sets the prices of fuel products; influences prices through state-owned enterprises and utilities, including electricity, telecommunications, water, and transportation services; determines guideline prices for maize; and subsidizes agricultural production. Consequently, an additional 10 percent is deducted from Namibia's monetary freedom score to account for these policies.

INVESTMENT FREEDOM — 40%

Namibia guarantees foreign investors national treatment for most sectors. Foreign-owned and non-productive farms are targets of the government's land reform program. Foreign investors are strongly encouraged to form a partnership with a local business as part of its Black Economic Empowerment policy. Companies that are 75 percent or more foreign-owned are subject to exchange controls. Residents may hold foreign exchange accounts, subject to prior approval and some restrictions. Non-residents may hold foreign currency accounts only if they operate in an export-processing zone. Capital transactions, transfers, and payments are subject to various restrictions, approvals, and quantitative limits. Investments abroad by residents are restricted.

FINANCIAL FREEDOM — 60%

Namibia's small but sound financial sector is closely tied to South Africa's financial system. There were four commercial banks in 2004, all at least partially foreign-owned. The largest two banks are South African. The government owns the Agricultural Bank of Namibia, the Development Bank of Namibia, and the National Housing Enterprise. It also affects the allocation of credit through subsidized credits for subsistence farmers. There were 22 insurance companies and two reinsurers in 2004. One of the reinsurers, the Namibia National Reinsurance Corporation (NamibRe), is state-owned and enjoys first option on reinsurance placed within Namibia. A 1998 law requiring that insurance companies must cede 20 percent of any policy, either issued or renewed, to NamibRe is not currently enforced and is under review. The Namibian Stock Exchange (NSX) opened in 1992 and listed 33 companies at the end of 2004.

PROPERTY RIGHTS — 30%

Expropriating land from white farm owners is now official policy. The government expropriated three large farms at the end of 2005 and by mid-2006 had begun to offer the land for resettlement. The lack of qualified magistrates, other court officials, and private attorneys causes a serious backlog of cases.

FREEDOM FROM CORRUPTION — 43%

Corruption is perceived as significant. Namibia ranks 47th out of 158 countries in Transparency International's Corruption Perceptions Index for 2005.

LABOR FREEDOM — 81.2%

The labor market operates under flexible employment regulations that enhance employment and productivity growth. The non-salary cost of employing a worker is very low, and dismissing a redundant employee is costless. Namibia's labor freedom is one of the 20 highest in the world.

NEPAL

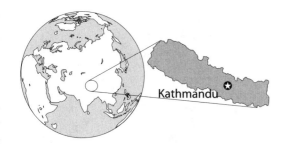

Kathmandu

Nepal's economy is 54 percent free, according to our 2007 assessment, which makes it the world's 121st freest economy. Its overall score is 1.5 percentage points lower than last year. Nepal is ranked 23rd out of 30 countries in the Asia–Pacific region, and its overall score is slightly lower than the regional average.

Nepal enjoys moderately high levels of fiscal freedom, freedom from government, and monetary freedom. Both the top income tax rate and the top corporate tax rate are moderate, and overall tax revenue is low as a percentage of GDP. Government expenditures are also low. Although Nepal receives 10 percent of its income from state-owned businesses, a plan for privatization has been in place since the 1990s, and there has been limited progress. The government is also working to eliminate price controls.

As a developing nation with widespread civil unrest, Nepal faces significant challenges. Investment freedom, financial freedom, trade freedom, property rights, and freedom from corruption are weak. There are many restrictions on foreign investment that put much of Nepal's economy off-limits to foreign capital. These regulations are enforced by an inefficient and corrupt bureaucracy. Property rights are not secured by the judiciary, which is also subject to substantial corruption and political influence.

BACKGROUND: Nepal's absolute monarchy ended in April 2006, but its transition to democracy faces many challenges. The interim government must find common ground with Maoist rebels and conduct new elections if it is to be successful. The Maoists are participating in negotiations and have honored a cease-fire, but the "people's government" continues to impose its own taxes and maintains a hard line in negotiations against both the monarchy and the interim government. There is little economic development against this backdrop; approximately three-quarters of the population works in agriculture, and services constitute the largest portion of GDP.

How Do We Measure Economic Freedom? See Chapter 3 (page 37) for an explanation of the methodology or visit the *Index* Web site at *heritage.org/index*.

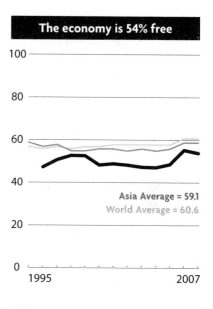

The economy is 54% free

Asia Average = 59.1
World Average = 60.6

QUICK FACTS

Population: 26.6 million

GDP (PPP): $39.6 billion
3.8% growth in 2004
3.6% 5-yr. comp. ann. growth
$1,490 per capita

Unemployment: 42% (2004 estimate)

Inflation (CPI): 4.5%

FDI (net inflow): $10.0 million (gross)

Official Development Assistance:
Multilateral: $164 million
Bilateral: $329 million (11% from the U.S.)

External Debt: $3.4 billion

Exports: $1.2 billion
Primarily carpets, clothing, leather goods, jute goods, grain

Imports: $2.2 billion
Primarily gold, machinery and equipment, petroleum products, fertilizer

NEPAL'S TEN ECONOMIC FREEDOMS

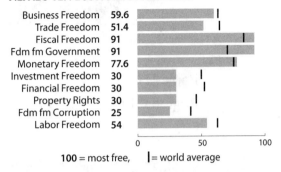

Business Freedom	59.6
Trade Freedom	51.4
Fiscal Freedom	91
Fdm fm Government	91
Monetary Freedom	77.6
Investment Freedom	30
Financial Freedom	30
Property Rights	30
Fdm fm Corruption	25
Labor Freedom	54

0   50   100

100 = most free, | = world average

BUSINESS FREEDOM — 59.6%

Starting a business takes an average of 31 days, compared to the world average of 48 days. Entrepreneurship should be easier for maximum job creation. Both obtaining a business license and closing a business are difficult. Other obstacles to entrepreneurial activities include inadequate and obscure commercial codes as well as bureaucratic delays. The overall freedom to start, operate, and close a business is restricted by the national regulatory environment.

TRADE FREEDOM — 51.4%

Nepal's weighted average tariff rate was 14.3 percent in 2004. Although Nepal has one of the region's more open economies, import bans, import restrictions, import taxes, red tape and procedural delays, and customs corruption add to the cost of trade. Consequently, an additional 20 percent is deducted from Nepal's trade freedom score to account for these non-tariff barriers.

FISCAL FREEDOM — 91%

Nepal has moderate tax rates. Both the top income tax rate and the top corporate tax rate are 25 percent. Other taxes include a value-added tax (VAT) and a property tax. In the most recent year, overall tax revenue as a percentage of GDP was 9.7 percent.

FREEDOM FROM GOVERNMENT — 91%

Total government expenditures in Nepal, including consumption and transfer payments, are low. In the most recent year, government spending equaled 15.5 percent of GDP, and the government received 10.2 percent of its total revenues from state-owned enterprises and government ownership of property. Nepal began to privatize state-owned enterprises in the early 1990s, but procedural problems and weak political will have retarded the overall process.

MONETARY FREEDOM — 77.6%

Inflation in Nepal is relatively high, averaging 7.5 percent between 2003 and 2005. Relatively high and unstable prices explain most of the monetary freedom score. While most price controls have been eliminated, the government regulates the prices of petroleum products and telecommunications services and subsidizes companies in strategic sectors. Consequently, an additional 5 percent is deducted from Nepal's monetary freedom score to account for these policies.

INVESTMENT FREEDOM — 30%

Foreign ownership is permitted in various sectors, but business and management consulting, accounting, engineering, legal services, defense, alcohol and cigarette production, travel and trekking agencies, and retail sales remain closed. Foreign investors complain about complex and opaque government procedures. Residents may hold foreign exchange accounts only in specific instances. Most non-residents may hold foreign exchange accounts. Most payments and transfers are subject to prior approval by the government. There are restrictions on most capital transactions, and all real estate transactions are subject to controls.

FINANCIAL FREEDOM — 30%

Nepal's financial system is dominated by banking and strongly influenced by the government. Financial supervision is insufficient, and efforts to prevent fraud are lacking. Regulations are not transparent and fall short of international standards. The government owns one commercial bank and 40 percent of another. Government-controlled banks account for approximately 60 percent of total banking sector lending. Foreign banks are permitted to own up to two-thirds of a joint venture but may not open a branch. The government sets commercial interest rates and directs credit to support state projects and state-owned enterprises. There were 18 insurance companies in mid-2004, the largest of which (the National Insurance Company) is majority-owned by the government. Capital markets are weak, trading on the government-owned stock exchange is moribund, and foreign participation is restricted.

PROPERTY RIGHTS — 30%

Nepal's judicial system suffers from corruption and inefficiency. Lower-level courts are vulnerable to political pressure, and bribery of judges and court staff is endemic.

FREEDOM FROM CORRUPTION — 25%

Corruption is perceived as widespread. Nepal ranks 117th out of 158 countries in Transparency International's Corruption Perceptions Index for 2005.

LABOR FREEDOM — 54%

The labor market operates under restrictive employment regulations that could be improved to enhance employment and productivity growth. The non-salary cost of employing a worker is moderate, but dismissing a redundant employee is costly. Rigid labor markets add to the cost of conducting business in Nepal.

THE NETHERLANDS

Amsterdam

The economy of the Netherlands is 77.1 percent free, according to our 2007 assessment, which makes it the world's 14th freest economy. Its overall score is 0.1 percentage point higher than last year, partially reflecting new methodological detail. The Netherlands is ranked 7th out of 41 countries in the European region, and its overall score is much higher than the regional average.

The Netherlands enjoys high levels of investment freedom, trade freedom, financial freedom, property rights, business freedom, freedom from corruption, and monetary freedom. The average tariff rate is low, although non-tariff barriers include distortionary European Union subsidies, and business regulation is efficient. Virtually all commercial operations are simple and transparent. Inflation is low, and investment in the Netherlands is actively promoted. The country's financial sector is highly developed, and it has been a European banking hub for centuries. The judiciary, independent of politics and free of corruption, has an exemplary ability to protect property rights.

The Netherlands could do better in freedom from government, fiscal freedom, and labor freedom. Total government spending is high: almost half of total GDP. The government has been working to liberalize the labor market, but impediments to reform, such as extensive unemployment benefits, still exist.

BACKGROUND: As a founding member of the European Union, the Netherlands stunned its fellow members by decisively rejecting the European Constitution in June 2005. Rotterdam remains the world's largest port as measured by tonnage of goods, and there are few restrictions on foreign direct investment. The governing coalition has pursued its reform program by trimming welfare benefits and trying to liberalize the labor market while scrapping tax breaks for early retirees. A robust, modern agricultural sector exports high-quality foodstuffs. Other exports include metal manufactures and chemicals.

How Do We Measure Economic Freedom? See Chapter 3 (page 37) for an explanation of the methodology or visit the *Index* Web site at *heritage.org/index*.

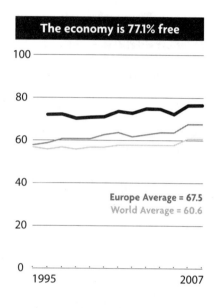

The economy is 77.1% free

Europe Average = 67.5
World Average = 60.6

QUICK FACTS

Population: 16.3 million

GDP (PPP): $517.6 billion
1.7% growth in 2004
1.3% 5-yr. comp. ann. growth
$31,789 per capita

Unemployment: 6.5%

Inflation (CPI): 1.3%

FDI (net inflow): −$6.1 million

Official Development Assistance:
Multilateral: None
Bilateral: None

External Debt: $1.7 trillion (2005)

Exports: $388.9 billion
Primarily machinery and equipment, chemicals, fuels, food

Imports: $341.6 billion
Primarily machinery and transport equipment, chemicals, fuels, food, clothing

THE NETHERLANDS' TEN ECONOMIC FREEDOMS

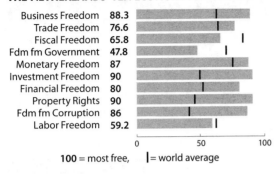

Business Freedom	88.3
Trade Freedom	76.6
Fiscal Freedom	65.8
Fdm fm Government	47.8
Monetary Freedom	87
Investment Freedom	90
Financial Freedom	80
Property Rights	90
Fdm fm Corruption	86
Labor Freedom	59.2

0   50   100

100 = most free, I = world average

BUSINESS FREEDOM — 88.3%

Starting a business takes an average of 10 days, compared to the world average of 48 days. Such ease of entrepreneurship is good for job creation. Obtaining a business license is relatively simple, and closing a business is easy. Regulations affecting entrepreneurial activities are transparent and applied evenly. The overall freedom to start, operate, and close a business is protected by the national regulatory environment.

TRADE FREEDOM — 76.6%

The Netherlands' trade policy is the same as those of other members of the European Union. The common EU weighted average tariff rate was 1.7 percent in 2005. Various non-tariff barriers are reflected in EU policy, including agricultural and manufacturing subsidies, regulatory and licensing restrictions, and other market access restrictions. The government further restricts trade by implementing supplementary biotechnology and pharmaceuticals rules that extend beyond EU policy. Consequently, an additional 20 percent is deducted from the Netherlands' trade freedom score.

FISCAL FREEDOM — 65.8%

The Netherlands has high income tax rates and moderate corporate tax rates. The top income tax rate is 52 percent, and the top corporate tax rate is 29.6 percent, which it is expected will be reduced to 29.1 percent in January 2007. Other taxes include a value-added tax (VAT), a tax on insurance contracts, and a real estate tax. In the most recent year, overall tax revenue as a percentage of GDP was 39.3 percent.

FREEDOM FROM GOVERNMENT — 47.8%

Total government expenditures in the Netherlands, including consumption and transfer payments, are very high. In the most recent year, government spending equaled 46.6 percent of GDP, and the government received 4.6 percent of its total revenues from state-owned enterprises and government ownership of property.

MONETARY FREEDOM — 87%

The Netherlands is a member of the euro zone. Inflation in the Netherlands is low, averaging 1.6 percent between 2003 and 2005. Relatively stable prices explain most of the monetary freedom score. As a participant in the EU's Com-

mon Agricultural Policy, the government subsidizes agricultural production, distorting the prices of agricultural products. The government also regulates energy prices, pharmaceutical prices, and housing rents. Consequently, an additional 5 percent is deducted from the Netherlands' monetary freedom score to account for these policies.

INVESTMENT FREEDOM — 90%

The Netherlands actively promotes foreign investment, except in railways, the national airport, and public broadcasting. Foreign firms receive national treatment. There is no screening process, 100 percent foreign ownership is allowed in the areas where foreign investment is permitted, and foreign investors receive national treatment. There are no restrictions or barriers on current transfers, repatriation of profits, purchase of real estate, or access to foreign exchange. Capital transactions are not restricted but are subject to reporting requirements under the External Financial Relations Act.

FINANCIAL FREEDOM — 80%

The Netherlands has been one of Europe's financial and banking centers for centuries, and its financial system operates freely, with little government regulation. Foreign investors face no restrictions on accessing domestic finance. Banks established in the Netherlands may engage in a variety of financial services, even real estate. Three Dutch bank conglomerates (ABN Amro, Rabobank, and ING Bank) dominate the market and account for about 75 percent of total lending. There are few formal barriers to foreign banks, but foreign participation in Dutch retail banking is minimal. The government is minimally involved in the banking sector but does guarantee loans for small to medium-size enterprises that lack sufficient collateral for securing credit lines. EU banks receive privileged treatment. Capital markets are well developed, and the Dutch stock exchange forms part of the Euronext alliance.

PROPERTY RIGHTS — 90%

Private property is secure. Contracts are very secure, and the judiciary is of high quality.

FREEDOM FROM CORRUPTION — 86%

Corruption is perceived as minimal. The Netherlands ranks 11th out of 158 countries in Transparency International's Corruption Perceptions Index for 2005.

LABOR FREEDOM — 59.2%

The labor market operates under restrictive employment regulations that could be improved to enhance employment and productivity growth. The non-salary cost of employing a worker is high, and dismissing a redundant employee is relatively costly. As modernization of the unemployment insurance program advances, changes will include reduction of the maximum duration of unemployment benefits from 60 months to 38 months.

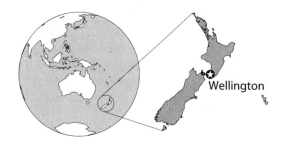
Wellington

NEW ZEALAND

N ew Zealand's economy is 81.6 percent free, according to our 2007 assessment, which makes it the world's 5th freest economy. Its overall score is 2.4 percentage points lower than last year, partially reflecting new methodological detail. New Zealand is ranked 4th out of 30 countries in the Asia–Pacific region, and its overall score is much higher than the regional average.

New Zealand rates highly in almost all areas of economic freedom but is most impressive in financial freedom, property rights, business freedom, labor freedom, and freedom from corruption. A globally competitive financial system based on market principles attracts many foreign banks, helped by low inflation and low tariff rates. A strong rule of law protects property rights, and New Zealand is the world's second most corruption-free country. Foreign and domestically owned businesses enjoy considerable flexibility in licensing, regulation, and employment practices.

New Zealand could do better in freedom from government and fiscal freedom. The top income tax rates are fairly high, as are tax revenue and government spending, but the overall effect is eclipsed by the amount of economic freedom that has been established. New Zealand's economy is a global competitor and a regional model of economic freedom.

BACKGROUND: Following two decades of sound economic policies and structural reforms, New Zealand has turned itself into a modern, flexible economy with the lowest unemployment rate of any Organisation for Economic Cooperation and Development member country. Agricultural commodities, which historically have thrived on privileged British market access, dominate the export market. New Zealand relies heavily on international trade, and its openness has helped to boost exports of goods and services, which now account for more than 30 percent of total output. Securing bilateral and regional free trade agreements is one of the government's major foreign policy goals, as is continuing to diversify the economy into industrial goods.

How Do We Measure Economic Freedom? See Chapter 3 (page 37) for an explanation of the methodology or visit the *Index* Web site at *heritage.org/index*.

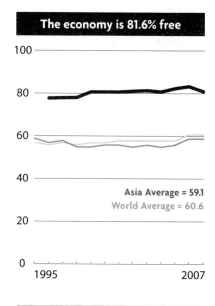

The economy is 81.6% free

Asia Average = 59.1
World Average = 60.6

1995 — 2007

QUICK FACTS

Population: 4.1 million

GDP (PPP): $95.1 billion
4.4% growth in 2004
3.8% 5-yr. comp. ann. growth
$23,413 per capita

Unemployment: 3.9% (end 2004)

Inflation (CPI): 2.3%

FDI (net inflow): $1.6 billion

Official Development Assistance:
Multilateral: None
Bilateral: None

External Debt: $42.8 billion (2005 estimate)

Exports: $28.3 billion
Primarily dairy products, meat, wood and wood products, fish, machinery

Imports: $28.8 billion
Primarily machinery and equipment, vehicles, aircraft, petroleum, electronics, textiles, plastics

NEW ZEALAND'S TEN ECONOMIC FREEDOMS

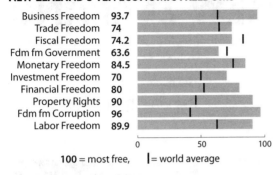

Business Freedom	93.7
Trade Freedom	74
Fiscal Freedom	74.2
Fdm fm Government	63.6
Monetary Freedom	84.5
Investment Freedom	70
Financial Freedom	80
Property Rights	90
Fdm fm Corruption	96
Labor Freedom	89.9

0   50   100

100 = most free, ∎ = world average

BUSINESS FREEDOM — 93.7%

Starting a business takes an average of 12 days, compared to the world average of 48 days. The business environment has allowed entrepreneurial activities to flourish. Obtaining a business license is simple, and closing a business is very easy. The overall freedom to start, operate, and close a business is strongly protected by the national regulatory environment.

TRADE FREEDOM — 74%

New Zealand's weighted average tariff rate was 3 percent in 2004. The government maintains a relatively open trade regime, but restrictive sanitary and phytosanitary regulations, import fees, import restrictions, import bans, issues involving the enforcement of intellectual property rights, protectionist pharmaceutical policies, and market access restrictions in some service sectors add to the cost of trade. Consequently, an additional 20 percent is deducted from New Zealand's trade freedom score to account for these non-tariff barriers.

FISCAL FREEDOM — 74.2%

New Zealand has high tax rates. The top income tax rate is 39 percent, and the top corporate tax rate is 33 percent, which is higher than those of most developing Asian countries. Other taxes include a value-added tax (VAT) and a tax on interest. In the most recent year, overall tax revenue as a percentage of GDP was 35.4 percent.

FREEDOM FROM GOVERNMENT — 63.6%

Total government expenditures in New Zealand, including consumption and transfer payments, are high. In the most recent year, government spending equaled 39.2 percent of GDP, and the government received 1.7 percent of its total revenues from state-owned enterprises and government ownership of property.

MONETARY FREEDOM — 84.5%

Inflation in New Zealand is relatively low, averaging 2.7 percent between 2003 and 2005. Relatively low and stable prices explain most of the monetary freedom score. There are no official price controls, but the government regulates the prices of utilities and subsidizes pharmaceuticals. Consequently, an additional 5 percent is deducted from New Zealand's monetary freedom score to account for these policies.

INVESTMENT FREEDOM — 70%

New Zealand encourages foreign investment, and barriers to investment are minimal. Foreign ownership is restricted in Telecom New Zealand, Air New Zealand, and fishing. The purchase of land and real estate is subject to strong restrictions. Foreign investments involving acquisition of an existing New Zealand business where foreign ownership would be 25 percent or greater or the investment exceeds NZ$50 million require approval from the Overseas Investment Commission. There are no restrictions on current transfers, repatriation of profits, or access to foreign exchange.

FINANCIAL FREEDOM — 80%

New Zealand's financial system is regulated minimally and transparently in accordance with international standards. The central bank is independent. Foreign banks are welcome, and all but two of the registered banks are predominantly foreign-owned. Foreign-owned banks account for approximately 90 percent of banking assets. The government owns one small bank, Kiwibank Limited, which began operations in late 2001. The government does not provide deposit insurance for financial institutions. Banks are required to provide full public disclosure of their financial condition. Banking services may be offered by nonbank financial institutions, provided they comply with banking regulations and public disclosure requirements. Capital markets are well developed, if small, and stocks are actively traded. Capital markets are open to foreign participation. The insurance sector is lightly regulated, and foreign participation is high. The government is involved in the accident and earthquake sectors of the insurance market.

PROPERTY RIGHTS — 90%

Private property is well protected in New Zealand. The judiciary is independent, and contracts are notably secure.

FREEDOM FROM CORRUPTION — 96%

Corruption is perceived as almost nonexistent. New Zealand ranks 2nd out of 158 countries in Transparency International's Corruption Perceptions Index for 2005.

LABOR FREEDOM — 89.9%

The labor market operates under flexible employment regulations that enhance employment and productivity growth. The non-salary cost of employing a worker is low, and dismissing a redundant employee is costless. Regulations related to increasing or contracting the number of work hours are flexible. New Zealand's labor freedom is one of the 20 highest in the world.

NICARAGUA

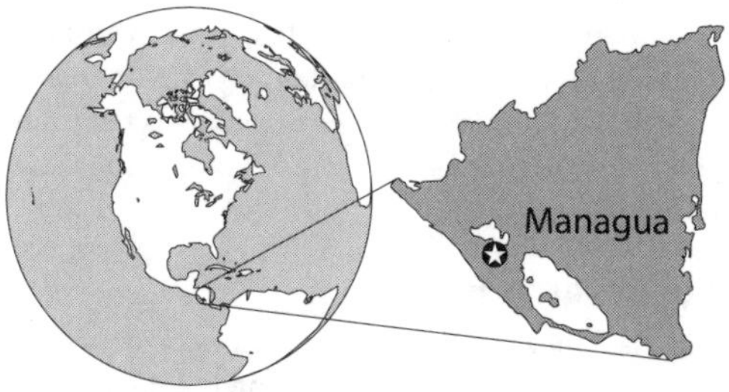

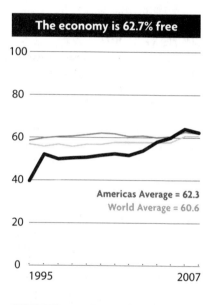

Managua

Rank: 61

Regional Rank: 14 of 29

Nicaragua's economy is 62.7 percent free, according to our 2007 assessment, which makes it the world's 61st freest economy. Its overall score is 1.7 percentage points lower than last year, partially reflecting new methodological detail. Nicaragua is ranked 14th out of 29 countries in the Americas, and its overall score is equal to the regional average.

Nicaragua enjoys high levels of fiscal freedom, freedom from government, labor freedom, investment freedom, financial freedom, and trade freedom. Personal and corporate tax rates are high, and overall tax revenue is low as a percentage of GDP. Government expenditures are also fairly low, and state-owned businesses account for less than 10 percent of total revenues. The labor market is flexible, and dismissing an employee is not costly. Nicaragua has liberalized its foreign investment procedures, and the law accords foreign capital equal treatment (although certain restrictions still exist).

Nicaragua could improve in property rights, freedom from corruption, and business freedom. The judicial system is rudimentary, inconsistent in contract enforcement, and subject to political interference. A significant amount of corruption also has a negative impact on the economic climate. Business freedom is fairly low because of difficult licensing procedures, but the government is working to streamline its regulatory process.

BACKGROUND: Nicaragua is the second-poorest country in the Western Hemisphere. Its economy depends on exports of coffee, seafood, and sugar but has also been diversified to include minerals and clothing manufacturing. The treasury was looted when the Sandinista National Liberation Front controlled the government during the 1980s. Since then, free elections have helped to restore order and promote growth. The economy has grown stronger thanks to President Enrique Bolaños's macroeconomic reforms and lower deficits through better tax collection. The outcome of presidential elections scheduled for November 2006 could have a major effect on economic policies.

How Do We Measure Economic Freedom? See Chapter 3 (page 37) for an explanation of the methodology or visit the *Index* Web site at *heritage.org/index*.

The economy is 62.7% free

Americas Average = 62.3
World Average = 60.6

1995 — 2007

QUICK FACTS

Population: 5.4 million

GDP (PPP): $19.5 billion
5.1% growth in 2004
3.0% 5-yr. comp. ann. growth
$3,634 per capita

Unemployment: 5.6% (2005 estimate)

Inflation (CPI): 8.4%

FDI (net inflow): $250 million (gross)

Official Development Assistance:
Multilateral: $410 million
Bilateral: $1.2 billion (7% from the U.S.)

External Debt: $5.2 billion

Exports: $1.7 billion
Primarily coffee, beef, shrimp, lobster, tobacco, sugar, gold, peanuts

Imports: $2.9 billion
Primarily consumer goods, machinery and equipment, raw materials, petroleum products

NICARAGUA'S TEN ECONOMIC FREEDOMS

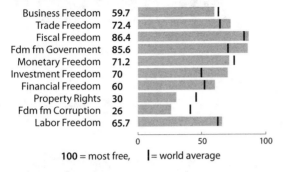

Business Freedom	59.7
Trade Freedom	72.4
Fiscal Freedom	86.4
Fdm fm Government	85.6
Monetary Freedom	71.2
Investment Freedom	70
Financial Freedom	60
Property Rights	30
Fdm fm Corruption	26
Labor Freedom	65.7

100 = most free, ▌ = world average

BUSINESS FREEDOM — 59.7%

Starting a business takes an average of 39 days, compared to the world average of 48 days. Entrepreneurship should be easier for maximum job creation. Obtaining a business license is difficult, but closing a business is relatively easy. The government has established a single window for investment in an attempt to streamline the bureaucracy, but the legal and regulatory framework remains cumbersome and lacks transparency. The overall freedom to start, operate, and close a business is restricted by the national regulatory environment.

TRADE FREEDOM — 72.4%

Nicaragua's weighted average tariff rate was 3.8 percent in 2004. The government has made progress in liberalizing the trade regime, but some prohibitive tariffs, import taxes, import fees, weak enforcement of intellectual property rights, corruption, import restrictions, import bans, and import licensing restrictions add to the cost of trade. Consequently, an additional 20 percent is deducted from Nicaragua's trade freedom score to account for these non-tariff barriers.

FISCAL FREEDOM — 86.4%

Nicaragua has burdensome tax rates. Both the top income tax rate and the top corporate tax rate are 30 percent. Other taxes include a value-added tax (VAT) and a capital gains tax. During the most recent year, overall tax revenue as a percentage of GDP was 15.5 percent.

FREEDOM FROM GOVERNMENT — 85.6%

Total government expenditures in Nicaragua, including consumption and transfer payments, are low. In the most recent year, government spending equaled 22.3 percent of GDP, and the government received 8.3 percent of its total revenues from state-owned enterprises and government ownership of property. Privatization has been rather slow.

MONETARY FREEDOM — 71.2%

Inflation in Nicaragua is relatively high, averaging 8.8 percent between 2003 and 2005. Unstable prices explain most of the monetary freedom score. Although most price controls have been eliminated, the government continues to set prices for pharmaceuticals, sugar, domestically produced soft drinks and cigarettes, and liquefied natural gas; regulates the retail price of butane gas and rates for electricity, energy, water, and telecommunications; and has been known to negotiate voluntary price restraints with domestic producers of important consumer goods. Consequently, an additional 10 percent is deducted from Nicaragua's monetary freedom score to account for these policies.

INVESTMENT FREEDOM — 70%

Nicaragua has liberalized its foreign investment sector. Investment is guaranteed equal treatment, is not screened, and faces no performance requirements. Investors are permitted to own and use property. Poor protection of property rights and cumbersome procedures are still disincentives for foreign investors. Residents may hold foreign exchange accounts, but the only non-residents who may hold such accounts are those with approved immigration status (such as diplomats). There are no controls or restrictions on payments and transfers. There are very few restrictions on capital transactions.

FINANCIAL FREEDOM — 60%

Nicaragua's underdeveloped financial system was the smallest in Central America in 2004. Foreign investors may access credit from domestic financial institutions on the same terms as domestic investors. The banking system has been stabilizing since regulators intervened to liquidate four banks between November 2000 and March 2002 and reforms introduced international standards. The state owns several development banks. There were 17 microfinance institutions in 2003, primarily serving rural areas. The insurance sector, once a state monopoly, now has four private insurance companies, though the state-owned firm remains the country's largest insurer and controls over half of the market. Capital markets are small, and the stock exchange trades primarily in government bonds.

PROPERTY RIGHTS — 30%

Protection of property rights is weak. Contracts are not strongly enforced, and the judiciary is politicized and subject to corruption.

FREEDOM FROM CORRUPTION — 26%

Corruption is perceived as widespread. Nicaragua ranks 107th out of 158 countries in Transparency International's Corruption Perceptions Index for 2005.

LABOR FREEDOM — 65.7%

The labor market operates under somewhat flexible employment regulations that could be improved to enhance employment and productivity growth. The non-salary cost of employing a worker is high, but dismissing a redundant employee is not costly. Workers are entitled to generous fringe benefits. Regulations on increasing or contracting the number of work hours are not flexible.

NIGER

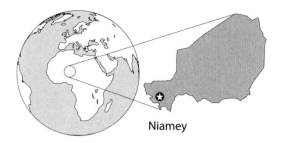

Niamey

Niger's economy is 53.5 percent free, according to our 2007 assessment, which makes it the world's 124th freest economy. Its overall score is virtually unchanged since last year. Niger is ranked 25th out of 40 countries in the sub-Saharan Africa region, and its overall score is roughly equal to the regional average.

Niger enjoys high levels of freedom from government and monetary freedom. Total government expenditures in Niger are fairly low, equaling roughly 20 percent of GDP, and state-owned businesses constitute a negligible source of revenue. Although the country has high tax rates, overall tax revenue is low as a percentage of GDP. Inflation is moderate at about 5 percent per year, and the market sets all prices for consumer goods except for petroleum.

Niger faces many challenges that are commonly found throughout Africa. Business freedom, labor freedom, property rights, and freedom from corruption are weak. Starting a business takes less time than the world average, but commercial operations overall are constrained by the national regulatory environment. The labor market is highly inelastic and one of the 20 least free in the world. The judicial system does not have enough qualified magistrates or independence from the executive branch and, like much of the rest of Niger's bureaucracy, is subject to corruption.

BACKGROUND: Niger is arid, landlocked, and one of the world's poorest countries. More than 80 percent of the population is engaged in subsistence farming and herding, and most economic activity is conducted informally. Drought is common and frequently leads to food shortages. The country possesses substantial mineral resources, including uranium and gold, and exploration for oil is underway. The infrastructure is poor and inadequate. Mamadou Tandja, first elected president in 1999, was reelected in 2004. Niger has strong economic ties with its neighbors, particularly Nigeria, which serves as a key trading partner and conduit to international markets.

How Do We Measure Economic Freedom? See Chapter 3 (page 37) for an explanation of the methodology or visit the *Index* Web site at *heritage.org/index*.

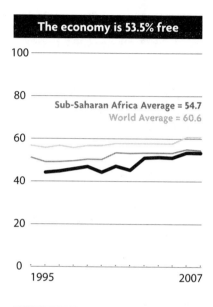

The economy is 53.5% free

Sub-Saharan Africa Average = 54.7
World Average = 60.6

1995 — 2007

QUICK FACTS

Population: 13.5 million

GDP (PPP): $10.5 billion
0.0% growth in 2004
2.8% 5-yr. comp. ann. growth
$779 per capita

Unemployment: n/a

Inflation (CPI): 0.3%

FDI (net inflow): $3.6 billion

Official Development Assistance:
Multilateral: $261 million
Bilateral: $339 million (6% from the U.S.)

External Debt: $2.0 billion

Exports: $415.1 million
Primarily uranium ore, livestock, cowpeas, onions

Imports: $681.0 million
Primarily food, machinery, vehicles and parts, petroleum, cereals

NIGER'S TEN ECONOMIC FREEDOMS

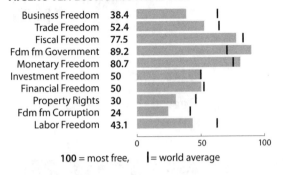

Business Freedom	38.4
Trade Freedom	52.4
Fiscal Freedom	77.5
Fdm fm Government	89.2
Monetary Freedom	80.7
Investment Freedom	50
Financial Freedom	50
Property Rights	30
Fdm fm Corruption	24
Labor Freedom	43.1

100 = most free, | = world average

BUSINESS FREEDOM — 38.4%

Starting a business takes an average of 24 days, compared to the world average of 48 days. Entrepreneurship should be easier for maximum job creation. Both obtaining a business license and closing a business can be very difficult. The overall freedom to start, operate, and close a business is significantly restricted by the national regulatory environment.

TRADE FREEDOM — 52.4%

Niger's weighted average tariff rate was 13.8 percent in 2004. Burdensome import licensing and certification regulations, inefficient and non-transparent customs implementation and regulation, and widespread corruption add to the cost of trade. Consequently, an additional 20 percent is deducted from Niger's trade freedom score to account for these non-tariff barriers.

FISCAL FREEDOM — 77.5%

Niger has high tax rates. The top income tax rate is 45 percent, and the top corporate tax rate is 35 percent. Other taxes include a value-added tax (VAT), a tax on interest, and an insurance tax. In the most recent year, overall tax revenue as a percentage of GDP was 11.4 percent.

FREEDOM FROM GOVERNMENT — 89.2%

Total government expenditures in Niger, including consumption and transfer payments, are low. In the most recent year, government spending equaled 21.4 percent of GDP, and the government received 0.3 percent of its total revenues from state-owned enterprises and government ownership of property.

MONETARY FREEDOM — 80.7%

Inflation in Niger is moderate, averaging 5.1 percent between 2003 and 2005. Relatively moderate and unstable prices explain most of the monetary freedom score. With the exception of petroleum products, market forces set prices in Niger. The government also influences prices through state-owned utilities. Consequently, an additional 5 percent is deducted from Niger's monetary freedom score to account for these policies.

INVESTMENT FREEDOM — 50%

Niger does not screen foreign investment and grants national treatment to foreign investors. All sectors are open except for national security purposes. Land ownership requires authorization. Barriers to investment include the small scale of the economy, limited buying power, high transport costs, and government bureaucracy. Residents may hold foreign exchange accounts, subject to some restrictions. Non-residents may hold foreign exchange accounts with prior approval. Payments and transfers to selected countries are subject to quantitative limits and approval. Some capital transactions to selected countries are subject to authorization. Real estate purchases by non-residents must be reported.

FINANCIAL FREEDOM — 50%

Niger's financial system is underdeveloped and the weakest in the Economic Community of West African States. The Central Bank of West African States (BCEAO) governs Niger's banking institutions. The eight BCEAO member countries use the CFA franc, pegged to the euro. Credit is allocated on market terms, but the cost is high, and credit generally is extended only to large businesses. Foreign investors have access to credit. At the beginning of 2005, nine commercial banks were in operation along with a large number of microfinance institutions. Banks offer only a limited number of financial instruments, generally letters of credit and loans. The government is a shareholder in a number of financial institutions, but private banks and foreign banks operate freely and account for most bank resources and deposits. Most capital market activity is centered in the regional stock exchange in the Ivory Coast. Although the stock market has a branch in Niger, trading is moribund and capital markets are minimal.

PROPERTY RIGHTS — 30%

Niger's judicial system is understaffed and subject to pressure from the executive. Corruption is pervasive, fuelled in part by low salaries and inadequate training programs.

FREEDOM FROM CORRUPTION — 24%

Corruption is perceived as widespread. Niger ranks 126th out of 158 countries in Transparency International's Corruption Perceptions Index for 2005.

LABOR FREEDOM — 43.1%

The labor market operates under highly restrictive employment regulations that hinder employment and productivity growth. The non-salary cost of employing a worker is high. Regulations on increasing or contracting the number of work hours are very rigid. Niger's labor freedom is one of the 20 lowest in the world.

NIGERIA

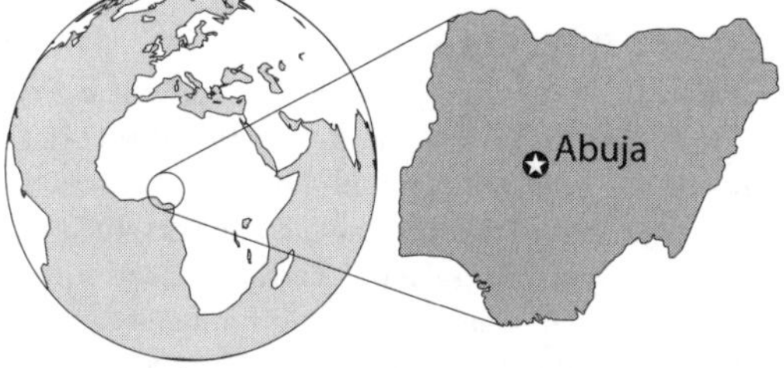

Nigeria's economy is 52.6 percent free, according to our 2007 assessment, which makes it the world's 131st freest economy. Its overall score is 3.8 percentage points higher than last year, partially reflecting new methodological detail. Nigeria is ranked 30th out of 40 countries in the sub-Saharan Africa region, and its overall score is slightly lower than the regional average.

Nigeria ranks moderately well in fiscal freedom and labor freedom and fairly well in business freedom. The top income and corporate tax rates are moderate, and overall tax revenue is low as a percentage of GDP. Regulatory commercial burdens exist, and inflation is fairly high, but the government does not distort market prices with subsidies (except for rail transport). The labor market is fairly elastic, and while firing an employee can be difficult, other factors are more flexible.

Nigeria faces significant economic challenges. Trade freedom, freedom from government, investment freedom, property rights, and freedom from corruption all need improvement. Non-tariff barriers are high, and regulations are enforced inconsistently. As in many other sub-Saharan African nations, judicial enforcement is rudimentary, corrupt, and subject to the political whims of the executive. Corruption is substantial throughout the civil service.

BACKGROUND: Nigeria has Africa's largest population, with nearly 130 million people, including 250 ethnic groups and the continent's second-largest Muslim population. Ethnic and religious tensions are volatile. Despite extensive oil resources, per capita income remains low because of corruption and mismanagement. Two-thirds of the population is engaged in agriculture, and the infrastructure is poor. In recent years, democratic processes have replaced coups and dictatorship. President Olusegun Obasanjo, who won re-election in April 2003 and is expected to leave office in 2007, has sought to reduce government involvement in the economy through privatization and deregulation, although progress has been slow.

How Do We Measure Economic Freedom? See Chapter 3 (page 37) for an explanation of the methodology or visit the *Index* Web site at *heritage.org/index*.

The economy is 52.6% free

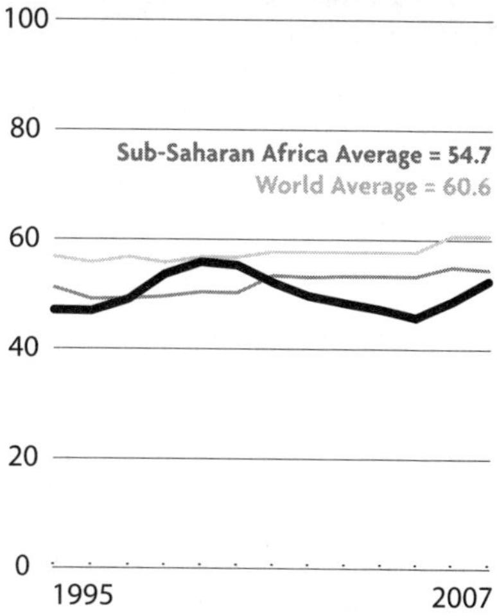

Sub-Saharan Africa Average = 54.7
World Average = 60.6

QUICK FACTS

Population: 128.7 million

GDP (PPP): $148.6 billion
6.0% growth in 2004
5.3% 5-yr. comp. ann. growth
$1,154 per capita

Unemployment: 2.9% (2005 estimate)

Inflation (CPI): 19.1%

FDI (net inflow): $1.9 billion

Official Development Assistance:
Multilateral: $284 million
Bilateral: $328 million (37% from the U.S.)

External Debt: $35.9 billion

Exports: $27.0 billion
Primarily petroleum and petroleum products, cocoa, rubber

Imports: $16.1 billion
Primarily machinery, chemicals, transport equipment, manufactured goods, food, live animals

NIGERIA'S TEN ECONOMIC FREEDOMS

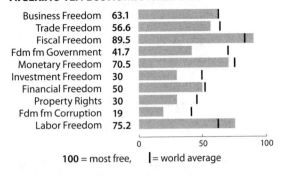

Business Freedom	63.1
Trade Freedom	56.6
Fiscal Freedom	89.5
Fdm fm Government	41.7
Monetary Freedom	70.5
Investment Freedom	30
Financial Freedom	50
Property Rights	30
Fdm fm Corruption	19
Labor Freedom	75.2

0   50   100

100 = most free,   ▌= world average

BUSINESS FREEDOM — 63.1%

Starting a business takes an average of 43 days, compared to the world average of 48 days. Entrepreneurship should be easier for maximum job creation. Obtaining a business license is difficult, but closing a business can be relatively easy. Regulation is uneven and lacks transparency. The overall freedom to start, operate, and close a business is restricted by the national regulatory environment.

TRADE FREEDOM — 56.6%

Nigeria's weighted average tariff rate was 11.7 percent in 2005. The government has made progress in liberalizing trade, but prohibitive tariffs, import fees, import and export taxes, import bans, export incentive programs, sanitary and phytosanitary regulations, weak enforcement of intellectual property rights, corruption, and inconsistent and non-transparent customs implementation add to the cost of trade. Consequently, an additional 20 percent is deducted from Nigeria's trade freedom score to account for these non-tariff barriers.

FISCAL FREEDOM — 89.5%

Nigeria has moderate tax rates. The top income tax rate is 25 percent, and the top corporate tax rate is 30 percent. Other taxes include a value-added tax (VAT), a tax on interest, and a capital gains tax. In the most recent year, overall tax revenue as a percentage of GDP was 7.2 percent.

FREEDOM FROM GOVERNMENT — 41.7%

Total government expenditures in Nigeria, including consumption and transfer payments, are moderate. In the most recent year, government spending equaled 35.4 percent of GDP, and the government received 87.2 percent of its total revenues from state-owned enterprises and government ownership of property. Privatization has progressed slowly and is behind schedule.

MONETARY FREEDOM — 70.5%

Inflation in Nigeria is high, averaging 15 percent between 2003 and 2005. Relatively high and unstable prices explain most of the monetary freedom score. With the exception of petroleum products, prices are set by the market. The government also subsidizes agriculture and manufacturing and influences prices through state-owned enterprises and utilities. Consequently, an additional 5 percent is deduct-ed from Nigeria's monetary freedom score to account for these policies.

INVESTMENT FREEDOM — 30%

Nigeria permits 100 percent foreign ownership in every industry, except for petroleum and national security. Investment disincentives include poor infrastructure, complex tax procedures, confusing land ownership laws, arbitrary application of regulations, corruption, and crime. Residents and non-residents may hold foreign exchange accounts. Some capital transactions are subject to documentation requirements and restrictions. Most payments and transfers must be conducted through banks.

FINANCIAL FREEDOM — 50%

Nigeria's financial sector is not as advanced as the size of the economy suggests. Supervision and regulation of financial institutions is bureaucratic. Nigeria has 25 licensed banks, down from 89 as a result of a new minimum capital requirement that forced many banks to merge or sell shares. Banks may offer a wide variety of financial services. Over 700 community banks focus on microfinance lending. Foreign banks must acquire licenses from the central bank. The government owns six development banks and affects the allocation of credit under the Small and Medium Industries Equity Investment Scheme, which requires banks to deposit 10 percent of their profit after tax to fund its loan programs. Nigeria has approximately 100 insurance companies. The government sold a majority of the dominant National Insurance Corporation of Nigeria to a domestic insurer in October 2005 but retains 49 percent of the Nigeria Reinsurance Corporation (scheduled for privatization in 2006), which automatically reinsures 20 percent of all direct business received by Nigerian insurance companies and 25 percent of all outward reinsurance business. Capital markets are underdeveloped.

PROPERTY RIGHTS — 30%

Nigeria's judiciary is subject to corruption and delays, partly because of insufficient funding. There is a severe lack of available court facilities, a lack of computerized systems to facilitate document processing, and arbitrary adjournment of court sessions caused by power outages.

FREEDOM FROM CORRUPTION — 19%

Corruption is perceived as widespread. Nigeria ranks 152nd out of 158 countries in Transparency International's Corruption Perceptions Index for 2005.

LABOR FREEDOM — 75.2%

The labor market operates under relatively flexible employment regulations that could be improved to enhance employment and productivity growth. The non-salary cost of employing a worker is low, and dismissing a redundant employee is relatively costless. Regulations related to increasing or contracting the number of work hours are flexible.

NORWAY

Oslo

Rank: 30

Regional Rank: 17 of 41

Norway's economy is 70.1 percent free, according to our 2007 assessment, which makes it the world's 30th freest economy. Its overall score is 0.7 percentage point lower than last year, partially reflecting new methodological detail. Norway is ranked 17th out of 41 countries in the European region, and its overall score is roughly equal to the regional average.

Norway enjoys high levels of business freedom, trade freedom, monetary freedom, property rights, and freedom from corruption. The average tariff rate is low, although some non-tariff barriers complicate trade. Starting a business takes only a few days, and the overall protection of business operations is high. Although Norway's overall monetary freedom score is harmed by government subsidizing of several goods, inflation is low. Norway has an efficient, independent judiciary that protects property rights effectively, and corruption is negligible.

Norway could do better in freedom from government, fiscal freedom, and labor freedom. Government spending is high as a percentage of GDP, as is income from state-owned businesses (mainly petroleum, although not relative to other oil-producing states). As in most other modern European welfare economies, the labor market is fairly rigid, but the government has been trying to introduce more flexibility into employment practices.

BACKGROUND: Norway has been a key force in development of the transatlantic alliance. In October 2005, Jens Stoltenberg and his Labor–Green coalition took office as the first majority government in nearly two decades. Although Norway is not a member of the European Union, the European Economic Area agreement has enabled it to benefit from close economic interaction with EU members. The country's welfare state is largely subsidized by high taxes and oil revenues. Fisheries, metal, and oil are the most important economic sectors.

How Do We Measure Economic Freedom? See Chapter 3 (page 37) for an explanation of the methodology or visit the *Index* Web site at *heritage.org/index*.

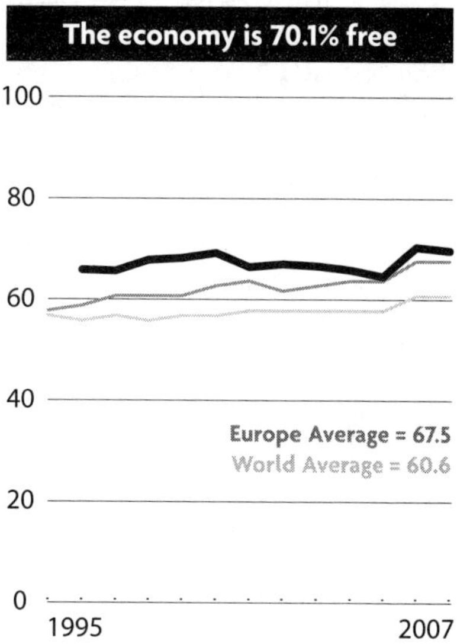

The economy is 70.1% free

Europe Average = 67.5
World Average = 60.6

1995 ———— 2007

QUICK FACTS

Population: 4.6 million

GDP (PPP): $176.5 billion
3.1% growth in 2004
2.2% 5-yr. comp. ann. growth
$38,454 per capita

Unemployment: 4.5%

Inflation (CPI): 0.5%

FDI (net inflow): $292.7 million

Official Development Assistance:
Multilateral: None
Bilateral: None

External Debt: $281.0 billion (2005)

Exports: $109.1 billion
Primarily petroleum, petroleum products, machinery and equipment, metals, chemicals, ships, fish

Imports: $73.6 billion
Primarily machinery and equipment, chemicals, metals, food

NORWAY'S TEN ECONOMIC FREEDOMS

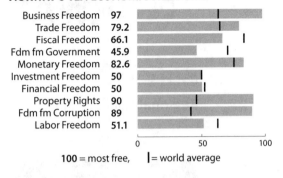

Business Freedom	97
Trade Freedom	79.2
Fiscal Freedom	66.1
Fdm fm Government	45.9
Monetary Freedom	82.6
Investment Freedom	50
Financial Freedom	50
Property Rights	90
Fdm fm Corruption	89
Labor Freedom	51.1

0   50   100

100 = most free, ▌ = world average

BUSINESS FREEDOM — 97%

Starting a business takes an average of 13 days, compared to the world average of 48 days. Such ease of entrepreneurship is good for job creation. Both obtaining a business license and closing a business are very simple. The overall freedom to start, operate, and close a business is strongly protected by the national regulatory environment.

TRADE FREEDOM — 79.2%

Norway's weighted average tariff rate was 0.4 percent in 2004. Although tariffs are relatively low, import licensing requirements, restrictive pharmaceutical policies, prohibitive and burdensome regulations and standards, agriculture and manufacturing subsidies, and inconsistent enforcement of intellectual property rights add to the cost of trade. Consequently, an additional 20 percent is deducted from Norway's trade freedom score to account for these non-tariff barriers.

FISCAL FREEDOM — 66.1%

Norway has a high income tax rate and a moderate corporate tax rate. The top income tax rate is 47.8 percent, and the top corporate tax rate is 28 percent. Other taxes include a value-added tax (VAT) and a tax on insurance contracts. In the most recent year, overall tax revenue as a percentage of GDP was 44.9 percent.

FREEDOM FROM GOVERNMENT — 45.9%

Total government expenditures in Norway, including consumption and transfer payments, are high. In the most recent year, government spending equaled 45.9 percent of GDP, and the government received 14.9 percent of its total revenues from state-owned enterprises and government ownership of property.

MONETARY FREEDOM — 82.6%

Inflation in Norway is low, averaging 1.4 percent between 2003 and 2005. Stable prices explain most of the monetary freedom score. The government controls prices for petroleum products, regulates prices for pharmaceuticals, influences prices through state-owned enterprises and utilities, and provides numerous agriculture and manufacturing subsidies. Consequently, an additional 10 percent is deducted from Norway's monetary freedom score to account for these policies.

INVESTMENT FREEDOM — 50%

The government restricts investment in sectors in which it has a monopoly, such as financial services, mining, hydropower, property acquisition, and areas considered politically sensitive. There are nationality restrictions in the fishing and maritime transport sectors. Existing regulations, standards, and practices often marginally favor Norwegian, Scandinavian, and European Economic Area (EEA) investors. Both residents and non-residents may hold foreign exchange accounts. There are no restrictions on payments, transfers, or repatriation of profits.

FINANCIAL FREEDOM — 50%

Supervision of the financial system is prudent, and regulations are largely consistent with international norms. Credit is allocated on market terms, and banks offer a wide array of financial services. Norway's banking system is composed of 15 commercial banks, 129 savings banks, and a number of specialized state-owned banks that provide medium-term and long-term credit to targeted industries. The government continues to own 34 percent of Den norske Bank, Norway's largest bank, which accounts for 40 percent of banking assets. The Norwegian Financial Supervisory Authority must grant permission for acquisition of financial institutions that exceed certain thresholds. Moreover, half of a bank's board and corporate assembly must be nationals or permanent residents of Norway or an EEA nation. There were eight registered foreign banks and two foreign subsidiary banks as of October 2005. The insurance sector is dominated by private insurers. The stock exchange is part of a regional integrated network of exchanges that covers all Nordic and most Baltic countries.

PROPERTY RIGHTS — 90%

Private property is safe from expropriation. Contracts are secure, and the judiciary is of high quality.

FREEDOM FROM CORRUPTION — 89%

Corruption is perceived as minimal. Norway ranks 8th out of 158 countries in Transparency International's Corruption Perceptions Index for 2005.

LABOR FREEDOM — 51.1%

The labor market operates under restrictive employment regulations that hinder employment and productivity growth. The non-salary cost of employing a worker is moderate, but dismissing a redundant employee is relatively costly. A new Working Environment and Worker Protection Act, passed in late 2005, mainly maintains the basic principles of a 1977 Act and aims to meet the need for flexibility in employment contracts and working hour periods.

OMAN

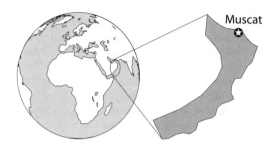

Muscat

Oman's economy is 63.9 percent free, according to our 2007 assessment, which makes it the world's 54th freest economy. Its overall score is 1.6 percentage points higher than last year, partially reflecting new methodological detail. Oman is ranked 4th freest among the 17 countries in the Middle East/North Africa region, and its overall score is higher than the regional average.

Oman has high levels of fiscal freedom, trade freedom, labor freedom, monetary freedom, and freedom from corruption. A business-friendly environment encourages the rapid growth of private enterprise. There are no taxes on private income, and the highest corporate tax rate is only 12 percent. The government imposes significant additional non-tariff barriers to trade, but a free trade agreement signed with the United States in 2006 should lead to the easing of some restrictions. Corruption is very low, particularly for a country that is not a democracy. Oman's labor market is flexible, but the practice of forcing foreign governments to hire Omanis is cumbersome.

Oman could primarily improve in freedom from government but also in investment freedom and financial freedom. Very high government spending is supported by a large state-owned energy sector.

BACKGROUND: The Arab monarchy of Oman has been trying to modernize its oil-dominated economy without diluting the ruling al-Said family's power. Oman is a relatively small oil producer, and production has declined steadily since 2001, but this has been offset by rising oil prices. To promote economic diversification, the government has sought to expand natural gas exports and develop gas-based industries. It has encouraged foreign investment in the petrochemical, electrical power, telecommunications, and other industries. Dangerously high unemployment has led the government to place a high priority on "Omanization," or the replacement of foreign workers with local staff. A new free trade agreement reached with the U.S. in 2006 should spur further growth and new opportunities.

How Do We Measure Economic Freedom? See Chapter 3 (page 37) for an explanation of the methodology or visit the *Index* Web site at *heritage.org/index*.

The economy is 63.9% free

Mideast/North Africa Average = 57.2
World Average = 60.6

(chart with y-axis from 0 to 100, x-axis from 1995 to 2007)

QUICK FACTS

Population: 2.5 million

GDP (PPP): $38.7 billion
4.5% growth in 2004
4.3% 5-yr. comp. ann. growth
$15,259 per capita

Unemployment: 15% (2004 estimate)

Inflation (CPI): 0.4%

FDI (net inflow): −$17.9 million

Official Development Assistance:
Multilateral: $1 million
Bilateral: $83 million (1% from the U.S.)

External Debt: $3.9 billion

Exports: $14.2 billion
Primarily petroleum, fish, metals, textiles

Imports: $10.6 billion
Primarily machinery, transport equipment, manufactured goods, food, livestock, lubricants

OMAN'S TEN ECONOMIC FREEDOMS

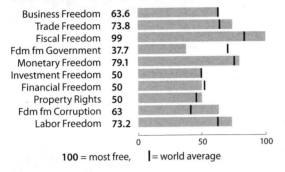

Business Freedom	63.6
Trade Freedom	73.8
Fiscal Freedom	99
Fdm fm Government	37.7
Monetary Freedom	79.1
Investment Freedom	50
Financial Freedom	50
Property Rights	50
Fdm fm Corruption	63
Labor Freedom	73.2

100 = most free, ▌= world average

BUSINESS FREEDOM — 63.6%

Starting a business takes an average of 34 days, compared to the world average of 48 days. Entrepreneurship should be easier for maximum job creation. Oman's regulatory system is not always transparent and consistent. Obtaining a business license can be difficult, but closing a business is relatively easy. The overall freedom to start, operate, and close a business is relatively well protected by the national regulatory environment.

TRADE FREEDOM — 73.8%

Oman's weighted average tariff rate was 3.1 percent in 2005. Prohibitive tariffs, import restrictions, import bans, burdensome licensing requirements, subsidies, and protectionist government procurement policies add to the cost of trade. Consequently, an additional 20 percent is deducted from Oman's trade freedom score to account for these non-tariff barriers.

FISCAL FREEDOM — 99%

Oman has low tax rates. There is no income tax on individuals, and the top corporate tax rate is 12 percent. Other taxes include a value-added tax (VAT) and a transfer tax. In the most recent year, overall tax revenue as a percentage of GDP was 1.9 percent.

FREEDOM FROM GOVERNMENT — 37.7%

Total government expenditures in Oman, including consumption and transfer payments, are high. In the most recent year, government spending equaled 40 percent of GDP, and the government received 74.9 percent of its total revenues from state-owned enterprises and government ownership of property.

MONETARY FREEDOM — 79.1%

Inflation in Oman is low, averaging 0.9 percent between 2003 and 2005. Stable prices explain most of the monetary freedom score. The government implements an extensive subsidy system, controlling the prices of a range of core goods and services, and influences prices through state-owned enterprises and utilities, including electricity and water. Consequently, an additional 15 percent is deducted from Oman's monetary freedom score to account for these policies.

INVESTMENT FREEDOM — 50%

Foreign ownership above 70 percent is allowed with the Minister of Commerce and Industry's approval. The official "Omanization" requirement that only Omanis may work in specified occupational categories is an impediment to foreign investment. The approval process for establishing a business can be difficult, particularly with respect to land acquisition and labor requirements. Both residents and non-residents may hold foreign exchange accounts. Restrictions on payments, transactions, and transfers generally apply only to Israel. Non-residents are generally not permitted to own land, but there are exceptions for citizens of Gulf Cooperation Council countries.

FINANCIAL FREEDOM — 50%

Supervision and regulation of the financial sector is often a burden. A 2000 banking law limited investments in foreign securities, raised capital requirements, and granted the central bank authority to reject candidates for senior positions in commercial banks. Since then, several banks have merged. Oman's banking sector consists of 14 commercial banks, nine of which are foreign bank branches. Three other specialized banks provide housing and industrial loans to Omani citizens at favorable terms. Although most credit is offered at market rates, the government intervenes in credit markets through subsidized loans to promote investment. The central bank also imposes restrictions on interest rates on personal housing loans. The central bank purchased a 35 percent stake in the National Bank of Oman in 2005. The Muscat Securities Market is very active and, unlike many other equity markets in the region, is open to foreign investors.

PROPERTY RIGHTS — 50%

The threat of expropriation is low, although the judiciary is subject to political influence. Since February 2006, foreigners may hold the title to homes inside specified tourism projects.

FREEDOM FROM CORRUPTION — 63%

Corruption is perceived as present. Oman ranks 28th out of 158 countries in Transparency International's Corruption Perceptions Index for 2005.

LABOR FREEDOM — 73.2%

The labor market operates under relatively flexible employment regulations that could be improved to enhance employment and productivity growth. The non-salary cost of employing a worker is low, and dismissing a redundant employee is not difficult. The labor laws, which enforce the "Omanization" requirement that private-sector firms must meet quotas for hiring native Omani workers, are burdensome.

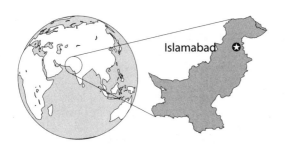

Islamabad ✪

PAKISTAN

Rank: 89

Regional Rank: 15 of 30

Pakistan's economy is 58.2 percent free, according to our 2007 assessment, which makes it the world's 89th freest economy. Its overall score is 1.3 percentage points lower than last year, partially reflecting new methodological detail. Pakistan is ranked 15th out of 30 countries in the Asia–Pacific region, and its overall score is slightly below the regional average.

Pakistan scores well in fiscal freedom, business freedom, freedom from government, and labor freedom. The top income and corporate tax rates are high (35 and 37 percent, respectively), but tax revenue and government spending are low relative to GDP. Commercial registration and licensing are historically inefficient, but the government's efforts to liberalize the business climate are producing results. The labor market is flexible, although firing procedures are costly.

Pakistan has weak trade freedom, financial freedom, property rights, and freedom from corruption. Imports are subject to a high average tariff rate and burdensome non-tariff barriers. The judicial system does not protect property rights effectively because of a serious case backlog, under-staffed facilities, and poor overall security. Serious corruption taints the judiciary and civil service, making Pakistan one of the 20 most corrupt nations rated by the *Index*. Pakistan's financial market, though advanced for the region, is similarly constrained by regulation and bureaucracy.

BACKGROUND: Pakistan is a vital crossroads between Central and South Asia. President Pervez Musharraf is expected to stay in office throughout the year; to retain his positions as chief of the army and chairman of the National Security Council, which gives him the power to dismiss Parliament and the prime minister; and to retain power after elections scheduled for October 2007. Active insurgencies in Baluchistan, Waziristan, and Kashmir and the attendant possibility of assassination threaten political stability. Wide-ranging macroeconomic reforms have spurred economic growth. Services comprise just over half the economy, with agriculture and industry evenly dividing the rest.

How Do We Measure Economic Freedom? See Chapter 3 (page 37) for an explanation of the methodology or visit the *Index* Web site at *heritage.org/index*.

The economy is 58.2% free

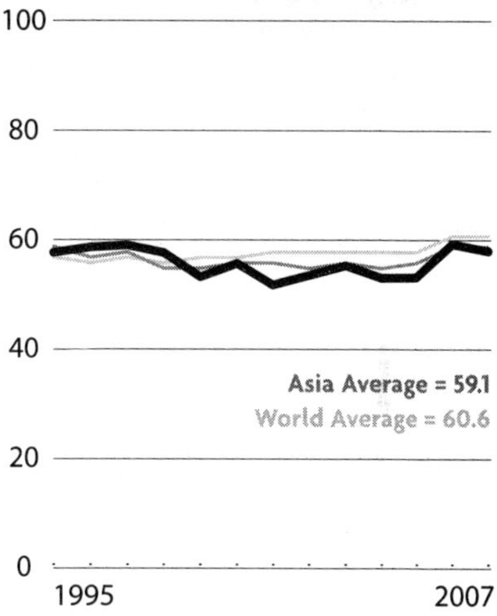

Asia Average = 59.1
World Average = 60.6

1995 — 2007

QUICK FACTS

Population: 152.1 million

GDP (PPP): $338.4 billion
7.1% growth in 2004
4.5% 5-yr. comp. ann. growth
$2,225 per capita

Unemployment: 6.5%

Inflation (CPI): 7.4%

FDI (net inflow): $896 million

Official Development Assistance:
Multilateral: $1.4 billion
Bilateral: $424 million (18% from the U.S.)

External Debt: $35.7 billion

Exports: $16.1 billion
Primarily textiles, rice, leather goods, sports goods, chemicals, manufactures, carpets and rugs

Imports: $22.1 billion
Primarily petroleum and petroleum products, machinery, plastics, transportation equipment, edible oils, paper and paperboard, iron and steel, tea

PAKISTAN'S TEN ECONOMIC FREEDOMS

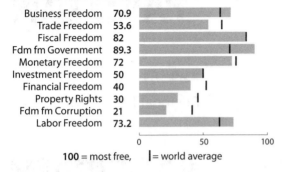

Business Freedom	70.9
Trade Freedom	53.6
Fiscal Freedom	82
Fdm fm Government	89.3
Monetary Freedom	72
Investment Freedom	50
Financial Freedom	40
Property Rights	30
Fdm fm Corruption	21
Labor Freedom	73.2

0   50   100

100 = most free, | = world average

BUSINESS FREEDOM — 70.9%

Starting a business takes an average of 24 days, compared to the world average of 48 days. Entrepreneurship should be easier for maximum job creation. Obtaining a business license is difficult, but closing a business is relatively easy. In recent years, the implementation of privatization, banking sector reforms, utility sector reform, and reductions in red tape have helped to create an environment within which the private sector has begun to thrive. The overall freedom to start, operate, and close a business is relatively well protected by the national regulatory environment.

TRADE FREEDOM — 53.6%

Pakistan's weighted average tariff rate was 13.2 percent in 2004. The government has made progress toward liberalizing the trade regime, but import bans, inconsistent and non-transparent regulations and standards, export subsidies, weak enforcement of intellectual property rights, and corruption add to the cost of trade. Consequently, an additional 20 percent is deducted from Pakistan's trade freedom score to account for these non-tariff barriers.

FISCAL FREEDOM — 82%

Pakistan has burdensome tax rates. The top income tax rate is 35 percent, and the top corporate tax rate is 37 percent. Other taxes include a value-added tax (VAT) and a property tax. In the most recent year, overall tax revenue as a percentage of GDP was 10.1 percent.

FREEDOM FROM GOVERNMENT — 89.3%

Total government expenditures in Pakistan, including consumption and transfer payments, are low. In the most recent year, government spending equaled 16 percent of GDP, and the government received 14.1 percent of its total revenues from state-owned enterprises and government ownership of property.

MONETARY FREEDOM — 72%

Inflation in Pakistan is relatively high, averaging 8.1 percent between 2003 and 2005. Relatively high and unstable prices explain most of the monetary freedom score. The government controls pharmaceutical and fuel prices and provides subsidies to agriculture. It also influences prices through state-owned enterprises and utilities, including electricity and water. Consequently, an additional 10 per-

cent is deducted from Pakistan's monetary freedom score to account for these policies.

INVESTMENT FREEDOM — 50%

Foreign investors are permitted to own 100 percent of most businesses, except in arms and munitions, high explosives, currency and mint operations, radioactive substances, finance, and new non-industrial alcohol plants. The government requires a minimum initial investment in agriculture, infrastructure, and social services; maintains local content requirements for 16 items in the automobile and motorcycle industries; and caps foreign ownership in agricultural investments at 60 percent. Foreign exchange accounts are subject to restrictions, including government approval in some cases. Payments and transfers are subject to approval, quantitative limits, and other restrictions. Most capital transactions are not permitted or require government approval.

FINANCIAL FREEDOM — 40%

Pakistan's financial system is well developed compared to those of other developing countries but remains vulnerable to government influence. The banking sector is dominated by five domestic banks that account for over 80 percent of assets. The government maintains a majority stake in the largest bank and controls several specialized banks. There were 14 foreign banks as of mid-2005. The central bank must approve all new bank branches, whether domestic or foreign. The underdeveloped insurance sector included 55 companies in 2003, but a state-owned firm controls 76 percent of the life insurance market. Foreign investors may not own more than 51 percent of a life or general insurance company. Domestic insurance companies are required to meet their reinsurance needs in Pakistan.

PROPERTY RIGHTS — 30%

Pakistan's judiciary was completely separated from the executive in mid-2001 but remains hampered by ineffective implementation of the laws, poor security for judges and witnesses, delays in sentencing, and a huge backlog of cases. Corruption is a serious impediment to the administration of justice.

FREEDOM FROM CORRUPTION — 21%

Corruption is perceived as widespread. Pakistan ranks 144th out of 158 countries in Transparency International's Corruption Perceptions Index for 2005.

LABOR FREEDOM — 73.2%

The labor market operates under relatively flexible employment regulations that could be improved to enhance employment and productivity growth. The non-salary cost of employing a worker is moderate, but dismissing a redundant employee is relatively costly. Regulations related to increasing or contracting the number of working hours are flexible.

PANAMA

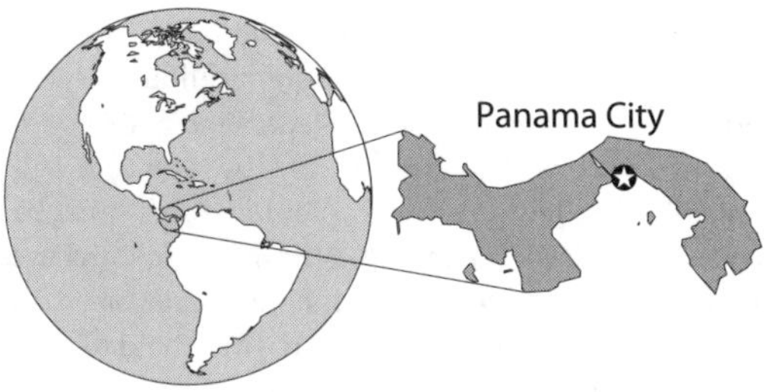

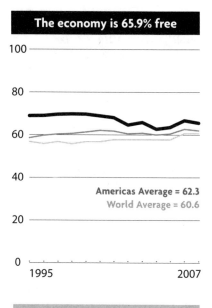

Panama City

Panama's economy is 65.9 percent free, according to our 2007 assessment, which makes it the world's 47th freest economy. Its overall score is 1.3 percentage points lower than last year, partially reflecting new methodological detail. Panama is ranked 10th out of 29 countries in the Americas, and its overall score is slightly higher than the regional average.

Panama receives high scores for business freedom, fiscal freedom, freedom from government, financial freedom, investment freedom, and monetary freedom. Commercial operations are generally subject to clear rules, although bureaucratic inefficiency worsens the regulatory environment. Personal and corporate income tax rates are moderate, and overall tax revenue is low as a percentage of GDP. Government expenditures are also fairly low, and the country experiences only a marginal amount of inflation. The law welcomes foreign capital and imposes only minor restrictions on investments. Panama is a regional financial hub and uses the U.S. dollar as its currency.

Panama suffers from weak property rights and freedom from corruption. The judicial system is backlogged with cases, not committed to contract enforcement, and subject to political interference. The economic climate is further hurt by a significant amount of corruption in the judiciary and civil service. Trade regulations are enforced inconsistently.

BACKGROUND: Once a part of Colombia, Panama has been independent since 1903. Its canal was built by the U.S. Army Corps of Engineers and operated jointly with the United States until 1999. Since then, Panama has managed the canal and has put former U.S. military zones to commercial use. President Martín Torrijos, elected in 2004, has enacted laws to curb corruption and has proposed expanding the canal to handle large container ships. Education needs to be improved so that youth will be better prepared for jobs in the service sector that dominates Panama's economy.

How Do We Measure Economic Freedom? See Chapter 3 (page 37) for an explanation of the methodology or visit the *Index* Web site at *heritage.org/index*.

The economy is 65.9% free

Americas Average = 62.3
World Average = 60.6

1995 — 2007

QUICK FACTS

Population: 3.2 million

GDP (PPP): $23.1 billion
7.6% growth in 2004
3.4% 5-yr. comp. ann. growth
$7,278 per capita

Unemployment: 9.8% (2005 estimate)

Inflation (CPI): 0.5%

FDI (net inflow): −$472.7 million

Official Development Assistance:
Multilateral: $21 million
Bilateral: $39 million (39% from the U.S.)

External Debt: $9.5 billion

Exports: $8.9 billion
Primarily bananas, shrimp, sugar, coffee, clothing

Imports: $9.2 billion
Primarily capital goods, food, consumer goods, chemicals

PANAMA'S TEN ECONOMIC FREEDOMS

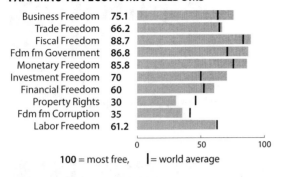

Business Freedom	75.1
Trade Freedom	66.2
Fiscal Freedom	88.7
Fdm fm Government	86.8
Monetary Freedom	85.8
Investment Freedom	70
Financial Freedom	60
Property Rights	30
Fdm fm Corruption	35
Labor Freedom	61.2

0   50   100

100 = most free, **|** = world average

BUSINESS FREEDOM — 75.1%

Starting a business takes an average of 19 days, compared to the world average of 48 days. Obtaining a business license is relatively simple, but closing a business is difficult. Regulations are generally transparent, but bureaucratic delays and red tape are obstacles to entrepreneurship. The overall freedom to start, operate, and close a business is relatively well protected by the national regulatory environment.

TRADE FREEDOM — 66.2%

Panama's weighted average tariff rate was 6.9 percent in 2001. Import taxes (including a 5 percent transfer tax levied on the CIF value of all imports), an arbitrary and non-transparent import licensing process, inconsistent and non-transparent regulations and standards, export subsidies, weak enforcement of intellectual property rights, and corruption add to the cost of trade. Consequently, an additional 20 percent is deducted from Panama's trade freedom score to account for these non-tariff barriers.

FISCAL FREEDOM — 88.7%

Panama has moderate income tax and corporate tax rates. The top income tax rate is 27 percent, and the top corporate tax rate is 30 percent. Other taxes include a value-added tax (VAT) and a transfer tax. In the most recent year, overall tax revenue as a percentage of GDP was 8.5 percent.

FREEDOM FROM GOVERNMENT — 86.8%

Total government expenditures in Panama, including consumption and transfer payments, are low. In the most recent year, government spending equaled 18.7 percent of GDP, and the government received 15.2 percent of its revenues from state-owned enterprises and government ownership of property.

MONETARY FREEDOM — 85.8%

Panama has used the U.S. dollar as its legal tender (i.e., has been fully dollarized) since its founding in 1904. Inflation in Panama is relatively low, averaging 2.1 percent between 2003 and 2005. The government controls pharmaceutical and fuel prices. It also influences prices through state-owned enterprises and utilities, including electricity and water. Consequently, an additional 5 percent is deducted from Panama's monetary freedom score to account for these policies.

INVESTMENT FREEDOM — 70%

Most sectors of the economy are open to foreign investment. The government imposes some limitations on foreign ownership—for example, in the retail and media sectors where ownership must be Panamanian, except in cases of franchising. Some professionals, such as medical practitioners, lawyers, and custom brokers, must be Panamanian citizens. Foreign investors may not purchase land within 10 kilometers of a national border or on an island. Both residents and non-residents may hold foreign exchange accounts. There are no restrictions or controls on payments, transactions, transfers, repatriation of profits, or capital transactions.

FINANCIAL FREEDOM — 60%

Panama is a financial hub in Latin America and home to numerous international companies and financial institutions. Because the U.S. dollar is legal tender, Panama does not have a central bank. Instead, an independent Banking Superintendency oversees the sector. A 1998 banking reform law brought Panamanian regulations largely into compliance with international standards. There are few restrictions on opening banks, and the government exercises little control over the allocation of credit. Domestic and foreign banks offer a wide variety of financial services. Foreign and domestic banks are treated equally, and there is considerable foreign participation in the banking sector. Of the country's 10 largest banks, two are state-owned. Capital markets are relatively sophisticated, although the stock market trades primarily in government debt.

PROPERTY RIGHTS — 30%

Panama's judiciary, although constitutionally independent, is influenced by the executive. Businesses do not trust the system as an objective, independent arbiter in legal or commercial disputes. Backlogs and corruption are severe.

FREEDOM FROM CORRUPTION — 35%

Corruption is perceived as significant. Panama ranks 65th out of 158 countries in Transparency International's Corruption Perceptions Index for 2005.

LABOR FREEDOM — 61.2%

The labor market operates under inflexible employment regulations that hinder overall productivity growth. The non-salary cost of employing a worker is high, and dismissing a redundant employee can be difficult. Regulations on increasing or contracting the number of work hours are flexible.

PARAGUAY

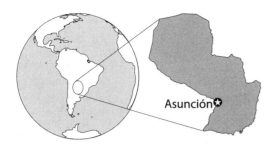

Asunción

Rank: 99

Regional Rank: 22 of 29

Paraguay's economy is 56.8 percent free, according to our 2007 assessment, which makes it the world's 99th freest economy. Its overall score is 1.4 percentage points higher than last year, partially reflecting new methodological detail. Paraguay is ranked 22nd out of 29 countries in the Americas, and its overall score is lower than the regional average.

Paraguay enjoys high levels of fiscal freedom, monetary freedom, and freedom from government. Income and corporate tax rates are extremely low, and overall tax revenue is low as a percentage of GDP. Government spending is also low. Even though the government has initiated a program of privatization, it still receives a large amount of income from state-owned businesses. Inflation is moderate, most prices are freely set by the market, and price intervention is minimal.

Paraguay has weak business freedom, labor freedom, property rights, and freedom from corruption. Opening a business is difficult, commercial regulations are extensive, and enforcement is the prerogative of an opaque bureaucracy. The labor market is similarly constrained by regulation and bureaucracy to the extent that Paraguay has one of the world's 20 most restricted labor systems. The rule of law is significantly influenced by the government, and corruption is rampant.

BACKGROUND: Since 1989, Paraguay has consolidated its democracy, though not without occasional violence, including the assassination of a vice president in 1999. President Nicanor Duarte Frutos, elected in 2003, launched fiscal and judicial reforms and has enjoyed broad support; but nearly half of the labor force still works in agriculture—the major export earner—and 36 percent of Paraguayans live below the poverty line. Better security cooperation with neighboring countries has resulted in a reduction in smuggling and better scrutiny of suspected Middle Eastern terrorist-support groups.

How Do We Measure Economic Freedom? See Chapter 3 (page 37) for an explanation of the methodology or visit the *Index* Web site at *heritage.org/index*.

The economy is 56.8% free

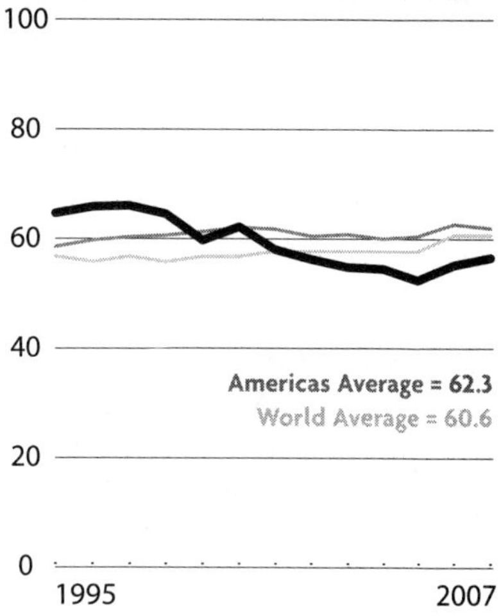

Americas Average = 62.3
World Average = 60.6

1995 — 2007

QUICK FACTS

Population: 6 million

GDP (PPP): $29.0 billion
4.1% growth in 2004
1.3% 5-yr. comp. ann. growth
$4,813 per capita

Unemployment: 16.2% (2004 estimate)

Inflation (CPI): 4.3%

FDI (net inflow): $113.4 million

Official Development Assistance:
Multilateral: $10 million
Bilateral: $91 million (18% from the U.S.)

External Debt: $3.4 billion

Exports: $3.4 billion
Primarily soybeans, feed, cotton, meat, edible oils, electricity, wood, leather

Imports: $3.5 billion
Primarily road vehicles, consumer goods, tobacco, petroleum products, electrical machinery

PARAGUAY'S TEN ECONOMIC FREEDOMS

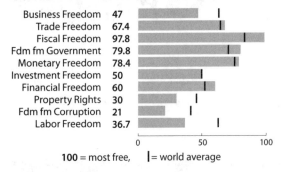

Business Freedom	47
Trade Freedom	67.4
Fiscal Freedom	97.8
Fdm fm Government	79.8
Monetary Freedom	78.4
Investment Freedom	50
Financial Freedom	60
Property Rights	30
Fdm fm Corruption	21
Labor Freedom	36.7

0   50   100

100 = most free, | = world average

BUSINESS FREEDOM — 47%

Starting a business takes an average of 74 days, compared to the world average of 48 days. To maximize entrepreneurship and job creation, it should be easier to start a company. Obtaining a business license can be difficult, and closing a business is difficult. Regulations are sometimes inconsistent and lack transparency. The overall freedom to start, operate, and close a business is seriously restricted by the national regulatory environment.

TRADE FREEDOM — 67.4%

Paraguay's weighted average tariff rate was 6.3 percent in 2004. Cumbersome and time-consuming customs procedures, import taxes, import fees, and burdensome labeling requirements add to the cost of trade. Import restrictions and prohibitions are imposed for economic development and balance-of-payments purposes or to protect domestic industry. Consequently, an additional 20 percent is deducted from Paraguay's trade freedom score to account for these non-tariff barriers.

FISCAL FREEDOM — 97.8%

Paraguay has very low income tax rates. A top income tax rate of 10 percent was introduced in 2006, and the corporate income tax rate is also 10 percent. Other taxes include a value-added tax (VAT) and a property tax. In the most recent year, overall tax revenue as a percentage of GDP was 11.2 percent.

FREEDOM FROM GOVERNMENT — 79.8%

Total government expenditures in Paraguay, including consumption and transfer payments, are low. In the most recent year, government spending equaled 21.1 percent of GDP, and the government received 29.5 percent of its revenues from state-owned enterprises and government ownership of property. Privatization has been slow and uneven.

MONETARY FREEDOM — 78.4%

Inflation in Paraguay is relatively high, averaging 6.9 percent between 2003 and 2005. Relatively high and unstable prices explain most of the monetary freedom score. Most prices are freely set in the market, but the government controls the price of fuel and is able to influence prices through state-owned enterprises and utilities, including electricity, telecommunications, transportation, and water.

Consequently, an additional 5 percent is deducted from Paraguay's monetary freedom score to account for these policies.

INVESTMENT FREEDOM — 50%

Paraguay guarantees equal treatment to foreign investors, as well as full repatriation of capital and profits. Foreigners may not purchase land along the country's borders, and foreign investment is deterred by legal insecurity, shortages of skilled labor, deficient infrastructure, and the absence of cheap and reliable transport. Both residents and non-residents may hold foreign exchange accounts. Most payments and transfers are permitted, although financial enterprises require central bank authorization to transfer earnings. Capital transactions are subject to minimal restrictions.

FINANCIAL FREEDOM — 60%

Although several domestic financial crises, including a number of bank closures, have hurt the financial sector and have led the government to restructure the banking sector and improve oversight, supervision of the financial system falls short of international standards. The central bank is not entirely independent. The state development bank, Banco Nacional de Fomento (BNF), is charged with channeling loans from international financial institutions to local banks and other financial institutions but is burdened with numerous non-performing loans. The two largest banks are foreign-owned. Any financial transaction may be conducted in foreign currency. Most companies protect themselves against risk through international reinsurance companies. Capital markets are negligible, and trading on the small stock market is slight.

PROPERTY RIGHTS — 30%

Because of widespread judicial corruption, protection of property is extremely weak. Commercial and civil codes cover bankruptcy and give priority for claims first to employees, then to the state, and finally to private creditors.

FREEDOM FROM CORRUPTION — 21%

Corruption is perceived as widespread. Paraguay ranks 144th out of 158 countries in Transparency International's Corruption Perceptions Index for 2005.

LABOR FREEDOM — 36.7%

The labor market operates under highly restrictive regulations that hinder overall productivity growth. The non-salary cost of employing a worker is moderate, but dismissing a redundant employee is costly. Regulations on increasing or contracting the number of work hours are not flexible. Paraguay's labor freedom is one of the 20 lowest in the world.

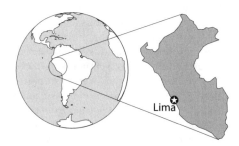

PERU

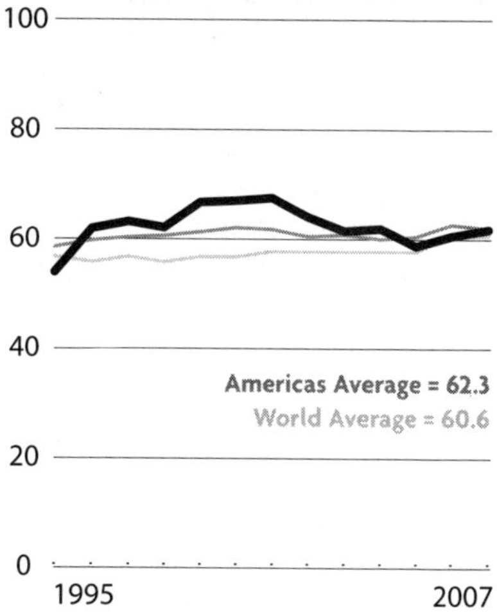

Peru's economy is 62.1 percent free, according to our 2007 assessment, which makes it the world's 63rd freest economy. Its overall score is 1.2 percentage points higher than last year, partially reflecting new methodological detail. Peru is ranked 15th out of 29 countries in the Americas, and its overall score is equal to the regional average.

Peru scores well in fiscal freedom, monetary freedom, and freedom from government. Personal income and corporate tax rates are moderate, and overall tax revenue is low as a percentage of GDP. Inflation is also low, and prices are not significantly influenced by the state. Peru is pushing forward its privatization efforts, particularly in infrastructure, and revenue from state-owned businesses is correspondingly low (as are overall government expenditures).

As a developing nation, Peru faces significant economic challenges, particularly in labor freedom, property rights, and freedom from corruption. The slowness and unpredictability of the court system have led to allegations of corruption. Corruption certainly is present, but it is not as serious in Peru as it is in other countries in the region. Economic development is also impeded by a restrictive labor market that regulates both costly employee dismissal procedures and inflexible weekly working hours.

BACKGROUND: Peru is Latin America's fifth most populous country and a growing industrial power. Exports include minerals, hydrocarbons, textiles, and clothing. Sound economic management under President Alejandro Toledo resulted in economic growth of 4 percent to 5 percent from 2002 to 2004. Trade liberalization has helped to reduce poverty, but half of all Peruvians are still considered poor. President Alan García, elected in 2006, promised to continue most of Toledo's economic policies but faces a Congress dominated by representatives from the rival populist Unión por el Perú.

How Do We Measure Economic Freedom? See Chapter 3 (page 37) for an explanation of the methodology or visit the *Index* Web site at *heritage.org/index*.

The economy is 62.1% free

Americas Average = 62.3
World Average = 60.6

1995 — 2007

QUICK FACTS

Population: 27.6 million

GDP (PPP): $156.5 billion
4.8% growth in 2004
3.3% 5-yr. comp. ann. growth
$5,678 per capita

Unemployment: 8.8%

Inflation (CPI): 3.7%

FDI (net inflow): $1.8 billion

Official Development Assistance:
Multilateral: $39 million
Bilateral: $620 million (33% from the U.S.)

External Debt: $31.3 billion

Exports: $14.5 billion
Primarily copper, gold, zinc, crude petroleum and petroleum products, coffee

Imports: $12.6 billion
Primarily petroleum and petroleum products, plastics, machinery, vehicles, iron and steel, wheat, paper

PERU'S TEN ECONOMIC FREEDOMS

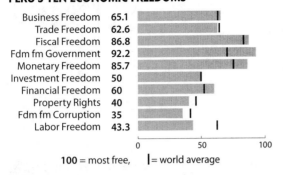

Business Freedom	65.1
Trade Freedom	62.6
Fiscal Freedom	86.8
Fdm fm Government	92.2
Monetary Freedom	85.7
Investment Freedom	50
Financial Freedom	60
Property Rights	40
Fdm fm Corruption	35
Labor Freedom	43.3

0   50   100

100 = most free,   ▌= world average

BUSINESS FREEDOM — 65.1%
Starting a business takes an average of 72 days, compared to the world average of 48 days. To maximize entrepreneurship and job creation, it should be easier to start a company. Obtaining a business license can be difficult, but closing a business can be relatively easy. Bureaucratic obstacles and delays are persistent problems. The overall freedom to start, operate, and close a business is relatively well protected by the national regulatory environment.

TRADE FREEDOM — 62.6%
Peru's weighted average tariff rate was 8.7 percent in 2004. Variable import levies for certain agricultural goods to maintain minimum import prices, export and import taxes, import restrictions, and restrictive sanitary and phytosanitary regulations add to the cost of trade. Consequently, an additional 20 percent is deducted from Peru's trade freedom score to account for these non-tariff barriers.

FISCAL FREEDOM — 86.8%
Peru has moderate income tax rates. Both the top income tax rate and the top corporate tax rate are 30 percent. Other taxes include a value-added tax (VAT), a real estate tax, and a vehicle tax. In the most recent year, overall tax revenue as a percentage of GDP was 13.3 percent.

FREEDOM FROM GOVERNMENT — 92.2%
Total government expenditures in Peru, including consumption and transfer payments, are low. In the most recent year, government spending equaled 16.9 percent of GDP, and the government received 3.5 percent of its revenues from state-owned enterprises and government ownership of property. Much of the progress made in privatization has been in the infrastructure sector.

MONETARY FREEDOM — 85.7%
Inflation in Peru is relatively low, averaging 2.2 percent between 2003 and 2005. Relatively low and stable prices explain most of the monetary freedom score. Most prices are freely set in the market, but the government is able to influence prices through regulation, state-owned enterprises, and utilities. A special government fund is used to stabilize changes in fuel prices. Consequently, an additional 5 percent is deducted from Peru's monetary freedom score to account for these policies.

INVESTMENT FREEDOM — 50%
Peru welcomes foreign investment and provides national treatment. There is no screening process for foreign investors, and only investments in banking and defense-related industries require prior approval. Both investment in broadcast media and the purchase of land are restricted to Peruvian citizens. National air and water transportation are restricted to domestic operators. Both residents and non-residents may hold foreign exchange accounts. There are no restrictions or controls on payments, transactions, transfers, or repatriation of profits. Capital transactions face minimal restrictions. There are limitations on hiring foreign employees.

FINANCIAL FREEDOM — 60%
Peru is open to foreign banks and insurance companies. The government has established capital requirements and has strengthened prudential standards and disclosure requirements. Credit is allocated on market terms, and foreign investors can obtain credit in the domestic market. At the end of 2005, foreigners were majority owners of nine of 14 commercial banks and held shares in three more. There are also three state-owned specialized financial institutions in addition to the central bank—the government's financial agent (Banco de la Nacion) and two development banks (Corporación Financiera de Desarrollo and the Agrarian Bank)—and several dozen microfinance institutions and savings banks. The insurance sector is small. Capital markets are centered on the small stock market and the pension system. Pension funds may not invest over 10.5 percent of their resources abroad.

PROPERTY RIGHTS — 40%
The judicial system is often extremely slow to hear cases and issue decisions. Court rulings and the degree of enforcement are difficult to predict. Allegations of corruption and outside interference in the judicial system are common.

FREEDOM FROM CORRUPTION — 35%
Corruption is perceived as significant. Peru ranks 65th out of 158 countries in Transparency International's Corruption Perceptions Index for 2005.

LABOR FREEDOM — 43.3%
The labor market operates under highly inflexible employment regulations that hinder overall productivity growth. The non-salary cost of employing a worker is low, but dismissing a redundant employee is very difficult. Regulations related to increasing or contracting the number of work hour are not flexible.

THE PHILIPPINES

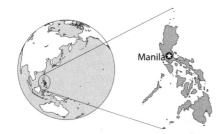

Manila

The economy of the Philippines is 57.4 percent free, according to our 2007 assessment, which makes it the world's 97th freest economy. Its overall score is 0.2 percentage point lower than last year, partially reflecting new methodological detail. The Philippines is ranked 16th out of 30 countries in the Asia–Pacific region, and its overall score is slightly lower than the regional average.

The Philippines scores well in fiscal freedom, trade freedom, and freedom from government. Income and corporate tax rates are burdensome, and overall tax revenue is low as a percentage of GDP. The average tariff rate is low, but non-tariff barriers are significant. Total government expenditures in the Philippines are equal to roughly 20 percent of national GDP, and state-owned businesses do not account for a large portion of overall revenue.

The Philippines is relatively weak in business freedom, investment freedom, monetary freedom, property rights, and freedom from corruption. The government imposes both formal and non-formal barriers to foreign investment. Inflation is fairly high, and the government subsidizes the prices of several basic goods. The judicial system is weak and subject to extensive political influence. Organized crime is a major deterrent to the administration of justice, and bureaucratic corruption is extensive.

BACKGROUND: Before gaining its independence in 1946, the Philippines had been a United States colony since 1898 and, before that, a Spanish colony since the 16th century. Current President Gloria Arroyo took power in 2001 after her predecessor's resignation and has weathered a number of coup attempts. GDP has grown annually by about 5 percent since 2002 as a result of success in the service sector, increased agricultural output, and improved exports. The Philippines is handicapped, however, by a major debt burden and an Islamic insurgency in the south. Industry, services, and remittances account for most of the country's GDP, and the majority of workers are employed in the service sector.

How Do We Measure Economic Freedom? See Chapter 3 (page 37) for an explanation of the methodology or visit the *Index* Web site at *heritage.org/index*.

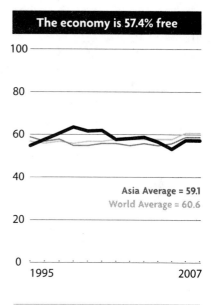

The economy is 57.4% free

Asia Average = 59.1
World Average = 60.6

1995   2007

QUICK FACTS

Population: 81.6 million

GDP (PPP): $376.6 billion
6.0% growth in 2004
4.5% 5-yr. comp. ann. growth
$4,614 per capita

Unemployment: 11.8%

Inflation (CPI): 6%

FDI (net inflow): $57 million

Official Development Assistance:
Multilateral: $49 million
Bilateral: $970 million (11% from the U.S.)

External Debt: $60.6 billion

Exports: $42.8 billion
Primarily electronic equipment, machinery, transport equipment, garments, optical instruments, coconut products, fruits and nuts, copper products, chemicals

Imports: $50.5 billion
Primarily raw materials, machinery, equipment, fuels, vehicles, vehicle parts, plastic, chemicals, grains

THE PHILIPPINES' TEN ECONOMIC FREEDOMS

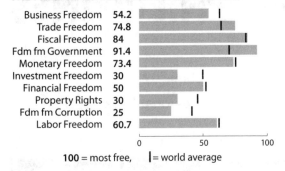

Business Freedom	54.2
Trade Freedom	74.8
Fiscal Freedom	84
Fdm fm Government	91.4
Monetary Freedom	73.4
Investment Freedom	30
Financial Freedom	50
Property Rights	30
Fdm fm Corruption	25
Labor Freedom	60.7

100 = most free, | = world average

BUSINESS FREEDOM — 54.2%

Starting a business takes an average of 48 days, which is equal to the world average of 48 days. To maximize entrepreneurship and job creation, it should be easier to start a company. Obtaining a business license is relatively simple, but closing a business can be difficult. Regulations are sometimes inconsistent and lacking in transparency. The overall freedom to start, operate, and close a business is restricted by the national regulatory environment.

TRADE FREEDOM — 74.8%

The Philippines' weighted average tariff rate was 2.6 percent in 2003. Complex and restrictive customs regulations, burdensome import licensing requirements, sanitary and phytosanitary restrictions, import and export taxes, import and export bans, numerous import restrictions, export subsidies, quotas, widespread corruption, and weak protection of intellectual property rights add to the cost of trade. Consequently, an additional 20 percent is deducted from the Philippines' trade freedom score to account for these non-tariff barriers.

FISCAL FREEDOM — 84%

The Philippines has burdensome tax rates. The top income tax rate is 32 percent, and the top corporate tax rate is 35 percent. Other taxes include a value-added tax (VAT) and a real property tax. In the most recent year, overall tax revenue as a percentage of GDP was 12.4 percent.

FREEDOM FROM GOVERNMENT — 91.4%

Total government expenditures in the Philippines, including consumption and transfer payments, are low. In the most recent year, government spending equaled 18.7 percent of GDP, and the government received 1.2 percent of its revenues from state-owned enterprises and government ownership of property. Although efforts to restructure and privatize state-owned companies have been made in recent years, privatization in the electricity generation and distribution network has not been significant.

MONETARY FREEDOM — 73.4%

Inflation in the Philippines is high, averaging 6.9 percent between 2003 and 2005. Relatively high and unstable prices explain most of the monetary freedom score. Additionally, the government is able to influence prices through state-owned enterprises and utilities. Price controls exist for elec-

tricity distribution, water, telecommunications, and most transportation services. Price ceilings are usually imposed only on basic commodities for emergencies. The president can impose price controls to check inflation or ease social tension, but this authority has rarely been exercised. An additional 10 percent is deducted from the score to account for these policies.

INVESTMENT FREEDOM — 30%

The Philippines maintains barriers to many foreign investments. Two negative lists restrict both foreign investment and the ability of foreigners to practice in numerous sectors. Unofficial barriers, like high levels of corruption, also impede foreign investment. The mining sector is now open to 100 percent foreign-owned companies. Both residents and non-residents may hold foreign exchange accounts, although non-residents may do so only with foreign currency deposits or proceeds from conversions of property in the Philippines. Payments, capital transactions, and transfers are subject to numerous restrictions, controls, quantitative limits, and authorizations.

FINANCIAL FREEDOM — 50%

The government has opened the financial system to foreign competition, has raised capital standards, and has improved oversight in the wake of a 1990s devaluation and financial crisis. Non-performing loans are declining. Two banks are fully state-owned, and one is partially state-owned, including the fourth and seventh largest domestic banks as of March 2005. Credit is generally available at market terms, but the government requires banks to lend specified portions of their funds to preferred sectors. Foreign banks are not permitted to own over 30 percent of banking assets. Foreign firms are allowed to fully own insurers and may set up local subsidiaries. Capital markets are centered on the stock exchange.

PROPERTY RIGHTS — 30%

The Philippine judicial system enforces the law weakly. Judges are supposed to be independent, but several are corrupt, having been appointed strictly for political reasons. Organized crime is a strong deterrent to the administration of justice.

FREEDOM FROM CORRUPTION — 25%

Corruption is perceived as widespread. The Philippines ranks 117th out of 158 countries in Transparency International's Corruption Perceptions Index for 2005.

LABOR FREEDOM — 60.7%

The labor market operates under inflexible employment regulations that could be improved to enhance overall productivity growth. The non-salary cost of employing a worker is low, but dismissing a redundant employee can be costly.

POLAND

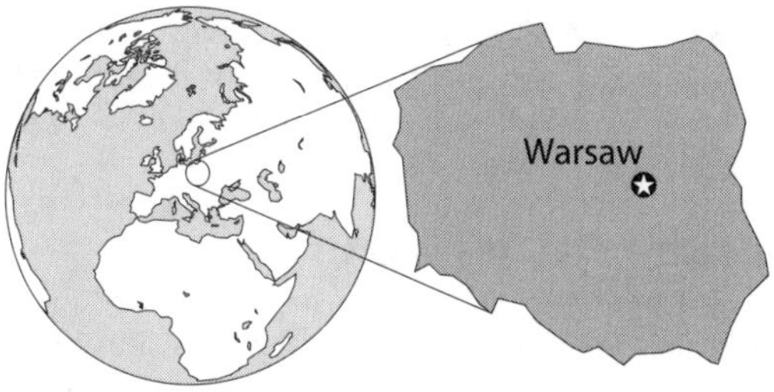

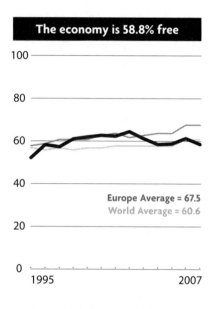

Warsaw

Rank: 87

Regional Rank: 35 of 41

Poland's economy is 58.8 percent free, according to our 2007 assessment, which makes it the world's 87th freest economy. Its overall score is 2.8 percentage points lower than last year, partially reflecting new methodological detail. Poland is ranked 35th out of 41 countries in the European region, and its overall score is much lower than the regional average.

Poland scores well in trade freedom and monetary freedom. The average tariff rate is low, but non-tariff barriers include distortionary EU subsidies of agricultural and other goods. Inflation is also low. Poland has a fairly high top personal income tax rate, but its corporate rate is relatively low.

Poland faces several economic challenges, as do other formerly Communist nations, but is progressing. Freedom from government, freedom from corruption, and labor freedom remain weak. The court system, though fairly reliable, is prone to inefficiency and sudden changes in laws or regulations. Foreign investment is generally welcome, but foreign ownership of companies in certain industries is limited. The financial sector, while subject to government interference, is well-regarded overall.

BACKGROUND: Poland's struggle for freedom from the Soviet Union ended in 1990, with Solidarity sweeping parliament and the presidency. A pioneer among countries making the transition from Communism to free markets, Poland has managed to tame inflation and achieve rapid real income growth and is now a member of the European Union. Many problems, like high unemployment, remain. The country continues to work on further economic liberalization through a robust but chaotic democratic process. Key Polish exports include foodstuffs, chemicals, steel, and transport equipment.

How Do We Measure Economic Freedom? See Chapter 3 (page 37) for an explanation of the methodology or visit the *Index* Web site at *heritage.org/index.*

The economy is 58.8% free

Europe Average = 67.5
World Average = 60.6

QUICK FACTS

Population: 38.2 million

GDP (PPP): $495.4 billion
5.3% growth in 2004
3.2% 5-yr. comp. ann. growth
$12,974 per capita

Unemployment: 19.6%

Inflation (CPI): 3.6%

FDI (net inflow): $5.4 billion

Official Development Assistance:
Multilateral: $1.1 billion
Bilateral: $433 million (1% from the U.S.)

External Debt: $99.2 billion

Exports: $95.3 billion
Primarily machinery, transport equipment, intermediate and miscellaneous manufactured goods, food, live animals

Imports: $99.9 billion
Primarily machinery, transport equipment, intermediate manufactured goods, chemicals, minerals, fuels, lubricants, related materials

POLAND'S TEN ECONOMIC FREEDOMS

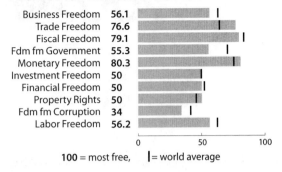

Business Freedom	56.1
Trade Freedom	76.6
Fiscal Freedom	79.1
Fdm fm Government	55.3
Monetary Freedom	80.3
Investment Freedom	50
Financial Freedom	50
Property Rights	50
Fdm fm Corruption	34
Labor Freedom	56.2

0   50   100

100 = most free, ▌= world average

BUSINESS FREEDOM — 56.1%

Starting a business takes an average of 31 days, compared to the world average of 48 days. To maximize entrepreneurship and job creation, it should be easier to start a company. Obtaining a business license and closing a business can be difficult, and regulations are sometimes inconsistent. The government has put more emphasis on reducing bureaucratic barriers to business. The overall freedom to start, operate, and close a business is restricted by the national regulatory environment.

TRADE FREEDOM — 76.6%

Poland's trade policy is the same as those of other members of the European Union. The common EU weighted average tariff rate was 1.7 percent in 2005. Various non-tariff barriers are reflected in EU and Polish government policy, including agricultural and manufacturing subsidies, regulatory and licensing restrictions, and other market access restrictions. The government also implements non-transparent pharmaceutical regulations. Consequently, an additional 20 percent is deducted from Poland's trade freedom score.

FISCAL FREEDOM — 79.1%

Poland has a high income tax rate and a low corporate tax rate. The top income tax rate is 40 percent, and the top corporate tax rate is 19 percent. Other taxes include a value-added tax (VAT) and a property tax. In the most recent year, overall tax revenue as a percentage of GDP was 34.3 percent.

FREEDOM FROM GOVERNMENT — 55.3%

Total government expenditures in Poland, including consumption and transfer payments, are high. In the most recent year, government spending equaled 42.9 percent of GDP, and the government received 5.2 percent of its revenues from state-owned enterprises and government ownership of property.

MONETARY FREEDOM — 80.3%

Inflation in Poland is relatively low, averaging 2.4 percent between 2003 and 2005. Relatively stable prices explain most of the monetary freedom score. As a participant in the EU's Common Agricultural Policy, the government subsidizes agricultural production, distorting the prices of agricultural products. The government also monitors utility rates and sets official prices for pharmaceutical and medical materials, taxi services, and any other goods or services as required to maintain the proper functioning of the economy. Consequently, an additional 10 percent is deducted from Poland's monetary freedom score to account for these policies.

INVESTMENT FREEDOM — 50%

Polish law allows for 100 percent foreign ownership of domestic businesses but sets ceilings on the share of foreign ownership in various industries. Foreign ownership of land is restricted. Both residents and non-residents may hold foreign exchange accounts, subject to certain restrictions, including government approval for resident accounts held abroad. Payments, transactions, and transfers over a specified amount must be conducted through a domestic bank. Capital transactions with nations outside the EU are subject to restrictions and government approval.

FINANCIAL FREEDOM — 50%

Poland's financial system is open and well regulated, but government influence is considerable. Credit is available on market terms, and foreign investors can access domestic financial markets. The banking sector is dominated by 12 commercial banks, two of which are government-controlled and the remaining 10 of which are foreign-controlled. Foreign banks control around 70 percent of banking assets. The government provides low-interest loans to farmers and homeowners. The insurance sector has been growing strongly. The Polish government controls the country's largest insurer. Capital markets are expanding, as is the stock exchange.

PROPERTY RIGHTS — 50%

Property rights are moderately well protected. The judicial system is slow to resolve cases, and investors complain about the unexpected issuance of or changes in laws and regulations.

FREEDOM FROM CORRUPTION — 34%

Corruption is perceived as significant. Poland ranks 70th out of 158 countries in Transparency International's Corruption Perceptions Index for 2005.

LABOR FREEDOM — 56.2%

The labor market operates under inflexible employment regulations that hinder overall productivity growth. The non-salary cost of employing a worker is high, and dismissing a redundant employee is relatively costly. Poland's small and medium-sized companies have cited the rigid labor code as a barrier to the creation of new jobs. In response to growing unemployment, there have been debates on means to increase labor flexibility.

PORTUGAL

Lisbon

Portugal's economy is 66.7 percent free, according to our 2007 assessment, which makes it the world's 43rd freest economy. Its overall score is 1.1 percentage points higher than last year, partially reflecting new methodological detail. Portugal is ranked 24th freest out of 41 countries in the European region, and its overall score is slightly lower than the regional average.

Portugal enjoys high levels of business freedom, trade freedom, monetary freedom, investment freedom, property rights, and freedom from corruption. The average tariff rate is low, but non-tariff barriers include distortionary EU subsidies on agriculture and other goods. Business formation is efficient, although other commercial operations are often slowed by bureaucracy. Inflation is low, and the government actively promotes foreign investment. Case resolution is slower than the EU average, but the judiciary is independent and free of corruption.

Portugal is weak in freedom from government and labor freedom. Total government spending equals almost 50 percent of GDP, and the labor sector is highly restrictive in all areas, from maximum workweek hours to employment severance procedures.

BACKGROUND: Since the 1974 "Revolution of the Carnations" that overthrew the country's long-running dictatorship, Portugal has been central to both European integration and the transatlantic alliance. In January 2006, Anibal Cavaco Silva became the first conservative president of the democratic era. Although his role is largely ceremonial, the president must deal with a Socialist Party that won its first overall parliamentary majority since the revolution. Currently, the public sector consumes the equivalent of 15 percent of gross domestic product in wages alone. Portugal's main exports include agricultural produce, textiles, wood products, and electrical equipment.

How Do We Measure Economic Freedom? See Chapter 3 (page 37) for an explanation of the methodology or visit the *Index* Web site at *heritage.org/index*.

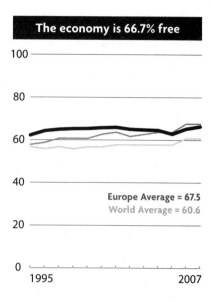

The economy is 66.7% free

Europe Average = 67.5
World Average = 60.6

QUICK FACTS

Population: 10.5 million

GDP (PPP): $206.1 billion
1.1% growth in 2004
1.3% 5-yr. comp. ann. growth
$19,629 per capita

Unemployment: 6.7%

Inflation (CPI): 2.4%

FDI (net inflow): −$5.1 billion

Official Development Assistance:
Multilateral: None
Bilateral: None

External Debt: $287.8 billion (2005 estimate)

Exports: $51.9 billion
Primarily clothing, footwear, machinery, chemicals, cork and paper products, hides

Imports: $65.4 billion
Primarily machinery, transport equipment, chemicals, petroleum, textiles, agricultural products

PORTUGAL'S TEN ECONOMIC FREEDOMS

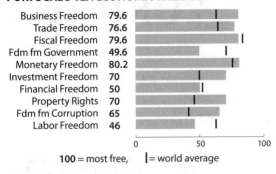

Business Freedom	79.6
Trade Freedom	76.6
Fiscal Freedom	79.6
Fdm fm Government	49.6
Monetary Freedom	80.2
Investment Freedom	70
Financial Freedom	50
Property Rights	70
Fdm fm Corruption	65
Labor Freedom	46

0   50   100

100 = most free,   ❙ = world average

BUSINESS FREEDOM — 79.6%

Starting a business takes an average of eight days, compared to the world average of 48 days. Such ease of entrepreneurship is good for job creation. Obtaining a business license can be difficult, but closing a business is easy. Bureaucratic obstacles and delays are ongoing problems. The overall freedom to start, operate, and close a business is relatively well protected by the national regulatory environment.

TRADE FREEDOM — 76.6%

Portugal's trade policy is the same as those of other members of the European Union. The common EU weighted average tariff rate was 1.7 percent in 2005. Various non-tariff barriers are reflected in EU and Portuguese government policy, including agricultural and manufacturing subsidies, regulatory and licensing restrictions, and other market access restrictions. The government also implements burdensome pharmaceutical regulations and non-transparent government procurement rules. Consequently, an additional 20 percent is deducted from Portugal's trade freedom score.

FISCAL FREEDOM — 79.6%

Portugal has a high income tax rate and a moderate corporate tax rate. The top income tax rate is 42 percent, and the top corporate tax rate is 27.5 percent. Other taxes include a value-added tax (VAT), a property tax, and a vehicle tax. In the most recent year, overall tax revenue as a percentage of GDP was 23.2 percent.

FREEDOM FROM GOVERNMENT — 49.6%

Total government expenditures in Portugal, including consumption and transfer payments, are high. The government's privatization plans include divestment of state holdings in such traditional industries as paper and pulp. In the most recent year, government spending equaled 46.4 percent of GDP, and the government received 0.6 percent of its revenues from state-owned enterprises and government ownership of property.

MONETARY FREEDOM — 80.2%

Portugal is a member of the euro zone. Inflation in Portugal is relatively low, averaging 2.4 percent between 2003 and 2005. Relatively low and stable prices explain most of the monetary freedom score. As a participant in the EU's Com-

mon Agricultural Policy, the government subsidizes agricultural production, distorting the prices of agricultural products. The government also influences prices through state-owned enterprises and utilities. Consequently, an additional 10 percent is deducted from Portugal's monetary freedom score to account for these policies.

INVESTMENT FREEDOM — 70%

Portugal does not discriminate against foreign investments. Foreigners may invest in almost all economic sectors that are open to private enterprise. Approval is required for non-EU investment in the defense industry, water management, public service telecommunications operators, railways, and maritime transportation. Portugal also restricts non-EU investment in regular air transport and television operations. Residents and non-residents may hold foreign exchange accounts. There are no controls or restrictions on repatriation of profits, current transfers, payments for invisible transactions, or real estate transactions.

FINANCIAL FREEDOM — 50%

Financial institutions may offer a variety of services, and banks increasingly sell insurance products. The government has been privatizing state financial institutions since the late 1980s, and the sole remaining state-owned financial services firm, Caixa Geral de Depósitos (CGD), is Portugal's largest financial group. Following a period of banking consolidation, CGD and four large private banks dominate the market and account for about 80 percent of banking assets. The government also influences the allocation of credit through a program that is designed to assist small and medium-size enterprises. The insurance sector is dominated by three firms, two of which are owned by CGD. Capital markets and the stock market were bolstered by government privatization in the 1990s but remain small by European standards. The stock exchange participates in Euronext, the common trading platform linking the bourses of Paris, Brussels, and Amsterdam.

PROPERTY RIGHTS — 70%

The judiciary is independent. The court system is slow and deliberate, and the number of years it takes to resolve cases is well above the EU average.

FREEDOM FROM CORRUPTION — 65%

Corruption is perceived as present. Portugal ranks 26th out of 158 countries in Transparency International's Corruption Perceptions Index for 2005.

LABOR FREEDOM — 46%

The labor market operates under inflexible employment regulations that hinder overall productivity growth. The non-salary cost of employing a worker is high, and dismissing a redundant employee is costly. Regulations related to increasing or contracting the number of work hours are not flexible. Portugal's labor freedom is one of the 20 lowest in the world.

QATAR

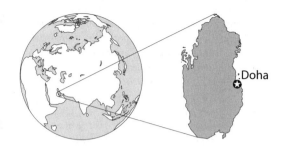

:Doha

Qatar's economy is 60.7 percent free, according to our 2007 assessment, which makes it the world's 72nd freest economy. Its overall score is 0.3 percentage point higher than last year, partially reflecting new methodological detail. Qatar is ranked 7th out of 17 countries in the North Africa/Middle East region, and its overall score is slightly higher than the regional average.

Qatar enjoys high levels of trade freedom, property rights, freedom from corruption, and fiscal freedom. The average tariff rate is reasonable, and business regulation is becoming more efficient as the government tries to streamline commercial procedures. There are no personal or corporate taxes on Qatari nationals, and overall tax revenue is very low as a percentage of GDP. The financial sector is fairly modern and supervised mostly according to government standards. Corruption is low, particularly for a developing nation.

Qatar has weak monetary freedom, freedom from government, and investment freedom. Total government spending is fairly high at one-third of GDP, and the government receives over half of its revenues from state-owned businesses. Inflation is fairly high, and prices are unstable. Investment in Qatar is hindered by rules that mandate the hiring of Qataris and limit the percentage of enterprises that foreigners may own.

BACKGROUND: Qatar has been ruled by the Al-Thani family ever since gaining its independence from Great Britain in 1971. Sheikh Hamad bin Khalifa al-Thani, who ousted his father in a bloodless coup in 1995, implemented a publicly approved constitution in 2005 that formalized the country's social and economic progress. The emir is pursuing a parliamentary election that is expected to grant direct legislative power to an advisory council elected by Qatari citizens. Despite efforts at diversification, the economy remains heavily dependent on oil and gas. Qatar recently overtook Indonesia to become the world's largest exporter of liquefied natural gas.

How Do We Measure Economic Freedom? See Chapter 3 (page 37) for an explanation of the methodology or visit the *Index* Web site at *heritage.org/index*.

The economy is 60.7% free

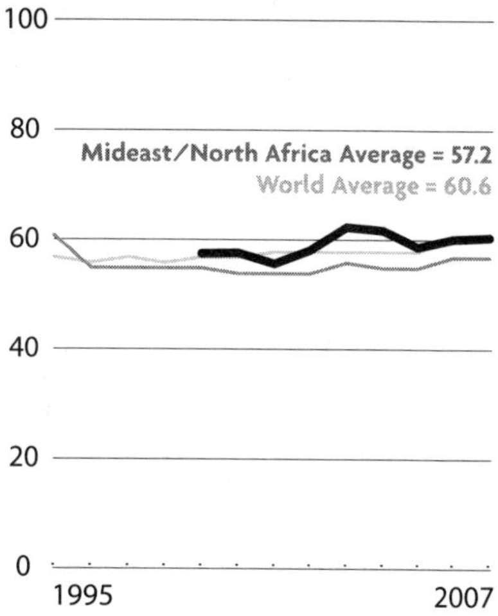

Mideast/North Africa Average = 57.2
World Average = 60.6

(chart, 1995–2007, scale 0 to 100)

QUICK FACTS

Population: 0.8 million

GDP (PPP): $23.6 billion (2005 estimate)
9.3% growth in 2004
7.8% 5-yr. comp. ann. growth
$27,400 per capita (2005 estimate)

Unemployment: 2.7% (2001)

Inflation (CPI): 6.8%

FDI (net inflow): $680.9 million

Official Development Assistance:
Multilateral: None
Bilateral: $2 million (0% from the U.S.)

External Debt: $21.13 billion (2005 estimate)

Exports: $18.7 billion
Primarily liquefied natural gas, petroleum products, fertilizers, steel

Imports: $5.4 billion
Primarily machinery, transport equipment, food, chemicals

QATAR'S TEN ECONOMIC FREEDOMS

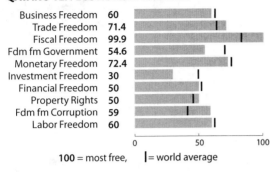

Business Freedom	60
Trade Freedom	71.4
Fiscal Freedom	99.9
Fdm fm Government	54.6
Monetary Freedom	72.4
Investment Freedom	30
Financial Freedom	50
Property Rights	50
Fdm fm Corruption	59
Labor Freedom	60

100 = most free, **I** = world average

BUSINESS FREEDOM — 60%

In recent years, the Qatari government has passed and updated a number of commercial laws to enhance the business environment and further economic development, but bureaucracy and a lack of transparency in procurement are problems. The overall freedom to start, operate, and close a business is restricted by the national regulatory environment.

TRADE FREEDOM — 71.4%

Qatar's average tariff rate was 4.3 percent in 2002. Prohibitive tariffs, import licensing requirements, import bans, service market access barriers, and non-transparent government procurement procedures add to the cost of trade. Consequently, an additional 20 percent is deducted from Qatar's trade freedom score to account for these non-tariff barriers.

FISCAL FREEDOM — 99.9%

Qatar imposes no income taxes on individuals and no corporate income tax on corporations that are wholly owned by Qatari nationals. The top corporate tax rate of 35 percent applies to foreign corporations operating in Qatar. Other than customs duties, there are no major taxes, as Qatar does not impose wealth taxes or consumption taxes. In the most recent year, overall tax revenue as a percentage of GDP was 3.6 percent.

FREEDOM FROM GOVERNMENT — 54.6%

Total government expenditures in Qatar, including consumption and transfer payments, are high. In the most recent year, government spending equaled 34 percent of GDP, and the government received 55.3 percent of its revenues from state-owned enterprises and government ownership of property. Despite some progress in privatization, the state is involved in such activities as oil and gas production and transportation.

MONETARY FREEDOM — 72.4%

Inflation in Qatar is high, averaging 7.7 percent between 2003 and 2005. Relatively unstable prices explain most of the monetary freedom score. The government influences prices through regulation, subsidies, and numerous state-owned enterprises and utilities. Consequently, an additional 10 percent is deducted from Qatar's monetary freedom score to account for these policies.

INVESTMENT FREEDOM — 30%

Full or majority foreign investment is permitted in agriculture, industry, health, education, tourism, and projects involved in the development of natural resources with prior approval. Other sectors are capped at 49 percent foreign ownership with prior approval. The law still requires foreign businesses to employ a local agent. The government screens all major foreign investment projects in the oil and gas industry. Foreign companies face a higher tax rate (up to 35 percent) than do domestic companies (0 percent). Both residents and non-residents may hold foreign exchange accounts. There are no controls or restrictions on payments and transfers.

FINANCIAL FREEDOM — 50%

Qatar has a relatively open financial system that permits the free flow of capital. Supervision is prudent, and the regulatory system is transparent and largely consistent with international standards. At the end of 2005, there were 15 commercial banks, seven of which were locally owned and accounted for approximately 80 percent of banking assets. The government owns 50 percent of Qatar National Bank, which holds nearly 50 percent of total deposits and handles most of the government's business. Loans to the government and to liquefied natural gas operations account for the majority of commercial bank loans. The government must approve foreign investment in the banking and insurance sectors and has shares in two prominent insurers. The Doha Securities Market has been opened to foreign investors, but their holdings are restricted to 25 percent of the issued capital of nearly all listed companies.

PROPERTY RIGHTS — 50%

Expropriation of property is not likely, but the judiciary is subject to inefficiencies and influence from the executive. The court system is slow, bureaucratic, and biased in favor of Qataris and the government.

FREEDOM FROM CORRUPTION — 59%

Corruption is perceived as present. Qatar ranks 32nd out of 158 countries in Transparency International's Corruption Perceptions Index for 2005.

LABOR FREEDOM — 60%

Qatar's labor force consists primarily of expatriate workers whose role in the economy is vital. In general, flexible immigration and employment rules to enable the import of foreign labor are offered to foreign and Qatari investors as an incentive. Over the past several years, Qatar has tightened the administration of its manpower programs to control the flood of expatriate workers. The government does not mandate a minimum wage.

ROMANIA

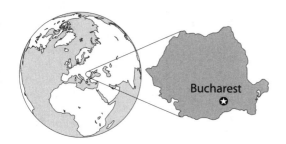

Bucharest ✪

Romania's economy is 61.3 percent free, according to our 2007 assessment, which makes it the world's 67th freest economy. Its overall score is 2.3 percentage points higher than last year, partially reflecting new methodological detail. Romania is ranked 31st out of 41 countries in the European region, and its overall score is well below the regional average.

Romania enjoys high levels of fiscal freedom, trade freedom, and financial freedom. The top income and corporate tax rates are a flat 16 percent, although overall tax revenue is fairly high as a percentage of GDP. Progress has been made in lowering tariffs, but non-tariff barriers remain significant. The financial system in Budapest is consistent with international standards and has been enhanced by a recent reform and privatization program.

As one of the poorer European countries, Romania faces several economic challenges. Its monetary freedom, property rights, and freedom from corruption are weak. Inflation is high, particularly for a European nation. There is significant corruption in most areas of the bureaucracy, particularly in the judiciary, which enforces commercial contracts only selectively.

BACKGROUND: In the run-up to joining the European Union, the Romanian government has implemented economic reform that is consistent with the Maastricht criteria. However, friction between Romania's two main governing coalition partners, the Democratic Party and National Liberal Party, could cause political deadlock, especially in the event of any delays in EU accession. Macroeconomic improvements have spurred the beginnings of a middle class and have helped to reduce poverty. Investment activity is expected to remain strong as accession approaches, with new and modernized production facilities being launched, large public investment projects getting underway, and healthy inflows of foreign direct investment continuing.

How Do We Measure Economic Freedom? See Chapter 3 (page 37) for an explanation of the methodology or visit the *Index* Web site at *heritage.org/index.*

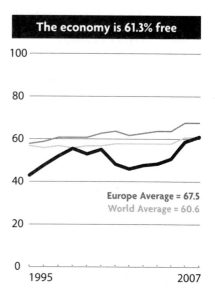

The economy is 61.3% free

Europe Average = 67.5
World Average = 60.6

QUICK FACTS

Population: 21.7 million

GDP (PPP): $183.9 billion
8.4% growth in 2004
5.3% 5-yr. comp. ann. growth
$8,480 per capita

Unemployment: 6.6%

Inflation (CPI): 11.9%

FDI (net inflow): $5.1 billion

Official Development Assistance:
Multilateral: $706 million
Bilateral: $215 million (19% from the U.S.)

External Debt: $30.0 billion

Exports: $27.1 billion
Primarily textiles, footwear, metals, metal products, machinery and equipment, minerals, fuels, chemicals, agricultural products

Imports: $34.0 billion
Primarily machinery and equipment, fuels, minerals, chemicals, textiles, basic metals, agricultural products

ROMANIA'S TEN ECONOMIC FREEDOMS

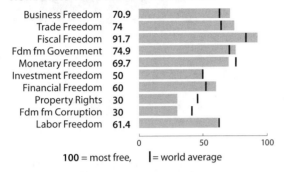

Business Freedom	70.9
Trade Freedom	74
Fiscal Freedom	91.7
Fdm fm Government	74.9
Monetary Freedom	69.7
Investment Freedom	50
Financial Freedom	60
Property Rights	30
Fdm fm Corruption	30
Labor Freedom	61.4

100 = most free, | = world average

BUSINESS FREEDOM — 70.9%

Starting a business takes an average of 11 days, compared to the world average of 48 days. Obtaining a business license can be difficult, and closing a business is likewise difficult. Cumbersome regulations are sometimes inconsistent and not always transparent, and the result is unreliability of interpretation. The overall freedom to start, operate, and close a business is relatively well protected by the national regulatory environment.

TRADE FREEDOM — 74%

Romania's weighted average tariff rate was 3 percent in 2005. Prohibitive tariffs, restrictive sanitary and phytosanitary regulations, customs fees, weak enforcement of intellectual property rights, and customs corruption all add to the cost of trade. Consequently, an additional 20 percent is deducted from Romania's trade freedom score to account for these non-tariff barriers.

FISCAL FREEDOM — 91.7%

Romania has low flat tax rates. Both the income tax rate and the corporate tax rate are a flat 16 percent. Other taxes include a value-added tax (VAT), a land tax, and a vehicle tax. In the most recent year, overall tax revenue as a percentage of GDP was 27.1 percent.

FREEDOM FROM GOVERNMENT — 74.9%

Total government expenditures in Romania, including consumption and transfer payments, are moderate. In the most recent year, government spending equaled 31.1 percent of GDP, and the government received 7.6 percent of its revenues from state-owned enterprises and government ownership of property. Privatization has proceeded slowly.

MONETARY FREEDOM — 69.7%

Inflation in Romania is high, averaging 10.3 percent between 2003 and 2005. Relatively high and unstable prices explain most of the monetary freedom score. The government is able to influence prices through regulation, subsidies, and numerous state-owned enterprises and utilities. Consequently, an additional 10 percent is deducted from Romania's monetary freedom score to account for these policies.

INVESTMENT FREEDOM — 50%

Although foreign investment is officially welcome in Romania, the country's weak rule of law and unpredictable regulatory environment are major deterrents. The government has simplified the procedures for obtaining permits and licenses and has implemented a flat tax to simplify tax reporting. Residents and non-residents may hold foreign exchange accounts, subject to restrictions and government approval in some cases. All payments and transfers must be documented. Most restrictions on capital transactions have been removed, and the few transactions that require central bank approval are those involving derivatives.

FINANCIAL FREEDOM — 60%

Romania's financial system is still developing. Supervision and regulation are largely consistent with international standards. The banking sector has undergone significant reform and restructuring, including privatization of many state-owned banks. Majority foreign-owned banks account for 23 of the country's 32 private banks, or three-fifths of sector assets. With the sale of Banca Comerciala Romana to an Austrian bank in December 2005, the state-owned banks' total share of banking assets fell to under 8 percent, down from 75 percent in 1998. Foreign insurers must form a partnership with a Romanian partner to enter the domestic market. Capital markets are underdeveloped compared to those of other Eastern European countries, and most trading involves government debt.

PROPERTY RIGHTS — 30%

Investors usually complain about unpredictable changes in legislation as well as weak enforcement of contracts and the rule of law. Judicial corruption is a serious problem.

FREEDOM FROM CORRUPTION — 30%

Corruption is perceived as significant. Romania ranks 85th out of 158 countries in Transparency International's Corruption Perceptions Index for 2005.

LABOR FREEDOM — 61.4%

The labor market operates under inflexible employment regulations that could be improved to enhance overall productivity growth. The non-salary cost of employing a worker is very high, and dismissing a redundant employee can be relatively easy. Regulations related to increasing or contracting the number of work hours are not flexible.

RUSSIA

Russia's economy is 54 percent free, according to our 2007 assessment, which makes it the world's 120th freest economy. Its overall score is 0.3 percentage point lower than last year, partially reflecting new methodological detail. Russia is ranked 39th out of 41 countries in the European region, and its overall score is much lower than the regional average.

Russia enjoys high levels of fiscal freedom, labor freedom, and business freedom. The top income and corporate tax rates are 13 percent and 24 percent, respectively, although overall tax revenue is relatively high as a percentage of GDP. The labor system is only partially flexible; dismissing a redundant employee is simple, but regulation in other areas is rigid.

Russia's significant weaknesses lie in monetary freedom, investment freedom, financial freedom, property rights, and freedom from corruption. Foreign investment in virtually all sectors faces both official and unofficial hurdles, including bureaucratic inconsistency, corruption, and outright restrictions in lucrative sectors like energy. Corruption engenders a weak rule of law, which in turn reinforces the transience of property rights and arbitrary law enforcement.

BACKGROUND: The 1991 collapse of the Soviet Union was a seminal event in Russian history. Russia seems to have moved to a "managed democracy"—a soft authoritarianism—under President Vladimir Putin. The economy continues to depend heavily on sales of natural resources, especially oil and natural gas. Russia has almost paid off its debts and is enjoying an impressive $200 billion hard currency reserve. Although Russia aspires to join the World Trade Organization, weak intellectual property rights and protectionism in the natural resources sector make accession difficult.

How Do We Measure Economic Freedom? See Chapter 3 (page 37) for an explanation of the methodology or visit the *Index* Web site at *heritage.org/index*.

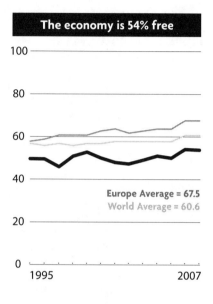

The economy is 54% free

Europe Average = 67.5
World Average = 60.6

QUICK FACTS

Population: 143.9 million

GDP (PPP): $1.4 trillion
7.2% growth in 2004
6.9% 5-yr. comp. ann. growth
$9,902 per capita

Unemployment: 8.2%

Inflation (CPI): 10.9%

FDI (net inflow): $2.1 billion

Official Development Assistance:
Multilateral: $189 million
Bilateral: $1.2 billion (64% from the U.S.)

External Debt: $197.3 billion

Exports: $203.7 billion
Primarily petroleum, petroleum products, natural gas, wood, wood products, metals, chemicals, civilian and military manufactures

Imports: $130.1 billion
Primarily machinery and equipment, consumer goods, medicines, meat, sugar, semi-finished metal products

RUSSIA'S TEN ECONOMIC FREEDOMS

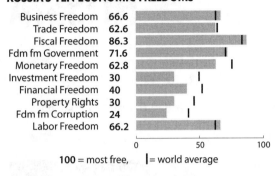

Business Freedom	66.6
Trade Freedom	62.6
Fiscal Freedom	86.3
Fdm fm Government	71.6
Monetary Freedom	62.8
Investment Freedom	30
Financial Freedom	40
Property Rights	30
Fdm fm Corruption	24
Labor Freedom	66.2

100 = most free, |= world average

BUSINESS FREEDOM — *66.6%*

Starting a business takes an average of 28 days, compared to the world average of 48 days. Both obtaining a business license and closing a business are difficult. Regulations are inconsistent, causing unreliability of interpretation, and laws are implemented unevenly. Bureaucratic obstacles are a particular problem for small businesses. The overall freedom to start, operate, and close a business is somewhat protected by the national regulatory environment.

TRADE FREEDOM — *62.6%*

Russia's weighted average tariff rate was 8.7 percent in 2002. Prohibitive tariffs, quotas, discriminatory and prohibitive taxes, charges and fees, non-transparent regulations and standards, discriminatory licensing, registration, and certification rules, and weak enforcement of intellectual property rights add to the cost of trade. Consequently, an additional 20 percent is deducted from Russia's trade freedom score to account for these non-tariff barriers.

FISCAL FREEDOM — *86.3%*

Russia has a low income tax rate and a moderate corporate tax rate. The income tax rate is a flat 13 percent, and the top corporate tax rate is 24 percent. Other taxes include a value-added tax (VAT), a property tax, and a transport tax. In the most recent year, overall tax revenue as a percentage of GDP was 36.1 percent.

FREEDOM FROM GOVERNMENT — *71.6%*

Total government expenditures in Russia, including consumption and transfer payments, are moderate. In the most recent year, government spending equaled 33.6 percent of GDP, and the government received 6.1 percent of its revenues from state-owned enterprises and government ownership of property. Privatization has been hasty and very chaotic.

MONETARY FREEDOM — *62.8%*

Inflation in Russia is high, averaging 12.3 percent between 2003 and 2005. Relatively high and unstable prices explain most of the monetary freedom score. The government influences prices through regulation, extensive subsidies, and numerous state-owned enterprises and utilities. Consequently, an additional 15 percent is deducted from Russia's monetary freedom score to account for these policies.

INVESTMENT FREEDOM — *30%*

Official and unofficial barriers impede foreign investment in Russia. Officially, Russia restricts investments in aerospace, natural gas, insurance, electric power, defense, natural resources, Russian liquor concerns, and large-scale construction projects. Corruption is a serious unofficial barrier to foreign investment. In 2005, the government announced a decision barring foreign-controlled companies from bidding on its most lucrative natural resources. Residents and non-residents may hold foreign exchange accounts, subject to restrictions and government approval in some cases. Payments and transfers are subject to restrictions and surrender requirements. Transactions involving capital and money market instruments, derivatives, and credit operations are subject to central bank authorization in many cases.

FINANCIAL FREEDOM — *40%*

Russia's financial system, which was strongly affected by a 1998 financial crisis, consists primarily of banking. Both supervision and transparency are insufficient. The 1,000 licensed and registered banks in Russia are generally small and undercapitalized. Patron relationships between industries and banks continue. The banking sector is dominated by two state-owned banks, which together account for a large minority of banking assets. Foreign banks may operate only as subsidiaries and must have a minimum number of Russian employees and board members. Foreign investment in the sector is capped at 12 percent of total banking capital. The state has a 25 percent stake in the largest insurer. Foreign insurers together may not control over 15 percent of the insurance market and are barred from the life insurance market. Capital markets are relatively small and are dominated by energy companies.

PROPERTY RIGHTS — *30%*

Protection of private property in Russia is weak. The judicial system is unpredictable and corrupt, and contracts are difficult to enforce.

FREEDOM FROM CORRUPTION — *24%*

Corruption is perceived as widespread. Russia ranks 126th out of 158 countries in Transparency International's Corruption Perceptions Index for 2005.

LABOR FREEDOM — *66.2%*

The labor market operates under somewhat flexible employment regulations that could be improved to enhance overall productivity growth. The non-salary cost of employing a worker is high, and dismissing a redundant employee can be easy. Characterized by limited and restricted labor mobility across regions, the labor market is still fragmented. Regulations on increasing or contracting the number of work hours are rigid.

RWANDA

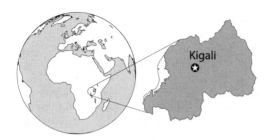

Kigali

Rank: 136

Regional Rank: 31 of 40

Rwanda's economy is 52.1 percent free, according to our 2007 assessment, which makes it the world's 136th freest economy. Its overall score is 2.2 percentage points lower than last year, partially reflecting new methodological detail. Rwanda is ranked 31st out of 40 countries in the sub-Saharan Africa region, and its overall score is slightly lower than the regional average.

Rwanda enjoys relatively high levels of fiscal freedom and freedom from government. Personal and corporate income tax rates are moderately high, but overall tax revenue is relatively low as a percentage of GDP. Recent government efforts to liberalize foreign trade include reducing some of Rwanda's non-tariff barriers. Total government expenditures are moderate, equaling slightly more than 25 percent of national GDP, and state-owned businesses do not constitute a large source of revenue.

Rwanda scores poorly in most areas: business freedom, investment freedom, financial freedom, monetary freedom, property rights, and freedom from corruption. The government officially welcomes foreign investment and has streamlined the relevant bureaucratic procedures, but political instability is still a major deterrent to capital. The judicial system does not have enough qualified magistrates or political independence, and legal procedures are subject to corruption. Inflation is high.

BACKGROUND: Over 80 percent of Rwanda's population is engaged in rain-fed subsistence agriculture that is supplemented by cash crops, particularly tea and coffee. Much economic activity is informal. Rwanda is still dealing with the social and legal aftermath of the 1994 genocide of an estimated 800,000 Tutsis and moderate Hutus. The largely Tutsi Rwandan Patriotic Front (RFP) seized power in 1994 and ruled through a transition government until 2003, when the RFP's Paul Kagame was elected president and the RFP won a majority in the legislature. Based partly on economic reform, including privatization and trade liberalization, the economy has surpassed pre-genocide levels.

How Do We Measure Economic Freedom? See Chapter 3 (page 37) for an explanation of the methodology or visit the *Index* Web site at *heritage.org/index.*

The economy is 52.1% free

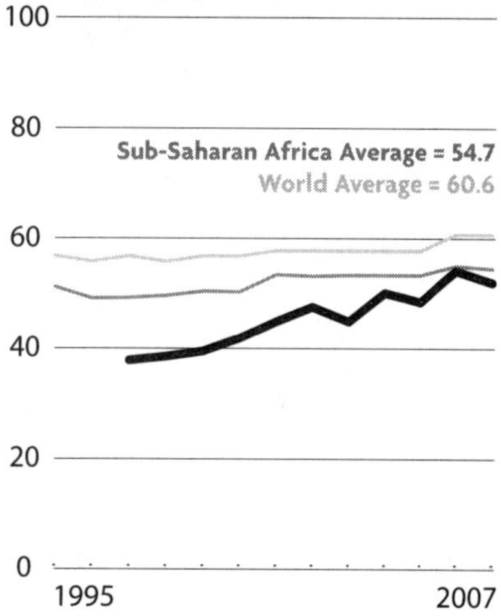

Sub-Saharan Africa Average = 54.7
World Average = 60.6

[Line chart showing economic freedom from 1995 to 2007, with values ranging from about 40 to 52]

QUICK FACTS

Population: 8.9 million

GDP (PPP): $11.2 billion
4.0% growth in 2004
5.4% 5-yr. comp. ann. growth
$1,263 per capita

Unemployment: n/a

Inflation (CPI): 11.7%

FDI (net inflow): $10.9 million

Official Development Assistance:
Multilateral: $279 million
Bilateral: $221 million (23% from the U.S.)

External Debt: $1.7 billion

Exports: $200.5 million
Primarily coffee, tea, hides, tin ore

Imports: $493.3 million
Primarily food, machinery and equipment, steel, petroleum products, cement, construction material

RWANDA'S TEN ECONOMIC FREEDOMS

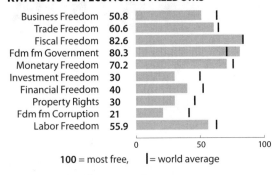

Business Freedom	50.8
Trade Freedom	60.6
Fiscal Freedom	82.6
Fdm fm Government	80.3
Monetary Freedom	70.2
Investment Freedom	30
Financial Freedom	40
Property Rights	30
Fdm fm Corruption	21
Labor Freedom	55.9

0   50   100

100 = most free, | = world average

BUSINESS FREEDOM — 50.8%

Starting a business takes an average of 16 days, compared to the world average of 48 days. However, both obtaining a business license and closing a business can be very difficult. Regulations are sometimes opaque and inconsistent, causing unreliability of interpretation. The overall freedom to start, operate, and close a business is restricted by the national regulatory environment.

TRADE FREEDOM — 60.6%

Rwanda's weighted average tariff rate was 9.7 percent in 2005. The government has made progress in liberalizing the trade regime, but import bans, prohibitive tariffs, and lack of transparency in some trade regulations and government procurement add to the cost of trade. Consequently, an additional 20 percent is deducted from Rwanda's trade freedom score to account for these non-tariff barriers.

FISCAL FREEDOM — 82.6%

Rwanda has moderately high tax rates. Both the top income tax rate and the top corporate tax rate are 35 percent. Other taxes include a value-added tax (VAT) and a property transfer tax. In the most recent year, overall tax revenue as a percentage of GDP was 12.8 percent.

FREEDOM FROM GOVERNMENT — 80.3%

Total government expenditures in Rwanda, including consumption and transfer payments, are moderate. In the most recent year, government spending equaled 26.1 percent of GDP, and the government received 11.5 percent of its revenues from state-owned enterprises and government ownership of property.

MONETARY FREEDOM — 70.2%

Inflation in Rwanda is high, averaging 9.8 percent between 2003 and 2005. Relatively unstable prices explain most of the monetary freedom score. The government influences prices through regulation and through state-owned enterprises and utilities, and it controls the prices of cement, electricity, water, telecommunications, petroleum, beer, and soft drinks. Consequently, an additional 10 percent is deducted from Rwanda's monetary freedom score to account for these policies.

INVESTMENT FREEDOM — 30%

Rwanda officially welcomes foreign investment and has adopted several initiatives, including a one-stop shop, to facilitate investment, but corruption and political instability are persistent unofficial barriers. The government relaxed some restrictions on foreign investment in June 2000. Both residents and non-residents may hold foreign exchange accounts, but only if they provide supporting documentation. Payments and transfers are subject to authorizations and maximum allowances and limits. Nearly all capital transactions require the central bank's approval.

FINANCIAL FREEDOM — 40%

The Rwandan financial sector is very small and burdened by serious shortcomings in supervision, regulation, auditing and oversight. Non-performing loans are a problem for the financial sector, which consists primarily of small banks and microfinance institutions. The government reduced its involvement in the banking sector in 2004 when it sold an 80 percent stake of the Banque Commerciale du Rwanda and 80 percent of Banque Continentale Africaine du Rwanda to foreign investors, but it remains extensively involved in the sector and, according to the International Monetary Fund, controls about 22 percent of total assets. The state also plays a large role in the insurance sector. It owns the largest insurer, Sonarwa, and controls another insurance parastatal, and these two companies together account for a majority of the insurance market. There are no capital markets in Rwanda.

PROPERTY RIGHTS — 30%

The Rwandan judiciary is influenced by the government and suffers from inefficiency, a lack of resources, and corruption.

FREEDOM FROM CORRUPTION — 21%

Corruption is perceived as significant. Rwanda ranks 83rd out of 158 countries in Transparency International's Corruption Perceptions Index for 2005.

LABOR FREEDOM — 55.9%

The labor market operates under restrictive employment regulations that could be improved to enhance overall productivity growth. The non-salary cost of employing a worker is low, but dismissing a redundant employee can be difficult. There are rigid regulations on increasing or contracting the number of work hours. The government sets minimum wages that vary by type of job.

SAUDI ARABIA

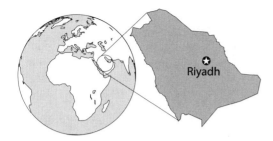

Riyadh

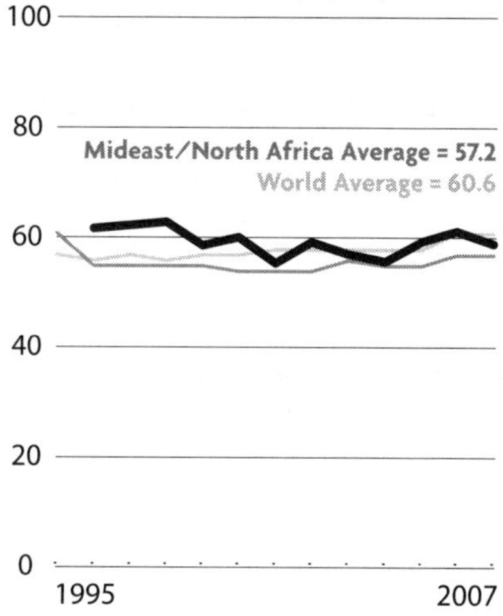

Saudi Arabia's economy is 59.1 percent free, according to our 2007 assessment, which makes it the world's 85th freest economy. Its overall score is 2.3 percentage points lower than last year, partially reflecting new methodological detail. Saudi Arabia is ranked 10th out of 17 countries in the Middle East/North Africa region, and its overall score is above the regional average.

Saudi Arabia has high levels of fiscal freedom, labor freedom, property rights, and monetary freedom. Except for a mandatory Islamic 2.5 percent *Zakat* charitable contribution, the government imposes no taxes on personal or corporate income. Saudi Arabia's labor market is flexible, as the government imposes few costs on employing or firing workers. Inflation is less than 1 percent, and the government maintains no direct price supports.

Saudi Arabia could improve its freedom from government, investment freedom, financial freedom, business freedom, and freedom from corruption. As in many other Gulf oil states, high government spending is supported by a large state-owned energy sector. The monarchy has begun to liberalize aspects of foreign investment, but immense barriers remain in effect. Financial markets in Saudi Arabia are distorted by government influence, and the legal system is similarly subject to political influence.

BACKGROUND: Saudi Arabia, the largest Persian Gulf oil kingdom, was founded in 1932 by King Abdul Aziz al-Saud and has been ruled as an absolute monarchy by the Saud dynasty ever since then. Crown Prince Abdullah officially became monarch in August 2005 following the death of King Fahd. As the world's leading oil producer and exporter, Saudi Arabia plays a dominant role in the Organization of Petroleum Exporting Countries. Its accession to the World Trade Organization in 2005 has led to gradual economic reforms, but recent debates about the king's successor have increased political tension and slowed the reform process.

How Do We Measure Economic Freedom? See Chapter 3 (page 37) for an explanation of the methodology or visit the *Index* Web site at *heritage.org/index*.

The economy is 59.1% free

Mideast/North Africa Average = 57.2

World Average = 60.6

(Chart: vertical axis 0 to 100, horizontal axis 1995 to 2007)

QUICK FACTS

Population: 24 million

GDP (PPP): $331.1 billion
5.2% growth in 2004
3.6% 5-yr. comp. ann. growth
$13,825 per capita

Unemployment: 6.9%

Inflation (CPI): 0.3%

FDI (net inflow): $1.8 billion

Official Development Assistance:
Multilateral: $15 million
Bilateral: $25 million (0.4% from the U.S.)

External Debt: $36.78 billion (2005 estimate)

Exports: $131.8 billion
Primarily petroleum and petroleum products

Imports: $66.7 billion
Primarily machinery and equipment, food, chemicals, motor vehicles, textiles

SAUDI ARABIA'S TEN ECONOMIC FREEDOMS

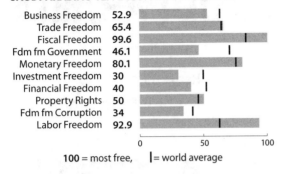

Business Freedom	52.9
Trade Freedom	65.4
Fiscal Freedom	99.6
Fdm fm Government	46.1
Monetary Freedom	80.1
Investment Freedom	30
Financial Freedom	40
Property Rights	50
Fdm fm Corruption	34
Labor Freedom	92.9

100 = most free, | = world average

BUSINESS FREEDOM — 52.9%

Starting a business takes an average of 39 days, compared to the world average of 48 days. To maximize entrepreneurship and job creation, it should be easier to start a company. Obtaining a business license is relatively simple, but closing a business is difficult. Cumbersome bureaucratic procedures are coupled with a lack of transparency. The overall freedom to start, operate, and close a business is restricted by the national regulatory environment.

TRADE FREEDOM — 65.4%

Saudi Arabia's weighted average tariff rate was 7.3 percent in 2004. Import bans, special approval for some imports, non-transparent regulations, service market access barriers, and weak protection of intellectual property rights add to the cost of trade. Consequently, an additional 20 percent is deducted from Saudi Arabia's trade freedom score to account for these non-tariff barriers.

FISCAL FREEDOM — 99.6%

Saudi Arabia has no income tax or corporate tax, either for Saudi nationals or for citizens of the Gulf Cooperation Council (GCC). However, a fixed 2.5 percent religious tax, called *Zakat*, is mandated by Islamic law and applied to Saudi and GCC individuals and corporations. Saudi Arabia has neither a value-added tax nor an estate tax. In the most recent year, overall tax revenue as a percentage of GDP was 7.7 percent.

FREEDOM FROM GOVERNMENT — 46.1%

Total government expenditures in Saudi Arabia, including consumption and transfer payments, are high. In the most recent year, government spending equaled 33.3 percent of GDP, and the government received 84.1 percent of its revenues from state-owned enterprises and government ownership of property.

MONETARY FREEDOM — 80.1%

Inflation in Saudi Arabia is low, averaging 0.6 percent between 2003 and 2005. Relatively low and stable prices explain most of the monetary freedom score. Although direct price controls are forbidden by Islamic law, the government influences prices across the economy through regulation, extensive subsidies, and state-owned enterprises and utilities, and a government purchasing agency controls prices for wheat and barley. Consequently, an additional

15 percent is deducted from Saudi Arabia's monetary freedom score to account for these policies.

INVESTMENT FREEDOM — 30%

Saudi Arabia has taken steps to open its economy to foreign investments, but substantial barriers remain. Many sectors are still off-limits to foreign investment. All foreign investment projects require a license from the government. Residents may hold foreign exchange accounts, but approval is required for non-residents. There are no controls or restrictions on payments and transfers. Only Saudi Arabian and Gulf Cooperation Council nationals and corporations may engage in portfolio investment in listed Saudi Arabian companies or buy securities, bonds, or money market instruments, and non-residents must have permission to issue them in Saudi Arabia. Credit operations must be approved.

FINANCIAL FREEDOM — 40%

Financial markets in Saudi Arabia are constrained by government influence, Islamic financial principles, and barriers to foreign participation. Regulatory, supervisory, and accounting standards are generally consistent with international norms. Foreign ownership of financial institutions is limited. Credit is available to domestic and foreign borrowers and is generally allocated on market terms. The banking sector includes 13 domestic commercial banks (nine majority privately owned) and eight foreign bank branches. The government owns a majority of the largest domestic bank and 34 percent of the majority foreign-owned Gulf International Bank and offers subsidized credit to preferred sectors. All insurance companies must be locally registered and must operate according to the principle of co-operative insurance. Insurance liberalization in 2005 led to 13 new insurance companies, including some foreign firms. Capital markets are relatively well developed.

PROPERTY RIGHTS — 50%

Investors question the ability of Saudi courts to enforce contracts efficiently. The court system is slow and non-transparent, and the judiciary is influenced by the ruling elite.

FREEDOM FROM CORRUPTION — 34%

Corruption is perceived as significant. Saudi Arabia ranks 70th out of 158 countries in Transparency International's Corruption Perceptions Index for 2005.

LABOR FREEDOM — 92.9%

The labor market operates under highly flexible employment regulations that enhance overall productivity growth. The non-salary cost of employing a worker is very high, but dismissing a redundant employee is not difficult. There is no legal minimum wage.

SENEGAL

⊙ Dakar

Senegal's economy is 58.8 percent free, according to our 2007 assessment, which makes it the world's 86th freest economy. Its overall score is 1.4 percentage points higher than last year, partially reflecting new methodological detail. Senegal is ranked 9th out of 40 countries in the sub-Saharan Africa region, and its overall score is slightly higher than the regional average.

Senegal enjoys high levels of freedom from government and monetary freedom. Total government expenditures in Senegal equal slightly more than 20 percent of GDP, and state-owned businesses constitute a negligible source of revenue. Inflation is very low, and the market sets virtually all prices for consumer goods.

As a developing African nation, Senegal faces many challenges. Business freedom, fiscal freedom, labor freedom, property rights, and freedom from corruption are all weak. Starting a business takes more time than the international average, and commercial operations overall are made more difficult by the national regulatory environment. Tax rates are high, particularly the top income tax rate. The labor market is highly inelastic and one of the 20 least free in the world. The judicial system does not have enough qualified magistrates or freedom from the executive branch and is subject to corruption, as is much of the rest of Senegal's bureaucracy.

BACKGROUND: Senegal is one of the few African countries with a long-standing democratic tradition. In March 2000, President Abdoulaye Wade was elected to a seven-year term. The peace process with a rebel group in the southern Casamance region is progressing fitfully. Infrastructure is fairly good by African standards, and Senegal serves as a regional gateway and business center. Senegal has limited natural resources and is predominantly rural, with agriculture and fishing occupying at least 60 percent of the population. Economic reforms aimed at liberalizing the economy are progressing slowly, and business is hindered by inconsistent or opaque regulation and corruption.

How Do We Measure Economic Freedom? See Chapter 3 (page 37) for an explanation of the methodology or visit the *Index* Web site at *heritage.org/index.*

The economy is 58.8% free

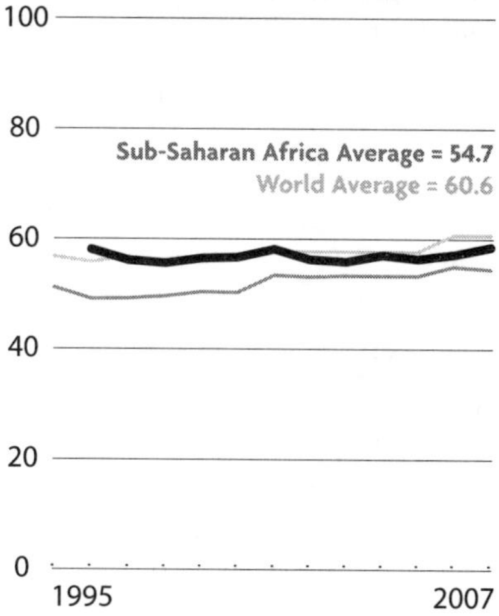

Sub-Saharan Africa Average = 54.7
World Average = 60.6

1995 — 2007

QUICK FACTS

Population: 11.4 million

GDP (PPP): $19.5 billion
6.2% growth in 2004
4.3% 5-yr. comp. ann. growth
$1,713 per capita

Unemployment: 48% (2001 estimate)

Inflation (CPI): 0.5%

FDI (net inflow): $66 million

Official Development Assistance:
Multilateral: $392 million
Bilateral: $880 million (6% from the U.S.)

External Debt: $3.9 billion

Exports: $1.8 billion
Primarily fish, groundnuts, petroleum products, phosphates, cotton

Imports: $2.7 billion
Primarily food and beverages, capital goods, fuels

SENEGAL'S TEN ECONOMIC FREEDOMS

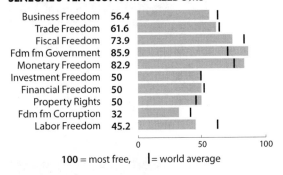

Business Freedom	56.4
Trade Freedom	61.6
Fiscal Freedom	73.9
Fdm fm Government	85.9
Monetary Freedom	82.9
Investment Freedom	50
Financial Freedom	50
Property Rights	50
Fdm fm Corruption	32
Labor Freedom	45.2

0   50   100

100 = most free, | = world average

BUSINESS FREEDOM — 56.4%

Starting a business takes an average of 58 days, compared to the world average of 48 days. To maximize entrepreneurship and job creation, it should be easier to start a company. Although obtaining a business license and closing a business can be relatively easy, the regulatory environment still lacks consistency and transparency. The overall freedom to start, operate, and close a business is restricted by the national regulatory environment.

TRADE FREEDOM — 61.6%

Senegal's weighted average tariff rate was 9.2 percent in 2004. Significant import taxes and fees, as well as inconsistent customs implementation and corruption, add to the cost of trade. Consequently, an additional 20 percent is deducted from Senegal's trade freedom score to account for these non-tariff barriers.

FISCAL FREEDOM — 73.9%

Senegal has high tax rates. The top income tax rate is 50 percent, and the top corporate tax rate is 33 percent. Other taxes include a value-added tax (VAT) and a vehicle tax. In the most recent year, overall tax revenue as a percentage of GDP was 18.1 percent.

FREEDOM FROM GOVERNMENT — 85.9%

Total government expenditures in Senegal, including consumption and transfer payments, are relatively low. In the most recent year, government spending equaled 23.2 percent of GDP, and the government received 4.6 percent of its revenues from state-owned enterprises and government ownership of property. The pace of privatization has been slow.

MONETARY FREEDOM — 82.9%

Inflation in Senegal is low, averaging 1.3 percent between 2003 and 2005. Relatively stable prices explain most of the monetary freedom score. Although many prices are freely determined, the government influences prices across the economy through state-owned enterprises and utilities, and the prices of pharmaceuticals and medical services are controlled. Consequently, an additional 10 percent is deducted from Senegal's monetary freedom score to account for these policies.

INVESTMENT FREEDOM — 50%

There is no legal discrimination against foreign investors, and 100 percent foreign ownership of businesses is permitted in most sectors except for electricity, telecommunications, mining, and water. The unofficial barriers to investment, such as corruption and judicial weakness, are substantial. The government must approve capital transfers to most countries. Other transfers are subject to numerous requirements, controls, and authorization, depending on the transaction. Residents and non-residents must receive official approval to hold foreign exchange accounts.

FINANCIAL FREEDOM — 50%

Senegal's financial system is underdeveloped. The Central Bank of West African States (BCEAO), a central bank common to eight countries, governs Senegal's financial institutions. The eight BCEAO member countries use the CFA franc, pegged to the euro. There were 10 commercial banks at the end of 2005. There were also two specialized banks providing credit for housing and agriculture. The largest banks are predominantly French-owned. The banking sector is highly concentrated, with three banks holding two-thirds of deposits. The government owns over 25 percent of the shares in seven banks, including a majority share in the agricultural bank. Banks are heavily exposed to a small number of borrowers, according to the International Monetary Fund. There also are several microfinance institutions. Senegal participates in a small regional stock market that is based in the Ivory Coast.

PROPERTY RIGHTS — 50%

Senegal lacks commercial courts staffed with trained judges, so court decisions can be arbitrary and inconsistent. An arbitration center administered by the Dakar Chamber of Commerce was established in 1998. Corruption is present in dispute settlement cases.

FREEDOM FROM CORRUPTION — 32%

Corruption is perceived as significant. Senegal ranks 78th out of 158 countries in Transparency International's Corruption Perceptions Index for 2005.

LABOR FREEDOM — 45.2%

The labor market operates under highly restrictive employment regulations that hinder overall productivity growth. The non-salary cost of employing a worker is high, and dismissing a redundant employee can be costly. Regulations related to increasing or contracting the number of work hours are rigid. Senegal's labor freedom is one of the 20 lowest in the world.

SERBIA AND MONTENEGRO

Belgrade

Rank: Not Ranked

Regional Rank: Not Ranked

Most of the economic freedom of Serbia and Montenegro cannot be graded because of the violence and political turmoil that the country has endured in recent years. The last time Serbia and Montenegro was wholly graded was in 2003, when it received a score of 39.5 percent.

Monetary freedom and trade freedom are weak. Inflation is high, particularly for a European country, and the government reserves the right to re-impose price supports that have been phased out in the past. Belgrade imposes a fairly high average tariff rate, although efforts are underway to liberalize the country's regulatory non-tariff barriers.

BACKGROUND: Following Montenegro's secession in May 2006, Serbia became a stand-alone state for the first time since the adoption of the 1835 constitution. After suffering from economic sanctions imposed throughout the 1990s, Serbia has started the long road to membership in the European Union by signing a Stability and Association Agreement. However, membership talks have been jeopardized by the failure of Serbian authorities to hand over indicted war criminal Ratko Mladic, and investor confidence is likely to remain stagnant until Mladic is captured. Serbia's exports include manufactured goods, machinery and transport equipment, and foodstuffs.

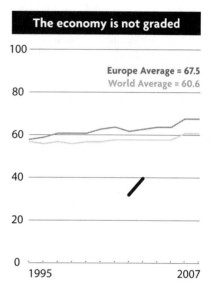

The economy is not graded

Europe Average = 67.5
World Average = 60.6

QUICK FACTS

Population: 8.1 million

GDP (PPP): n/a
8.8% growth in 2004
5.2% 5-yr. comp. ann. growth
n/a

Unemployment: 31.6%

Inflation (CPI): 9.5%

FDI (net inflow): $966 million (gross)

Official Development Assistance:
Multilateral: $563 million
Bilateral: $611 million (30% from the U.S.)

External Debt: $15.9 billion

Exports: $4.0 billion (2004 estimate)
Primarily manufactured goods, food, live animals, machinery, transport equipment

Imports: $11.4 billion (2004 estimate)
Primarily machinery, transport equipment, fuels and lubricants, manufactured goods, chemicals, food, live animals, raw materials (2003 data)

How Do We Measure Economic Freedom? See Chapter 3 (page 37) for an explanation of the methodology or visit the *Index* Web site at *heritage.org/index*.

BUSINESS FREEDOM — NOT GRADED

Starting a business takes an average of 18 days in Serbia and an average of 24 days in Montenegro, compared to the world average of 48 days. Obtaining a business license can be difficult: It involves 20 procedures in Serbia and 22 procedures in Montenegro. Regulations can be inconsistent and lacking in transparency.

TRADE FREEDOM — NOT GRADED

The weighted average tariff rate in Serbia and Montenegro was 7.9 percent in 2002. Progress has been made toward liberalizing the trade regime, but import licensing, import bans, and corruption still add to the cost of trade. Consequently, if Serbia and Montenegro were graded this year, an additional 20 percent would be deducted from its trade freedom score to account for these non-tariff barriers.

FISCAL FREEDOM — NOT GRADED

Different tax rates exist in Serbia and Montenegro. Serbia has a flat tax rate of 10 percent for both individual and corporate income. Montenegro's top income tax rate is 22 percent, and its corporate tax rate is a flat 9 percent. Other taxes include a value-added tax (VAT), which Serbia introduced in 2005 and Montenegro introduced in 2003.

FREEDOM FROM GOVERNMENT — NOT GRADED

Total government expenditures in Serbia and Montenegro, including consumption and transfer payments, are high. In the most recent year, government spending was estimated to equal about 46 percent of GDP.

MONETARY FREEDOM — NOT GRADED

Inflation in Serbia and Montenegro is high, averaging 14.2 percent between 2003 and 2005. For most goods, state subsidies and price supports have been eliminated, and prices are determined by market forces. However, the government retains the right to control the prices of certain basic products, including milk, bread, flour, and cooking oil; directly controls the prices of utilities, public transit, telecommunications services, and petroleum; and influences prices through numerous state-owned enterprises. Consequently, if Serbia and Montenegro were graded this year, an additional 15 percent would be deducted from its monetary freedom score to account for these policies.

INVESTMENT FREEDOM — NOT GRADED

Serbian law eliminates previous investment restrictions, provides for national treatment, permits transfer and repatriation of profits and dividends, guarantees against expropriation, and provides investment incentives. Montenegro's Foreign Investment Law incorporates these same protections for foreign investors. However, the business environment is still weak. Excessive bureaucracy, red tape, and corruption are major impediments to existing enterprises and to the creation of new enterprises. Both residents and non-residents may hold foreign exchange accounts, subject to central bank permission or conditions. Payments and transfers are subject to restrictions, and most capital transactions are subject to controls.

FINANCIAL FREEDOM — NOT GRADED

Serbia and Montenegro have two separate banking systems with central banks for each republic. A 2005 banking law requires that Serbia's central bank approve purchases of 5 percent or more in any bank. The government has been privatizing state-owned banks, including selling Jubanka, Novosadska Banka, and Kulska Banka in 2005. Serbia enjoys significant participation by foreign banks. Montenegro also has participation and investment by foreign banks. The government privatized the last bank with direct majority state ownership in 2005. Serbia's insurance sector is dominated by state-owned insurers, although the government has announced its intention to privatize them. Capital markets in Serbia are vigorous, and takeovers are common on the Belgrade Stock Exchange. Montenegro's capital markets are less developed.

PROPERTY RIGHTS — NOT GRADED

The constitutions of the Serbian Union and the Republic of Montenegro serve as the foundation of the legal system and create independent judiciaries in Serbia and Montenegro. The judicial system is inefficient, judges are poorly trained, and corruption is present.

FREEDOM FROM CORRUPTION — NOT GRADED

Corruption is perceived as widespread. Serbia and Montenegro ranks 97th out of 158 countries in Transparency International's Corruption Perceptions Index for 2005.

LABOR FREEDOM — NOT GRADED

Labor costs are relatively low in Serbia and Montenegro. Labor laws have improved the ability of businesses to dismiss non-performing employees without high severance costs. Serbia's adoption of a new labor law in 2005 was viewed as a step back toward labor market rigidity, but amendments are under consideration. Permitting direct talks between workers and employers, Montenegro has amended its labor code to increase labor market flexibility.

SIERRA LEONE

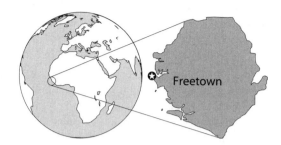

Freetown

Rank: 141

Regional Rank: 34 of 40

Sierra Leone's economy is 48.4 percent free, according to our 2007 assessment, which makes it the world's 141st freest economy. Its overall score is 1.6 percentage points higher than last year, partially reflecting new methodological detail. Sierra Leone is ranked 34th out of 40 countries in the sub-Saharan Africa region, and its overall score is below the regional average.

Sierra Leone scores well in fiscal freedom and freedom from government. The government imposes high tax rates, but overall tax revenue is relatively low as a percentage of GDP. Total government expenditures in Sierra Leone are equal to about 25 percent of GDP, and state-owned businesses are a relatively small source of revenue.

Recovering from a civil war, Sierra Leone faces many challenges. Investment freedom, financial freedom, labor freedom, property rights, and freedom from corruption are all weak. The government faces political instability, which discourages foreign investment, as do legal restrictions and devastated infrastructure. Sierra Leone's financial system is small. The judicial system is riddled with corruption (as is virtually all of the country's civil service) and often supplemented by traditional tribal courts in areas outside of the government's jurisdiction. The labor market is highly inflexible and one of the 20 least free in the world.

BACKGROUND: Sierra Leone's decade-long civil war ended in 2002. President Ahmed Tejan Kabbah was re-elected in 2002, and his party won a majority in parliament. The demobilization and disarmament of rebel forces and militias are proceeding, but stability is fragile. Sierra Leone could also be affected by regional instability. Per capita income is very low, and the economy and infrastructure were seriously damaged by the civil war. Minerals, particularly diamonds, are central to the economy. Agriculture accounts for about 40 percent of the economy, and two-thirds of the population is engaged in subsistence agriculture. Corruption is pervasive.

How Do We Measure Economic Freedom? See Chapter 3 (page 37) for an explanation of the methodology or visit the *Index* Web site at *heritage.org/index*.

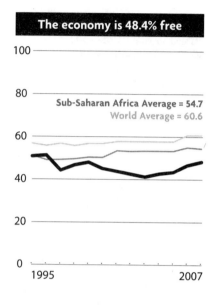

The economy is 48.4% free

Sub-Saharan Africa Average = 54.7
World Average = 60.6

QUICK FACTS

Population: 5.3 million

GDP (PPP): $3.0 billion
7.4% growth in 2004
12.9% 5-yr. comp. ann. growth
$561 per capita

Unemployment: n/a

Inflation (CPI): 14.2%

FDI (net inflow): $4.9 million (gross)

Official Development Assistance:
Multilateral: $239 million
Bilateral: $166 million (19% from the U.S.)

External Debt: $1.7 billion

Exports: $215.5 million
Primarily diamonds, rutile, cocoa, coffee, fish

Imports: $341.9 million
Primarily food, machinery and equipment, fuels, lubricants, chemicals

SIERRA LEONE'S TEN ECONOMIC FREEDOMS

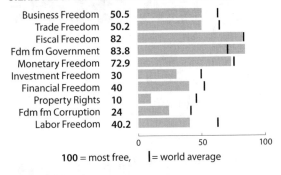

Business Freedom	50.5
Trade Freedom	50.2
Fiscal Freedom	82
Fdm fm Government	83.8
Monetary Freedom	72.9
Investment Freedom	30
Financial Freedom	40
Property Rights	10
Fdm fm Corruption	24
Labor Freedom	40.2

0   50   100

100 = most free, **I** = world average

BUSINESS FREEDOM — 50.5%

Starting a business takes an average of 26 days, compared to the world average of 48 days. To maximize entrepreneurship and job creation, it should be easier to start a company. Obtaining a business license can be difficult, and closing a business is very difficult. Regulations are inconsistent and applied unevenly, causing unreliability of interpretation. The overall freedom to start, operate, and close a business is restricted by the national regulatory environment.

TRADE FREEDOM — 50.2%

The weighted average tariff rate in Sierra Leone was 14.9 percent in 2005. The government is making progress toward liberalizing the trade regime, but non-transparent customs valuation, customs fees, inefficient and burdensome customs implementation, import bans and restrictions, export taxes, and complex export regulations all add to the cost of trade. Consequently, an additional 20 percent is deducted from Sierra Leone's trade freedom score to account for these non-tariff barriers.

FISCAL FREEDOM — 82%

Sierra Leone has relatively high tax rates. Both the top income tax rate and the top corporate tax rate are 35 percent. Other taxes include a vehicle tax and a tax on interest. In the most recent year, overall tax revenue as a percentage of GDP was 15.7 percent.

FREEDOM FROM GOVERNMENT — 83.8%

Total government expenditures in Sierra Leone, including consumption and transfer payments, are moderate. In the most recent year, government spending equaled 24.8 percent of GDP, and the government received 5.4 percent of its revenues from state-owned enterprises and government ownership of property.

MONETARY FREEDOM — 72.9%

Inflation in Sierra Leone is high, averaging 12.2 percent between 2003 and 2005. Such unstable prices explain most of the monetary freedom score. While most prices are freely set in the market, the government influences prices through state-owned enterprises and utilities. Consequently, an additional 5 percent is deducted from Sierra Leone's monetary freedom score to account for these policies.

INVESTMENT FREEDOM — 30%

Foreign and local businesses face a shortage of foreign exchange, corruption, devastated infrastructure, and uncertainty in the wake of the civil war. Non-citizens and foreign investors are not permitted to participate in certain economic activities. Both residents and non-residents may hold foreign exchange accounts, subject to some restrictions. Payments and transfers are generally permitted but face quantitative limits and approval requirements in some instances. Most capital transactions involving capital and money market instruments and credit operations require the Bank of Sierra Leone's approval. Direct investment abroad by residents, including the purchase of real estate, is prohibited.

FINANCIAL FREEDOM — 40%

Sierra Leone's financial system is small and recovering from civil war, during which the system collapsed. Sierra Leone is a member of the Economic Community of West African States (ECOWAS), which promotes regional trade and economic integration. Poor enforcement of contracts discourages lending, and non-performing loans are a problem. The banking sector, composed of the central bank and seven commercial banks, is relatively sound. Foreign and domestic borrowers have access to credit at market rates. Government-owned banks, taken together, account for a majority of banking assets. There are also several dozen small, non-bank financial institutions. The government holds frequent bond auctions, which tend to crowd out credit to other markets. There were 10 insurance companies as of January 2004. The government is in the process of setting up a stock market.

PROPERTY RIGHTS — 10%

Property is not secure in Sierra Leone. The level of judicial corruption is significant. Traditional tribal justice systems continue to serve as a frequently used supplement to the central government's judiciary, especially in rural areas.

FREEDOM FROM CORRUPTION — 24%

Corruption is perceived as widespread. Sierra Leone ranks 126th out of 158 countries in Transparency International's Corruption Perceptions Index for 2005.

LABOR FREEDOM — 40.2%

The labor market operates under highly inflexible employment regulations that hinder overall productivity growth. The non-salary cost of employing a worker is moderate, but dismissing a redundant employee is costly. Sierra Leone's labor freedom is one of the 20 lowest in the world.

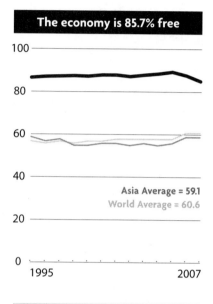

SINGAPORE

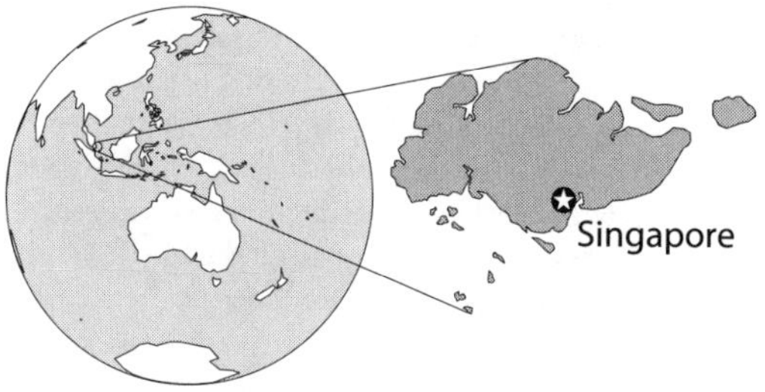

Singapore's economy is 85.7 percent free, according to our 2007 assessment, which makes it the world's 2nd freest economy. Its overall score is 2.8 percentage points lower than last year, partially reflecting new methodological detail. Singapore is ranked 2nd out of 30 countries in the Asia–Pacific region, and its overall score is much higher than the regional average.

Singapore is a world leader in all 10 areas of economic freedom. Virtually all commercial operations are performed with transparency and speed, and private enterprise has boomed. Inflation is low, and foreign investment is welcomed and given equal treatment. There are no tariffs. Singapore's legal system is efficient and highly protective of private property, and corruption is almost nonexistent. The labor market is highly flexible, and dismissing workers is costless.

Singapore could do slightly better in financial freedom, which at 50 percent is the only one of 10 economic freedoms below 80 percent. It is a world leader in foreign exchange transactions, and the government is promoting Singapore as a global financial hub, but state influence in the banking system persists.

BACKGROUND: Singapore gained its independence in 1965, and the People's Action Party has controlled its parliament ever since then. One of the foundations of Singapore's attractiveness to business is the integrity of its courts, but there is a growing perception that the judiciary may reflect the views of the ruling party. In 2006, a Canadian appeals court was asked to determine whether rulings in Singapore were sufficiently fair and impartial. Regardless of how the court rules, this case could well affect the decisions of foreign investors. Manufacturing makes up the largest portion of the economy, followed by business and financial services.

How Do We Measure Economic Freedom? See Chapter 3 (page 37) for an explanation of the methodology or visit the *Index* Web site at *heritage.org/index*.

The economy is 85.7% free

Asia Average = 59.1
World Average = 60.6

1995 — 2007

QUICK FACTS

Population: 4.2 million

GDP (PPP): $119.1 billion
8.7% growth in 2004
4.6% 5-yr. comp. ann. growth
$28,077 per capita

Unemployment: 3.4%

Inflation (CPI): 1.7%

FDI (net inflow): $5.4 billion

Official Development Assistance:
Multilateral: None
Bilateral: $9 million (0% from the U.S.)

External Debt: $23.76 billion (2005 estimate)

Exports: $238.5 billion
Primarily machinery and equipment (including electronics), consumer goods, chemicals, mineral fuels

Imports: $206.8 billion
Primarily machinery and equipment, mineral fuels, chemicals, food

SINGAPORE'S TEN ECONOMIC FREEDOMS

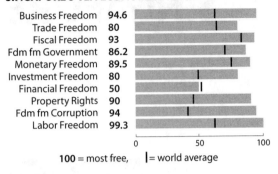

Business Freedom	94.6
Trade Freedom	80
Fiscal Freedom	93
Fdm fm Government	86.2
Monetary Freedom	89.5
Investment Freedom	80
Financial Freedom	50
Property Rights	90
Fdm fm Corruption	94
Labor Freedom	99.3

100 = most free, ▌ = world average

BUSINESS FREEDOM — 94.6%

Starting a business takes an average of six days, compared to the world average of 48 days. The business environment has allowed entrepreneurship to flourish. Obtaining a business license is simple, and closing a business is very easy. The overall freedom to start, operate, and close a business is strongly protected by the national regulatory environment.

TRADE FREEDOM — 80%

Singapore's weighted average tariff rate was zero percent in 2003. Although tariffs are generally low, import restrictions, import taxes, import licensing, export incentive programs, issues involving the enforcement of intellectual property rights, service market barriers, sanitary and phytosanitary rules, and non-transparent regulations add to the cost of trade. Consequently, an additional 20 percent is deducted from Singapore's trade freedom score to account for these non-tariff barriers.

FISCAL FREEDOM — 93%

Singapore enjoys low income tax rates. The top income tax rate is 22 percent, and the top corporate tax rate is 20 percent. Other taxes include a value-added tax (VAT) and a property tax. In the most recent year, overall tax revenue as a percentage of GDP was 13 percent.

FREEDOM FROM GOVERNMENT — 86.2%

Total government expenditures, including consumption and transfer payments, are low. In the most recent year, government spending equaled 14.6 percent of GDP, and the government received 26.4 percent of its revenues from state-owned enterprises and government ownership of property.

MONETARY FREEDOM — 89.5%

Inflation in Singapore is low, averaging 0.8 percent between 2003 and 2005. Relatively low and stable prices explain most of the monetary freedom score. The government influences prices through regulation and state-supported enterprises and can impose controls as it deems necessary. Consequently, an additional 5 percent is deducted from Singapore's monetary freedom score to account for these policies.

INVESTMENT FREEDOM — 80%

Singapore's investment laws are clear and fair. Foreign

and domestic businesses are treated equally, there are no production or local content requirements, and nearly all sectors are open to 100 percent foreign ownership. Foreign investment is still limited in broadcasting (up to 49 percent unless waived); newspaper services (5 percent); foreign law firms and foreign lawyers practicing in Singapore; and some sectors in which government-linked companies are dominant (for example, foreign equity in the PSA Corporation, one of two main managers of Singapore's ports, is restricted to 49 percent). Foreign ownership of certain landed properties is subject to approval by the relevant authority. Residents and non-residents may hold foreign exchange accounts. There are no controls or requirements on current transfers, payments, or repatriation of profits.

FINANCIAL FREEDOM — 50%

The financial system is sound and well regulated, and Singapore is among the world's top five foreign exchange trading centers. The Monetary Authority of Singapore, owned and controlled by the Ministry of Finance, acts as the central bank. Credit is readily available and generally allocated at market rates. The government controls the Development Bank of Singapore (the largest domestic bank group and publicly listed) and indirectly holds significant minority shares in the other two domestic bank groups. The government launched the SME Access Loan Program, a new financing scheme for small and medium-sized enterprises, in 2005. Foreign banks have been granted greater freedom to open branches and offer services, but the government seeks to maintain the domestic bank share of deposits above 50 percent and requires that the majority of board members of domestic banks must be Singapore citizens and residents. Six foreign banks possess "qualifying full bank" licenses. Other foreign banks face more restrictions on their activities. A free trade agreement between Singapore and the U.S. has greatly loosened restrictions on U.S. banks in Singapore. Foreign financial firms compete aggressively in insurance, fund management, and venture capital. Capital markets are sophisticated and well developed, and the Singapore Exchange is increasing its ties with other Asian exchanges.

PROPERTY RIGHTS — 90%

The court system is very efficient and strongly protects private property. There is no threat of expropriation, and contracts are very secure.

FREEDOM FROM CORRUPTION — 94%

Corruption is perceived as almost nonexistent. Singapore ranks 5th out of 158 countries in Transparency International's Corruption Perceptions Index for 2005.

LABOR FREEDOM — 99.3%

The labor market operates under highly flexible employment regulations that enhance overall productivity growth. The non-salary cost of employing a worker is low, and dismissing a redundant employee is costless. Regulations on increasing or contracting the number of work hours are very flexible.

SLOVAK REPUBLIC

Bratislava

Rank: 40

Regional Rank: 21 of 41

The Slovak Republic's economy is 68.4 percent free, according to our 2007 assessment, which makes it the world's 40th freest economy. Its overall score is 0.8 percentage point lower than last year, partially reflecting new methodological detail. The Slovak Republic is ranked 21st out of 41 countries in the European region, and its overall score is equal to the regional average.

The Slovak Republic enjoys high levels of investment freedom, trade freedom, financial freedom, and business freedom. The average tariff rate is low, although non-tariff barriers include distortionary EU subsidies, and business regulation is efficient. Foreign investment is actively promoted, and foreigners are subject to remarkably few regulations in almost all areas of the economy. The financial sector has benefited significantly from an aggressive privatization campaign by the government.

The Slovak Republic is weak in freedom from government, property rights, and freedom from corruption. Total government spending equals almost two-fifths of GDP. The judiciary is independent of political influence, but cases take years to resolve, both for citizens and for foreign investors. The level of corruption in the judiciary and civil service is significant by modern European standards.

BACKGROUND: Slovakia became independent following its peaceful "Velvet Divorce" from the former Czechoslovakia in 1993. Elections scheduled for September 2006 were moved up to June because of the departure of the New Citizen Party and the Christian Democratic Movement from the coalition government. Although Robert Fico's Smer–Socialist Democratic Party failed to gain an overall majority, he announced that he would form a coalition. The reforms implemented by former Prime Minister Mikulas Dzurinda have led to low labor costs, low taxes, and political stability that make Slovakia one of Europe's most attractive economies, especially for automobile and other manufacturing.

How Do We Measure Economic Freedom? See Chapter 3 (page 37) for an explanation of the methodology or visit the *Index* Web site at *heritage.org/index*.

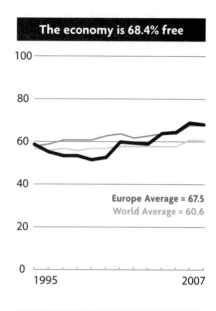

The economy is 68.4% free

Europe Average = 67.5
World Average = 60.6

1995 — 2007

QUICK FACTS

Population: 5.4 million

GDP (PPP): $78.7 billion
5.5% growth in 2004
4.1% 5-yr. comp. ann. growth
$14,623 per capita

Unemployment: 14.3%

Inflation (CPI): 7.5%

FDI (net inflow): $1.3 billion

Official Development Assistance:
Multilateral: $171 million
Bilateral: $64 million (2% from the U.S.)

External Debt: $22.1 billion

Exports: $25.2 billion
Primarily vehicles, machinery, electrical equipment, base metals, chemicals, minerals, plastics

Imports: $25.6 billion
Primarily machinery, transport equipment, intermediate and other manufactured goods, fuels, chemicals

SLOVAK REPUBLIC'S TEN ECONOMIC FREEDOMS

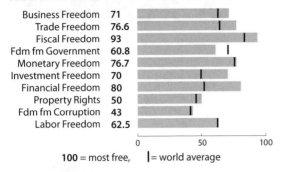

Business Freedom	71
Trade Freedom	76.6
Fiscal Freedom	93
Fdm fm Government	60.8
Monetary Freedom	76.7
Investment Freedom	70
Financial Freedom	80
Property Rights	50
Fdm fm Corruption	43
Labor Freedom	62.5

0   50   100

100 = most free, | = world average

BUSINESS FREEDOM — 71%

The Slovak Republic has been making considerable progress in improving its business environment. Starting a business takes an average of 25 days, compared to the world average of 48 days. Obtaining a business license is relatively simple, but closing a business can be somewhat difficult and time-consuming. The overall freedom to start, operate, and close a business is relatively well protected by the national regulatory environment.

TRADE FREEDOM — 76.6%

The Slovak Republic's trade policy is the same as those of other members of the European Union. The common EU weighted average tariff rate was 1.7 percent in 2005. Various non-tariff barriers are reflected in EU policy, including agricultural and manufacturing subsidies, regulatory and licensing restrictions, and other market access restrictions. The enforcement of intellectual property rights is weak, licensing and government procurement regulations are burdensome and non-transparent, and corruption can be a problem. Consequently, an additional 20 percent is deducted from the Slovak Republic's trade freedom score.

FISCAL FREEDOM — 93%

The Slovak Republic enjoys relatively low and flat tax rates. Both the income and corporate tax rates are a flat 19 percent. Other taxes include a value-added tax (VAT) and a property tax. In the most recent year, overall tax revenue as a percentage of GDP was 18 percent.

FREEDOM FROM GOVERNMENT — 60.8%

Total government expenditures in the Slovak Republic, including consumption and transfer payments, are high. In the most recent year, government spending equaled 39.3 percent of GDP, and the government received 9.4 percent of its revenues from state-owned enterprises and government ownership of property.

MONETARY FREEDOM — 76.7%

Inflation in the Slovak Republic is moderate, averaging 4.4 percent between 2003 and 2005. Relatively unstable prices explain most of the monetary freedom score. As a participant in the EU's Common Agricultural Policy, the government subsidizes agricultural production, distorting the prices of agricultural products. The government also influences prices through regulation and state-owned enterprises and utilities. Consequently, an additional 10 percent is deducted from the Slovak Republic's monetary freedom score to account for these policies.

INVESTMENT FREEDOM — 70%

There is no screening process for foreign investment, and full foreign ownership is permitted in some cases. Foreign ownership is limited to 49 percent of the natural gas company, the electric power producer, electricity distributors, and an oil pipeline, and the state retains ownership of the railroad rights of way, postal services, water supplies (but not suppliers), and forestry companies. Residents may establish foreign exchange accounts when staying abroad or with permission of the National Bank of Slovakia; non-residents may hold foreign exchange accounts. There are very few controls on capital transactions, except for rules governing commercial banking and credit institutions, which must abide by existing banking laws.

FINANCIAL FREEDOM — 80%

The Slovak Republic has implemented an aggressive privatization program and has adopted reforms to bring its financial sector into line with European standards. Interest rates have been completely liberalized, and credit limits have been abolished. The banking sector, which dominates the financial sector, was composed of 18 Slovak incorporated banks and six licensed branches of foreign banks as of December 2005. The Slovak Republic has sold most state-owned banks, and only one medium-size bank remains fully owned by domestic owners. Foreign capital controls 97 percent of the banking sector. The insurance sector is growing but remains limited. Capital markets are small, and trading on the two exchanges is relatively light. Pension administration companies are required to invest at least 30 percent of their assets in Slovakia.

PROPERTY RIGHTS — 50%

The judiciary is independent and effective, although decisions can take years. Slovak courts recognize and enforce foreign judgments, subject to the same delays. Corruption is present in the court system.

FREEDOM FROM CORRUPTION — 43%

Corruption is perceived as significant. The Slovak Republic ranks 47th out of 158 countries in Transparency International's Corruption Perceptions Index for 2005.

LABOR FREEDOM — 62.5%

The labor market operates under relatively flexible employment regulations that could be further improved to enhance overall productivity growth. The non-salary cost of employing a worker is high, but dismissing a redundant employee is not costly. The government's efforts to reform the labor codes, which began in 2003, have contributed to increasing labor market flexibility.

SLOVENIA

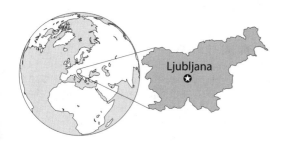

Ljubljana

Slovenia's economy is 63.6 percent free, according to our 2007 assessment, which makes it the world's 58th freest economy. Its overall score is 0.1 percentage point higher than last year, partially reflecting new methodological detail. Slovenia is ranked 27th out of 41 countries in the European region, and its overall score is lower than the regional average.

Slovenia enjoys high levels of business freedom, investment freedom, trade freedom, and freedom from corruption. The average tariff rate is low, although non-tariff barriers include distortionary EU subsidies, and business regulations are transparent. Foreign investment is encouraged, and the streamlining of investment rules has left virtually no restrictions on foreign capital. Slovenia has low levels of corruption but, as a member of the European Union, could still improve.

Slovenia is weak in freedom from government, labor freedom, and property rights. Total government spending equals more than two-fifths of GDP. Slovenia's labor market, like those of many other EU social democracies, is highly rigid. The judiciary is constitutionally protective of private property but suffers from understaffing, long delays in case resolution, and traces of corruption.

BACKGROUND: As the first entity to secede from the former Yugoslavia in 1991, Slovenia managed to avoid the bloody conflict that followed Croatia's secession. As a result, Slovenia's economic infrastructure was left intact, and it continues to be the richest country in East Central Europe. The nation was invited to join both NATO and the EU in 2002, which it did by referendum approvals in 2004. In 2007, Slovenia is expected to become the first former Communist state to join the European single currency, the euro.

How Do We Measure Economic Freedom? See Chapter 3 (page 37) for an explanation of the methodology or visit the *Index* Web site at *heritage.org/index*.

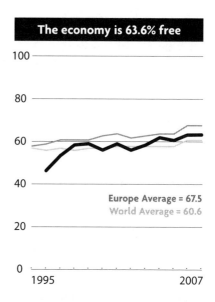

The economy is 63.6% free

Europe Average = 67.5
World Average = 60.6

QUICK FACTS

Population: 2 million

GDP (PPP): $41.8 billion
4.2% growth in 2004
3.4% 5-yr. comp. ann. growth
$20,939 per capita

Unemployment: 10.6%

Inflation (CPI): 3.6%

FDI (net inflow): $18.2 million

Official Development Assistance:
Multilateral: $58 million
Bilateral: $9 million (10% from the U.S.)

External Debt: $19.0 billion (2005 estimate)

Exports: $19.5 billion
Primarily manufactured goods, machinery, transport equipment, chemicals, food

Imports: $19.9 billion
Primarily machinery, transport equipment, manufactured goods, chemicals, fuels and lubricants, food

SLOVENIA'S TEN ECONOMIC FREEDOMS

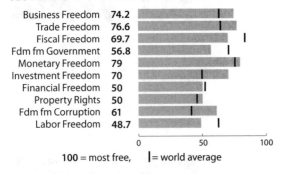

Business Freedom	74.2
Trade Freedom	76.6
Fiscal Freedom	69.7
Fdm fm Government	56.8
Monetary Freedom	79
Investment Freedom	70
Financial Freedom	50
Property Rights	50
Fdm fm Corruption	61
Labor Freedom	48.7

0   50   100

100 = most free,   ▌= world average

BUSINESS FREEDOM — 74.2%

Starting a business takes an average of 60 days, compared to the world average of 48 days. To maximize entrepreneurship and job creation, it should be easier to start a company. Obtaining a business license and closing a business are relatively simple. The overall freedom to start, operate, and close a business is relatively well protected by the national regulatory environment.

TRADE FREEDOM — 76.6%

Slovenia's trade policy is the same as those of other members of the European Union. The common EU weighted average tariff rate was 1.7 percent in 2005. Various non-tariff barriers are reflected in EU policy, including agricultural and manufacturing subsidies, regulatory and licensing restrictions, and other market access restrictions. The government also implements burdensome pharmaceutical and non-transparent government procurement regulations. Consequently, an additional 20 percent is deducted from Slovenia's trade freedom score.

FISCAL FREEDOM — 69.7%

Slovenia has a very high income tax rate and a moderate corporate tax rate. The top income tax rate is 50 percent, and the top corporate tax rate is 25 percent. Other taxes include a value-added tax (VAT), a property transfer tax, and a tax on insurance. In the most recent year, overall tax revenue as a percentage of GDP was 37.6 percent.

FREEDOM FROM GOVERNMENT — 56.8%

Total government expenditures in Slovenia, including consumption and transfer payments, are high. In the most recent year, government spending equaled 42.7 percent of GDP, and the government received 2 percent of its revenues from state-owned enterprises and government ownership of property.

MONETARY FREEDOM — 79%

Inflation in Slovenia is moderate, averaging 3 percent between 2003 and 2005. Relatively moderate and unstable prices explain most of the monetary freedom score. As a participant in the EU's Common Agricultural Policy, the government subsidizes agricultural production, distorting the prices of agricultural products. The government also controls pharmaceutical prices and influences prices through regulation and state-owned enterprises and utili-

ties. Consequently, an additional 10 percent is deducted from Slovenia's monetary freedom score to account for these policies.

INVESTMENT FREEDOM — 70%

Foreign investors are accorded national treatment, restrictions on portfolio investment have been abolished, and the government has streamlined the investment process. Residents and non-residents may hold foreign exchange accounts after proving their identity. There are no restrictions on payments and transfers. Nearly all restrictions on capital and money market instruments were removed in 2003. Most direct investment is unrestricted, but a license is required to invest in the trading or producing of armaments or military equipment. Non-EU foreigners may face restrictions on investment in real estate.

FINANCIAL FREEDOM — 50%

Slovenia has been pursuing privatization and financial reform to meet EU standards. The banking system is relatively well developed and sound, although concentrated, with the top three banks accounting for a majority of banking assets. At the end of 2004, there were 20 banks and two savings institutions. The government owns a majority share in Slovenia's two largest banks and sold 39 percent of the largest bank in 2002. The state also owns 85 percent of the country's largest insurer, Zavarovalnica Triglav, which dominates the general and life insurance markets. Capital markets are relatively small and centered on the Ljubljana Stock Exchange.

PROPERTY RIGHTS — 50%

Private property is guaranteed by Slovenia's constitution, but the courts are inadequately staffed and procedurally slow, and there are reports of corruption. Investors are usually frustrated about the weak protection afforded by the judiciary.

FREEDOM FROM CORRUPTION — 61%

Corruption is perceived as present. Slovenia ranks 31st out of 158 countries in Transparency International's Corruption Perceptions Index for 2005.

LABOR FREEDOM — 48.7%

The labor market operates under highly inflexible employment regulations that retard overall productivity growth. The non-salary cost of employing a worker is moderate, but dismissing a redundant employee is relatively costly. Regulations related to increasing or contracting the number of work hours are not flexible. Comprehensive overhauls to reduce labor market rigidities are necessary to foster productivity and job creation.

SOUTH AFRICA

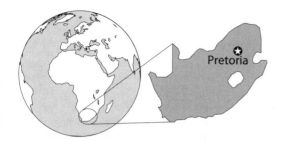

Pretoria

Rank: 52

Regional Rank: 3 of 40

South Africa's economy is 64.1 percent free, according to our 2007 assessment, which makes it the world's 52nd freest economy. Its overall score is 2.2 percentage points lower than last year, partially reflecting new methodological detail. South Africa is ranked 3rd out of 40 countries in the sub-Saharan Africa region, and its overall score is much higher than the regional average.

South Africa enjoys fairly high levels of business freedom, fiscal freedom, monetary freedom, freedom from government, and financial freedom. The government has been working to increase the transparency of commercial regulations. Income tax rates are high, but corporate taxes are relatively moderate, and overall tax revenue is moderate as a percentage of GDP. Inflation is low, and the government actively subsidizes the market prices of only a few staple goods. South Africa's financial system is the most developed in Africa.

South Africa's investment freedom, property rights, and freedom from corruption could be improved. The judicial system is slow, primarily because of understaffing and inefficiency. Race laws and unclear regulation hamper foreign investment, but the legal environment is free from political interference and the threat of expropriation.

BACKGROUND: South Africa is the economic hub of sub-Saharan Africa, accounting for one-third of regional GDP. South Africa is the world's largest producer of gold and platinum, and its well-developed mining, services, manufacturing, and agriculture sectors rival those in the developed world. The government has implemented economic reform over the past decade, and growth has improved. Obstacles to long-term growth and stability include crime, HIV/AIDS, and high unemployment. Powerful unions oppose labor market liberalization, and privatization is undermined by failure to include major state-owned enterprises. President Thabo Mbeki and the African National Congress have a commanding majority in parliament.

How Do We Measure Economic Freedom? See Chapter 3 (page 37) for an explanation of the methodology or visit the *Index* Web site at *heritage.org/index*.

The economy is 64.1% free

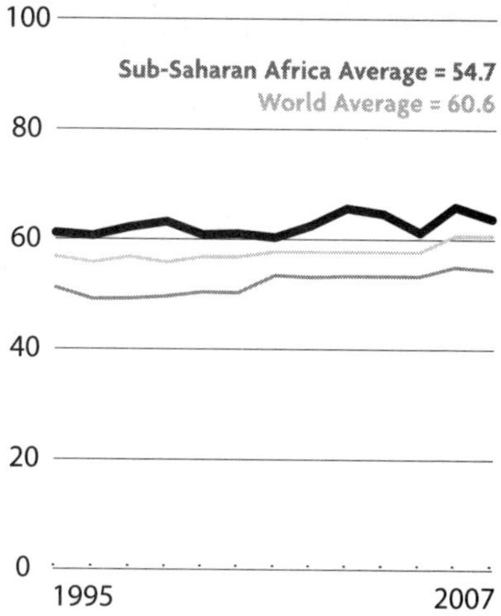

Sub-Saharan Africa Average = 54.7
World Average = 60.6

100
80
60
40
20
0

1995 — 2007

QUICK FACTS

Population: 45.5 million

GDP (PPP): $509.3 billion
4.5% growth in 2004
3.6% 5-yr. comp. ann. growth
$11,191 per capita

Unemployment: 27.1%

Inflation (CPI): 1.4%

FDI (net inflow): −$1 billion

Official Development Assistance:
Multilateral: $156 million
Bilateral: $493 million (19% from the U.S.)

External Debt: $28.5 billion

Exports: $56.7 billion
Primarily gold, diamonds, platinum, other metals and minerals, machinery and equipment

Imports: $57.9 billion
Primarily machinery and equipment, chemicals, petroleum products, scientific instruments, food

SOUTH AFRICA'S TEN ECONOMIC FREEDOMS

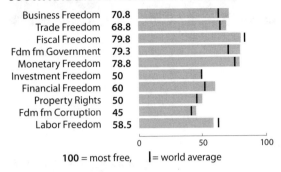

Business Freedom	70.8	
Trade Freedom	68.8	
Fiscal Freedom	79.8	
Fdm fm Government	79.3	
Monetary Freedom	78.8	
Investment Freedom	50	
Financial Freedom	60	
Property Rights	50	
Fdm fm Corruption	45	
Labor Freedom	58.5	

0   50   100

100 = most free, | = world average

BUSINESS FREEDOM — 70.8%

Starting a business takes an average of 35 days, compared to the world average of 48 days. To maximize entrepreneurship and job creation, it should be easier to start a company. Obtaining a business license and closing a business are relatively simple. Despite efforts to increase regulatory transparency, bureaucratic obstacles and delays persist. The overall freedom to start, operate, and close a business is relatively well protected by the national regulatory environment.

TRADE FREEDOM — 68.8%

South Africa's weighted average tariff rate was 5.6 percent in 2001. Import restrictions, weak enforcement of intellectual property rights, service market barriers, sanitary and phytosanitary rules, non-transparent and inefficient bureaucracy, excessive regulation, and corruption add to the cost of trade. Consequently, an additional 20 percent is deducted from South Africa's trade freedom score to account for these non-tariff barriers.

FISCAL FREEDOM — 79.8%

South Africa has a high income tax rate and a moderate corporate tax rate. The top income tax rate is 40 percent, and the top corporate tax rate is 29 percent. Other taxes include a value-added tax (VAT), a property tax, and a capital gains tax. In the most recent year, overall tax revenue as a percentage of GDP was 24.3 percent.

FREEDOM FROM GOVERNMENT — 79.3%

Total government expenditures in South Africa, including consumption and transfer payments, are moderate. In the most recent year, government spending equaled 26.3 percent of GDP, and the government received 13.7 percent of its revenues from state-owned enterprises and government ownership of property. The state still exerts monopolistic controls over enterprises in some sectors.

MONETARY FREEDOM — 78.8%

Inflation in South Africa is moderate, averaging 3.1 percent between 2003 and 2005. Relatively moderate and unstable prices explain most of the monetary freedom score. Prices are generally set by the market, the exceptions being the prices of petroleum products, coal, paraffin, and utilities, and the government influences prices through regulation, state-owned enterprises, and support programs. Conse-

quently, an additional 10 percent is deducted from South Africa's monetary freedom score to account for these policies.

INVESTMENT FREEDOM — 50%

South Africa permits foreign investment in most sectors and generally does not restrict the form or extent of foreign investment. The Black Economic Empowerment strategy establishes a scorecard with targets for equity ownership, management, procurement, and equality in employment for "historically disadvantaged" individuals. Unclear regulations in key sectors and rigid labor laws are disincentives. Residents may establish foreign exchange accounts through authorized dealers, subject to government approval and quantitative limits. Non-residents may hold them with authorized dealers. Many payments, capital transactions, and transfers are subject to restrictions, controls, quantitative limits, and prior approval.

FINANCIAL FREEDOM — 60%

South Africa's financial system is the most advanced in Africa. Financial regulations are generally consistent with international standards. However, under the Financial Services Charter, which establishes a scorecard to measure progress in empowering "historically disadvantaged" individuals and communities, banks must have black ownership of 25 percent by 2010, direct a portion of after-tax profits to specific projects, and employ a fair representation of disadvantaged individuals in management. Banking is dominated by the "Big Four" banks, which together account for about 80 percent of assets. There are 65 foreign banks. Foreign ownership must be approved by the government. A large number of microfinance institutions are active. The insurance industry is well-capitalized and has 166 firms. Capital markets are well developed, and the JSE Securities Exchange is one of the world's 20 largest.

PROPERTY RIGHTS — 50%

The threat of expropriation is low. The judiciary is independent, and contractual arrangements are generally secure. However, the judiciary is understaffed, underfunded, and overburdened.

FREEDOM FROM CORRUPTION — 45%

Corruption is perceived as significant. South Africa ranks 46th out of 158 countries in Transparency International's Corruption Perceptions Index for 2005.

LABOR FREEDOM — 58.5%

The labor market operates under inflexible employment regulations that hinder overall productivity growth. The non-salary cost of employing a worker is low, but dismissing a redundant employee can be cumbersome. Businesses characterize South Africa's labor market as overly regulated and have urged the government to amend some of the recently passed labor codes.

SPAIN

Madrid

Spain's economy is 70.9 percent free, according to our 2007 assessment, which makes it the world's 27th freest economy. Its overall score is 0.3 percentage point higher than last year, partially reflecting new methodological detail. Spain is ranked 16th out of 41 countries in the European region, and its overall score is slightly higher than the regional average.

Spain enjoys high levels of business freedom, trade freedom, monetary freedom, investment freedom, property rights, and freedom from corruption. The average tariff rate is low, but non-tariff barriers include distortionary European Union subsidies on agriculture and other goods. The government has tried to streamline business red tape and has improved licensing procedures. Inflation is low, and foreign investment is subject to few government restrictions. The judiciary is independent of politics, as in most other EU countries, but case resolution is extremely slow.

Spain is relatively weak in freedom from government and labor freedom. Total government spending equals almost two-fifths of GDP. Spain's labor market is highly restrictive in many ways, from a strict limit on the number of workweek hours to employment severance procedures.

BACKGROUND: Many years of brisk growth characterized by strong job creation, structural reforms, and sound fiscal policy are a major part of former Spanish Prime Minister José María Aznar's legacy from 1996 to 2004. The new premier, José Luis Rodríguez Zapatero, won office in the wake of the pre-election al-Qaeda bombings in Madrid in 2004. The new socialist government has not undermined Aznar's economic achievement, however. Gross domestic product has continued to grow respectably, and unemployment—long the scourge of modern Spain—continues to decline. The key to continued growth lies in improving sluggish labor productivity.

How Do We Measure Economic Freedom? See Chapter 3 (page 37) for an explanation of the methodology or visit the *Index* Web site at *heritage.org/index*.

The economy is 70.9% free

Europe Average = 67.5
World Average = 60.6

1995 — 2007

QUICK FACTS

Population: 42.7 million

GDP (PPP): $1.1 trillion
3.1% growth in 2004
3.5% 5-yr. comp. ann. growth
$25,047 per capita

Unemployment: 11%

Inflation (CPI): 3.03%

FDI (net inflow): −$35.9 billion

Official Development Assistance:
Multilateral: None
Bilateral: None

External Debt: $970.7 billion (2005 estimate)

Exports: $269.0 billion
Primarily machinery, motor vehicles, food, pharmaceuticals, medicines, other consumer goods

Imports: $307.4 billion
Primarily machinery and equipment, fuels, chemicals, semi-finished goods, food, consumer goods, measuring and medical control instruments

SPAIN'S TEN ECONOMIC FREEDOMS

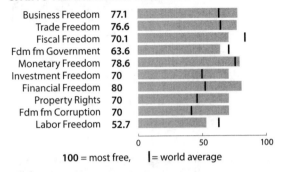

Business Freedom	77.1
Trade Freedom	76.6
Fiscal Freedom	70.1
Fdm fm Government	63.6
Monetary Freedom	78.6
Investment Freedom	70
Financial Freedom	80
Property Rights	70
Fdm fm Corruption	70
Labor Freedom	52.7

0   50   100

100 = most free, ▮ = world average

BUSINESS FREEDOM — 77.1%

Starting a business takes an average of 47 days, compared to the world average of 48 days. To maximize entrepreneurship and job creation, it should be easier to start a company. Obtaining a business license can be relatively simple, and closing a business is easy. Although the government has streamlined its regulatory regime, bureaucratic obstacles and delays remain problems. The overall freedom to start, operate, and close a business is relatively well protected by the national regulatory environment.

TRADE FREEDOM — 76.6%

Spain's trade policy is the same as those of other members of the European Union. The common EU weighted average tariff rate was 1.7 percent in 2005. Various non-tariff barriers are reflected in EU policy, including agricultural and manufacturing subsidies, regulatory and licensing restrictions, and other market access restrictions. The government also implements burdensome pharmaceutical and biotechnology regulations and service market access barriers, and the protection of intellectual property rights can be problematic. Consequently, an additional 20 percent is deducted from Spain's trade freedom score.

FISCAL FREEDOM — 70.1%

Spain has burdensome tax rates. The top income tax rate is 45 percent, and the top corporate tax rate is 35 percent. Other taxes include a value-added tax (VAT), a property tax, and a transportation tax. In the most recent year, overall tax revenue as a percentage of GDP was 35.1 percent.

FREEDOM FROM GOVERNMENT — 63.6%

Total government expenditures in Spain, including consumption and transfer payments, are moderate. In the most recent year, government spending equaled 38.8 percent of GDP, and the government received 3.7 percent of its revenues from state-owned enterprises and government ownership of property.

MONETARY FREEDOM — 78.6%

Spain is a member of the euro zone. Inflation in Spain is moderate, averaging 3.3 percent between 2003 and 2005. Nearly stable prices explain most of the monetary freedom score. As a participant in the EU's Common Agricultural Policy, the government subsidizes agricultural production, distorting the prices of agricultural products. The government also influences prices through regulation and state-owned enterprises and utilities. Consequently, an additional 10 percent is deducted from Spain's monetary freedom score to account for these policies.

INVESTMENT FREEDOM — 70%

Spain maintains few restrictions on foreign investment. Spanish law permits foreign investment of up to 100 percent of equity, and capital movements have been completely liberalized. Activities related to national defense require prior approval. In May 2006, a decree law was approved allowing the government to stop public offers from foreign companies to acquire domestic firms. There are no restrictions or controls on resident or non-resident foreign exchange accounts, repatriation of profits, and proceeds from invisible transactions. Current transfers are not restricted but must be declared to deposit institutions. The Bank of Spain requires reporting on most credit and lending activities.

FINANCIAL FREEDOM — 80%

Spain's financial sectors are diverse, modern, and fully integrated into international financial markets. Spain has 348 credit entities, including private banks, savings banks, credit unions, finance houses, and branches of foreign banks headquartered in non-EU countries. Two large private commercial banks, Banco Santander Central Hispano and Banco Bilbao Vizcaya Argentaria, dominate the banking sector and account for over half of banking assets. Sixty-one foreign banks together account for less than 15 percent of total banking assets. The government provides subsidized financing through several modest credit institutions. The insurance sector has over 300 insurers, and foreign companies are among the industry leaders. Capital markets are well developed and open to foreign investors.

PROPERTY RIGHTS — 70%

The judiciary is independent in practice, but bureaucratic obstacles at the national and state levels are significant. Contracts are secure, although the courts are very slow to enforce contracts when they are not honored.

FREEDOM FROM CORRUPTION — 70%

Corruption is perceived as minimal. Spain ranks 23rd out of 158 countries in Transparency International's Corruption Perceptions Index for 2005.

LABOR FREEDOM — 52.7%

The labor market operates under inflexible employment regulations that hinder overall productivity growth. Regulations on increasing or contracting the number of work hours are rigid. The non-salary cost of employing a worker is high, and dismissing a redundant employee is relatively costly.

SRI LANKA

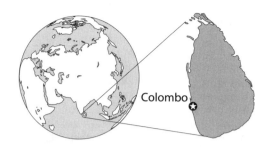

Colombo

Rank: 84

Regional Rank: 14 of 30

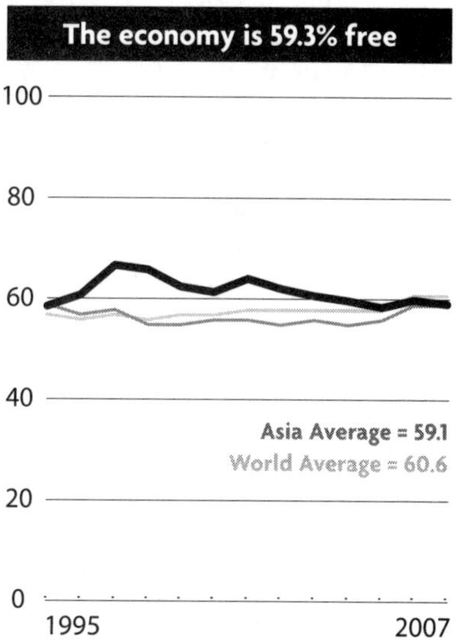

S ri Lanka's economy is 59.3 percent free, according to our 2007 assessment, which makes it the world's 84th freest economy. Its overall score is 0.8 percentage point lower than last year, partially reflecting new methodological detail. Sri Lanka is ranked 14th out of 30 countries in the Asia–Pacific region, and its overall score is equal to the regional average.

Sri Lanka scores well in fiscal freedom and freedom from government. Income and corporate tax rates are moderate, and overall tax revenue is relatively low as a percentage of GDP. Total government expenditures in Sri Lanka equal slightly more than one-fifth of GDP, and state-owned businesses generate only a small portion of total tax revenue.

As a developing Asian nation with widespread civil unrest, Sri Lanka faces serious challenges. Investment freedom, financial freedom, monetary freedom, property rights, and freedom from corruption all score poorly. The government generally welcomes foreign capital, but a host of formal restrictions and the security situation are deterrents. Sri Lanka's financial system is small but growing and would benefit from greater transparency. Inflation is high, and the government directly subsidizes a wide array of goods. The judicial system is not independent of political interference and is subject to corruption as well as extensive delays in resolving cases.

BACKGROUND: As of August 2006, Sri Lanka's shaky cease-fire was holding, and both sides remained engaged in negotiations. But President Mahinda Rajapske, elected in November 2005, is considered a hard-liner on negotiations with the Liberation Tigers of Tamil Eelam, and negotiations have progressed slowly. The civil war continues to hinder development, as reflected by the high number of people still involved in agriculture and the fact that industry still contributes little to the economy. Services contribute a fair amount to GDP and to opportunities in the labor pool.

How Do We Measure Economic Freedom? See Chapter 3 (page 37) for an explanation of the methodology or visit the *Index* Web site at *heritage.org/index*.

The economy is 59.3% free

Asia Average = 59.1
World Average = 60.6

1995 — 2007

QUICK FACTS

Population: 19.4 million

GDP (PPP): $85.2 billion
5.4% growth in 2004
3.9% 5-yr. comp. ann. growth
$4,390 per capita

Unemployment: 8.3%

Inflation (CPI): 7.6%

FDI (net inflow): $227 million

Official Development Assistance:
Multilateral: $246 million
Bilateral: $552 million (4% from the U.S.)

External Debt: $10.9 billion

Exports: $7.3 billion
Primarily textiles, apparel, tea, spices, diamonds, emeralds, rubies, coconut products, rubber manufactures, fish

Imports: $9.1 billion
Primarily textile fabrics, mineral products, petroleum, foodstuffs, machinery, transportation equipment

SRI LANKA'S TEN ECONOMIC FREEDOMS

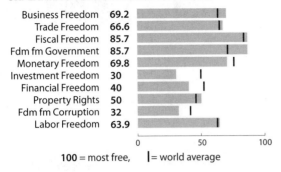

Business Freedom	69.2	
Trade Freedom	66.6	
Fiscal Freedom	85.7	
Fdm fm Government	85.7	
Monetary Freedom	69.8	
Investment Freedom	30	
Financial Freedom	40	
Property Rights	50	
Fdm fm Corruption	32	
Labor Freedom	63.9	

0   50   100

100 = most free, **|** = world average

BUSINESS FREEDOM — 69.2%
Starting a business takes an average of 50 days, compared to the world average of 48 days. To maximize entrepreneurship and job creation, it should be easier to start a company. Both obtaining a business license and closing a business are relatively simple. However, enforcement of commercial codes can be deficient, and transparency is lacking. The overall freedom to start, operate, and close a business is relatively well protected by the national regulatory environment.

TRADE FREEDOM — 66.6%
Sri Lanka's weighted average tariff rate was 6.7 percent in 2004. Import restrictions, restrictive import taxes, numerous import fees, weak enforcement of intellectual property rights, service market barriers, non-transparent government procurement policies, export subsidies, and export controls add to the cost of trade. Consequently, an additional 20 percent is deducted from Sri Lanka's trade freedom score to account for these non-tariff barriers.

FISCAL FREEDOM — 85.7%
Sri Lanka has burdensome tax rates. The top income tax rate is 30 percent, and the top corporate tax rate is 32.5 percent. Other taxes include a value-added tax (VAT), a property tax, and a tax on interest. In the most recent year, overall tax revenue as a percentage of GDP was 13.9 percent.

FREEDOM FROM GOVERNMENT — 85.7%
Total government expenditures in Sri Lanka, including consumption and transfer payments, are moderate. In the most recent year, government spending equaled 23.5 percent of GDP, and the government received 4.3 percent of its revenues from state-owned enterprises and government ownership of property.

MONETARY FREEDOM — 69.8%
Inflation in Sri Lanka is high, averaging 10.2 percent between 2003 and 2005. Such unstable prices explain most of the monetary freedom score. The government influences prices through regulation, state-owned enterprises, and subsidies for a wide array of goods, including petroleum products, fertilizer, and electricity. Consequently, an additional 10 percent is deducted from Sri Lanka's monetary freedom score to account for these policies.

INVESTMENT FREEDOM — 30%
Foreign investment, although generally welcomed, is prohibited in non-bank lending, pawnbroking, and retail trade with a capital investment of less than $1 million (with some exceptions). Foreign investment is screened and approved on a case-by-case basis when foreign equity exceeds 40 percent in several sectors. Outward direct investment must be approved by the government. Residents and non-residents may hold foreign exchange accounts subject to requirements, including government approval in some cases. There are strict reporting requirements and limits on payments and transfers. Capital transactions are subject to many restrictions and government approval in some cases.

FINANCIAL FREEDOM — 40%
Sri Lanka's financial system remains subject to extensive government influence but has been growing rapidly as the government has pursued privatization and liberalization. Regulations are largely consistent with international standards, but supervision and enforcement are insufficient. The central bank is not independent. Foreign investors are free to access domestic capital markets, and the government allows 100 percent foreign ownership of commercial banks, insurance services, and stockbroker services. The government influences the allocation of credit and has a virtual monopoly on the management of long-term savings, using half of domestic financial resources to finance government borrowing. The two state-owned banks control 45 percent of banking assets. The insurance sector has 13 insurers, and the largest firm, which controls 40 percent of premiums, was privatized in 2003. Capital markets are centered on the Colombo Stock Exchange, which is modern but relatively small.

PROPERTY RIGHTS — 50%
The judiciary is influenced by other branches of government. The system is subject to extensive delays in litigation that lead investors most often to pursue out-of-court settlements.

FREEDOM FROM CORRUPTION — 32%
Corruption is perceived as significant. Sri Lanka ranks 78th out of 158 countries in Transparency International's Corruption Perceptions Index for 2005.

LABOR FREEDOM — 63.9%
The labor market operates under relatively flexible employment regulations that could be improved to enhance overall productivity growth. The non-salary cost of employing a worker is moderate, but dismissing a redundant employee can be difficult.

SUDAN

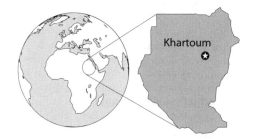

Khartoum

Rank: Not Ranked

Regional Rank: Not Ranked

Most of Sudan's economic freedom cannot be graded because of the violence and genocide that have wracked the country in recent years. The last time Sudan was wholly graded was in 2000, when it received a score of 46.8 percent.

Trade freedom, monetary freedom, and freedom from corruption are all weak. Sudan's average tariff rate is very high, and significant non-tariff barriers further impede trade. Inflation is also high, and the state subsidizes a wide array of goods. Khartoum's government is rife with corruption: Sudan is one of the world's 20 most corrupt nations.

BACKGROUND: Sudan is Africa's largest country and has a long history of internal conflict. President Omar Hassan al-Bashir's government has ruled since a 1989 military coup. A January 2005 peace agreement ended the decades-long civil war between the government in Khartoum and the Sudan People's Liberation Movement/Army. In the western Darfur region, conflict between government-supported militia groups and rebels has resulted in 200,000 deaths and 2 million displaced persons. Sudan's economy is hindered by instability, poor infrastructure, economic mismanagement, and corruption. Until significant oil production began in 2000, the economy was predominantly agrarian, and most Sudanese remain engaged in agriculture.

How Do We Measure Economic Freedom? See Chapter 3 (page 37) for an explanation of the methodology or visit the *Index* Web site at *heritage.org/index.*

The economy is not graded

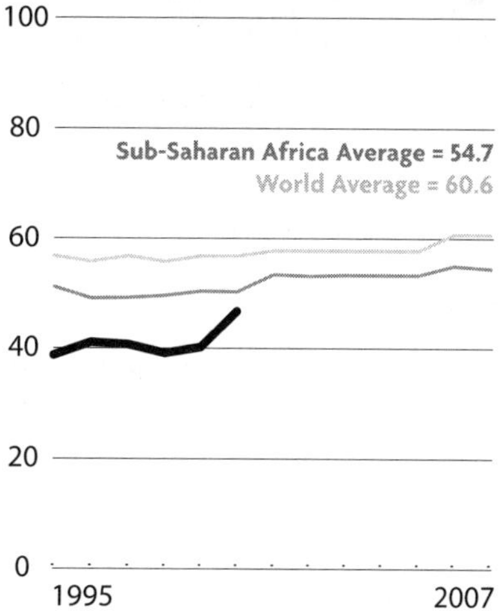

Sub-Saharan Africa Average = 54.7
World Average = 60.6

1995 — 2007

QUICK FACTS

Population: 35.5 million

GDP (PPP): $69.2 billion
5.2% growth in 2004
6.3% 5-yr. comp. ann. growth
$1,949 per capita

Unemployment: 18.7% (2002 estimate)

Inflation (CPI): 8.4%

FDI (net inflow): $1.5 billion (gross)

Official Development Assistance:
Multilateral: $136 million
Bilateral: $789 million (48% from the U.S.)

External Debt: $19.3 billion

Exports: $3.8 billion
Primarily oil and petroleum products, cotton, sesame, livestock, groundnuts, gum arabic, sugar

Imports: $4.7 billion
Primarily food, manufactured goods, refinery and transport equipment, medicines, chemicals, textiles, wheat

BUSINESS FREEDOM — NOT GRADED

Starting a business takes an average of 39 days, compared to the world average of 48 days. It takes 17 days to obtain a business license in Sudan. Regulations are often characterized as inconsistent, uneven, and lacking in transparency.

TRADE FREEDOM — NOT GRADED

Sudan's weighted average tariff rate was 19.6 percent in 2002. The government has made some progress in liberalizing the trade regime, but non-transparent and burdensome customs implementation, discriminatory taxes, significant delays in customs clearance, and corruption add to the cost of trade. Consequently, if Sudan were graded this year, an additional 20 percent would be deducted from its trade freedom score to account for these non-tariff barriers.

FISCAL FREEDOM — NOT GRADED

Sudan has a low income tax rate but a burdensome corporate tax rate. The top income tax rate is 20 percent, but the top corporate tax rate is 35 percent. In the most recent year, overall tax revenue as a percentage of GDP was 7.8 percent.

FREEDOM FROM GOVERNMENT — NOT GRADED

Total government expenditures in Sudan, including consumption and transfer payments, are low. In the most recent year, government spending equaled 18.9 percent of GDP.

MONETARY FREEDOM — NOT GRADED

Inflation in Sudan is high, averaging 8.4 percent between 2003 and 2005. The government is able to influence prices through regulation, a wide range of subsidies, and state-owned enterprises and utilities, and petroleum products are both subsidized and subject to price controls. Consequently, if Sudan were graded this year, an additional 10 percent would be deducted from its monetary freedom score to account for these policies.

INVESTMENT FREEDOM — NOT GRADED

Foreign investment in Sudan is restricted by cumbersome regulations, political instability, and corruption. The government is seeking foreign investment for the privatization of state-owned enterprises, but SOEs are in such poor shape and the level of corruption is so high that investors do not find them an attractive prospect. All residents (except the government, public institutions, and public enterprises) may hold foreign exchange accounts. Non-residents may hold foreign exchange accounts only with government approval. Controls apply to all transactions involving capital market securities, money market instruments, credit operations, and outward direct investment.

FINANCIAL FREEDOM — NOT GRADED

Sudan's financial system is underdeveloped, small, and largely bound by Islamic financial principles that include a prohibition on charging interest. Under the North–South peace agreement, banks operating in the South do not have to abide by Islamic principles. Supervision and regulation are weak. There are 26 commercial banks in Sudan, including 17 that are completely or majority privately owned and seven that are state-owned. The government continues to direct the allocation of credit, and non-performing loans are a problem. The insurance sector is small. Capital markets are very small and focused on trading bank shares on the Khartoum Stock Exchange.

PROPERTY RIGHTS — NOT GRADED

There is little respect for private property in Sudan. The government influences the judiciary. The military and civil authorities do not follow due process to protect private property rights.

FREEDOM FROM CORRUPTION — NOT GRADED

Corruption is perceived as widespread. Sudan ranks 144th out of 158 countries in Transparency International's Corruption Perceptions Index for 2005.

LABOR FREEDOM — NOT GRADED

The non-salary cost of employing a worker is high, and dismissing a redundant employee is costly. Regulations related to increasing or contracting the number of work hours are not flexible.

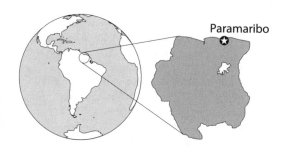

Paramaribo

SURINAME

Rank: 133

Regional Rank: 26 of 29

Suriname's economy is 52.6 percent free, according to our 2007 assessment, which makes it the world's 133rd freest economy. Its overall score is 0.6 percentage point lower than last year, partially reflecting new methodological detail. Suriname is ranked 26th out of 29 countries in the Americas, and its overall score is lower than the regional average.

Suriname scores well in only one area: labor freedom. The country's labor market is flexible, and the combination of no minimum wage and low non-salary costs of employment gives Suriname a high labor freedom score. Corruption is present in the civil service, although not as extensively as it is in other developing countries.

Most economic freedoms are weak in Suriname. Opening a business takes almost 15 times the world average time, and commercial operations are hamstrung by red tape. The government dominates economic activities. One central authority has been set up to coordinate foreign investment, but foreign investors still do not receive equal treatment under the law. Tax rates, inflation, and government spending are all high. Suriname's financial system is small, and the regulations that exist are antiquated. Banking is subject to substantial political interference. The judicial system is understaffed, and case backlogs are extensive.

BACKGROUND: Suriname has gone through five peaceful changes of government since becoming a presidential democracy in 1991. Ronald Venetiaan won the presidency in September 2005. Suriname is rich in natural resources, especially timber and minerals, and has reserves of bauxite, gold, nickel, and silver. However, it remains one of the region's poorest and least-developed countries. Agriculture accounts for 8.6 percent of gross domestic product, and mining accounts for over 10 percent of GDP. The public sector is the primary employer, with half of the labor force on its rolls. Fiscal budget deficits remain the most pressing economic problem.

How Do We Measure Economic Freedom? See Chapter 3 (page 37) for an explanation of the methodology or visit the *Index* Web site at *heritage.org/index*.

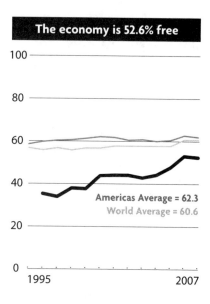

The economy is 52.6% free

Americas Average = 62.3
World Average = 60.6

1995 — 2007

QUICK FACTS

Population: 0.5 million

GDP (PPP): $2.8 billion (2005 estimate)
7.8% growth in 2004
4.1% 5-yr. comp. ann. growth
$4,100 per capita (2005 estimate)

Unemployment: 9.5%

Inflation (CPI): 9.1%

FDI (net inflow): −$60 million (gross)

Official Development Assistance:
Multilateral: $8 million
Bilateral: $40 million (3% from the U.S.)

External Debt: $503.4 million (2005 estimate)

Exports: $923.5 million
Primarily alumina, crude oil, lumber, shrimp, fish, rice, bananas

Imports: $1.0 billion
Primarily capital equipment, petroleum, food, cotton, consumer goods

SURINAME'S TEN ECONOMIC FREEDOMS

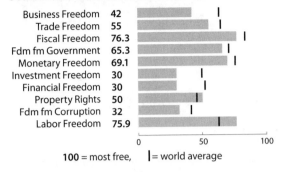

Business Freedom	42
Trade Freedom	55
Fiscal Freedom	76.3
Fdm fm Government	65.3
Monetary Freedom	69.1
Investment Freedom	30
Financial Freedom	30
Property Rights	50
Fdm fm Corruption	32
Labor Freedom	75.9

100 = most free, | = world average

BUSINESS FREEDOM — 42%

Starting a business takes an average of 694 days, compared to the world average of 48 days. To maximize entrepreneurship and job creation, it should be easier to start a company. Closing a business is very difficult. The overall freedom to start, operate, and close a business is seriously restricted by the national regulatory environment.

TRADE FREEDOM — 55%

Suriname's weighted average tariff rate was 12.5 percent in 2000. The government has made progress toward liberalizing the trade regime, but non-transparent regulations and standards, import and export taxes, and import and export restrictions add to the cost of trade. Consequently, an additional 20 percent is deducted from Suriname's trade freedom score to account for these non-tariff barriers.

FISCAL FREEDOM — 76.3%

Suriname has high tax rates. The top income tax rate is 38 percent, and the top corporate tax rate is 36 percent. Other taxes include a property tax and a tax on dividends. In the most recent year, overall tax revenue as a percentage of GDP was 28.5 percent.

FREEDOM FROM GOVERNMENT — 65.3%

Despite some reforms, the state still dominates economic activity in Suriname. Total government expenditures in Suriname, including consumption and transfer payments, are high. In the most recent year, government spending equaled 37.1 percent of GDP, and the government received 7.8 percent of its revenues from state-owned enterprises and government ownership of property.

MONETARY FREEDOM — 69.1%

Inflation in Suriname is high, averaging 10.9 percent between 2003 and 2005. Highly unstable prices explain most of the monetary freedom score. The government is able to influence prices through regulation and state-owned enterprises and utilities, and prices of basic food items are controlled. Consequently, an additional 10 percent is deducted from Suriname's monetary freedom score to account for these policies.

INVESTMENT FREEDOM — 30%

The government has created a new institute, InvestSur, to process applications for investment requests, settle disputes, and help investors. Foreign companies do not receive equal treatment. Residents may hold foreign exchange accounts provided that the funds did not come from sales of real estate in Suriname. Non-residents may open foreign exchange accounts in U.S. dollars and with the approval of the Foreign Exchange Commission. Payments and transfers face various quantitative limits and approval requirements. Capital transactions involving outward remittances of foreign exchange require the approval of the Foreign Exchange Commission.

FINANCIAL FREEDOM — 30%

Suriname's financial system is underdeveloped and subject to extensive government influence. Financial regulations are antiquated, and supervision is poor. Of the country's eight banks, three controlled over 85 percent of banking deposits as of 2004. The state owns a majority of two of the three major banks. The financial health of these banks is poor, and non-performing loans are a problem. The third major bank is owned by a parent company in Trinidad and Tobago. The non-banking financial sector, including insurance and pension funds, is small and underdeveloped. Capital markets are slight and focused on the small stock market, which listed 11 companies as of May 2006.

PROPERTY RIGHTS — 50%

Private property is not well protected in Suriname. There is a severe shortage of judges, and dispute settlement can be extremely time-consuming.

FREEDOM FROM CORRUPTION — 32%

Corruption is perceived as significant. Suriname ranks 78th out of 158 countries in Transparency International's Corruption Perceptions Index for 2005.

LABOR FREEDOM — 75.9%

The labor market operates under relatively flexible employment regulations that could be improved to enhance overall productivity growth. The non-salary cost of employing a worker is low, but dismissing a redundant employee can be costly. There is no minimum wage legislation in Suriname.

SWAZILAND

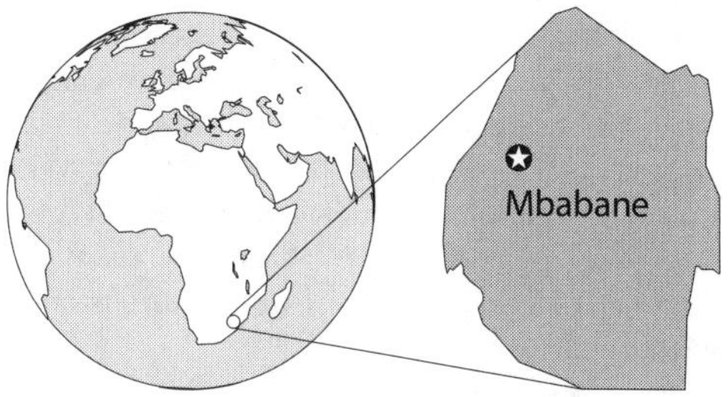

Rank: 64

Regional Rank: 6 of 40

Mbabane

Swaziland's economy is 61.6 percent free, according to our 2007 assessment, which makes it the world's 64th freest economy. Its overall score is 0.6 percentage point lower than last year, partially reflecting new methodological detail. Swaziland is ranked 6th out of 40 countries in the sub-Saharan Africa region, and its overall score is higher than the regional average.

Swaziland scores highly in several areas, including business freedom, fiscal freedom, and labor freedom. The government maintains a business-friendly environment, and licensing procedures are simple, although opening an enterprise takes longer than the world average. The top income and corporate tax rates in Swaziland are moderate, and overall tax revenue is not overwhelmingly high as a percentage of GDP. The labor sector in Swaziland is flexible, but dismissing a redundant employee can be costly.

Swaziland is weak in freedom from corruption, freedom from government, investment freedom, property rights, trade freedom, and financial freedom. Though inflation is fairly low, the government distorts the price of certain goods through direct subsidies. Total government expenditures equal about a third of national GDP. Corruption is rampant. Swaziland's financial sector is extremely small and subject to political interference and unclear rules.

BACKGROUND: The economy of this landlocked Southeast African nation is dependent on South Africa, which is the source of most imports and the destination for most exports. Most of the population is rural and engages in subsistence agriculture or herding. Progress toward economic liberalization and privatization has been slow, and corruption remains a problem. Under the new constitution, King Mswati III of Swaziland holds supreme executive, legislative, and judiciary powers. However, much authority is delegated to the prime minister, his cabinet, and traditional government structures. Swaziland has one of the world's highest HIV/AIDS rates: an estimated 42 percent of adults.

How Do We Measure Economic Freedom? See Chapter 3 (page 37) for an explanation of the methodology or visit the *Index* Web site at *heritage.org/index*.

The economy is 61.6% free

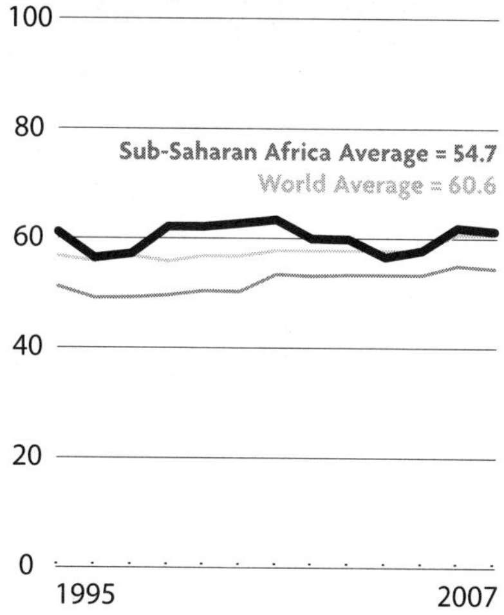

Sub-Saharan Africa Average = 54.7
World Average = 60.6

QUICK FACTS

Population: 1.1 million

GDP (PPP): $6.3 billion
2.1% growth in 2004
2.3% 5-yr. comp. ann. growth
$5,638 per capita

Unemployment: 40% (2005 estimate)

Inflation (CPI): 3.4%

FDI (net inflow): $65.1 million

Official Development Assistance:
Multilateral: $15 million
Bilateral: $112 million (1.4% from the U.S.)

External Debt: $470.0 million

Exports: $2.4 billion
Primarily soft drink concentrates, sugar, wood pulp, cotton yarn, refrigerators, citrus, canned fruit

Imports: $2.4 billion
Primarily motor vehicles, machinery, transport equipment, food, petroleum products, chemicals

349

SWAZILAND'S TEN ECONOMIC FREEDOMS

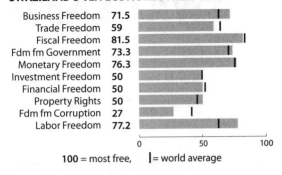

Business Freedom	71.5	
Trade Freedom	59	
Fiscal Freedom	81.5	
Fdm fm Government	73.3	
Monetary Freedom	76.3	
Investment Freedom	50	
Financial Freedom	50	
Property Rights	50	
Fdm fm Corruption	27	
Labor Freedom	77.2	

0   50   100

100 = most free, ❙**= world average**

BUSINESS FREEDOM — 71.5%

Starting a business takes an average of 61 days, compared to the world average of 48 days. To maximize entrepreneurship and job creation, it should be easier to start a company. Both obtaining a business license and closing a business can be simple. The overall freedom to start, operate, and close a business is relatively well protected by the national regulatory environment.

TRADE FREEDOM — 59%

Swaziland's weighted average tariff rate was 10.5 percent in 2005. Select import permit requirements and weak enforcement of intellectual property rights also add to the cost of trade. Consequently, an additional 20 percent is deducted from Swaziland's trade freedom score to account for these non-tariff barriers.

FISCAL FREEDOM — 81.5%

Swaziland has moderately high tax rates. The top income tax rate is 33 percent, and the top corporate tax rate is 30 percent. Other taxes include a real estate tax and a fuel tax. In the most recent year, overall tax revenue as a percentage of GDP was 28 percent.

FREEDOM FROM GOVERNMENT — 73.3%

Total government expenditures in Swaziland, including consumption and transfer payments, are high. In the most recent year, government spending equaled 33.6 percent of GDP, and the government received 1 percent of its revenues from state-owned enterprises and government ownership of property.

MONETARY FREEDOM — 76.3%

Inflation in Swaziland is moderate, averaging 4.7 percent between 2003 and 2005. Relatively moderate and unstable prices explain most of the monetary freedom score. The government is able to influence prices through regulation and numerous state-owned enterprises and utilities, and government administered prices account for approximately 16 percent of the consumer price index. Consequently, an additional 10 percent is deducted from Swaziland's monetary freedom score to account for these policies.

INVESTMENT FREEDOM — 50%

The foreign investment laws are not clear and are highly affected by government statements and decrees. All foreign workers must have permits, and the process involved in obtaining these permits can be both time-consuming and cumbersome. Both residents and non-residents may hold foreign exchange accounts, but residents face restrictions. Payments and transfers, while not usually restricted, are subject to quantitative limits and government approval in some cases. The central bank must approve most inward capital transfers. Most other capital transactions require documentation or face restrictions. Real estate transactions by non-residents must be approved.

FINANCIAL FREEDOM — 50%

Swaziland's financial system is very small and subject to considerable government influence. The banking sector is composed of three foreign-owned private banks, a state-owned bank, and a state-owned housing bank. There also are over 150 microfinance institutions. Supervision of the banking sector is insufficient. The non-bank financial sector is dominated by the government. As of September 2005, the government owned 41 percent of the Swaziland Royal Insurance Corporation, which has a monopoly in the insurance sector. Two state-owned pension funds dominate the pension sector. Capital markets are slight and centered on the Swaziland Stock Exchange, which listed six companies in September 2005, and a small bond market.

PROPERTY RIGHTS — 50%

The judiciary suffers from inadequate training, low salaries, and a small budget. Delays are common. The executive exerts significant influence over judges' decisions.

FREEDOM FROM CORRUPTION — 27%

Corruption is perceived as widespread. Swaziland ranks 103rd out of 158 countries in Transparency International's Corruption Perceptions Index for 2005.

LABOR FREEDOM — 77.2%

The labor market operates under relatively flexible employment regulations that could be improved to enhance overall productivity growth. The non-salary cost of employing a worker is low, but dismissing a redundant employee can be costly.

SWEDEN

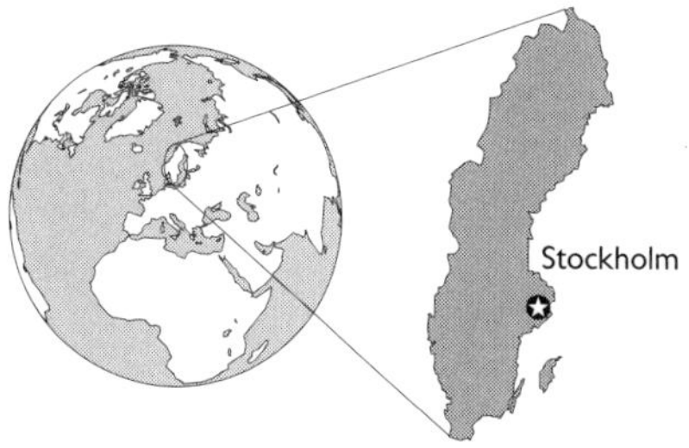

Rank: 21

Regional Rank: 13 of 41

S weden's economy is 72.6 percent free, according to our 2007 assessment, which makes it the world's 21st freest economy. Its overall score is 1.4 percentage points lower than last year, partially reflecting new methodological detail. Sweden is ranked 13th out of 41 countries in the European region, and its overall score is higher than the regional average.

Sweden enjoys high levels of investment freedom, trade freedom, financial freedom, property rights, business freedom, freedom from corruption, and monetary freedom. The average tariff rate is low, although non-tariff barriers include distortionary European Union subsidies, and business regulation is efficient. Virtually all commercial operations are simple and transparent. Inflation is low. Foreign investment is permitted without government approval, though capital is subject to restrictions in some areas. Sweden's financial sector is highly developed, and the Stockholm stock market is open to foreign investment. The judiciary, independent of politics and free of corruption, has an exemplary ability to protect property rights.

Sweden is weaker in fiscal freedom, freedom from government, and labor freedom. The top income tax rate of 60 percent is one of the highest in the world, and total government spending equals more than half of GDP. The labor market is over-regulated, and the costs of employing and dismissing workers are significant.

BACKGROUND: Renowned for its economic model of public–private partnerships, Sweden has enjoyed a buoyant economy since becoming a member of the EU in 1995. Sweden relies heavily on international trade, with total trade accounting for more that 50 percent of GDP. Job creation in the private sector remains low, and as of this writing, this was seen as a possible catalyst for the removal of Goran Persson's Social Democratic–led coalition government in September 2006. Sweden's main exports include paper products, machinery and transport equipment, and chemicals.

How Do We Measure Economic Freedom? See Chapter 3 (page 37) for an explanation of the methodology or visit the *Index* Web site at *heritage.org/index*.

The economy is 72.6% free

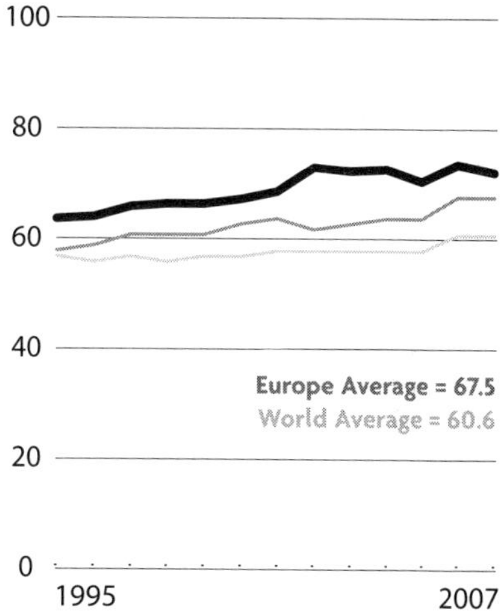

Europe Average = 67.5
World Average = 60.6

QUICK FACTS

Population: 9 million

GDP (PPP): $265.6 billion
3.7% growth in 2004
2.6% 5-yr. comp. ann. growth
$29,541 per capita

Unemployment: 5.5%

Inflation (CPI): 0.4%

FDI (net inflow): −$15.5 billion

Official Development Assistance:
Multilateral: None
Bilateral: None

External Debt: $516.1 billion (2005)

Exports: $163.9 billion
Primarily machinery, motor vehicles, paper products, pulp and wood, iron and steel products, chemicals

Imports: $134.9 billion
Primarily machinery, petroleum and petroleum products, chemicals, motor vehicles, iron and steel, food, clothing

SWEDEN'S TEN ECONOMIC FREEDOMS

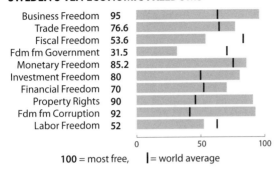

Business Freedom	95
Trade Freedom	76.6
Fiscal Freedom	53.6
Fdm fm Government	31.5
Monetary Freedom	85.2
Investment Freedom	80
Financial Freedom	70
Property Rights	90
Fdm fm Corruption	92
Labor Freedom	52

0   50   100

100 = most free, | = world average

BUSINESS FREEDOM — 95%

Starting a business takes an average of 16 days, compared to the world average of 48 days. The business environment has allowed entrepreneurship to flourish in Sweden. Obtaining a business license is very simple, and closing a business is easy. The overall freedom to start, operate, and close a business is strongly protected by the national regulatory environment.

TRADE FREEDOM — 76.6%

Sweden's trade policy is the same as those of other members of the European Union. The common EU weighted average tariff rate was 1.7 percent in 2005. Various non-tariff barriers are reflected in EU policy, including agricultural and manufacturing subsidies, regulatory and licensing restrictions, and other market access restrictions. The government also implements burdensome sanitary and phytosanitary regulations, and the enforcement of intellectual property rights can be problematic. Consequently, an additional 20 percent is deducted from Sweden's trade freedom score.

FISCAL FREEDOM — 53.6%

Sweden has a very high income tax rate and a moderate corporate tax rate. The top income tax rate is 60 percent, making Sweden's income tax burden one of the heaviest in the world, and the top corporate tax rate is 28 percent. Other taxes include a value-added tax (VAT) and a capital gains tax. There has been debate over the wealth tax. In the most recent year, overall tax revenue as a percentage of GDP was 50.7 percent.

FREEDOM FROM GOVERNMENT — 31.5%

Total government expenditures in Sweden, including consumption and transfer payments, are very high. In the most recent year, government spending equaled 56.7 percent of GDP, and the government received 5.5 percent of its revenues from state-owned enterprises and government ownership of property.

MONETARY FREEDOM — 85.2%

Inflation in Sweden is low, averaging 0.6 percent between 2003 and 2005. Such stable prices explain most of the monetary freedom score. As a participant in the EU's Common Agricultural Policy, the government subsidizes agricultural production, distorting the prices of agricultural products.

Prices are generally set by market forces, but oligopolies may hinder price competition, and the government influences prices through regulation and state-owned enterprises and utilities. Consequently, an additional 10 percent is deducted from Sweden's monetary freedom score to account for these policies.

INVESTMENT FREEDOM — 80%

Sweden presents few barriers to foreign investment. Foreign companies may purchase Swedish companies without government approval, although they are subject to controls in fishing, civil aviation, and transport and communications. Both domestic and foreign investors are prohibited from investing in the retail sale of pharmaceuticals and alcoholic beverages, in which the government maintains a monopoly. Residents and non-residents may hold foreign exchange accounts. There are no controls on payments and transfers or repatriation of profits. A permit may be required for the purchase of real estate by non-residents.

FINANCIAL FREEDOM — 70%

Sweden's financial system is sophisticated and dynamic. Credit is allocated on market terms, and financial regulation is transparent and largely consistent with international norms. Banks offer a full range of financial services. Foreign-owned banks and insurance companies may open branch offices. Nearly all commercial banks in Sweden are privately owned and operated. The banking sector is highly concentrated, with four banks, including one in which the government holds a 19.5 percent stake, accounting for over 80 percent of banking assets. The government also owns a mortgage company and a number of development funds and continues to offer concessional funds through various government agencies. The insurance sector is sophisticated, and foreign insurers are well-represented. The Stockholm Stock Exchange is modern, active, and open to domestic and foreign investment.

PROPERTY RIGHTS — 90%

The judiciary is independent and provides citizens with a fair judicial process. Contracts are highly respected, and the judiciary is of high quality.

FREEDOM FROM CORRUPTION — 92%

Corruption is perceived as almost nonexistent. Sweden ranks 6th out of 158 countries in Transparency International's Corruption Perceptions Index for 2005.

LABOR FREEDOM — 52%

The labor market operates under inflexible employment regulations that hinder overall productivity growth. The non-salary cost of employing a worker is high, and dismissing a redundant employee is costly. Rigid labor market regulations, including high statutory overtime payment, have contributed to Sweden's failure to create jobs, particularly in the private service sector.

SWITZERLAND

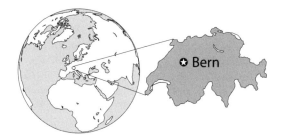

⊙ Bern

Switzerland's economy is 79.1 percent free, according to our 2007 assessment, which makes it the world's 9th freest economy. Its overall score is 1 percentage point lower than last year, partially reflecting new methodological detail. Switzerland is ranked 4th out of 41 countries in the European region, and its overall score is much higher than the regional average.

Switzerland has high levels of investment freedom, trade freedom, financial freedom, property rights, business freedom, and freedom from corruption. The average tariff rate is low, and commercial operations are protected by the regulatory environment and aided by a flexible labor market. Inflation is extremely low, and foreign investment is welcome and subject to only a few restrictions. The national financial sector leads the world and is both protective of privacy and open to foreign institutions. The judiciary, independent of politics, enforces contracts reliably. Corruption is virtually nonexistent.

Switzerland could improve its fiscal freedom and freedom from government. As in many other European social democracies, personal income taxes are high, particularly at the provincial level, and in some areas are nearly 42 percent. Unsurprisingly, total government spending equals more than a third of GDP.

BACKGROUND: Stable currency and politics, low taxes, secure banking, and incentives for new investors make Switzerland an attractive investment location, particularly for small manufacturing. In general, there are no overall restrictions on the percentage of equity that foreign firms may hold, and some cantons waive taxes on new firms for up to 10 years. Larger businesses are highly competitive, but the protection of smaller businesses, particularly those related to agriculture, has led to higher food prices. Although the growth in GDP has been weak during the past two decades, reflecting the low growth in productivity, per capita income remains high.

How Do We Measure Economic Freedom? See Chapter 3 (page 37) for an explanation of the methodology or visit the *Index* Web site at *heritage.org/index.*

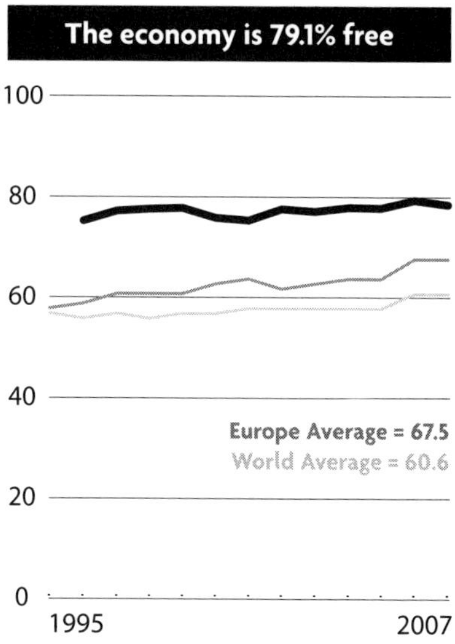

The economy is 79.1% free

100

80

60

40

Europe Average = 67.5
World Average = 60.6

20

0

1995   2007

QUICK FACTS

Population: 7.4 million

GDP (PPP): $244.1 billion
2.1% growth in 2004
1.3% 5-yr. comp. ann. growth
$33,040 per capita

Unemployment: 3.9%

Inflation (CPI): 0.8%

FDI (net inflow): −$20.7 billion

Official Development Assistance:
Multilateral: None
Bilateral: None

External Debt: $856 billion (2005)

Exports: $181.6 billion
Primarily machinery, chemicals, metals, watches, agricultural products

Imports: $146.3 billion
Primarily machinery, chemicals, vehicles, metals, agricultural products, textiles

SWITZERLAND'S TEN ECONOMIC FREEDOMS

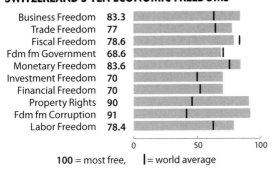

Business Freedom	83.3
Trade Freedom	77
Fiscal Freedom	78.6
Fdm fm Government	68.6
Monetary Freedom	83.6
Investment Freedom	70
Financial Freedom	70
Property Rights	90
Fdm fm Corruption	91
Labor Freedom	78.4

0   50   100

100 = most free, | = world average

BUSINESS FREEDOM — 83.3%

Starting a business takes an average of 20 days, compared to the world average of 48 days. Both obtaining a business license and closing a business can be relatively easy. The overall freedom to start, operate, and close a business is protected by the national regulatory environment.

TRADE FREEDOM — 77%

Switzerland's weighted average tariff rate was 1.5 percent in 2001. Prohibitive agriculture tariffs and quotas, restrictive biotechnology regulations, import taxes, export subsidies, and service market access barriers add to the cost of trade. Consequently, an additional 20 percent is deducted from Switzerland's trade freedom score to account for these non-tariff barriers.

FISCAL FREEDOM — 78.6%

Taxation in Switzerland is more burdensome at the cantonal levels than it is at the federal level. In addition, tax rates vary widely between regions. The top income tax rate can be as high as 41.5 percent, and the top corporate tax rate can be as high as 25 percent. Other taxes include a value-added tax (VAT), a property tax, and a vehicle tax. In the most recent year, overall tax revenue as a percentage of GDP was 29.4 percent.

FREEDOM FROM GOVERNMENT — 68.6%

Total government expenditures in Switzerland, including consumption and transfer payments, are high. In the most recent year, government spending equaled 36.6 percent of GDP, and the government received 0.6 percent of its revenues from state-owned enterprises and government ownership of property.

MONETARY FREEDOM — 83.6%

Inflation in Switzerland is low, averaging 1 percent between 2003 and 2005. Such stable prices explain most of the monetary freedom score. The prices of some products, primarily agricultural goods and pharmaceutical products, are directly influenced by government measures, and the government is also able to influence prices through regulation, subsidies, and state-owned utilities. Consequently, an additional 10 percent is deducted from Switzerland's monetary freedom score to account for these policies.

INVESTMENT FREEDOM — 70%

Switzerland is generally open to foreign investment. Formal approval is not required, and screening applies only to foreign investment in real estate and national security establishments. Cantonal laws generally require 51 percent Swiss ownership in mining activities, and foreign firms must have less than 51 percent ownership in petroleum exploitation operations. Both residents and non-residents may hold foreign exchange accounts. There are no restrictions on repatriation of profits, payments for invisible transactions, or current transfers. Purchases of real estate by non-residents must be approved by the canton in which the property is located.

FINANCIAL FREEDOM — 70%

Switzerland is a leading international financial center, and its institutions are highly developed and well regulated. The credit, currency, and equity markets are open to foreign investors without restriction. The federal government is not a shareholder in the central bank but does have authority over appointments and approves its regulations. Banks may offer a wide range of financial services, and credit is allocated on market terms. Banking secrecy has been loosened to prevent money laundering and tax evasion. Switzerland's two biggest banks, UBS and Credit Suisse, dominate the Swiss market and rank among the world's top 10 financial institutions. Twenty-four cantonal banks, owned by the cantonal governments, are involved in savings deposits, mortgages, and lending to public authorities. Approximately 44 percent of all banks in Switzerland are foreign controlled, and they can operate only if their country of origin grants reciprocal privileges to Swiss banks. The insurance industry is well developed. The state-owned postal service is a leader in the payments system through its Postfinance operation, which offers mutual funds, insurance products, and interest-earning savings accounts. Capital markets are strong, and Switzerland has Europe's fourth largest stock exchange.

PROPERTY RIGHTS — 90%

The judiciary is independent, and the government respects this independence in practice. Contracts are secure, and the judiciary is of high quality.

FREEDOM FROM CORRUPTION — 91%

Corruption is perceived as almost nonexistent. Switzerland ranks 7th out of 158 countries in Transparency International's Corruption Perceptions Index for 2005.

LABOR FREEDOM — 78.4%

The labor market operates under relatively flexible employment regulations that could be improved to enhance overall productivity growth. The non-salary cost of employing a worker is moderate, but dismissing a redundant employee is relatively costly.

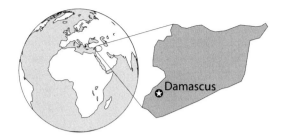

SYRIA

Rank: 142

Regional Rank: 15 of 17

Syria's economy is 48.2 percent free, according to our 2007 assessment, which makes it the world's 142nd freest economy. Its overall score is 2.3 percentage points lower than last year, partially reflecting new methodological detail. Syria is ranked 15th out of 17 countries in the Middle East/North Africa region, and its overall score is lower than the regional average.

Syria scores well in only one area: fiscal freedom. The top income tax is relatively low, and the corporate tax is moderate. Overall tax revenue is low as a percentage of GDP.

Syria is weak in trade freedom, investment freedom, financial freedom, monetary freedom, freedom from government, property rights, and freedom from corruption. The government maintains a high average tariff rate, as well as non-tariff barriers such as an opaque regulatory process. Significant state influence in most areas of the economy taints the civil service and makes court rulings subject to the diktats of the Ba'athist government. This interference bleeds into the Syrian financial market, which is unsophisticated and dominated by the state. Inflation is high, and the government directly subsidizes a wide array of goods. State expenditures are also high, and over half of Syria's revenue comes from state-owned businesses.

BACKGROUND: Syria has been ruled by the Assad regime since Minister of Defense Hafez al-Assad seized power in 1970. Assad was succeeded in 2000 by his son Bashar, who has failed to deliver on his promises to reform Syria's socialist economy. Foreign investment has been dampened by U.S. economic sanctions and Syria's growing isolation as a result of its involvement in the February 2005 assassination of former Lebanese Prime Minister Rafiq Hariri. Military withdrawal from Lebanon has deprived Syrian officials of substantial opportunities for graft and the smuggling of illicit goods.

How Do We Measure Economic Freedom? See Chapter 3 (page 37) for an explanation of the methodology or visit the *Index* Web site at *heritage.org/index*.

The economy is 48.2% free

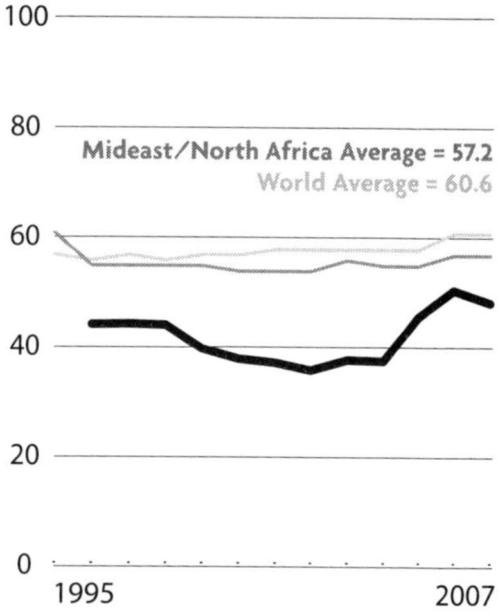

Mideast/North Africa Average = 57.2
World Average = 60.6

[Line graph showing economic freedom scores from 1995 to 2007, y-axis from 0 to 100]

QUICK FACTS

Population: 18.6 million

GDP (PPP): $67.1 billion
2.5% growth in 2004
2.4% 5-yr. comp. ann. growth
$3,610 per capita

Unemployment: 12.3% (2004 estimate)

Inflation (CPI): 4.6%

FDI (net inflow): $1.2 billion (gross)

Official Development Assistance:
Multilateral: $126 million
Bilateral: $134 million (0% from the U.S.)

External Debt: $21.5 billion

Exports: $8.2 billion
Primarily crude oil, petroleum products, fruits, vegetables, cotton fiber, clothing, meat, live animals, wheat

Imports: $7.9 billion
Primarily machinery, transport equipment, electric power machinery, food, livestock, metal, metal products, chemicals, chemical products, plastics, yarn, paper

355

SYRIA'S TEN ECONOMIC FREEDOMS

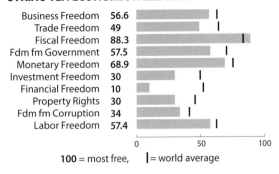

Business Freedom	56.6
Trade Freedom	49
Fiscal Freedom	88.3
Fdm fm Government	57.5
Monetary Freedom	68.9
Investment Freedom	30
Financial Freedom	10
Property Rights	30
Fdm fm Corruption	34
Labor Freedom	57.4

0   50   100

100 = most free, | = world average

BUSINESS FREEDOM — 56.6%

Starting a business takes an average of 43 days, compared to the world average of 48 days. To maximize entrepreneurship and job creation, it should be easier to start a company. Obtaining a business license is relatively simple, but closing a business can be difficult. Bureaucratic obstacles and delays are ongoing problems. The overall freedom to start, operate, and close a business is restrained by the national regulatory environment.

TRADE FREEDOM — 49%

Syria's weighted average tariff rate was 15.5 percent in 2002. Prohibitive tariffs, import taxes, non-transparent trade regulations, import bans and restrictions, burdensome standards requirements, restrictive biotechnology regulations, import taxes, and corruption all add to the cost of trade. Consequently, an additional 20 percent is deducted from Syria's trade freedom score to account for these non-tariff barriers.

FISCAL FREEDOM — 88.3%

Syria has a low income tax rate and a moderately high corporate tax rate. The top income tax rate is 20 percent, and the top corporate tax rate is 35 percent. Other taxes include a tax on insurance and a property transfer tax. In the most recent year, overall tax revenue as a percentage of GDP was 11.6 percent.

FREEDOM FROM GOVERNMENT — 57.5%

Total government expenditures in Syria, including consumption and transfer payments, are moderate. In the most recent year, government spending equaled 31.6 percent of GDP, and the government received 57.7 percent of its revenues from state-owned enterprises and government ownership of property. The state maintains its controls over a large part of economic activity.

MONETARY FREEDOM — 68.9%

Inflation in Syria is relatively high, averaging 6.5 percent between 2003 and 2005. Relatively high and unstable prices explain most of the monetary freedom score. The government controls product prices for many goods and sets prices, provides subsidies, and controls marketing in the agricultural sector. Prices are also influenced through state-owned enterprises and utilities, and private participation in manufacturing remains constrained by input and output pricing limits. Consequently, an additional 15 percent is deducted from Syria's monetary freedom score to account for these policies.

INVESTMENT FREEDOM — 30%

Officially, foreigners may own 100 percent of a company and may own land. New laws guarantee against expropriation and permit repatriation. Almost all sectors of the economy are open to foreign direct investment, except for power generation and distribution, air transport, port operation, water bottling, telephony, and oil and gas production and refining. However, a weak and arbitrary legal environment is a strong disincentive for foreign investors. Many capital transactions are subject to controls, and foreign exchange and trade are severely hampered by a requirement for government approval of all transactions.

FINANCIAL FREEDOM — 10%

Syria's financial system is subject to heavy state influence, and financial services are so unsophisticated that they inhibit development. Regulations are cumbersome and unclear, and interest rates are fixed by the government. Although private banks are now permitted, the banking system remains dominated by five state-owned banks, which focus on certain economic sectors. Three private banks were licensed to operate in January 2004, and three more were licensed to operate in June 2004. However, state-owned banks account for 92 percent of private-sector lending, and the central bank is not independent. Foreign banks have been allowed to establish offices in free trade zones since 2000, but only six foreign banks, mostly Lebanese, have done so. The public sector is given priority in lending, and private borrowers find it difficult to obtain loans. The insurance sector is controlled almost entirely by a government-owned firm. The first private insurers were permitted to operate in June 2006. Capital markets are negligible and restricted to small amounts of government debt. There is no stock market.

PROPERTY RIGHTS — 30%

Protection of property rights is weak. The government, political connections, and bribery influence court decisions.

FREEDOM FROM CORRUPTION — 34%

Corruption is perceived as significant. Syria ranks 70th out of 158 countries in Transparency International's Corruption Perceptions Index for 2005.

LABOR FREEDOM — 57.4%

The labor market operates under inflexible employment regulations that hinder overall productivity growth. The non-salary cost of employing a worker is high, and dismissing a redundant employee is relatively costly.

TAIWAN

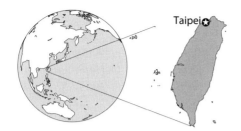

Taipei

Taiwan's economy is 71.1 percent free, according to our 2007 assessment, which makes it the world's 26th freest economy. Its overall score is 0.5 percentage point higher than last year, partially reflecting new methodological detail. Taiwan is ranked 6th out of 30 countries in the Asia–Pacific region, and its overall score is much higher than the regional average.

Taiwan has high levels of investment freedom, trade freedom, property rights, fiscal freedom, freedom from corruption, and freedom from government. The average tariff rate, inflation rate, and level of corruption are all low. Although Taiwan's personal income tax is high, the corporate tax rate is moderate, and overall tax revenue is low as a percentage of GDP. Government spending is similarly low. Taiwan's investment climate is healthy, and 100 percent foreign ownership is permitted in most sectors. Property rights are protected by the judiciary, although there are minor problems with case delays and corruption associated with organized crime.

Taiwan is relatively weak in labor freedom and business freedom. The country's labor market is not as flexible as it could be, and dismissing a redundant worker is costly. Starting a business takes as long as the global average, but commercial licensing can be difficult.

BACKGROUND: Taiwan is Asia's fifth largest economy and one of its most dynamic democracies. Despite Taiwan's long-standing autonomy from the People's Republic of China, Beijing's "One China" policy has isolated Taipei from the international community and pressured it to accept PRC suzerainty. Taiwan seeks to participate in the World Health Organization and to maintain a presence in international trade and financial organizations with the help of such democratic partners as the United States and Japan. The service industry leads the Taiwanese economy, and both the agricultural and manufacturing sectors are gradually declining.

How Do We Measure Economic Freedom? See Chapter 3 (page 37) for an explanation of the methodology or visit the *Index* Web site at *heritage.org/index.*

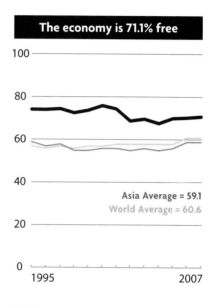

The economy is 71.1% free

Asia Average = 59.1
World Average = 60.6

QUICK FACTS

Population: 23 million (2006 estimate)

GDP (PPP): $631.2 billion (2005 estimate)
6.1% growth in 2004
3.4% 5-yr. comp. ann. growth
$27,600 per capita (2005 estimate)

Unemployment: 4.4%

Inflation (CPI): 1.6%

FDI (net inflow): −$5.2 billion

Official Development Assistance:
Multilateral: n/a
Bilateral: $15 million (4% from the U.S.)

External Debt: $87.5 billion (2005 estimate)

Exports: $199.6 billion
Primarily computer products, electrical equipment, metals, textiles, plastics, rubber products, chemicals

Imports: $188.3 billion
Primarily machinery, electrical equipment, minerals, precision instruments

TAIWAN'S TEN ECONOMIC FREEDOMS

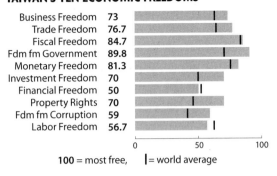

Business Freedom	73
Trade Freedom	76.7
Fiscal Freedom	84.7
Fdm fm Government	89.8
Monetary Freedom	81.3
Investment Freedom	70
Financial Freedom	50
Property Rights	70
Fdm fm Corruption	59
Labor Freedom	56.7

0   50   100

100 = most free, | = world average

BUSINESS FREEDOM — 73%

Starting a business takes an average of 48 days, which is about the world average. To maximize entrepreneurship and job creation, it should be easier to start a company. Obtaining a business license can be difficult, but closing a business is easy. The overall freedom to start, operate, and close a business is relatively well protected by the national regulatory environment.

TRADE FREEDOM — 76.7%

Taiwan's weighted average tariff rate was 1.67 percent in 2005. Prohibitive agriculture tariffs, import bans and restrictions, import taxes, export subsidies, burdensome standards and certification requirements, complex regulations, restrictive sanitary and phytosanitary rules, service market access barriers, and weak enforcement of intellectual property rights all add to the cost of trade. Consequently, an additional 20 percent is deducted from Taiwan's trade freedom score to account for these non-tariff barriers.

FISCAL FREEDOM — 84.7%

Taiwan has a high income tax rate and a moderate corporate tax rate. The top income tax rate is 40 percent, and the top corporate tax rate is 25 percent. Other taxes include a value-added tax (VAT) and a capital gains tax. In the most recent year, overall tax revenue as a percentage of GDP was 8.5 percent.

FREEDOM FROM GOVERNMENT — 89.8%

Total government expenditures in Taiwan, including consumption and transfer payments, are moderate. In the most recent year, government spending equaled 15.3 percent of GDP, and the government received 14.4 percent of its revenues from state-owned enterprises and government ownership of property.

MONETARY FREEDOM — 81.3%

Inflation in Taiwan is low, averaging 1.9 percent between 2003 and 2005. Relatively stable prices explain most of the monetary freedom score. The government regulates the prices of pharmaceutical and medical products and is also able to influence prices through regulation, subsidies, and state-owned utilities. Consequently, an additional 10 percent is deducted from Taiwan's monetary freedom score to account for these policies.

INVESTMENT FREEDOM — 70%

Repatriation of profits is not restricted, and 100 percent ownership is permitted in most sectors. However, foreign investment is prohibited in a handful of industries such as agriculture, wireless broadcasting, oil exploration of Taiwan's coastal area, public utilities, and postal services. Foreign investment is limited in the telecommunications sector, electricity transmission and distribution, and high-speed railway transportation. Restrictions on capital flows relating to portfolio investment have been removed. The insurance and securities industries have been liberalized and opened to foreign investment. Access to Taiwan's securities markets by foreign institutional investors has also been broadened.

FINANCIAL FREEDOM — 50%

Taiwan has liberalized the traditionally over-regulated financial sector. Among other things, the government has reduced many restrictions on financial activities, particularly the activities of foreign financial institutions. A wide variety of financial instruments are available to foreign and domestic investors on market terms. Four state-owned banks were privatized in 1998, four more in 1999, and one more in 2005. Four state-controlled banks remain, including two of the three largest domestic banks, which together account for 16 percent of bank assets. Banks offer a wide range of services, and foreign banks are treated essentially the same as domestic banks. The insurance and securities industries have been opened to foreign participation and ownership, although foreign participation remains relatively low. The only reinsurance company was privatized in 2002. Capital markets are sophisticated, and the stock market is open to foreign participation, except for select industries.

PROPERTY RIGHTS — 70%

Property rights are generally protected, and the judiciary enforces contracts, although the court system is very slow. One of the judiciary's biggest problems is corruption associated with organized crime.

FREEDOM FROM CORRUPTION — 59%

Corruption is perceived as present. Taiwan ranks 32nd out of 158 countries in Transparency International's Corruption Perceptions Index for 2005.

LABOR FREEDOM — 56.7%

The labor market operates under inflexible employment regulations that hinder overall productivity growth. The non-salary cost of employing a worker is moderate, but dismissing a redundant employee is relatively costly.

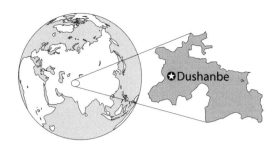

TAJIKISTAN

Tajikistan's economy is 56.9 percent free, according to our 2007 assessment, which makes it the world's 98th freest economy. Its overall score is 1.1 percentage points higher than last year, partially reflecting new methodological detail. Tajikistan is ranked 17th out of 30 countries in the Asia–Pacific region, and its overall score is lower than the regional average.

Tajikistan scores well in fiscal freedom, freedom from government, and labor freedom. The government imposes low tax rates, including a 13 percent personal income rate. Total government expenditures in Tajikistan are equal to about 20 percent of national GDP, and state-owned businesses constitute a relatively minor source of overall tax revenue. Tajikistan's labor market is flexible, and both dismissing redundant employees and changing the number of workweek hours are easy.

As a nation still recovering from a civil war, Tajikistan faces significant challenges. Business freedom, monetary freedom, investment freedom, financial freedom, property rights, and freedom from corruption all score poorly. The regulatory environment is not protective of business, and laws are both restrictive and inconsistent. Foreign investment in Tajikistan faces many regulatory hurdles as well as outright corruption. Tajikistan is rated one of the world's 20 most corrupt nations, and corruption seeps into most aspects of official life, from the courts to customs.

BACKGROUND: After it gained its independence from the Soviet Union in 1991, Tajikistan was wracked by civil war from 1992 to 1997. Since then, it has struggled with political and economic reforms. While progress toward a market economy is clearly evident, Tajikistan's transition to a multi-party democracy and pluralism remains bumpy, with parliamentary elections in February 2005 failing to meet international standards. The combination of uneven implementation of structural reforms, weak governance, high unemployment, external debt, and drug trafficking has left Tajikistan with an extremely fragile economy.

How Do We Measure Economic Freedom? See Chapter 3 (page 37) for an explanation of the methodology or visit the *Index* Web site at *heritage.org/index*.

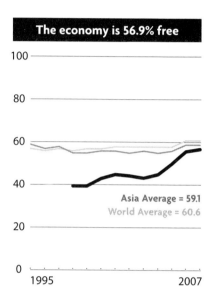

The economy is 56.9% free

Asia Average = 59.1
World Average = 60.6

QUICK FACTS

Population: 6.4 million

GDP (PPP): $7.7 billion
10.6% growth in 2004
9.6% 5-yr. comp. ann. growth
$1,202 per capita

Unemployment: 12% (2004 estimate)

Inflation (CPI): 7.1%

FDI (net inflow): $272 million (gross)

Official Development Assistance:
Multilateral: $149 million
Bilateral: $105 million (46% from the U.S.)

External Debt: $896.0 million

Exports: $1.2 billion
Primarily aluminum, electricity, cotton, fruits, vegetable oil, textiles

Imports: $1.4 billion
Primarily electricity, petroleum products, aluminum oxide, machinery and equipment, food

TAJIKISTAN'S TEN ECONOMIC FREEDOMS

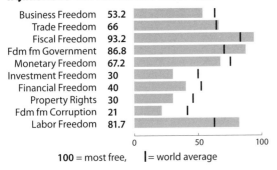

Business Freedom	53.2
Trade Freedom	66
Fiscal Freedom	93.2
Fdm fm Government	86.8
Monetary Freedom	67.2
Investment Freedom	30
Financial Freedom	40
Property Rights	30
Fdm fm Corruption	21
Labor Freedom	81.7

100 = most free, I = world average

BUSINESS FREEDOM — 53.2%

Starting a business takes an average of 67 days, compared to the world average of 48 days. To maximize entrepreneurship and job creation, it should be easier to start a company. Both obtaining a business license and closing a business can be relatively simple. Regulations are sometimes inconsistent, causing unreliability of interpretation. The overall freedom to start, operate, and close a business is restricted by the national regulatory environment.

TRADE FREEDOM — 66%

Tajikistan's weighted average tariff rate was 7 percent in 2005. Excessive and non-transparent standards and certification requirements, burdensome and corrupt customs implementation, quotas, import bans and restrictions, and weak enforcement of intellectual property rights all add to the cost of trade. Consequently, an additional 20 percent is deducted from Tajikistan's trade freedom score to account for these non-tariff barriers.

FISCAL FREEDOM — 93.2%

Tajikistan has relatively low tax rates. The top income tax rate is 13 percent, and the top corporate tax rate is 25 percent. Other taxes include a value-added tax (VAT) and a tax on immovable property. (Effective January 1, 2005, Tajikistan abolished its property tax while introducing the tax on immovable property.) In the most recent year, overall tax revenue as a percentage of GDP was 15.2 percent.

FREEDOM FROM GOVERNMENT — 86.8%

Total government expenditures in Tajikistan, including consumption and transfer payments, are moderate. In the most recent year, government spending equaled 20.3 percent of GDP, and the government received 10.7 percent of its revenues from state-owned enterprises and government ownership of property.

MONETARY FREEDOM — 67.2%

Inflation in Tajikistan is high, averaging 7.9 percent between 2003 and 2005. Relatively unstable prices explain most of the monetary freedom score. The government is able to influence prices through regulation, subsidies, and numerous state-owned enterprises and utilities. Consequently, an additional 15 percent is deducted from Tajikistan's monetary freedom score to account for these policies.

INVESTMENT FREEDOM — 30%

Tajikistan presents substantial barriers to foreign investment, including corruption and a lack of transparency in government contracts and privatizations. Investors face ownership restrictions, especially in the banking sector, and cumbersome procedures with regard to tax and business registrations. Both residents and non-residents may hold foreign exchange accounts, although residents are subject to some restrictions. Payments and transfers are subject to documentary requirements. Most capital transactions, including all direct investment transactions, require central bank approval.

FINANCIAL FREEDOM — 40%

Tajikistan's financial sector is small and underdeveloped. The government is pursuing reforms to increase transparency and to improve supervision and the regulatory regime, but substantial weaknesses remain. The financial system is dominated by banking, which includes the central bank and 12 commercial banks. Four large banks hold approximately 80 percent of deposits and 70 percent of non-government loans. All banks, except for Amonat Bank (one of the country's four largest) are privately owned. Non-performing loans remain a problem. The government increased minimum capital requirements for banks in January 2006 and opened the banking sector to foreign banks in late 2005. The non-banking financial sector is very small, including a number of small insurance companies and one pension fund. Capital markets are negligible, and a securities market has been established, although it was not yet functioning as of March 2006.

PROPERTY RIGHTS — 30%

Protection of private property is weak in Tajikistan. Judicial corruption is widespread, and the courts are sensitive to pressure from the government and paramilitary groups.

FREEDOM FROM CORRUPTION — 21%

Corruption is perceived as widespread. Tajikistan ranks 144th out of 158 countries in Transparency International's Corruption Perceptions Index for 2005.

LABOR FREEDOM — 81.7%

The labor market operates under flexible employment regulations that enhance overall productivity growth. The non-salary cost of employing a worker is high, but dismissing a redundant employee is relatively easy. Regulations on increasing or contracting the number of work hours are flexible.

2007 Index of Economic Freedom

TANZANIA

Dar es Salaam◉

Rank: 103
Regional Rank: 15 of 40

Tanzania's economy is 56.4 percent free, according to our 2007 assessment, which makes it the world's 103rd freest economy. Its overall score is 2.9 percentage points lower than last year, partially reflecting new methodological detail. Tanzania is ranked 15th out of 40 countries in the sub-Saharan Africa region, and its overall score is slightly higher than the regional average.

Tanzania enjoys strong fiscal freedom and freedom from government. The top personal income and corporate tax rates are moderate, and overall tax revenue is relatively low as a percentage of GDP. Government expenditures are fairly low, and state-owned businesses produce only a small portion of overall tax revenue.

Economic development has been hurt by weak property rights, freedom from corruption, financial freedom, and business freedom. The overall regulatory environment is poor, and most business operations are seriously restricted. A slow civil service hurts Tanzania's trade score, as fairly high tariff rates are complemented by an inefficient customs service. As in many other sub-Saharan African nations, Tanzania's judiciary is underdeveloped and subject to the political whims of the executive. Exacerbating these problems is a high level of corruption, although the problem is not as acute in Tanzania as it is in some other African nations.

BACKGROUND: The United Republic of Tanzania is composed of mainland Tanzania and the Zanzibar archipelago. Despite an impressive growth rate averaging nearly 7 percent since 2001, it remains very poor. More than 80 percent of the population is rural, and agriculture accounts for nearly 50 percent of GDP. President Jakaya Kikwete won the 2005 election, succeeding President Benjamin Mkapa. The historically state-led economy is becoming more market-based, and efforts to improve economic management and privatize public enterprises continue. The business and investment climate remains challenging, however, and the economy is hindered by corruption, poor infrastructure, and HIV/AIDS.

How Do We Measure Economic Freedom? See Chapter 3 (page 37) for an explanation of the methodology or visit the *Index* Web site at *heritage.org/index*.

The economy is 56.4% free

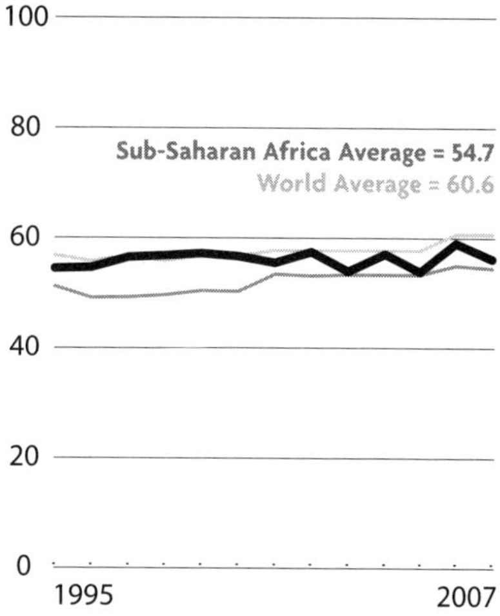

Sub-Saharan Africa Average = 54.7
World Average = 60.6

1995 — 2007

QUICK FACTS

Population: 37.6 million

GDP (PPP): $25.4 billion
6.7% growth in 2004
6.5% 5-yr. comp. ann. growth
$674 per capita

Unemployment: n/a

Inflation (CPI): 0.03%

FDI (net inflow): $469.9 million (gross)

Official Development Assistance:
Multilateral: $830 million
Bilateral: $1.2 billion (8% from the U.S.)

External Debt: $7.8 billion

Exports: $2.2 billion
Primarily gold, coffee, cashew nuts, manufactures, cotton

Imports: $3.2 billion
Primarily consumer goods, machinery, transportation equipment, industrial raw materials, crude oil

TANZANIA'S TEN ECONOMIC FREEDOMS

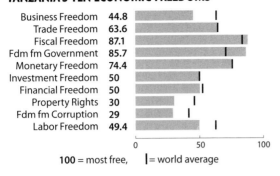

Business Freedom	44.8
Trade Freedom	63.6
Fiscal Freedom	87.1
Fdm fm Government	85.7
Monetary Freedom	74.4
Investment Freedom	50
Financial Freedom	50
Property Rights	30
Fdm fm Corruption	29
Labor Freedom	49.4

0   50   100

100 = most free, | = world average

BUSINESS FREEDOM — 44.8%

Starting a business takes an average of 30 days, compared to the world average of 48 days. To maximize entrepreneurship and job creation, it should be easier to start a company. Obtaining a business licenses can be very difficult, and closing a business is difficult. Regulations are not always transparent and consistent, causing unreliability of interpretation. The overall freedom to start, operate, and close a business is seriously restricted by the national regulatory environment

TRADE FREEDOM — 63.6%

Tanzania's weighted average tariff rate was 8.2 percent in 2003. Inefficient and corrupt customs implementation, import taxes, some prohibitive tariffs, and weak enforcement of intellectual property rights add to the cost of trade. Consequently, an additional 20 percent is deducted from Tanzania's trade freedom score to account for these non-tariff barriers.

FISCAL FREEDOM — 87.1%

Tanzania has moderate tax rates. Both the top income tax rate and the top corporate tax rate are 30 percent. Other taxes include a value-added tax (VAT), a property tax, and a tax on interest. In the most recent year, overall tax revenue as a percentage of GDP was 11.7 percent.

FREEDOM FROM GOVERNMENT — 85.7%

Total government expenditures in Tanzania, including consumption and transfer payments, are low. In the most recent year, government spending equaled 22.2 percent of GDP, and the government received 8.4 percent of its revenues from state-owned enterprises and government ownership of property. Privatization and restructuring of public enterprises have progressed in recent years.

MONETARY FREEDOM — 74.4%

Inflation in Tanzania is relatively high, averaging 6.1 percent between 2003 and 2005. Relatively high and unstable prices explain most of the monetary freedom score. The government influences prices through regulation, subsidies, and state-owned enterprises and utilities. Consequently, an additional 10 percent is deducted from Tanzania's monetary freedom score to account for these policies.

INVESTMENT FREEDOM — 50%

Tanzania generally welcomes foreign investment, although investors must overcome many bureaucratic obstacles. There is no limit on foreign ownership or control, but land ownership is restricted. Residents may hold foreign exchange accounts only for funds acquired outside of Tanzania; otherwise, such accounts are restricted. Non-residents temporarily residing in Tanzania may hold foreign exchange accounts. All transfers of foreign currency from residents to non-residents must be approved by the central bank. Most capital transactions are subject to reporting requirements, and some are restricted. Foreign purchase of real estate in Tanzania and purchase of real estate abroad by residents must be approved by the government.

FINANCIAL FREEDOM — 50%

Tanzania's financial system is relatively small and under-developed. The central bank lists 22 commercial banks that are licensed to operate. Credit is allocated largely at market rates. There are minimal restrictions on foreign banks, and international banks are expanding their Tanzanian operations. Privatization of remaining government-owned banks is continuing. In September 2005, the government selected a consortium led by Rabobank of the Netherlands to buy 49 percent of the National Microfinance Bank, although the government will retain 30 percent. There are three non-bank financial institutions, including the government-owned Tanzania Investment Bank and Tanzania Postal Bank. The insurance sector is small, with 12 insurance companies licensed as of the beginning of 2004. The state-owned National Insurance Corporation is the largest insurer and controls 25 percent of premiums. Capital markets are rudimentary. The Dar es Salaam Stock Exchange is open to foreign investors, but foreign ownership of listed companies is restricted to 60 percent. Foreign investors may not participate in government securities.

PROPERTY RIGHTS — 30%

The legal system is slow and subject to corruption. A commercial court has been established to improve the capacity of the legal system to resolve commercial disputes.

FREEDOM FROM CORRUPTION — 29%

Corruption is perceived as widespread. Tanzania ranks 88th out of 158 countries in Transparency International's Corruption Perceptions Index for 2005.

LABOR FREEDOM — 49.4%

The labor market operates under very restrictive employment regulations that hinder overall productivity growth. The non-salary cost of employing a worker is moderate, but dismissing a redundant employee can be difficult.

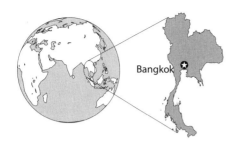

Bangkok

THAILAND

Thailand's economy is 65.6 percent free, according to our 2007 assessment, which makes it the world's 50th freest economy. Its overall score is 0.5 percentage point higher than last year, partially reflecting new methodological detail. Thailand is ranked 9th out of 30 countries in the Asia–Pacific region, and its overall score is higher than the regional average.

Thailand enjoys high levels of business freedom, fiscal freedom, freedom from government, monetary freedom, and labor freedom. Opening a business takes less time than the world average, and overall licensing procedures are simple and transparent. Thailand imposes fairly high tax rates, and overall tax revenue is low as a percentage of GDP. Government spending is also low as a percentage of GDP, and state-owned businesses account for a small portion of overall revenue. Thailand's labor market is highly flexible, and firing a redundant worker is costless.

Thailand could do better in monetary freedom, investment freedom, and freedom from corruption. Though inflation is low, Bangkok directly subsidizes the prices of a number of staple goods. Foreign investment is subject to a variety of restrictions, and these restrictions are not enforced uniformly. Corruption is significant, although it is not as great a problem as it is in many neighboring countries.

BACKGROUND: Thailand has a strong and business-friendly economy. The only Southeast Asian state never to be colonized, it has been independent for over 600 years and a constitutional monarchy since 1932. Thai politics were already in turmoil in early 2006, and then the military deposed Prime Minister Thaksin Shinawatra in September as this publication was being prepared for printing. Consistent annual growth rates of 4 percent–6 percent in recent decades and relatively high GDP per capita are largely the result of free-market economic policies, manufacturing and agricultural exports, and tourism. In 2004, Thailand began negotiating a free trade agreement with the United States that has yet to be finalized.

How Do We Measure Economic Freedom? See Chapter 3 (page 37) for an explanation of the methodology or visit the *Index* Web site at *heritage.org/index*.

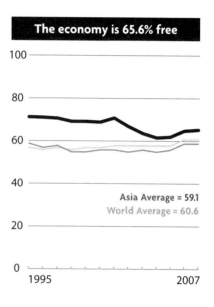

The economy is 65.6% free

Asia Average = 59.1
World Average = 60.6

QUICK FACTS

Population: 63.7 million

GDP (PPP): $515.3 billion
6.2% growth in 2004
5.1% 5-yr. comp. ann. growth
$8,090 per capita

Unemployment: 2.1%

Inflation (CPI): 2.8%

FDI (net inflow): $702 million

Official Development Assistance:
Multilateral: $30 million
Bilateral: $971 million (1% from the U.S.)

External Debt: $51.3 billion

Exports: $114.0 billion
Primarily textiles, footwear, fishery products, rice, rubber, jewelry, automobiles, computers, electrical appliances

Imports: $107.5 billion
Primarily capital goods, intermediate goods and raw materials, consumer goods, fuels

THAILAND'S TEN ECONOMIC FREEDOMS

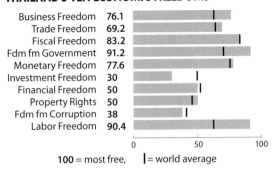

Business Freedom	76.1
Trade Freedom	69.2
Fiscal Freedom	83.2
Fdm fm Government	91.2
Monetary Freedom	77.6
Investment Freedom	30
Financial Freedom	50
Property Rights	50
Fdm fm Corruption	38
Labor Freedom	90.4

0   50   100

100 = most free, | **= world average**

BUSINESS FREEDOM — *76.1%*

Starting a business takes an average of 33 days, compared to the world average of 48 days. To maximize entrepreneurship and job creation, it should be easier to start a company. Obtaining a business license is simple, but closing a business is difficult. The overall freedom to start, operate, and close a business is relatively well protected by the national regulatory environment.

TRADE FREEDOM — *69.2%*

Thailand's weighted average tariff rate was 5.4 percent in 2005. Some prohibitive tariffs, import bans, significant and complex import taxes and fees, export subsidies, burdensome standards and import licensing requirements, restrictive sanitary and phytosanitary rules, service market access barriers, non-transparent government procurement procedures, and weak enforcement of intellectual property rights add to the cost of trade. Consequently, an additional 20 percent is deducted from Thailand's trade freedom score to account for these non-tariff barriers.

FISCAL FREEDOM — *83.2%*

Thailand has burdensome tax rates. The top income tax rate is 37 percent, and the top corporate tax rate is 30 percent. Other taxes include a value-added tax (VAT) and a property tax. In the most recent year, overall tax revenue as a percentage of GDP was 15.9 percent.

FREEDOM FROM GOVERNMENT — *91.2%*

Total government expenditures in Thailand, including consumption and transfer payments, are low. In the most recent year, government spending equaled 17 percent of GDP, and the government received 6.2 percent of its revenues from state-owned enterprises and government ownership of property.

MONETARY FREEDOM — *77.6%*

Inflation in Thailand is low, averaging 3.9 percent between 2003 and 2005. Relatively unstable prices explain most of the monetary freedom score. The government retains authority to set price ceilings for 20 goods and services, including medicines, sound recordings, milk, sugar, fuel oil, and fertilizer, and influences prices through regulation, subsidies, and state-owned utilities. Consequently, an additional 10 percent is deducted from Thailand's monetary freedom score to account for these policies.

INVESTMENT FREEDOM — *30%*

The law permits 100 percent foreign ownership except in 32 restricted service occupations. Non-Thai businesses and citizens may not own land in Thailand unless it is on government-approved industrial estates. Regulations are not enforced consistently or predictably and remain an obstacle to investment. Residents and non-residents may hold foreign exchange accounts, subject to approval in some cases and maximum limits. Foreign exchange transactions, repatriation, some outward direct investments, and transactions involving capital market securities, bonds, debt securities, money market instruments, real estate, and short-term money securities are regulated and require government approval in most cases.

FINANCIAL FREEDOM — *50%*

Following the 1997 Asian financial crisis, Thailand pursued reform of its financial system. Financial regulation and supervision are largely transparent and have improved, although they remain short of international standards. Credit is generally allocated on market terms. Financial regulations can be burdensome. The government holds 56 percent of Krung Thai Bank, 48 percent of Siam City Bank, and 49 percent of BankThai, all of which are among the top 10 domestic banks. Foreign ownership of Thai financial institutions is restricted in some cases. The government's establishment of an investment fund in June 2003 raises questions of impartiality. Roughly 100 insurance companies are registered in Thailand, including many competitive foreign firms. Capital markets are relatively well developed and sophisticated. The stock exchange is active and open to foreign investors.

PROPERTY RIGHTS — *50%*

Thailand generally protects private property, but there are indications of inefficiency and corruption. The legal process is slow, and litigants or third parties sometimes affect judgments through extra-legal means.

FREEDOM FROM CORRUPTION — *38%*

Corruption is perceived as significant. Thailand ranks 59th out of 158 countries in Transparency International's Corruption Perceptions Index for 2005.

LABOR FREEDOM — *90.4%*

The labor market operates under highly flexible employment regulations that enhance overall productivity growth. The non-salary cost of employing a worker is low, and dismissing a redundant employee is relatively costless.

TOGO

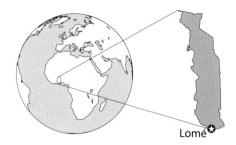

Lomé

Rank: 139
Regional Rank: 33 of 40

Togo's economy is 49.8 percent free, according to our 2007 assessment, which makes it the world's 139th freest economy. Its overall score is 1.4 percentage points higher than last year, partially reflecting new methodological detail. Togo is ranked 33rd out of 40 countries in the sub-Saharan Africa region, and its overall score is far below the regional average.

Togo scores best in monetary freedom and freedom from government. Government spending is low, and state-run businesses produce a moderate amount of revenue. Inflation is moderate, and petroleum is the only good that the government subsidizes directly.

Virtually all areas of economic freedom in Togo are restricted. Opening a business takes longer than the world average, and commercial operations are hamstrung by red tape. Despite efforts at liberalization during the 1990s, foreign investment is allowed only in certain sectors. The judiciary is not free from political influence, and corruption pervades much of the economy. Both formal and informal barriers to trade are high, and the financial system is rudimentary. Despite a smoothly functioning bureaucracy, labor regulations are extensive and make Togo one of the world's 20 least free labor markets.

BACKGROUND: Togo has an agrarian economy, and a majority of the population is engaged in subsistence agriculture. The principal exports are cotton and phosphates. Services are also important, particularly the re-export of goods through the Lomé port facility to landlocked states in the region. Following the death of President Gnassingbé Eyadéma, the military appointed his son Faure Gnassingbé president. After protests, international condemnation, and the imposition of sanctions, an election was held in April 2005. Gnassingbé won this election, but international pressure led him to establish a government of national unity with opposition party leader Edem Kodjo as prime minister.

How Do We Measure Economic Freedom? See Chapter 3 (page 37) for an explanation of the methodology or visit the *Index* Web site at *heritage.org/index*.

The economy is 49.8% free

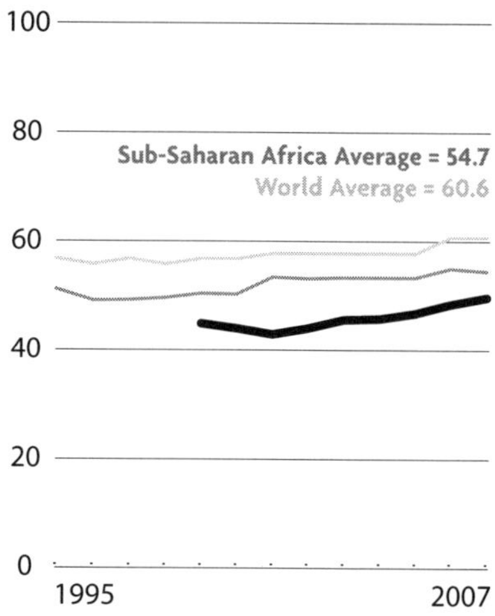

Sub-Saharan Africa Average = 54.7
World Average = 60.6

1995 — 2007

QUICK FACTS

Population: 6 million

GDP (PPP): $9.2 billion
3.0% growth in 2004
2.0% 5-yr. comp. ann. growth
$1,536 per capita

Unemployment: n/a

Inflation (CPI): 0.4%

FDI (net inflow): $63 million

Official Development Assistance:
Multilateral: $26 million
Bilateral: $59 million (6% from the U.S.)

External Debt: $1.8 billion

Exports: $0.7 billion
Primarily re-exports, cotton, phosphates, coffee, cocoa

Imports: $1.0 billion
Primarily machinery and equipment, food, petroleum products

TOGO'S TEN ECONOMIC FREEDOMS

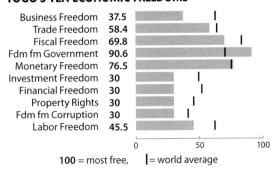

Business Freedom	37.5
Trade Freedom	58.4
Fiscal Freedom	69.8
Fdm fm Government	90.6
Monetary Freedom	76.5
Investment Freedom	30
Financial Freedom	30
Property Rights	30
Fdm fm Corruption	30
Labor Freedom	45.5

0   50   100

100 = most free, | **= world average**

BUSINESS FREEDOM — 37.5%

Starting a business takes an average of 53 days, compared to the world average of 48 days. To maximize entrepreneurship and job creation, it should be easier to start a company. Obtaining a business license can be very difficult, and closing a business is difficult. Regulations are sometimes inconsistent, causing unreliability of interpretation. Lack of transparency and bureaucratic delays are ongoing problems. The overall freedom to start, operate, and close a business is seriously restricted by the national regulatory environment.

TRADE FREEDOM — 58.4%

Togo's weighted average tariff rate was 10.8 percent in 2004. Significant import taxes and fees, import bans, and weak enforcement of intellectual property rights add to the cost of trade. Consequently, an additional 20 percent is deducted from Togo's trade freedom score to account for these non-tariff barriers.

FISCAL FREEDOM — 69.8%

Togo has burdensome tax rates. The top income tax rate is 55 percent, and the top corporate tax rate is 37 percent. Other taxes include a value-added tax (VAT), a property tax, and a vehicle tax. In the most recent year, overall tax revenue as a percentage of GDP was 11.7 percent.

FREEDOM FROM GOVERNMENT — 90.6%

Total government expenditures in Togo, including consumption and transfer payments, are moderate. In the most recent year, government spending equaled 13.7 percent of GDP, and the government received 15.1 percent of its revenues from state-owned enterprises and government ownership of property.

MONETARY FREEDOM — 76.5%

Inflation in Togo is moderate, averaging 4.5 percent between 2003 and 2005. Relatively unstable prices explain most of the monetary freedom score. The government is able to influence prices through regulation and state-owned enterprises and utilities, and prices for petroleum products are controlled. Consequently, an additional 10 percent is deducted from Togo's monetary freedom score to account for these policies.

INVESTMENT FREEDOM — 30%

Togo's foreign investment code was liberalized in 1990, but investors still face barriers. The 1990 code includes local content restrictions, and there is an overall lack of administrative transparency. Investment is permitted only in certain sectors and is screened on a case-by-case basis. Residents and non-residents may hold foreign exchange accounts after obtaining government approval. Payments and transfers to certain countries are subject to authorization and quantitative limits in some cases. Purchases of real estate by non-residents for purposes other than business are subject to controls. Most capital transactions are subject to controls or require government approval.

FINANCIAL FREEDOM — 30%

Togo's financial system is underdeveloped. The Central Bank of West African States (BCEAO), a central bank common to eight countries, governs Togo's financial institutions. The eight BCEAO member countries use the CFA franc, pegged to the euro. Four of Togo's six commercial banks are state-controlled. Government involvement in banking and lending decisions has caused the banking sector to deteriorate in recent years, particularly for these four state-dominated banks, which have substantial levels of non-performing loans. Togo has pursued privatization of the four state-run banks, but only one had found a private partner as of mid-2005. The government offered two-thirds of the national savings bank to the public in March 2005 as part of the process of converting the institution into a commercial bank. A new bank opened in December 2005: the Banque Régionale de Solidarité, owned by the BCEAO and regional private investors. Togo participates in a small regional stock market based in the Ivory Coast.

PROPERTY RIGHTS — 30%

The judicial system does not protect private property sufficiently and is subject to strong influence from the executive. Contracts are difficult to enforce.

FREEDOM FROM CORRUPTION — 30%

Togo has a large informal market in computer software, video, and cassette recordings, as well as beauty products. Informal retail accounts for much of the country's entrepreneurial activity.

LABOR FREEDOM — 45.5%

The labor market operates under highly restrictive employment regulations that hinder overall productivity growth. The non-salary cost of employing a worker is high, and dismissing a redundant employee can be difficult. There are rigid regulations related to increasing or contracting the number of work hours. Togo's labor freedom is one of the 20 lowest in the world.

TRINIDAD AND TOBAGO

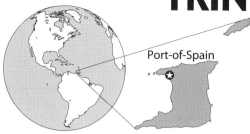

Port-of-Spain

Rank: 23

Regional Rank: 4 of 29

Trinidad and Tobago's economy is 71.4 percent free, according to our 2007 assessment, which makes it the world's 23rd freest economy. Its overall score is 0.4 percentage point lower than last year, partially reflecting new methodological detail. Trinidad and Tobago is ranked 4th out of 29 countries in the Americas, and its overall score is higher than the regional average.

Trinidad and Tobago enjoys high levels of fiscal freedom, freedom from government, financial freedom, investment freedom, property rights, and labor freedom. The tax system has been simplified, and both the corporate and income tax rates have been lowered to 25 percent. Government expenditures equal about one-fourth of GDP. The government welcomes foreign investment, and the financial market is generally transparent. Flexible labor regulations contribute to an elastic employment market with no major regulatory distortions. Property rights are secured by an independent judiciary, although the legal system is burdened by a years-long backlog of cases.

Business freedom, monetary freedom, and corruption could be improved. Regulation of commercial operations makes licensing procedures difficult, and the enforcement of applicable regulations is uneven. Although inflation is moderate, the government subsidizes the prices of several goods. Corruption is minimal for a developing nation.

BACKGROUND: Investor-friendly Trinidad and Tobago is the largest supplier of liquefied natural gas in the Americas and has one of the largest economies in the Caribbean Community. The former British colony is a parliamentary democracy, practices sound fiscal management, and has embraced free-market policies. It has a stabilization fund to save windfall revenues when oil and gas prices are high so that it can meet expenses when prices are low. Exports also include petrochemicals, and there is potential for growth in financial services. Trinidad and Tobago leads Caribbean integration efforts and supports the proposed Caribbean Single Market and Economy.

How Do We Measure Economic Freedom? See Chapter 3 (page 37) for an explanation of the methodology or visit the *Index* Web site at *heritage.org/index*.

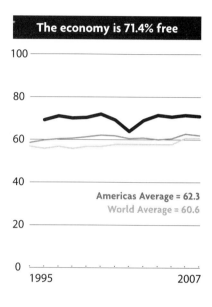

The economy is 71.4% free

Americas Average = 62.3
World Average = 60.6

QUICK FACTS

Population: 1.3 million

GDP (PPP): $15.9 billion
6.6% growth in 2004
7.7% 5-yr. comp. ann. growth
$12,182 per capita

Unemployment: 8.4%

Inflation (CPI): 3.7%

FDI (net inflow): $972.7 million

Official Development Assistance:
Multilateral: $5 million
Bilateral: $7 million (25% from the U.S.)

External Debt: $2.9 billion

Exports: $5.9 billion
Primarily petroleum, petroleum products, chemicals, steel products, fertilizer, sugar, cocoa, coffee, citrus, flowers

Imports: $4.3 billion
Primarily machinery, transportation equipment, manufactured goods, food, live animals

TRINIDAD & TOBAGO'S TEN ECONOMIC FREEDOMS

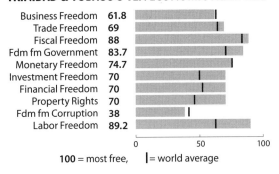

Business Freedom	61.8
Trade Freedom	69
Fiscal Freedom	88
Fdm fm Government	83.7
Monetary Freedom	74.7
Investment Freedom	70
Financial Freedom	70
Property Rights	70
Fdm fm Corruption	38
Labor Freedom	89.2

100 = most free, | = world average

BUSINESS FREEDOM — *61.8%*

Starting a business takes an average of 43 days, compared to the world average of 48 days. To maximize entrepreneurship and job creation, it should be easier to start a company. Both obtaining a business license and closing a business can be difficult. Regulations are sometimes inconsistent, causing unreliability of interpretation. The overall freedom to start, operate, and close a business is restricted by the national regulatory environment.

TRADE FREEDOM — *69%*

The weighted average tariff rate in Trinidad and Tobago was 5.5 percent in 2003. Certain prohibitive tariffs, import taxes and fees, export support programs, and import licensing requirements add to the cost of trade. Consequently, an additional 20 percent is deducted from Trinidad and Tobago's trade freedom score to account for these non-tariff barriers.

FISCAL FREEDOM — *88%*

Trinidad and Tobago enjoys low tax rates, and the tax system has been simplified through tax rate reductions in recent years. Both the top income tax rate and the standard corporate tax rate are 25 percent. Other taxes include a value-added tax (VAT) and a property tax. In the most recent year, overall tax revenue as a percentage of GDP was 23.4 percent.

FREEDOM FROM GOVERNMENT — *83.7%*

Total government expenditures in Trinidad and Tobago, including consumption and transfer payments, are moderate. In the most recent year, government spending equaled 25.4 percent of GDP, and the government received 3.8 percent of its revenues from state-owned enterprises and government ownership of property.

MONETARY FREEDOM — *74.7%*

Inflation in Trinidad and Tobago is moderate, averaging 5.8 percent between 2003 and 2005. Relatively moderate and unstable prices explain most of the monetary freedom score. The government retains price ceilings for a number of goods; controls prices for sugar, schoolbooks, and some pharmaceuticals; and influences prices through regulation, subsidies, and state-owned enterprises and utilities, including oil, electricity, and chemicals. Consequently, an addi-

tional 10 percent is deducted from Trinidad and Tobago's monetary freedom score to account for these policies.

INVESTMENT FREEDOM — *70%*

Trinidad and Tobago is open to foreign investment, which receives national treatment and is welcome in the privatization program. Foreign investment in private business is not subject to limitations, but a foreigner must obtain a license to purchase more than 30 percent of a publicly held business. Foreign ownership of land is limited to one acre for residential purposes and five acres for trade purposes. Both residents and non-residents may hold foreign exchange accounts. There are no restrictions or controls on payments, transactions, transfers, or repatriation of profits.

FINANCIAL FREEDOM — *70%*

Trinidad and Tobago has one of the region's more advanced financial systems. Financial regulations and supervision are generally transparent. There are no restrictions on foreign banks or foreign borrowers, and all banks are free to engage in a wide range of services. There are six commercial banks, including one state-owned bank and several foreign banks. Many of Trinidad and Tobago's banks have expanded into neighboring countries. The country's approximately 130 credit unions are growing in importance, and the government is considering tightening their regulation and oversight. In 2004, the insurance sector included over 40 firms but was dominated by CL Financial, which controlled over half of total assets. Capital markets are well developed, if rather small, and centered around the stock exchange in Port-of-Spain.

PROPERTY RIGHTS — *70%*

The judiciary is independent and provides a fair judicial process. However, court cases are time-consuming, and there is a several-year backlog of cases waiting to be heard.

FREEDOM FROM CORRUPTION — *38%*

Corruption is perceived as significant. Trinidad and Tobago ranks 59th out of 158 countries in Transparency International's Corruption Perceptions Index for 2005.

LABOR FREEDOM — *89.2%*

The labor market operates under flexible employment regulations that enhance overall productivity growth. The non-salary cost of employing a worker is low, but dismissing a redundant employee can be costly. Regulations related to increasing or modifying the number of work hours are flexible.

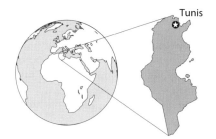

Tunis

TUNISIA

Rank: 69

Regional Rank: 6 of 17

Tunisia's economy is 61 percent free, according to our 2007 assessment, which makes it the world's 69th freest economy. Its overall score is 1.8 percentage points higher than last year, partially reflecting new methodological detail. Tunisia is ranked 6th out of 17 countries in the Middle East/North Africa region, and its overall score is slightly higher than the regional average.

Tunisia enjoys high levels of business freedom, monetary freedom, fiscal freedom, freedom from government, and labor freedom, especially for a Middle Eastern country. Inflation is low, although the state retains the right to set prices in some circumstances. Tunisia maintains moderately high tax rates, but overall tax revenue is not particularly large as a percentage of GDP. There are regulatory obstacles, but businesses can be opened and closed without undue difficulty. The labor market is fairly flexible, and redundant workers can be fired without significant cost.

Tunisia faces challenges in trade freedom, investment freedom, and financial freedom. The government maintains complex trade regulations and opaque bureaucratic practices. Protectionist economic policies have limited the opportunities for foreign investment. The financial sector is subject to heavy political influence, and much of its regulation and oversight falls short of international standards.

BACKGROUND: Tunisia gained its independence from France in 1956 and developed a socialist economy. President Zine al-Abidine Ben Ali has undertaken gradual free-market economic reforms since the early 1990s, including privatization of state-owned firms, simplification of the tax code, and more prudent fiscal restraint. The country's diverse economy includes significant agricultural, mining, energy, tourism, and manufacturing sectors. Tunisia's 1998 association agreement with the European Union, which has helped to create jobs and modernize the economy, was the first such agreement between the EU and a Maghreb country. The economy has also benefited from expanded trade and tourism.

How Do We Measure Economic Freedom? See Chapter 3 (page 37) for an explanation of the methodology or visit the *Index* Web site at *heritage.org/index*.

The economy is 61% free

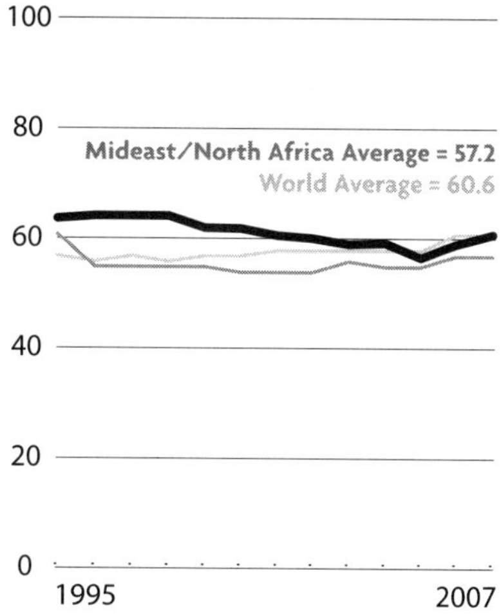

Mideast/North Africa Average = 57.2
World Average = 60.6

100
80
60
40
20
0
1995   2007

QUICK FACTS

Population: 9.9 million

GDP (PPP): $77.2 billion
6.0% growth in 2004
4.6% 5-yr. comp. ann. growth
$7,768 per capita

Unemployment: 14.2%

Inflation (CPI): 3.6%

FDI (net inflow): $634.7 million

Official Development Assistance:
Multilateral: $116 million
Bilateral: $423 million (0.1% from the U.S.)

External Debt: $18.7 billion

Exports: $13.3 billion
Primarily textiles, mechanical goods, phosphates, chemicals, agricultural products, hydrocarbons

Imports: $14.1 billion
Primarily textiles, machinery, equipment, hydrocarbons, chemicals, food

TUNISIA'S TEN ECONOMIC FREEDOMS

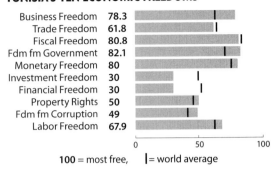

Business Freedom	78.3
Trade Freedom	61.8
Fiscal Freedom	80.8
Fdm fm Government	82.1
Monetary Freedom	80
Investment Freedom	30
Financial Freedom	30
Property Rights	50
Fdm fm Corruption	49
Labor Freedom	67.9

0   50   100

100 = most free, | = world average

BUSINESS FREEDOM — 78.3%

Starting a business takes an average of 11 days, compared to the world average of 48 days. Obtaining a business license can be difficult, but closing a business can be easy. Bureaucratic obstacles and delays can be problems. The overall freedom to start, close, and operate a business is relatively well protected by the national regulatory environment.

TRADE FREEDOM — 61.8%

Tunisia's weighted average tariff rate was 9.1 percent in 2005. A complex tariff structure, significant and complex import taxes and fees, export subsidies and other export promotion programs, and delays in customs all add to the cost of trade. Consequently, an additional 20 percent is deducted from Tunisia's trade freedom score to account for these non-tariff barriers.

FISCAL FREEDOM — 80.8%

Tunisia has burdensome tax rates. Both the top income tax rate and the top corporate tax rate are 35 percent. Other taxes include a value-added tax (VAT) and a vehicle tax. In the most recent year, overall tax revenue as a percentage of GDP was 20.7 percent.

FREEDOM FROM GOVERNMENT — 82.1%

Total government expenditures in Tunisia, including consumption and transfer payments, are moderate. In the most recent year, government spending equaled 26.8 percent of GDP, and the government received 3.4 percent of its revenues from state-owned enterprises and government ownership of property.

MONETARY FREEDOM — 80%

Inflation in Tunisia is low, averaging 2.5 percent between 2003 and 2005. Relatively low and stable prices explain most of the monetary freedom score. The government retains authority to set prices for subsidized goods and influences prices through regulation, subsidies, and state-owned utilities and enterprises. Consequently, an additional 10 percent is deducted from Tunisia's monetary freedom score to account for these policies.

INVESTMENT FREEDOM — 30%

Tunisia is open to foreign investment generally but does restrict it in some sectors to minimize the impact on domestic competitors. The Investment Code Law covers all major sectors of economic activity except mining, energy, the financial sector, and domestic trade. Foreign ownership of agricultural land is prohibited. Onshore companies outside the tourism sector with a capital share larger than 49 percent require government authorization. Residents and non-residents may hold foreign exchange accounts, subject to restrictions and approval. There are some controls, quantitative limits, and other restrictions on payments and transfers. There are many restrictions and controls on capital transactions.

FINANCIAL FREEDOM — 30%

Tunisia's financial system is subject to heavy government involvement. Supervision and regulation are slowly being brought up to international standards, but they remain insufficient. The banking sector includes 14 commercial banks. The government sold its stake in two banks in 2002 and late in 2005 but remains the controlling shareholder in at least four banks that together account for about 42 percent of bank assets. In 2005, the government established a state-owned financial institution to improve access to capital by small and medium-size enterprises. The small insurance sector had 20 insurance companies in 2005 (15 Tunisian and five foreign), four of which were wholly or partly state-owned, including the largest, which controlled one-third of the market. Capital markets are nominal, although the stock market is active, and the number of investment funds is growing.

PROPERTY RIGHTS — 50%

The executive branch is the supreme arbiter of events in the cabinet, government, judiciary, and military. Commercial cases take long to resolve and face complex legal procedures.

FREEDOM FROM CORRUPTION — 49%

Corruption is perceived as significant. Tunisia ranks 43rd out of 158 countries in Transparency International's Corruption Perceptions Index for 2005.

LABOR FREEDOM — 67.9%

The labor market operates under somewhat flexible employment regulations that could be improved to enhance overall productivity growth. The non-salary cost of employing a worker is high, but dismissing a redundant employee is not costly.

TURKEY

Ankara

Rank: 83

Regional Rank: 34 of 41

Turkey's economy is 59.3 percent free, according to our 2007 assessment, which makes it the world's 83rd freest economy. Its overall score is 0.9 percentage point higher than last year, partially reflecting new methodological detail. Turkey is ranked 34th out of 41 countries in the European region, and its overall score is lower than the regional average.

Turkey enjoys strong trade freedom, business freedom, and fiscal freedom. The government maintains a business-friendly environment for young companies, although licensing and bankruptcy procedures are difficult. Turkey's average tariff rate is low, but there are significant non-tariff barriers and complex regulations. The top income and corporate tax rates are moderately high, and overall tax revenue is relatively moderate as a percentage of GDP.

Turkey faces some challenges in freedom from corruption, freedom from government, monetary freedom, and labor freedom. Inflation is fairly high, and the government distorts the prices of a variety of agricultural goods through direct subsidies. Total government expenditures equal more than a third of national GDP. Corruption is present, although it is not as serious a problem in Turkey as it is in some nearby Middle Eastern countries. Turkey's labor freedom is exceptionally low, and its labor market is one of the 20 least free in the world.

BACKGROUND: Ever since Mustafa Kemal Ataturk founded modern Turkey in 1923, the country has sought a more Western-oriented approach to policy, especially in its vigorous attempts to join the European Union. Prime Minister Recep Tayyip Erdogan is seeking to reverse decades of corruption, economic mismanagement, and authoritarian intervention, but Turkey still faces challenges in decreasing the role of the state. The public sector dominates energy, telecommunications, transport, and banking. The EU agreed to start formal accession talks with Turkey in October 2005. Turkey's main exports include foodstuffs, textiles, clothing, iron, and steel.

How Do We Measure Economic Freedom? See Chapter 3 (page 37) for an explanation of the methodology or visit the *Index* Web site at *heritage.org/index*.

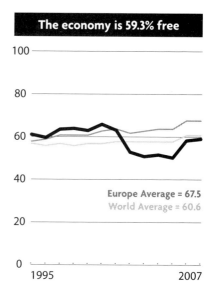

The economy is 59.3% free

Europe Average = 67.5
World Average = 60.6

1995 — 2007

QUICK FACTS

Population: 71.7 million

GDP (PPP): $556.1 billion
8.9% growth in 2004
4.3% 5-yr. comp. ann. growth
$7,753 per capita

Unemployment: 10.3%

Inflation (CPI): 8.6%

FDI (net inflow): $1.9 billion

Official Development Assistance:
Multilateral: $326 million
Bilateral: $394 million (2% from the U.S.)

External Debt: $161.6 billion

Exports: $91.0 billion
Primarily apparel, food, textiles, metal manufactures, transport equipment

Imports: $102.2 billion
Primarily machinery, chemicals, semi-finished goods, fuels, transport equipment

TURKEY'S TEN ECONOMIC FREEDOMS

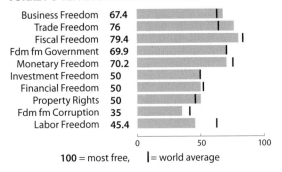

Business Freedom	67.4	
Trade Freedom	76	
Fiscal Freedom	79.4	
Fdm fm Government	69.9	
Monetary Freedom	70.2	
Investment Freedom	50	
Financial Freedom	50	
Property Rights	50	
Fdm fm Corruption	35	
Labor Freedom	45.4	

0   50   100

100 = most free, I = world average

BUSINESS FREEDOM — 67.4%

Starting a business takes an average of nine days, compared to the world average of 48 days. Both obtaining a business license and closing a business are difficult. Red tape and bureaucratic delays are persistent problems. The overall freedom to start, operate, and close a business is relatively well protected by the national regulatory environment.

TRADE FREEDOM — 76%

Turkey's weighted average tariff rate was 2 percent in 2003. Prohibitive tariffs for agriculture and food products, significant import taxes and fees, export subsidies and other export promotion programs, import licensing, non-transparent and complex standards and regulations, service market access barriers, weak enforcement of intellectual property rights, and corruption all add to the cost of trade. Consequently, an additional 20 percent is deducted from Turkey's trade freedom score to account for these non-tariff barriers.

FISCAL FREEDOM — 79.4%

Turkey has burdensome tax rates. The top income tax rate is 35 percent, and the top corporate tax rate is 30 percent. Other taxes include a value-added tax (VAT), a property tax, and a tax on interest. In the most recent year, overall tax revenue as a percentage of GDP was 31.1 percent.

FREEDOM FROM GOVERNMENT — 69.9%

Total government expenditures in Turkey, including consumption and transfer payments, are moderate. In the most recent year, government spending equaled 35.4 percent of GDP, and the government received 2.6 percent of its revenues from state-owned enterprises and government ownership of property.

MONETARY FREEDOM — 70.2%

Inflation in Turkey is high, averaging 9.8 percent between 2003 and 2005. Such unstable prices explain most of the monetary freedom score. The government sets prices for many agricultural products and pharmaceuticals and influences prices through regulation, subsidies, and state-owned utilities and enterprises. Municipalities fix ceilings on the retail price of bread. Permission for price increases traditionally has depended more on political than on economic criteria. Consequently, an additional 10 percent is deducted from Turkey's monetary freedom score to account for these policies.

INVESTMENT FREEDOM — 50%

Turkey welcomes foreign investment but maintains a number of formal and informal barriers in broadcasting, aviation, maritime transportation, and value-added telecommunications services companies, and port facilities must be at least 51 percent Turkish-owned. Significant deterrents to foreign investment include excessive bureaucracy, a weak judicial system, and frequent changes in the legal environment. Both residents and non-residents may hold foreign exchange accounts. There are few restrictions on payments and transfers. Reporting requirements apply to some capital transactions. Non-residents are subject to restrictions on the purchase of real estate, but foreign companies may acquire real estate through a Turkish legal entity or local partnership.

FINANCIAL FREEDOM — 50%

Turkey's financial system is well developed and has largely recovered from the 2000–2001 financial crisis. Following the crisis, the government increased transparency, strengthened regulatory and accounting standards, and improved oversight. As of November 2005, there were 34 commercial banks, including three state-owned banks, 18 private domestic banks, and 13 majority foreign-owned banks. Three state-owned commercial banks control over 30 percent of banking assets, whereas foreign banks account for only 6 percent. The insurance sector is growing and includes 60 insurance companies, five of which are foreign-owned and two of which are state-owned. Capital markets are relatively small and dominated by government securities. The stock exchange is state-owned but autonomous.

PROPERTY RIGHTS — 50%

Property rights are generally enforced, although the court system is overburdened and slow to reach decisions, and judges are not well trained for commercial cases. The judiciary is subject to government influence.

FREEDOM FROM CORRUPTION — 35%

Corruption is perceived as significant. Turkey ranks 65th out of 158 countries in Transparency International's Corruption Perceptions Index for 2005.

LABOR FREEDOM — 45.4%

The labor market operates under highly inflexible employment regulations that hinder overall productivity growth. Turkey's Labor Law 4857, enacted in 2003, has provided some increased flexibility to employers. However, the non-salary cost of employing a worker is high, and dismissing a redundant employee is still costly. Turkey's labor freedom is one of the 20 lowest in the world.

TURKMENISTAN

Ashgabat

Turkmenistan's economy is 42.5 percent free, according to our 2007 assessment, which makes it the world's 152nd freest economy. Its overall score is 1.3 percentage points lower than last year, partially reflecting new methodological detail. Turkmenistan is ranked 28th out of 30 countries in the Asia–Pacific region, and its overall score is much lower than the regional average.

Turkmenistan scores well in fiscal freedom, freedom from government, and trade freedom. The top income tax is only 10 percent, and the corporate tax is 20 percent. Government spending equals slightly more than one-fifth of national GDP. While there are non-tariff barriers, including cumbersome regulations, the average tariff rate is low.

Turkmenistan's business freedom, investment freedom, financial freedom, labor freedom, property rights, and freedom from corruption are all weak. Although total government spending is fairly low relative to GDP, a non-transparent regulatory system discourages both local businesses and foreign investment. The national financial market is unsophisticated, and most operations are dominated by the state; accordingly, many people keep their money in cash. The judicial system is wholly controlled by the state, and corruption pervades the judiciary and civil service. Inflation is fairly high, and the government subsidizes a wide array of goods. The labor market is highly inflexible, with the government providing most of the country's jobs.

BACKGROUND: Since gaining its independence in 1991, Turkmenistan has remained impoverished and largely closed to the outside world. Its government, led by President Saparmurat Niyazov, is composed mainly of former Communists who resist reform. Turkmenistan's large external debt is due to low export prices and a heavy reliance on imports. Its main exports are gas, oil, and oil products, which are sold primarily to Russia. A recent agreement with Russia will double the export price of Turkmen gas. The other main industry, agriculture, is concentrated in cotton, the price of which is kept artificially low.

How Do We Measure Economic Freedom? See Chapter 3 (page 37) for an explanation of the methodology or visit the *Index* Web site at *heritage.org/index*.

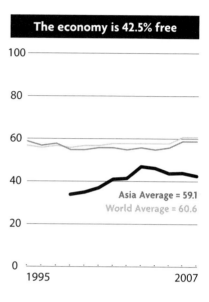

The economy is 42.5% free

Asia Average = 59.1
World Average = 60.6

QUICK FACTS

Population: 4.8 million

GDP (PPP): $39.5 billion
17.2% growth in 2004
17.8% 5-yr. comp. ann. growth
$8,000 per capita

Unemployment: 60% (2004 estimate)

Inflation (CPI): 5.9%

FDI (net inflow): $150 million (gross)

Official Development Assistance:
Multilateral: $7 million
Bilateral: $32 million (22% from the U.S.)

External Debt: $2.4 (2001 estimate)

Exports: $3.9 billion
Primarily gas, crude oil, petrochemicals, cotton fiber, textiles

Imports: $3.2 billion
Primarily machinery and equipment, chemicals, food

TURKMENISTAN'S TEN ECONOMIC FREEDOMS

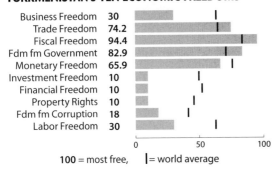

Business Freedom	30
Trade Freedom	74.2
Fiscal Freedom	94.4
Fdm fm Government	82.9
Monetary Freedom	65.9
Investment Freedom	10
Financial Freedom	10
Property Rights	10
Fdm fm Corruption	18
Labor Freedom	30

100 = most free, | = world average

BUSINESS FREEDOM — 30%

The non-transparency of the entire regulatory system is a great challenge to entrepreneurial activities in Turkmenistan. Businesses have difficulty getting copies of laws and regulations as government officials routinely refuse even to provide them. Personal relations with government officials often help to determine how and when government regulations are applied. Considering the private sector a competitor, government entities use regulations as an excuse for restricting private business. The overall freedom to start, operate, and close a business is seriously restricted by the national regulatory environment.

TRADE FREEDOM — 74.2%

Turkmenistan's weighted average tariff rate was 2.9 percent in 2002. Prohibitive tariffs for agricultural and food products, import taxes and fees, export bans, and customs procedures that are bureaucratic, slow, and subject to corruption add to the cost of trade. Consequently, an additional 20 percent is deducted from Turkmenistan's trade freedom score to account for these non-tariff barriers.

FISCAL FREEDOM — 94.4%

Turkmenistan enjoys low tax rates. The top income tax rate is 10 percent, and the top corporate tax rate is 20 percent. Other taxes include a value-added tax (VAT) and an excise tax. Important gaps in the available data include figures for government finance. In the most recent year, overall tax revenue as a percentage of GDP was 18.3 percent.

FREEDOM FROM GOVERNMENT — 82.9%

Total government expenditures in Turkmenistan, including consumption and transfer payments, are moderate. In the most recent year, government spending equaled 22.1 percent of GDP. Turkmenistan has made very limited progress in economic reforms. Government intervention has been pervasive in the economy, and privatization has stalled. There are still mandatory state plans.

MONETARY FREEDOM — 65.9%

Inflation in Turkmenistan is high, averaging 9.1 percent between 2003 and 2005. Relatively high and unstable prices explain most of the monetary freedom score. A system of subsidies, price controls, and free provision of utilities underpins the government's economic policies, and the government also influences prices through numerous state-owned utilities and enterprises. Consequently, an additional 15 percent is deducted from Turkmenistan's monetary freedom score to account for these policies.

INVESTMENT FREEDOM — 10%

The government controls most of Turkmenistan's economy and restricts foreign participation. Investors face currency and trade restrictions, and the state continues to interfere in companies that have been privatized. The government chooses its investment partners selectively. Deficient rule of law, excessive and inconsistent regulation, and corruption are strong disincentives to foreign investment. Foreign exchange accounts require government approval. All payments and transfers require government approval. Capital transactions face restrictions and central bank approval in some cases.

FINANCIAL FREEDOM — 10%

Turkmenistan's financial system is subject to very heavy government influence. A financial crisis led the number of banks in operation to fall from 67 to 12 in mid-2004. Many banks are insolvent by international standards, and the financial sector is dominated by state-owned or state-influenced institutions. An estimated 95 percent of all loans go to state-owned enterprises. The government directs credit allocation, often at subsidized rates. Most individuals hold their wealth in cash, preferably foreign currency. The central bank is not independent. Private enterprises have little access to credit. There are no significant non-bank financial institutions, and the state-owned insurance company is the sole insurer. There is no private capital market.

PROPERTY RIGHTS — 10%

The legal system does not strongly enforce contracts and rights. Laws are poorly developed, and judicial employees and judges are poorly trained and open to bribery.

FREEDOM FROM CORRUPTION — 18%

Corruption is perceived as widespread. Turkmenistan ranks 155th out of 158 countries in Transparency International's Corruption Perceptions Index for 2005.

LABOR FREEDOM —30%

The labor market operates under highly inflexible employment regulations that hinder overall productivity growth. The government provides the majority of jobs. Minimum wages are mandated by the state.

UGANDA

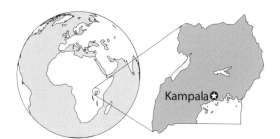

Kampala○

Uganda's economy is 63.4 percent free, according to our 2007 assessment, which makes it the world's 59th freest economy. Its overall score is 1.5 percentage points lower than last year, partially reflecting new methodological detail. Uganda is ranked 5th out of 40 countries in the sub-Saharan Africa region, and its overall score is much higher than the regional average.

Uganda scores highly in fiscal freedom, freedom from government, financial freedom, and labor freedom. The top income and corporate tax rates are moderate, and overall tax revenues are not large as a percentage of GDP. Government expenditures are also fairly low, and government-owned businesses do not account for a significant portion of total tax revenues. Uganda has a small but developed financial sector that is dominated by banking. The labor sector is elastic in workweek hours and workforce flexibility.

Uganda is weaker in freedom from corruption, property rights, and business freedom. Regulations make commercial licensing burdensome and are not always enforced consistently. Closing a business is also difficult. Uganda opened its first commercial court several years ago, but slow resolution and understaffing lead most investors to seek settlements or outside arbitration. Corruption is a problem, but no more so than for other African nations.

BACKGROUND: Uganda remains poor despite market reforms that contributed to economic growth averaging over 6 percent annually during the past decade. The government's "abstinence, be faithful, and condoms" (ABC) program has reduced HIV prevalence to 6.5 percent in 2005 from 18 percent in the 1990s. President Yoweri Museveni, who has ruled since leading a successful insurgency that seized power in 1986, was elected to a third five-year term in 2006 following the adoption of a controversial constitutional amendment that removed the two-term limit. The agricultural sector employs most Ugandans and accounted for over one-third of gross domestic product in 2004.

How Do We Measure Economic Freedom? See Chapter 3 (page 37) for an explanation of the methodology or visit the *Index* Web site at *heritage.org/index*.

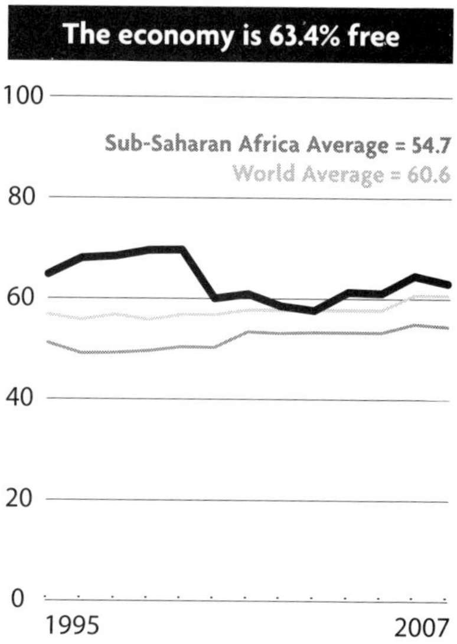

The economy is 63.4% free

Sub-Saharan Africa Average = 54.7
World Average = 60.6

100

80

60

40

20

0

1995 — 2007

QUICK FACTS

Population: 27.8 million

GDP (PPP): $41.1 billion
5.6% growth in 2004
5.4% 5-yr. comp. ann. growth
$1,478 per capita

Unemployment: n/a

Inflation (CPI): 3.3%

FDI (net inflow): $237.2 million (gross)

Official Development Assistance:
Multilateral: $585 million
Bilateral: $751 million (28% from the U.S.)

External Debt: $4.8 billion

Exports: $1.2 billion
Primarily coffee, fish, fish products, tea, cotton, flowers, horticultural products, gold

Imports: $2.2 billion
Primarily capital equipment, vehicles, petroleum, medical supplies, cereals

UGANDA'S TEN ECONOMIC FREEDOMS

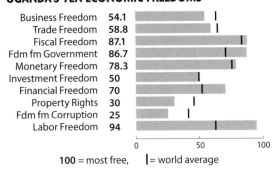

Business Freedom	54.1
Trade Freedom	58.8
Fiscal Freedom	87.1
Fdm fm Government	86.7
Monetary Freedom	78.3
Investment Freedom	50
Financial Freedom	70
Property Rights	30
Fdm fm Corruption	25
Labor Freedom	94

0   50   100

100 = most free, | = world average

BUSINESS FREEDOM — 54.1%

Starting a business takes an average of 30 days, compared to the world average of 48 days. To maximize entrepreneurship and job creation, it should be easier to start a company. Obtaining a business license can be very difficult, and closing a business is difficult. Regulations are sometimes inconsistent, causing unreliability of interpretation. The overall freedom to start, operate, and close a business is restricted by the national regulatory environment.

TRADE FREEDOM — 58.8%

Uganda's weighted average tariff rate was 10.6 percent in 2005. The government has made progress toward liberalizing the trade regime, but inefficient and non-transparent customs implementation, import restrictions, weak enforcement of intellectual property rights, and corruption still add to the cost of trade. Consequently, an additional 20 percent is deducted from Uganda's trade freedom score to account for these non-tariff barriers.

FISCAL FREEDOM — 87.1%

Uganda has moderate tax rates. Both the top income tax rate and the top corporate tax rate are 30 percent. Other taxes include a value-added tax (VAT), a property tax, and a vehicle tax. In the most recent year, overall tax revenue as a percentage of GDP was 11.7 percent.

FREEDOM FROM GOVERNMENT — 86.7%

Total government expenditures in Uganda, including consumption and transfer payments, are low. In the most recent year, government spending equaled 23.8 percent of GDP, and the government received 0.1 percent of its revenues from state-owned enterprises and government ownership of property. Many state-owned companies have been privatized or divested.

MONETARY FREEDOM — 78.3%

Inflation in Uganda is relatively high, averaging 6.9 percent between 2003 and 2005. Relatively high and unstable prices explain most of the monetary freedom score. The government is able to influence prices through state-owned utilities and enterprises. Consequently, an additional 5 percent is deducted from Uganda's monetary freedom score to account for these policies.

INVESTMENT FREEDOM — 50%

Foreign investment is allowed in privatized industries. Foreign investors may form 100 percent foreign-owned companies and majority or minority joint ventures with local investors with no restrictions. They also may acquire or take over domestic enterprises. Foreign investors, however, do not receive equal treatment, especially for performance obligations. A slow land registry and complex land regulations make it difficult for foreign companies to buy land. Both residents and non-residents may hold foreign exchange accounts. There are no restrictions or controls on payments, transactions, or transfers.

FINANCIAL FREEDOM — 70%

Uganda's small financial system is dominated by its banking sector. The banking industry generally is sound and well capitalized. The central bank has tightened supervision and increased regulatory requirements in the wake of several bank closures in the late 1990s. Uganda had 16 commercial banks and two development banks in 2004. Most banks are foreign-owned. New banks are not allowed unless they offer completely new financial services or take over existing banks. As of 2004, there also were seven savings and loan institutions and a number of microfinance institutions. The insurance sector is small and comprised 15 companies in 2003, including the state-owned National Insurance Company, which is undergoing privatization. Capital markets are relatively small and underdeveloped. Foreign investors may participate in capital markets, and foreign-owned companies may trade on the stock market subject to some restrictions.

PROPERTY RIGHTS — 30%

Uganda opened its first commercial court about six years ago, but a shortage of judges and funding drives most commercial cases to outside arbitration or settlement. The judiciary suffers from corruption.

FREEDOM FROM CORRUPTION — 25%

Corruption is perceived as widespread. Uganda ranks 117th out of 158 countries in Transparency International's Corruption Perceptions Index for 2005.

LABOR FREEDOM — 94%

The labor market operates under highly flexible employment regulations that enhance overall productivity growth. The non-salary cost of employing a worker is moderate, and dismissing a redundant employee is not difficult. Regulations on increasing or contracting the number of work hours are flexible.

UKRAINE

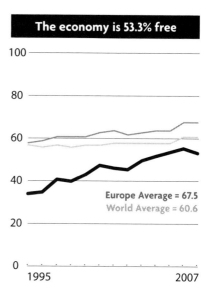
Kiev ★

Ukraine's economy is 53.3 percent free, according to our 2007 assessment, which makes it the world's 125th freest economy. Its overall score is 2.2 percentage points lower than last year, partially reflecting new methodological detail. Ukraine is ranked 40th out of 41 countries in the European region, and its overall score is much lower than the regional average.

Ukraine scores well in trade freedom and fiscal freedom. The average tariff rate is low, although highly complex regulations constitute significant non-tariff barriers. The top personal income and corporate tax rates are relatively low, and overall revenue from taxes is not high as a percentage of GDP.

Ukraine is weaker in freedom from government, monetary freedom, investment freedom, property rights, and freedom from corruption. Inflation is high, and government expenditures equal nearly two-fifths of GDP. While foreign investment is officially welcomed, corruption and arcane regulations are de facto deterrents to capital. The judiciary, subject to pressure from both the government and organized crime, does not always enforce contracts and is tarnished with corruption. Corruption is a major problem throughout the civil service, particularly for a European nation, and the bureaucracy's inefficiency makes many commercial operations difficult.

BACKGROUND: Promises of market openness and economic reform after Ukraine's 2004 "Orange Revolution" have fallen short, and April 2006 elections produced a weak coalition led by the pro-reform "Our Ukraine" party and the more populist Tymoshenko Bloc. Prominent sectors of the economy include services, mining, metals, and manufacturing. Ukraine has benefited heavily from recent price increases for metal and ore. Despite lucrative opportunities for foreign direct investment, economic progress in the near term may be slowed by persistent corruption, steadily increasing gas prices, deteriorating infrastructure, and political deadlock.

How Do We Measure Economic Freedom? See Chapter 3 (page 37) for an explanation of the methodology or visit the *Index* Web site at *heritage.org/index*.

The economy is 53.3% free

100

80

60

40

Europe Average = 67.5
World Average = 60.6

20

0

1995   2007

QUICK FACTS

Population: 47.5 million

GDP (PPP): $303.4 billion
12.1% growth in 2004
8.3% 5-yr. comp. ann. growth
$6,394 per capita

Unemployment: 3.5% (end 2004)

Inflation (CPI): 9.0%

FDI (net inflow): $1.7 billion

Official Development Assistance:
Multilateral: $92 million
Bilateral: $275 million (41% from the U.S.)

External Debt: $21.7 billion

Exports: $39.7 billion
Primarily ferrous and nonferrous metals, fuel, petroleum products, chemicals, machinery, transport equipment, food products

Imports: $34.8 billion
Primarily energy, machinery and equipment, chemicals

UKRAINE'S TEN ECONOMIC FREEDOMS

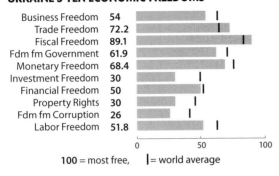

Business Freedom	54
Trade Freedom	72.2
Fiscal Freedom	89.1
Fdm fm Government	61.9
Monetary Freedom	68.4
Investment Freedom	30
Financial Freedom	50
Property Rights	30
Fdm fm Corruption	26
Labor Freedom	51.8

0   50   100

100 = most free, | = world average

BUSINESS FREEDOM — 54%

Starting a business takes an average of 33 days, compared to the world average of 48 days. Obtaining a business license is relatively simple, but closing a business is difficult. Cumbersome regulations are sometimes inconsistent and lacking in transparency. The overall freedom to start, operate, and close a business is restricted by the national regulatory environment.

TRADE FREEDOM — 72.2%

Ukraine's weighted average tariff rate was 3.9 percent in 2002. Import taxes and fees, import licensing requirements, restrictive sanitary and phytosanitary regulations, export subsidies, burdensome and complex standards and certification regulations, and weak enforcement of intellectual property rights add to the cost of trade. Consequently, an additional 20 percent is deducted from Ukraine's trade freedom score to account for these non-tariff barriers.

FISCAL FREEDOM — 89.1%

Ukraine enjoys low tax rates. The top income tax rate is a flat 13 percent, and the top corporate tax rate is 25 percent. Other taxes include a value-added tax (VAT), a land tax, and a vehicle tax. In the most recent year, overall tax revenue as a percentage of GDP was 29.1 percent.

FREEDOM FROM GOVERNMENT — 61.9%

Total government expenditures in Ukraine, including consumption and transfer payments, are high. In the most recent year, government spending equaled 39.4 percent of GDP, and the government received 5.6 percent of its revenues from state-owned enterprises and government ownership of property. Ukraine's economy is still shackled by lingering government interference in private-sector decision-making.

MONETARY FREEDOM — 68.4%

Inflation in Ukraine is high, averaging 11.7 percent between 2003 and 2005. Relatively high and unstable prices explain most of the monetary freedom score. The executive branch is allowed by law to establish high minimum prices for goods and services, and the government further influences prices through regulation and state-owned enterprises and utilities. Consequently, an additional 10 percent is deducted from Ukraine's monetary freedom score to account for these policies.

INVESTMENT FREEDOM — 30%

Foreign investment laws provide equal treatment, with some restrictions in publishing, broadcasting, energy and insurance. Foreign investment is prohibited in weapons manufacturing and alcoholic spirits. Complex regulations and corruption are major deterrents to foreign investment. Resident and non-resident foreign exchange accounts are subject to restrictions and government approval in some cases. Payments and transfers are subject to various requirements and quantitative limits. Some capital transactions are subject to controls and licenses.

FINANCIAL FREEDOM — 50%

Ukraine's financial system is small but growing. Financial regulation and supervision are weak. Banks may offer a wide range of services. Ukraine has 166 licensed banks, most of which are very small, including 28 wholly or partially foreign-owned banks. There are two state-owned banks, and the 10 largest banks account for about half of the net banking assets. A 2002 law eliminated restrictions on foreign participation in the banking system, which may now include 100 percent foreign-owned subsidiaries that operate on par with domestic banks, but foreign bank branches are not permitted. Several large Ukrainian banks have been purchased by foreign investors in recent years, including the second largest Ukrainian bank, which was purchased by an Austrian bank in 2005. Despite 338 registered insurance companies, the insurance sector is small. Foreign insurers may operate in Ukraine but are subject to more restrictions than domestic insurers. Capital markets are underdeveloped and poorly regulated.

PROPERTY RIGHTS — 30%

Protection of property is weak. The judiciary is subject to pressure from the executive and organized crime, and corruption is a serious problem. Contracts are not well enforced, and expropriation is possible.

FREEDOM FROM CORRUPTION — 26%

Corruption is perceived as widespread. Ukraine ranks 107th out of 158 countries in Transparency International's Corruption Perceptions Index for 2005.

LABOR FREEDOM — 51.8%

The labor market operates under inflexible employment regulations that hinder overall productivity growth. The non-salary cost of employing a worker is very high, and dismissing a redundant employee is not easy.

UNITED ARAB EMIRATES

Abu Dhabi

The economy of the United Arab Emirates (UAE) is 60.4 percent free, according to our 2007 assessment, which makes it the world's 74th freest economy. Its overall score is 0.7 percentage point higher than last year, partially reflecting new methodological detail. The UAE is ranked 8th out of 17 countries in the Middle East/North Africa region, and its overall score is higher than the regional average.

The UAE scores well in fiscal freedom, labor freedom, freedom from corruption, and trade freedom. The average tariff rate is not high, but the government issues general import licenses only to nationals. Individual emirates impose their own corporate taxes, but there are no income or corporate taxes at the federal level. The labor market is highly flexible, and there is no minimum wage. The level of corruption is low for a developing nation.

The UAE is weak in business freedom, freedom from government, investment freedom, financial freedom, and property rights. Total government spending equals less than 25 percent of GDP, but state-owned businesses account for more than 75 percent of total tax revenues. Foreign investment is restricted, and even in the free zones, rules mandate majority emirati ownership. Though the UAE is a regional financial hub, its financial sector is subject to considerable government interference. The state also interferes with the courts, which are dominated by the UAE's rulers.

BACKGROUND: The United Arab Emirates is a federation of seven Arab monarchies (Abu Dhabi, Ajman, Dubai, Fujairah, Ras Al-Khaimah, Sharjah, and Umm al-Qaiwain) that gained their independence from Great Britain in 1971. Abu Dhabi accounts for about 90 percent of UAE oil production and has taken a leading role in political and economic decision-making, but many economic policy decisions are made by the rulers of the individual emirates. Dubai has developed into the UAE's foremost center of finance, commerce, transportation, and tourism. UAE nationals continue to rely heavily on a bloated public sector for employment, subsidized services, and government handouts.

How Do We Measure Economic Freedom? See Chapter 3 (page 37) for an explanation of the methodology or visit the *Index* Web site at *heritage.org/index*.

The economy is 60.4% free

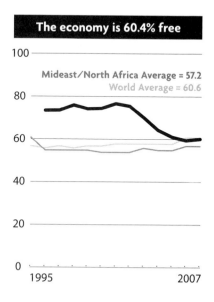

Mideast/North Africa Average = 57.2
World Average = 60.6

QUICK FACTS

Population: 4.3 million

GDP (PPP): $103.9 billion
7.8% growth in 2004
7.1% 5-yr. comp. ann. growth
$24,056 per capita

Unemployment: 2.4% (2001)

Inflation (CPI): 4.6%

FDI (net inflow): $870 million

Official Development Assistance:
Multilateral: None
Bilateral: $5 million (6% from the U.S.)

External Debt: $34.5 billion (2005 estimate)

Exports: $90.6 billion
Primarily crude oil, natural gas, re-exports, dried fish, dates

Imports: $63.4 billion
Primarily machinery, transport equipment, chemicals, food

UAE'S TEN ECONOMIC FREEDOMS

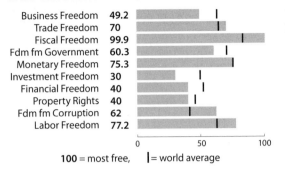

Business Freedom	49.2
Trade Freedom	70
Fiscal Freedom	99.9
Fdm fm Government	60.3
Monetary Freedom	75.3
Investment Freedom	30
Financial Freedom	40
Property Rights	40
Fdm fm Corruption	62
Labor Freedom	77.2

100 = most free, ❙ = world average

BUSINESS FREEDOM — 49.2%

Starting a business takes an average of 63 days, compared to the world average of 48 days. To maximize entrepreneurship and job creation, it should be easier to start a company. Obtaining a business license is relatively simple, but closing a business can be difficult. The overall freedom to start, operate, and close a business is seriously restricted by the national regulatory environment.

TRADE FREEDOM — 70%

The weighted average tariff rate in the UAE was 5 percent in 2005. Non-transparent standards, sanitary and phyto-sanitary regulations, service market access barriers, and inconsistent government procurement regulations add to the cost of trade. Only firms with a trade license may engage in importation, and only UAE nationals may obtain such a license (this provision does not apply to goods imported into free zones). Consequently, an additional 20 percent is deducted from the UAE's trade freedom score to account for these non-tariff barriers.

FISCAL FREEDOM — 99.9%

The UAE has no income tax and no federal-level corporate tax, but different corporate tax rates exist in some emirates (for example, a 55 percent corporate tax rate for foreign oil companies and a 20 percent corporate tax rate for foreign banks. The government also levies a rental tax, and a 7 percent–12 percent federal-level value-added tax is under consideration. In the most recent year, overall tax revenue as a percentage of GDP was 1.7 percent.

FREEDOM FROM GOVERNMENT — 60.3%

Total government expenditures in the UAE, including consumption and transfer payments, are moderate. In the most recent year, government spending equaled 24.3 percent of GDP, and the government received 77.7 percent of its revenues from state-owned enterprises and government ownership of property.

MONETARY FREEDOM — 75.3%

Inflation in the UAE is moderate, averaging 5.4 percent between 2003 and 2005. Relatively moderate and unstable prices explain most of the monetary freedom score. The government influences prices through regulation, subsidies, and numerous state-owned enterprises and utilities, including oil, gas, electricity, and telecommunications.

Consequently, an additional 10 percent is deducted from the UAE's monetary freedom score to account for these policies.

INVESTMENT FREEDOM — 30%

Foreign investment in the UAE is restricted, and foreign investors do not receive national treatment. Except for companies located in the free zones, at least 51 percent of a business establishment must be owned by a UAE national. Non–Gulf Cooperation Council nationals may not own land, and only 22 out of 53 stocks on the UAE stock market are open to foreign investment. There are no controls or requirements on current transfers, access to foreign exchange, or repatriation of profits.

FINANCIAL FREEDOM — 40%

Financial supervision has been strengthened to address money laundering. There are 21 domestic banks (some with federal or local government ownership), 26 foreign bank entities, two investment banks, and 49 representative bank offices. The central bank stopped issuing licenses for new foreign bank branches in the mid-1980s but announced that it would consider permitting new branches if they employed UAE citizens. There is a 20 percent tax on foreign bank profits. In early 2006, the insurance sector had 47 companies, about half of them foreign. The government closed the insurance sector to new foreign entries in 1989 but has announced that it intends to reopen it. Capital markets are relatively developed, and the two stock markets are open to foreign investment, but foreign ownership of companies listed on the stock market is limited to 49 percent, and some companies prohibit foreign ownership. A new regional exchange opened in September 2005.

PROPERTY RIGHTS — 40%

The ruling families exercise considerable influence on the judiciary. Incompetence and corruption are rarely challenged. All land in Abu Dhabi, the largest of the UAE's seven emirates, is owned by the government.

FREEDOM FROM CORRUPTION — 62%

Corruption is perceived as present. The United Arab Emirates ranks 30th out of 158 countries in Transparency International's Corruption Perceptions Index for 2005.

LABOR FREEDOM — 77.2%

The labor market operates under relatively flexible employment regulations that could be improved to enhance overall productivity growth. The non-salary cost of employing a worker is moderate, but dismissing a redundant employee is relatively costly. There is no minimum wage.

2007 Index of Economic Freedom

UNITED KINGDOM

London

Rank: 6

Regional Rank: 1 of 41

The United Kingdom's economy is 81.6 percent free, according to our 2007 assessment, which makes it the world's 6th freest economy. Its overall score is 0.7 percentage point lower than last year, partially reflecting new methodological detail. The United Kingdom is ranked 1st out of 41 countries in the European region, and its overall score is much higher than the regional average.

The United Kingdom scores highly in virtually all areas: investment freedom, trade freedom, financial freedom, property rights, business freedom, and freedom from corruption. The average tariff rate is low, although the government does implement distortionary European Union agricultural tariffs, and business regulation is highly efficient. Almost all commercial operations are simple and transparent, and support for private enterprise is a world model. Inflation is fairly low, and foreign investment is welcome and attracted by a favorable business climate. The United Kingdom's financial sector is modern and a historic world hub. The judiciary, independent of politics and highly trained, should be the envy of the world. Corruption is almost nonexistent, and the labor market is highly flexible, particularly for the European Union.

The U.K. could do slightly better in freedom from government. Total government spending equals more than two-fifths of GDP, although almost none of the government's total tax revenues is received from state-owned businesses.

BACKGROUND: Since implementation of the market reforms instituted by former Prime Minister Margaret Thatcher in the 1980s, the United Kingdom has experienced steady economic growth. The U.K., particularly the City of London, remains one of the world's leading centers of commerce, and exports of manufactured goods, chemicals, and foodstuffs remain strong. However, the fall-off in North Sea oil production has left the U.K. as a net importer of oil, making its economy more susceptible to disruptions in the global energy market.

How Do We Measure Economic Freedom? See Chapter 3 (page 37) for an explanation of the methodology or visit the *Index* Web site at *heritage.org/index*.

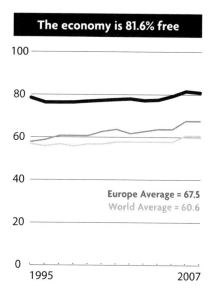

The economy is 81.6% free

100

80

60

40

Europe Average = 67.5
World Average = 60.6

20

0

1995   2007

QUICK FACTS

Population: 59.9 million

GDP (PPP): $1.8 trillion
3.1% growth in 2004
2.8% 5-yr. comp. ann. growth
$30,821 per capita

Unemployment: 4.7%

Inflation (CPI): 3%

FDI (net inflow): $13 billion

Official Development Assistance:
Multilateral: None
Bilateral: None

External Debt: $7.1 trillion (2005)

Exports: $533.2 billion
Primarily manufactured goods, fuels, chemicals, food, beverages, tobacco

Imports: $604.6 billion
Primarily manufactured goods, machinery, fuels, food

UNITED KINGDOM'S TEN ECONOMIC FREEDOMS

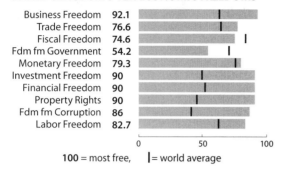

Business Freedom	92.1
Trade Freedom	76.6
Fiscal Freedom	74.6
Fdm fm Government	54.2
Monetary Freedom	79.3
Investment Freedom	90
Financial Freedom	90
Property Rights	90
Fdm fm Corruption	86
Labor Freedom	82.7

0   50   100

100 = most free, | = world average

BUSINESS FREEDOM — 92.1%

Starting a business takes an average of 18 days, compared to the world average of 48 days. To maximize entrepreneurship and job creation, it should be easier to start a company. Obtaining a business license is simple, and closing a business is very easy. The overall freedom to start, operate, and close a business is strongly protected by the national regulatory environment.

TRADE FREEDOM — 76.6%

The United Kingdom's trade policy is the same as those of other members of the European Union. The common EU weighted average tariff rate was 1.7 percent in 2005. Various non-tariff barriers are reflected in EU policy, including agricultural and manufacturing subsidies, regulatory and licensing restrictions, and other market access restrictions. Consequently, an additional 20 percent is deducted from the U.K.'s trade freedom score.

FISCAL FREEDOM — 74.6%

The United Kingdom has a high income tax rate and a moderate corporate tax rate. The top income tax rate is 40 percent, and the top corporate tax rate is 30 percent. Other taxes include a value-added tax (VAT), a tax on insurance contracts, and a vehicle tax. In the most recent year, overall tax revenue as a percentage of GDP was 36.1 percent.

FREEDOM FROM GOVERNMENT — 54.2%

Total government expenditures in the United Kingdom, including consumption and transfer payments, are very high. In the most recent year, government spending equaled 44 percent of GDP, and the government received 1.8 percent of its revenues from state-owned enterprises and government ownership of property.

MONETARY FREEDOM — 79.3%

Inflation in the United Kingdom is low, averaging 2.9 percent between 2003 and 2005. Relatively low and stable prices explain most of the monetary freedom score. As a participant in the EU's Common Agricultural Policy, the government subsidizes agricultural production, distorting the prices of agricultural products. Prices in the United Kingdom are generally set by market forces, but pharmaceutical prices are capped, and the government influences prices through regulation and state-owned utilities. Consequently, an additional 10 percent is deducted from

the U.K.'s monetary freedom score to account for these policies.

INVESTMENT FREEDOM — 90%

Foreign investors receive the same treatment as domestic businesses. The most attractive features of the business environment are deep and sophisticated capital markets, strong macroeconomic fundamentals, and a relatively flexible labor market. The government has the power to block foreign acquisitions but rarely does so in practice. Both residents and non-residents may hold foreign exchange accounts. Payments and proceeds on invisible transactions and current transfers are not subject to restrictions, profits can be repatriated freely, and there are no controls on real estate transactions. The government can prohibit the transfer of control of important domestic manufacturing to a non-resident if the transaction is determined not to be in the national interest.

FINANCIAL FREEDOM — 90%

The U.K. has a well-developed, competitive financial system that offers all forms of financial services. Credit is allocated on market terms. Supervision is prudent, regulations are transparent and undemanding, and the sector is overseen by an independent institution. Universal banking is permitted. The banking sector is the third largest in the world, and nearly 100 British banks and nearly 400 foreign-controlled banks were operating in 2005. There were also a number of credit unions. There are no government banks, although some government agencies provide grants and financing, and the Post Office provides some personal banking services. The insurance market is the world's third largest. Most large foreign insurers are represented in the U.K., and many account for significant market shares. The London Stock Exchange is one of the world's largest exchanges.

PROPERTY RIGHTS — 90%

Property rights are highly respected and well enforced. Contracts are secure, and the judiciary is of very high quality.

FREEDOM FROM CORRUPTION — 86%

Corruption is perceived as minimal. The United Kingdom ranks 11th out of 158 countries in Transparency International's Corruption Perceptions Index for 2005.

LABOR FREEDOM — 82.7%

The labor market operates under flexible employment regulations that enhance overall productivity growth. The non-salary cost of employing a worker is moderate, but dismissing a redundant employee can be relatively costly.

UNITED STATES

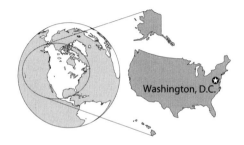

Washington, D.C.

Rank: 4

Regional Rank: 1 of 29

The economy of the United States is 82 percent free, according to our 2007 assessment, which makes it the world's 4th freest economy. Its overall score is 0.4 percentage point lower than last year, partially reflecting new methodological detail. The United States is ranked 1st out of 29 countries in the Americas, and its overall score is much higher than the regional average.

The United States enjoys high levels of investment freedom, trade freedom, financial freedom, property rights, business freedom, and freedom from corruption. The average tariff rate is low, although there are several non-tariff barriers. Almost all commercial operations are simple and transparent. Foreign investment is welcome and subject to the same rules as national capital. Financial markets are open to foreign competition and are the world's most dynamic and modern. The judiciary is independent and of consistently high quality. Corruption is low, as befits a Western democracy, and the labor market is highly flexible.

America could do slightly better in fiscal freedom and freedom from government. Total government spending equals more than a third of GDP, although the percentage of total revenue received from state-owned enterprises and government ownership of property is low. Corporate and personal taxes are moderately high.

BACKGROUND: The United States is the world's dominant economy. With over two centuries of a fundamentally free, constitutionally protected economy, America benefits from its massive scale and intrastate competition. Trade barriers among the 50 states are unconstitutional, for example, allowing for the free movement of goods and labor. However, troubling changes include the weakening of property rights caused by the Supreme Court's 2005 ruling in *Kelo v. City of New London*. Burdensome accounting regulations under Sarbanes–Oxley legislation are also a concern. Most alarming, America's major political parties are unwilling to curb growing government expenditures, particularly public entitlements.

How Do We Measure Economic Freedom? See Chapter 3 (page 37) for an explanation of the methodology or visit the *Index* Web site at *heritage.org/index*.

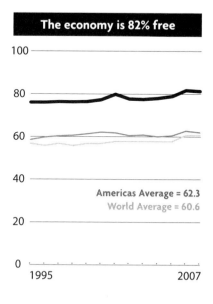

The economy is 82% free

100

80

60

40

Americas Average = 62.3
World Average = 60.6

20

0

1995   2007

QUICK FACTS

Population: 293.7 million

GDP (PPP): $11.7 trillion
    4.2% growth in 2004
    2.6% 5-yr. comp. ann. growth
    $39,676 per capita

Unemployment: 5.5%

Inflation (CPI): 2.7%

FDI (net inflow): −$133.4 billion

Official Development Assistance:
Multilateral: None
Bilateral: None

External Debt: $8.8 trillion (2005 estimate)

Exports: $1.2 trillion
Primarily soybeans, fruit, corn, industrial supplies, transistors, aircraft, motor vehicle parts, computers

Imports: $1.8 trillion
Primarily agricultural products, industrial supplies, computers, telecommunications, motor vehicle parts, electric power machinery, automobiles

UNITED STATES' TEN ECONOMIC FREEDOMS

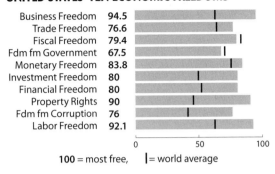

Business Freedom	94.5
Trade Freedom	76.6
Fiscal Freedom	79.4
Fdm fm Government	67.5
Monetary Freedom	83.8
Investment Freedom	80
Financial Freedom	80
Property Rights	90
Fdm fm Corruption	76
Labor Freedom	92.1

100 = most free, | = world average

BUSINESS FREEDOM — 94.5%

Starting a business takes an average of five days, compared to the world average of 48 days. The business environment has allowed entrepreneurship to flourish. Obtaining a business license is simple, and closing a business is very easy. The overall freedom to start, operate, and close a business is strongly protected by the national regulatory environment.

TRADE FREEDOM — 76.6%

The weighted average U.S. tariff rate was 1.7 percent in 2005. High out-of-quota tariffs, anti-dumping provisions, countervailing duties, export controls, service market access restrictions, and export promotion programs and subsidies add to the cost of trade. Consequently, an additional 20 percent is deducted from the U.S. trade freedom score to account for these non-tariff barriers.

FISCAL FREEDOM — 79.4%

The United States has burdensome tax rates. Both the top income tax rate and the top corporate tax rate are 35 percent. Other taxes include a property tax, an estate tax, and excise taxes. In the most recent year, overall tax revenue as a percentage of GDP was 25.4 percent.

FREEDOM FROM GOVERNMENT — 67.5%

Total government expenditures in the U.S., including consumption and transfer payments, are high. In the most recent year, government spending equaled 36.4 percent of GDP, and the government received 4.8 percent of its revenues from state-owned enterprises and government ownership of property.

MONETARY FREEDOM — 83.8%

Inflation in the U.S. is moderate, averaging 3.1 percent between 2003 and 2005. Relatively moderate and unstable prices explain most of the monetary freedom score. Price controls apply to some regulated monopolies; certain states and localities control residential rents; Hawaii imposes caps on gasoline prices; and the government influences prices through subsidies, particularly for the agricultural sector, dairy products, and some forms of transportation. Consequently, an additional 5 percent is deducted from the United States' monetary freedom score to account for these policies.

INVESTMENT FREEDOM — 80%

Foreign and domestic enterprises are treated equally under the law, and foreign investors are not required to register with or seek approval from the federal government. However, foreign investors face restrictions in banking, mining, defense contracting, certain energy-related industries, fishing, shipping, communications, and aviation. The government also restricts foreign acquisitions that threaten to impair national security. There are no controls or requirements on current transfers, access to foreign exchange, or repatriation of profits. Purchase of real estate is unrestricted on a national level, but the purchase of agricultural land by foreign nationals or companies must be reported to the government.

FINANCIAL FREEDOM — 80%

The United States has the world's most dynamic and developed financial markets. Reform in 1999 eliminated barriers to entry; removed barriers between commercial banks, insurance companies, and securities firms; and permitted a wider range of services. The reforms facilitated consolidation, led to universal financial services companies, and enhanced the competitiveness of U.S. banking. Federal and state governments share regulatory responsibility for banks. Regulations are generally straightforward, undemanding, and consistent with international standards, although concerns have been raised about the intrusive nature and cost of the 2002 Sarbanes–Oxley Act. Foreign financial institutions are subject to the same restrictions as domestic banks. Direct government involvement in banking and finance prominently includes the Federal National Mortgage Association (Fannie Mae) and Federal Home Mortgage Loan Corporation (Freddie Mac), which enjoy privileged treatment and account for about half of U.S. home mortgages. Foreign participation in the equities and insurance markets is substantial and competitive.

PROPERTY RIGHTS — 90%

Property rights are guaranteed. Contracts are very secure, and the judiciary is independent and of high quality. The courts recognize foreign arbitration and court rulings.

FREEDOM FROM CORRUPTION — 76%

Corruption is perceived as minimal. The United States ranks 17th out of 158 countries in Transparency International's Corruption Perceptions Index for 2005.

LABOR FREEDOM — 92.1%

The labor market operates under highly flexible employment regulations that enhance overall productivity growth. The non-salary cost of employing a worker is low, and dismissing a redundant employee is costless.

URUGUAY

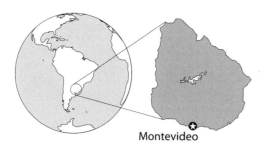

Montevideo

Rank: 33
Regional Rank: 8 of 29

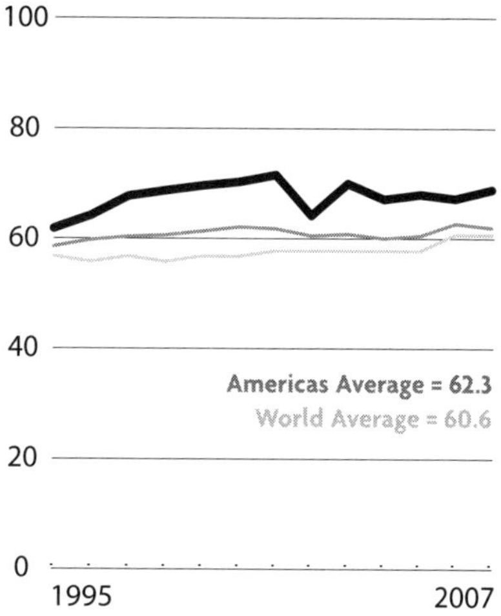

U ruguay's economy is 69.3 percent free, according to our 2007 assessment, which makes it the world's 33rd freest economy. Its overall score is 1.8 percentage points higher than last year, partially reflecting new methodological detail. Uruguay is ranked 8th out of 29 countries in the Americas, and its overall score is higher than the regional average.

Uruguay enjoys high levels of investment freedom, trade freedom, property rights, freedom from corruption, and fiscal freedom. The average tariff rate is fairly low, although non-tariff barriers are extensive, and while bureaucratic procedures can be time-consuming, business regulation is relatively simple. The boom in private enterprise and lack of a personal income tax have given Uruguay Latin America's fourth highest GDP per capita. Foreign investment is permitted in almost all sectors, and the government has never expropriated foreign capital. The judiciary is independent of politics and free of corruption but can be subject to bureaucratic delays. Uruguay's labor market is highly flexible, and firing a redundant worker is easy.

Uruguay could do slightly better in financial freedom and monetary freedom. Inflation is fairly high, and the government fixes the prices of a few staples. The financial sector is small and subject to government interference, although this is partially a response to financial crises in nearby Argentina and Brazil.

BACKGROUND: Uruguay has a history of stable democratic government and a small economy based largely on beef and wool exports. Today, wood and software are gaining market share, and the government is increasingly trade-friendly. Despite being a founding member of MERCO-SUR (the Southern Cone Common Market), Uruguay has signed a bilateral investment treaty with the United States, which is now its major trade partner, and has proposed free-trade accords with the U.S. and China. Uruguay's rule of law rivals Chile's, and the country has Latin America's fourth highest GDP per capita.

How Do We Measure Economic Freedom? See Chapter 3 (page 37) for an explanation of the methodology or visit the *Index* Web site at *heritage.org/index*.

The economy is 69.3% free

Americas Average = 62.3
World Average = 60.6

1995 — 2007

QUICK FACTS

Population: 3.4 million

GDP (PPP): $32.4 billion
12.3% growth in 2004
−0.6% 5-yr. comp. ann. growth
$9,421 per capita

Unemployment: 12.2% (2005 estimate)

Inflation (CPI): 9.2%

FDI (net inflow): $299.5 million

Official Development Assistance:
Multilateral: $15 million
Bilateral: $19 million (3% from the U.S.)

External Debt: $12.4 billion

Exports: $4.0 billion
Primarily meat, rice, leather products, wool, fish, dairy products

Imports: $3.7 billion
Primarily machinery, chemicals, road vehicles, crude petroleum

URUGUAY'S TEN ECONOMIC FREEDOMS

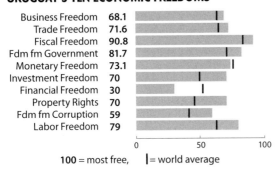

Business Freedom	68.1
Trade Freedom	71.6
Fiscal Freedom	90.8
Fdm fm Government	81.7
Monetary Freedom	73.1
Investment Freedom	70
Financial Freedom	30
Property Rights	70
Fdm fm Corruption	59
Labor Freedom	79

0   50   100

100 = most free, | = world average

BUSINESS FREEDOM — *68.1%*

Starting a business takes an average of 43 days, compared to the world average of 48 days. To maximize entrepreneurship and job creation, it should be easier to start a company. Both obtaining a business license and closing a business are relatively simple, although bureaucratic obstacles and delays remain problems. The overall freedom to start, operate, and close a business is relatively well protected by the national regulatory environment.

TRADE FREEDOM — *71.6%*

Uruguay's weighted average tariff rate was 4.2 percent in 2004. Import bans and restrictions, import taxes and fees, quotas, import licensing requirements, protectionist anti-dumping and safeguard provisions, and customs delays all add to the cost of trade. Consequently, an additional 20 percent is deducted from Uruguay's trade freedom score to account for these non-tariff barriers.

FISCAL FREEDOM — *90.8%*

Uruguay imposes no income tax, and its top corporate tax rate is 30 percent. Other taxes include a value-added tax (VAT), a capital tax, and a property transfer tax. In the most recent year, overall tax revenue as a percentage of GDP was 21.9 percent.

FREEDOM FROM GOVERNMENT — *81.7%*

Total government expenditures in Uruguay, including consumption and transfer payments, are moderate. In the most recent year, government spending equaled 27.2 percent of GDP, and the government received 3 percent of its revenues from state-owned enterprises and government ownership of property.

MONETARY FREEDOM — *73.1%*

Inflation in Uruguay is high, averaging 7.1 percent between 2003 and 2005. Relatively high and unstable prices explain most of the monetary freedom score. Uruguay has eliminated most price controls, but the executive branch continues to fix prices on certain staples, including milk, and the government influences prices through regulation and numerous state-owned enterprises and utilities, including energy, petroleum products, and telecommunications. Consequently, an additional 10 percent is deducted from Uruguay's monetary freedom score to account for these policies.

INVESTMENT FREEDOM — *70%*

Foreign investors face few restrictions outside of state-monopoly sectors. Uruguay has traditionally met all of its commitments to foreign investors and has never confiscated any foreign capital. State monopolies include electricity, hydrocarbons, railroads, some minerals, port administration, and telecommunications, although the government permits some of these monopolies to forge private partnerships. Both residents and non-residents may hold foreign exchange accounts. There are no restrictions or controls on payments, transactions, transfers, or repatriation of profits. Non-residents may purchase real estate.

FINANCIAL FREEDOM — *30%*

Uruguay's small financial system is subject to heavy government influence. Economic crises in Argentina and Brazil spurred a financial crisis in Uruguay and led to the closing of four major banks. The assets of those banks were grouped into the new state-owned (but privately managed) Nuevo Banco Comercial in 2003. Uruguay's banking system now includes the central bank, three state-owned banks, 23 private banks, and 15 other financial institutions. The state-owned Banco de la República Oriental del Uruguay is the country's largest bank, and the state-owned Banco Hipotecario del Uruguay is the leading mortgage lender. Most private banks are foreign bank branches. Long-term banking credit has been scarce since the 2002 financial crisis. Insurance was a government monopoly until 1996, when the government opened most insurance sectors to private competition. The government-owned Banco de Seguros del Estadoize still dominates the sector, accounting for over half of the market. Capital markets are underdeveloped and concentrated in government debt. The two stock exchanges listed only 19 firms in 2006, and trading is negligible.

PROPERTY RIGHTS — *70%*

Private property is generally secure, and expropriation is unlikely. Contracts are enforced properly, although the judiciary tends to be slow. The government has established a Settlement and Arbitration Center to improve investment relations.

FREEDOM FROM CORRUPTION — *59%*

Corruption is perceived as present. Uruguay ranks 32nd out of 158 countries in Transparency International's Corruption Perceptions Index for 2005.

LABOR FREEDOM — *79%*

The labor market operates under relatively flexible employment regulations that enhance overall productivity growth. The non-salary cost of employing a worker is low, and dismissing a redundant employee is relatively easy.

UZBEKISTAN

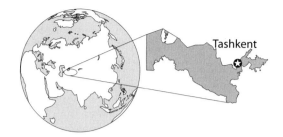
Tashkent

U zbekistan's economy is 52.6 percent free, according to our 2007 assessment, which makes it the world's 132nd freest economy. Its overall score is 2.2 percentage points higher than last year, partially reflecting new methodological detail. Uzbekistan is ranked 24th out of 30 countries in the Asia–Pacific region, and its overall score is lower than the regional average.

Uzbekistan enjoys high levels of fiscal freedom, labor freedom, business freedom, and trade freedom. The top personal income tax rate is moderately high, but the top corporate tax rate is low, and overall tax revenue equals little more than 20 percent of national GDP. Uzbekistan's labor market is flexible. Commercial licensing and bankruptcy procedures are costly, but opening a business is easy, and the average tariff rate is moderate.

Uzbekistan is weaker in monetary freedom, investment freedom, financial freedom, property rights, and freedom from corruption. Inflation is disastrously high, and the government controls the prices of a variety of goods through state monopolies. While foreign investment is officially welcome, opaque bureaucratic procedures and political interference are disincentives. The courts are subject to political interference, and corruption is rampant throughout the civil service.

BACKGROUND: Uzbekistan, created after the Bolshevik occupation of Turkestan in the 1920s, achieved its independence from the Soviet Union in 1991 after over 120 years of Russian and Soviet rule. President Islam Karimov has ruled since the late 1980s and, since the violent Islamist insurrection in Andijan in May 2005, has intensified the suppression of opponents. Uzbekistan relies heavily on natural gas, gold, and cotton production as sources of export revenue. Efforts at privatization are expected to remain sluggish because of the harsh investment environment and the government's reluctance to cede majority control over strategic enterprises.

How Do We Measure Economic Freedom? See Chapter 3 (page 37) for an explanation of the methodology or visit the *Index* Web site at *heritage.org/index.*

The economy is 52.6% free

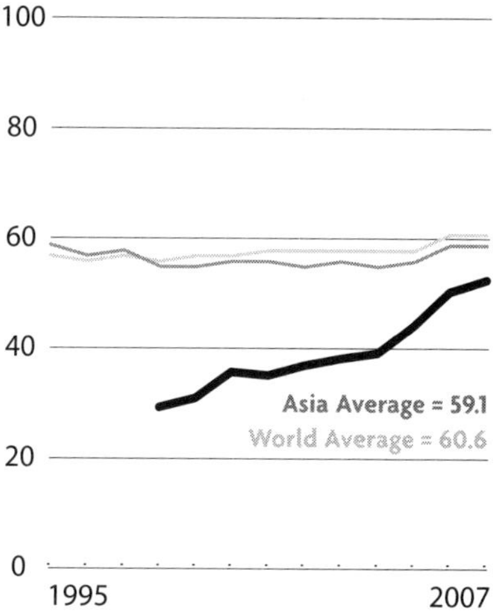

100

80

60

40

Asia Average = 59.1
World Average = 60.6

20

0

1995   2007

QUICK FACTS

Population: 26.2 million

GDP (PPP): $49.0 billion
7.4% growth in 2004
3.9% 5-yr. comp. ann. growth
$1,869 per capita

Unemployment: 0.6% (2004 estimate)

Inflation (CPI): 8.8%

FDI (net inflow): $140 million (gross)

Official Development Assistance:
Multilateral: $25 million
Bilateral: $222 million (28% from the U.S.)

External Debt: $5.0 billion

Exports: $4.3 billion
Primarily cotton, gold, energy products, mineral fertilizers, ferrous metals, textiles, food products, automobiles

Imports: $3.1 billion
Primarily machinery and equipment, food, chemicals, metals

UZBEKISTAN'S TEN ECONOMIC FREEDOMS

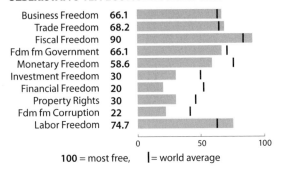

Business Freedom	66.1
Trade Freedom	68.2
Fiscal Freedom	90
Fdm fm Government	66.1
Monetary Freedom	58.6
Investment Freedom	30
Financial Freedom	20
Property Rights	30
Fdm fm Corruption	22
Labor Freedom	74.7

0   50   100

100 = most free, | = world average

BUSINESS FREEDOM — 66.1%

Starting a business takes an average of 29 days, compared to the world average of 48 days. Both obtaining a business license and closing a business are difficult. The regulatory burden makes it costly for small companies to operate in the formal economy. Regulations are sometimes inconsistent and unevenly applied, lacking transparency. The overall freedom to start, operate, and close a business is relatively well protected by the national regulatory environment.

TRADE FREEDOM — 68.2%

Uzbekistan's weighted average tariff rate was 5.9 percent in 2001. Discriminatory import taxes and fees, import licensing requirements, currency controls, non-transparent and burdensome standards and certification regulations, export subsidies, service market access barriers, weak enforcement of intellectual property rights, and inefficient customs implementation add to the cost of trade. Consequently, an additional 20 percent is deducted from Uzbekistan's trade freedom score to account for these non-tariff barriers.

FISCAL FREEDOM — 90%

Uzbekistan has a moderate income tax rate and a low corporate tax rate. The top income tax rate is 29 percent, and the top corporate tax rate is 12 percent. The government is considering reducing the top tax rates to 25 percent and 10 percent, respectively. Other taxes include a value-added tax (VAT) and a property tax. In the most recent year, overall tax revenue as a percentage of GDP was 22.7 percent.

FREEDOM FROM GOVERNMENT — 66.1%

Total government expenditures in Uzbekistan, including consumption and transfer payments, are moderate. In the most recent year, government spending equaled 32 percent of GDP, and the government received 30.1 percent of its revenues from state-owned enterprises and government ownership of property. State control of the economy is still extensive and hinders development of the private sector.

MONETARY FREEDOM — 58.6%

Inflation in Uzbekistan is very high, averaging 17.5 percent between 2003 and 2005. Highly unstable prices explain most of the monetary freedom score. The government influences prices through extensive regulation, subsidies, and numerous state-owned enterprises and utilities. The government controls prices primarily by declaring companies or certain products national or regional monopolies, which automatically requires official review and approval of prices for such products. Consequently, an additional 15 percent is deducted from Uzbekistan's monetary freedom score to account for these policies.

INVESTMENT FREEDOM — 30%

Officially, all sectors of the economy are open to foreign investment except for industries the government deems "strategic" (mining, agriculture, and machinery manufacturing). In practice, investors face numerous unofficial barriers, including cumbersome procedures, the threat of expropriation, and corruption. Residents and non-residents may hold foreign exchange accounts, subject to some restrictions. Payments and transfers face quantitative limits and bona fide tests. Some capital transactions, including credit operations and real estate transactions, are subject to controls.

FINANCIAL FREEDOM — 20%

Uzbekistan's financial sector is underdeveloped and subject to heavy government intervention. The banking sector includes 29 banks, most of which are privately owned. The government controls three large banks, totaling about 70 percent of the country's foreign exchange business and 60 percent of banking sector assets. Government-controlled banks support the government's economic priorities through subsidized loans offered to specific sectors. The government uses the banking system to collect and enforce taxes by freezing the accounts of those who are believed to be evading taxes. The government withdrew the license of the largest private joint-stock commercial bank in 2005. Foreign banks may operate only in a subsidiary status, and all routine banking operations require government permission. The insurance sector is minimal. Uzbek law grants state-owned companies a monopoly over certain forms of insurance. Capital markets are virtually nonexistent, and the stock market is very small.

PROPERTY RIGHTS — 30%

The government influences the judiciary. Judicial procedures fall short of international standards, corruption is extensive, and expropriation is possible.

FREEDOM FROM CORRUPTION — 22%

Corruption is perceived as widespread. Uzbekistan ranks 137th out of 158 countries in Transparency International's Corruption Perceptions Index for 2005.

LABOR FREEDOM — 74.7%

The labor market operates under relatively flexible employment regulations that could be improved to enhance overall productivity growth. The non-salary cost of employing a worker is high, but dismissing a redundant employee is relatively easy.

VENEZUELA

Caracas

Rank: 144
Regional Rank: 28 of 29

Venezuela's economy is 47.7 percent free, according to our 2007 assessment, which makes it the world's 144th freest economy. Its overall score is 2.6 percentage points higher than last year, partially reflecting new methodological detail. Venezuela is ranked 28th out of 29 countries in the Americas, and its overall score is much lower than the regional average.

Venezuela scores fairly well only in fiscal freedom. The top income and corporate taxes are relatively high, but overall tax revenue is relatively low as a percentage of GDP.

As a staunchly socialist nation, Venezuela is weak in labor freedom, financial freedom, investment freedom, monetary freedom, freedom from government, property rights, and freedom from corruption. The commercial regulatory process is burdensome and confusing. The judiciary is heavily influenced by the government and does not enforce contracts well. The labor market is rigid, and the financial market, though sophisticated, has become more vulnerable to political interference. Corruption pervades the civil service and, along with the likelihood of expropriation, helps to deter foreign investment. Inflation is extremely high, and the government has the power to set prices.

BACKGROUND: Since his initial election in 1998, President Hugo Chávez has engaged in a military buildup, adopted draconian libel laws to constrain the media, hobbled opponents through electoral manipulation, imposed foreign exchange controls on the private sector, and politicized the state oil industry, which dominates the economy. Manufacturing and agricultural products like cocoa and coffee comprise a small share of GDP. Although Chávez promised to help the poor, Venezuela's National Statistics Institute has calculated that poverty rose from 43.9 percent to 55.1 percent from 1998 to 2003.

How Do We Measure Economic Freedom? See Chapter 3 (page 37) for an explanation of the methodology or visit the *Index* Web site at *heritage.org/index*.

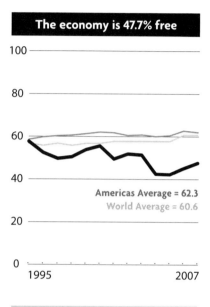

The economy is 47.7% free

Americas Average = 62.3
World Average = 60.6

1995 — 2007

QUICK FACTS

Population: 26.1 million

GDP (PPP): $157.9 billion
17.9% growth in 2004
1.2% 5-yr. comp. ann. growth
$6,043 per capita

Unemployment: 15.1%

Inflation (CPI): 21.8%

FDI (net inflow): $1.9 billion

Official Development Assistance:
Multilateral: $20 million
Bilateral: $34 million (26% from the U.S.)

External Debt: $35.6 billion

Exports: $39.8 billion
Primarily crude oil, marine products, rice, coffee, rubber, tea, garments, shoes

Imports: $22 billion
Primarily machinery and equipment, petroleum products, fertilizer, steel products, raw cotton, grain, cement, motorcycles

VENEZUELA'S TEN ECONOMIC FREEDOMS

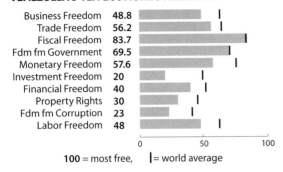

Business Freedom	48.8
Trade Freedom	56.2
Fiscal Freedom	83.7
Fdm fm Government	69.5
Monetary Freedom	57.6
Investment Freedom	20
Financial Freedom	40
Property Rights	30
Fdm fm Corruption	23
Labor Freedom	48

0   50   100

100 = most free, | = world average

BUSINESS FREEDOM — 48.8%

Starting a business takes an average of 141 days, compared to the world average of 48 days. To maximize entrepreneurship and job creation, it should be easier to start a company. Obtaining a business license can be difficult, and closing a business is very difficult. Complicated regulations are sometimes inconsistent, causing unreliability of interpretation. The overall freedom to start, operate, and close a business is seriously restricted by the national regulatory environment.

TRADE FREEDOM — 56.2%

Venezuela's weighted average tariff rate was 11.9 percent in 2004. Discriminatory import licensing requirements, import bans and restrictions, mismanagement of tariff rate quotas, currency controls, non-transparent and burdensome standards and labeling regulations, export subsidies, service market access barriers, weak enforcement of intellectual property rights, and inefficient customs implementation add to the cost of trade. Consequently, an additional 20 percent is deducted from Venezuela's trade freedom score to account for these non-tariff barriers.

FISCAL FREEDOM — 83.7%

Venezuela has burdensome tax rates. Both the top income tax rate and the top corporate tax rate are 34 percent. Other taxes include a value-added tax (VAT) and a property tax. In the most recent year, overall tax revenue as a percentage of GDP was 11.5 percent.

FREEDOM FROM GOVERNMENT — 69.5%

Total government expenditures in Venezuela, including consumption and transfer payments, are moderate. In the most recent year, government spending equaled 26.7 percent of GDP, and the government received 41.6 percent of its revenues from state-owned enterprises and government ownership of property.

MONETARY FREEDOM — 57.6%

Inflation in Venezuela is high, averaging 18.7 percent between 2003 and 2005. Relatively high and unstable prices explain most of the monetary freedom score. The government has the authority to control most prices through extensive regulation, subsidies, and numerous state-owned enterprises and utilities and protects agricultural producers through a non-legislated system of guaranteed minimum

prices. Consequently, an additional 15 percent is deducted from Venezuela's monetary freedom score to account for these policies.

INVESTMENT FREEDOM — 20%

The government restricts certain types of investment and requires that certain professions be licensed in Venezuela. Foreign equity participation in media companies is limited to 20 percent, and the number of foreign workers that foreign companies may hire is limited. The government controls key sectors of the economy, including oil, petrochemicals, and much of the mining and aluminum industries. Expropriation is likely. The government controls foreign exchange and fixes the exchange rate. Special regulations exist for a range of transactions including foreign investment, remittances, foreign private debt, imports, exports, insurance and reinsurance, and the airline industry.

FINANCIAL FREEDOM — 40%

Venezuela's financial system is relatively well developed but subject to growing government influence. As of November 2005, there were 51 financial institutions (43 private and eight state-owned). Foreign banks may acquire existing banks, create a new wholly owned foreign bank, or establish a branch; and they accounted for over 30 percent of loans as of March 2005. The government created a new bank in 2005 to centralize public-sector resources, now largely held in private institutions, and act as its financial agent. The government increasingly directs financial institutions to provide credit in accordance with its requirements, and even the central bank is subject to government influence. Maximum and minimum levels for lending and deposit interest rates were established in 2005. There were 50 insurance companies as of April 2005, and the top two insurers were foreign-owned. Capital markets are relatively small. Foreign companies may participate legally in capital markets and may buy shares in Venezuelan companies, either directly or on the stock exchange.

PROPERTY RIGHTS — 30%

Property rights are weakly protected. The judiciary is influenced by the executive, and the government routinely backs off from "inconvenient" contracts, particularly in the oil sector.

FREEDOM FROM CORRUPTION — 23%

Corruption is perceived as widespread. Venezuela ranks 130th out of 158 countries in Transparency International's Corruption Perceptions Index for 2005.

LABOR FREEDOM — 48%

The labor market operates under highly inflexible employment regulations that hinder overall productivity growth. The non-salary cost of employing a worker is moderate, but dismissing a redundant employee is costly. Regulations related to increasing or contracting the number of work hours are rigid.

VIETNAM

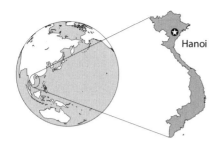

Hanoi

Rank: 138

Regional Rank: 25 of 30

Vietnam's economy is 50 percent free, according to our 2007 assessment, which makes it the world's 138th freest economy. Its overall score is unchanged since last year. Vietnam is ranked 25th out of 30 countries in the Asia–Pacific region, and its overall score is much lower than the regional average.

Vietnam has high levels of fiscal freedom and freedom from government. While the government imposes high personal tax rates, overall tax revenue is not large as a percentage of GDP. Total government expenditures equal about a fourth of national GDP, and state-owned businesses constitute a minor source of revenue. Commercial licensing is fairly simple, although other business regulatory procedures can be difficult.

Vietnam suffers from weak trade freedom, investment freedom, financial freedom, property rights, and freedom from corruption. Although it is undergoing reform, the financial sector is neither well-regulated nor independent of the government. Foreign investment is subject to an array of opaque regulations and cannot be guaranteed legally. The judiciary is subject to political influence, and commercial cases often take years to reach resolution. Corruption is a serious problem in the legal system, as well as for the civil service as a whole. Tariffs are extremely high and supplemented by regulatory non-tariff barriers.

BACKGROUND: The Socialist Republic of Vietnam continues to reform its economy while maintaining a single-party state. The most significant development during 2006 was an agreement in principle with the United States on a bilateral market access agreement that will clear the way for Vietnam to join the World Trade Organization. The economy is liberalizing slowly. Services and industry account for a large share of GDP even though they employ less than half the population. The majority of Vietnamese still work in agriculture.

How Do We Measure Economic Freedom? See Chapter 3 (page 37) for an explanation of the methodology or visit the *Index* Web site at *heritage.org/index*.

The economy is 50% free

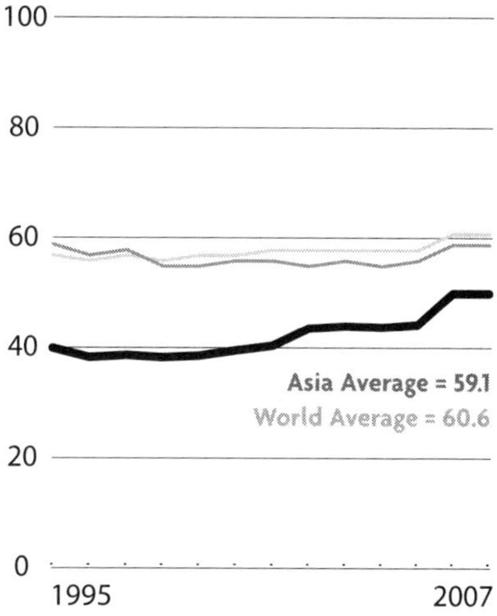

Asia Average = 59.1
World Average = 60.6

1995 — 2007

QUICK FACTS

Population: 82.2 million

GDP (PPP): $225.5 billion
7.7% growth in 2004
7.2% 5-yr. comp. ann. growth
$2,745 per capita

Unemployment: 2.4% (2005 estimate)

Inflation (CPI): 7.8%

FDI (net inflow): $1.6 billion (gross)

Official Development Assistance:
Multilateral: $701 million
Bilateral: $1.3 billion (3% from the U.S.)

External Debt: $17.8 billion

Exports: $29.9 billion
Primarily crude oil, marine products, rice, coffee, rubber, tea, garments, shoes

Imports: $33.3 billion
Primarily machinery and equipment, petroleum products, fertilizer, steel products, raw cotton, grain, cement, motorcycles

VIETNAM'S TEN ECONOMIC FREEDOMS

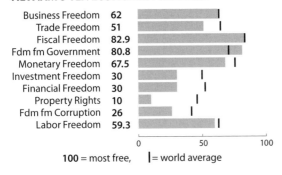

Business Freedom	62
Trade Freedom	51
Fiscal Freedom	82.9
Fdm fm Government	80.8
Monetary Freedom	67.5
Investment Freedom	30
Financial Freedom	30
Property Rights	10
Fdm fm Corruption	26
Labor Freedom	59.3

100 = most free, I = world average

BUSINESS FREEDOM — 62%

Starting a business takes an average of 50 days, compared to the world average of 48 days. To maximize entrepreneurship and job creation, it should be easier to start a company. Obtaining a business license is relatively simple, but closing a business can be difficult. Although the government has started to streamline the regulatory process in recent years, the process is still characterized by a general lack of transparency. The overall freedom to start, operate, and close a business is restricted by the national regulatory environment.

TRADE FREEDOM — 51%

Vietnam's weighted average tariff rate was 14.5 percent in 2004. The government has made progress toward liberalizing the trade regime, but import bans and restrictions, export restrictions, import licensing requirements, burdensome pharmaceutical standards, restrictive sanitary and phytosanitary regulations, export subsidies, service market access barriers, weak enforcement of intellectual property rights, corruption, and inconsistent customs implementation add to the cost of trade. Consequently, an additional 20 percent is deducted from Vietnam's trade freedom score to account for these non-tariff barriers.

FISCAL FREEDOM — 82.9%

Vietnam has a high income tax rate and a moderate corporate tax rate. The top income tax rate is 40 percent, and the top corporate tax rate is 28 percent. Other taxes include a value-added tax (VAT) and a business licensing tax. In the most recent year, overall tax revenue as a percentage of GDP was 13.6 percent.

FREEDOM FROM GOVERNMENT — 80.8%

Total government expenditures in Vietnam, including consumption and transfer payments, are moderate. In the most recent year, government spending equaled 26.7 percent of GDP, and the government received 7.8 percent of its revenues from state-owned enterprises and government ownership of property. Progress in reforming state enterprises has been confined mainly to the smaller ones.

MONETARY FREEDOM — 67.5%

Inflation in Vietnam is high, averaging 7.7 percent between 2003 and 2005. Such unstable prices explain most of the monetary freedom score. The government controls prices to stem inflation and also influences prices through regulation, subsidies, and state-owned enterprises and utilities, including electricity, gasoline, telecommunications, water, and fares for train and air travel. Consequently, an additional 15 percent is deducted from Vietnam's monetary freedom score to account for these policies.

INVESTMENT FREEDOM — 30%

Vietnam's regulatory and financial system is cumbersome and corrupt. Obtaining a license is a lengthy process. The courts are unable to enforce rules transparently and consistently. The government limits the employment of foreign workers. Both residents and non-residents may hold foreign exchange accounts, subject to restrictions and government approval for resident accounts held abroad. Payments and transfers are subject to restrictions, including requirements for government approval over established amounts. Most transactions in money market and capital instruments, derivatives, commercial credits, and direct investments either are prohibited or require government approval. Foreigners may not own land but can lease it from the government.

FINANCIAL FREEDOM — 30%

Despite reform efforts, the government remains heavily involved in the financial sector. Regulations, supervision, and transparency fall short of international standards. The central bank is not independent. Of 63 commercial banks, five are state-run, and four of them provide about 70 percent of all lending. A March 2006 decree permits fully foreign-owned banks to open in Vietnam, subject to some restrictions and conditions. Lending from state banks is still used as an arm of government policy in some cases, particularly with subsidized interest rates and debt relief to farmers and large state-owned enterprises. Non-performing loans are a problem. The insurance sector is small, and the largest insurer is state-owned. Capital markets are very small. Trading on Vietnam's first stock market, founded in 2000, has been light.

PROPERTY RIGHTS — 10%

The judiciary is not independent. Corruption among judges and court clerks is common. Contractual agreements are weakly enforced, and disputes can take years to resolve.

FREEDOM FROM CORRUPTION — 26%

Corruption is perceived as widespread. Vietnam ranks 107th out of 158 countries in Transparency International's Corruption Perceptions Index for 2005.

LABOR FREEDOM — 59.3%

The labor market operates under inflexible employment regulations that hinder overall productivity growth. The non-salary cost of employing a worker is high, and dismissing a redundant employee is relatively costly.

YEMEN

Sanaa

Yemen's economy is 53.8 percent free, according to our 2007 assessment, which makes it the world's 122nd freest economy. Its overall score is 3 percentage points higher than last year, partially reflecting new methodological detail. Yemen is ranked 12th out of 17 countries in the Middle East/North Africa region, and its overall score is slightly lower than the regional average.

Yemen scores well in fiscal freedom and somewhat well in labor freedom. The top income tax is relatively low, but the corporate tax rate is more burdensome. Overall tax revenue is low as a percentage of GDP. The labor market is relatively flexible, and employing and dismissing workers is easy.

Yemen faces major challenges in financial freedom, monetary freedom, freedom from government, property rights, and freedom from corruption. State influence makes the regulatory process opaque and court rulings subject to the demands of the government. Political interference bleeds into the financial market, which is unsophisticated, dominated by the state, and not subject to standard oversight and international regulations. Corruption is prevalent throughout the civil service. Inflation is high, although the government directly subsidizes only a few goods. State expenditures equal almost two-fifths of national GDP.

BACKGROUND: Yemen, in addition to being a poor country with few natural resources, suffers from political instability. President Ali Abdallah Saleh's government continues to face intermittent challenges from some of Yemen's often unruly tribes and Islamic radicals, who oppose the government's economic reform program and cooperation with the United States in the war against terrorism. Saleh's government has placed economic reforms on the back burner while it has waged war against Islamic extremists. In recent years, the economy has been hurt by declining oil production, terrorist attacks, and kidnappings, which have undermined tourism and foreign investment. The government has acknowledged the problem of corruption and has taken some steps to combat it, but needs to do more.

How Do We Measure Economic Freedom? See Chapter 3 (page 37) for an explanation of the methodology or visit the *Index* Web site at *heritage.org/index*.

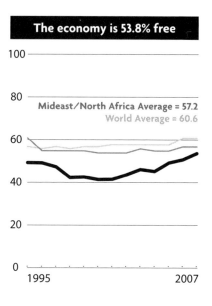

The economy is 53.8% free

Mideast/North Africa Average = 57.2
World Average = 60.6

QUICK FACTS

Population: 20.3 million

GDP (PPP): $17.9 billion
2.6% growth in 2004
3.7% 5-yr. comp. ann. growth
$879 per capita

Unemployment: 35% (2003 estimate)

Inflation (CPI): 12.5%

FDI (net inflow): −$20.9 million (gross)

Official Development Assistance:
Multilateral: $171 million
Bilateral: $176 million (25% from the U.S.)

External Debt: $5.5 billion

Exports: $5 billion
Primarily crude oil, coffee, dried and salted fish

Imports: $4.9 billion
Primarily food, live animals, machinery and equipment, chemicals

YEMEN'S TEN ECONOMIC FREEDOMS

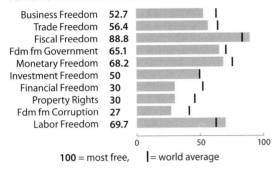

Business Freedom	52.7
Trade Freedom	56.4
Fiscal Freedom	88.8
Fdm fm Government	65.1
Monetary Freedom	68.2
Investment Freedom	50
Financial Freedom	30
Property Rights	30
Fdm fm Corruption	27
Labor Freedom	69.7

100 = most free, | = world average

BUSINESS FREEDOM — 52.7%

Starting a business takes an average of 63 days, compared to the world average of 48 days. To maximize entrepreneurship and job creation, it should be easier to start a company. Both obtaining a business license and closing a business are relatively simple. The implementation and enforcement of investment codes is not always transparent. The overall freedom to start, operate, and close a business is restricted by the national regulatory environment.

TRADE FREEDOM — 56.4%

Yemen's weighted average tariff rate was 11.8 percent in 2000. Import taxes, import licensing requirements, import bans and restrictions, weak enforcement of intellectual property rights, and customs corruption add to the cost of trade. There is some progress in making customs more transparent, but not enough. Consequently, an additional 20 percent is deducted from Yemen's trade freedom score to account for these non-tariff barriers.

FISCAL FREEDOM — 88.8%

Yemen has a low income tax rate but a burdensome corporate tax rate. The top income tax rate is 20 percent, and the top corporate tax rate is 35 percent. Other taxes include a property tax and a fuel tax. In the most recent year, overall tax revenue as a percentage of GDP was 7.1 percent.

FREEDOM FROM GOVERNMENT — 65.1%

Total government expenditures in Yemen, including consumption and transfer payments, are high. In the most recent year, government spending equaled 38.2 percent of GDP, and the government received 2.5 percent of its revenues from state-owned enterprises and government ownership of property. Unlike other regional oil producers, Yemen depends heavily on foreign oil companies. The relationship with these private companies is based on production-sharing agreements.

MONETARY FREEDOM — 68.2%

Inflation in Yemen is high, averaging 11.9 percent between 2003 and 2005. Relatively high and unstable prices explain most of the monetary freedom score. The government controls the prices of pharmaceuticals and petroleum products and also influences prices through regulation, subsidies, and state-owned enterprises and utilities. Consequently, an

additional 10 percent is deducted from Yemen's monetary freedom score to account for these policies.

INVESTMENT FREEDOM — 50%

The government officially permits foreign investment in most sectors and grants equal treatment to all investors, both domestic and foreign. Foreign investment in the exploration for and production of oil, gas, and minerals is subject to production-sharing agreements. Foreign investment is not permitted in the arms and explosive materials industries, industries that could cause environmental disasters, or wholesale and retail imports. Foreign exchange accounts are permitted. There are no restrictions on payments and transfers, and capital transactions are subject to few restrictions. Yemen has a significant and widely acknowledged corruption problem.

FINANCIAL FREEDOM — 30%

Yemen's financial system is small, underdeveloped, and dominated by the state. Despite efforts at improvement, financial supervision and regulation remain insufficient, and enforcement of prudential standards is poor. Non-performing loans are a problem. There were 15 commercial banks (including four Islamic banks) in October 2005, of which nine were private domestic banks, four were foreign banks, and two were state-owned banks. The state wholly owns the country's largest bank, the National Bank of Yemen, and owns a majority of the Yemen Bank for Reconstruction and Development. Efforts to privatize these banks have foundered. The state also owns a large majority of two specialized development banks focused on housing and agriculture. The Embassy of Yemen reports that the state is a very small shareholder in three other private banks. The insurance sector is small and included 10 insurance and reinsurance companies in 2004. Capital markets are negligible, and there is no stock market.

PROPERTY RIGHTS — 30%

The judiciary is subject to government pressure and corruption. Contracts are weakly enforced.

FREEDOM FROM CORRUPTION — 27%

Corruption is perceived as widespread. Yemen ranks 103rd out of 158 countries in Transparency International's Corruption Perceptions Index for 2005.

LABOR FREEDOM — 69.7%

The labor market operates under relatively flexible employment regulations that could be improved to enhance overall productivity growth. The non-salary cost of employing a worker is low, and dismissing a redundant employee is relatively easy.

ZAMBIA

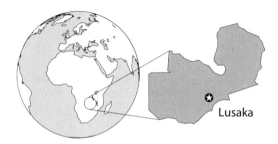

Lusaka

Zambia's economy is 57.9 percent free, according to our 2007 assessment, which makes it the world's 92nd freest economy. Its overall score is 1.2 percentage points lower than last year, partially reflecting new methodological detail. Zambia is ranked 12th out of 40 countries in the sub-Saharan Africa region, and its overall score is slightly higher than the regional average.

Zambia scores fairly well in fiscal freedom, freedom from government, and labor freedom. Personal and corporate tax rates are moderately high, but overall tax revenue is relatively low as a percentage of GDP. Total government expenditures equal about one-fourth of national GDP, and state-owned businesses constitute a minor source of revenue. Zambia's labor market is somewhat flexible, if uneven; hiring an employee is easy, but firing a redundant employee is more difficult.

Zambia's scores in most of the other economic factors are at best mediocre. The judicial process is slow, and many courts cannot arbitrate commercial suits effectively. Corruption is a serious problem. The regulatory environment is not protective of business, and commercial licensing procedures are notably slow. The government has streamlined foreign investment procedures, but capital is still subject to extensive restrictions.

BACKGROUND: Zambia experienced steadily declining income from 1974 to 1990 as a result of falling copper prices, a bloated civil service, HIV/AIDS, government mismanagement, inefficient state-owned enterprises, and corruption. Beginning in 1991, the government began to implement reforms to improve macroeconomic policies and reduce its intervention in the economy, including privatizing Zambia Consolidated Copper Mines. Nevertheless, the public sector remains excessive, efforts to improve the business climate and adopt a new investment code have stalled, and an anti-corruption initiative has had only limited success. Most of the population relies on subsistence agriculture, and copper accounts for most export earnings.

How Do We Measure Economic Freedom? See Chapter 3 (page 37) for an explanation of the methodology or visit the *Index* Web site at *heritage.org/index*.

The economy is 57.9% free

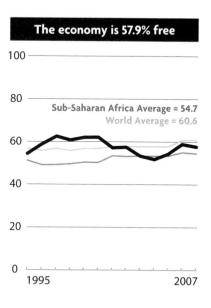

Sub-Saharan Africa Average = 54.7
World Average = 60.6

QUICK FACTS

Population: 11.5 million

GDP (PPP): $10.8 billion
5.4% growth in 2004
4.5% 5-yr. comp. ann. growth
$943 per capita

Unemployment: 50% (2000 estimate)

Inflation (CPI): 18%

FDI (net inflow): $334 million (gross)

Official Development Assistance:
Multilateral: $622 million
Bilateral: $757 million (11% from the U.S.)

External Debt: $7.3 billion

Exports: $1.8 billion
Primarily copper, cobalt, electricity, tobacco, flowers, cotton

Imports: $1.7 billion
Primarily machinery, transportation equipment, petroleum products, electricity, fertilizer, food, clothing

ZAMBIA'S TEN ECONOMIC FREEDOMS

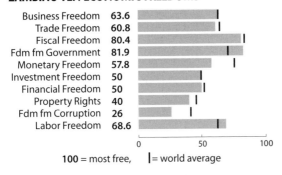

Business Freedom	63.6
Trade Freedom	60.8
Fiscal Freedom	80.4
Fdm fm Government	81.9
Monetary Freedom	57.8
Investment Freedom	50
Financial Freedom	50
Property Rights	40
Fdm fm Corruption	26
Labor Freedom	68.6

0   50   100

100 = most free, | = world average

BUSINESS FREEDOM — 63.6%

Starting a business takes an average of 35 days, compared to the world average of 48 days. To maximize entrepreneurship and job creation, it should be easier to start a company. Obtaining a business license can be very difficult, and closing a business is difficult. Bureaucratic obstacles and delays are persistent problems. The overall freedom to start, operate, and close a business is restricted by the national regulatory environment.

TRADE FREEDOM — 60.8%

Zambia's weighted average tariff rate was 9.6 percent in 2005. Import certification, export licensing requirements, import restrictions, and corruption all add to the cost of trade. Consequently, an additional 20 percent is deducted from Zambia's trade freedom score to account for these non-tariff barriers.

FISCAL FREEDOM — 80.4%

Zambia has burdensome tax rates. The top income tax rate is 37.5 percent, and the top corporate tax rate is 35 percent. Other taxes include a value-added tax (VAT), a tax on services, and a property transfer tax. In the most recent year, overall tax revenue as a percentage of GDP was 17.6 percent.

FREEDOM FROM GOVERNMENT — 81.9%

Total government expenditures in Zambia, including consumption and transfer payments, are moderate. In the most recent year, government spending equaled 26.8 percent of GDP, and the government received 4.1 percent of its revenues from state-owned enterprises and government ownership of property.

MONETARY FREEDOM — 57.8%

Inflation in Zambia is high, averaging 18.5 percent between 2003 and 2005. Relatively high and unstable prices explain most of the monetary freedom score. The government strongly influences agriculture prices by purchasing and selling agricultural input products and crops from the private sector, thereby significantly distorting the economy. The government also influences prices through subsidies and state-owned enterprises and utilities. Consequently, an additional 15 percent is deducted from Zambia's monetary freedom score to account for these policies.

INVESTMENT FREEDOM — 50%

The Zambian Investment Center was established as a one-stop resource for international investors interested in Zambia. An investment board screens all investments for which incentives are requested. The retail sector is closed to foreigners. There are no local content, equity, financing, employment, or technology transfer requirements. Red tape is extensive, and corruption remains common despite government efforts to clamp down on it. Both residents and non-residents may hold foreign exchange accounts. There are no controls on payments, transfers, capital transactions, or repatriation of profits.

FINANCIAL FREEDOM — 50%

Zambia's financial sector is small and dominated by banking. Zambia has one of Southern Africa's more liberal banking regimes. Banking supervision and regulation have improved. There were 11 operational commercial banks in mid-2006, including several majority foreign-owned banks. The government-owned Zambia National Commercial Bank, which was in the process of being privatized in 2006, controlled about 24 percent of the banking retail market. The poor loan repayment records of many borrowers and difficulty seizing loan collateral have led banks to invest in government debt. The government opened the insurance market to competition in the early 1990s. Privatization efforts for the state-owned Zambia State Insurance Corporation have stalled. Capital markets are small, and the stock exchange listed only 13 companies in mid-2006. There are no restrictions on foreign investment in the stock exchange.

PROPERTY RIGHTS — 40%

Zambia's judicial system suffers from inefficiency, government influence, and a lack of resources. Contracts are weakly enforced, and courts are relatively inexperienced in commercial litigation.

FREEDOM FROM CORRUPTION — 26%

Corruption is perceived as widespread. Zambia ranks 107th out of 158 countries in Transparency International's Corruption Perceptions Index for 2005.

LABOR FREEDOM — 68.6%

The labor market operates under relatively flexible employment regulations that could be improved to enhance overall productivity growth. The non-salary cost of employing a worker is moderate, but dismissing a redundant employee can be costly.

ZIMBABWE

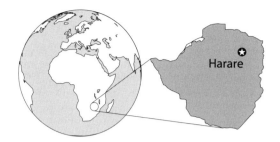

Harare

Rank: 154

Regional Rank: 40 of 40

Zimbabwe's economy is 35.8 percent free, according to our 2007 assessment, which makes it the world's 154th freest economy. Its overall score is 1.8 percentage points higher than last year, partially reflecting new methodological detail. Zimbabwe is ranked 40th out of 40 countries in the sub-Saharan Africa region, and its overall score is much lower than the regional average.

Zimbabwe scores somewhat well in fiscal freedom. The top income tax rate is high, but the corporate tax rate is somewhat lower. The government imposes an additional 3 percent AIDS surcharge on all taxes.

Zimbabwe has transformed itself from the "breadbasket of Africa" into a starving, destitute tyranny. Virtually all areas of economic freedom score poorly. The government maintains a high average tariff rate, as well as non-tariff barriers embedded in its labyrinthine customs service. National expenditures are also high. State influence in most areas of the economy is stifling, and expropriation is common as the political executive pushes forward with its resource-redistribution-by-angry-mob economic plan. Political interference has wrecked the once-prosperous financial market, and the state has made a point of not welcoming foreign investment. Inflation is crippling, and the government directly subsidizes a wide array of goods.

BACKGROUND: Upon gaining its independence from Rhodesia in 1980, Zimbabwe had ample natural resources, a diversified economy, a well-developed infrastructure, and an advanced financial sector. Since then, economic mismanagement and state intervention have undermined the economy. President Robert Mugabe has ruled since 1980, and economic policies designed to strengthen his hold on power have led to chaos and economic collapse. Mugabe has sanctioned violent acts of political repression, and many Zimbabweans have fled to neighboring countries. Corruption is endemic, inflation is in triple digits, most economic activity is informal, and controversial land reform has seriously undermined agricultural production.

How Do We Measure Economic Freedom? See Chapter 3 (page 37) for an explanation of the methodology or visit the *Index* Web site at *heritage.org/index*.

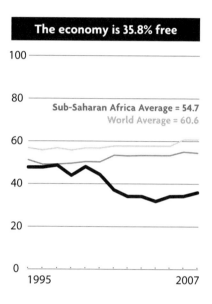

The economy is 35.8% free

Sub-Saharan Africa Average = 54.7
World Average = 60.6

1995 — 2007

QUICK FACTS

Population: 12.9 million

GDP (PPP): $26.7 billion
−3.8% growth in 2004
−5.7% 5-yr. comp. ann. growth
$2,065 per capita

Unemployment: 80% (2005 est.)

Inflation (CPI): 350%

FDI (net inflow): $60 million (gross)

Official Development Assistance:
Multilateral: $47 million
Bilateral: $167 million (18% from the U.S.)

External Debt: $4.8 billion

Exports: $1.7 billion
Primarily cotton, tobacco, gold, ferroalloys, textiles, clothing

Imports: $2.0 billion
Primarily machinery, transport equipment, other manufactures, chemicals, fuels

ZIMBABWE'S TEN ECONOMIC FREEDOMS

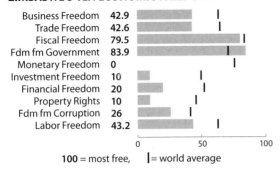

Business Freedom	42.9
Trade Freedom	42.6
Fiscal Freedom	79.5
Fdm fm Government	83.9
Monetary Freedom	0
Investment Freedom	10
Financial Freedom	20
Property Rights	10
Fdm fm Corruption	26
Labor Freedom	43.2

100 = most free, I = world average

BUSINESS FREEDOM — 42.9%

Starting a business takes an average of 96 days, compared to the world average of 48 days. To maximize entrepreneurship and job creation, it should be easier to start a company. Obtaining a business license can be very difficult, and closing a business is very difficult. Regulations are sometimes inconsistent, causing unreliability of interpretation. The overall freedom to start, operate, and close a business is seriously restricted by the national regulatory environment.

TRADE FREEDOM — 42.6%

Zimbabwe's weighted average tariff rate was 18.7 percent in 2003. Customs corruption, import taxes, import bans, import restrictions, and government controls on the export and domestic trading of major agricultural commodities add to the cost of trade. Consequently, an additional 20 percent is deducted from Zimbabwe's trade freedom score to account for these non-tariff barriers.

FISCAL FREEDOM — 79.5%

Zimbabwe has burdensome tax rates. The top income tax rate is 40 percent, and the top corporate tax rate is 30 percent. Other taxes include a 3 percent AIDS surcharge on all taxes, a value-added tax (VAT), and a capital gains tax. In the most recent year, overall tax revenue as a percentage of GDP was 24 percent.

FREEDOM FROM GOVERNMENT — 83.9%

Total government expenditures in Zimbabwe, including consumption and transfer payments, are very high. In the most recent year, government spending equaled 25.3 percent of GDP, and the government received 3.6 percent of its revenues from state-owned enterprises and government ownership of property.

MONETARY FREEDOM — 0%

Inflation in Zimbabwe is high, averaging 276.7 percent between 2003 and 2005. Relatively high and unstable prices explain most of the monetary freedom score. The government sets price ceilings for essential commodities such as agricultural seeds, bread, maize meal, sugar, beef, stock feeds, and fertilizer; imposes price controls on a wide array of basic goods and food staples, including energy; and influences prices through subsidies and state-owned enterprises and utilities. Consequently, an additional 15

percent is deducted from Zimbabwe's monetary freedom score to account for these policies.

INVESTMENT FREEDOM — 10%

The government will consider foreign investment up to 100 percent in high-priority projects but applies pressure for eventual majority ownership by Zimbabweans. The government's increasingly hostile attitude toward foreign investment and its support for economic nationalism have led to growing cronyism and corruption. Expropriation is very common. The government controls foreign exchange. Foreign exchange accounts are subject to government approval and restrictions. Payments and transfers are subject to government approval and numerous restrictions, and all outward capital transactions are controlled.

FINANCIAL FREEDOM — 20%

Zimbabwe's once relatively sophisticated financial system has deteriorated due to government intervention, lack of adequate supervision, and repeated crises. The government has used the Reserve Bank of Zimbabwe to finance deficit spending and direct loans to state-owned enterprises. Many banks are illiquid, and fears of a banking collapse have caused a flight to quality service that benefits foreign-owned banks. The government also owns a savings bank and development banks devoted to financing specific economic sectors. There were nine life insurance companies, 26 general insurance companies, and six re-insurance companies operating in 2003. Capital markets have been greatly diminished by financial turmoil, the stock market is small, and trading is thin. Foreign ownership of any locally listed company is capped at 40 percent, with a single investor capped at 10 percent. Foreign participation in the bond market is restricted.

PROPERTY RIGHTS — 10%

The executive branch exerts strong influence on the judiciary and openly challenges court outcomes when they run afoul of government action. Corruption and expropriation are common.

FREEDOM FROM CORRUPTION — 26%

Corruption is perceived as widespread. Zimbabwe ranks 107th out of 158 countries in Transparency International's Corruption Perceptions Index for 2005.

LABOR FREEDOM — 43.2%

The labor market operates under highly restrictive employment regulations that hinder overall productivity growth. The non-salary cost of employing a worker can be burdensome, and dismissing a redundant employee is costly. Zimbabwe's labor freedom is one of the 20 lowest in the world.

Appendix

Index of Economic Freedom Scores, 1995–2007

Country	1995	1996	1997	1998	1999	2000	2001	2002	2003	2004	2005	2006	2007
Albania	46.4	50.8	54.2	54.4	51.5	51.0	53.1	53.2	53.2	56.1	56.6	62.0	61.4
Algeria	54.3	52.9	53.4	54.4	55.8	58.4	55.4	60.0	54.0	54.9	50.3	53.4	52.2
Angola	27.2	24.4	24.3	24.7	23.9	24.3	*	*	*	*	*	43.3	43.5
Argentina	67.3	73.9	74.1	74.3	76.9	74.1	70.5	64.9	55.5	53.0	54.0	57.3	57.5
Armenia	*	38.9	43.0	48.7	55.7	62.4	65.7	67.0	67.0	67.7	67.7	74.6	69.4
Australia	73.8	73.7	73.2	75.8	76.4	77.1	77.4	77.6	77.6	78.1	78.8	81.5	82.7
Austria	71.6	71.7	72.1	69.5	67.9	71.1	70.7	68.5	68.8	68.7	67.6	71.4	71.3
Azerbaijan	*	27.2	31.7	40.7	44.9	47.1	47.5	51.0	51.3	49.9	52.5	54.0	55.4
Bahamas	72.2	75.0	75.3	75.0	75.6	74.2	75.2	75.7	74.8	73.0	73.4	72.7	71.4
Bahrain	80.7	80.8	80.6	79.4	78.9	79.2	79.0	78.3	77.7	77.8	73.0	71.0	68.4
Bangladesh	39.5	50.6	49.7	43.9	48.2	47.1	47.2	46.7	49.0	49.7	47.1	54.4	47.8
Barbados	*	60.4	64.9	68.3	67.0	69.8	72.4	72.9	74.2	72.4	72.9	75.2	70.5
Belarus	41.2	41.7	40.8	37.9	35.3	37.8	34.1	37.8	33.9	41.6	45.3	48.5	47.4
Belgium	*	68.5	68.7	68.8	68.8	65.9	69.6	68.9	69.6	69.9	70.0	74.2	74.5
Belize	63.1	63.0	65.3	60.6	62.0	62.5	64.2	63.0	62.2	61.4	63.1	65.5	63.7
Benin	*	53.1	57.7	58.2	58.7	59.8	58.3	54.4	52.3	52.5	49.7	54.3	54.8
Bolivia	53.7	62.4	61.9	67.3	66.1	65.4	68.5	65.0	64.2	62.2	59.1	59.1	55.0
Bosnia and Herzegovina	*	*	*	28.8	24.0	40.5	34.0	33.6	40.1	43.9	49.5	56.9	54.7
Botswana	55.1	59.6	58.8	61.9	62.0	61.2	62.7	60.9	68.5	69.5	69.8	70.3	68.4
Brazil	51.4	46.0	50.6	50.1	58.2	57.2	57.9	58.8	60.3	58.7	59.0	61.7	60.9
Bulgaria	47.8	48.2	47.2	47.2	45.0	50.4	52.7	55.9	55.6	57.1	59.9	64.3	62.2
Burkina Faso	*	47.1	51.6	52.1	53.2	53.3	53.9	56.3	55.4	55.8	54.6	55.7	55.0
Burma (Myanmar)	*	42.1	42.2	36.9	37.8	46.4	44.9	42.9	41.3	38.8	37.1	39.6	40.1
Burundi	*	*	43.7	35.7	41.9	43.6	*	*	*	*	*	49.6	46.8
Cambodia	*	*	54.6	58.9	59.4	58.5	61.0	62.0	65.0	62.1	58.7	59.2	56.5
Cameroon	50.8	45.8	44.7	46.5	48.7	47.6	50.8	50.8	50.1	50.1	49.7	54.2	54.4
Canada	72.6	73.3	69.7	70.0	70.6	71.4	71.9	74.5	74.6	75.0	75.6	78.7	78.7
Cape Verde	*	48.7	46.4	46.8	49.9	51.1	56.2	56.8	53.5	59.5	59.7	60.3	58.4

Index of Economic Freedom Scores, 1995–2007

Country	1995	1996	1997	1998	1999	2000	2001	2002	2003	2004	2005	2006	2007
Central African Republic	*	*	*	*	*	*	*	57.0	57.3	54.7	53.6	54.8	50.3
Chad	*	*	42.9	44.4	45.0	44.5	44.2	45.9	49.3	49.8	48.7	49.4	46.4
Chile	69.5	70.5	73.4	76.3	76.4	76.1	76.5	79.0	76.7	77.5	79.0	81.2	78.3
China, People's Republic of	52.1	51.5	52.9	54.1	55.3	54.1	50.6	51.2	51.1	51.0	52.4	55.4	54.0
Colombia	63.1	62.1	61.5	64.0	61.9	62.3	61.9	62.4	62.4	61.7	60.1	62.9	60.5
Congo, Democratic Republic of	44.8	37.8	37.8	32.3	25.6	26.4	*	*	*	*	*	*	*
Congo, Republic of	*	38.0	39.9	33.8	41.6	40.4	42.2	40.9	42.4	41.2	43.0	43.6	43.0
Costa Rica	66.3	64.3	63.6	63.5	63.8	65.6	67.3	67.7	65.1	64.6	65.1	67.4	65.1
Croatia	*	46.6	47.8	53.2	54.6	52.7	52.7	50.8	52.5	52.9	52.5	56.2	55.3
Cuba	28.0	28.0	28.0	28.1	28.1	30.7	31.1	29.5	32.0	31.8	35.1	32.2	29.7
Cyprus	*	66.8	67.1	67.4	67.1	65.3	72.5	75.3	73.4	74.1	71.6	73.3	73.1
Czech Republic	71.8	72.1	70.4	68.9	72.3	71.6	70.9	66.6	67.2	66.8	66.6	70.0	69.7
Denmark	*	72.5	70.5	66.2	66.2	66.4	68.6	73.7	76.3	75.7	75.7	76.2	77.6
Djibouti	*	*	52.9	54.5	55.9	53.7	57.0	56.3	54.1	55.3	56.4	55.0	52.6
Dominican Republic	55.1	55.4	53.0	55.1	55.4	56.2	56.4	56.8	55.0	54.1	52.9	56.7	56.7
Ecuador	54.9	57.4	58.3	59.6	59.6	58.0	52.5	49.9	51.0	51.1	51.2	55.6	55.3
Egypt	46.4	52.9	55.2	58.8	58.6	51.3	48.7	50.5	51.7	53.5	52.7	52.2	53.2
El Salvador	66.8	68.0	68.3	67.9	73.1	76.2	72.6	71.4	72.2	72.0	73.1	71.0	70.3
Equatorial Guinea	*	*	*	*	41.8	42.4	44.7	42.2	49.0	49.2	50.6	50.2	53.2
Estonia	65.2	67.4	71.2	72.6	75.8	74.2	79.0	79.5	79.4	79.0	76.6	75.9	78.1
Ethiopia	42.1	46.8	46.6	47.4	47.5	50.1	48.6	47.1	46.6	52.3	50.1	53.4	54.4
Fiji	52.5	55.7	56.0	56.1	57.0	56.7	51.3	53.5	54.0	56.0	55.0	57.0	59.8
Finland	*	65.4	67.5	68.7	68.6	66.7	69.5	74.7	74.8	74.4	72.7	75.6	76.5
France	65.6	65.6	64.0	64.0	64.4	61.7	62.1	59.6	60.5	62.1	62.9	65.2	66.1
Gabon	58.2	56.4	59.5	59.8	61.1	58.7	54.7	55.9	56.5	54.3	52.3	54.9	53.0
Gambia	*	*	51.0	50.7	52.7	50.2	54.1	56.3	54.8	53.7	56.3	57.9	57.6
Georgia	*	40.1	42.8	44.8	49.3	51.1	53.7	51.1	53.3	56.2	55.6	64.8	68.7
Germany	68.8	67.1	68.9	62.7	64.6	65.2	71.4	70.8	70.3	70.0	69.0	74.0	73.5

Index of Economic Freedom Scores, 1995–2007

Country	1995	1996	1997	1998	1999	2000	2001	2002	2003	2004	2005	2006	2007
Ghana	55.4	57.1	56.0	58.6	59.5	61.8	61.7	56.6	56.0	56.5	55.1	56.7	58.1
Greece	55.4	57.8	58.3	58.2	58.5	60.2	61.1	56.9	57.3	57.3	55.6	58.2	57.6
Guatemala	59.1	63.2	63.0	63.1	63.4	63.8	64.3	59.0	59.8	56.9	58.2	60.7	61.2
Guinea	57.4	56.4	52.7	58.5	57.2	55.7	56.2	52.9	54.7	54.0	55.8	53.7	55.1
Guinea-Bissau	*	*	*	*	32.5	35.1	40.3	38.2	40.0	39.3	41.2	47.1	45.7
Guyana	43.2	49.5	52.9	50.1	50.6	49.5	50.7	50.9	49.8	51.4	55.8	59.6	58.2
Haiti	38.1	37.8	42.7	42.5	42.8	42.5	43.9	43.6	46.3	48.1	45.8	49.8	52.2
Honduras	54.6	54.2	53.6	53.9	54.4	56.1	55.4	56.5	57.3	52.2	54.4	59.6	60.3
Hong Kong	88.8	90.4	90.1	90.4	90.4	90.8	91.4	88.9	89.3	90.1	90.2	90.9	89.3
Hungary	58.2	58.9	58.4	58.8	59.8	66.4	67.3	64.6	63.3	63.1	63.4	67.1	66.2
Iceland	*	*	70.4	71.0	71.2	73.0	72.7	73.4	73.8	72.7	77.1	77.7	77.1
India	46.4	47.8	47.9	44.9	48.1	45.7	47.1	51.4	51.6	51.8	54.4	52.3	55.6
Indonesia	54.6	60.8	60.6	61.1	59.0	51.7	49.2	52.4	52.6	49.8	52.1	54.1	55.1
Iran	*	32.8	31.6	33.2	34.0	34.7	33.0	33.3	39.4	38.7	43.9	43.3	43.1
Iraq	*	14.4	14.4	14.4	14.4	15.3	16.5	15.1	*	*	*	*	*
Ireland	69.6	69.5	69.8	75.1	75.9	77.1	82.4	80.1	80.5	79.9	78.2	81.2	81.3
Israel	62.8	63.1	63.7	63.7	63.8	62.9	62.3	67.2	64.0	63.1	63.8	66.7	68.4
Italy	64.3	63.8	64.3	64.4	65.0	65.7	66.5	64.3	65.1	65.0	63.5	62.7	63.4
Ivory Coast	54.2	50.1	50.8	51.5	52.0	50.1	53.8	55.9	55.2	56.2	54.9	56.8	55.5
Jamaica	62.1	66.5	67.6	67.0	64.3	66.7	62.9	60.5	66.7	65.5	66.5	67.7	66.1
Japan	73.9	72.7	72.9	71.2	71.9	73.8	74.0	66.0	67.0	63.9	65.7	74.5	73.6
Jordan	61.8	60.5	64.5	65.1	65.7	64.0	65.1	64.3	63.7	64.4	64.7	63.8	64.0
Kazakhstan	*	*	*	39.1	44.8	47.5	48.1	50.2	50.0	47.3	51.1	61.2	60.4
Kenya	53.8	53.5	58.4	59.6	59.4	60.4	55.8	55.3	55.8	55.4	56.0	60.0	59.4
Korea, North (DPRK)	5.6	5.6	5.6	5.6	5.6	5.6	5.6	4.4	4.4	4.4	4.0	4.0	3.0
Korea, South (ROK)	70.3	71.3	71.3	73.9	71.3	71.2	71.2	67.4	66.1	66.2	65.0	68.1	68.6
Kuwait	*	62.6	62.5	62.6	66.2	65.5	63.3	61.6	62.6	60.4	59.2	62.6	63.7
Kyrgyz Republic	*	*	*	49.0	52.2	53.2	52.2	50.5	54.7	55.7	54.7	62.8	59.9

Index of Economic Freedom Scores, 1995–2007

Country	1995	1996	1997	1998	1999	2000	2001	2002	2003	2004	2005	2006	2007
Laos	*	32.8	30.9	25.4	25.4	28.1	30.4	32.9	36.9	37.7	39.2	46.8	49.1
Latvia	*	54.6	61.9	62.4	63.3	63.0	64.9	64.3	65.0	66.2	63.0	69.2	68.2
Lebanon	*	62.3	63.7	58.9	58.9	56.9	61.1	55.5	55.1	53.1	55.8	58.5	60.3
Lesotho	*	44.1	46.4	47.5	50.0	49.9	52.3	49.1	50.7	48.6	52.9	57.0	54.1
Libya	*	25.7	25.9	26.8	27.1	32.1	32.2	31.7	31.8	28.9	28.4	34.3	34.5
Lithuania	*	47.4	56.3	60.9	62.8	63.3	65.7	67.2	68.2	70.9	69.5	73.0	72.0
Luxembourg	*	73.6	73.9	73.9	74.0	77.0	80.8	78.0	80.2	79.6	78.5	80.3	79.3
Macedonia	*	*	*	*	*	*	*	53.2	54.0	55.2	55.6	60.7	60.8
Madagascar	51.7	52.9	52.2	52.3	53.0	54.5	54.0	56.5	62.9	59.1	61.6	63.0	61.4
Malawi	51.9	53.5	50.9	51.4	53.8	53.7	52.3	54.1	51.3	52.0	53.4	57.9	55.5
Malaysia	70.2	68.3	67.1	70.7	69.7	66.5	60.2	57.8	58.7	57.4	61.9	63.7	65.8
Mali	52.8	58.0	57.3	58.2	59.5	60.8	60.6	60.3	57.8	55.7	56.6	54.1	53.7
Malta	55.0	54.9	57.0	60.3	58.6	57.9	62.5	58.9	60.7	64.6	69.3	69.4	67.8
Mauritania	*	43.7	47.4	44.1	43.0	46.4	48.9	52.3	56.0	59.0	57.0	55.6	53.2
Mauritius	*	*	*	*	69.4	67.5	66.7	65.4	64.5	64.3	64.3	66.5	69.0
Mexico	62.8	61.0	59.2	57.5	58.6	60.8	60.2	60.8	63.8	63.4	63.8	64.6	65.8
Moldova	33.0	50.1	46.6	51.4	54.0	58.1	51.0	55.1	57.5	54.8	55.1	59.6	59.5
Mongolia	48.7	48.6	52.7	59.0	59.4	59.4	58.1	58.5	59.8	58.0	60.1	63.2	60.1
Morocco	62.1	63.4	62.9	62.3	64.6	63.1	63.7	59.3	59.4	58.1	54.0	53.0	57.4
Mozambique	43.1	45.8	40.8	42.2	48.2	51.4	55.7	56.8	58.1	55.5	54.6	55.1	56.6
Namibia	*	*	60.3	63.8	65.4	64.6	63.7	64.2	66.5	61.6	60.0	60.9	63.8
Nepal	*	47.3	50.8	52.8	52.7	48.3	48.9	48.3	47.3	47.1	48.6	55.4	54.0
Netherlands	*	72.5	72.7	70.7	71.2	71.5	74.1	73.2	75.4	75.2	72.7	77.0	77.1
New Zealand	*	78.3	78.5	78.6	81.3	81.3	81.3	81.7	82.0	81.4	83.0	84.0	81.6
Nicaragua	39.5	52.2	50.0	50.5	50.8	51.8	52.5	51.8	54.0	58.2	60.2	64.4	62.7
Niger	*	44.2	44.8	45.9	47.0	44.3	47.2	45.3	51.1	51.4	51.2	53.6	53.5
Nigeria	47.1	47.1	49.2	53.8	56.1	55.5	52.3	49.8	48.5	47.3	45.8	48.8	52.6
Norway	*	66.2	66.0	68.2	68.6	69.6	66.8	67.4	67.1	66.2	64.9	70.8	70.1

Index of Economic Freedom Scores, 1995–2007

Country	1995	1996	1997	1998	1999	2000	2001	2002	2003	2004	2005	2006	2007
Oman	67.5	62.8	62.1	62.6	61.1	59.9	63.3	62.9	61.8	63.3	62.3	62.3	63.9
Pakistan	57.9	58.9	59.3	57.9	53.4	55.9	51.9	53.7	55.5	53.2	53.3	59.5	58.2
Panama	69.3	69.4	70.0	70.2	70.1	69.3	68.5	65.0	66.2	63.0	63.9	67.1	65.9
Paraguay	65.0	66.2	66.4	64.9	60.0	62.5	58.3	56.5	55.0	54.7	52.6	55.4	56.8
Peru	54.1	62.2	63.5	62.4	67.1	67.4	67.9	64.4	61.8	62.2	59.0	60.9	62.1
Philippines	54.9	57.9	60.8	63.8	61.9	62.2	57.9	58.4	59.0	56.7	53.3	57.5	57.4
Poland	52.3	58.5	57.5	61.3	62.2	63.0	62.6	64.8	61.5	58.7	59.0	61.6	58.8
Portugal	62.5	64.6	65.3	65.6	65.7	66.1	66.3	65.4	65.1	64.9	63.1	65.6	66.7
Qatar	*	*	*	*	57.7	57.8	55.8	58.3	62.6	62.0	58.9	60.4	60.7
Romania	42.9	47.7	52.1	55.7	53.1	55.3	48.3	46.0	47.7	48.4	50.8	58.9	61.3
Russia	49.7	49.6	45.9	50.9	52.9	50.1	48.0	47.3	49.1	51.1	50.1	54.3	54.0
Rwanda	*	*	37.7	38.4	39.4	41.8	44.9	47.6	44.9	50.2	48.5	54.3	52.1
Saudi Arabia	*	61.9	62.5	63.1	58.8	60.3	55.5	59.4	57.2	55.8	59.5	61.4	59.1
Senegal	*	58.3	56.3	55.8	56.7	56.9	58.4	56.5	56.1	57.3	56.6	57.4	58.8
Serbia and Montenegro	*	*	*	*	*	*	*	31.7	39.5	*	*	*	*
Sierra Leone	50.9	51.4	44.2	46.8	48.1	45.1	*	*	41.1	42.6	43.4	46.7	48.4
Singapore	87.3	87.8	88.0	88.2	88.0	88.6	88.6	87.9	88.6	89.2	90.1	88.4	85.7
Slovak Republic	58.9	55.3	53.5	53.5	51.6	52.7	60.1	59.6	59.2	64.2	64.7	69.2	68.4
Slovenia	*	46.3	53.5	58.6	59.2	56.2	59.2	56.2	58.6	62.2	60.9	63.5	63.6
South Africa	61.4	60.9	62.5	63.5	61.1	61.3	60.6	62.8	66.0	65.1	61.5	66.3	64.1
Spain	65.7	60.4	63.3	66.2	66.8	65.0	66.5	66.8	68.8	68.9	67.5	70.6	70.9
Sri Lanka	58.7	61.0	67.0	66.1	62.7	61.6	64.3	62.3	60.9	59.9	58.6	60.1	59.3
Sudan	38.6	41.0	40.6	39.0	40.1	46.8	*	*	*	*	*	*	*
Suriname	*	35.1	33.7	37.8	37.5	43.8	44.1	44.1	42.8	44.2	47.8	53.2	52.6
Swaziland	61.4	56.6	57.4	62.4	62.4	63.0	63.7	60.2	60.1	56.8	58.0	62.2	61.6
Sweden	63.9	64.3	66.2	66.7	66.7	67.6	69.0	73.5	72.8	73.1	70.9	74.0	72.6
Switzerland	*	75.8	77.8	78.2	78.4	76.4	75.9	78.2	77.7	78.5	78.4	80.0	79.1
Syria	*	44.1	44.2	44.0	39.6	37.7	37.0	35.6	37.5	37.3	45.5	50.5	48.2

Index of Economic Freedom Scores, 1995–2007

Country	1995	1996	1997	1998	1999	2000	2001	2002	2003	2004	2005	2006	2007
Taiwan	74.6	74.5	74.9	73.0	74.2	76.4	74.9	69.1	70.0	67.9	70.3	70.6	71.1
Tajikistan	*	*	*	39.2	39.2	42.9	44.8	44.2	43.1	44.8	49.9	55.8	56.9
Tanzania	54.6	54.8	56.7	57.0	57.4	56.9	55.7	57.7	54.1	57.3	54.0	59.3	56.4
Thailand	71.6	71.4	71.0	69.5	69.5	69.2	71.2	67.2	63.9	61.8	62.2	65.1	65.6
Togo	*	*	*	*	44.9	44.0	42.9	44.0	45.6	45.8	46.8	48.5	49.8
Trinidad and Tobago	*	69.6	71.5	70.5	70.8	72.4	69.6	64.2	69.4	71.9	71.1	71.9	71.4
Tunisia	63.9	64.4	64.4	64.4	62.2	62.1	60.8	60.3	59.2	59.4	56.7	59.2	61.0
Turkey	61.3	59.8	63.8	64.2	63.2	66.2	63.4	53.0	50.9	51.7	50.3	58.5	59.3
Turkmenistan	*	*	*	33.6	34.7	36.8	40.9	41.3	47.0	46.2	43.7	43.9	42.5
Uganda	65.1	68.4	68.8	70.0	70.1	60.3	61.2	58.8	57.9	61.6	61.4	64.9	63.4
Ukraine	33.7	34.5	40.6	39.7	42.9	47.4	46.1	45.4	49.7	51.8	53.7	55.5	53.3
United Arab Emirates	*	73.9	74.0	76.5	74.7	74.9	77.2	76.0	70.6	64.6	61.3	59.7	60.4
United Kingdom	79.1	76.9	76.9	77.0	77.5	77.9	78.3	78.6	77.8	78.1	79.9	82.2	81.6
United States	76.6	76.6	76.9	76.8	77.0	77.9	80.5	78.3	78.1	78.6	79.6	82.4	82.0
Uruguay	62.1	64.5	68.1	69.1	70.0	70.7	72.0	64.5	70.4	67.5	68.4	67.6	69.3
Uzbekistan	*	*	*	29.0	30.7	35.5	34.9	36.7	38.0	39.0	44.2	50.4	52.6
Venezuela	57.9	52.6	49.8	50.6	54.0	55.8	49.6	52.0	51.5	42.4	42.2	45.1	47.7
Vietnam	39.8	38.1	38.5	38.1	38.4	39.4	40.3	43.5	43.9	43.7	44.2	50.0	50.0
Yemen	49.3	49.2	47.3	42.2	42.5	41.3	41.4	43.5	46.1	45.2	49.3	50.8	53.8
Zambia	54.5	59.0	62.8	61.0	62.3	62.4	57.4	57.7	53.5	51.9	54.5	59.1	57.9
Zimbabwe	47.8	47.8	48.8	43.9	48.1	44.4	37.0	33.9	33.9	31.6	33.9	34.0	35.8

* Not graded for that year.

Source: Tim Kane, Kim R. Holmes, and Mary Anastasia O'Grady, *2007 Index of Economic Freedom* (Washington, D.C.: The Heritage Foundation and Dow Jones & Company, Inc., 2007), at *www.heritage.org/index*.

Major Works Cited

The following sources provided the basis for the country factor analyses in the 2007 *Index of Economic Freedom*. In addition, the authors and analysts of the various elements of the *Index* relied on supporting documentation and information from various government agencies and sites on the Internet, news reports and journal articles, and official responses to inquiries. All statistical and other information received from government sources was verified with independent, internationally recognized nongovernmental sources as well.

African Development Bank, *Selected Statistics on African Countries 2006*; available at *www.afdb.org/pls/portal/docs/page/adb_admin_pg/documents/statistics/selected%202006_web.pdf*.

Asian Development Bank, *Key Indicators 2005: Labor Markets in Asia: Promoting Full, Productive, and Decent Employment*; available at */www.adb.org/Documents/Books/Key_Indicators/2005/default.asp*.

Central Intelligence Agency, *The World Factbook 2005*, at *www.cia.gov/cia/publications/factbook/index.html*.

Country statistical agencies, central banks, and ministries of finance, economy, and trade; available at *www.un.org/Depts/unsd/gs_natstat.htm*; *www.census.gov/main/www/stat_int.html* and *www.bis.org/cbanks.htm*.

Deloitte, *Country Snapshots*; available at *www.deloitte.com/dtt/section_node/0,1042,sid%253D11410,00.html*.

Economist Intelligence Unit Limited, *Country Profile*, London, U.K., 2004, 2005, and 2006.

———, *EIU Country Report*, London, U.K., 1996 through 2006.

———, *Country Commerce*, London, U.K., 2004, 2005, and 2006.

Ernst & Young International, Ltd., *The Global Executive*, New York, N.Y., 2004, 2005, and 2006.

———, *Worldwide Corporate Tax Guide*, New York, N.Y., 2004, 2005, and 2006.

———, direct correspondence with Country Office.

European Bank for Reconstruction and Development, *Country Strategies*, 2004, 2005, and 2006; available at *www.ebrd.org/about/strategy/index.htm#country*.

First Initiative, *Information Exchange*; available at *www.firstinitiative.org/informationExchange/countries/index.cfm*.

Inter-American Development Bank; available at *www.iadb.org*.

International Monetary Fund, *Annual Report on Exchange Arrangements and Exchange Restrictions, 2005*, Washington, D.C., September 2005.

———, *Article IV Staff Reports*, various countries, Washington, D.C., 2002 through 2006; available at *www.imf.org/external/ns/cs.aspx?id=51*.

———, *Government Finance Statistics* CD–ROM 2006, Washington, D.C., 2006.

———, *International Financial Statistics Online*, Washington, D.C., 2006; available by subscription at *http://ifs.apdi.net/imf/logon.aspx*.

———, *Selected Issues and Statistical Appendix*, various countries, Washington, D.C., 2001 through 2006.

———, *World Economic Outlook: Globalization and Inflation*, Washington, D.C., April 2006; available at *www.imf.org/Pubs/FT/weo/2006/01/index.htm*.

———, *Country Information*; available at *www.imf.org/external/country/index.htm*.

Miles, Marc A., Edwin J. Feulner, and Mary Anastasia O'Grady, *2006 Index of Economic Freedom* (Washington, D.C.: The Heritage Foundation and Dow Jones & Company, Inc., 2006).

Organisation for Economic Co-operation and Development, *OECD Economic Outlook*, No. 78 (December 2005) and No. 79 (May 2006).

———, *OECD Statistics*; available at *http://cs4hq.oecd.org/oecd/*.

———, *OECD Web site*; available at *www.oecd.org/statsportal/0,2639,en_2825_293564_1_1_1_1_1,00.html*.

Transparency International, *The Corruption Perceptions Index*, Berlin, Germany, 2005, 2004, 2003, 2002, 2001, 2000, and 1999; available at *www.transparency.org/policy_research/surveys_indices/cpi*.

United Nations, *National Account Statistics Databases*; available at *http://unstats.un.org/unsd/snaama/Introduction.asp*.

United States Department of Commerce, *Country Commercial Guides*, Washington, D.C., 2003, 2004, 2005, and 2006; available at *www.buyusainfo.net/adsearch.cfm?search_type=int&loadnav=no*.

United States Department of State, *Country Reports on Human Rights Practices for 2005*, released by the Bureau of Democracy, Human Rights, and Labor, March 2006; available at *www.state.gov/g/drl/rls/hrrpt/2005/*.

———, *Investment Climate Statements: 2006*, released by the Bureau of Economic and Business Affairs, February 2006; available at *www.state.gov/e/eb/ifd/2006/*.

United States Trade Representative, Office of the, *2006 National Trade Estimate Report on Foreign Trade Barriers*, 2006; available at *www.ustr.gov/Document_Library/Reports_Publications/2006/2006_NTE_Report/Section_Index.html*.

World Bank, *World Bank World Development Indicators Online*, Washington, D.C., 2006; available by subscription at *http://publications.worldbank.org/WDI/*.

———, *Doing Business*, available at *www.doingbusiness.org/*.

World Trade Organization, *Trade Policy Reviews*, 1995 through 2006; available at *www.wto.org/english/tratop_e/tpr_e/tpr_e.htm*.